PRESIDENTS AND CIVIL LIBERTIES FROM WILSON TO OBAMA

This book is a history of the civil liberties records of American presidents from Woodrow Wilson to Barack Obama. It examines the full range of civil liberties issues: First Amendment rights of freedom of speech, press, and assembly; due process; equal protection, including racial justice, women's rights, and lesbian and gay rights; privacy rights, including reproductive freedom; and national security issues. The book argues that presidents have not protected or advanced civil liberties, and that several have perpetrated some of the worst violations. Some Democratic presidents (Woodrow Wilson and Franklin D. Roosevelt), moreover, have violated civil liberties as badly as some Republican presidents (Richard Nixon and George W. Bush). This is the first book to examine the full civil liberties record of each president, allowing us to place a president's record on civil rights, for example, in the context of his record on national security issues and to compare the performance of all the presidents covered on particular issues.

Samuel Walker is Professor Emeritus of Criminal Justice at the University of Nebraska at Omaha. He is author of thirteen books on civil liberties, criminal justice, and policing. They include *In Defense of American Liberties: A History of the ACLU* (1990), *Hate Speech* (1994), and *Sense and Nonsense about Crime* (7th ed., 2012). He is a frequent commentator on criminal justice and police issues in the national news media and has appeared on CNN, NBC, NPR, PBS *Frontline*, and the History Channel. He has served as a consultant to the U.S. Justice Department and local community groups on police problems.

PRESIDENTS AND CIVIL LIBERTIES FROM WILSON TO OBAMA

A STORY OF POOR CUSTODIANS

Samuel Walker

University of Nebraska at Omaha

CAMBRIDGE
UNIVERSITY PRESS

CAMBRIDGE UNIVERSITY PRESS
Cambridge, New York, Melbourne, Madrid, Cape Town,
Singapore, São Paulo, Delhi, Mexico City

Cambridge University Press
32 Avenue of the Americas, New York, NY 10013-2473, USA

www.cambridge.org
Information on this title: www.cambridge.org/9781107016606

First published 2012

Printed in the United States of America

A catalog record for this publication is available from the British Library.

Library of Congress Cataloging in Publication data
Walker, Samuel, 1942–
Presidents and civil liberties from Wilson to Obama : a story of poor
custodians / Samuel Walker.
p. cm.

Includes bibliographical references and index.
ISBN 978-1-107-01660-6 (hardback)
1. Presidents – United States. 2. Civil rights – United States. 3. Executive
power – United States. I. Title.
KF5053.W35 2012
342.7308′5–dc23 2011048914

ISBN 978-1-107-01660-6 Hardback

To

Elizabeth Emlen Walker

January 13, 1913–June 15, 2011

My mother was born two months before the events in this book begin, and she died almost exactly a year before it was published. She had a long and happy life, never complaining, even though at times we certainly gave her plenty of reason to do so. The summer before her death, at age ninety-seven, she was working in the garden at the assisted living center. She worked in a garden almost every day of her adult life. Everyone should tend his or her own chosen garden with the same determination and contentment.

Contents

Preface

This book was initially conceived in 2005 in response to the presidency of George W. Bush. Many people at that time were calling Bush the worst president ever on civil liberties, if not on all issues, because of the Iraq War, the human rights abuses at Abu Ghraib, the secrecy, the lying, and many other assaults on established rights. While I joined in that judgment, it soon occurred to me that you cannot legitimately call anything the "worst" unless you have studied others in the same category. I then realized that no historian had ever undertaken a systematic study of modern presidents and civil liberties. Thus was born this book.

This book examines the civil liberties records of all the presidents beginning with Woodrow Wilson and covers the full range of civil liberties issues: freedom of speech and press, religious liberty, due process of law, equal protection of the law, privacy, and all of the civil liberties issues raised by national security considerations. From the outset, I determined to be rigorously even-handed and to examine Democratic presidents as critically as their Republican counterparts. In my personal life I am a liberal Democrat (although most often a very disappointed one). I began well aware that Democratic presidents were responsible for some of the worst violations of civil liberties in American history: Woodrow Wilson's suppression of dissent in World War I and Franklin D. Roosevelt's evacuation and internment of Japanese Americans in World War II. So I was prepared to be critical of famous liberal Democrats. I believe that readers will find that I have held to my original commitment, including reaching favorable judgments about Republican presidents where the evidence warrants them.

Readers have a right to know that parts of my personal history inevitably shape my perspective on particular episodes in this book. In summer 1964, I was a volunteer in the Mississippi Summer Project, a historic effort to register African American voters in that state, and I eventually spent most of the next two years in Mississippi. This was a transformative experience, which has shaped my life and scholarly work ever since. Inevitably, that experience gives this book a special focus on how presidents have dealt with racial justice. Given the salience of race in American history, it is an appropriate focus. I am also a member of the Vietnam War–era generation and was active in the antiwar movement. Lyndon Johnson was the first president I ever voted for, and I did so in 1964 because we believed he was not going to do something reckless like get the United States involved in a war, particularly in Asia. The escalation of the Vietnam War in early 1965 generated a strong sense of betrayal and anger at Johnson. The tragedy of the war overshadowed for me, as I believe it continues to do for many Americans, his great accomplishments on civil rights and civil liberties. In researching and writing this book it took a while to get past the legacy of that anger and appreciate the great things he did accomplish, but without forgetting or excusing his responsibility for the tragedy of the Vietnam War. I was also a strong critic of President George W. Bush, for his two wars, the way he prosecuted the war on terrorism, and the assaults on civil liberties at home. Thus, presidential decisions to involve this country in wars are another special focus of this book. Again, the subject warrants this attention, and readers will find that I am sharply critical of presidents of both parties.

Readers should also know that my commitment to civil liberties includes a long involvement with the American Civil Liberties Union (ACLU). I served for about a decade on the ACLU Board of Directors and for about as many years on the Board of Directors of the ACLU of Nebraska, and was President of that board in 1981 and 1982. I then wrote a history of the ACLU: *In Defense of American Liberties* (Oxford University Press, 1990; second edition, Southern Illinois University Press, 1999). Inevitably, some skeptics will question my capacity to be objective about the ACLU as it appears in this book. They should take a look at my book on the ACLU, and in particular the chapters on the cold war, and then make their judgments about my capacity for objectivity.

With respect to the research that went into this book, I would like to point out that I conducted no original interviews. This reflected a choice about the kind of book I wanted to write. The written record available for this book is enormous, including the material in twelve presidential libraries, the archives of many other individuals and organizations, innumerable memoirs of and biographies of key figures; the relevant scholarly articles by historians, political scientists, legal scholars, and others; news media accounts, including notably the entire record of the *New York Times*, which is conveniently available online. I realized that if I began conducting interviews, the only responsible approach was to be systematic and to interview nearly everyone of importance who is alive and willing. That would be an enormous undertaking, given the fact that there are people still alive who are knowledgeable about Presidents Lyndon Johnson and Richard Nixon. Such an undertaking by itself would be virtually impossible to complete within my lifetime. Selective interviewing would open the door to potentially impermissible bias, or at least the perception of bias. And so I made a difficult, but I feel necessary, decision to rely entirely on the available written record.

Acknowledgments

No one writes a book of this size and scope without a lot of help from many people. Some of that help is practical, and some of it is encouragement and moral support during difficult times.

I would particularly like to thank Emily Whitfield, who has functioned as both a good friend and my agent. She helped shaped my prospectus, which involved thinking about how the book would be presented to its audiences, and she made the initial contact with Cambridge University Press. At Cambridge, my editor, John Berger, was immediately enthusiastic about the book and has been completely supportive, including through some difficult moments. His assistant, David Jou, also provided practical assistance on some important points in the production process.

At the University of Nebraska at Omaha (UNO), Jim Shaw, Government Documents Librarian, was extraordinarily helpful in tracking down documents that I could not locate. On several occasions I would call him about, for example, a set of congressional hearings, and fifteen minutes later a PDF copy would appear in my e-mail in-box. Jim also arranged an early opportunity for me to present on the subject of this book at the UNO Library and was also the first to arrange a presentation after the book is published.

The History News Network published a short piece online early in my research when I had an opportunity to develop my thoughts on the issue of ranking presidents. Through the courtesy of Professor Jack Call, I had the privilege of being the Centennial Speaker at Radford University in Virginia in 2010. Two of the three presentations I gave were based on material from this book. The UNO History Department invited me to be its Centennial Speaker in the fall of 2009, and it afforded me an opportunity to give a presentation on the speeches presidents did not give, which proved to be an interesting way to approach failures in presidential leadership. The ACLU of Nebraska invited me to speak on Obama and civil liberties in the fall of 2010, and that gave me an opportunity to refine my position on that issue. Martha P. Noonan, organizer of a conference on the fiftieth anniversary of the Freedom Rides in Chicago in 2011, invited me to give a paper on President Kennedy's response to the Rides.

The staffs at all of the Presidential Libraries where I conducted the most important research were always extremely helpful. Several gave me very valuable tips on particular sets of files that I should examine. Some were more than happy to track down later information or documents that I discovered I had missed during my visit. In chronological order of the presidents, I would like to thank the staff at the Herbert Hoover Presidential Library, the Franklin D. Roosevelt Presidential Library, the Harry Truman Presidential Library, the Dwight D. Eisenhower Presidential Library, the John F. Kennedy Presidential Library, the Lyndon B. Johnson Presidential Library, the Gerald Ford Presidential Library, the Jimmy Carter Presidential Library, the Ronald Reagan

Presidential Library, and the George H. W. Bush Library. At the time of my research, the Richard Nixon Papers were still housed at the National Archives, in College Park, Maryland, and I would like to thank the staff there for their assistance with that collection and several others. As with previous books, I found the Library of Congress to be a wonderful place to conduct research, and I would like to thank the staff there for their help during repeated visits. For my trip to the Kennedy Library I would like to thank Ruth Purtillo and Vard Johnson for graciously hosting me in Boston. And in Albany, New York, Julie Horney hosted me while I was working in the Roosevelt Library in Hyde Park.

I would like to express special appreciation for the directors of the American Presidency Project at the University of California at Santa Barbara. Its online archive has nearly 100,000 documents related to the presidency, including speeches, press conferences, executive orders, political party platforms, and many other relevant documents. It is a truly magnificent resource that saved me far more hours than I could possibly estimate. Congratulations and thanks to everyone involved with the project. I would also like to thank the directors of the National Security Archive at George Washington University. The online archive contains an estimated 500,000 pages of previously classified documents, usually with explanatory introductions. The archive made an enormous contribution to the research for this book.

Several people read various chapters of the manuscript. In particular, I would like to thank Leigh Ann Wheeler of Binghamton University. She took time out from her important forthcoming book on civil liberties to offer helpful comments. It has also been a great pleasure to be able to share the travails of completing a book with someone in the midst of the same experience.

I owe a special debt to Greg Robinson, of the Universite du Quebec a Montreal, who carefully read the chapter on Franklin D. Roosevelt and caught some errors of fact and interpretation that I had allowed to slip into the manuscript. Louis Fisher, now retired from the Library of Congress, meanwhile, read the chapters on Bill Clinton and George W. Bush and also caught some points that needed clarification and had other very helpful comments regarding national security issues. Phillipa Strum, then at the Woodrow Wilson Center, a longtime colleague on the ACLU National Board of Directors and the author of books on Louis Brandeis, read the chapter on Wilson and offered some valuable suggestions. Athan Theoharis, now retired from Marquette University and the leading expert on the FBI and the cold war, read the Truman and Eisenhower chapters and provided some important critical comments. Kathyrn Olmsted, University of California at Davis, provided valuable comments on the Gerald Ford chapter, with some good suggestions on the complex topic of the post-Watergate investigations of the intelligence agencies. Christopher Smith of Michigan State University read several chapters and had some helpful comments on the role of the Supreme Court. David Harris of the University of Pittsburgh Law School, who has been a longtime close colleague on issues of police accountability, my primary area of activity when I am not doing history, read the first chapter I wrote and made some encouraging comments. Roger Goldman of St. Louis University Law School, another friend and colleague on police accountability issues, also made some helpful comments on several chapters.

In Omaha, the UNO History Professor Bill Pratt, a colleague and friend for more than forty years, read the chapter on Harry Truman and forced me to rethink what had been my initial treatment of his presidency. Some friends who are not historians also read the manuscript, as I was interested in whether it was written in a style that would appeal to the nonhistorian. Nora Bacon, Professor of English at UNO, gave me a very helpful reading. She is the author of *The Well-Crafted Sentence*, and her book helped me avoid a number of common lapses in writing. Any poorly crafted sentences that remain are my own responsibility. John Else, my longest-standing friend, also read two chapters and offered helpful comments.

Carol Grant Gould obtained the photographs for the book in an extremely efficient manner, saving me much time and enormous headaches. Working with her was a real pleasure.

I have had a long involvement of more than thirty years with the ACLU at both the state and national levels. Over those years I have had many discussions with many leaders and members of the organization on issues covered in this book: presidential power, First and Fourth Amendment questions, church and state, and so on. This has been a major part of my continuing education, and it has directly informed this book. I would particularly like to express my appreciation to Norman Dorsen, former President of the ACLU, who has been enormously supportive of this and other books. In addition to his vast knowledge of civil liberties issues, he has always been a wise counsel. Nadine Strossen, Norman's successor as President of the ACLU, has been a great friend and colleague, and provided special support for this book. I first met Emily Whitfield, whom I have already mentioned as my agent for this book, when she was the news media person in the ACLU national office. In 2010 I worked with Mia Nitchun on the materials for the ACLU's ninetieth anniversary. Her probing questions helped to clarify fine points about exactly who did what in particular major cases.

At the office, our computer specialist, Angela Patton, has always been there to solve my computer problems quickly and with a smile. I cannot thank her enough for explaining to me the mysteries of the "On" button, which seems to solve about half of all computer problems. Holi Samieva, a graduate student and now UNO staff member from Uzbekistan, edited the footnotes and made many important corrections in the citations.

Finally, I would like to thank my companion, Mary Ann Lamanna. In late September of 2011 we spent a week in Paris to celebrate thirty years together. It was a wonderful week. So were the thirty years. She works tirelessly on her own books but always knows there is time for a movie.

Abbreviations

AARC	Assassination Archive Research Center
AAUM	American Union against Militarism
ACLU	American Civil Liberties Union
ACLUP	American Civil Liberties Union Papers, Mudd Library, Princeton University
ACLUPME	ACLU Papers, Microfilm edition
ACW	Ann C. Whitman, Secretary to President Dwight D. Eisenhower
APP	American Presidency Project, University of California, Santa Barbara
APRP	A. Philip Randolph Papers, Library of Congress
BOI	Bureau of Investigation. Predecessor of the Federal Bureau of Investigation
CIA	Central Intelligence Agency
CLB	Civil Liberties Bureau
COHC	Columbia University Oral History Collection, Columbia University
CORE	Congress of Racial Equality
CSI	Center for the Study of Intelligence
DDE	Dwight D. Eisenhower
DDEPL	Dwight D. Eisenhower Presidential Library, Abilene, Kansas
DOJ	Department of Justice
DPC	Domestic Policy Council
EHLP	Edward H. Levi Papers, University of Chicago
ER	Eleanor Roosevelt
EROHP	Eleanor Roosevelt Oral History Project, Franklin D. Roosevelt Presidential Library
ERP	Eleanor Roosevelt Papers, Franklin D. Roosevelt Presidential Library
FAOH	Foreign Affairs Oral History Project, Library of Congress
FBI	Federal Bureau of Investigation
FBIERR	Federal Bureau of Investigation Electronic Reading Room
FDR	Franklin D. Roosevelt
FDRPL	Franklin D. Roosevelt Presidential Library, Hyde Park, New York
FFPLOC	Felix Frankfurter Papers, Library of Congress
FOR	Fellowship of Reconciliation

FPBP	Francis P. Biddle Papers, Franklin D. Roosevelt Presidential Library
FPBP-GU	Francis P. Biddle Papers, Georgetown University
GFPL	Gerald Ford Presidential Library, Ann Arbor, Michigan
GHWBPL	George H. W. Bush Presidential Library, College Station, Texas
GID	General Intelligence Division, Bureau of Investigation
GUL	Georgetown University Library, Washington, D.C.
HHPL	Herbert Hoover Presidential Library, West Branch, Iowa
HST	Harry S. Truman
HSTPL	Harry S. Truman Presidential Library, Independence, Missouri
HU	Human Rights (category within White House Central Files [WHCF])
JCPL	Jimmy Carter Presidential Library, Atlanta, Georgia
JFKPL	John F. Kennedy Presidential Library, Boston, Massachusetts
JL	Judicial Legal (category within White House Central Files [WHCF])
LBJ	Lyndon B. Johnson
LBJPL	Lyndon B. Johnson Library, Austin, Texas
LOC	Library of Congress
MCPA	Miller Center of Public Affairs, University of Virginia
NA	National Archives
NAACP	National Association for the Advancement of Colored People
NAACPP	National Association for the Advancement of Colored People Papers, Library of Congress. Also, Microfilm edition
NCLB	National Civil Liberties Bureau
NSA	National Security Agency
NSArch	National Security Archive, George Washington University
NSC	National Security Council
NWPP	National Woman's Party Papers, Library of Congress
NYT	The *New York Times*
OH	Oral History
OHAS	Oral History of the American South, University of North Carolina Library
OPL	Office of Public Liaison
PWW	Papers of Woodrow Wilson
RFK	Robert F. Kennedy
RMNP	Richard M. Nixon Papers, National Archives (The Nixon Papers have since been moved to the Richard M. Nixon Presidential Library, Yorba Linda, California.)
ROHO	Regional Oral History Office, Bancroft Library, University of California
RRRPL	Ronald Reagan Presidential Library, Simi Valley, California
SCLC	Southern Christian Leadership Council

SNCC	Student Non-violent Coordinating Committee
SWPC	Swarthmore Peace Collection, Swarthmore College
UC	University of Chicago
WHCF	White House Central Files
WJCPL	William J. Clinton Presidential Library, Little Rock, Arkansas

1 Introduction

Presidents and Civil Liberties

SCENES FROM THE WHITE HOUSE

February 19, 1942

For his signature, Attorney General Francis Biddle presented President Franklin D. Roosevelt with Executive Order 9066, authorizing the military to evacuate people from the West Coast of the United States. Roosevelt promptly signed it. Within months the government removed 117,116 Japanese Americans and interned them in Relocation Centers, which have been properly called concentration camps. At least seventy thousand of the internees were bona fide American citizens. Many lost their homes and businesses. Historians generally regard the treatment of the Japanese Americans as the greatest single violation of civil liberties in American history.

President Roosevelt had no qualms about signing Executive Order 9066. He expressed no concerns about its legality and ignored information on his desk that the overwhelming majority of Japanese Americans were loyal to this country.

Nor did he ever express regrets about his decision. Nearly three thousand Americans had died in the Japanese attack on Pearl Harbor just two and a half months earlier, and many feared that the Japanese might attack the continental United States itself. Military officials argued that security required evacuating all people of Japanese origin from the West Coast to prevent espionage and sabotage. Several Justice Department lawyers objected, arguing that it would be wrong and unnecessary. Both the Federal Bureau of Investigation (FBI) director, J. Edgar Hoover, and the Office of Naval Intelligence reported that there were only a few potential spies or saboteurs among the Japanese Americans. Roosevelt sided with the military, however, and signed the order, setting in motion a terrible tragedy.

November 26, 1963

Four days after being sworn in as president after the assassination of John F. Kennedy, Lyndon Johnson consulted White House advisers about his forthcoming speech to Congress and the nation the evening of November 27. He wanted the speech to heal the nation and define the goals of his presidency. The group was a mixture of his own staff and Kennedy advisers. Musing out loud, he said he was thinking about making the pending civil rights bill his top legislative priority. Although it eventually became the historic 1964 Civil Rights Act, the bill at that point faced a very uncertain prospect in Congress, with strong opposition from southern segregationists and Republican conservatives.

Abe Fortas, the future Supreme Court justice, who was at the meeting, recalled that "one of the wise, fine, practical people around the table" advised against making the bill his top priority. Others agreed, arguing that a president has only so much "coinage to expend," and that he should not risk it all on a bill that might not pass. Silence fell over the room, as Johnson pondered this advice. Finally rousing himself, he said, "Well, what the hell's the presidency for?"

Johnson understood power, and the special power of the presidency. Since his first days as a public official in 1936 he had been deeply committed to ending racial segregation in America. The day after consulting his advisers, he told the nation that the civil rights bill was his top priority and that he wanted it to be a memorial to the slain former president. Congress passed it the following year, and the 1964 Civil Rights Act is today regarded as one of the most important laws in American history, defining racial equality as national policy. A year later Johnson again used his special influence as president to secure passage of the 1965 Voting Rights Act, an equally important law in the cause of racial justice.

POOR CUSTODIANS OF AMERICAN LIBERTIES

These two episodes dramatize the role regarding civil liberties presidents have played in American democracy. In the first, a president authorized the violation of fundamental liberties with little regard for the rights of the 117,116 victims. In his view, national security trumped all other considerations. Over the last one hundred years, other presidents have violated constitutional rights. Rarely have presidents taken strong stands to defend individual rights, on national security questions, free speech controversies, church and state questions, or other freedoms guaranteed by the Bill of Rights.

In the second episode, a president understood that the country faced a historic moment involving the rights of Americans and chose to use his power to secure legislation ending an ancient wrong. It would have been easy for President Johnson to heed counsels of caution and hope for a more promising political moment in the future, but he rejected that advice and did what he knew was right. Regrettably, American presidents have been poor custodians of the Bill of Rights. Too often, they have knowingly authorized violations of individual rights or looked away and failed to speak out or prevent abuses that were occurring. Few have been willing to use the enormous power of the White House to defend or advance the protections of individual liberties enshrined in the Bill of Rights.

There is exactly one instance when a president risked his political future in defense of civil rights. Harry Truman was the first to appoint a presidential civil rights commission and to send Congress a comprehensive legislative program. In summer 1948 he issued an executive order ending racial segregation in the Armed Services. He was far ahead of white American opinion on racial justice at that time, and his actions jeopardized his reelection chances in November 1948. Yet, he not only did what was right, but won a stunning upset reelection victory.

PRESIDENTS AND AMERICA'S CORE VALUES

The failure of most presidents to defend or advance civil liberties is a matter of great importance in assessing presidential performance. The principles in the Bill of Rights represent the core values of American democracy. The freedoms of speech and press, religious liberty, due process of law even for the most heinous suspect, equal protection for all people, and privacy are at the core of our constitutional law. The United States is unique in the world for its commitment to expanding and protecting those liberties. No other country extends such protection to free speech, no matter how offensive it might be, or to guarding against government sponsorship of religion.

The president in America is more than just the person who won the last election; he or she is the national leader and spokesperson for the country in world affairs. When historians attempt to rank presidential performance, they consider how they led the country through times of crisis, including wars, economic difficulties, and other critical moments. Given the centrality of the Bill of Rights in American democracy, it is important to assess how presidents have done in protecting the rights it enshrines. Curiously, no historian has undertaken such an assessment. Indeed, civil liberties tend to vanish in the traditional efforts to rank presidential importance. This book seeks to fill that void.

From Wilson to Obama

This book examines in detail the records of American presidents on civil liberties from Woodrow Wilson through Barack Obama. Wilson is the proper starting point because the suppression of free speech and other rights during World War I put civil liberties on the American political and legal agenda on a permanent basis. Over the previous century and a half, there had been only episodic civil liberties crises: over the Alien and Sedition Acts between 1798 and 1800, the suppression of anti-lavery activity prior to the Civil War, and Abraham Lincoln's suspension of habeas corpus during the Civil War. In each case, however, the crisis passed and the country returned to its normal course of business without undertaking an ongoing debate over the constitutional questions about individual liberties that had arisen.

All that changed in the crucible of World War I, when thoughtful Americans suddenly discovered the awesome power of the federal government to suppress freedom and the capacity of the American people to be stampeded by patriotic hysteria into accepting such actions. Two events mark the emergence of civil liberties as an ongoing national issue: First, the Supreme Court's wartime free speech cases set in motion a debate over the First Amendment and the entire Bill of Rights that continues today. That debate focuses on the scope of the First Amendment, whether there is a right to criticize the government during wartime, the meaning of due process, equal protection and other rights enumerated in the Bill of Rights, and the role of the Court in defining those rights.

The second watershed event was the founding of the American Civil Liberties Union (ACLU) in January 1920. The ACLU became the first permanent national organization devoted to civil liberties and over the years aggressively fought for an expanded protection of individual rights. The aggressive pursuit of rights by public interest groups – the ACLU, the National Association for the Advancement of Colored People (NAACP), and in time a host of other rights groups – shaped the social and political context of America over the next eighty-plus years. The role of advocacy groups is crucial to understanding presidents and civil liberties. As this book makes clear, presidents have generally not played a leading role in defending the principles of freedom of speech and press, the right to due process, equal protection, and individual privacy. In several tragic episodes, in fact, presidents have authorized gross violations of those rights.

Presidential performance: The major themes

Why has presidential performance been so poor in this area? Several themes emerge from this examination of the records of the seventeen presidents from Woodrow Wilson to Barack Obama. The first is that in a democratic society, presidents inevitably shy away from unpopular issues that are likely to cost them votes. This melancholy fact is inherent in the very nature of democracy itself and is why the generation that fashioned the Constitution added a Bill of Rights to remove certain issues from the passions of conventional politics.

Examples of presidential leadership in defense of civil liberties have been extremely rare. As indicated, President Harry Truman's initiative on civil rights in 1946 and 1948 is the only example of a president's risking his political future in defense of the rights of Americans; no other president has demonstrated a similar kind of courage. Beginning in the 1970s, presidents – almost always Democrats – supported civil rights, women's rights, and reproductive rights but largely because by then these issues had powerful political constituencies.

A second theme is that the failure to defend American liberties has been decidedly bipartisan. Democratic presidents have as poor a record as do Republicans. It is particularly important to emphasize this point in the wake of the presidency of George W. Bush, whose record on civil liberties was truly appalling. Many people – liberal Democrats and others – have framed his presidency in a narrative that incorporates Richard Nixon and Ronald Reagan and views Republicans as hostile to civil liberties and Democratic presidents as sympathetic to and protective of individual rights. The record does not support that narrative. Most glaringly, Woodrow Wilson and Franklin D. Roosevelt, two of the most famous and celebrated liberal Democratic presidents of the twentieth century, were responsible for two of the worst violations of civil liberties in American history: Wilson's suppression of free speech during World War I and Roosevelt's evacuation and internment of the Japanese Americans in the Second World War.

A third theme is that the record of many presidents on civil liberties is filled with contradictions, with a good or even outstanding record on one issue but a terrible one on another. Roosevelt ordered the evacuation of the Japanese Americans, but his Supreme Court appointments established the first significant body of civil liberties case law in American history in the late 1930s and 1940s, laying the groundwork for the more famous Warren Court of the 1960s. Truman deserves great credit for his leadership on civil rights, but he also launched the 1947 Federal Loyalty Program, which embodied the principle of guilt by association, was a terrible assault on freedom of belief and association, and in the view of many historians helped set the stage for Senator Joe McCarthy's reckless anticommunist demagoguery beginning in 1950. President Eisenhower has been deservedly criticized for failing to endorse the Supreme Court's historic school desegregation decision, *Brown v. Board of Education*, in 1954. And yet, his administration moved aggressively to desegregate the nation's capital, Washington, D.C. On that issue, he had a far superior civil rights record to Truman, who had ignored the racial segregation in the nation's seat of government.

As we shall see, contradictions mark the records of many if not most of the presidents under consideration. Among other things, they create a serious problem for making any final assessment of individual presidents on civil liberties and then comparing different presidents. To be sure, some presidents have been clearly better than others. Woodrow Wilson, for example, has perhaps the worst record on freedom of speech and press and on racial justice, with only a few positive actions on the other side of the ledger. Lyndon Johnson, meanwhile, was clearly the greatest civil libertarian, with a strong record on civil rights, reproductive rights, the rights of criminal suspects, and other issues. But he too perpetrated serious violations of the Constitution, wiretapping civil rights activists and lying to secure congressional authorization to escalate American involvement in Vietnam.

A fourth theme involves national security. Beginning with Franklin D. Roosevelt in the late 1930s, as the world headed for another global conflict, national security considerations repeatedly trumped constitutional considerations. From FDR to the present, national security has been a rationale for military adventures overseas, excessive government secrecy, illegal spying on Americans, and violations of law and human rights overseas. Democratic and Republican presidents alike have been guilty of these abuses.

Surprises

The history of presidents and civil liberties is filled with surprises. Woodrow Wilson, the most accomplished scholar ever to serve as president, was a prominent authority on American democracy. His 1908 book, *Constitutional Government*, however, contains not a word about the Bill of Rights, free speech, or other civil liberties, and his other writings indicate he was oblivious to hard questions about the scope of the Bill of Rights.

Warren G. Harding is generally regarded as one of the most incompetent presidents, who presided over a terribly corrupt administration. Yet, in 1921 he gave a speech in Birmingham, Alabama, that was the strongest call for racial justice by any president between Abraham Lincoln and Harry Truman. Calvin Coolidge, meanwhile, is generally remembered for doing almost nothing as president, but in 1924 he cleaned up the FBI and ended the practice of political spying that had begun under Wilson during World War I. Franklin D. Roosevelt in 1936 gave J. Edgar Hoover the green light for political spying by the FBI, sweeping away the reforms established by President Coolidge. Hoover's campaign of massive illegal spying on Americans dates from FDR's presidency.

Richard Nixon has a reputation for hostility to civil rights, but through the first twenty-two years of his public life he had one of the best records on the issue among all leading Republicans. In 1960 the Reverend Martin Luther King initially preferred him to John F. Kennedy for president. Nixon was also a staunch supporter of the Equal Rights Amendment, which would guarantee equality to women, from the beginning of his political career to the day he left office on August 9, 1974. Jimmy Carter is generally regarded as a failure as president, but he was the first president to invite lesbian and gay rights activists to the White House and had by far the strongest record on women's rights of any previous president.

A dialogue about America

Exploring the history of presidents and civil liberties is more than a matter of simply reviewing and grading presidential performance. When we ask how well a president has done with regard to freedom of speech, religious liberty, or racial justice, we are asking some basic questions about what is important to us as a country, about what we expect of our leaders. We are asking how important, in the larger scheme of things, is protecting freedom of speech for dissenters in wartime. How we answer that question reflects the value we place on the First Amendment, and it will determine how we evaluate certain presidents. How important is it to preserve civil liberties vis-à-vis considerations of national security? Our answer to that question has implications for every president from Franklin D. Roosevelt to Barack Obama.

American presidents have had such a weak record on defending civil liberties because of the very nature of those rights in a democratic society. Civil liberties inherently involve unpopular issues: free speech for the radical critic of the free enterprise system or the dissenter in time of war; the due process rights of the mass murderer; equal protection for an unpopular minority group; the privacy right to engage in a sexual activity that many people find abhorrent. These are not the issues a candidate for political office is likely to champion. And they are precisely the kind of issues that are likely to get an officeholder soundly rejected at the next election.

In the end, while this book examines in detail the performance of seventeen presidents with regard to civil liberties, it ultimately becomes a dialogue about American democracy. Although presidents have not been strong defenders of the Bill of Rights, in fact the rights of Americans have expanded enormously in the century covered here. Americans today enjoy freedoms of speech, press, and assembly, of equality and due process, that in most cases were unimaginable the day Woodrow Wilson entered the White House in 1913. This book examines the generally poor performance of the sixteen presidents during this period, but this story is only a part of the larger drama of civil liberties in America.

PART I

The Early Years

Feminist pickets the White House in support of women's suffrage, summer of 1917. The United States had entered World War I in April, and calling the president "Kaiser Wilson" was highly inflammatory.
Source: National Archives.

2 Woodrow Wilson and the Suppression of Civil Liberties in World War I

"SUCH CREATURES ... MUST BE CRUSHED OUT"

"Such creatures of passion, disloyalty, and anarchy must be crushed out." Speaking to a joint session of Congress, President Woodrow Wilson warned of a grave internal threat to the nation. "There are citizens of the United States ... born under other flags ... who have poured forth the poison of disloyalty into the very arteries of our national life; who have sought to bring the authority and good name of our Government into contempt." To solve the problem of dangerous immigrants Wilson urged Congress to enact laws "by which we may be purged of their corrupt distempers."[1]

Wilson's inflammatory attack on the "poison of disloyalty" occurred on December 7, 1915, sixteen months before the United States entered World War I. The massive suppression of freedom of speech and press, along with other violations of individual rights by his administration during the war, is one of the major attacks on civil liberties in American history. Historians have generally portrayed it as an unfortunate aberration, a sudden eruption of excessive wartime patriotic hysteria that was unrelated to Wilson's attitudes and policies as president. As we shall see, however, intolerance of dissent was an integral part of Wilson's view of American society and progressive reform. The wartime suppression of free speech was no aberration, and he bears direct responsibility for it.[2]

WILSON, PROGRESSIVISM, AND CIVIL LIBERTIES

A stark paradox lies at the heart of Woodrow Wilson's presidency, one that few historians have confronted. Wilson consistently ranks among the few "near-great" presidents. That ranking rests on the important domestic reforms he secured before the war. Only Presidents Franklin D. Roosevelt and Lyndon B. Johnson exceed his achievements in that regard. And yet, he also perpetrated terrible violations of individual rights

1 Woodrow Wilson, 3rd Annual Message to Congress, December 7, 1915, APP.

2 The literature on Woodrow Wilson is unbalanced, with much on foreign affairs, less on domestic policy, and little on the suppression of free speech. The latter is addressed largely by civil liberties specialists, and few historians have seriously addressed the relationship between the wartime civil liberties issues and the rest of Wilson's public and private career. Arthur Link's five-volume biography (Princeton, NJ: Princeton University Press, 1947–65) ends with U.S. entry into the war. A short but insightful biography is John Morton Blum, *Woodrow Wilson and the Politics of Morality* (Boston: Little, Brown, 1956); see also Blum's comparative analysis, *The Progressive Presidents* (New York: W. W. Norton, 1980). Daniel D. Stid, *The President as Statesman: Woodrow Wilson and the Constitution* (Lawrence: University of Kansas, 1998) contains almost no mention of freedom of speech or other civil liberties issues. John M. Mulder, *Woodrow Wilson: The Years of Preparation* (Princeton, NJ: Princeton University Press, 1978) is valuable.

during the war. Wilson's legislative accomplishments were extraordinary. They included creation of the Federal Reserve System, the Department of Labor, and the Federal Trade Commission; major tariff reform; and the Clayton Anti-Trust Act. Progressive social legislation included the 1915 LaFollette Seaman's Act, which ended dreadful and unsafe working conditions; the first workmen's compensation law; a ban on children working in coal mines; and the 1916 Adamson Act establishing the eight-hour workday in the railroad industry.[3]

Wilson's record on civil liberties, however, is among the worst of all modern presidents. In addition to wartime violations of free speech and press, which included the notorious postwar Palmer Raids in 1919–20, he instituted racial segregation among federal employees and opposed women's suffrage until political expediency forced him to switch and support it. The appointment of Louis Brandeis to the Supreme Court is his lone contribution to the protection of individual rights.

The crisis of Wilson's suppression of civil liberties during World War I was a watershed in American history, transforming the issue of individual rights into a permanent controversy in American law and politics. Previous civil liberties crises – the 1798 Alien and Sedition Acts, the suppression of antislavery speech prior to the Civil War, Lincoln's suspension of habeas corpus during that war – had been temporary affairs that soon disappeared. The World War I crisis, by contrast, launched the modern civil liberties era. As the First Amendment scholar Zechariah Chafee put it in 1920, "Never in the history of our country, since the Alien and Sedition Acts of 1798, has the meaning of free speech been the subject of such sharp controversy as today."[4] The controversy continued after the war, and the debate over the scope of the First Amendment and the entire Bill of Rights remains a central part of American law and politics. For this reason, Wilson's presidency is the proper starting point for examining presidents and civil liberties.

WAR AND REPRESSION BEGIN, 1917

Just three months into the war, Max Eastman, Amos Pinchot, and John Reed of the Civil Liberties Bureau wrote to President Wilson to protest the Post Office ban on antiwar publications, including the radical magazine *Masses*. Congress had declared war on April 6, and already the administration was cracking down on dissent. Wilson asked Postmaster General Albert S. Burleson, one of his closest political advisers, for response to their objections. Burleson disingenuously told him that neither the *Masses* nor any other publications had been "suppressed nor suspended," although conceding that "particular issues of them which were unlawful" had been banned. In fact, he had excluded virtually the entire antiwar press from the mail. Wilson was satisfied with his assurances and did

3 James Lindgren and Steven G. Calabresi, "Rating the Presidents of the United States, 1789–2000: A Survey of Scholars in Political Science, History, and Law," *Constitutional Commentary* 18 (Winter 2001): 583–605. Arthur S. Link, *Woodrow Wilson and the Progressive Era, 1910–1917* (New York: Harper, 1954). Wilson's 1912 campaign views: Woodrow Wilson, *The New Freedom* (Englewood Cliffs, NJ: Prentice-Hall, 1961). James Chace, *1912: Wilson, Roosevelt, Taft and Debs – The Election That Changed the Country* (New York: Simon & Schuster, 2004).

4 Zechariah Chafee, *Freedom of Speech* (New York: Harcourt, Brace, and Howe, 1920), p. 1. Geoffrey Stone, *Perilous Times: Free Speech in Wartime* (New York: W. W. Norton, 2004). Samuel Walker, *In Defense of American Liberties* (New York: Oxford University Press, 1990). See also Paul Murphy, *World War I and the Origin of Civil Liberties in the United States* (New York: W. W. Norton, 1979).

not inquire further. Over the next three years, he consistently approved the violations of civil liberties in the name of the war effort.[5]

Such repression should have been no surprise to anyone who listened closely to Wilson's war message to Congress the night of April 2, 1917. Thousands lined the streets that rainy night, including antiwar pickets and suffragists outside the Capitol, as he spoke. Alice Paul and her militant women's suffrage allies carried banners asking, "How long must American women wait for liberty?" Inside, Wilson had a fit of nervous trembling before stepping out to speak. The war called forth all the righteous, crusading zeal for which he is famous. He inspired millions of Americans that night by declaring that "the world must be made safe for democracy." Such a noble crusade, he cautioned, was also filled with great risks, and "It is a fearful thing to lead this great peaceful people into war." Then, he candidly warned that "if there should be disloyalty, it will be dealt with a firm hand of stern repression." Few people that night realized how savage that repression would be.[6]

Once war began, Wilson wasted not a minute cracking down on dissent. The day after Congress declared war, he issued a secret executive order authorizing federal agencies to "forthwith remove any employee" whose "conduct, sympathies or utterances" were "inimical to the public welfare." Little known today, his order was the first loyalty test for government employees in American history, anticipating by thirty years President Harry Truman's well-known Federal Loyalty Program during the cold war.[7]

Wartime hysteria began even before Congress declared war. The day before Wilson addressed Congress, a Baltimore mob led by prominent businessmen and Johns Hopkins University faculty disrupted an antiwar meeting at the Academy of Music. In Philadelphia that night, the police chief banned a meeting of the Emergency Peace Federation, "as a precaution against disorder." Four days later, sailors and civilians in the city attacked antiwar protesters at a military recruiting rally, beating one protester unconscious. Police then arrested him and not his attackers. The next day, the University of Pennsylvania told the pacifist economics professor Simon N. Patten that his contract would not be renewed.[8]

Wilson and Congress quickly began creating the machinery for the war effort. On April 13, he issued an executive order creating the Committee on Public Information (CPI) as an official propaganda agency to sell the war to the American people. Led by the crusading progressive reformer and journalist George Creel, the CPI issued a flood of material, including pamphlets with inflammatory titles such as *The Beast of Berlin*

[5] Eastman, Pinchot, Reed to Wilson, July 12, 1917, in Arthur S. Link, ed., *Papers of Woodrow Wilson* [hereinafter cited as Link, *PWW*] (Princeton, NJ: Princeton University Press, 1966–94), 43, p. 165. Burleson, letter to Wilson, July 16, 1917, ibid., pp. 187–8.

[6] Wilson, Address to a Joint Session of Congress, April 2, 1917, APP. "Picket White House Again," *NYT*, April 3, 1917. In an often quoted statement, Wilson allegedly told the *New York World* editor Frank Cobb on the night of his message to Congress, "Once lead this people into war, and they'll forget there ever was such a thing as tolerance ... and the spirit of ruthless brutality will enter into every fibre of our national life." Some historians argue that Cobb invented the quote years later: Jerold S. Auerbach, "Woodrow Wilson's 'Prediction' to Frank Cobb: Words Historians Should Doubt Ever Got Spoken," *Journal of American History*, 54, no. 3 (1967): 608–17.

[7] Executive Order 2587-A, April 7, 1917, *PWW*, 41, pp. 546–8.

[8] "Riot at Baltimore Ends Peace Meeting," *NYT*, April 2, 1917. Bill Lynskey, "Reinventing the First Amendment in Wartime Philadelphia," *Pennsylvania Magazine of History and Biography* 131 (1): 33–80. Online at www.historycooperative.org/journals/pmh/131/lynskey.html. "Ousts Pacifist Professor," *NYT*, April 7, 1917.

and *The Claw of the Hun*. To mobilize ordinary citizens, it organized seventy-five thousand "Four Minute Men," who delivered an estimated 750,000 short speeches promoting the war in community settings. The CPI effort whipped up popular hysteria against all things German, dissenters, and alleged "slackers," young men suspected of evading military service. As Creel explained in his memoirs, "It was the fight for the minds of men." Indeed it was. A "conscription of thought" enforcing conformity of opinion paralleled drafting men into military service. Signing the Selective Service bill into law, Wilson said, "It is not an army that we must shape and train for war, it is a nation." Norman Thomas, a leading pacifist opponent of the war (and later Socialist Party leader and presidential candidate) worried, "It will take hard work to defend free thought and speech" in this political climate.[9]

The military draft was the first comprehensive conscription in American history. Young men could not buy their way out of military service, as they did during the Civil War, and 2.8 million men were eventually drafted. The day the draft became law in mid-May, the famous anarchist Emma Goldman addressed ten thousand people at her No Conscription League meeting in New York City:. "You cannot have democracy and have compulsory military training," she charged, arguing that the draft violated the Thirteenth Amendment ban on slavery. Police agents mingled with the crowd, and a month later she was arrested for conspiracy to obstruct the draft. Nineteen months later, at dawn on December 21, 1919, the government placed her and 248 other radicals on the aging ship *Buford* (the "Red Ark") and deported them to the Soviet Union.[10]

Two civil liberties crises: The draft and the Espionage Act

The rights of conscientious objectors (CO) under the draft joined freedom of speech as the first great civil liberties crises of the war. Only members of a "well-recognized" religious group whose creed "forbade its members to participate in war in any form" were eligible for CO status. They were nonetheless required to serve in noncombat military units. Many people were outraged that the law excluded both members of the major religious denominations and young men who on religious grounds objected to any cooperation with the military. Many religious leaders who supported the war felt the law violated freedom of conscience, which they regarded as part of America's great heritage of religious liberty. In response to these concerns, the American Union against Militarism (AUAM), which had led the fight against American entry into the war, created a Civil Liberties Bureau to assist young men seeking advice about CO status. Organized and led by Crystal Eastman and Roger Baldwin, the bureau marked the beginning of a permanent fight for civil liberties in America, and in 1920 it became the American Civil Liberties Union.[11]

[9] Executive Order 2594 – Creating Committee on Public Information, April 13, 1917, APP. George Creel, *How We Advertised America* (1920, reprint, New York: Arno Press, 1969). "Creel to Direct Nation's Publicity," *NYT*, April 15, 1917. Proclamation – Conscription, May 18, 1917, APP. "Plans for National Army," *NYT*, May 19, 1917. Norman Thomas, Letter to Membership of Fellowship of Reconciliation, April 23, 1917, John Nevin Sayre Papers, Series E, Box 1, SPC.

[10] Goldman's speeches: http://sunsite.berkeley.edu/Goldman/. "We Don't Believe in Conscription," Harlem River Casino, New York City, May 18, 1917. Transcribed by police officer. Alice Wexler, *Emma Goldman in America* (Boston: Beacon Press, 1984), Ch. 14.

[11] Pacifist materials: Edward W. Evans Papers, Box 2, SPC. Birth of ACLU: Walker, *In Defense of American Liberties*, pp. 30–47.

Many young men who were denied CO status and then convicted of violating the law were brutalized in federal military camps: beaten, pricked with bayonets, made to stand at attention for hours, confined to unheated cells, yanked around with ropes around their necks, threatened with summary execution, and subjected to the "water Cure" that a later generation called water boarding. When the Civil Liberties Bureau protested, the War Department directed its inspector general to investigate, and the report confirmed many of the allegations.[12]

Faced with widespread antiwar protests, Congress on June 15 passed the Espionage Act, which quickly became a potent weapon of repression. Section 3 of the law made it illegal to cause "insubordination, disloyalty, mutiny, [or] refusal of duty" in the armed forces, or to "obstruct" recruitment or enlistment. Violators faced up to twenty years in prison. Critics argued that the terms "causing" and "disloyalty" could cover mere opposition to the war, and events quickly confirmed their fears. The government eventually convicted an estimated 1,956 people under the Espionage Act and the 1918 Sedition Act, but this number does not include state prosecutions.[13]

The Espionage Act also banned from the mail any material violating the law, and Postmaster General Burleson immediately used this and other established Post Office powers to suppress virtually the entire antiwar press. Demands for censorship had arisen a year earlier, with President Wilson's full support. Attorney General Thomas Gregory proposed a bill in 1916 allowing the government to censor the news, and offered a new bill appeared immediately after war was declared. It provoked a storm of opposition from the news media, congressional Republicans, and opponents of the war. One section criminalized attempting to obtain information about military matters. The *New York Times* denounced the bill as "an insidious assault upon the very foundations which underlie our free institutions -freedom of thought and freedom of speech." Republicans feared giving broad censorship power to a Democratic president, while antiwar activists argued that the prohibition on causing "disaffection" among military personnel could cover any opposition to the war. Characteristically self-righteous about his motives, a defensive President Wilson tried to assure critics he would never use the law as "a shield against criticism" of his administration. "I can imagine no greater disservice to the country," he wrote, "than to establish a system of censorship that would deny to the people of a free republic like our own their indisputable right to criticize their own public officials."[14] During the war, however, his administration disregarded these principles. The 1917 censorship bill did not pass, but the terms of the Espionage and Sedition Acts proved more than adequate. The Republican leaders and news media who had criticized the bill fell silent in the heat of the war effort.

Arguably, the most celebrated victim of the Espionage Act was the Socialist Party leader Eugene V. Debs, convicted and sentenced to ten years in prison for a June 16, 1918,

[12] National Civil Liberties Bureau, *Political Prisoners in Federal Military Prisons* (New York: NCLB, November 1918), ACLUP (1977) MF Ed., Reel 90. Norman Thomas, *Is Conscience a Crime?* (New York: Vanguard Press, 1927), "Brutalities," pp. 143–64.

[13] Chafee, *Freedom of Speech*, p. 387.

[14] Stone, *Perilous Times*, pp. 146–53. Harry N. Scheiber, *The Wilson Administration and Civil Liberties, 1917–1921* (Ithaca, NY: Cornell University Press, 1960), pp. 12, 20–41. "Senators See Peril in Espionage Bill," *NYT*, April 15, 1917. "Undermining Democracy," ibid., April 20, 1917. Seward Livermore, *Politics Is Adjourned: Woodrow Wilson and the War Congress, 1916–1918* (Middletown, CT: Wesleyan University Press, 1966). Wilson, letter to Arthur Brisbane, April 25, 1917, *PWW*, 42, p. 129.

speech in Canton, Ohio. The case dramatized how broadly the government interpreted the Espionage Act to punish dissent. Speaking to more than a thousand people at an Ohio Socialist Party picnic, Debs began by saying he would have to be "exceedingly careful, prudent, about what I say," and he studiously did not criticize either the war, the draft, or the Wilson administration, giving only a generic socialist critique of war as a symptom of capitalism. Justice Department officials in Washington felt there was no case against Debs, but the local U.S. attorney prosecuted him anyway. The historian David Shannon observed dryly that in the fevered atmosphere of the times, "there was no such thing as a poor case against a Socialist."[15]

The September 17 Trading with the Enemy Act, meanwhile, made it illegal to publish "in any foreign language" anything regarding the conduct of the war unless the Post Office had approved an English translation. The law became a powerful tool for silencing the large foreign-language press, which was an important center of opposition to the war. The May 1918 Sedition Act was potentially the heaviest weapon against dissent. Closely resembling the notorious 1798 Sedition Act, the law made it a crime to speak or write "any disloyal, profane, scurrilous, or abusive language" about the government, the Constitution, or the military. These elastic terms could cover any critical comment about the war. In truth, the Sedition Act was hardly necessary, given the reach of the Espionage Act. Mere passage of the Sedition Act, however, further inflamed the already overheated public. Even John Lord O'Brian, special assistant for war matters in the Justice Department, worried that it "fanned animosities into flame, vastly increasing the amount of suspicion and complaints throughout the country."[16]

Burleson, the Post Office, and the scope of freedom of the press

The day Congress declared war, President Wilson and his cabinet discussed the question of press censorship. Postmaster General Burleson proposed a sweeping policy of "excluding papers from the mail, papers that criticized [the war effort]." Secretary of State Robert Lansing argued for allowing no papers to be printed in German, while Secretary of War Newton Baker would "only exclude publication of military news that would aid the enemy." Wilson advised caution and "spoke strongly against action that was more than moderate," although without explaining what that meant.[17] Burleson became the key player in the government's policy of repression. While Justice Department prosecutions attacked prominent leaders such as Debs, Post Office censorship made it impossible for organizations to communicate with their members. Burleson, moreover, hardly needed the Espionage Act because the 1879 Classification Act gave him unfettered

15 Ernest Freeberg, *Democracy's Prisoner: Eugene V. Debs, the Great War, and the Right to Dissent* (Cambridge, MA: Harvard University Press, 2008), pp. 67–82. *Debs v. United States*, 249 U.S. 211 (1919). David A. Shannon, *The Socialist Party of America: A History* (Chicago: Quadrangle Books, 1967), p. 115.

16 Trading with the Enemy Act, Oct. 6, 1917, 40 Stat. 411, Ch. 106. For a sympathetic postwar analysis of the government's use of the law: William Bernard, ed., *Americanization Studies* [1920–4], V. 7, Robert Park, *The Immigrant Press and Its Control* (New York: Arno Press, 1971), pp. 412–47. Sedition Act: Stone, *Perilous Times*, pp. 184–92. Debs was technically indicted under the amended Espionage Act that included the new Sedition Act. The appeal to the Supreme Court, however, involved two counts related to the original Espionage Act. John Lord O'Brian, "Civil Liberty in War Time," U.S. Senate, 65th Cong, 3rd Sess., Doc No. 434, p. 18.

17 E. David Cronon, ed., *The Cabinet Diaries of Josephus Daniels* (Lincoln: University of Nebraska Press, 1963), p. 130. "Socialist Paper Barred," *NYT*, July 7, 1917.

discretion over second-class mailing privileges (which were necessary for the survival of any publication).

In June 1917, postal officials began revoking the permits of socialist, antiwar, and foreign-language publications. They included the *American Socialist*, the most important antiwar publication, and the *Masses*, the *Milwaukee Leader*, Emma Goldman's *Mother Earth*, *Arbeiter Zeitung*, *Novy Mir*, *Il Proletario*, and Civil Liberties Bureau publications. Victor Berger, editor of the *Milwaukee Leader*, later indicted under the Espionage Act and barred from his seat in Congress, wrote to Burleson asking for a meeting, pleading that "After all – Woodrow Wilson, you and I are all striving for the same goal: the greatest good for the greatest mass in our country." Burleson told him a meeting was "impossible." Prowar zealots in the Post Office went even further and refused to deliver first-class mail to the *Leader*'s office, forcing the paper's staff to have mail sent to their homes. The once-strong Socialist Party never recovered from the wartime assault and was reduced to a fringe party.[18]

Burleson was quite candid about his view of permissible speech in wartime. He informed the publisher of the *New York World*, "Nothing will be excluded from the mails because of being politically or personally offensive to the administration," but then adding that no criticism of the government during wartime would be tolerated. The "limit is reached," he explained, when a newspaper says the country "got into war wrong, that it is there for a wrong purpose, or anything else that impugns the motives of the Government, thereby encouraging insubordination." And especially, "newspapers cannot say that this Government is the tool of Wall Street, or of the munitions makers, or of anybody." A Boston attorney representing several newspapers sarcastically complained to President Wilson that it is "like telling a child that he may go swimming but must not go near the water." Burleson holds the dubious distinction of being the worst member of the entire Wilson administration on civil liberties. In addition to censoring the mails, he initiated the 1913 campaign to impose racial segregation among federal employees. Enjoying special status as one of Wilson's closest political confidants, he was consulted on a wide variety of issues and counted likely votes on key issues in the Senate for the president. Wilson always deferred to him, writing in November 1917, for example, that "you know that I am willing to trust your judgment."[19]

Hostility to war critics, it should be noted, was a bipartisan affair. The former president Theodore Roosevelt in May 1918 denounced opposition to the draft or sending troops to Europe as a form of "moral sedition." The Wilson administration, he complained, had been too lenient "in dealing with such acts." He also "heartily" approved of dismissing "all teachers who refuse to sign the loyalty pledge or who in any way have shown the slightest

18 Third Assistant Post Master General, Memorandum, May 8, 1918, Burleson Papers, Container 20, LOC. Berger to Burleson, July 12, 1917; Burleson to Berger, July 19, 1917, Burleson Papers, Container 19, LOC. Shannon, *Socialist Party of America*, p. 110. The law on the power of the postmaster general prior to the war: David Rabban, *The First Amendment in Its Forgotten Years* (New York: Cambridge University Press, 1997), pp. 149–52.

19 Burleson to Editor and Publisher, World Building, October 3, 1917; Grenville S. MacFarland to Wilson, October 12, 1917, Burleson Papers, Container 19, LOC. Scheiber, *Wilson Administration and Civil Liberties*, p. 31. *U.S. Ex Rel. Milwaukee Social Democratic Pub. Co. v. Burleson*, 255 U.S. 407 (1921). Sally Miller, *Victor Berger and the Promise of Constructive Socialism, 1910–1920* (Westport, CT: Greenwood Press, 1973), Ch. 9, "The Crucifixion of Berger," pp. 191–26. Wilson to Burleson, September 4, 1917, Burleson Papers, Container 19, LOC. The Burleson Papers have many examples of Wilson's relying on him for political advice. Scheiber, *Wilson Administration and Civil Liberties*, p. 39.

symptoms of disloyalty to this nation."[20] Republican leaders in Congress who had vigorously denounced censorship before the war did not challenge the suppression of dissent once the war began.

Government-sponsored vigilantism

An epidemic of vigilante violence by private citizens reinforced government actions in bludgeoning the American people into silence. Mobs in Baltimore and Philadelphia attacked war critics as soon as Congress declared war, and on July 2 a Boston mob that included soldiers and sailors attacked a Socialist Party peace parade. Similar acts occurred all across the country. The purge of German cultural items became the stuff of American folklore: sauerkraut became "liberty cabbage," symphony orchestras dropped Beethoven and other German composers, and German language courses almost disappeared from the schools. Arguably the largest vigilante action involved the forced deportation of 1,185 men from the copper mining town of Bisbee, Arizona, on July 12, 1917, after miners, supported by the radical Industrial Workers of the World (IWW) went out on strike. The mining companies had about two thousand volunteers in the Citizens Defense League deputized by the sheriff, and on July 12 they rounded up strikers and many others, herded them onto railroad cars, and dumped them in New Mexico. The Bisbee deportations caused such outrage that President Wilson created the Federal Mediation Commission to investigate. No action against the mining companies resulted, however. The IWW became a special target of government prosecution, and it was destroyed during the war. The Civil Liberties Bureau protested the denial of First Amendment and due process rights of the IWW and other radical unions, but to no avail.[21]

The Justice Department, with President Wilson's approval, actually sponsored vigilantism through the American Protective League (APL). Wilson tacitly endorsed the brainchild of the Chicago advertising executive Albert M. Briggs at a March 30 cabinet meeting, a week before Congress declared war. The APL eventually had six hundred local chapters, with between 100,000 and 250,000 volunteers carrying official badges that read, "Secret Service, U.S." In summer 1917, APL volunteers swept through city streets rounding up alleged "slackers" (young men suspected of evading the draft), guided only by their own prejudices. A. Bruce Bielaski, head of the Bureau of Investigation, ordered a nationwide crackdown on July 3d, and APL volunteers seized about six thousand young men. The APL's official historian, Emerson Hough, boasted that they conducted illegal entries of houses "thousands of times."

President Wilson and some cabinet members expressed reservations about the legality of government-sanctioned amateurs' enforcing the law. Treasury Secretary William Gibbs McAdoo (Wilson's son-in-law) told the president the "scheme" was "fraught with the gravest danger." Two days later Wilson himself wrote to Attorney General Gregory that it would be "very dangerous to have such an organization operating in

20 Roosevelt to Senator Miles Poindexter, May 22, 1918, in Elting E. Morison et al., eds., *The Letters of Theodore Roosevelt*, V. 8 (Cambridge, MA: Harvard University Press, 1954), pp. 1320–1.

21 Vigilante violence: Shannon, *The Socialist Party of America*. National Civil Liberties Bureau, *War-Time Prosecutions and Mob Violence* (July 1918); National Civil Liberties Bureau, *The Truth about the I.W.W.* (1918), ACLUP-MF, [1977] Reel 90. Melvyn Dubofsky, *We Shall Be All: A History of the Industrial Workers of the World* (Urbana: University of Illinois Press, 1988). Bisbee deportations materials: www.library.arizona.edu/exhibits/bisbee/history/overview.html.

the United States." Curiously and rather pathetically, he asked Gregory whether there was some way it could be stopped, apparently not understanding that as president he could just order it ended. Gregory declared the APL "patriotic" and very "useful" to the understaffed Justice Department. Wilson dropped the matter, again deferring to the judgment of a cabinet official over a major matter of policy, in this case over his own doubts.[22]

The worst APL abuses occurred in the massive "slacker raids" in the summer of 1918. In Chicago, ten thousand APL agents stopped nearly 150,000 people over a period of three days, arresting sixteen thousand men, only twelve hundred of whom proved to be genuine draft evaders. APL agents in New York City rounded up twenty thousand men on September 3 alone. The *Nation* magazine proclaimed "Civil Liberty Dead" in its next issue. The roundups provoked the first significant expressions of outrage among prominent officials. Senators Hiram Johnson of California and George Chamberlain of Oregon denounced the raids, and other senators called for an investigation. President Wilson, in one of the rare instances when he questioned a cabinet member over a civil liberties matter, asked Attorney General Gregory for a "full report." The Justice Department backed off, and on September 19, 1918, Bielaski informed APL volunteers they did not have arrest power. This step was too little and too late, however. The damage was already done, and the war ended two months later.[23]

To put the events in the United States in perspective, it is important to note that a similar civil liberties crisis occurred in England in the two and a half years before the United States entered the war. In an insightful account, *To End All Wars*, Adam Hochschild describes a massive outburst of prowar fever, even among the working class; a vast government propaganda effort to maintain public support and crush dissent, vigilante attacks against opponents of the war, government spying on dissenters, the jailing of conscientious objectors, and public protests against that action. It remains for some future historian to examine in more detail the drive for political conformity in the two countries.[24]

WILSON'S ROLE IN THE REPRESSION

"Would you be kind enough to have the enclosed carefully examined?" President Wilson asked Attorney General Thomas Gregory about an August 10, 1917, memo from the Civil Liberties Bureau alleging massive violations of constitutional rights. The memo cited many incidents, including the cases of thirteen people in Philadelphia charged with treason for circulating a pamphlet entitled *Long Live the Constitution of the United States*, a postal employee in St. Paul fired for simply posting bond for three friends arrested for not registering for the draft, and a Chicago meeting of conscientious objectors broken up by federal agents. Wilson noted that the memo was signed by "people whom I personally

[22] Wilson to Gregory, June 4, 1917, 42, *PWW*, p. 446. McAdoo's criticisms: McAdoo to Wilson, June 2, 1917, ibid., p. 440; McAdoo to Gregory, June 2, 1917, ibid., pp. 441–3. Gregory's defense of the APL proposal: Gregory to Wilson, June 14, 1917, ibid., pp. 509–10; Gregory to McAdoo, June 12, 1917, ibid., pp. 510–18.

[23] "Seize 20,000 Here in Slacker Search," *NYT*, September 4, 1918. "Civil Liberty Dead," *The Nation*, September 14, 1918, p. 382. Jensen, *The Price of Vigilance*, pp. 195–6, 215. "Draft Raids Here Anger Senators," *NYT*, September 6, 1918.

[24] Adam Hochschild, *To End All Wars: A Story of Loyalty and Rebellion, 1914–1918* (Boston: Houghton Mifflin Harcourt, 2011).

esteem, but I am not always sure that they know what they are talking about."[25] As he did in almost every other instance, Wilson deferred to his cabinet member, accepting his explanation that there was no real problem without further inquiry. In virtually all biographies and accounts of the war years, historians have glossed over Wilson's personal responsibility for the repression, as if he was somehow insulated from the events. Nothing could be further from the truth. Wilson received and read mail about the violations of civil liberties, much of it from people he knew or knew of, and he consistently refused to stop the abuses. Nor did he provide his cabinet members with specific guidelines for protecting legitimate dissent. And as we shall see, the suppression of civil liberties was no wartime aberration but was fully consistent with his vision of progressive reform.

One of the striking aspects of the protests reaching Wilson was the extraordinary access to him enjoyed by Crystal Eastman and other civil libertarians. Before the United States entered the war, Eastman personally lobbied Wilson to keep America out of the European conflict, leading an AUAM group that met with him in the White House on May 8, 1916. The *New York Times* characterized it as a "running conversation" over American preparations for war. The civil libertarians also knew key figures in the administration, notably Secretary of War Newton D. Baker, the former progressive reform mayor of Cleveland, Ohio, and Assistant Secretary of War Frederick Keppel, a dean at Columbia University. These previous relationships convinced Eastman, Baldwin, and others that Wilson and members of his administration would give them a sympathetic hearing. As fellow progressive reformers, they knew of each other's work and had at times collaborated in prewar campaigns to transform America. After the country entered the war, however, the White House door eventually slammed shut. Joseph Tumulty, the president's chief aide, told Amos Pinchot of the Civil Liberties Bureau in July 1917 that a meeting would be "literally impossible."[26]

In response to another protest from the Civil Liberties Bureau, Wilson asked Solicitor General John W. Davis for his assessment. (Almost four decades later, Davis argued the segregationist case before the Supreme Court in *Brown v. Board of Education.*) Davis dismissed the charges of illegal government actions as "unfounded" and "untrue," with the possible exception of a "few isolated instances of excess of zeal" by some officials. As always, that assurance from a top official was enough for Wilson. Some administration insiders cautioned him about the excesses of suppression. Walter Lippmann, who would become the nation's preeminent political columnist after the war, told Wilson in October 1917, "I have no doctrinaire belief in free speech," and "in the interest of the war it is necessary to sacrifice some of it." Nonetheless, he worried that the administration's current "method" was "breaking down liberal support of the war" and counseled restraint in censorship, although mainly on the grounds that opponents of the war posed no real threat. Wilson ignored his advice.[27]

On just a few occasions Wilson did express concern that censorship might be going too far. He worried about a Post Office action against the *Milwaukee Leader* and

25 Wald, Eastman, Baldwin, and Wood to Wilson, August 10, 1917, *PWW*, 43, pp. 420–4; Wilson to Gregory, August 17, 1917, ibid., pp. 420, 503.

26 "President on Defenses," *NYT*, May 9, 1916. Pinchot letter to Tumulty, July 14, 1917; The President to Tumulty, July 14, 1917, *PWW*, 43, pp. 175–6. See also Baldwin, letter to Keppel, March 13, 1918; Baldwin, letter to Keppel, August 3, 1918, ACLUP (1996), MF ED, Reel 2.

27 John William Davis to Mr. President, September 13, 1917, *PWW*, 44, pp. 192–4. Lippmann to Colonel House, October 17, 1917, *PWW*, 44, pp. 393–4.

told Burleson in October 1917 that he did not find the government's position "very convincing." While some items "probably cross the line," he explained, "I must frankly say that I do not think that most of what is quoted ought to be regarded as unmailable ... [and] doubt ought always to be resolved in favor of the utmost freedom of speech." Such sentiments were rare, however, and in any event he never acted on them. More typical of his attitude was his suggestion to Attorney General Gregory a month earlier that a treason prosecution against an obscure antiwar publication would "probably scotch a great many snakes."[28]

The only instance when Wilson overruled Burleson involved the pacifist magazine *The World Tomorrow,* on which Wilson quickly had a Post Office ban lifted. A close family connection undoubtedly explains this exception to his normal hands-off policy. One of the magazine's top officials was John Nevin Sayre, brother of Wilson's son-in-law Francis B. Sayre. When the Post Office declared the September 1918 issue of *The World Tomorrow* unmailable, Nevin Sayre and Norman Thomas met with the postmaster general on September 13, and that evening, Sayre "managed to have a long talk about it with President Wilson in the White House. I gave him the offending copy." At a cabinet meeting the next day Wilson "brought the matter up" and overruled his postmaster general. The Post Office banned two subsequent issues, but Sayre recalled that "each time we managed to get free."[29]

Wilson opposed repressive legislation only once, speaking out against a 1918 proposal to try spies and "disloyalists" by courts-martial. In a public letter he declared it unnecessary and unconstitutional, and the proposal was immediately withdrawn. Courts-martial for ordinary citizens apparently violated his view of American legal procedures, although prosecuting dissenters in regular criminal courts was fully consistent with his understanding of the First Amendment.[30]

Wilson rebuffed requests by civil libertarians that he speak out against repressive actions. When the AUAM asked him in August 1917 to condemn the ban on the *Masses,* he replied, "You will understand, I am sure," that a such public statement "would undoubtedly be taken advantage of by those with whom neither you nor I have been in sympathy at all." A year later they asked for a statement against "these invasions of established rights," assuring him, "We are not pleading for those who desire to obstruct the war or embarrass the government," but only for "those whose minds and hearts like yours long for a world order in which all peoples may be really free." Wilson declined to issue a public statement. Mob violence actually encouraged administration officials to call for more repressive legislation. Attorney General Gregory supported the 1918 Sedition Act because he felt vigilantism arose from public perceptions that the government had failed to suppress traitors. Stronger government action, he believed, would convince citizens they need not take the law into their own hands. The *New York Times* agreed and endorsed the sedition law.[31]

28 Wilson to Burleson, October 18, 1917, *PWW,* 44, pp. 396–7. Wilson to Gregory, September 25, 1917, ibid., p. 247.

29 John Nevin Sayre, "Supplemental Notes" [circa 1960s], handwritten date estimate, regarding the Fellowship of Reconciliation, 1917–19; John Nevin Sayre, "Twenty Years of the Fellowship of Reconciliation," *Fellowship* 1, no. 5 (September 1935): 6, copy in JNSP, Series E, Box 1, SPC. Scheiber, *Wilson Administration and Civil Liberties,* p. 37.

30 Wilson to [Senator] Overman, April 20, 1918, *PWW,* 47, pp. 381–2. "Wilson Opposes New Spy Bill," *NYT,* April 23, 1918.

31 Lillian Wald and others to Mr. President, August 10, 1917, *PWW,* 43, pp. 420–4. Wilson, letter to Amos Pinchot, July 13, 1917, ibid., p. 164. Thomas Gregory, "Suggestions of Attorney General Gregory to Executive

Apart from a brief comment in a November 1917 speech Wilson did not speak out on mob violence until the summer of 1918, when he finally issued a written statement condemning racist mob violence. On July 26, he declared "There have been many lynchings, and every one of them has been a blow to the heart of ordered law and humane justice." Mob violence only "contributes to German lies about the United States," and he "very earnestly and solemnly" called on local officials to end "this disgraceful evil."[32] The statement was late and did not involve a public speech that would have given it more force. Wilson's reputation in history rests in great part on capacity for memorable phrase making, most famously his 1917 call to make the world safe for democracy. An eloquent denunciation of domestic lawlessness might have curbed vigilantism, but he remained silent.

THE MIND OF THE PROGRESSIVE REFORMER

The question demands a definitive answer: How could Woodrow Wilson, one of the great reformers in modern American history and a scholar of American constitutional democracy, countenance the suppression of free speech and other violations of civil liberties? The answer lies in several practical, personal, and ideological factors.

As a practical matter, Wilson was immediately overwhelmed by the crushing demands of mobilizing the country for war. In May, only one month into the war, he complained, "My days are so full now as to come near to driving me to distraction." The federal government was very small in those years, and virtually every matter came to his desk. At the outset of the war there was no machinery for raising an army and mobilizing the economy for a foreign war. The economy almost broke down under the strain. The novelist John Dos Passos recalled winter 1917: "As Christmas approached, news came to Washington daily of plants shutting down for lack of fuel, of finished goods essential to the war effort jammed into warehouses or deteriorating on open docks, of ships tied up in frozen harbors." Congress, moreover, steadily granted Wilson greater executive authority, in what one historian has called "one of the most sweeping grants of power in American history." The many emergency war measures, which ended after the war, were a prevue of the vast and permanent expansion of the role of the federal government that would begin in the 1930s.[33] In the context of this emergency, with his dreams of remaking the world at stake, an overwhelmed Wilson saw civil liberties protests as minor and illegitimate nuisances.

Wilson also had a character flaw that hurt him in other important moments in his career. The Wilson scholar Arthur Link found a "temperamental inability to cooperate with men who were not willing to follow his lead completely," compounded by a habit of "making his political opponents also his personal enemies." These traits exacerbated conflicts when he was president of Princeton University and governor of New

Committee in Relation to the Department of Justice," *American Bar Association Journal* 4 (1918): 305–16. "The Sedition Bill," *NYT*, April 10, 1918. Stone, *Perilous Times*, pp. 184–91.

32 Wilson, An Address in Buffalo to the American Federation of Labor, November 12, 1917, *PWW*, 45, p. 16. "President Deplores Mob Spirit in War," *NYT*, July 23, 1918. Woodrow Wilson, "A Statement to the American People," July 26, 1918, PWW, 49, pp. 97–8. NCLB, *The President on Mob Violence* (July 26, 1918), ACLUP-MF (1977), Reel 90.

33 Ronald Schaffer, *America in the Great War: The Rise of the War Welfare State* (New York: Oxford, 1991), p. 35. Wilson distracted: *PWW*, 42, p. 292. John Dos Passos, *Mr. Wilson's War* (Garden City, NY: Doubleday, 1962), p. 97. Peter Zavondnyik, *The Rise of the Federal Colossus: The Growth of Federal Power from Lincoln to F.D.R.* (Santa Barbara: Praeger, 2011), pp. 331–55.

Jersey, and most famously in his failure to win Senate ratification of the Versailles Treaty after the war.[34]

Most important, however, Wilson's vision of progressive reform did not include tolerance of dissent. Historians have largely treated the wartime repression as an aberration, but in fact it was fully consistent with his earlier ideas, particularly as he moved into the political arena after 1900. Wilson left an extensive record of his thinking, in voluminous personal correspondence and acclaimed academic writings, his actions as president of Princeton University (1902–10) and governor of New Jersey (1910–12), and finally in four and a half years as president before the war. They clearly reveal that he never thought about the hard questions of civil liberties.[35] It is not that he rejected modern concepts of freedom of speech or due process – he simply did not think about them at all. His 1908 book *Constitutional Government in the United States* does not mention political and civil rights, concentrating on the formal structure of American government. The only mention of the Bill of Rights, in fact, refers to the 1689 English document. Nor did he discuss civil liberties in his earlier best seller, *Congressional Government*, the book that established his professional reputation, or in *The New Freedom*, a full statement of his views for the 1912 presidential election campaign.[36] In this respect, Wilson was typical of the leading progressive reformers of his day. As we shall see, two progressive reformers who later became pioneers in the field of civil liberties, the ACLU founder Roger Baldwin and the Supreme Court justice Louis Brandeis, also did not think about civil liberties in their prewar careers. An examination of Wilson's prewar views on democracy and progressive reform illuminates not just his actions as president but progressivism itself.

Wilson on national unity, democracy, and liberty

"What is liberty?" Wilson asked in the 1912 presidential election campaign. Answering his own question, he portrayed American society as "a great piece of powerful machinery," an "engine," "a locomotive." The challenge of modern society was to maintain each part in "absolutely perfect alignment and adjustment with the other parts of the machine." Individual liberty meant being an active part of this vast enterprise, playing one's proper role. The machine metaphor is a revealing clue to Wilson's thinking: Despite his soaring rhetoric about democracy and individualism, he saw the individual as subordinate to the broad goals of society. For Wilson, Theodore Roosevelt, and other progressive reformers, the great machine of society had a common national purpose. The rapid growth of

[34] Arthur S. Link, *Wilson, The Road to the White House* (Princeton, NJ: Princeton University Press, 1947), pp. 277–309 (quote, p. 307).

[35] Woodrow Wilson, *Congressional Government: A Study in American Politics* (Boston: Houghton Mifflin, 1885). Wilson never set foot in Congress itself, even though Johns Hopkins University is less than 50 miles away. Mulder, *Years of Preparation*, p. 79. Niels Aage Thorsen, *The Political Thought of Woodrow Wilson, 1875–1910* (Princeton, NJ: Princeton University Press, 1988), p. 288. The historian John Morton Blum regards Wilson's scholarship as "often shallow or derivative." Blum, *Woodrow Wilson*, p. 19. Wilson as governor of New Jersey: Arthur S. Link, *Woodrow Wilson: The Road to the White House* (Princeton, NJ: Princeton University Press, 1947).

[36] Woodrow Wilson, *Constitutional Government in the United States* (1908, reprint, New York: Columbia University Press, 1961). Wilson, *Congressional Government*, pp. 34–6. Wilson, *New Freedom*. In passing, he did write that "the people must control the judiciary" (ibid., p. 141), suggesting that he would be hostile to the modern practice of judicial review on controversial civil liberties issues. Scholars have also ignored Wilson's disinterest: Stid, *The President as Statesman: Woodrow Wilson and the Constitution* contains almost no mention of freedom of speech and press and other basic civil liberties issues.

industrial capitalism, however, threatened national unity, introducing the threat of class conflict and the specter of foreign ideas such as socialism. A progressive America, they believed, created opportunity for every person and every group, politically and economically. To ensure those opportunities, reformers sought to eliminate political machines that prevented the majority from expressing its will; abolish the "trusts" (the giant corporations such as Standard Oil and U.S. Steel) that blocked economic opportunity for small business enterprise; provide protection for workers, women, and children against the excesses of capitalism; and "Americanize" immigrants.[37]

The advent of war only reinforced Wilson's views about national unity. Announcing the new draft law in May 1917, he declared, "The whole nation must be a team, in which each man shall play the part for which he is best fitted." Military service, moreover, was a new way of "accepting and vitalizing our duty to give ourselves with thoughtful devotion to the common purpose of us all." The draft, in this regard, "is in no sense a conscription of the unwilling; it is, rather, selection from a nation which has volunteered in mass." In fact, there were many people very unwilling to be conscripted, often on the basis of sincere religious belief, and their resistance launched the civil liberties crisis of the war. Majoritarian democracy was the crux of the matter for Wilson. Once the American people had spoken through a congressional declaration of war, he believed, the issue was settled. At that point, Americans had a duty to end debate and close ranks. As Postmaster General Burleson put it in an open letter during the war: Once "the majority has spoken in legal and proper terms, every loyal member of the minority should become one with the majority."[38]

The challenge of immigration

Immigration posed a special challenge to Wilson's vision of a national unity, as it did for other progressives. While many Americans wanted to stop the flood of Eastern and Southern European immigrants, Wilson welcomed them, but only on certain conditions. Most important, immigrants must put aside Old World customs and attachments and become "Americanized." He and others made a clear distinction between deserving and undeserving immigrants. Vetoing a 1915 immigration bill because it included a literacy test, he explained that it was a "radical" departure from America's historic rejection of tests of "quality or character or of personal fitness." People of good character who could not pass a literacy test simply because they had never had educational opportunities should not be excluded.[39]

The war in Europe only heightened his concern about immigration. In his December 1915 message to Congress, he pronounced "hyphenated" Americans (a commonly used term in those years) a dangerous threat to national unity. And in the 1916 presidential

37 Wilson, *New Freedom*, pp. 49, 57. On some occasions, Wilson characterized society as organic rather than mechanistic.

38 "Draft of a Proclamation," *PWW*, 42, pp. 180–2. "A Proclamation Message by the President," *NYT*, May 19, 1917. Third Assistant Postmaster General, Memorandum, May 8, 1918, Burleson Papers, Container 20, LOC. Scheiber, *Wilson Administration and Civil Liberties*, p. 34.

39 Veto Message, January 28, 1915, APP. "Immigration Veto Sent to Congress," *NYT*, January 29, 1915. Wilson and immigration: Hans P. Vought, *The Bully Pulpit and the Melting Pot: American Presidents and the Immigrant, 1897–1933* (Macon, GA: Mercer University Press, 2004), Ch. 4, "Woodrow Wilson and Hyphenated Americans," pp. 94–120.

election campaign, he repeatedly advocated suppressing the "disloyalty" associated with immigrant allegiances to their native lands. The *New York Times* reported his June 14, 1916, Flag Day address with a headline screaming, "Crush Disloyalty Cries the President." Speaking to a crowd of twenty-five thousand at the Washington Monument, he declared that Americans would "repudiate" the threats to "wreak vengeance at the polls," a reference to strong antiwar sentiment among German Americans. He did not specifically mention them by name, but the *Times* reported that "no one within earshot mistook the President's meaning." Wilson made his own threat: "There is disloyalty active in the United States, and it must be crushed." A month later at a July 13 Conference on Americanization he confessed he was "disturbed" by people "born in other lands, [who] have in recent months thought more of those lands than they have of" the United States. Such attitudes, he declared, are "absolutely incompatible with the fundamental idea of loyalty." Wilson took a personal interest in inserting a loyalty plank in the 1916 Democratic Party platform, condemning anyone who seeks to "promote the interest of a foreign power" or arouses "prejudices of a racial, religious or other nature [and] creates discord and strife among our people so as to obstruct the wholesome process of unification." Any such person "is disloyal to his country." (He did not, however, condemn the Ku Klux Klan for its racial and religious prejudice.)[40]

To be fair, other leading Americans shared Wilson's attitudes toward immigration. The former president Theodore Roosevelt, for example, declared, "There is no room in this country for hyphenated Americanism" and called for "a common language" and "an increase in our social loyalty ... which emphatically repudiates all duality of national loyalty." The antiimmigrant feeling of the prewar years closely parallels the attitudes of many Americans in the early twenty-first century. In lending his powerful voice to these prejudices, Wilson as president bears direct personal responsibility for whipping up the patriotic hysteria that swept the country once the United States entered the war.[41]

The prewar views of Louis Brandeis, progressive reformer, adviser to Wilson, and eventually one of the greatest civil libertarians on the Supreme Court, are particularly revealing. In a July 4, 1915, address on "True Americanism" at Boston's historic Faneuil Hall, he asked, "What is Americanization?" Only superficially, he explained, did it involve adopting "the clothes, the manners and the customs" of this country. Learning to speak English was important, but "we properly demand" even more. The immigrant "must be brought into complete harmony with our ideals and aspirations." Wilson shared this coercive view of Americanization, and it followed that in a time of crisis – especially wartime – the nation could legitimately force conformity, including by suppressing dissenting opinions. Brandeis's vision of a conformist Americanism is all the more striking because he was an ardent Zionist who simultaneously urged Jewish immigrants to retain and indeed cherish their religious and cultural heritage.[42]

40 "Hungarians Pledge Loyalty to America," *NYT*, January 31, 1916. "Calls Hyphen a Failure," ibid., February 1, 1916. "Crush Disloyalty Cries the President," *NYT*, June 15, 1916. "President Chides American Boasters," ibid., July 14, 1916. Democratic platform: Scheiber, *Wilson Administration and Civil Liberties*, p. 8. Party platforms are available at APP.

41 Theodore Roosevelt, "Americanism," in *The Works of Theodore Roosevelt: National Edition*, XVIII (New York: Charles Scribner's Sons, 1926), pp. 388–405.

42 Louis Brandeis, "True Americanism," in Philippa Strum, ed., *Brandeis on Democracy* (Lawrence: University Press of Kansas, 1995), pp. 25–30. Vought, *Bully Pulpit*, offers an illuminating discussion of this issue.

Brandeis was also innocent of the difficult civil liberties questions before and during much of the war. His prewar letters contain virtually no discussions of freedom of speech. In one revealing incident during the war, he complained to his wife about an August 1917 dinner at the Cosmos Club in Washington, where he became "inextricably attached" to Oswald Garrison Villard before escaping. He added that he "should like to consign [Villard] to burning oil." Villard was a key spokesperson for both the Civil Liberties Bureau and the National Association for the Advancement of Colored People (NAACP) in dealing with the Wilson administration, and in August 1917 there was certainly nothing else on his mind than the mounting repression of civil liberties and racist mob violence. Brandeis evidently did not want to hear about these issues. He later confessed to Felix Frankfurter that even by the time of the March 1919 *Schenck* decision, in which the Court upheld Charles Schenck's conviction for radical opinions, he had not "thought the issue of freedom of speech out." Once he did, however, he moved quickly toward a strong defense of free speech, joining Justice Oliver Wendell Holmes in a pivotal dissent in the 1919 *Abrams v. United States* decision, arguing that the First Amendment protected unpopular speech.[43]

The vision of a monocultural America that Wilson and other progressives envisioned contrasts sharply with the modern concept of a multicultural America that respects diversity. Multiculturalism in those years was a radical idea, advocated only by a few isolated thinkers such as Horace Kallen and Randolph Bourne. In 1916, Bourne wrote prophetically in the *Atlantic Monthly* that despite all the efforts to mold immigrants into Americans, "the immigrant will have a hand in making" what "American shall be." As we shall see, Bourne also leveled the most scathing attack on the Progressive Era reformers who uncritically supported the war and refused to question the suppression of civil liberties.[44]

"The social possibilities of war"

A particularly disturbing aspect of Wilson's prewar thinking was his enthusiasm for war as a vehicle for promoting national unity. In a revealing but neglected episode years before World War I, he was galvanized by the Spanish-American War. While other Americans hotly debated American imperialism and the nasty war in the Philippines (including controversy over the use of the "water cure" by American soldiers, a practice that under President George W. Bush would later be known as water boarding), Wilson found a noble purpose in the war. The greatness of democracy, he wrote, was in "its tendency to exalt the purposes of the average man to some higher level of endeavor." The "accidental possession of the Philippines" by the United States called for "a singular unity in our national task," creating a "national feeling" that put aside the old political conflicts of sectionalism, the legacy of the Civil War, and the battle over the gold standard versus the coinage of silver. In his elitist and thoroughly racist view of America's global mission, the United

43 Brandeis to Alice Goldmark Brandeis, September 1, 1917, in Melvin Urofsky and David W. Levy, eds., *The Family Letters of Louis D. Brandeis* (Norman: University of Oklahoma Press, 2002), pp. 310–11. Comment to Frankfurter, quoted in Philippa Strum, *Louis D. Brandeis: Justice for the People* (New York: Schocken Books, 1989), p. 316; and see the entire chapter, "Law and Civil Liberties," pp. 309–38. See also Melvin Urofsky and David W. Levy, eds., *The Letters of Louis D. Brandeis*, 4 Vols. (Albany: State University Press of New York, 1971–8).

44 Horace M. Kallen, "Democracy versus the Melting Pot: A Study of American Nationality," *The Nation*, February 25, 1915). Randolph Bourne, "Trans-National America," *War and the Intellectuals*, pp. 107–23.

States would "extend self-government to Porto Rico" as "soon as they can be made fit" and teach the Philippines "order as a condition precedent to liberty, self control as a condition precedent to self-government." As one scholar put it, Wilson embraced "the role of crisis in distilling the public mind" on a common national purpose, and he developed this view sixteen years before he led the country into World War I.[45]

Just as coercive measures were appropriate to introduce democracy to the Philippines in the 1890s, so they would be appropriate and necessary at home in 1917. The Spanish-American War also transformed his view of the presidency. In the preface to the fifteenth edition of *Congressional Government* in 1900, he wrote that "the most important change" resulting from the Spanish-American War was "the greatly increased power and opportunity for constructive statesmanship given the President."[46] As president, he would welcome the opportunity to use that power.

Wilson was not alone in imagining the social utility of war. The most famous, if not notorious statement of this idea was expressed by the philosopher John Dewey, one of the giants of American intellectual history, in his 1918 essay "The Social Possibilities of War." A year into the war, Dewey explained how a national war effort could foster reform at home and peace around the world. Government intervention in the economy provided the opportunity for controlling private corporations for public benefit, while wartime regulations could give a "public aspect [to] every social enterprise." That included "physical training, industrial education, better housing, and the setting up of agencies for securing a public service and function from private industries." This grand enterprise would, of course, be directed by an intellectual and managerial elite - that is, people like Dewey himself and other progressives- and involve the "systematic utilization of the scientific expert." Social control by an elite would also occur at the international level. Anticipating the League of Nations, Dewey envisioned an "international state" that could control conflict between nations and ensure world peace. Dewey's essay was in many respects a very prescient analysis, anticipating what we today call globalization. It resembles, for example, George Orwell's frightening *1984* vision of a world divided into two large forces in a state of permanent conflict[47]

Inspired by a similar vision of using wartime controls to remake America, numerous progressive reformers eagerly enlisted in the war effort. George Creel, head of the Committee on Public Information, had been a crusading reform journalist. The Women's Committee of the Council of National Defense included the leading suffragist Carrie

[45] Woodrow Wilson, "Democracy and Efficiency," *Atlantic Monthly* LXXXVII (March 1901), pp. 289-99: in *PWW*, 12, pp. 6-20. For this point, which few biographers have noted, I am indebted to Thorsen, *The Political Thought of Woodrow Wilson, 1875-1910*, pp. 164-7. C. Eric Schulzke, "Wilsonian Crisis Leadership, the Organic State, and the Modern Presidency," *Polity* 37 (April 2005): 262-85. Paul Kramer, "The Water Cure," *The New Yorker*, February 28, 2008.

[46] Woodrow Wilson, *Congressional Government: A Study in American Politics* (Boston: Houghton Mifflin, 1885), "Preface to Fifteenth Edition, August 15, 1900," pp. v-xiii; especially pp. xi-xii.

[47] John Dewey, "The Social Possibilities of War," *The Independent* (June 22, 1918), in John Dewey, *Characters and Events*, 2 (New York: Henry Holt, 1929), pp. 551-60. An invaluable analysis of Dewey is Peter Beinart, *The Icarus Syndrome: A History of American Hubris* (New York: HarperCollins, 2010), pp. 39-43. See also Rabban, *The First Amendment in Its Forgotten Years*, pp. 211-47. Also: Alan Cywar, "John Dewey in World War I: Patriotism and International Progressivism," *American Quarterly* 21 (Autumn 1969): 578-94. Critique of intellectuals' enthusiasm for war: Charles Forcey, *Crossroads of Liberalism* (New York: Oxford University Press, 1961). To his credit, Dewey publicly criticized the dismissal of New York City high school teachers for alleged "disloyalty": "Arraigns Methods in Trying Teachers," *NYT*, December 16, 1917. A chastened Dewey became a founding member of the ACLU in 1920.

Chapman Catt, the feminist Anna Shaw, and the famous muckraking journalist Ida M. Tarbell. Walter Lippmann, a prewar socialist, became a Wilson adviser. Protestant leaders, believers in the Social Gospel idea that Christians had a duty to reform society, embraced the war as an opportunity to attack prostitution and venereal disease, and to promote prohibition.[48] Federal officials, for example, forced the closing of Storyville, the red light district in New Orleans, because of its proximity to a military base. In his essay, Dewey saw the prohibition of alcohol as an example of the "new lessons of social regulation for purposes of moral prophylaxis." Dewey also explicitly subordinated the individual to the needs of the state. The draft, he explained, embodied "the supremacy of public need over private possession," countering the deeply ingrained "individualist tradition" in America. Significantly, he said nothing about the bitter controversy then raging over the rights of conscientious objectors who did not wish to be conscripted by the state.

Dewey's vision of war as an engine of reform drew a savage attack from one of his own students, Randolph Bourne. A prominent prewar progressive, who had published widely about school reform, Bourne was a lonely but prophetic voice during the war. With devastating insight, he skewered Dewey and other prowar progressives for naively thinking they could control events, particularly the war. Even worse, Bourne argued, they compromised their intellectual integrity in pursuit of political influence. The price of enlisting in the war effort was not criticizing the government on civil liberties or anything else. They "put themselves into a terrifying strategic position," he explained. If they criticized the administration, they would lose their access to power; if they kept silent, they lost their integrity. The tragedy of these highly respected activists and intellectuals is that they traded their integrity for a dream of power and influence. They ended up with neither.[49]

In the cold bitter light of the postwar years, Bourne's criticisms proved very prescient. Far from promoting national unity, the war inflamed prejudice against dissenters and "foreigners" and provoked mob violence. Dewey's naive vision of social control of the economy evaporated as wartime controls were immediately dismantled, and the following decade marked the triumph of a probusiness culture in America. The Versailles Treaty was a disaster that betrayed Wilson's grand principles about the self-determination of people and open treaties. Finally, the traumatic events of the war years shattered the optimism of prewar reformers and killed the spirit of progressivism.

Tragically, Bourne did not live to enjoy his vindication. Always in poor health, he died of pneumonia in December 1918. A pariah when alive, he became a hero for subsequent generations of radicals for his stinging criticisms of intellectuals seduced by the lure of power. His writings resurfaced during World War II, and with even greater force during the Vietnam War. Noam Chomsky's influential 1967 essay "The Responsibility of Intellectuals" was essentially a restatement of Bourne's 1918 views. And finally, Bourne offered one of the best critiques of the intellectuals who embraced President George W. Bush's war on terrorism and invasion of Iraq.[50]

[48] Donald K. Gorrell, *The Age of Social Responsibility: The Social Gospel in the Progressive Era, 1900–1920* (Macon, GA: Mercer University Press, 1988), Ch. 17, "Wartime Service," pp. 279–89.

[49] Randolph Bourne, "The War and the Intellectuals," in Carl Resek, ed., *Randolph Bourne, War and the Intellectuals: Collected Essays, 1915–1919* (New York: Harper & Row, 1964), pp. 3–14. Bruce Clayton, *Forgotten Prophet: The Life of Randolph Bourne* (Baton Rouge: Louisiana State University Press, 1984).

[50] The issues raised by Bourne resonated in two later wars. Louis Filler, *Randolph Bourne* (Washington, DC: American Council on Public Affairs, 1943). Writing during World War II, Filler speculates that Bourne's

A different path: The odyssey of Roger Baldwin

The odyssey of Roger Baldwin, founder of the ACLU, provides an illuminating contrast to Woodrow Wilson with regard to progressive reform and civil liberties. Both began as reformers, sharing the same boundlessly optimistic faith in the capacity of good people to reshape society. Neither of them thought about difficult civil liberties issues before the war. The crucible of war, however, drove them in very different directions. It only hardened Wilson's views on national unity and the obligations of citizenship, while it shattered Baldwin's progressive faith and forced him to think for the first time about how to protect individual liberties from the coercive power of government.

As a social worker in St. Louis between 1906 and early 1917, Baldwin was a classic progressive reformer, throwing himself into innumerable causes: directing a settlement house among the poor; creating the St. Louis Juvenile Court; campaigning for civil service reform, the initiative, referendum and recall; and championing racial justice. Soon he had a national reputation as a reformer, helped organize the National Probation Association, and coauthored *Juvenile Courts and Probation* (1916), which became the standard text on the subject. Interestingly, however, when scheduled speeches by the celebrated anarchist Emma Goldman and the birth control pioneer Margaret Sanger provoked free speech controversies in St. Louis, he did not see the larger First Amendment issues at stake. Both were initially barred from speaking, and Baldwin helped arrange alternative venues, but he did not become a civil libertarian. In her memoirs, Goldman remembered Baldwin then as "rather confused in his social views, a person who tried to be all things to all men," and "a social lion surrounded by society girls."[51]

Two events jarred Baldwin loose from his progressive moorings. The European war in 1914 shattered his faith in progress, as it did for many other people in the United States and around the world. Then, in 1916 St. Louis voters passed a referendum permitting racial segregation in residential housing. Baldwin fought it and was devastated when it passed, particularly because he had helped create the referendum process as an instrument of democracy. The experience shattered his easy optimism about progressive reform and forced him to reflect on the dangers of majoritarian democracy.[52]

American entry into the war led Baldwin to make a dramatic break. In February 1917 he wrote to the AUAM's Crystal Eastman to ask how he might help in the effort to keep America out of the war. Such was his national reputation that the AUAM had offered him a position in 1915. On March 23, 1917, with American entry into the war imminent, he again wrote to Eastman asking, "How and where in your judgment could you best use

principled stand would be inadequate in the face of fascism. Dwight Macdonald restates Bourne's position in the context of World War II in "The Responsibility of Peoples," *Politics*, V. 2 (1945), as does Noam Chomsky in the Vietnam War in "The Responsibility of Intellectuals," *The New York Review of Books*, February 23, 1967, reprinted in Noam Chomsky, *American Power and the New Mandarins* (New York: Pantheon, 1969), pp. 323–66. Daniel Patrick Moynihan, on the other hand, expressed a view similar to Dewey's in the Vietnam War, in "Who Gets in the Army?" *The New Republic*, November 5, 1966, 19–22; also January 7, 1967, 43–4.

51 Robert C. Cottrell, *Roger Nash Baldwin and the American Civil Liberties Union* (New York: Columbia University Press, 2000), pp. 22–45. Walker, *In Defense of American Liberties*, pp. 30–7. Bernard Flexner and Roger N. Baldwin, *Juvenile Courts and Probation* (New York: Century, 1914). Emma Goldman, *Living My Life* (1931, reprint, New York: Dover, 1970), V. 1, p. 477; V. 2, p. 665.

52 This interpretation of Baldwin is developed in Walker, *In Defense of American Liberties*, pp. 33–4. The pivotal referendum: Roger Baldwin, "Negro Segregation by Initiative Election in St. Louis," *American City* 14 (April 1916): 356. Cottrell, *Roger Nash Baldwin and the American Civil Liberties Union*, pp. 46–8.

me?" Ten days later, just as President Wilson asked Congress to declare war, he was at her side in the AUAM's New York office.[53] Little did he know that within a few months he would become a political outcast because of his criticisms of the government, that he would go to prison within eighteen months, and by the mid-1920s would be the most famous civil libertarian in the country.

Launching the fight for civil liberties

In their cramped office on lower Fifth Avenue in New York City, Eastman and Baldwin responded to the wartime crisis with a sense of great alarm, boundless energy, and precious few resources. They initially created the Civil Liberties Bureau as an AUAM committee to advise young men about conscientious objection and to lobby the Wilson administration for a more tolerant interpretation of the law on COs.

At the outset, they had good reason to believe they could use their personal contacts to work closely behind the scenes with administration officials and influence government policies. They knew Secretary of War Newton D. Baker and his assistant Frederick Keppel from prewar reform campaigns and had a personal connection to the White House in John Nevin Sayre, brother of Wilson's son-in-law, Francis B. Sayre. Crystal Eastman had met with President Wilson in the White House on May 8, 1916, and had a serious "Colloquy" with him about the American arms buildup. "We sat in a circle around his desk," recalled her brother, Max Eastman. Engaging the president in the Oval Office on a matter of urgent national policy was a heady experience that encouraged their belief they could change the administration's war policies. An early Civil Liberties Bureau pamphlet explained that they were "working with the departments in Washington ... for a liberal solution of the problem" of conscientious objectors. Their faith proved to be extremely naive. The administration regarded any criticism as disloyalty and turned on its old friends.[54]

Within just a few weeks, Eastman and Baldwin discovered they were under suspicion. The Post Office banned their publications in July, and in November they told their supporters, "You have not heard from us since last July" because the Post Office action. On two occasions, the Post Office threatened to ban the prowar *The New Republic* if it even published a Civil Liberties Bureau advertisement.[55]

An even greater shock occurred when the leaders of the parent AUAM, Lillian D. Wald and Paul U. Kellogg, sought to curb their civil liberties work. Wald bluntly told Eastman and Baldwin, "We cannot plan continuance of our program which entails friendly government relations, and at the same time drift into being a party of opposition to the government." Wald was one of the very people Randolph Bourne attacked when he

[53] Baldwin, letter to Crystal Eastman, March 23, 1917, ACLU, FBI File, Doc #21058. Baldwin's FBI file was obtained by Samuel Walker and subsequently donated to the Mudd Library, Princeton University.

[54] "Memorial to the President ... by the American Union against Militarism," and "Transcript of a Colloquy with a Group of Antipreparedness Leaders," May 8, 1916: *PWW*, 36, pp. 632–48. "President on Defenses," *NYT*, May 9, 1916. Max Eastman, *Enjoyment of Living* (New York: Harper, 1948), p. 546. See cordial correspondence between Baldwin and the War Department in June and early July, 1917, in ACLUP-MF (1996), Reel 2. ACLU Papers for the years 1917–1920 were placed online in the summer of 2011. National Civil Liberties Bureau, *The Conscientious Objector: A Special Statement by the Civil Liberties Bureau* (August, 1917). ACLUP-MF (1977), Reel 90.

[55] National Civil Liberties Bureau, Pamphlet, November 1, 1917. ACLU-MF (1977), Reel 90. Walter Nelles, *A Liberal in Wartime: The Education of Albert DeSilver* (New York: W. W. Norton, 1940), pp. 146–7. Scheiber, *Wilson Administration and Civil Liberties*, p. 33.

denounced intellectuals for trading their principles for influence with the administration. She finally forced the issue by threatening to resign from the AUAM if Eastman and Baldwin did not cease. They resolved the conflict by accepting her proposal to create a "separate enterprise," which became the National Civil Liberties Bureau (NCLB) in July 1917. The aggressively prowar *New York Times* greeted the NCLB with the stern warning "Jails Are Waiting for Them," explaining that in wartime, "good citizens willingly submit."[56]

Baldwin went on to become famous and influential in American life, but Wald failed disastrously with all of her goals. She compromised her principles by ignoring the suppression of civil liberties, watched helplessly as the Versailles Treaty betrayed Wilson's idealistic war aims, and in January 1919 was herself "named" before a Senate investigating committee as one of sixty-two dangerous radicals in the country. Thus, she ended under the very cloud of suspicion she had so desperately sought to avoid.[57]

Military spying and attacks on the Civil Liberties Bureau

Within a year, Roger Baldwin's friends in the administration cut him off and Military Intelligence intensified its investigation of the Civil Liberties Bureau. (Eastman withdrew from active work in late 1917 because of health problems.) Confused and desperate, Baldwin tried to maintain relations with his principal contact, Assistant Secretary of War Frederick Keppel. In the first of several compromises, he assured Keppel in March 1918, "we are entirely willing to discontinue any practices" the government found objectionable. Two months later, Keppel cut him off, explaining that talking with Secretary of War Baker indicated that it was not in their interest "to cooperate in any way with the Civil Liberties Bureau." Baldwin suggested a ruse of corresponding as private individuals, but Keppel finally told the NCLB that their relationship was "very embarrassing to him."[58]

Baldwin's situation was far worse than he imagined, as the Military Intelligence Section (MIS) began investigating the NCLB in early 1918. On March 6, Major Nicholas Biddle, head of MIS in New York, burglarized the bureau's office and stole some materials. Two days later, Biddle interviewed Baldwin and demanded that he admit that his organization "may open an opportunity for the 'slacker' to avoid his duty." Baldwin refused to see that his inquisitor had already answered his own question. In a later interview, Baldwin tried to assure another interrogator of his loyalty by pointing out that the bureau had "withdrawn" one pamphlet because "Major Biddle objected to it" and had burned the remaining fifty copies. Then, in a move that would shock later generations of civil libertarians, he "offered to throw open … all his files of correspondence," and even let MIS take them. They included the mailing list and names of financial supporters, a disclosure that potentially exposed people to prosecution under the Espionage Act. Baldwin added that their private correspondence with draft age men was "entirely at the disposal" of the War Department. Baldwin's naive gestures not only betrayed confidences, but accomplished nothing. On March 18 the New York MIS office advised Washington that "this

56 AUAM Executive Committee, Minutes, June 1, 1917, June 4, 1917. AUAM Papers (1996), MF ED, Reel 1. "Jails Are Waiting for Them," *NYT*, July 4, 1917. "Bureau to Defend Lovers of Peace," ibid., July 3, 1917. Walker, *In Defense of American Liberties*, pp. 11, 19, 37–8.

57 "Lists Americans as Pacifists," *NYT*, January 25, 1919. Ann Hagedorn, *Savage Peace: Hope and Fear in America, 1919* (New York: Simon & Schuster, 2007), pp. 56–7.

58 Baldwin, letter to Keppel, March 13, 1918; Keppel, letter to Baldwin, May 19, 1918; Keppel, letter to Wood, May 22, 1918; Baldwin, letter to Keppel, August 3, 1918. ACLUP-MF (1996), Reel 2.

organization serves no good purpose and their activities should be stopped."[59] There is no record of President Wilson's being informed of this military surveillance, but all the evidence suggests he would have deferred to the judgment of military officials.

The final crackdown occurred on August 30, 1918, when Justice Department agents raided the NCLB office at 80 Fifth Avenue and the offices of allied groups in the building. In Chicago and other cities, government officials also raided the offices of the Socialist Party, the IWW, and other radical groups, serving a reported three hundred search warrants and seizing more than two million documents. As the authorities ransacked the Civil Liberties Bureau office, throwing the files into complete disarray, the usually self-possessed Baldwin became hysterical, throwing up his hands in despair and telling them to go ahead and shoot him. Government agents proceeded to cart away all of the files.[60]

For several weeks the threat of prosecution under the Espionage Act hung over the entire NCLB leadership, including Baldwin, board members, contributors, and cooperating attorneys. Had they been indicted, there is little doubt they would have been convicted, given Debs's conviction, and like him probably given a ten-year prison sentence. For reasons that are not clear, however, they were spared. Perhaps the prospect of indicting the brother of the president's son-in-law gave the Justice Department pause. There is, however, no record that either of the Sayre brothers contacted the president. Nonetheless, the department in November warned Americans not to contribute "to so-called 'civil liberties [or] liberty defense" organizations. Had Baldwin and his colleagues spent the early 1920s in prison, the history of the ACLU and the course of civil liberties in America would certainly have been very different. Baldwin did go to prison in November 1918 for refusing to register for the draft (Congress had just extended the draft to men up to age thirty-five). After serving nine months, he organized the ACLU in January 1920.[61]

THE FINAL ORGY: THE RED SCARE, 1919–1920

On the night of June 2, 1919, bombs exploded on the doorstep of Attorney General A. Mitchell Palmer's house on R Street in Washington, D.C. Across the street, another bomb went off on the doorstep of Assistant Secretary of the Navy Franklin D. Roosevelt, future president of the United States. Alice Roosevelt Longworth, daughter of Franklin's cousin and former president Theodore Roosevelt, recalled that "a leg lay in the path to the house next to theirs, another leg farther up the street ... [and] a head was on the roof of yet

59 Biddle, "Interrogation," of Baldwin, March 8, 1918; Col. Mastellar, Baldwin interview, August, 22, 1918, *U.S. Military Intelligence Reports: Surveillance of Radicals in the United States, 1917–1941*, MF Ed. (Frederick, MD: University Publications of America, 1984), Reel 9. Roy Talbert, Jr., *Negative Intelligence: The Army and the American Left, 1917–1941* (Jackson: University of Mississippi Press, 1991), pp. 78–81. Memo, Grant Squires to Maj. Nicholas Biddle, Military Intelligence Section, March 16, 1918, Baldwin interview, March 15, 3:45 pm, at NCLB office. Baldwin to Biddle, March 8, 1918, *U.S. Military Intelligence Reports. Surveillance of Radicals in the United States, 1917–1941*, Reel 9. Office of Military Intelligence Section, New York City to Chief, Military Intelligence Branch, March 18, 1918, ibid.

60 "Letters Seized by Millions in Raids," *NYT*, August 30, 1918. "Federal Agents Raid Legal Advice Bureau," ibid., August 31, 1918. Walker, *In Defense of American Liberties*, pp. 38–9.

61 George Foster Peabody to Wilson, October 31, 1918, *PWW*, 51, pp. 534–5; Thomas W. Gregory to Wilson, November 9, 1918, ibid., V. 53, pp. 282–3. Justice Department warning: "Not Cruel to Slackers," *NYT*, November 20, 1918. Possible NCLB prosecution: Minutes, NCLB Directing Committee, September 23, 1918, ACLUP-MF (1996), Reel 14.

another house."[62] The future president never mentioned the bombing, and we can only speculate on its impact on his attitude toward political radicals.

The anarchists' bombs sparked the final orgy of repression, popularly known as the Red Scare or the Palmer Raids. The war ended in November 1918, but the June 1919 bombs inflamed fears of a revolution in America similar to the Bolshevik Revolution in Russia. In late April 1919, a Post Office employee in New York City discovered a set of bombs destined for Attorney General Palmer, Postmaster General Burleson, and other prominent figures, thwarting that plot. Summer 1919 was one of the grimmest and most conflict-ridden periods in American history. Major strikes occurred in the coal and steel industries, and race riots erupted in Chicago, Washington, D.C., Omaha (where martial law prevailed for a week), and other cities. In September, Boston police officers went out on strike, raising fears of a total collapse of law and order. President Wilson denounced the police strike as a "crime against civilization," and Calvin Coolidge, governor of Massachusetts and a future president, enhanced his national reputation declaring, "There is no right to strike against the public safety, anywhere, anytime."[63]

With the end of the war President Wilson moderated his views on dissent only slightly. He pardoned some people convicted of wartime offenses, but in other ways his attitude hardened. He refused to pardon Eugene V. Debs despite a recommendation to do so by Attorney General Palmer. In his December 1919 Message to Congress (delivered in writing because of the stroke he suffered in September), he called for a peacetime sedition law, pointing to "the widespread condition of political restlessness in our body politic" and "the transfusion of radical theories from seething European centers." He paid the standard homage to freedom of speech ("With the free expression of opinion and with the advocacy of orderly political change ... there must be no interference") but promised "no leniency" "towards passion and malevolence tending to incite crime and insurrection." Congress did not pass the sedition bill, but twenty states enacted criminal syndicalism or criminal anarchy laws, which became the principal legal weapon against alleged radicals over the next twenty years.[64]

Alarmed by the anarchist bombings, Attorney General Palmer set in motion a massive roundup of suspected radicals. "Like a prairie fire," he explained, "the blaze of revolution was sweeping over every American institution of law and order." Assisting him was a twenty-three-year-old employee of the Bureau of Investigation named John Edgar Hoover, who took charge of the General Intelligence Division and soon compiled files on 200,000 alleged radicals. The infamous Palmer Raids actually consisted of two separate roundups. On November 7 (the second anniversary of the Bolshevik Revolution) the Justice Department conducted coordinated raids in twelve cities. The New York City crackdown focused on the Russian Peoples House, a center for immigrant labor radicals in Lower Manhattan, and lasted from 9 p.m. until 4:30 the next morning. The 211

62 "Palmer and Family Safe," *NYT*, June 4, 1919. Alice Roosevelt Longworth, *Crowded Hours: Reminiscences* (New York: Charles Scribner's Sons, 1933), pp. 282–3.

63 Wilson, PWW, 63, p. 196 An excellent account of the year is Hagedorn, *Savage Peace: Hope and Fear in America, 1919.* Robert K. Murray, *Red Scare: A Study in National Hysteria, 1919–1920* (Minneapolis: University of Minneapolis Press, 1955). Francis Russell, *A City in Terror: 1919, The Boston Police Strike* (New York: Viking, 1975).

64 Debs: Palmer to Wilson, January 29, 1921, *PWW*, 67, pp. 98–102. 7th Annual Message, December 2, 1919, APP. The Ohio Criminal Syndicalism law was struck down by the Supreme Court in *Brandenburg v. Ohio,* 395 U.S. 444 (1969).

people seized were held incommunicado, unable to see friends, family, or lawyers. The November raids were only a prelude to the larger and more famous raids on January 2, 1920, when the government arrested 2,585 people in more than forty cities. All pretense of due process was cast aside, as people were arrested because they looked "foreign" or were alleged to belong to a radical labor union. Most were confined to overcrowded jails for months without seeing a lawyer. President Wilson bears no direct responsibility for the Palmer Raids. By then he was incapacitated by his stroke and cloistered by his wife, doctors, and a few close aides. He apparently did not even learn about the raids until a cabinet meeting in mid-April 1920.[65]

The outrages of the Palmer Raids provoked a backlash that marked the first turn in public opinion about government repression. The Harvard Law School professors Felix Frankfurter and Zechariah Chafee and ten other prominent attorneys issued the blistering *Report on the Illegal Practices of the United States Department of Justice*. Published by the National Popular Government League (NPGL) and circulated by the ACLU, the report condemned the "continual illegal acts," which included "wholesale arrests ... without warrant," holding people incommunicado "without access of friends or counsel," warrantless searches, destruction of property, and physical abuse of prisoners. The historian Kenneth D. Ackerman observes that "no one had seen anything quite like it before in America: twelve of the country's most prominent lawyers accusing the attorney general of breaking the law he was sworn to enforce."[66]

In part because of the *Illegal Practices* report, the term "Palmer Raids" entered the American political lexicon as shorthand for government abuse of power. The NPGL actively lobbied Congress, and the Senate Judiciary Committee cited its report in hearings on the raids in early 1921. Two decades later, as American entry into World War II loomed, key officials in Franklin D. Roosevelt's administration, including notably the attorneys general Frank Murphy, Robert Jackson, and Francis Biddle, remembered the abuses and vowed not to repeat them. The future president Harry Truman, according to one colleague, returned from combat in Europe disgusted by the hysteria and abuses of people's rights at home.[67]

AN OMINOUS LEGACY: ORIGINS OF THE NATIONAL SECURITY STATE

President Wilson's secret executive order authorizing federal agencies to dismiss any employee whose "sympathies or utterances" were "inimical to the public welfare" was just one part of something new in American life: the creation of the national security state, a vast apparatus of laws and practices designed to enforce political conformity.

65 Hoover and the Red Scare: Kenneth D. Ackerman, *Young J. Edgar: Hoover, the Red Scare, and the Assault on Civil Liberties* (New York: Carroll & Graf, 2007); January raid, pp. 180–6. Murray, *Red Scare*. On Hoover's appointment: John Lord O'Brian, COHC, pp. 293–4, 323–5. Josephus Daniels Diary, April 14, 1920, in *PWW*, 65, pp. 186–7.

66 National Popular Government League, *Report on the Illegal Practices of the United States Department of Justice* (New York: ACLU, May 1920). "12 Lawyers Renew Attack on Palmer," *NYT*, January 19, 1921. NPGL materials: FFP, Box 159, LOC. Palmer's defense: A. Mitchell Palmer, "The Case against the Reds," *The Forum* 63 (1920): 173–85. Wilson's lack of knowledge: Josephus Daniels, *The Cabinet Diaries of Josephus Daniels* (Lincoln: University of Nebraska Press, 1963), April 14, 1920, p. 188. Ackerman, *Young J. Edgar*, p. 309, and see the entire section on the *Illegal Practices* report, pp. 306–11.

67 NPGL: FFP, Box 159, LOC. "Palmer Defends His War on Reds," *NYT*, February 19, 1921. On FDR's attorneys general, see Chapter 3 of this book.

Although much of it went into abeyance during the 1920s, it returned with a vengeance in the late 1930s under President Franklin D. Roosevelt and became a permanent part of American political life.[68]

The apparatus included laws that criminalized opinions the government deemed suspect: the Espionage and Sedition Acts, the Trading with the Enemy Act, various restrictive immigration laws, and state criminal syndicalism or criminal anarchy laws. The Supreme Court sanctioned punishing unpopular speech in the pivotal 1919 *Schenck v U.S.* decision. Charles T. Schenck, secretary of the Socialist Party, was convicted of printing and distributing leaflets opposing the draft, including the argument that the draft was a form of slavery prohibited by the Thirteenth Amendment. The Court held that the allegations incited insubordination and were not protected by the First Amendment and formulated the "clear and present danger" test regarding the boundaries of free speech. Political spying by Military Intelligence and the Bureau of Investigation began during the war and continued afterward.[69] Legislative investigations into political beliefs and associations began with Senator Lee Overman's 1919 investigation of Bolshevik propaganda in the United States and continued with the more famous Lusk Committee of the New York legislature, which issued the five-volume report *Revolutionary Radicalism*, which indiscriminately labeled as suspect socialists, pacifists, civil libertarians, and opponents of the recent war. Private individuals arose as "professional patriots" and developed their own lists of alleged radicals. The most famous in the post–World War I years was Archibald Stevenson, who named sixty-two prominent pacifists and radicals, including Roger Baldwin (then in prison) and Lillian Wald, before the Overman Committee.[70]

All of the mechanisms of the national security state assumed that national security trumped considerations of freedom of speech and due process of law. They all used vague and elastic terms, such as "un-American," "subversive," or "disloyal," that did not involve specific criminal acts such as espionage or sabotage. The principle of guilt by association linked people and groups because of common ideas or affiliations. The violations of civil liberties during the cold war in the 1950s are well known, particularly the excesses of Senator Joe McCarthy. But it all began during World War I under the administration of President Woodrow Wilson.

In addition to the calamitous impact on civil liberties, the war years marked an unprecedented shift in power to the presidency. The historian Harry Scheiber lists eleven new

68 Garry Wills, *Bomb Power: The Modern Presidency and the National Security State* (New York: Penguin, 2010) dates the creation of the national security state from the invention of the atomic bomb. Most of the major elements, however, were created during World War I.

69 Executive Order, 2587-A, *PWW*, 41, pp. 547–8. Because of its confidential status, the order does not appear in many conventional sources. The order and the letter from the Civil Service Commission are on a Web site maintained by the Conservative Caucus: www.conservative usa.org/co/eo/eo2587a.htm. Scheiber, *The Wilson Administration and Civil Liberties*, Ch. 2, "Security Measures," pp. 15–28. *Schenck v. United States*, 249 U.S. 47. Joan M. Jensen, *Army Surveillance in America, 1775–1980* (New Haven, CT: Yale University Press, 1991), pp. 160–77. Athan G. Theoharis and John Stuart Cox, *The Boss: J. Edgar Hoover and the Great American Inquisition* (Philadelphia: Temple University Press, 1988), p. 56. The best overall history of Hoover and the FBI is Curt Gentry, *J. Edgar Hoover: The Man and the Secrets* (New York: W. W. Norton, 1991).

70 "Lists Americans as Pacifists," *NYT*, January 25, 1919. Overman Committee: Bolshevik Propaganda. "Plan Bolshevism Hearing," ibid., May 3, 1919. Hagedorn, *Savage Peace: Hope and Fear in America, 1919*, "The List," pp. 53–60. New York State legislature, Joint Commitee Investigating Seditious Activities [Lusk Committee], *Revolutionary Radicalism*, 4 Vols. (Albany, NY: J. B. Lyon, 1920). HUAC: Walter Goodman, *The Committee: The Extraordinary Career of the House Committee on Un-American Activities* (New York: Farrar, Straus & Giroux, 1968). HUAC was abolished in 1975, in part as a consequence of the Watergate scandal.

measures between February 1917 and October 1918 granting vast powers to the president, and Wilson issued seventeen hundred executive orders while president. The 1918 Overman Act, for example, gave Wilson virtually unlimited power to regulate the entire economy. Although most were temporary wartime measures and acts of Congress rather than unilateral presidential acts, they established the precedent of the relying on presidential power in an emergency. The habit became deeply ingrained and led to what later generations called the "Imperial Presidency."[71]

MOVING BACKWARD ON RACE

On behalf of the NAACP, Oswald Garrison Villard wrote to President Wilson in August 1913 to protest the imposition of racial segregation among federal employees. Wilson replied that he believed "segregation to be in the interest of the colored people," because it reduced "friction" among employees. Moreover, he said "a number of colored people" "agreed with us" on this issue.[72] Race discrimination stands as a second great blemish on Wilson's civil liberties record. In addition to segregating federal employees, he remained passive in the face of racial mob violence, especially the 1917 East St. Louis riot, despite widespread calls for federal action to protect African Americans.

Postmaster General Burleson initiated the idea of segregation at the April 11, 1913, cabinet meeting, soon after Wilson took office. The presence of four African-American railway clerks created a "very unpleasant" situation for white employees, he explained, particularly without "different drinking vessels and different towels" in the railroad cars. Burleson was a Texan whose father and grandfather had been generals in the Confederate army in the Civil War. Secretary of the Treasury William Gibbs McAdoo, a southerner and Wilson's son-in-law, supported Burleson's proposal. Burleson cited support from moderate African-American leaders such as Bishop Alexander Walters, president of the National Colored Democratic League. With Wilson's tacit approval, the Post Office began separating employees by race, downgrading and discharging African-American employees, and creating separate window service for whites and African Americans at local post offices.[73]

As word of the new policy spread, the NAACP undertook an investigation. "In the Dead Letter Office," it found, "colored men and women have been segregated back of lockers in one corner of the room." White employees ate in a nice lunch room, while African Americans had no meal area at all. One African-American employee was placed behind a screen to shield white employees from him. Some administration officials refused to go along with the new policy, however. The most adamant opponent was Assistant Secretary of Labor Louis Post, a founding member of the NAACP who was nearly impeached for

71 Scheiber, *The Wilson Administration and Civil Liberties, 1917–1921*. A comprehensive analysis of executive orders and other forms of presidential authority is Phillip J. Cooper, *By Order of the President: The Use and Abuse of Executive Direct Action* (Lawrence: University Press of Kansas, 2002); on Wilson, pp. 8, 13. Cooper argues persuasively that the mere number of executive orders is meaningless, and the content of particular orders is more important (pp. 13–14). Wilson, Address to a Joint Session of Congress on the Demands of Railway Employees, August 29, 1916, APP. Arthur M. Schlesinger, Jr., *The Imperial Presidency*. Rev. ed. (Boston: Houghton Mifflin, 2004).

72 Wilson to Villard, August 29, 1913, *PWW*, 28, pp. 245–6.

73 Cronon, ed., *The Cabinet Diaries of Josephus Daniels*, pp. 32–3.

protesting the Palmer Raids. But his was a lonely voice of opposition. Assistant Secretary of the Navy Franklin D. Roosevelt willingly complied.[74]

Segregating federal agencies was just one symptom of the worst period of American race relations since the Civil War. Beginning around 1890, southern states institutionalized racial segregation in education, employment, and transportation, and African-American voters were almost completely disenfranchised in the Deep South. The pattern of lynchings also changed. Lynchings of whites and of people outside the South declined significantly, leaving southern African Americans as the principal victims. The racial crisis finally provoked the creation of the NAACP, the first national civil rights organization and the model for subsequent rights-oriented public interest groups, in 1909.[75]

In approving segregation, Wilson betrayed a vague campaign promise he had made to several African American leaders, including W. E. B. DuBois, in the 1912 election campaign. Although he made "no promises in particular to negroes, except to do them justice," it was a small but hopeful sign. When he met with NAACP leaders again in the White House in early 1913, they expressed alarm about the worsening racial situation and asked him to create a National Race Commission to address the problem. Oswald Garrison Villard, publisher of the *New York Evening Post*, left the meeting feeling confident Wilson would accept their proposal. He was quickly disappointed. Wilson soon told him it was politically impossible because it would offend powerful southern Democrats in Congress and jeopardize his ambitious legislative agenda. He candidly explained that he was "absolutely blocked by the sentiments of Senators," and that a race commission would be a "blunder on my part." In later decades, Presidents Franklin D. Roosevelt and John F. Kennedy would also say that the power of southern congressional members prevented them from initiating civil rights measures.[76] President Harry Truman defied the southerners and created the first presidential commission on race relations in 1946. We can only speculate on the course of American race relations had Wilson created one in 1913.

Race intruded into the White House in 1915 in a famous incident when Wilson was given a private showing of the film *Birth of a Nation*. Generally regarded as the first film to demonstrate the artistic potential of the new medium, it also embodied a deeply racist view of Reconstruction and portrayed the Ku Klux Klan as the savior of the South. Initial screenings prompted angry protests: Five hundred African Americans protested the Boston premier. Alarmed by the reaction, Thomas Dixon, author of the original novel, *The Clansman*, decided he might gain some favorable publicity by showing it to an old Johns Hopkins University graduate school friend who now just happened to be the president of the United States.[77]

[74] Villard to Wilson, October 14, 1913 [with report by May Childs Nerney], *PWW*, 28, pp. 401–10. Louis F. Post, *The Deportations Delirium of Nineteen-Twenty* (Chicago: Charles H. Kerr, 1923). Nancy J. Weiss, *Farewell to the Party of Lincoln: Black Politics in the Age of FDR* (Princeton, NJ: Princeton University Press, 1983), p. 20.

[75] Racial climate of the period: C. Vann Woodward, *The Strange Career of Jim Crow*, 3rd ed. (New York: Oxford University Press, 1974), and Jack T. Kirby, *Darkness at the Dawning* (Philadelphia: J. B. Lippincott, 1972). Charles Flint Kellogg, *NAACP: A History of the National Association for the Advancement of Colored People* (Baltimore: Johns Hopkins University Press, 1967).

[76] Villard to Prof. Leavell, May 15, 1913, *PWW*, 27, p. 442. Villard to Wilson, August, 18, 1913, *PWW*, 38, p. 185–6. Wilson to Villard, August 21, 1913, *PWW*, 28, p. 202. Link, *Woodrow Wilson and the Progressive Movement*, p. 64.

[77] Raymond A. Cook, *Thomas Dixon* (New York: Twayne, 1974), p. 114. "Negroes Mob Photo Play," *NYT*, April 17, 1915.

Apparently not familiar with the new medium of film, Wilson was "puzzled" by the offer. Nonetheless, he accepted, and on the night of February 18, 1915, viewed the film in the East Room of the White House with his family and some other officials. In a famous but undoubtedly apocryphal quote, Wilson allegedly pronounced the film "like writing history with lightning." Dixon probably invented the comment, but Wilson's 1902 five-volume *History of the American People* incorporated the southern view that the post–Civil War Reconstruction of the South had been a disaster by empowering the newly freed slaves. Born in Virginia in 1856, he inherited the region's deeply racist view of African Americans.[78]

Racism also affected Wilson's appointments to federal offices. He appointed only two African Americans in his first two years in office, and named whites to twelve positions previously held by African Americans. Secretary of State William Jennings Bryan broke with established precedent by appointing a white person as ambassador to Haiti.[79]

War and race riots

In the fevered summer of 1917, just as Wilson was overwhelmed with mobilizing the country for war, a bloody race riot erupted in East St. Louis, Illinois. Suddenly, he was faced with a national race crisis and demands for federal action. The July 2 riot was the most serious in a series of violent racial incidents that had begun around 1900. A labor dispute aggravated racial tensions in the city, as the major employers recruited African Americans to replace white union members. Tensions finally boiled over on July 1 when whites assaulted African Americans on the street, and some whites drove through the African-American neighborhood firing guns. African Americans shot back and killed two white police officers, setting off mob violence. Early on July 2, in a pattern that characterized almost all race riots prior to the 1960s, mobs of whites invaded the African-American community, while the police and the National Guard stood by passively and in some cases joined the attacks themselves. When it was over, thirty-nine African Americans and nine whites were dead.[80]

The scale of the violence shocked the nation. The former president Theodore Roosevelt angrily denounced the "appalling brutality" and demanded "the fullest investigation into these murders." The NAACP organized an impressive silent march of eight thousand people down New York City's Fifth Avenue on July 28. Thousands of people watched from the sidewalks as muffled drums provided the only sound, and marchers carried signs reading, "Mother, do lynchers go to heaven?" and in a pointed reference to Wilson's war aims, "Mr. President, why not make America safe for democracy?" March organizers petitioned Wilson for a federal law against "lynching and mob violence." He consulted Attorney General Gregory but was told the facts of the riot did not "present a proper predicate" for federal action. He then met quietly with a few African-American leaders but

[78] D. W. Griffith to Wilson, March 2, 1915, *PWW*, 32, p. 301. Thomas Dixon to Wilson, February 20, 1915, ibid., p. 267. Melvyn Stokes, *D. W. Griffith's* The Birth of a Nation*: A History of "The Most Controversial Motion Picture of All Time"* (New York: Oxford University Press, 2007), p. 111. Woodrow Wilson, *A History of the American People*, 5 Vols. (New York: Harper and Brothers, 1902).

[79] Judson MacLaury, "The Federal Government and Negro Workers under President Woodrow Wilson," Paper, Annual Meeting, Society for History in the Federal Government, Washington, DC, March 16, 2000, www.dol.gov.

[80] Elliott M. Rudwick, *Race Riot at East St. Louis, July 2, 1917* (Cleveland: World, 1966).

did not issue a public statement until a year later and never took any action. Pressure on Wilson continued to mount. Roosevelt declared that the federal government and local officials "should take notice now, and act now." Senator Joseph France, Republican from Maryland, wrote to Wilson demanding action, and a group of African-American leaders begged for a three- to five-minute meeting. "In the name of God, and SUFFERING HUMANITY," pleaded Alfred B. Cosey, "Mr. President see us." Through an intermediary, Wilson expressed sympathy but told Senator France that it was "imperative for me to conserve my time as much as is practicable."[81]

Wilson certainly failed in his responsibility as president to issue a public statement condemning mob violence in 1917. He could easily have couched it in terms of the war effort and the importance of respect for law and order. Perhaps he worried that any statement condemning racial mob violence might be interpreted as a criticism of attacks on antiwar activists. A year later he finally issued a written statement condemning mob violence, but it was far too late. Even more serious racial violence erupted in 1919.

"Civil liberty in the United States is dead," proclaimed a young African-American activist in 1918, claiming it was even worse for African Americans. "Civil liberty for the Negro, however, was dead even before the war, killed by the combination of a hypocritical North and an unregenerate South." The writer was A. Philip Randolph, then only twenty-five years old, a socialist and a vocal opponent of the war. On August 10, 1918, Special Agent Sawken of the Bureau of Investigation heard Randolph and other socialists speak in Cleveland, bought a copy of Randolph's magazine the *Messenger*, and arrested him for violating the Espionage Act. The judge dismissed the charge, allegedly because he did not believe Randolph was old enough to have written the offending material. The Post Office then suspended the *Messenger*'s second-class mailing privilege. Randolph would prove to be a voice for presidents to reckon with. On three separate occasions, in 1941, 1948, and 1963, he challenged presidents in the White House, in each case eventually inducing them to grant his demands.[82]

African Americans and the war effort

Wilson took some positive steps to encourage African-American participation in the war. The Selective Service Act authorized drafting African Americans, although on a strictly segregated basis. In response to pressure from the NAACP, Secretary of War Newton D. Baker allowed the training of some African-American officers and established African-American combat units, the most famous of which was the 369th Regiment, known as the Harlem Hellfighters. On the home front, Wilson created the Division of Negro Economics in the War Labor Administration to mobilize African-American workers. He was more

[81] "Negroes in Protest March in Fifth Av.," *NYT*, July 29, 1917. Tumulty to Wilson, with Enclosure [from Committee of the Negro Silent Protest], August 1, 1917, *PWW*, 43, pp. 342–3. Gregory to Wilson, July 27, 1917, *PWW*, 43, pp. 297–8. Meeting: Cosey to Wilson, August 9, 1917, *PWW*, 43, p. 412, n. 4, pp. 412–13. Roosevelt to Victor A. Olander, July 17, 1917, in Morison, ed., *The Letters of Theodore Roosevelt*, pp. 1208–11. Tumulty to Wilson, July 10, 1917, *PWW*, 43, p. 139. Alfred B. Cosey to Wilson, August 9, 1917, ibid., p. 412. Wilson to [U.S. senator] Joseph Irwin France [of Maryland], July 11, 1917, ibid., p. 146.

[82] Randolph, "Civil Liberties," *The Messenger* (March 1919), MF Ed. (New York: Negro Universities Press, 1969). Special Agent Sawken, Report on Socialist Meeting, Cleveland, August 10, 1918, APRP, Box 29, LOC. FBI Memorandum, Re: A. Philip Randolph, July, 1942, in Kenneth O'Reilly, *Black Americans: The FBI Files* (New York: Carroll & Graf, 1994), pp. 310–16. Jervis Anderson, *A. Philip Randolph: A Biographical Portrait* (New York: Harcourt Brace, 1973), pp. 106–9.

concerned with promoting wartime productivity, however, than racial justice. George Haynes, an African American and the educational secretary of the Urban League, became head of the division in May 1918. Much of the division's work involved building morale. On July 4, 1918, for example, an estimated two thousand speakers around the country spoke on "Labor and Victory," promoting the African-American role in the "world struggle for democracy." The commitment to African-American employment did not survive the war, however. The division's budget was drastically cut when the war ended, and it disappeared altogether under President Warren G. Harding.[83]

In one of the most curious and still controversial aspects of wartime race relations, the great African-American intellectual W. E. B. Dubois published an editorial urging African Americans to "Close Ranks" behind the war effort. In the July 1918 issue of the NAACP's magazine *The Crisis*, he counseled African Americans to put aside their "special grievances" and support the president. Given DuBois's long career as a radical social critic and Wilson's prewar record on segregation, this appeal seems inexplicable. Perhaps he too was caught up in the same patriotic fever that caused white progressive reformers to join the war effort enthusiastically, and some historians suggest that he was influenced by a tentative offer of a commission with the military.[84]

1919: More riots and an antilynching campaign

A wave of racial violence erupted across the country in 1919, with a major riots in Chicago and Omaha and disturbances in Washington, D.C., and seventeen other cities. All of the riots involved white-initiated violence against African Americans, with police officers passively tolerating it or in some instances participating in the violence themselves. The week-long Chicago riot left thirty-eight people dead, including twenty-three African Americans, and one thousand people homeless. About six thousand National Guard troops were mobilized to restore order. In Washington, D.C., violence took place very close to the White House itself. As they had in 1917, African Americans demanded that President Wilson act to stop the violence. "How long," an NAACP telegram asked Wilson in late August, will the government "tolerate anarchy in the United States?" Wilson was then consumed by his effort to persuade the Senate to ratify the Versailles Treaty and did not respond. African-American leaders began demanding a federal law making lynching a crime, and in the 1920s the NAACP made such a law one of its top priorities.[85]

Aside from the few wartime measures, President Wilson's record of racial equality was as shameful as his record on free speech. He betrayed his vague 1912 promises to the NAACP, countenanced segregation in federal agencies, and remained silent in the face of racist violence across the country. His failure is highlighted by the fact that the three Republican presidents of the 1920s were far more responsive to the cause of racial justice.

83 Bernard C. Nalty, *Strength for the Fight: A History of Black Americans in the Military* (New York: Free Press, 1986). MacLaury, "The Federal Government and Negro Workers under President Woodrow Wilson."

84 "Editorial: Close Ranks," *The Crisis* 16 (July 1918). Mark Ellis, "'Closing Ranks' and 'Seeking Honors': W. E. B. DuBois in World War I," *Journal of American History* 79 (June 1992): 96–124. Much controversy at the time and today among historians surrounds the editorial and the fact that DuBois was offered a commission with the Military Intelligence Branch (although it was withdrawn) around the time it was published. See Shane A. Smith, "The Crisis in the Great War: W. E. B. DuBois and His Perception of African American Participation in World War I," *The Historian* 70 (Summer 2008): 239–62.

85 "Negro Protest to Wilson," *NYT*, August 30, 1919. Chicago riot and other cities: William Tuttle, Jr., *Race Riot: Chicago in the Red Summer of 1919* (New York: Atheneum, 1970).

A RELUCTANT PATH TO WOMEN'S SUFFRAGE

Pickets outside the White House on August 11, 1917, carried signs denouncing the president as "Kaiser Wilson." In an atmosphere of rising wartime hysteria, no accusation could have been more inflammatory than equating the president with the nation's enemy. The protesters were members of Alice Paul's National Woman's Party, demanding a constitutional amendment guaranteeing women the right to vote. Paul is most famous for drafting the Equal Rights Amendment in 1923. On this occasion she was arrested, convicted, jailed, and then transferred to a psychiatric hospital, where she went on a highly publicized hunger strike.[86]

Wilson initially opposed women's suffrage but changed his mind in late 1917 only out of political expediency. As a socially conservative southerner, he was uncomfortable with the very idea of women's rights, and according to one biographer he had a genuine "distaste" for suffragists and their tactics. He left his first teaching job at the noted women's college Bryn Mawr (1885–8) in part because he did not like teaching women. Lecturing to women about politics, he confided in his diary in 1887, was "about as appropriate and profitable as would be lecturing to stone-masons on the evolution of fashion in dress." His female students, he complained, had a "painful *absenteeism* of mind" [Wilson's italics]. Given his attitudes, it is a mystery why he ever accepted the Bryn Mawr job in the first place.[87]

Wilson first confronted the suffrage issue as governor of New Jersey (1911–13), and when questioned either said he did not support it or evaded the question. In June 1911, he told a reporter, "I must say very frankly that my personal judgment is strongly against it." A few months earlier, when a female reporter brought up the subject, he abruptly ended the interview by exclaiming, "Ah, there's my wife. I must speak to her for a moment." As the 1912 Democratic Party candidate for president, he faced powerful conflicting pressures from suffrage supporters in the North and West and opposition from southern conservatives (and some northerners as well). In the campaign he again dodged the issue, telling one group of suffragists he really had not thought about it, which of course was patently untrue. (His closest confidant, Edward M. House, privately noted Wilson's habit of giving "evasive or foolish answers" on issues he wanted to avoid.) At a banquet in Syracuse, New York, he was seated beside Max Eastman, an ardent suffragist (and future antiwar radical). Turning to Eastman, he admitted, "I am badly in need of instruction about" suffrage but immediately added, "I have the feeling that these women are avoiding their duties rather than demanding their rights."[88]

The moment Wilson entered the White House in March 1913, Paul and her allies launched an aggressive campaign, joining the Inauguration Day Parade uninvited. Years

86 "Suffragettes Lose Two More Banners," *NYT*, August 12, 1917. Katherine H. Adams and Michael L. Keene, *Alice Paul and the American Suffrage Campaign* (Urbana: University of Illinois Press, 2008), pp. 157–90.

87 Wilson, Excerpt from Confidential Journal, October 20, 1887, *PWW*, 5, p. 619. Mulder, *Woodrow Wilson: The Years of Preparation*, pp. 91–101.

88 Wilson to Witter Bynner, June 20, 1911, *PWW*, 23, p. 160. Virginia Tyler Hudson in *New York Globe and Commercial Advertiser*, January 17, 1911, *PWW*, 22, p. 356. Blum, *Woodrow Wilson*, p. 116. House, Diary excerpt, July 26, 1917, *PWW*, 43, p. 290. Max Eastman, *Enjoyment of Living* (New York: Harper and Brothers, 1948), p. 386; Max Eastman, *Love and Revolution: My Journey through an Epoch* (New York: Random House, 1964), p. 32. Christine A. Lunardini, *From Equal Suffrage to Equal Rights: Alice Paul and the National Woman's Party, 1910–1928* (New York: New York University Press, 1986), p. 32. Sally Hunter Graham, "Woodrow Wilson, Alice Paul, and the Woman Suffrage Movement," *Political Science Quarterly* 98 (Winter 1983–4): 665–79.

later, Paul proudly recalled, "There had never been a procession of women for [*sic*] any corner of the world or in Washington, probably." The National American Woman Suffrage Association, the largest suffrage organization, bitterly attacked her confrontational tactics, fearing they would alienate hard-won support. Most of Paul's followers were wealthy Republicans and were regarded with suspicion by most feminists, who focused on legislation regulating the hours and working conditions for women in industrial jobs. Just two weeks after his inauguration in March, Wilson met with Paul and her associates in the White House. Again, he falsely claimed he had not thought about the issue. And in a December 1913 statement to the National Woman Suffrage Convention, he was completely evasive, taking no position on the issue.[89]

The National Woman's Party dramatically escalated its campaign at Wilson's second inaugural on March 4, 1917. About two thousand suffragists circled the White House in the rain, demanding support for the suffrage amendment. A heavy police presence surrounded them, mainly to protect them from attacks by angry opponents. "Silent Sentinels" stood at each of the main gates, holding signs reading, "Mr. President, How Long Must Women Wait for Liberty?" "That's when our militancy really began," Paul recalled. Wilson ignored their demands, but in a gesture of conciliation invited them into the White House as shelter from the freezing rain. They declined the offer. Suffragists were feeling extremely confident that year, with recent victories in New York, South Dakota, Oklahoma, North Dakota, Indiana, Nebraska, and Michigan. The suffrage campaign involved two separate issues: an amendment to the U.S. Constitution and similar state amendments. A month later, Paul led another group of pickets on the night of April 2, when Wilson delivered his war message to Congress.[90]

After Congress declared war, Paul seized on the strategy of linking suffrage to Wilson's grand promise to make the world safe for democracy. Why should Americans fight overseas, she asked, when half the population at home were denied the right to vote? (During World War II, African Americans adopted a similar strategy, with a "Double V" standing for victory abroad and equality at home.) Picketing the White House as prowar hysteria was growing was highly provocative, and government employees, soldiers, and sailors attacked them and ripped up their banners. The police either stood by passively or tore up signs themselves. There was speculation the picketers might be prosecuted under the Espionage Act, a not unreasonable fear given the arrests of antiwar militants such as Emma Goldman. Paul recalled that the police warded off one mob, but the chief of police told the Woman's Party that evening that they could no longer "hold banners of any kind before the White House."[91]

Paul and others were eventually arrested for unlawful assembly. The law at that time afforded them no First Amendment protection for peaceable assembly. In jail, Paul and

89 Alice Paul, *Conversations with Alice Paul: Woman Suffrage and the Equal Rights Amendment*, ROHO, BL, UCal, p. 76. Wilson, Remarks to Delegation from National Woman Suffrage Convention, December 8, 1913, PWW, 29, pp. 21–2. Lucy G. Barber, *Marching on Washington: The Forging of an American Political Tradition* (Berkeley: University of California Press, 2002), Ch. 2.

90 "President Ignores Suffrage Pickets," *NYT*, January 11, 1917. "President Offers Shelter to 'Pickets,'" ibid., January 12, 1917. "Suffragists Girdle White House in Rain," ibid., March 5, 1917. "Picket White House Again," ibid., April 3, 1917. Graham, "Woodrow Wilson, Alice Paul, and the Woman Suffrage Movement."

91 Graham, "Woodrow Wilson, Alice Paul, and the Woman Suffrage Movement," 667–73. Paul, *Conversations with Alice Paul*, p. 216. National Woman's Party, Report to the Legislative Department Month of August, 1917, NWP, MF ED., Reel 87, LOC.

others began hunger strikes, and she was transferred to a psychiatric hospital. The resulting public outcry embarrassed President Wilson, who already felt overwhelmed by the war effort. The national economy almost collapsed under the strain of wartime mobilization, criticism of the war was growing, and the July 1917 race riot in East St. Louis, Illinois, posed a national race crisis. Mainstream suffragists, appalled by Paul's tactics and worried that the entire suffrage movement might be accused of disloyalty, tried to assure Wilson of their support. Elizabeth Bass told him that she, Lillian Wald, Jane Addams, and others had "agreed to waive the whole matter [of conscientious objectors] and follow you wherever you had to lead them." Wald, of course, had already dissociated herself from the Civil Liberties Bureau. Bass asked Wilson for a five-minute interview and "reassurance" that in return for their support of the war he would maintain his commitments on "the most vital questions of social legislation," particularly enforcement of labor standards.[92]

Despite the criticisms, Alice Paul's militant tactics quickly brought about a change. Embarrassed by the publicity over the arrests and hunger strikes, Wilson suddenly shifted his position on suffrage. A *New York Times* headline on July 19 said it all: "Wilson, Shocked at Jailing Militants, May Advocate 'Votes for Women' as Part of War Emergency Program." Jailed suffragists were unexpectedly released and pardoned on July 20 (although some refused to accept a pardon and remained in jail). The National Woman's Party declared the pardons "a tacit acknowledgment by the President of the Constitutionality of peaceful picketing." On October 25, Wilson endorsed a New York referendum granting women suffrage in that state. It was approved on November 6. Press accounts noted that this was his strongest support ever for suffrage, and he now defined it as a "fundamental question." At a huge prosuffrage parade of twenty thousand people down Fifth Avenue on November 27, suffragists prominently heralded his statement. Paul's jail sentence was commuted on November 28, and six weeks later, on January 9, 1918, Wilson announced his support for the Nineteenth Amendment.[93]

In addition to Paul's tactics, several war-related and political factors prompted Wilson's dramatic about-face. Many women, including prominent feminists, eagerly volunteered for the war effort, and he publicly acknowledged their contribution in this time of national crisis. On September 30, 1918, he told a joint session of Congress that women's suffrage was "vitally essential to the successful prosecution of the great war of humanity in which we are engaged." He also worried about losing Democratic Party seats in Congress in the upcoming off-year elections, and support for suffrage was designed to shore up support among liberals. Finally, in his Annual Message to Congress on December 2, 1918, just two weeks after the war ended, he paid a glowing tribute to the contributions of women, praising "their instant intelligence, quickening every task that they touched; their capacity for organization and cooperation, which gave their action discipline and enhanced the effectiveness of everything they attempted." They deserved a proper reward, and

92 "Miss Alice Paul on Hunger Strike," *NYT*, November 7, 1917. Paul, *Conversations with Alice Paul*, p. 223. "Peace Party Ousts Mrs. Carrie Catt," *NYT*, March 7, 1917. Paul, *Conversations with Alice Paul*. Elizabeth Bass, letter to Wilson, May 3, 1917, *PWW*, 42, p. 208.

93 "Wilson Shocked at Jailing Militants," *NYT*, July 19, 1917. Alison Turnbull Hopkins to Wilson, July 20, 1917, *PWW*, 43, p. 235. National Woman's Party, Report of the Legislative Department, Month of July, 1917, NWP, MF ED, Reel 87, LOC. "President Speeds Suffrage in State," *NYT*, August 30, 1917. "New Suffrage Drive Planned by Women," ibid., November 7, 1917. "President Puts Suffrage to Fore," ibid., October 26, 1917. "20,000 March in Suffrage Line," ibid., October 28, 1917. Graham, "Woodrow Wilson, Alice Paul, and the Woman Suffrage Movement," 678.

"the least tribute we can pay them is to make them the equals of men in political rights" (England granted women the right to vote in 1918 in large part because of their contribution to the war effort). With Wilson's support, the Nineteenth Amendment was ratified on August 18, 1920, and women voted for president for the first time that November. Suffrage marked the end of one era in the status of women in America and the beginning of a new era. To be sure, women already voted in many states, but denial of the vote for president represented both a real and a symbolic exclusion of women from full citizenship. Granting the vote to half the population was one of the greatest expansions of liberty in American history. The Nineteenth Amendment might not have passed when it did without Wilson's support, and for this, he deserves proper credit. Nonetheless, that support was late, was driven by the militant protests, and was heavily influenced by pragmatic political considerations.[94]

BRANDEIS TO THE SUPREME COURT

Without any question, Woodrow Wilson's greatest contribution to civil liberties was his appointment of Louis Brandeis to the Supreme Court, which remains one of the most significant appointments in the entire history of the Court. Although Brandeis became one of the most influential justices in the development of civil liberties, Wilson did not choose him because of that issue. Brandeis was a prominent progressive reformer on jurisprudence and social and economic issues and is most famous for originating the "Brandeis Brief," which employed empirical data rather than abstract legal theory to argue a case. Wilson met Brandeis early in the 1912 presidential campaign, and Brandeis played a significant role in shaping the candidate's views on regulating the trusts, which was the dominant issue in the campaign. Civil liberties did not enter into their discussions.[95]

Brandeis's confirmation process turned ugly, however, and became "one of the most controversial in the history of the Supreme Court," according to the Brandeis biographer Philippa Strum. Opponents questioned his alleged "radicalism" on economic policy. In fact, he was a firm believer in the free enterprise system, arguing as did other progressives that reform would aid its survival by creating greater opportunities for individuals. More serious were the charges of "unprofessional" legal conduct, which had strong anti-semitic overtones. Brandeis would be the first Jew to serve on the Court. No less a figure than the Harvard University president A. Lawrence Lowell joined other prominent Bostonians in declaring him "unfit" for the Court. The historian John Morton Blum credits Wilson for overcoming his southern prejudices, which included a tradition of anti-semitism, in choosing Brandeis and standing behind him during the confirmation controversy.[96]

On the Court, Brandeis was instrumental in shaping modern First Amendment law. At some point in summer 1919 he began for the first time to think seriously about freedom of speech, as did Justice Oliver Wendell Holmes. Both had joined the unanimous opinion

[94] Wilson, Address to the Senate, September 30, 1918, *PWW*, 51, pp. 158–61. Wilson, *Sixth Annual Message to Congress*, December 2, 1918, APP. Hochschild, *To End All Wars*, pp. 315–16. "Tennessee Completes Suffrage Victory," *NYT*, August 19, 1920. Lunardini, *From Equal Suffrage to Equal Rights*, p. 147.

[95] Melvin Urofsky, *Louis D. Brandeis: A Life* (New York: Pantheon, 2009). See also Philippa Strum, *Brandeis: Beyond Progressivism* (Lawrence: University Press of Kansas, 1993), Philippa Strum, *Louis D. Brandeis: Justice for the People* (Cambridge, Ma: Harvard University Press, 1984), and Melvin I. Urofsky, *Louis D. Brandeis and the Progressive Tradition* (Boston: Little, Brown, 1981).

[96] Blum, *Woodrow Wilson: The Politics of Morality*, p. 116.

in *Schenck v. United States* that March, upholding Schenck's conviction and articulating the clear and present danger test. Just eight months later they switched and dissented in *Abrams v. United States*, and Holmes's opinion that the First Amendment protected unpopular speech became one of the most famous statements about freedom of speech in the history of the Court. Brandeis's concurring opinion in the 1927 *Whitney v. California* case, which was virtually a dissent, carried the *Abrams* argument further, arguing that the government could limit speech only in the case of imminent lawless action. His dissent in *Olmstead v. United States*, a 1928 wiretapping case arising from Prohibition enforcement, meanwhile, was an early and eloquent statement of a right to privacy. We can only speculate on the course of constitutional law and the right to privacy in America had he been joined by just one other Justice in the 5–4 decision.[97]

Brandeis had the misfortune, however, to join the most notorious anti-semite ever to sit on the Court. Wilson's 1914 appointee James C. McReynolds, his first attorney general, refused even to speak to Brandeis for three years, made many blatantly anti-semitic remarks, insulted other justices, and was universally regarded as an utterly unpleasant individual. He is mainly remembered as one of the archconservative justices who struck down President Franklin D. Roosevelt's New Deal measures in the 1930s. Nonetheless, he wrote two of the earliest pro–civil liberties decisions in the 1920s (*Meyer v. Nebraska*; *Pierce v. Society of Sisters*), which enunciated a limited constitutional right to privacy. Additionally, he joined the majority in the pivotal 1925 decision *Gitlow v. New York*, where the Court for the first time incorporated the First Amendment into the due process clause of the Fourteenth Amendment and laid the foundation for the civil liberties revolution in later years.[98] One is tempted to argue that McReynolds and Brandeis cancel each other out in terms of an overall assessment of Wilson Court appointments. McReynolds's influence was temporary, however, while Brandeis's legacy has been an enduring one.

END OF A PRESIDENCY – DAWN OF THE CIVIL LIBERTIES ERA

Through his last eighteen months as president, Woodrow Wilson was disabled by his stroke, participating only minimally in his official responsibilities. He was at least aware enough to order Democrats in the Senate not to compromise on the League of Nations, thereby guaranteeing its rejection. Even, if he fully comprehended the tragic events of the war years at home, it is absolutely certain that he had no second thoughts about his handling of dissent. Ever self-righteous, he remained convinced that it was proper and served the democratic process. Walter Lippmann, who had eagerly enlisted in the war effort, did understand the damage, however, and expressed second thoughts in the *Atlantic Monthly*. Surveying the trauma of the war years in December 1919, he somberly concluded that "the traditional liberties of speech and opinion rest on no solid foundation."[99]

97 *Schenck v. United States*, 249 U.S. 47 (1919). *Abrams v. United States*, 250 U.S. 616 (1919). Richard Polenberg, *Fighting Faiths: The Abrams Case, The Supreme Court, and Free Speech* (New York: Viking, 1987). *Whitney v. California*, 274 U.S. 357 (1927). *Olmstead v. United States*, 277 U.S. 438 (1928).

98 Henry J. Abraham, *Justices, Presidents, and Senators*. 5th ed. (Lanham, MD: Rowman & Littlefield, 2008), pp. 139–41; Wilson's third appointee, John H. Clarke, resigned after only six years on the Court and made no mark as a Justice (pp. 144–5).

99 Walter Lippmann, "The Basic Problem of Democracy," *Atlantic Monthly* 124 (December 1919): 616.

The trauma of the World War I years was a watershed in American life, exposing how weak was the support for freedom of speech and thrusting civil liberties to the forefront of American law and politics. The wartime repression and the reaction to it marked the dawn of the civil liberties era in American history. The period also marked the first appearance of the apparatus of the national security state that resurfaced in the late 1930s to become a permanent part of American life and one of the most serious threats to civil liberties.

President Woodrow Wilson's contribution to this watershed moment was entirely negative. He uncritically approved the suppression of freedom of speech and press, issued only one weak statement critical of mob violence, and even before the war fanned the flames of antiimmigrant fever that boiled over into an attack on all suspected disloyalty during the war. His legacy of repression lasted for decades, and the attack on dissent continued through the 1920s and beyond. Had Wilson established a tone of tolerance for dissent, the course of American history might well have been very different. Additionally, Wilson introduced racial segregation into federal agencies and opposed women's suffrage until political exigencies forced him to reverse course. Historians consistently rate Wilson among the few "near-great" presidents in American history, but while his domestic legislative accomplishments were truly impressive, his record on civil liberties is among the worst of all modern presidents. The historian John Morton Blum summed it up with the comment "In the name of republican institutions, the Wilson administration violated the Constitution; in the name of law, it allowed license; in the name of democracy, it practiced autocracy.[100]

The blame, of course, cannot be laid entirely at Wilson's feet. His insistence on national unity and intolerance of dissent were shared by almost all Progressive Era reformers. It required the trauma of the wartime events to provoke a rethinking of the meaning of the Bill of Rights. The Supreme Court, meanwhile, afforded no protection for dissenting opinion. The modern civil liberties era in American history that was born during Wilson's presidency was signaled by two events. First, with the 1919 *Abrams* case, the Supreme Court embarked on a reconsideration of the meaning of the First Amendment, and ultimately of the entire Bill of Rights, in American life. That process continues to unfold today as a central part of our legal and political life. Second, a few thoughtful Americans realized that it was necessary to launch a continuing fight for civil liberties, and that insight led to the formation of the American Civil Liberties Union in 1920. It ultimately would be joined by a host of other rights advocacy groups related to race, women, the disabled, reproductive rights, and virtually every aspect of American life. All that lay decades in the future, however. The day Woodrow Wilson left the White House, civil liberties - freedom of speech, press, and assembly; racial justice; and due process - appeared to have no place in America.[101]

[100] Lindgren and Calabresi, "Rating the Presidents." Blum, *The Progressive Presidents*, p. 98.
[101] Walker, *In Defense of American Liberties*, pp. 46–7.

J. Edgar Hoover, December 1924, after being appointed director of the Bureau of Investigation, later renamed the Federal Bureau of Investigation, by President Calvin Coolidge. Beginning in 1936, Hoover maintained perhaps the longest-running violation of civil liberties in American history. *Source*: Library of Congress.

3 Harding, Coolidge, and Hoover

Civil Liberties in the Wilderness

CIVIL LIBERTIES IN A CHANGING AMERICA

The most famous civil liberties event of the 1920s occurred 560 miles from Washington, D.C., in the otherwise obscure town of Dayton, Tennessee. The celebrated defense attorney Clarence Darrow mercilessly grilled William Jennings Bryan, a leader of the Christian fundamentalist movement, over the literal interpretation of the Old Testament. The occasion was the Scopes "Monkey Trial" involving a new Tennessee law banning the teaching of evolution in public schools, which eventually became one of the most famous courtroom confrontations in American history.[1]

The Scopes case did not impinge on presidential politics. President Calvin Coolidge said nothing about it. Nonetheless, the trial was a harbinger of a bitter controversy over the place of religion in American life that would eventually take center stage in national politics, the first gun in a long-running "culture war" between traditional religion and the new secular, scientific culture.[2]

Presidents and civil liberties in the twenties

At first glance, the decade of the 1920s appears to be a complete blank with respect to presidents and civil liberties, a period of calm following the trauma of World War I. The three Republican presidents, Warren G. Harding (1921–3),[3] Calvin Coolidge (1923–9,[4] and Herbert Hoover (1929–33),[5] were passive chief executives, committed to the GOP belief in limited government. (Coolidge wrote in his *Autobiography*, "Never do anything you can get someone else to do for you.") Coolidge declared in 1924 that the Constitution "is the

[1] Edward L. Larson, *Summer for the Gods: The Scopes Trial and America's Continuing Debate over Science and Religion* (New York: Basic Books, 1997); older but still valuable is Ray Ginger, *Six Days or Forever* (Boston: Beacon Press, 1958).

[2] James Davison Hunter, *Culture Wars: The Struggle to Define America* (New York: Basic Books, 1991).

[3] Robert K. Murray, *The Harding Era: Warren G. Harding and His Administration* (Minneapolis: University of Minnesota Press 1969). Robert K. Murray, *The Politics of Normalcy: Governmental Theory and Practice in the Harding-Coolidge Era* (New York: W. W. Norton, 1973). John W. Dean, *Warren G. Harding* (New York: Times Books, 2004).

[4] Robert H. Ferrell, *The Presidency of Calvin Coolidge* (Lawrence: University Press of Kansas, 1998). Donald R. McCoy, *Calvin Coolidge: The Quiet President* (New York, Macmillan, 1967). Thomas B. Silver, *Coolidge and the Historians* (Durham, NC: Carolina Academic Press, 1982). Robert Sobel, *Coolidge: An American Enigma* (Washington, DC: Regnery, 1998).

[5] Joan Hoff Wilson, *Herbert Hoover: Forgotten Progressive* (Prospect Heights, IL: Waveland Press, 1992). David Burner, *Herbert Hoover: A Public Life* (New York: Knopf, 1979). George H. Nash, *The Life of Herbert Hoover*, 3 Vols. (New York: W. W. Norton, 1983–96).

sole source of American freedom," but he represented the prevailing view that the document did not include protection for political and civil rights. Similarly, Herbert Hoover's 1922 book *American Individualism* is silent on individual rights.[6]

The traditional image of the twenties as a period of peace and prosperity – "normalcy," as Harding put it – is too facile, however. Conflicts over "Americanism," censorship, racial justice, women's rights, sexuality, privacy, and police misconduct percolated across America. The dominant culture of business and consumerism generated changes that ultimately had powerful effects on civil liberties. Such mundane items as the washing machine and other home appliances, for example, promised to liberate the housewife from hours of toil; the automobile gave people new personal freedoms; the movies defined national standards of dress, behavior, and sexuality; the movies and the radio (KDKA in Pittsburgh began broadcasting as the first commercial station on November 2, 1920) broke down regional, ethnic, and religious traditions of morality. These changes had a deeply corrosive effect on the traditional culture of self-restraint and conformity to the standards of community, church, and family, redefining the norms of personal conduct, sexuality, and marriage. The culture of the twenties, in short, planted civil liberties land mines that would begin to explode in the decades ahead.[7]

When NAACP leaders met with the GOP presidential candidate Warren G. Harding during the 1920 presidential election campaign and won a promise of support for most of their civil rights agenda, it marked the arrival of another new feature of America politics. Powerless and outcast groups organized to claim their rightful place in America, challenging the dominant one-dimensional view of America as a white, male, and Protestant country. The NAACP lobbied Congress for a federal antilynching law, and the National Woman's Party introduced an Equal Rights Amendment (ERA) to the Constitution in 1923 to guarantee equality for women. The ACLU took up the Scopes case, the free speech rights of working people and communists, and other civil liberties issues.[8] Advocacy by public interest rights groups first appeared in the 1920s and eventually expanded into a major force in American life.

Contrary to later political stereotypes, the three Republican presidents of the twenties were more sympathetic to civil liberties than were most Democrats. In addition to cautious support for a federal antilynching law and the ERA, on a few notable issues they ended some of the worst repressive measures begun during the war years.

6 Address at the Dedication of the Monument to the First Division of the American Expeditionary Forces, Washington, DC, October 4, 1924, APP. Calvin Coolidge, *Autobiography* (New York: Cosmopolitan Books, 1929), pp. 196–7. Herbert Hoover, *American Individualism* (Garden City, NY: Doubleday, Page, 1922).

7 Lynn Dumenil, "Reshifting Perspectives on the 1920s: Recent Trends in Social and Cultural History," in John Earl Haynes, ed., *Calvin Coolidge and the Coolidge Era: Essays on the History of the 1920s* (Washington, DC: Library of Congress, 1998), pp. 63–96. See also Ronald Allen Goldberg, *America in the Twenties* (Syracuse, NY: Syracuse University Press, 2003).

8 Meeting with Harding and efforts to meet with Cox: NAACP, Board of Directors, Minutes, September 13, 1920, NAACPP, MF ED, Reel 1. Charles F. Kellogg, *NAACP: A History of the National Association for the Advancement of Colored People* (Baltimore: Johns Hopkins University, 1967). Christine A. Lunardini, *From Equal Suffrage to Equal Rights: Alice Paul and the National Woman's Party, 1910–1928* (New York: NYU Press, 1986). Samuel Walker, *In Defense of American Liberties: A History of the ACLU* (New York: Oxford University Press, 1990), Ch. 3. See ACLU, *Black Justice* (New York: ACLU, 1931), ACLUP MF (1977), Reel 90.

THE RED SCARE "HANGOVER"

"Normalcy" and repression

The prominent novelist Upton Sinclair began reading the Bill of Rights at a May 15, 1923, labor rally in San Pedro, California, but was arrested before he could finish. The Los Angeles police chief declared, "None of the Constitution stuff here, see?" Sinclair's arrest dramatized the national pattern of suppression of free speech by antilabor and antiradical forces. Sinclair's arrest on what became known as "Liberty Hill" led to the founding of the Los Angeles chapter of the ACLU.[9]

"The fear of radicalism persisted almost undiminished" after the war, observed the ACLU in 1923. "The heresy-hunt went on, with changing phases.... Intolerance organized in the Ku Klux Klan extended its area of militant activity from the South and Southwest to the North and Middle West." The ACLU counted fifty Klan chapters in New Jersey, and in Oregon the Klan sponsored a law that would put parochial schools out of business. The immediate civil liberties conflicts of the early 1920s were largely a hangover from World War I and the Red Scare.[10]

Roger Baldwin began each weekly ACLU Executive Committee meeting with a report on the "Civil Liberty Situation for the Week," providing a grim recital of violations of freedom of speech and assembly and vigilante violence. His August 15, 1921, report cited a Post Office ban on Carlo Tresca's Italian socialist paper, *Il Martello* (The Hammer), the denial of a permit for a Sacco-Vanzetti protest meeting on Boston Common, and an American Legion mob attack on a Socialist Party meeting in Shenandoah, Iowa. Los Angeles police arrested an atheist in 1925, with the police chief announcing, "I will not allow any man to deny the existence of God down there on the plaza." Mob violence continued unchecked across the country. Between September 1, 1920, and September 1, 1922, the ACLU reported 102 lynchings, which killed sixty-nine African Americans and thirty-three whites. Sixty-three people were tarred and feathered in the same period, only two of whom were African American, and mobs drove 460 people, most of them members of radical labor unions, out of their communities.[11]

Fear of immigrants continued at a high pitch, culminating in the 1924 Immigration Act with a national origins quota system that discriminated against Italians, Poles, Jews, and other Southern and Eastern Europeans. Accepting the Republican nomination for president in 1924, Calvin Coolidge endorsed the law, saying, "We cast no aspersions on any race or creed, but we must remember that every object of our institutions of society and government will fail unless America be kept American." That meant keeping new immigrants out.[12]

[9] "Upton Sinclair Held for 'Breach of Peace,'" *NYT*, May 17, 1923. Anthony Arthur, *Radical Innocent: Upton Sinclair* (New York: Random House, 2006), pp. 180–97. Liberty Hill is now a registered historic site in California.

[10] ACLU, *Annual Report, 1923* (New York: Arno Press, 1970), p. 3. "The 'hangover' Theme: Howard Zinn," in *La Guardia in Congress* (Ithaca, NY: Cornell University Press, 1959), p. 97.

[11] ACLU, *Mob Violence in the United States* (New York: ACLU, 1922), ACLUP-MF (1977), Reel 90. LAPD: ACLU, *Annual Report 1925*, p. 16.

[12] Hans P. Vought, *The Bully Pulpit and the Melting Pot: American Presidents and the Immigrant, 1897–1933* (Macon, GA: Mercer University Press, 2004) contains chapters on each of the three Republican presidents.

The continuing crusade against "reds"

Reaction to the Red Scare shadowed the 1920 presidential elections, and some thoughtful Americans had second thoughts about the violations of civil liberties. The Democratic Party was acutely sensitive about criticisms of Woodrow Wilson and refused to concede he had done anything wrong. The party's 1920 platform rejected "unfounded" criticisms of "alleged interference with the freedom of the press and freedom of speech." Blandly ignoring all the evidence, it claimed that "no utterance … and no publication has been repressed," apart from treason or threats to "the nation's peace, order and security in time of war." The Republican Platform demanded "that every American citizen shall enjoy the ancient and constitutional right of free speech, free press and free assembly," but quickly added that "no man may advocate resistance to the law, and no man may advocate violent overthrow of the government." Republican leaders had not protested the violations of free speech or press during the war, and the party's criticisms of abuse of presidential power now referred to the unprecedented government regulation of the economy during the war (which it had then supported).[13]

President Harding expressed the now standard pieties about freedom from government regulation in his March 1921 inaugural but also warned about political radicalism, advising Americans to be "no less alert in guarding against dangers from within than it is watchful against dangers from without." Other countries had made a "tragic experiment" with revolution, but "there is no place for it in America." Ignoring all the evidence, he assured his audience that under our "constitutional freedom," "minorities are sacredly protected." Harding's speech captured perfectly the vast gap between the conventional rhetoric about liberty and the realities of intolerance and repression.[14] Right-wing zealots across the country led a relentless campaign to impose their notion of "Americanism." The defense of free speech was regarded as advocating communism, anarchism, or revolution, and the ACLU topped their list of "un-American" groups. Paranoia about communists' power was often comical. A July 1923 headline in the *Los Angeles Times* warned that "Reds Collect Millions" for their planned U.S. revolution. Private groups rather than the federal government led the attack on dissent, with the American Legion, organized in November 1919, the most aggressive. The Daughters of the American Revolution (DAR) circulated a list of "Doubtful Speakers" to be avoided that included the famous social worker Jane Addams, the birth control leaders Mary Ware Dennett and Margaret Sanger, the ERA advocate Alice Paul (a "Revolutionary Feminist"), and Lillian Wald (a "communist," despite her loyalty to President Wilson during the war). In response, the ACLU tried to reframe the issue of free speech in terms of "Old Fashioned America Liberties." New York City public schools in October 1927, however, denied the ACLU permission to speak on the topic. The ACLU had virtually no victories in these years, however. The 1925 Scopes case was its first breakthrough regarding public opinion about civil liberties.[15]

13 Democratic Party platform of 1920; Republican Party platform of 1920, APP.

14 Harding, Inaugural Address, March 4, 1921, APP.

15 *Los Angeles Times*, July 9, 1923, clipping in ACLUP-MF (1996), Reel 32. Daughters of the American Revolution, *Doubtful Speakers* (1927), available online, Women and Social Movements in the United States, 1600–2000: http://womhist.alesanderstreet.com. ACLU, Board of Directors, Minutes, October 10, 1927, ACLUP-MF (1977), Reel 1. "School Board Bars Free Speech Rally by Liberties Union," *NYT*, May 22, 1926. "Baldwin to Appeal to School Board," ibid., April 24, 1929. Walker, *In Defense of American Liberties*, p. 59.

Federal prosecution of radicals virtually ended in the 1920s, but state and local authorities continued the antiradical crusade. Thirty-five states enacted variations of criminal syndicalism laws directed at communists and other radicals. The ACLU, meanwhile, concluded in 1921 that "the chief interference with free speech and assemblage ... is now practiced by city police." Eight years later little had changed; the ACLU reported that in 1929 "nine-tenths of all the attacks on freedom of speech and assembly are made by the local police." California was the center of the most aggressive repression, and its most celebrated case involved Charlotte Anita Whitney, convicted of violating the state's 1919 Criminal Syndicalism law. Her 1927 appeal to the U.S. Supreme Court (*Whitney v. California*), however, led to an opinion by Justice Louis Brandeis that ultimately shaped the direction of First Amendment law in the direction of broad protection for unpopular political speech.[16]

In truth, arrests and prosecution were only one part of the campaign to silence dissent in the 1920s. The ACLU's Walter Nelles concluded in August 1920 that the wartime repression lived on. The enforced "mobilization of the mind of America" had terrorized the country and left people "somewhat incapacitated for independent thinking."[17]

AMNESTY FOR THE VICTIMS OF WARTIME PROSECUTIONS

A lingering issue from the war years was the fate of the victims of Espionage Act prosecutions. The term "political prisoner" has no precise definition, and the estimated number of wartime victims fluctuated over the years. They included William Powell of Lansing, Michigan, serving a twenty-year prison term for denying reports of German atrocities, denouncing the war as a rich man's war, and saying he "could not believe in the president." All of these comments were in a conversation with relatives in his own home. (President Wilson reduced his sentence but refused to grant a pardon.) In his last months in office, disabled by his stroke and bitter over the Senate's rejection of the Versailles Treaty, Wilson remained unforgiving toward critics of the war. While he reduced the sentences of some prisoners, he rejected all pleas for pardons and amnesty. Most famously, he refused to pardon the aged and ailing Socialist Party leader Eugene V. Debs, who was serving a ten-year prison sentence in Atlanta. The genial Warren G. Harding, however, pardoned Debs on Christmas Day 1921. The terms of the pardon called for Debs to visit the White House, allegedly because Harding, despite his status as president, was excited about meeting this famous person.[18]

Amnesty for Espionage Act victims became one of the ACLU's major campaigns. The distinction between amnesty and pardon complicated the matter, however. Many prisoners demanded amnesty, a "forgetting" of any wrongdoing, and rejected pardons, which simply forgave them for their offenses. The ACLU organized the Joint Amnesty

16 ACLU, *The Police and the Radicals: What 88 Police Chiefs Think and Do about Radical Meetings* (New York: ACLU, March 1921); ACLU, *Blue Coats and Reds* (New York: ACLU, June 1929), ACLU-MF (1977), Reel 90. Civil liberties in the Twenties: Paul L. Murphy, *The Meaning of Freedom of Speech: First Amendment Freedoms from Wilson to FDR* (Westport, CT: Greenwood Press, 1972). ACLU, *State Political Prisoners* (New York: ACLU, May 1924); ACLU, *Who May Safely Advocate Force and Violence?* (New York: ACLU, November 1922), ACLUP-MF (1977), Reel 90.

17 Walter Nelles, *Seeing Red: Civil Liberty and Law in the Period Following the War* (New York: ACLU, August 1920), ACLUP-MF (1977), Reel 90.

18 Nick Salvatore, *Eugene V. Debs: Citizen and Socialist* (Urbana: University of Illinois Press, 1982), pp. 326–8.

Committee with pacifist groups in 1922 to lead the fight. The committee picketed the White House and promised to "picket the Golf Club where the President goes every day." Lucy Branham, Vassar graduate and feminist, who had picketed President Wilson, heckled President Harding on his cross-country trip in summer 1923. "Mr. President," she asked, "all other countries have released their political prisoners, why not America?" The ACLU's Roger Baldwin conceded in 1923 that picketing had "no perceptible effect" but nonetheless proposed stepping up the pressure by "picketing and annoying the Attorney General" outside the Justice Department.[19]

Despite the repressive national climate, pockets of support for amnesty appeared. The Idaho senator William G. Borah promised six formal hearings around the country. The Joint Amnesty Committee's demonstrations during Harding's cross-country trip to Alaska included local Episcopal, Methodist, Catholic, and Jewish leaders, and even the governor of Montana. The persistent lobbying eventually paid off, and President Calvin Coolidge released most of the prisoners from the war years on Christmas Day 1923.[20] The releases did not completely settle the issue, however. When Herbert Hoover became president in 1929, the ACLU sought restoration of full citizenship rights – mainly the right to vote – for all the estimated fifteen hundred victims of the wartime repression, labeling them "political prisoners." Hoover took a sincere interest in the matter and asked Attorney General William Mitchell to investigate. Mitchell, however, rejected the concept of "political prisoner" as "unknown to American law" and pointed out that pardons had been granted to all who applied for them. He estimated that 206 prisoners remained but advised Hoover that a general pardon would be an "admission" that they were political prisoners. Jane Addams wrote to Hoover to plea for amnesty and a public statement, but he replied that it would only result in "acrimonious discussion."[21]

POLITICAL SPYING CONTINUES

Anonymous bureaucrats in the War Department's Chemical Warfare Service in 1923 produced a document designed to frighten Americans about a massive radical conspiracy in America. Their "Spiderweb" chart purported to show a network of personal and organizational ties among communists, socialists, pacifists, the ACLU, and a host of others. Variations of the spiderweb became popular among right-wing anti-communists for decades. The propaganda work of the Chemical Warfare Service had burst into a public controversy the year before, when its director publicly accused the pacifist National Council for the Prevention of War of supporting communism. The group demanded and received an apology from Secretary of War John Weeks, but they alleged that the Chemical Service did not follow his order to end its attacks on pacifists and other liberal groups.[22]

19 Letters, Marguerite Tucker to Amy Woods, October 25, 1922, JACP, SPC.

20 Joint Amnesty Committee, Minutes, October 27, 1922; Report of Joint Amnesty Committee, June 1923, JACP, SPC. Baldwin to Joint Amnesty Committee, March 9, 1923, ACLUP-MF (1996), Reel 8. ACLU, *Amnesty for Political Prisoners* (New York: ACLU, October, 1920), ACLUP-MF (1977), Reel 90. Branham: "Radicals: Three Riddles," *Time*, June 25, 1923. Coolidge: ACLU, *Annual Report*, 1923, p. 5.

21 Attorney General Mitchell to Mr. President, August 23, 1929; William D. Mitchell, to President, August 8, 1929, Amnesty File, Box 63, HHPL. ACLU, *Restore the Rights of Citizenship to the 1500 Espionage Act Victims!* (New York: ACLU, 1928), ACLUP-MF (1977), Reel 90.[Unsigned letter, but clearly Hoover] to "My Dear Miss Adams, August 29, 1929, Amnesty File, Box 63, HHPL.

22 Spiderweb chart in Henry Ford's newspaper: *The Dearborn Independent*, XXIV (March 1924), p. 11, available online at http://womhist.alexadnerstreet.com. Joan Jensen, *Army Surveillance in America, 1775–1980*

Political spying by the War Department also continued through the Corps of Intelligence Police (CIP), organized in 1920 with a staff of forty-one. The CIP's 1920 Emergency Plan White outlined military occupation and control of military corps areas in case of an emergency. Ordered to cease surveillance of American citizens in March 1922, the War Department persisted nonetheless. In 1932, for example, it monitored communist involvement in the Bonus Army, a march on Washington by thousands of veterans demanding early payment of scheduled bonuses.[23]

The Bureau of Investigation, meanwhile, continued its own political spying, undeterred by criticisms of the Palmer Raids. A 1922 incident exposed its covert practices and provoked new protests. On August 22, bureau agents raided a secret Workers Party (the official name of the Communist Party at that time) meeting in the little town of Bridgman, Michigan, about 120 miles from Chicago on the shores of Lake Michigan. The bureau was hopelessly corrupt and inefficient in those years, and the inept agents gave themselves away. Thus, when four bureau agents and about twenty local volunteers arrived, most of the top leaders had already fled. Eventually, Earl Browder and Charles Ruthenberg and other communist leaders were arrested and prosecuted.[24]

The ACLU protested the Justice Department's involvement in the raid, pointing out that the Bridgman arrestees had not violated any federal law and, in fact, were being prosecuted under the Michigan Criminal Syndicalism law. An assistant U.S. attorney responded by accusing the ACLU of inhibiting a fair trial because of its "propaganda." The ACLU's pamphlet condemning *The Nationwide Spy System Centering in the Department of Justice* may have had some effect. In 1924 the newly appointed attorney general Harlan Fiske Stone ordered spying ended. Stone warned that "there is always the possibility that a secret police may become a menace to free government and free institutions, because it carries with it the possibility of abuses of power." He then issued guidelines ordering an end to political spying by the bureau.[25]

Although Calvin Coolidge is best known for doing very little as president and for not supporting civil liberties, he made one notable contribution to the protection of individual rights by appointing a politically independent attorney general, who cleaned up the Bureau of Investigation. Scandals in the Justice Department under Attorney General Harry Daugherty tainted the Harding administration, along with the highly publicized Teapot Dome scandal in the Interior Department. The Bureau of Investigation director,

(New Haven, CT: Yale University Press, 1991), pp. 190–9. Christine K. Erickson, "'I Have Not Had One Fact Disproven': Elizabeth Dilling's Crusade against Communism in the 1930s," *Journal of American Studies* 36, no. 3 (2002): 473–89. "Anti-War Council Again Asks Apology," *NYT*, July 7, 1924. Carrie Chapman Catt, "The Lie Factory," *The Woman Citizen*, 20 (September 1924): 24–5, available at http://womhist.alexanderstreet.com.

23 Military Intelligence reports: W. C. Grooms, Memorandum to Capt. J. A. Sullivan, Crime Prevention Division [presumably District of Columbia police], June 2, 1932, Re "Communist Meeting," War Veterans – Bonus Files, Box 375, HHPL. Jensen, *Army Surveillance in America*, pp. 192–207. Paul Dickson and Thomas B. Allen, *The Bonus Army: An American Epic* (New York: Walker and Co., 2004).

24 "Seek 30 More Reds," *NYT*, August 25, 1922. ACLU, *The Michigan Communist Trials* (New York: ACLU, October 1922), ACLUP-MF (1977), Reel 90. Theodore Draper, *The Roots of American Communism* (New York: Viking, 1957), pp. 363–75.

25 ACLU, Press Release, March 15, 1923; Nelles to Frankfurter, March 21, 1923, FFP, Box 124, LOC. ACLU, *The Nationwide Spy System Centering in the Department of Justice* (New York: ACLU, May 1924), ACLUP-MF (1977), Reel 90. Walker, *In Defense of American Liberties*, pp. 51–71. Stone quoted in *NYT*, May 10, 1924, cited in U.S. Senate, Select Committee to Study Governmental Operations with Respect to the Intelligence Activities, *Final Report, Book II, Intelligence Activities and the Rights of Americans* (April 23, 1976), p. 23.

William J. Burns, appointed politically connected people as "Dollar a Year Men" and countenanced political spying, while President Harding remained indifferent.

All of that changed when Harding suddenly died in August 1923, and President Coolidge appointed Stone attorney general. Then dean of Columbia University Law School and a future Supreme Court Justice (1925–46) and chief justice (1941–6), Stone had genuine civil liberties concerns. During World War I he served on a commission to examine conscientious objector cases and developed an appreciation for how the law failed to accommodate many sincere young men requesting CO status. He later testified against the Palmer Raids before the Senate in 1921, arguing that "any system" that allows the government "to restrain the liberty of individuals, without safeguards . . . will result in abuse of power."[26]

To head the Bureau of Investigation, however, Stone made a fateful choice, with disastrous consequences for civil liberties. He selected twenty-nine-year-old John Edgar Hoover, who had somehow escaped being tainted by the Palmer Raids, even though he had been a key figure in them. By 1924 Hoover had a reputation as a dutiful, low-key, and efficient bureaucrat. The historian Kenneth Ackerman argues that the normally thorough Stone simply gave him "the benefit of every doubt." Perhaps he thought the young man was raw material he could mold in the proper direction. Ackerman titles the applicable chapter in his book on Hoover, "Fooled."[27]

Stone gave Hoover a set of operating principles that included ending political spying. Point 1 of his May 13 memo directed that the bureau would limit itself "strictly to investigations of violation of law," which meant no investigations of purely political activities. He also ordered an end to warrantless wiretapping and directed Hoover to reduce the size of the bureau, terminate the "Dollar a Year Men," fire "incompetent and unreliable" employees, and seek job applicants with legal training. For the most part, Hoover dutifully complied, significantly raising personnel standards. Decades later, bureau files released under the Freedom of Information Act indicated that political spying almost completely ceased and did not resume until the late 1930s. Most historians have failed to see this change. The voluminous FBI files on the ACLU, for example, contain only a few scattered items between late 1924 and the late 1930s, while the files on the African-American leaders W. E. B. Dubois and A. Philip Randolph do not begin until the early 1940s. President Coolidge, in short, deserves credit for ending FBI spying, although he probably knew little about the details. As we shall see, spying revived in the late 1930s at the direction of President Franklin D. Roosevelt.[28]

[26] The best account of Hoover's appointment is Kenneth D. Ackerman, *Young J. Edgar: Hoover, the Red Scare, and the Assault on Civil Liberties* (New York: Carroll & Graf, 2007), pp. 372–81; Stone quote on p. 373. Laton McCartney, *The Teapot Dome Scandal: How Big Oil Bought the Harding White House and Tried to Steal the Country* (New York: Random House, 2008). Alpheus Thomas Mason, *Harlan Fiske Stone: Pillar of the Law* (New York: Viking, 1956), pp. 150–3. "Restoring Confidence: Harlan Fiske Stone," in Nancy V. Baker, *Conflicting Loyalties: Law and Politics in the Attorney General's Office, 1789–1990* (Lawrence: University Press of Kansas, 1992), pp. 135–9.

[27] Curtis Gentry, *J. Edgar Hoover: The Man and the Secrets* (New York: W. W. Norton, 1991). John Lord O'Brian recommendation of Hoover as a "very hard working man:" O'Brian, COHC, pp. 293, 323.

[28] Mason, *Harlan Fiske Stone*, p. 151, citing Memorandum, Attorney General to J. Edgar Hoover, May 13, 1924. U.S. Senate, Select Committee to Study Governmental Operations with Respect to the Intelligence Activities, *Final Report, Book III, Supplementary Detailed Staff Reports on Intelligence Activities and the Rights of Americans* (April 23, 1976). pp. 277–9, 388–9. ACLU FBI files are in the ACLU Archives at Princeton University and in the FBI Reading Room in Washington, DC. *FBI file on W. E. B. DuBois* (Wilmington, De: Scholarly Resources, 1996).

The most curious aspect of Hoover's appointment was the enthusiastic endorsement by none other than the ACLU director, Roger Baldwin, who traveled to Washington, met with both Stone and Hoover, and went away mightily impressed. He wrote to Stone that the reform of the bureau "meets every suggestion which any of us could possibly make" and then spread word among his liberal friends that the bureau was now in good hands and they should tone down their criticisms. The tragedy of this episode is not just that Baldwin was fooled - after all, Stone was too - but that it caused him to temper his criticisms of the bureau in later years when there was abundant evidence of revived spying. As a result, ACLU criticisms of the FBI during the 1940s and 1950s were muted. (Hoover did not return the favor, however, and even targeted Baldwin for custodial detention in 1940). The long-term price for civil liberties of Stone and Baldwin's failure regarding Hoover was enormous.[29]

KEEPING DANGEROUS IDEAS OUT OF THE UNITED STATES

Federal government attacks on political dissent in the 1920s included keeping allegedly "dangerous" ideas out of the country and barring American pacifists and radicals from traveling abroad. All three Republican presidents of the decade supported restricting the free flow of ideas. In 1929, for example, the State Department denied a passport to Dorothy Detzer, pacifist and executive director of the Women's International League for Peace and Freedom (WILPF), preventing her from attending an international pacifist conference. The required oath included a phrase about defending the United States. Detzer refused on the grounds that the word "defend" implied taking up arms, which would violate her pacifist principles. Officials eventually relented and allowed her to take an oath without the offending word. In the course of this dispute, it was revealed that the State Department had quietly granted the same option to the ACLU's Roger Baldwin for his trip to Europe in 1927.[30]

The case of the Hungarian refugee and pacifist Rosika Schwimmer became the most celebrated of the government's attack on political beliefs. In her citizenship application she freely testified that she would not comply if the United States tried to compel her "to take up arms in the defense of the country" but would "do everything that an American citizen has to do except fighting." The Supreme Court upheld the denial of her citizenship in 1929, ruling that "[I]t is the duty of citizens by force of arms to defend our government against all enemies." Restating the argument the government had used against many dissenters during World War I, the Court argued that "the influence of conscientious objectors [like Schwimmer] against the use of military force in defense of the principles of our Government is apt to be more detrimental than their mere refusal to bear arms."[31]

Athan Theoharis, *Spying on Americans: Political Surveillance from Hoover to the Huston Plan* (Philadelphia: Temple University Press, 1978), pp. 65–77.

29 Baldwin to Stone, August 7, 1924, August 11, 1924; Baldwin, Memorandum on the Department of Justice, October 17, 1924, ACLUP, MF Ed (1996), Reel 38. Walker, *In Defense of American Liberties*, pp. 65–6. In 1942 Baldwin withdrew an article critical of the FBI, ibid., pp. 165–6. On the ACLU and the FBI in the 1950s, see ibid., pp. 191–4.

30 "Pacifist Obtains Special Passport," *NYT*, July 13, 1929. Dorothy Detzer, *Appointment on the Hill* (New York: Henry Holt, 1948). Rosemary Rainbolt, "Women and War in the United States: The Case of Dorothy Detzer, National Secretary W.I.L.P.F.," *Peace and Change* IV, no. 3 (Fall 1977): 18–22.

31 *United States v. Schwimmer*, 279 U.S. 644 (1929). ACLU, *The Case of Rosika Schwimmer* (New York: ACLU, 1929), ACLUP, MF Ed (1977), Reel 90. Ronald B. Flowers and Nadia M. Lahutsky, "The Naturalization of Rosika Schwimmer," *Journal of Church and State* 32 (Spring 1990): 343–66.

The most notable part of the *Schwimmer* decision was Justice Oliver Wendell Holmes's eloquent dissent. In perhaps the most memorable statement in defense of unpopular ideas, he wrote that "if there is any principle of the Constitution that more imperatively calls for attachment than any other it is the principle of free thought – not free thought for those who agree with us but freedom for the thought that we hate." The phrase "freedom for the thought we hate" would resonate in the years ahead, exerting a powerful impact on thinking about the First Amendment.[32]

Glimmers of hope – and a nascent right to privacy

The fevered attack on all things "un-American" in the twenties provoked two Supreme Court decisions that offered a small glimmer of hope of legal protection for civil liberties. The first involved a 1919 Nebraska law prohibiting teaching classes in foreign languages up through the seventh grade in both public and private schools. The law was primarily directed at parochial schools teaching in German. The Nebraska Supreme Court upheld the conviction of Robert Meyer, a teacher at the Zion Evangelical Lutheran parochial school in Hamilton County, Nebraska, on the grounds that allowing "foreigners ... to rear and educate their children in the language of their native land" is "inimical to our own safety." The Supreme Court declared the law unconstitutional in *Meyer v. Nebraska* (1923), arguing that it violated the privacy rights of the parents to direct their children' education. Justice James C. McReynolds, arguably the most conservative member of the Court, held that the liberty guaranteed by the Fourteenth Amendment included the right "to engage in any of the common occupations of life, to acquire useful knowledge, to marry, establish a home and bring up children, to worship God according to the dictates of his own conscience," and this included Meyer's "right thus to teach and the right of parents to engage him so to instruct their children." Although it lay dormant for years, this novel and expansive reading of the Fourteenth Amendment was pregnant with implications for a right to privacy.[33]

The second case, *Pierce v. Society of Sisters*, involved a KKK-sponsored Oregon referendum that required schoolchildren between the ages of eight and sixteen years to attend public schools. The law was mainly an attack on Catholic parochial schools and grim testimony to the Klan's power outside the Deep South. The ACLU condemned the law as an "an infringement of religious and civil liberty" and promised to challenge it. The Supreme Court declared the law unconstitutional in 1925, again finding a limited right to privacy in the Fourteenth Amendment, holding that the law "unreasonably interferes with the liberty of parents and guardians to direct the upbringing and education of children under their control."[34]

The two decisions were arguably the only formal rebukes to the hysteria in the early twenties. Curiously, however, there was virtually no follow-up to these decisions regarding a right to privacy, and they lay fallow until the revolution in privacy law in the 1960s. Nonetheless, they were harbingers of new thinking about civil liberties by the Supreme Court.

32 *United States v. Schwimmer*, 279 U.S. 644 (1929).
33 *Meyer v. Nebraska*, 262 U.S. 390 (1923). ACLU, *Annual Report, 1923*, p. 5
34 ACLU, *Annual Report, 1922*, p. 19. *Pierce v. Society of Sisters*, 268 U.S. 510 (1925).

A NATIONAL CAMPAIGN FOR RACIAL JUSTICE

Dressed in their Klan robes (albeit without masks) and singing "Onward Christian Soldiers," thirty-five thousand Ku Klux Klan members paraded down Washington's Constitution Avenue on August 8, 1925. The three-hour and forty-minute parade was a brazen display of the racist organization's political power in the mid-1920s. The "Sight Astonishes Capital," headlined the *New York Times*. Speakers attacked "Catholics, Jews, Scientists, Bootleggers and Newspapers," and on the final day Klansmen burned a huge cross on the Virginia side of the Potomac River. Klan leaders asked President Coolidge to address the march, but he did not respond.[35]

The Klan was on the march in the 1920s, literally and figuratively, emerging as a powerful force not just in the South but also in Ohio, Indiana, and Oregon. The passions of the war years spurred racial violence across the country, notably in summer 1919, when there were twenty-six racial riots. In the 1921 Tulsa race riot, estimates of the number of people killed ranged from thirty-nine to possibly three hundred, and ten thousand people homeless. Seventy-nine African Americans were lynched in 1919, an increase from the average of about sixty in the previous three years. The NAACP and the ACLU protested the violence, but with little effect. The best they could do was to issue press releases publicizing lynchings and demand that local police enforce the law against the perpetrators. KKK terrorism silenced virtually all calls for racial tolerance in the South. William Pickens, an NAACP field organizer, reported in 1921, "In the South today no man, white or black, is really free publicly to speak the truth about the race problem."[36]

The political power of the Klan was nowhere more evident than at the 1924 Democratic Party convention, where the party nearly self-destructed over a proposal to denounce the racist organization by name. The initial draft of the platform condemned "any efforts to arouse religious or racial dissension," but without mentioning the Klan. The advocates of tolerance, led mainly by Catholic delegates from the North and Midwest, offered an amendment condemning "political secret societies" "of all kinds" and opposing "any effort on the part of the Ku Klux Klan or any other organization to interfere with the religious liberty or political freedom of any citizen." Wild applause and hisses greeted the proposal, and delegates who had left during a boring debate over the League of Nations rushed back into the auditorium. A *New York Times* reporter "witnessed dozens of verbal duels so impassioned and beyond reason that one moved [through the convention hall] in terror of a rain of blows or bullets." "Could intolerance so primal and menacing boil under the skin of America?" she asked. The honest answer was yes, and the spectacle dramatized the strength of racist feeling in one of the two major political parties during the twenties.[37]

35 "Sight Astonishes Capital," *NYT*, August 9, 1925. "Klan's Big Rally Ends with Oratory," ibid., August 10, 1925. David M. Chalmers, *Hooded Americanism: The History of the Ku Klux Klan* (New York: Frederick Watts, 1981), pp. 286–8.

36 Willliam M. Tuttle, *Race Riot: Chicago in the Red Summer of 1919* (New York: Atheneum, 1970). Oregon Law: *Pierce v. Society of Sisters*, 268 U.S. 510 (1925). Alfred L. Brophy, *Reconstructing the Dreamland: The Tulsa Riot of 1921: Race, Reparations, and Reconciliation* (New York: Oxford University Press, 2002). A contemporary account of lynching by the head of the NAACP is Walter White, *Rope and Faggot: A Biography of Judge Lynch* (New York: Knopf, 1929). Data on lynching is in the appendix. William Pickens, *Lynching and Debt Slavery* (May 1921), copy in ACLUP-MF (1977), Reel 90.

37 Anne O'Hare McCormick, "Convention's Most Thrilling Moments," *NYT*, July 6, 1924. Robert K. Murray, *The 103rd Ballot: Democrats and the Disaster in Madison Square Garden* (New York: Harper & Row, 1976).

Klan supporters had not wanted a public debate but now rose to defend the organization. Significantly, the delegate Franklin D. Roosevelt, the future president, played a major role at the convention and advised other party leaders against naming the Klan and becoming too closely identified with the anti-Klan forces. (As president, FDR never supported civil rights and always deferred to southerners in Congress.) The last speaker of the night, William Jennings Bryan, the aging hero of the party as its three-time presidential candidate, delivered what he regarded as his most important speech ever (disregarding his famous "Cross of Gold" speech at the 1896 Democratic Party convention), recommending an antiintolerance amendment without naming the Klan. Chaos erupted on the floor, and he was interrupted three times by cheers and boos.[38]

The battle over the Klan was not confined to the convention at Madison Square Garden that summer. About forty thousand Klan members held a giant rally in Long Branch, New Jersey, while the Democrats argued in New York City. Another fifteen hundred paraded in Binghamton, New York. The Georgia senator Thomas W. Hardwick said the Klan "rules" the state. The Democrats finally reached a compromise on the platform that condemned "any effort to arouse religious or racial dissension." Incredibly, the vote at 2 a.m. was settled by a single vote - 541 and 3/20 to 542 and 3/20. Amid a deafening roar, Roosevelt adjourned the convention.[39]

Civil rights enters national politics

As the 1920 presidential election campaign began, the NAACP's W. E. B. DuBois prepared a list of seven questions for candidates. Topping the list was a federal antilynching law, followed by ending racial segregation in federal agencies. In September, NAACP leaders had a "cordial" meeting with the GOP candidate Warren G. Harding, who expressed his support for all seven of their points, although with reservations on some. Efforts to meet with the Democratic Party candidate, James M. Cox, were unsuccessful.[40]

Led by the NAACP, civil rights entered national politics in the 1920s. Its persistent activism forced presidents, presidential candidates, and Congress to take a stand on lynching and racial segregation. Republicans, who still honored the memory of Abraham Lincoln, gave far more public support to racial justice than Democrats, who were beholden to the South. Although the NAACP won at best only one victory, it succeeded in putting civil rights on the national political agenda for the first time since Reconstruction.

The 1920 GOP platform urged Congress to end lynching, "which continues to be a terrible blot on our American civilization." The party repeated the call in 1924 and 1928. President Coolidge in his first year in office recommended creating a commission to investigate "the promotion of mutual understanding and confidence," a variation of the national race commission President Wilson had rejected in 1913. The Democratic Party platforms in the twenties, however, ignored lynching and other racial justice issues.[41]

38 Murray, *The 103rd Ballot*, pp. 153–64.

39 "40,000 Klansmen to Rally in Jersey," *NYT*, July 3, 1924. "Binghamton Sees Only 1,540 of Klan," ibid., July 5, 1924. "Hardwick Declares Klan Rules Georgia," ibid., July 7, 1924. Murray, *The 103rd Ballot*, pp. 144–7, 153–64. Chalmers, *Hooded Americanism*, pp. 202–12.

40 DuBois's seven issues: NAACP, Board of Directors, Minutes, February 9, 1920; Meeting with Harding and efforts to meet with Cox: NAACP, Board of Directors, Minutes, September 13, 1920, NAACPP-MF, Reel 1. Dean, *Warren G. Harding*, pp. 123–4.

41 Republican and Democratic Party platforms, APP.

President Harding's great – but brief– moment

Deep in the heart of the segregated South, before a racially mixed audience of 100,000 in Birmingham, Alabama, President Warren G. Harding stunned the crowd by declaring that "the negro is entitled to full economic and political rights as an American citizen." For whites in the audience he offered a tribute to the "lost cause" of the Confederacy but matched it with a tribute to the contributions of African-American soldiers during the Civil War. On the key issue of the right to vote, he declared, "let the black man vote when he is fit to vote; prohibit the white man voting when he is unfit to vote." Whites in the audience sat in stony silence.[42] Although consistently regarded as one of the worst presidents ever, Harding deserves credit for the strongest statement on equal rights by any sitting president until Harry S Truman a quarter-century later. Moreover, he delivered it in the face of a large and hostile southern audience, on the occasion of Birmingham's fiftieth anniversary celebration on October 26, 1921. The Harding biographer John W. Dean (of Watergate fame) calls the speech a "bold and atypical in-your-face move," "the most daring and controversial speech of Harding's political career."[43]

Harding was genuinely concerned about racial injustice, and his Birmingham speech was no aberration. Twice during the 1920 presidential campaign and again after the election he met with the NAACP's James Weldon Johnson. Harding listened thoughtfully to pleas for action on lynching, voting, and segregation and promised to act. He honored that commitment a month after taking office and to a special session of Congress called for antilynching legislation. In forthright language, he urged Congress to "wipe out the stain of barbaric lynching." Initial applause was quickly followed by silence from the assembled members of Congress, however. He also favored a Justice Department investigation of Klan violence but did not press the issue. On appointments to federal positions, his record was considerably better than Woodrow Wilson's, appointing 140 African American to federal jobs. He did not, however, follow through on a vague promise to end racial segregation in federal agencies.[44]

The Birmingham speech and the 1921 civil rights message to Congress proved to be Harding's brief shining moment, however. Finding little support and much opposition in Congress, he dropped racial justice completely in 1922. On May 30 he was the main speaker at the dedication of the Lincoln Memorial. In a bizarre setting by today's standards, the huge crowd of fifty thousand was segregated by race (the nation's capital was a segregated southern town in the 1920s). Harding spoke passionately about Lincoln's greatness as a president, and about slavery and the Civil War, but on this occasion he said nothing about segregation and other racial injustices. The NAACP took notice. "Disappointment," James Weldon Johnson noted in February 1922, "has grown into resentment," as Harding was now offering not even a "sop."[45]

42 "Harding Says Negro Must Have Equality," *NYT*, October 27, 1921.

43 Dean, *Warren G. Harding*, p. 125.

44 "Tells Congress of Policy," *NYT*, April 13, 1921. Dean, *Warren G. Harding*, pp. 123–4. "Harding Approves Ku Klux Inquiry," *NYT*, September 22, 1921. "Negro Appeal to Coolidge," ibid., June 29, 1926.

45 "Harding Dedicates Lincoln Memorial," *NYT*, May 31, 1922. National Park Service web site: www.nps.gov/linc/memorial/dedication.htm. Johnson to Storey, February 4, 1922, Storey Papers, Box 2, LOC.

The campaign for a federal antilynching law

The NAACP put its energies into a campaign for a federal law making lynching a crime. Their ally in Congress was Representative Leonidas Dyer, a Republican from St. Louis, Missouri, who had earlier demanded that President Wilson respond to the bloody East St. Louis race riot. In 1918 he introduced what became known as the Dyer bill making it a felony for any state or local official to fail "to make all reasonable efforts" to prevent someone in his custody from being killed "by any mob or riotous assemblage." The NAACP organized a National Conference on Lynching in May 1919 at Carnegie Hall, New York, and made the antilynching bill its top priority. Over the next forty years seven presidents were compelled to respond to this demand.[46]

Not everyone in the NAACP thought the Dyer bill was good law, however. The organization's own president, Moorefield Storey, white and a prominent Boston attorney, doubted the constitutionality of using the Fourteenth Amendment to create a new federal crime. During World War I he and the NAACP chairperson, Joel Spingarn, also white, proposed basing an antilynch law on the president's war powers, citing the wartime need to preserve the "morale and self-respect and the peace of the citizen-soldier." The end of the war in November 1918, however, eliminated the possibility of that novel and expansive use of the president's war powers. After much debate, Storey finally changed his mind and supported the Dyer bill in 1921, now persuaded that southern officials would not protect African Americans from lynching. The newly formed ACLU, meanwhile, also thought a federal antilynching law was unconstitutional. Not wishing to embarrass its ally on other racial justice issues, it maintained a discreet silence on the issue through the twenties and finally supported a federal law only in the 1930s.[47]

President Harding honored his campaign promise and supported the Dyer bill. His attorney general, the famously corrupt Harry Daugherty, sent a supportive letter to the House Judiciary Committee, and Assistant Attorney Guy D. Goff gave a lengthy defense of its legal rationale and constitutionality. Harding conceded there were unresolved constitutional questions but urged Congress to pass it so they could be put "squarely to the courts for determination."[48] President Coolidge later met with A. Philip Randolph in the White House over the bill but never publicly supported it. Nor did his successor, Herbert Hoover. Ultimately, of course, southerners in the Senate could kill any bill with a filibuster.

Although no antilynching bill ever passed Congress (for which the Senate officially apologized on June 13, 2005), the NAACP's campaign paid important dividends. It put civil rights on the political agenda for the first time since Reconstruction, laying the

[46] Robert L. Zangrando, *The NAACP Crusade against Lynching, 1909–1950* (Philadelphia: Temple University Press, 1980).

[47] NAACP, Board of Directors, Minutes, October 13, 1919, NAACPP, MF ED, V. 1, Reel 1. Materials on the constitutional questions regarding a federal law: Storey Papers, Box 2, LOC. War powers proposal: J. E. Spingarn to Storey, [with attached memorandum], June 18, 1918, Storey Papers, Box 2, LOC. Zangrando, *The NAACP Crusade,* pp. 44, 55, 59–60. William B. Hixson, Jr., *Moorfield Storey and the Abolitionist Tradition* (New York: Oxford, 1972), pp. 164–6. ACLU's role: see ACLU, *Annual Report 1922.* ACLU, *Civil Liberty Issues in Congress* (New York: ACLU, September 1926), ACLUP-MF (1977), Reel 90.

[48] Daugherty and Goff: "Antilynching Bill," House of Representatives, 67th Cong., 1st Sess. October 31, 1921, Report No. 452. Harding on constitutionality: J. W. Johnson to George B. Christian, September 8, 1922, WGHP, Reel 193.

groundwork for later successes. It also probably had some impact on lynchings by putting them in the national spotlight. Lynchings of African Americans dropped to an all-time low of sixteen in 1924 (also the first year no whites were lynched) and continued to fall in the following years. Social and political pressure probably achieved more results than a federal law would have.[49]

Herbert Hoover's tangled position on race

Herbert Hoover had a very mixed record on racial justice issues, as president and earlier. As did many Republicans, he sincerely sought to honor the memory of Abraham Lincoln and made some gestures in the direction of equality. His good intentions, however, were limited by conformity to the dominant racism of the period.

While secretary of commerce under Harding and Coolidge, Hoover distinguished himself by quietly reversing Woodrow Wilson's segregation policy and integrating employees in the department. No other cabinet member appears to have taken a similar step in the 1920s, and in the next decade his efforts would be matched by Roosevelt's interior secretary, Harold Ickes. Word of Hoover's action got around, and while it won him respect among African Americans it also roused opposition among southerners in the 1928 presidential election campaign. Although he won in a landslide, the issue negated his dream of winning over southern whites from the Democrats.[50]

Herbert Hoover's reputation on race was seriously damaged by his handling of the 1927 Mississippi River flood while secretary of commerce. The flood was arguably the most extensive natural disaster in America in the twentieth century. Beginning on New Year's Day 1927, the Mississippi breached its levees in 145 different places, flooding twenty-seven thousand square miles in seven states, killing 246 people, and causing more than $400 million in damage. The 700,000 displaced people were about equally divided among whites and African Americans. In one refugee camp near Greenville, Mississippi, more than thirteen thousand people were stranded for days without food or clean water.[51]

In those pre–New Deal days, the federal government had almost no capacity to respond to such calamities, and the Red Cross assumed primary responsibility for providing food and shelter and transporting people to safe ground. President Coolidge felt compelled to act, however, and appointed Hoover to chair a Special Mississippi Flood Committee and coordinate relief efforts. He was an ideal choice, as he had established his national reputation directing the enormously successful European food relief program during World War I. He thought the flood relief assignment would enhance his quest for the 1928 Republican presidential nomination. As expected, his efforts were effective and efficient, as he raised more than $17 million, helped organize the first Red Cross radio appeal, and even secured $10 million in federal relief funds. An engineer by profession, he also convinced President Coolidge and Congress to support a long-term plan to control the Mississippi River that ultimately reduced the number of disastrous floods.

49 Lynching Data: White, *Rope and Faggot*, Appendix. Coolidge: Andrew E. Kersten, *A. Philip Randolph: A Life in the Vanguard* (Lanham, MD: Rowman & Littlefield, 2007), pp. 53–4. "A Senate Apology for History on Lynching; Vote Condemns Past Failure to Act," *Washington Post*, June 14, 2005.

50 "Order on Negroes Bothering Hoover," *NYT*, August 30, 1928, clipping in HHPL. Hoover did not mention this issue in his memoirs: Herbert Hoover, *The Memoirs of Herbert Hoover*, V. 2, *The Cabinet and the Presidency, 1920–1933* (New York: Macmillan, 1952).

51 Pete Daniel, *Deep'n as It Come: The 1927 Mississippi River Flood* (New York: Oxford University Press, 1977).

These federal efforts might appear to be inconsistent with the conservative, small government ethos of the Republicans in the twenties, but Hoover was in fact a progressive in the pre–World War mode, firmly believing that government should act to meet important social needs. And as an engineer, he instinctively thought in terms of practical solutions to pressing problems. The historian Joan Hoff Wilson properly labels him the *Forgotten Progressive*.[52]

Flood relief efforts, however, were marred by pervasive race discrimination that Hoover countenanced. In several instances, boats rescued stranded whites while African Americans were held off at gunpoint. In some camps African Americans were forced to work virtually as slaves, at times at gunpoint. When African-American leaders protested, Hoover appointed a Colored Advisory Commission to investigate, chaired by Robert Russa Moton, president of Tuskegee Institute. He hoped the commission would defuse any potential controversy, but its reports only confirmed the acts of discrimination. Hoover responded with a cynical political deal. Not wanting to alienate white southerners in the 1928 elections by openly challenging racism, he promised Moton that if the commission would keep its reports quiet, he would support programs for African Americans as president. Moton accepted the deal, but Hoover delivered little as president, deeply alienating Moton and other moderate African Americans.[53]

Hoover on race as president

Although he failed to honor fully his promise to Robert Moton, Hoover took some creditable steps on race as president. He fully supported the creation of a National Memorial to the Negro People and appointed more African Americans to federal positions than any previous president. An engineer who always wanted facts and expert opinions to guide public policy, he sponsored a report on the economic status of African Americans in 1930. (In his twelve years as secretary of commerce and then president, he sponsored an estimated three thousand conferences on various issues.) By then, however, the Great Depression had overwhelmed the country and his presidency, and he could not follow through with any special programs for African Americans.[54]

One incident early in his presidency dramatized the political costs of even the slightest gesture on behalf of racial equality. First Lady Lou Henry Hoover arranged a series of White House tea parties for the wives of members of Congress. Politically astute, she had actively supported a number of reform efforts before entering the White House and intended the teas to help her husband with Congress. One guest was Mrs. Oscar DePriest, wife of the Illinois congressman Oscar DePriest, the first African American in Congress since Reconstruction. Predictably, southern segregationists were outraged and loudly protested this breech of the color line. "Society Shocked," screamed one headline, and angry letters poured into the White House. The first lady was deeply hurt and brought

52 Hoff Wilson, *Herbert Hoover: Forgotten Progressive.*

53 Zangrando, *The NAACP Crusade*, pp. 105–6. Hoover discusses the Mississippi relief effort in his memoirs but not the racial controversy: Hoover, *The Memoirs of Herbert Hoover*, V. 2.

54 Clippings and other materials, November 14, 1930; Press release, October 29, 1930; Report: Dr. T. J. Woofter, Jr., "Industrial Background of Study of the Economic Status of the Negro," Colored Question File, Subject Files, Box 106, HHPL. Hoover, conferences and social scientists: Hoff Wilson, *Herbert Hoover: Forgotten Progressive*, pp. 82, 138.

to tears by the personal attacks on her. The president was equally offended and in a very public rebuke to his critics, promptly invited the Tuskegee president, Robert Moton, to lunch at the White House. If he never delivered much in the way of programs, this one gesture indicated he had a strong sense of the symbols of racial justice.[55]

Disappointed civil rights leaders criticized Hoover for not delivering tangible programs. The most public controversy was his nomination of Judge John Parker for the Supreme Court in 1930. The NAACP vigorously fought the nomination because he had made racially insensitive remarks. The main opposition was from the labor movement, because of an opinion in which he held that unions were an illegal conspiracy. Parker's nomination failed by one vote in the Senate. Although not the primary factor in the vote, the NAACP nonetheless received considerable notice for its role and was credited with its first real political victory.[56]

Although he expressed concern about lynchings, Hoover never supported the Dyer Anti-Lynching Bill (fifteen lynchings were reported between December 1929 and July 1930). In his characteristic style, he sought expert opinion and asked Attorney General William Mitchell for a memo on the Dyer bill. Mitchell advised him that it rested on a very "strained" legal theory about the Fourteenth Amendment (the ACLU's position at the time), that it "would do more harm than good" and be "utterly impracticable" because southern juries would never convict white offenders. The only sound approach, he advised, was to rouse local public opinion in the South about racial violence and try to develop a sense of responsibility among state authorities. To that end, he suggested Hoover issue a special message condemning lynching. Despite similar pleas from the NAACP and others, however, Hoover never gave a public speech on race.[57]

Had the country not been overtaken by the Great Depression, it is possible Hoover might have done more for African Americans in the areas of education and employment training. He was not averse to using the federal government to solve problems, and these areas fit comfortably into his view of America's future and how government programs could advance it. It is extremely unlikely, however, that he would have challenged the racist status quo with regard to de jure segregation, voter disenfranchisement, or lynching.

ALICE PAUL, THE ERA, AND A NEW DIRECTION FOR WOMEN'S RIGHTS

At the seventy-fifth anniversary of the 1848 Women's Rights Convention in Seneca Falls, New York, on July 21, 1923, the movement for women's equality took a dramatic new turn.

55 "White House Has Negress as Tea Guest," *Daily Democrat*, June 16, 1929; Brooks to Hoover, June 17, 1929, Colored Question, Subject Files, Box 106, HHPL. Nancy Beck Young, *Lou Henry Hoover: Activist First Lady* (Lawrence: University of Kansas Press, 2004), pp. 65–71. Moton: Hoover, *The Memoirs of Herbert Hoover, V. 2*, p. 324.

56 African American criticisms in *Cleveland Call*, July 19, 1930, clipping, Colored Question File, Subject Files, Box 106, HHPL. Kenneth W. Goings, *The NAACP Comes of Age: The Defeat of Judge John J. Parker* (Bloomington: University of Indiana Press, 1990).

57 William D. Mitchell, Memorandum for the President on the Dyer Anti-Lynching Bill, January 6, 1932; NAACP to Hoover, August 15, 1930; Walter Newton, Secretary to the President, to Walter White, August 20, 1930; White to Hoover, October 3, 1930; George Akerson, Secretary to President to White, October 21, 1930; White to Akerson, October 22, 1930; Memo (list of lynchings, 1930), Walter White to The President, November 13, 1930; Monroe Trotter to Hoover, November 12, 1930; Thanks from Trotter: Akerson to Mr. Spencer [Trotter aide], November 18, 1930; Trotter to The President, November 20, 1930; Trotter to Hoover, February 7, 1931, Colored Question Files, Box 107, HHPL.

Alice Paul, founder of the National Woman's Party, drafted an Equal Rights Amendment to the U.S. Constitution, which read simply, "Men and women shall have equal rights throughout the United States and every place subject to its jurisdiction." Introduced in Congress that year and almost every session until it passed in 1972, the ERA represented a new vision of women's rights.[58]

Paul's ERA provoked a bitter split among feminists, just as her aggressive White House picketing had in 1917. The vast majority denounced it as a threat to their major goal of securing protective legislation on hours and working conditions for women workers. Her prominent critics included Florence Kelley, who called her a "fiend," while others pointed out that she and her small band of followers were mostly wealthy Republicans who did not care about working women. Paul, of course, was no stranger to attacks from moderate feminists, and she could legitimately claim that her White House picketing had forced President Wilson to reverse his position and support the suffrage amendment.[59]

The head of the U.S. Women's Bureau summed up for Congress the feminist and liberal criticisms of the ERA. Citing wages and hours laws covering women in every state except Florida, she warned that "all labor legislation will be endangered," and the ERA "is likely to take away these safeguards" for women. These fears were well founded. The Supreme Court was busily striking down laws regulating hours, wages, or working conditions under the doctrine that such laws infringed on the Fourteenth Amendment "liberty of contract." One of the most controversial decisions of the decade was *Adkins v. Children's Hospital* in 1923, declaring unconstitutional a Washington, D.C., law establishing minimum wages of women and children (since Washington was a federal enclave, the Fourteenth Amendment did not apply).[60]

President Coolidge expressed interest in the ERA and on November 17, 1923, met with a National Woman's Party delegation. The group included Mrs. Victor Du Pont (of the DuPont Corporation family) and the famous poet Edna St. Vincent Millay. He assured them "he had not the slightest doubt Congress would respond favorably" to their proposal. Other factors apparently intervened to change his mind, however. Three week later, in his Annual Message to Congress, he reversed himself and supported protective legislation for women and children without mentioning the ERA. Fully aware that the Supreme Court was hostile to wages and hours legislation, he endorsed both a constitutional amendment and federal legislation allowing the federal government to establish minimum wages for women – but nothing beyond that on behalf of women's rights.[61]

Republicans in the twenties were generally more supportive of women's issues. Their 1920 platform supported protective legislation for women, "to limit the hours of employment of women engaged in intensive industry," and endorsed "the principle of equal pay for equal service" among federal employees. Similar planks appeared in the 1924 and

58 "Women Adopt Form for Equal Rights," *NYT*, July 22, 1923. Christine A. Lunardini, *From Equal Suffrage to Equal Rights: Alice Paul and the National Woman's Party, 1910–1928* (New York: New York University Press, 1986), p. 164.

59 Lunardini, *From Equal Suffrage to Equal Rights*, p. 162. The ACLU opposed the ERA and did not change its position until the very different social and political climate of the 1970s. Walker, *In Defense of American Liberties*, pp. 166–7.

60 Testimony, February 4–5, 1924, in *Records of the Women's Bureau of the Department of Labor, 1918–1965* (Frederick, MD: University Publications of America, 1986), MF ed., Reel 14. *Adkins v. Children's Hospital*, 262 U.S. 525 (1923).

61 "Coolidge Assures Women of Victory," *NYT*, November 18, 1923. "Women Laud and Criticize," ibid., December 7, 1923. Coolidge, First Annual Address to Congress, December 6, 1923, APP.

1928 platforms. There is little evidence, however, that Presidents Harding, Coolidge, and Hoover gave them anything more than lip service. In the Democratic Party, the sizable southerner block opposed all women's issues, while northern and western liberals supported protective wages and hours legislation for women, opposed the ERA because they feared it would undermine such laws, but did endorse equal pay for equal work.[62]

Herbert Hoover was possibly even more liberal on women's issues than most Republicans and Democrats and as president was a very strong supporter of protective legislation. He told feminist leaders, "I am absolutely with you in your efforts to get adequate labor legislation for women." Women, he went on, "must have safeguards additional to those provided for men," particularly laws limiting the permissible hours women could work. Paul's National Woman's Party lobbied him heavily but could not persuade him to endorse the ERA.[63]

SEX AND CENSORSHIP: THE POST OFFICE AND THE CUSTOMS BUREAU

"The national book censor"

Although it was not his official job title, J. D. Nevius became "the national book censor." As deputy commissioner of the Customs Bureau he enforced Section 305 of the Tariff Act directing Customs to bar obscene materials from entering the country. Federal censorship efforts shifted significantly in the 1920s, with less emphasis on political ideology and a preoccupation with sexuality.[64] The new focus on sexually oriented foreign literature in the 1920s was in response to changing public attitudes about sexuality in both the United States and Europe. Many fiction and nonfiction works with treatments of sex that exceeded prevailing norms were rejected by American publishers and published in France (but not in England). The result was a small but thriving import business that necessarily involved some smuggling (that continued until the U.S. courts struck down censorship laws in the early 1960s). Nevius compiled a list of several hundred books that Customs collectors in 250 American cities were directed to seize. The list included such recognized classics as Boccaccio's *Decameron*, Balzac's *Droll Stories*, and several works by Rabelais. Seized copies were locked away, and so Customs held probably the largest collections of sexually oriented material in the country. None of the three Republican presidents in the twenties objected to or limited the bureau's efforts.

By the late twenties, however, the ACLU and other advocates of freedom of expression began to win some notable victories. Radclyffe Hall's novel about lesbianism, *The Well of Loneliness,* won several court decisions, culminating in a Customs Court ruling in July 1929 that it did not contain "one word, phrase, sentence or paragraph" that was "offensive." The case was handled by Morris Ernst, ACLU general counsel and a pioneering attorney on censorship and reproductive rights, who scored an even greater victory in overturning the ban on James Joyce's great novel *Ulysses*.[65]

62 Republican and Democratic platforms, APP.

63 Meeting with Hoover materials, October 26, 1928; petitions and correspondence from Women's Party; Woman's Party meeting with President Hoover, January 5, 1931, Women Files, Box 370, HHPL.

64 "Our National Book Censor," *NYT*, December 8, 1929.

65 "'Well of Loneliness' Held Not Offensive," *NYT*, July 27, 1929. Radclyffe Hall, *The Well of Loneliness* (New York: Covici and Friede, 1928). *United States v. One Book Entitled Ulysses*, 5 F.Supp. 182, aff'd, 72 F.2d 705.

Post Office censorship of political works, on the other hand, dropped substantially in 1921 under President Harding's postmaster general, Will Hays. In May he restored the mail privileges of two major socialist newspapers, the *New York Call* and the *Milwaukee Leader*. The Supreme Court belatedly upheld the wartime ban on the *Leader* in March, affirming the unfettered power of the Post Office to decide what could be mailed. Hays felt otherwise, however, and announced, "The war is over and it has been the purpose of the department to return to the ordered freedom." He objected to the Supreme Court's decision in the *Milwaukee Leader* case and in restoring the mailing rights of the *Liberator*, also banned during the war, declared that "the arbitrary power to decide what is and what is not information of a public benefit was never intended to be lodged in the Postmaster General."[66]

The ACLU hailed Hays's actions, declaring the Post Office completely "cleaned up" and asserting that no periodicals were now barred from the mails "for their expression of economic or political opinion." The ACLU had good reason to celebrate, since this was the first positive step on behalf of freedom of expression by the federal government. The last banned political book, Alexander Berkman's *Prison Memoirs of an Anarchist*, had its mailing privileges restored on September 7, 1922. The ACLU tempered its celebration, however, by conceding that the censorship of sexually oriented materials, particularly on birth control and abortion, continued unabated.[67]

Hays deserves full credit for ending censorship of political works, and there is no record of President Harding's views on the subject. Hays resigned in 1922, however, to become the first president of the Motion Picture Producers and Distributors Association. Ironically, in that position he enforced the film industry's program of self-censorship, as the head of what became known as the Hays Office. Initially advisory and quite ineffective, the office acquired real muscle in 1934 when Hollywood adopted the Production Code that for five years imposed rigid censorship on American movies.

Banning *the Sex Side of Life*

The government attack on sexually oriented materials culminated in a self-inflicted disaster in 1929 with the prosecution of Mary Ware Dennett for her pamphlet *The Sex Side of Life*. Although largely forgotten today, Dennett was an important feminist and political activist before and after World War I. During the war she had been closely allied with the Civil Liberties Bureau, and in the twenties she was Margaret Sanger's chief rival for leadership of the birth control movement. Her confrontation with the Comstock Act originated in 1915 when her fourteen-year-old son, Carl, began asking questions about sex. Finding no suitable sex education material (not one, she recalled, ever explained "*just what* the sex act is"), she decided to write something herself. It was first published in the *Medical Review of Reviews* in 1918, but as she began receiving many requests for copies, she published it herself as a pamphlet. With changing public

66 "Call and Leader Restored to Mail," *NYT*, June 1, 1921. Quote: "Hays Removes Ban on The Liberator," ibid., May 26, 1921. Hays did not discuss these actions in his memoirs: Will H. Hays, *Memoirs* (Garden City, NY: Doubleday, 1955). Harry N. Scheiber, *The Wilson Administration and Civil Liberties, 1917–1921* (Ithaca, NY: Cornell University Press, 1960), p. 35.

67 ACLU, *Annual Report*, 1922, pp. 16–17.

attitudes about sexuality creating a demand for information, it sold well with virtually no advertising.[68]

Traditional moralists struck back with a scheme to entrap her. In 1929 Dennett received a request for a copy from a "Mrs. Carl A. Miles" of Grottoes, Virginia, and she was then arrested under the 1873 Comstock Act, which prohibited the publication, sale, or possession of any "obscene book, pamphlet, paper, writing, advertisement" about contraception or abortion.[69] Dennett's prosecution provoked outrage among prominent Americans, and the trial became a national cause celebre and a focal point for emerging public support for sex education and birth control. The national defense committee organized by the ACLU included such wealthy individuals as the publisher Roy Howard (of the Scripps-Howard newspaper chain) and Mrs. Marshall Field (of the Chicago department store family). At Dennett's trial "Mrs. Miles" was exposed as a fictitious creation of postal authorities. An unsympathetic judge threw out all the expert opinion on her behalf, however, and Dennett was convicted by a jury that deliberated only forty-two minutes.

In a dramatic reversal, the Second Circuit Court of Appeals overturned her conviction. The opinion by Judge August Hand (cousin of the more famous Judge Learned Hand, of the World War I *Masses* case) rejected the prevailing *Hicklin* test, which held that a work could be deemed objectionable it if had a "bad tendency," and ruled that it should be judged in terms of its full context or "main effect." Reflecting a modern view of sexuality, Hand wrote that "an accurate exposition of the relevant facts of the sex side of life in decent language and in manifest serious and disinterested spirit cannot ordinarily be regarded as obscene." Federal officials, evidently embarrassed by the case, decided not to appeal Hand's decision. The Dennett decision hardly ended Post Office censorship of sexually oriented materials, and it continued to ban materials through the mid-1960s, as did the Customs Bureau. Nonetheless, the case was a great victory that gave hope regarding freedom from federal censorship generally and with respect to birth control materials in particular.[70]

ATTACKING THE FIRST AMENDMENT RIGHTS OF ORGANIZED LABOR

Feeling desperate about the worsening attacks on the rights of labor unions and working people, the ACLU's Roger Baldwin wrote to the Harvard Law professor Felix Frankfurter in late 1920 seeking help. He confessed that the ACLU was completely at a loss on how to fight the increasing use of federal court injunctions prohibiting the rights of freedom of speech and assembly to union organizers. Some injunctions barred union meetings or even discussion of unions. The Supreme Court justice Louis Brandeis argued that labor injunctions "endow[ed] property with active, militant power which would make it dominant over men," but his was a distinctly minority view at the time. Frankfurter was the right choice. He was well on his way to establishing himself as the nation's foremost

[68] Constance M. Chen, *The Sex Side of Life: Mary Ware Dennett's Pioneering Battle for Birth Control and Sex Education* (New York: New Press, 1996). Mary Ware Dennett, *Who's Obscene?* (New York: Vanguard Press, 1930).

[69] Chen, *The Sex Side of Life*. ACLU, *Annual Report 1930*, pp. 153–4. Heywood Broun and Margaret Leech, *Anthony Comstock: Roundsman of the Lord* (New York: A. and C. Boni, 1927).

[70] *United States v. Dennett*, 39 F. 2d. 564 (1930). Impact of the case on the ACLU: Walker, *In Defense of American Liberties*, pp. 84–6.

expert on labor injunctions and would coauthor the major book on the subject in 1930. But even he had no formula for how to protect the rights of labor at that time.[71]

The three Republican presidents of the period fully supported the attack on labor and expressed no sympathy for the First Amendment rights of workers. In the probusiness climate of the twenties, they embraced the idea that "liberty" meant freedom of contract, which meant individual workers should negotiate the terms of their employment free of the "interference" of labor union contracts or laws regulating hours and wages.

The issue of labor injunctions came to a head in the 1922 railroad workers' strike. On July 1, 256,435 skilled railroad workers – machinists, boilermakers, blacksmiths, sheet metal workers, car men, helpers, and apprentices – went out on strike. This included 25,000 in the New York City area and 100,000 in the Chicago region. Railroads were then the linchpin of the national economy, and the strike threatened to paralyze the country. On September 1, the U.S. District Court judge James H. Wilkerson issued a sweeping injunction that, for all practical purposes, gagged everyone associated with the strike, forbidding anyone to attempt to persuade others not to work by "threats of violence or abusive language," and incredibly also by "jeers, entreaties, arguments, persuasions." Nor could they seek to persuade workers through "letters printed or other circulars, telegrams, telephones, word of mouth, oral persuasion or suggestion, or through interviews to be published in newspaper." In short, people could not talk to friends, strangers, or the press. The injunction also wiped out freedom of assembly near workplaces, banning "loitering or being unnecessarily in the vicinity of the points and places of ingress or egress of the employees of said railway companies."[72] Judge Wilkerson's injunction destroyed the railroad strike and dealt a severe blow to the entire labor movement. Union membership fell 40 percent, from five million in 1920 to three million in 1929.

The tide finally turned in labor's favor in the early 1930s, through legislation rather than the courts. The catastrophe of the depression sent to Congress liberal majorities sympathetic to organized labor. The 1932 Norris-LaGuardia Act outlawed the worst abuses of labor injunctions, prohibiting federal courts from issuing injunctions against unions or labor leaders regarding joining or organizing a union, assembling for union purposes, striking or refusing to work or advising others to strike or organize, publicizing acts of a labor dispute, or offering lawful legal assistance to anyone involved in a labor dispute. In 1935 at the high tide of the New Deal, the Wagner Act guaranteed working people the right to join unions "of their own choosing" and put an end to the nearly-century-long legal hostility to their freedom of association.[73]

Rousting the Bonus Army: President Hoover and freedom of assembly

When U.S. Army cavalry and troops with fixed bayonets charged into the encampment of World War I veterans late in the afternoon on July 28, 1932, it was an assault on freedom

71 Baldwin, Ward, DeSilver to Frankfurter, December 11, 1920, Frankfurter Papers, LOC. Felix Frankfurter and Nathan Greene, *The Labor Injunction* (New York: Macmillan, 1930); Brandeis quoted, pp. 132–3. Irving Bernstein, *The Lean Years: A History of the American Worker, 1920–1933* (Boston: Houghton Mifflin, 1960), pp. 194–202.

72 Colin J. Davis, *Power at Odds: The 1922 National Railroad Shopmen's Strike* (Urbana: University of Illinois Press, 1997), pp. 130–2. "Text of Rail Strike Injunction Defining the Acts Now Restrained," *NYT*, September 2, 1922.

73 Bernstein, *The Lean Years*, pp. 397–414.

of assembly and an event that forever tarnished the image of President Herbert Hoover. The Bonus Army, as it was called, included seventeen thousand veterans accompanied by another twenty-three thousand family members and friends, who marched on Washington to demand immediate payment of bonuses that were scheduled for 1945. As they proceeded across the country, they enjoyed considerable popular support. National Guard trucks transported them in some states. By July, they were encamped in the nation's capitol, mainly in the swampy Anacostia flats in Southeast Washington, where they created a well-organized community, with marked streets, recreational activities, schools, and medical facilities. Bonus Army leaders developed a cordial and professional relationship with the Washington Police chief Pelham Glassford, and both sides worked to maintain order.[74]

Military Intelligence and the Bureau of Investigation, convinced it was a communist plot and a prelude to revolution, spied on the Bonus Army. Surveillance began as the first caravans left their hometowns. Some communists were indeed associated with the army, but they were mainly trying to capitalize on a spontaneous protest by the impoverished veterans who had no radical goals beyond obtaining their bonus payments. Undercover agents attended meetings in Washington, taking special note of "voices of Jewish accent," "local Colored Communists," and "certain Russian girls [who] were openly obscene."[75]

In late July a series of incidents led to tragic violence. On July 28, the police tried to remove some protesters from a federal construction site where they were in fact trespassing. The confrontation escalated, and two police officers were shot and killed. President Hoover then ordered the military to clear out the entire Bonus Army. General of the Army Douglas MacArthur led the operation on horseback, accompanied by his aide, Dwight D. Eisenhower. (Eisenhower gained a jaundiced view of MacArthur as a supreme egotist and drew a lesson about avoiding confrontations whenever possible.) Troops from several military units, with fixed bayonets and tear gas, supported by six tanks commanded by General George S. Patton, advanced on the settlements, destroying tents and rousting people. The morning after the rout, the Secret Service rounded up 130 alleged communists "and ran them out of the District, together with nearly four hundred veterans."[76]

The assault on the veterans' encampment provoked a storm of nationwide protest. The ACLU's Roger Baldwin fired off a telegram to President Hoover to "emphatically protest[s] your action in calling out army to disperse starving veterans." Hoover was unapologetic and reassured one District of Columbia commissioner that they had a duty to find the instigators of the violence (who were not the military, in his mind) and bring them to justice. In his memoirs, published in the 1950s, he still adamantly maintained that the march had been "largely organized and managed by Communists."[77]

74 Paul Dickson and Thomas B. Allen, *Bonus Army: An American Epic* (New York: Walker and Company, 2004).

75 W. C. Grooms, memo to Capt. J. A. Sullivan, Crime Prevention Division, June 2, 1932, Re "Communist Meeting;" Memo, July 11, 1932, re Workers Ex-Servicemen's League Meeting, July 10, 1932; Nugent Dodds, Assistant Attorney General, Memorandum for the Attorney General, September 9, 1932, War Veterans - Bonus Files, Box 375, HHPL.

76 Nugent Dodds, Asst. AG, Memorandum for the Attorney General, September 9, 1932, War Veterans - Bonus Files, Box 375, HHPL.

77 Roger Baldwin to Hoover, July 29, 1932; Hoover to Hon. Luther H. Reichelderfer, Commissioner, DC, July 29, 1932, World War Veterans - Bonus Files, Presidential Papers, Box 373, HHPL. Herbert Hoover, *The Memoirs of Herbert Hoover, V. 3, The Great Depression, 1929–1941* (New York: Macmillan, 1952), p. 230.

The routing of the Bonus Army has become fixed in popular memory as a symbol of President Hoover's heartlessness toward human suffering in the depths of the depression. It should be noted, however, that his successor as president, Franklin D. Roosevelt, also opposed paying the bonuses. He was simply more tactful when a much smaller group of veterans returned to Washington in 1933, dispatching his wife, Eleanor, to chat with them and serve coffee. New Deal officials persuaded many of the veterans to sign up for jobs building a highway in the Florida Keys. In 1935, however, a disastrous hurricane struck and inflicted more suffering on the veterans. Newsreels of the disaster aroused public opinion, and in 1936 Congress authorized payment of the bonus. When President Roosevelt vetoed the bill, Congress overrode him.[78]

LAWLESS POLICING: PROHIBITION ENFORCEMENT

The colorful exploits of the enforcement agents Izzie and Moe are part of the popular folklore of Prohibition (1920–33), which outlawed the manufacture and sale of alcoholic beverages in the United States. Working as local agents for the New York City Police in the early twenties (until they were fired), Izzie Einstein and Moe Smith used a variety of imaginative schemes to gain entrance to speakeasies: dressing as women, as a Yiddish couple, as cowboys; pretending to be baseball players; and so on. They allegedly made 4,392 arrests, with 95 percent resulting in convictions.[79]

Izzie and Moe's antics, together with the popular image of speakeasies and bathtub gin, distracted attention from the serious violations of civil liberties associated with Prohibition. The United States officially went "dry" at midnight, January 16, 1920, when the Eighteenth Amendment took effect. The "noble experiment," as it was called, was a disaster, inflicting long-term damage on American society. While it did reduce the consumption of alcohol, it also undermined respect for the law by encouraging massive lawbreaking and stimulated the growth of organized crime as national syndicates formed to exploit the enormous profits to be made through bootlegging. Enforcement involved widespread civil liberties violations, as Prohibition agents routinely conducted raids without warrants, broke down doors, and wiretapped suspects. Izzie and Moe's clever tricks were the exception; agents generally just broke down doors and barged in illegally. Legal restraints on police tactics were limited at best in those years. The Supreme Court had imposed the exclusionary rule on federal authorities in the 1914 *Weeks v. United States* case, but it did not apply to local police. The result was the ruse of the "silver platter" doctrine whereby local police conducted illegal searches and seizures and then handed off the evidence to federal agents.[80]

Since Prohibition was authorized by a constitutional amendment and a federal enabling statute (the Volstead Act), primary responsibility for enforcement lay with federal agencies, which made it a matter of presidential policy. Presidents Harding, Coolidge, and Hoover all failed to address the rampant violations of civil liberties, steadfastly supporting Prohibition as a nobel venture and complaining that the problem was inefficient

78 Dickson and Allen, *Bonus Army: An American Epic,* pp. 207–15, 229–34 (Roosevelts), 224–51 (Hurricane).

79 Dismissal: "Izzie and Moe," *Time*, November 23, 1925.

80 National Commission on Law Observance and Enforcement [Wickersham Commission], *Prohibition* (1931, reprint, New York: Arno Press, 1968). Norman H. Clark, *Deliver Us from Evil: An Interpretation of American Prohibition* (New York: W. W. Norton, 1976). *Weeks v. United States*, 232 U.S. 383 (1914).

enforcement. Democrats, except for a growing "wet" faction based in the big cities, took the same position. The 1924 Democratic Party platform, for example, condemned the Harding and Coolidge administrations for failing "to enforce the prohibition law" and becoming "the protector of violators of this law." It did not mention lawless enforcement actions.[81]

President Hoover's response to Prohibition was notably ambivalent. As secretary of commerce in early 1923 he saw that it was not working and resulted in abuses of law and suggested a national study to solve these problems. Alone among major political figures he mentioned the "undoubted abuses" related to enforcement in his 1929 presidential inaugural address. He put the blame, however, on the failure of state authorities to do their part, and on citizens who continued to buy and drink illegal alcohol. Despite his evident doubts, he pledged to maintain strict enforcement and to make Washington, D.C., the model dry city.[82]

Searching for a way out of a politically difficult solution, he created the National Commission on Law Observance and Enforcement in 1929 to conduct the first comprehensive survey of the American criminal justice system. The Wickersham Commission, as it was called, devoted one of its fourteen reports in 1931 to Prohibition. The report was thoroughly contradictory, acknowledging the problems with Prohibition enforcement, but in the end concluding that repeal was "not advisable." Arthur Krock, the prominent columnist in the *New York Times*, derided it as a "wet" report with a "dry" conclusion and attacked Hoover for not acting on either the report or his own good instincts.[83]

A Supreme Court case arising from Prohibition-related wiretapping resulted in a near-miss on a constitutional right to privacy. Federal agents placed wiretaps on eight phones in the home of Roy Olmstead, a Seattle, Washington, bootlegger. Convicted and sentenced to four years in prison, he appealed on the grounds that the wiretaps violated both the Fourth and Fifth Amendments. The Supreme Court, in *Olmstead v. United States*, rejected his argument and upheld the convictions in a narrow 5–4 decision.[84]

In dissent, however, Justice Louis Brandeis wrote one of the most eloquent statements about individual liberty in the history of the Court. "The makers of our Constitution," he wrote, "undertook to secure conditions favorable to the pursuit of happiness.... They sought to protect Americans in their beliefs, their thoughts, their emotions and their sensations." Then, breaking new ground, he argued for a constitutional right to privacy: "They conferred, as against the government, the right to be let alone – the most comprehensive of rights and the right most valued by civilized men. To protect, that right, every unjustifiable intrusion by the government upon the privacy of the individual, whatever the means employed, must be deemed a violation of the Fourth Amendment."[85]

Nor was Brandeis finished. He went on to articulate one of the most eloquent statements on the role of law in a democracy. "Decency, security, and liberty alike demand

[81] Democratic Party platform of 1924, APP.

[82] David E. Kyvig, *Repealing National Prohibition*. 2nd ed. (Kent, OH: Kent State University Press, 2000).

[83] National Commission on Law Observance and Enforcement, *Prohibition*, p. 76. Arthur Krock, "The Week in America: The Report Came In," *NYT*, January 25, 1931. Samuel Walker, *Popular Justice: A History of American Criminal Justice*, 2nd ed. (New York: Oxford University Press, 1998), pp. 154–7.

[84] *Olmstead v. United States*, 277 U.S. 438 (1928). Walter F. Murphy, *Wiretapping on Trial: A Case Study in the Judicial Process* (New York: Random House, 1965).

[85] *Olmstead v. United States*, 277 U.S. 438 (1928).

that government officials shall be subjected to the same rules of conduct that are commands to the citizen.... Our government is the potent, the omnipresent teacher. For good or for ill, it teaches the whole people by its example." And in a passage that had special relevance for the impact of Prohibition, he wrote, "Crime is contagious. If the government becomes a lawbreaker, it breeds contempt for law; it invites every man to become a law unto himself; it invites anarchy. To declare that in the administration of the criminal law the end justifies the means-to declare that the government may commit crimes in order to secure the conviction of a private criminal-would bring terrible retribution. Against that pernicious doctrine this court should resolutely set its face."

We can only speculate on the course of American constitutional law, indeed the history of American society as a whole, had only one other justice joined Brandeis and converted his dissent into a majority opinion. To be sure, the case at hand was limited to searches and seizures, but the Court had already established a narrow right of privacy in the *Meyer* and *Pierce* cases. Brandeis's vision of a right of privacy was so expansive that it is difficult to imagine that subsequent cases would have not have expanded it. Curiously, the ACLU took no part in the case and almost completely ignored the lawlessness associated with Prohibition enforcement.[86]

Report on the "third degree": Attacking police misconduct

If the Wickersham Commission dodged the issue of repealing Prohibition, it made a historic contribution to civil liberties regarding police misconduct. Its report *Lawlessness in Law Enforcement* was the most celebrated of all of its fourteen reports. In the long run it represented President Hoover's greatest contribution to civil liberties.

Based on field investigations in fifteen cities, *Lawlessness in Law Enforcement* minced no words, concluding that the third degree, "the inflicting of pain, physical or mental, to extract confessions or statements – is widespread throughout the country." Specifically, "Physical brutality is extensively practiced." This was a powerful indictment from such a high-level source. The commission found numerous examples of blatant disregard for constitutional rights. Without embarrassment, the chief of police in Buffalo, New York, said, "If I have to violate the Constitution or my oath of office, I'll violate the Constitution." The report was written by three lawyers with ACLU connections: Walter Pollak, who had argued the pivotal 1925 *Gitlow v. New York* case for the ACLU in the Supreme Court; Zechariah Chafee, author of the influential 1920 book *Free Speech in the United States*; and Carl Stern, an attorney with civil liberties concerns.[87]

As the first national study highlighting police abuse as a pervasive problem in America, the report received considerable attention and had a significant impact on public attitudes and police practices. Most important, it strengthened the hand of a new generation of police reformers who used it to professionalize their departments. One member of that generation, O. W. Wilson, became the leading authority on police management for more than three decades. President Hoover certainly never intended this result, although

86 Walker, *In Defense of American Liberties*, p. 68.

87 Walker, *In Defense of American Liberties*, pp. 87–8. National Commission on Law Observance and Enforcement, *Lawlessness in Law Enforcement* (1931, reprint, New York: Arno Press, 1968).

he was surely aware of police misconduct in Prohibition enforcement. Nonetheless, he deserves credit for a singular presidential contribution to protecting the rights of citizens at the hands of the police. The *Lawlessness* report embodied his basic approach to presidential leadership – creating commissions of experts that would study social problems and make responsible recommendations.[88]

FREEDOM TO TEACH: THE SCOPES CASE

"Cranks and Freaks Flock to Dayton," headlined the *New York Times*. At the very outset, the trial of John T. Scopes, prosecuted for teaching evolution in a Dayton, Tennessee, high school, was characterized as a circus side show. While it certainly had its bizarre aspects, the publicized aspects have often distracted attention from its very serious meaning for twentieth-century America. The Scopes case is one of the most famous trials in American history, mentioned in many history textbooks and now a part of American legal and popular folklore. With the hindsight of over eight decades, it looms as the opening gun of what became a continuing struggle over the place of religion in American life. If the case did not touch the White House in 1925, the underlying church-state controversy would nevertheless become a central issue in presidential politics.[89]

The Scopes case involved a 1925 Tennessee law making it unlawful "to teach any theory that denies the story of the Divine Creation of man as taught in the Bible, and to teach instead that man has descended from a lower order of animals." The ACLU promptly offered to represent anyone prosecuted under the law, and the Dayton businessman George Rappleyea organized a test case, mainly as a scheme to promote the city and attract new businesses. Little did he and his friends realize the kind of attention it would bring. Rappleyea persuaded the twenty-four-year-old biology teacher John T. Scopes to break the law and arranged his arrest.

The case took a dramatic and unexpected turn when William Jennings Bryan, three-time Democratic Party presidential candidate, announced he would testify for the prosecution. His intervention transformed the case into a national-level controversy over religious fundamentalism. Tradition-minded Protestants felt threatened by the forces of science and secularism that were sweeping through America in the twentieth century. The flash point became Darwin's theory of evolution, which directly challenged the literal interpretation of the creation story in the book of Genesis. Religious conservatives drew a line in the sand against modernism by organizing a new movement known as fundamentalism. A four-volume treatise, *The Fundamentals*, appeared in 1909.[90] In response to Bryan's intervention, Clarence Darrow, the most famous defense attorney in

[88] National Commission on Law Observance and Enforcement, *Lawlessness in Law Enforcement*, pp. 152–3; Buffalo, p. 103. The context of the report: Walker, *Popular Justice*, pp. 154–7.

[89] "Cranks and Freaks Flock to Dayton," *NYT*, July 11, 1925. Larson, *Summer for the Gods*. Ginger, *Six Days or Forever*. The play and the film *Inherit the Wind* present caricatures of Darrow and civil libertarians as heroes and Bryan as a fool.

[90] R. A. Torrey, ed., *The Fundamentals: A Testimony to the Truth* (Los Angeles: Bible Institute of Los Angeles, 1909). An extremely valuable history and analysis of fundamentalism is Karen Armstrong, *The Battle for God: A History of Fundamentalism* (New York: Knopf, 2000). George M. Marsden, *Fundamentalism and American Culture: The Shaping of Twentieth Century Evangelicalism, 1870–1925* (New York: Oxford University Press, 1980).

the country and an aggressively outspoken atheist, announced that he would assist the Scopes defense.

The trial became a media circus. Hundreds of journalists from around the country and the world descended on Dayton, and the trial was broadcast by Chicago radio station WGN in one of the earliest examples of such coverage of a major event by the new medium of radio. The most famous part of the trial was Darrow's ruthless cross-examination of Bryan, where the famed atheist forced Bryan to admit that he believed in the literal truth of the biblical stories about Adam and Eve, Noah and the Flood, and Jonah being swallowed by a whale. In the pivotal moment of the entire trial, he led Bryan to concede that the "days" in the Genesis story were not necessarily days of twenty-four hours in the modern sense. People in the audience gasped when they heard their fundamentalist hero yield on the literal reading of the Creation story.

Deeply embarrassed by Bryan's testimony, the judge and prosecutor quickly ended the trial. The jury readily convicted Scopes, but Judge John Raulston made a small error in setting the punishment. The mistake allowed the Tennessee Supreme Court to overturn Scopes's conviction on appeal. Eager to put the entire affair behind them, Tennessee officials did not retry the case. As a result, the ACLU was denied the opportunity to bring the case before the U.S. Supreme Court to test the underlying First Amendment issues. (The Court eventually ruled a similar Arkansas law unconstitutional in the 1968 *Epperson v. Arkansas* case.)[91]

President Coolidge did not comment on the case, and no one saw it as having national political implications. A half-century later, however, Christian fundamentalism emerged as a central force in national politics. The historian Karen Armstrong argues in her insightful history of fundamentalism *The Battle for God* that fundamentalists withdrew from the political arena in the mid-1920s, in part because of embarrassment over the Scopes case. In retreat they organized a counterculture with their own churches and colleges, separate from the modernist trends in mainstream American Protestantism and quite out of step with the increasing secularism of American society.[92]

Armstrong observes that "liberal Christians assumed that the fundamentalist crisis was over" after the Scopes case. She might have added that civil libertarians also thought they had won a great victory. In his 1966 memoirs, John T. Scopes observed that "the war cries of the Fundamentalists sound archaic" forty-one years after the trial. He was very wrong. Fundamentalists drew strength from their outsider status, and their righteous opposition to evolution, sex outside marriage, and the other hallmarks of modern secular culture. In the 1970s they emerged from their political isolation and threw their support to neoconservative Republicans, beginning with Ronald Reagan in 1980, and became a powerful political force. Along with abortion, pornography, and gay rights, the battle over teaching evolution in the schools moved to the forefront of American politics.[93]

[91] *Epperson v. Arkansas*, 393 U.S. 97 (1968). Long-term impact of the Scopes case: Edward J. Larson, *Trial and Error: The American Legal Controversy over Creation and Evolution* (New York: Oxford University Press, 1985).

[92] Armstrong, *The Battle for God*, pp. 199–232. Armstrong's explores the parallel fundamentalist trends among Christians, Jews, and Muslims.

[93] Armstrong, *The Battle for God*, p. 214; Chapter 9, "The Offensive (1974–1979)," pp. 278–316; Ch. 10 "Defeat?" (1979–99), pp. 317–64. John T. Scopes and James Presley, *Center of the Storm: Memoirs of John T. Scopes* (New York: Holt, Reinhart & Winston, 1967), p. 271.

STRAWS IN THE WIND: THE SUPREME COURT SHIFTS

The twelve years from 1920 to 1932 under three Republican presidents were bleak for civil liberties. One harbinger of possibly better days ahead was a shift in the Supreme Court, the full significance of which became evident only in retrospect.[94]

Although the Court upheld the conviction of Benjamin Gitlow for violating the New York state criminal anarchy law, the 1925 decision in *Gitlow v. New York* incorporated the First Amendment into the due process clause of the Fourteenth Amendment: "For present purposes we may and do assume that freedom of speech and of the press - which are protected by the First Amendment from abridgment by Congress - are among the fundamental personal rights and 'liberties' protected by the due process clause of the Fourteenth Amendment from impairment by the States." The decision was a historic breakthrough, as the incorporation principle became the foundation for the revolution in civil liberties in subsequent decades.[95]

Six years later, the Court gave meaning to the *Gitlow* principle in two pathbreaking First Amendment decisions. In *Stromberg v. California*, it struck down a state law banning the display of red flags (a symbol of communism), holding that "the maintenance of the opportunity for free political discussion ... is a fundamental principle of our constitutional system." The decision struck at the heart of the full panoply of antiradical laws that had proliferated in the twenties. In *Near v. Minnesota* (1931) it affirmed a right of freedom of the press under the First Amendment. Jay Near was a truly unsavory person, an anti-semite and vicious political scandalmonger but the Court ruled that the state could not restrain his expression of opinion, no matter how offensive many people found much of what he published. The two decisions marked the first tentative beginnings of the revolution in constitutional law protecting civil liberties.[96]

President Harding appointed four justices to the Supreme Court, beginning with William Howard Taft as chief justice, all of whom were anti-civil libertarian. George Sutherland, his second appointment, became one of the most conservative justices on the Court in the twentieth century, and famous as one of the "four horsemen" who blocked New Deal social legislation in the 1930s. Pierce Butler joined him as a solid member of the conservative block. Edward Terry Sanford was also very conservative but wrote the majority opinion in the pivotal *Gitlow* case.[97]

President Coolidge elevated Harlan Fiske Stone from attorney general to the Court in 1925. He had strong civil liberties commitments (having cleaned up the Bureau of Investigation as attorney general) and joined Louis Brandeis as an active liberal and civil libertarian on the Court. He is perhaps most notable for writing the famous "Footnote Four" in *United States v. Carolene Products* (1938), where he provided a rationale for the Court's emerging activism on civil liberties and civil rights. President Herbert Hoover

94 Threats to American democracy from radical movements in the 1930's: Alan Brinkley, *Voices of Protest: Huey Long, Father Coughlin, and the Great Depression* (New York: Knopf, 1982). Sinclair Lewis, *It Can't Happen Here: A Novel* (New York: Doubleday, Doran, 1935).

95 *Gitlow v. New York*, 268 U.S. 652 (1925).

96 *Stromberg v. California*, 283 U.S. 359 (1931). *Near v. Minnesota*, 283 U.S. 697 (1931). Fred Friendly, *Minnesota Rag: The Dramatic Story of the Landmark Case That Gave New Meaning to Freedom of the Press* (New York: Random House, 1981).

97 Henry J. Abraham, *Justices, Presidents, and Senators*, 5th ed. (Lanham, MD: Rowman & Littlefield, 2008), pp. 145-52.

added three justices. He reappointed Charles Evans Hughes to the Court in 1930 (having left to run for president in 1916) and Owen Roberts in 1930. Most important was his 1932 appointment of Benjamin Cardozo, widely regarded as one of the most distinguished jurists to sit on the Court. His opinion in *Palko v. Connecticut* (1937) developed a theory of the Fourteenth Amendment that established a foundation for future decisions protecting civil liberties. Roberts, meanwhile, executed a critical about-face in 1937 that ended the Court's hostility to New Deal legislation and helped set the Court on a new path of defending political and civil rights.[98]

END OF THE REPUBLICAN ERA

The twelve years of Republican presidents between 1921 and 1933 began in the midst of the grim hangover of World War I and the Red Scare and ended in the depths of the Great Depression. For civil liberties, these were the years in the wilderness. Free speech was equated with "un-American" ideologies, the First Amendment rights of working people were systematically suppressed, prohibition enforcement agents routinely committed violations of due process, while lynchings and other racist violence continued unchecked. The ACLU's Roger Baldwin was so dispirited in 1927 that he considered resigning to pursue other causes.[99]

In this period there were no tumultuous civil liberties crises comparable to the World War I years earlier or the upheavals of Franklin D. Roosevelt's presidency in the years that followed. With a few notable exceptions, the three Republican presidents tolerated the repressive atmosphere of the period. Nonetheless, on a few issues they were more sympathetic to civil liberties than their subsequent reputations suggest. The Harding administration ended political censorship by the Post Office and was far more compassionate toward the victims of World War I repression than President Wilson had been. He also for a brief moment championed racial justice. President Coolidge's attorney general ended political spying by the Bureau of Investigation. President Hoover made a notable contribution to curbing police misconduct. All three presidents were modestly sympathetic to women's rights.

Contrary to popular mythology, the Republican era was not a period of peace and tranquility. Across the country one could see the early stirrings of fights for civil liberties, racial justice, and women's rights. The 1925 Scopes case, the NAACP's campaign for a federal antilynching law, and the introduction of the Equal Rights Amendment in 1923 were all harbingers of controversies and change in the decades ahead. Particularly important, the Supreme Court took the first tentative steps toward giving meaning to the Bill of Rights, in the 1925 *Gitlow* decision and the two 1931 First Amendment cases. These were all straws in the wind. The next dozen years would witness a revolution in civil liberties in the United States, and when the next president left office in 1945, Americans would enjoy the first substantial body of protection of individual liberties.

[98] Ibid., pp. 151–61.
[99] Walker, *In Defense of American Liberties*, pp. 69, 71.

Japanese Americans being evacuated from the West Coast, spring 1942. A total of 117,116 people were evacuated and then interned in relocation centers until the Supreme Court ruled in December 1944 that the government could not constitutionally detain people it conceded were loyal to the United States.

Source: Library of Congress.

4 Franklin D. Roosevelt

The Mixed Legacy of a Strong President

"THE GREATEST VIOLATION OF CIVIL LIBERTIES IN AMERICAN HISTORY"

The climactic meeting occurred the night of February 17, 1942, at the home of Attorney General Francis Biddle. Three lawyers from the War Department presented their case for evacuating all Japanese Americans from the West Coast. The Justice Department lawyer Ed Ennis, who had strenuously argued against it, was shocked to discover that his boss had already conceded and accepted the plan. He left the meeting in tears, and friends had to talk him out of resigning from his job. Two days later President Franklin D. Roosevelt (FDR) issued Executive Order 9066 authorizing the military to designate areas on the West Coast and remove people from them. Over the next few weeks, the government forcibly evacuated 117,116 Japanese Americans and detained them in concentration camps. An estimated two-thirds, or about seventy-two thousand, were native born American citizens.[1]

FDR and civil liberties

The evacuation and internment of the Japanese Americans arguably constitute the greatest violation of civil liberties in American history, and they cast a deep shadow over FDR's presidency. Other presidents violated civil liberties in various ways, but he is the only one who ever put Americans in concentration camps. Despite this enormous outrage, however, historians consistently rank FDR with George Washington and Abraham Lincoln as the only three "great" presidents in American history. Roosevelt certainly deserves great credit for his leadership during the Great Depression, giving people hope and instituting lasting reforms, and during World War II, when he led the nation and the allies in a two-front world conflict. It is difficult, however, to reconcile his traditional high ranking with the Japanese-American tragedy.[2]

FDR's record on civil liberties is a tangle of contradictions. On the positive side, his 1941 Four Freedoms speech is arguably the greatest tribute to freedom of speech and

[1] Firsthand account of the meeting: James Rowe, Interview, October 15, 1942, Densho Archives, Document i67-00083. Legal aspects of the evacuation and internment: Peter H. Irons, *Justice at War* (New York: Oxford University Press, 1983). Indispensable on the internment: Greg Robinson, *By Order of the President: FDR and the Internment of Japanese Americans* (Cambridge, MA: Harvard University Press, 2001). Francis Biddle, *In Brief Authority* (Garden City, NY: Doubleday, 1962), pp. 212–26.

[2] James Lindgren and Steven G. Calabresi, "Rating the Presidents of the United States, 1789–2000: A Survey of Scholars in Political Science, History, and Law," *Constitutional Commentary* 18 (Winter 2001): 583–606. The Roosevelt literature is vast. The starting point is the three-volume *Age of Roosevelt* by Arthur M. Schlesinger, Jr., although the author is a strong Roosevelt partisan and longtime adviser to other leading Democrats.

religious liberty ever given by a sitting president. His attorney general, Frank Murphy, created the forerunner of today's Civil Rights Division in 1939, launching the active federal enforcement of individual rights. And most important, his Supreme Court appointees created the first substantial body of constitutional law protecting individual liberty. On the day FDR died, April 12, 1945, Americans enjoyed meaningful protections of individual rights as never before in American history.

At the same time, however, Roosevelt perpetrated several serious violations of civil liberties. In addition to the Japanese-American tragedy, he reauthorized political spying by the FBI, after it had been in abeyance for more than a decade. On several occasions he made claims of presidential power that set a dangerous precedent for the future. In the 1942 case of eight captured German saboteurs, he expressed blatant contempt for the Supreme Court and the rule of law. Until the very last minute he opposed the Wagner Act, the "magna carta" for working people, which guaranteed them freedom of speech and assembly. FDR was also indifferent to the demands of the rising civil rights movement. Unraveling the profound contradictions in Roosevelt's civil liberties record is a major challenge.

THE JAPANESE-AMERICAN TRAGEDY: FDR DECIDES

Secretary of War Henry L. Stimson desperately tried to schedule a meeting with FDR on February 11, 1942, for a final decision about the Japanese Americans on the West Coast. Military authorities and West Coast politicians were campaigning loudly for total evacuation. Consumed by the war effort, however, FDR was too busy to meet and over the phone told Stimson to do what he thought necessary. What about those Japanese Americans who were bona fide American citizens?, Stimson asked. FDR replied, "we will take care of them too." Eight days later, Roosevelt signed Executive Order 9066.[3]

Roosevelt's personal responsibility for the Japanese-American tragedy is clear: Only he as commander in chief had the authority to issue such an order affecting the liberties of Americans. The important question is how and why he made this fateful decision. Lawyers in the Justice Department told him it was unnecessary and raised serious legal questions for the American citizens involved. The FBI director, J. Edgar Hoover, reported that there was no "Japanese problem" on the West Coast, and that judgment was reiterated by both FDR's personal emissary, the businessman Curtis B. Munson, and Lt. Commander Kenneth Ringle in the Office of Naval Intelligence. Fears of a possible Japanese invasion, which were probably exaggerated, together with other political and personal factors, however, led FDR to ignore these objections.[4]

Immediately after the bombing of Pearl Harbor there was good reason to believe the United States would not repeat the massive suppression of civil liberties that occurred under President Wilson in World War I. Attorney General Biddle and other top administration officials remembered that episode and vowed not to repeat it. In June 1940, with the world alarmed by the Nazi conquest of France, he counseled against hysteria, advising, "We shall not defeat the Nazi evil by emulating its methods." Roosevelt's Four Freedoms speech in early 1941 was an unprecedented presidential clarion call to

[3] Robinson, *By Order of the President*, p. 106.

[4] Schlesinger impermissibly deflect's FDR's responsibility by arguing that it "was not a unilateral act." Arthur M. Schlesinger, Jr., *The Imperial Presidency*. Rev. ed. (Boston: Houghton Mifflin, 2004), p. 116.

respect individual rights in a world of totalitarianism. In his first public statement about the Japanese Americans on January 2, 1942, moreover, he called for tolerance, asking employers not to fire people simply because of the "accident of [their] birth." "Remember the Nazi technique," he counseled; they "pit race against race, religion against religion, prejudice against prejudice.... We must not let that happen here. We must not forget what we are defending: liberty, decency, justice." It was an impressive declaration of tolerance, especially delivered so soon after Pearl Harbor. That same day, the United States joined twenty-five other allied nations in a call to defeat the Axis powers and protect "life, liberty, independence and religious freedom." Had FDR held to these principles in the weeks ahead, the tragedy of the evacuation and detention might never have occurred.[5] History did not repeat itself in exactly the same way, however. In World War I there had been no surprise attack on a U.S. military base with three thousand people killed. Nor was there an element of racial prejudice, as was the case with the Japanese Americans. The immediate crisis following Pearl Harbor involved a toxic brew of war and race, for which neither President Roosevelt nor the country was prepared.

Months before Pearl Harbor, the Roosevelt administration wrestled with the question of the Japanese Americans on the West Coast in the event of war with Japan. In October 1941 FDR dispatched Curtis Munson to assess the situation privately for him. On the basis of interviews with Japanese Americans, the FBI, and military officials, Munson first sent in a preliminary report on October 19, and other reports on the situation both on the West Coast and in Hawaii, culminating in a final report in December. He consistently found the Japanese Americans to be "very good citizen[s]," who are "98% loyal." Those few Japanese Americans who posed any threat of espionage or sabotage could be readily controlled. Munson recommended that their loyalty be encouraged by a "statement from *high* government authority" (presumably the president), that their offers to assist in the war effort (e.g., through the Red Cross) be accepted, and that businesses owned by Issei (Japanese-born) be taken over by the government or managed by Nisei (American-born). A January 29 report by Lt. Commander Ringle of the Office of Naval Intelligence in Los Angeles agreed that the Japanese Americans were overwhelmingly loyal to the United States, and that there were at most about thirty-five hundred potential "saboteurs or agents" in the entire country ("less than three percent of the total," he noted). Both aliens and citizens deemed dangerous should be placed in "custodial detention," after a "review of individual cases" by boards composed of the military and the Department of Justice. As did Munson, he believed the "Japanese problem" had been "magnified out of its true proportion" and that the best solution was to encourage the loyalty of the vast majority actively and offer them a place in the war effort. In particular, they would be excellent sources of information about potential saboteurs. William J. Donovan, who in July became head of the Office of Strategic Services, forerunner of the Central Intelligence Agency (CIA), agreed.[6]

5 "Bars Nazi Methods in U.S. Spy Hunts," *NYT*, June 17, 1940. Statement against Discharging Loyal Aliens from Jobs, January 2, 1942, APP. "Call Allies' Pact 'Freedom Charter,'" *NYT*, January 3, 1942. "Roosevelt Limits Film Restrictions," ibid., January 4, 1942. Biddle, Cabinet Minutes, FPBP, Box 1, FDRPL.

6 Curtis B. Munson, Report and Suggestions Regarding Handling Japanese Question on the West Coast, December 20, 1941, John Franklin Carter File, Box 97, PSF, FDRPL. Munson's final report was preceded by several preliminary reports on both the West Coast and Hawaii, beginning with Munson to Carter ("Dear John"), October 19, 1941, PSF, John Franklin Carter, Box 97, FDRPL. Ringle Report on Japanese Internment, January 29, 1942: www.history.navy.mil/library//online/jap%20intern.htm.

The FBI director, J. Edgar Hoover, consistently opposed mass evacuation. He was undoubtedly flattered by Munson's October report that both the FBI and Naval Intelligence had "ticketed" the few real threats. Within twenty-four hours after the Pearl Harbor attack, in fact, the FBI arrested 736 suspected spies or saboteurs and had 3,000 in custody within a few weeks and 5,589 by 1943. On February 2 Hoover told Attorney General Biddle that the demands for evacuation were "based primarily on public and political pressure rather than on factual data," an assessment since vindicated by history.[7]

Attorney General Biddle emerges as a tragic figure in the Japanese-American affair. A committed civil libertarian who had handled ACLU cases in the late 1930s, he initially told FDR mass evacuation was unnecessary. (In his 1962 memoirs, the clearly regretful Biddle all but called it unconstitutional but never used the word.) His two key Justice Department lawyers, Edward J. Ennis and James Rowe, opposed it even more vigorously. Years later, Ennis recalled telling Biddle to "please say it [evacuation] is unconstitutional" to FDR, but that he was "not prepared" to do that. On the other side within the Justice Department, Tom Clark, future attorney general and Supreme Court justice, actively supported evacuation. Caught between conflicting pressures, Biddle sought outside advice and consulted the Washington lawyers Benjamin Cohen, Joseph L. Rauh, and Oscar Cox about the constitutionality of evacuation. Cohen had been a key member of FDR's "Brains Trust" in the early years of the New Deal, and Joe Rauh later became one of the nation's most important civil rights and civil liberties attorneys. They advised Biddle that in a time of "national peril" the issue had to be "resolved in favor of action to preserve the national security."[8]

The political atmosphere changed quickly in late January 1942, as West Coast politicians began demanding removal of the Japanese Americans. The War Department joined in, and after it was discussed at a January 30 cabinet meeting Biddle began to yield, suggesting they make some "arrangement" to remove Japanese Americans from West Coast military zones. He also told the Senate that evacuation would be legal as a military necessity. Still, at a February 7 meeting with the president, he said that evacuation was "inadvisable." Five days later, however, he gave up, and in a February 12h memo he advised Secretary of War Stimson that he had "no doubt" that the military could legally remove "all persons" from an area if it was "deemed essential from a military point of view." In his memoirs he explained that as the newest member of the cabinet (appointed only three months before the Pearl Harbor attack) he felt very uneasy about challenging the formidable Stimson, the most influential member of the cabinet at that time, or the military. (Stimson's diary, meanwhile, indicates that he regarded Biddle as a nuisance on this and other issues.) General John L. DeWitt sent his formal recommendation to the secretary of war recommending evacuation on February 14, and with Stimson's earlier February 11

Lt. K. D. Ringle, to Chief of Naval Operations, Report on the Japanese Question, January 26, 1942, www.history.navy.mil/library. Loyalty and the Japanese Americans: Eric L. Muller, *American Inquisition: the Hunt for Japanese American Disloyalty in World War II* (Chapel Hill: University of North Carolina Press, 2007).

7 J. Edgar Hoover to Francis M. Shea, assistant attorney general, December 17, 1941, Densho Archives, Document #i67-00020. Hoover, Memorandum for the Attorney General, February 2, 1942, Densho Archives, Document #i67-00102.

8 Edward J. Ennis, Interview for the Commission on Wartime Relocation, Densho Archives, Document #i67-00097. Benjamin Cohen, Joseph L. Rauh, and Oscar Cox, "The Japanese Situation on the West Coast" [circa February 1942], quoted in Irons, *Justice at War*, p. 54.

phone call to FDR, the debate was over. Ennis and Rowe continued to plead with Biddle, but without success. Ennis remembered Biddle as "almost a saint-like fair man," who just could not stand up to the president. (And as we shall see, he yielded to FDR on some other civil liberties issues as well.) Nor would he embarrass the president by resigning in protest in the midst of a national crisis.[9]

FDR's decision making

Despite his ultimate decision, President Roosevelt was only fitfully engaged in the debate over the Japanese Americans after Pearl Harbor. Several factors shaped his response. Most important were the demands of the war effort. The urgent challenge of raising an army, mobilizing the entire economy, and rallying the American people for a two-front world war took every ounce of his energy. Even Stimson could not meet with him to talk about the Japanese-American question. If fears of a Japanese invasion were exaggerated (and possibly manipulated by the military), it was difficult to dismiss them in the atmosphere following Pearl Harbor. During a critical three-week period in January 1942, moreover, FDR was consumed by a visit by the British prime minister, Winston Churchill, for intense discussions about war strategy. Two firsthand accounts vividly describe the war's impact on FDR's health. On the morning of December 8, Supreme Court Justice James Byrnes visited the White House and later recalled that FDR's "appearance shocked me." Milton Eisenhower, brother of the future president, Dwight D. Eisenhower, was called to the Oval Office in early March and given overall responsibility for the evacuation. He "was startled by the change in the President.... I had never seen him without his jaunty air ... buoyant, smiling, and confident." Now, "his face lacked color, his lips were a tight grim line, and, as he looked up at me, I saw his eyes were bloodshot." In the year before his death, Roosevelt's blood pressure went as high as 300 (something only a handful of people knew). Finally, Japanese forces made rapid advances in Asia after Pearl Harbor. Secretary of War Stimson noted in his diary on February 16 that "a somber tone pervades all [White House] conferences now." A sense of alarm about the military situation in Asia undoubtedly affected the decision on the Japanese Americans.[10]

Despite his January 2 call for tolerance, Roosevelt shared some of the anti-Japanese prejudices that permeated American society. He and other Americans believed the Japanese were different from German and Italian Americans. General DeWitt told the House Naval Affairs Subcommittee on April 13, 1943, "You needn't worry about the Italians at all except in certain cases. Also, the same for the Germans except in individual cases. But we must worry about the Japanese all the time until he is wiped off the map." FDR reportedly told guests at a White House dinner, "I don't care about the Italians. They're all opera singers. The Germans are different. They are dangerous." Group prejudices were a

[9] Biddle to Stimson, February 12, 1942, Densho Archive, Document i6700099. Robinson, *By Order of the President*, pp. 97–104. Henry L. Stimson Diaries, MF Ed., Yale University, January 16, 1942, March 2, 1942 (critical of Biddle regarding anti-trust enforcement against war industries); April 15, 1942 (critical of Biddle on possible east coast evacuations). Ennis, Interview; Rowe, Interview, www.archive.densho.org.

[10] Robinson, *By Order of the President*, Ch. 3, pp. 73–124. James F. Byrnes, *All in One Lifetime* (New York: Harper and Brothers, 1958), p. 147. Milton S. Eisenhower, *The President Is Calling* (Garden City, NY: Doubleday, 1974), pp. 95–6. Blood pressure: *Robert H. Ferrell, Presidential Leadership: From Woodrow Wilson to Harry S. Truman* (Columbia: University of Missouri Press, 2006), pp. 5, 119. Stimson, Diary, February 16. 1942.

part of his outlook, and as we shall see, he responded to African-American demands only when pressured to do so.[11]

Perhaps most important for the always politically minded FDR were the rising calls for total evacuation on the West Coast, supported by the military. Anti-Japanese prejudice had a long history on the coast, and by mid-January it began running at fever pitch. Caleb Foote, West Coast staff person for the pacifist Fellowship of Reconciliation, warned at the end of January, "The situation with regard to the Japanese has gotten worse with alarming rapidity in the last few days." He was one of the few who grasped the implications of mass evacuation, warning that "nothing could be more Hitlerian." Opponents of evacuation were taken by surprise and not able to organize an effective response at least to counterbalance the calls for evacuation. The writer and civil rights advocate Carey McWilliams later speculated that strong vocal opposition might have caused the president to choose a less drastic alternative.[12] The California attorney general, Earl Warren, was a particularly influential voice, announcing his support for evacuation on January 29. He fully understood that he did not have the legal authority to remove Japanese Americans and that only the president could do it as a war measure. Japan, he claimed, had planned "fifth column activities, or sabotage, or war behind the lines upon civilians," and it was no "coincidence" that many Japanese Americans owned or occupied land near military installations. In a complete reversal of ordinary logic, he argued that the absence of sabotage so far was "the most ominous sign" of all, indicating a plan to coordinate sabotage with the eventual invasion.[13]

It is impossible not to note the enormous irony in the positions taken by J. Edgar Hoover and Earl Warren in the crisis. Hoover, who violated the rights of Americans for a longer period than any government official in American history, was in this instance a voice for restraint. (Secretary of War Stimson did not believe him and noted in his diary on January 20 that the FBI had not gotten into the "secret thoughts" of the Japanese and the "great potential danger" they posed.) Warren, a civil liberties icon today for his role as chief justice of the Supreme Court and author of the *Brown v. Board of Education* decision, on the other hand, advocated evacuation and indulged in the worst anti-Japanese stereotypes. Warren never fully addressed his responsibility for the removals and in his memoirs said only that he "deeply regretted the removal order and my testimony in advocating it," before moving on.[14]

The long-standing west Coast prejudice against the Japanese was only part of the problem with public opinion. All across the country, Americans refused to speak out against the evacuation. The motives of different groups were mixed, but racial insensitivity and the need for national unity in wartime were common factors. Criticism of the government action was extremely limited, involving primarily the ACLU and its West Coast affiliates, the American Friends Service Committee, and other pacifist and religious leaders. With America at war, their voices went unheeded. Liberals refused to criticize FDR, conservatives rallied to national defense, and leftists supported the war effort uncritically because

11 FDR: Biddle, *In Brief Authority*, p. 207.

12 Foote to A. J. Muste, January 31, 1942, FORP, Section II, Series A-3, Box 2, SPC. Carey McWilliams, *The Education of Carey McWilliams* (New York: Simon & Schuster, 1979), p. 102.

13 Warren calls for martial law: "West Coast Widens Martial Law Call," *NYT*, February 12, 1942.

14 Stimson, Diary, January 20, 1942. Irons, *Justice at War*, pp. 41, 213–14. Earl Warren, *The Memoirs of Chief Justice Earl Warren* (New York: Doubleday, 1977), p. 149.

of Hitler's attack on Russia. Even the Japanese American Citizens League (JACL) initially refused to protest the evacuation, partly out of legitimate fear of vigilante attacks or even worse government actions. The ACLU affiliates on the West Coast had difficulty finding plaintiffs for the court challenges that eventually reached the Supreme Court. (The JACL recovered its footing and filed a brief in *Korematsu*, the challenge to the removal order in the Supreme Court.) Attorney General Biddle and Eleanor Roosevelt were among those otherwise thoughtful Americans who thought evacuation was actually in the best interests of the Japanese Americans, to protect them from vigilante attacks by California superpatriots.[15]

Even First Lady Eleanor Roosevelt was ambivalent, despite her high-profile support for racial justice before the war. She initially argued against evacuation until FDR curtly told her he did not want to discuss it anymore. At a White House dinner, however, she rebuked a guest, saying, "But some of the Japanese on the Coast *have* been caught as spies of the Japanese government." Three months later she wrote to the popular novelist Pearl Buck that while she regretted the evacuation, "it has to be done." Along with some other liberals, she thought it might be good social policy to scatter Japanese Americans around the country so as to integrate them better into American society (and in fact even proposed this for southern African Americans).[16] Her position on the evacuation was an exception to her otherwise strong record on civil rights, although it should also be noted that neither she nor FDR spoke out against the Holocaust. In short, the evacuation had the near-complete backing of the American people. It was a melancholy testimony of the willingness of Americans – including the president – to put civil liberties aside in a time of war.

FDR, THE CONSTITUTION, AND PRESIDENTIAL POWER

Military and political considerations aside, the question remains regarding what FDR thought about the constitutionality of the evacuation. In fact, he had very strong ideas about the Constitution and presidential power in a national emergency, which he explained in a revealing speech on the occasion of the 150th anniversary of the Constitution on September 17, 1937. Amazingly, despite its enormous significance, historians have almost completely overlooked this speech.[17]

The Constitution, FDR explained, is "a layman's document, not a lawyer's contract." It is a "charter of general principles," not filled with a lot of lawyers' "whereases," which permits "flexible statesmanship" in a crisis. Extremely well read in American history, he cited several critical episodes where presidents exercised extraordinary power that some at the time thought questionable if not unconstitutional. They included Thomas Jefferson's

15 Biddle: "Army Gets Power to Move Citizens or Aliens Inland," *NYT*, February 21, 1942. Irons, *Justice at War*, pp. 79–81, 112. Opponents: Robert Shaffer, "Cracks in the Consensus: Defending the Rights of Japanese Americans during World War II," *Radical History Review* 72 (1998): 84–120.

16 Louis Adamic, *Dinner at the White House* (New York: Harper and Brothers, 1946), p. 41. Eleanor Roosevelt, *It Seems to Me* (New York: W. W. Norton, 1954), pp. 39–40. "Scattering of Negro People": Eleanor Roosevelt to Pauli Murray, July 23, 1944, FDRPL, ERP, MF Ed., Reel 14.

17 Address on Constitution Day, Washington, DC, September 17, 1937, APP. Felix Frankfurter suggested the speech and wrote an initial draft: Frankfurter to Roosevelt, August 9, 1937, FFP, Box 243, LOC. Background on the speech: Joseph P. Lash, *Dealers and Dreamers: A New Look at the New Deal* (New York: Doubleday, 1988), pp. 310–11. The "general theme" of the speech was developed by FDR's aide, Tommy Corcoran; Samuel I. Rosenman, *Working with Roosevelt* (New York: Harper, 1952), pp. 163–4.

Louisiana Purchase and Abraham Lincoln's suspension of habeas corpus during the Civil War. A strict lawyer's view of the Constitution, he continued, would have prevented action vital to the national interest on those occasions. He also pointedly mentioned the recent constitutional crisis when the Supreme Court had invalidated New Deal economic measures, paralyzing the government's response to the depression. A "flexible" interpretation of the Constitution, he argued, would allow for "the [economic] reforms which the mass of the American people now demand."

To modern ears, FDR's view of constitutional "flexibility" contradicts the very principle of the Constitution as a constraint on the power of the federal government. His interpretation was nothing less than a license for unlimited presidential power that would have sanctioned Wilson's suppression of free speech during World War I, approved national security spying by federal agencies, and, of course, permitted his own subsequent order to evacuate the Japanese Americans.

FDR directly addressed the question of civil liberties but glibly turned the issue on its head. Assuring his audience, "No one cherishes more deeply than I the civil and religious liberties achieved by so much blood and anguish through many centuries," he said that the Bill of Rights existed to "protect minorities against intolerance of majorities" but immediately added that it was also designed to "protect majorities against the enthronement of minorities." The latter point clearly referred to the recent controversy where a majority of five Supreme Court justices had declared unconstitutional the principal New Deal economic measures designed to address the Great Depression. The crisis had just ended a few months earlier in 1937, and it was a bitter issue for him.[18]

The political pragmatism for which FDR is renowned underpinned his idea of a flexible Constitution. Robert Jackson, a close political ally who served as attorney general and was appointed to the Supreme Court, had a keen insight into Roosevelt's mind. FDR, he said, thought "in terms of right and wrong, instead of terms of legal and illegal." Always assuming his motives were good, FDR "found difficulty in thinking that there could be legal limitations on them."[19]

The well-read Roosevelt took his view of the Constitution as a layperson's document directly from none other than Woodrow Wilson, who in his 1908 book *Constitutional Government* wrote, "the Constitution ... is not a mere lawyers' document" and called for strong presidential leadership. In World War I, of course, he proceeded to exercise such leadership.[20] FDR earlier stated his views about presidential power in his famous first inaugural address in 1933. The speech is celebrated for his ringing statement that "the only thing we have to fear is fear itself," but few have noticed his later warning that if Congress failed to act on the economic crisis, he would make a "temporary departure" from the "normal balance of Executive and legislative authority" and "wage a war" on the crisis as "if we were in fact invaded by a foreign foe." He never elaborated on what such a "temporary departure" might involve, and he implicitly assumed that he as president had

[18] FDR reiterated his argument a year later. Radio Address on Constitution Day, Washington, DC September 17, 1938, APP. Court crisis: William Leuchtenburg, *The Supreme Court Reborn: The Constitutional Revolution in the Age of Roosevelt* (New York: Oxford University Press, 1995).

[19] Robert H. Jackson, *That Man: An Insider's Portrait of Franklin D. Roosevelt* (New York Oxford University Press, 2003), p. 74.

[20] Woodrow Wilson, *Constitutional Government in the United States* (New York: Columbia University Press, 1908), p. 69.

the sole power to determine that a sufficient national crisis existed. He also expressed his contempt for legal procedures when eight German saboteurs landed in the United States in 1942. He told Attorney General Biddle he would execute them no matter what the Supreme Court said about the constitutionality of his planned military tribunal and stated flatly, "I won't hand them over to any United States Marshall armed with a writ of habeas corpus. Understand?"[21]

It is impossible to avoid comparing FDR's claims of presidential power with those made more than sixty years later by President George W. Bush in the war on terrorism. In fact, FDR's claims were far broader, as Bush limited his to the president's role as commander in chief of the armed forces. FDR's claims extended to any aspect of government in a national emergency. To be sure, he used this power rarely apart from the Japanese American tragedy, but that event and the theory itself cast a deep shadow over Roosevelt's presidency.

THE TRAGEDY UNFOLDS

Empowered by Executive Order 9066, military officials began evacuating the Japanese Americans in March 1942. Often overlooked is the fact that the order did not specifically mention the Japanese Americans and said nothing about what would happen to them after removal. In a sweeping delegation of power to the military, the order authorized them to designate military zones, remove people from those areas, and establish regulations about entering or leaving the zones. In his first comments on the evacuation, Attorney General Biddle argued that evacuation was "for the protection of the Japanese themselves" against local vigilantes. Given the intense prejudice on the West Coast, vigilante attacks were a very real possibility, but it is impossible now and was difficult even then to justify a gross violation of individual rights in the name of protecting the victims. By voice vote in both houses, Congress on March 19 passed Public Law 503 providing criminal penalties for violating the president's order or any related military regulations.

The Japanese Americans were detained in Relocation Centers, run by the War Relocation Authority, as an ad hoc response to the loud protests by officials in mountain and midwestern states. Anti-Japanese prejudice was not confined to the West Coast, and leaders in other states did not want the evacuees. The centers have been properly labeled concentration camps. The legal, human, and economic consequences of the government's actions were enormous. In addition to the stigma of evacuation and detention, the victims suffered massive property losses, estimated at $4 to $5 billion in today's dollars. A 1943 War Relocation Authority report described the camps as "tar paper–covered barracks of simple frame construction without plumbing or cooking facilities of any kind." Finally, legal challenges led to two of the most shameful decisions in the Supreme Court.[22]

The ACLU immediately denounced Roosevelt's "unprecedented order" at its next board meeting on March 2, citing "grave" constitutional questions and arguing that people could be evacuated only "after individual examinations." On March 20, it sent a letter

[21] Inaugural Address, March 4, 1933, APP. Biddle, *In Brief Authority*, p. 331.

[22] Biddle: "Army Gets Power to Move Citizens or Aliens Inland," *NYT*, February 21, 1942. Irons, *Justice at War*, pp. 64–8. Robinson, *By Order of the President*, pp. 125–76. There are a many firsthand accounts of the evacuation experience.

of protest to FDR. It was a lonely protest, however, and had no effect on the unfolding events. Gripped by racism, fear of a Japanese invasion, raw patriotism in a time of war, Americans across the political spectrum - liberals, leftists, and conservatives - for their own varied reasons chose not to protest. Even the ACLU was deeply divided, as some members of its National Board did not want any legal challenges at all. After the board passed a limited policy, a bitter dispute between the national office and its West Coast affiliates erupted. That the ACLU was gravely divided was grim testimony to the impact of war and racism on concern for basic civil liberties among the American people.[23]

The Justice Department argued that individual loyalty hearings, as suggested by Lt. Commander Ringle and the ACLU, would be impossible. Its actions told a different story, however. The FBI arrested 736 suspected spies and saboteurs by December 8, about three thousand people within a few weeks. Naval intelligence and the FBI had been closely monitoring the Japanese Americans and had a list of suspects. In short, individualized hearings were quite feasible.[24]

Disaster in the Supreme Court

Challenges to the government's program reached the Supreme Court. In the first case, *Hirabayashi v. United States*, the ACLU challenged only Public Law 503 as an unconstitutional delegation of power to the military, and not FDR's Executive Order per se. The Court, however, immediately addressed the underlying order and in June 1943 unanimously upheld the curfew on Gordon Hirabayashi and other Japanese Americans in Seattle. Chief Justice Harlan Fiske Stone, generally a good civil libertarian, found the curfew not "an unconstitutional delegation by Congress of its legislative power" and asserted that it did not unconstitutionally discriminate against persons of Japanese ancestry. Expressing great deference to military authority, he argued that the government's war effort "extends to every matter and activity so related to war as substantially to affect its conduct and progress." The Justice Department, however, withheld from the Court Lt. Commander Ringle's report that there was no serious threat among the Japanese Americans on the West Coast, a finding that undermined the government's main argument about military necessity. While conceding that "distinctions between citizens solely because of their ancestry are, by their very nature, odious to a free people whose institutions are founded upon the doctrine of equality," Stone accepted the military's warnings about the threat of

23 ACLU, Board of Directors, Minutes, March 2, 1942; Baldwin et al. to Roosevelt, March 20, 1942, ACLUP-MF (1996), Reel 204. ACLU, *Annual Report, 1942*, p. 26. The split within the ACLU is covered in Samuel Walker, *In Defense of American Liberties: A History of the ACLU* (New York: Oxford, 1990), pp. 136–49, and Irons, *Justice at War*, pp. 128–38. Both Walker and Irons have been active in the ACLU, and both served on the National Board of Directors. The Fellowship of Reconciliation was also divided over the evacuation: "Whether or not we should oppose this forced migration is still questionable in our minds." Foote to Muste, March 17, 1942, FORP, Sec II, Series A-3, SPC. The Federal Council of Churches, forerunner of today's National Council of Churches, saw some advantages in the relocation. Muste to Foote, February 10, 1942, ibid.

24 J. Edgar Hoover, Memorandum for the Attorney General, March 1, 1943, FBI ERR, "Custodial Detention." Irons, *Justice at War*, p. 19. Ringle, Report on the Japanese Question. The fact that the FBI and military intelligence had a short list of suspected spies undercuts the government's argument that it could not make distinctions between loyal and disloyal Japanese-Americans. Defense of the internment: Michelle Malkin, *In Defense of Internment: The Case for "Racial Profiling" in World War II and the War on Terror* (Washington, DC: Regnery, 2004); and critique by Samuel Walker, Memorandum to ACLU, "Talking Points," December 10, 2004, copy available from the author.

invasion. William O. Douglas, one of the greatest civil libertarians ever to sit on the Court, also deferred to the military, declaring flatly, "we cannot override the military judgment which lay behind these orders."[25]

Justice Frank Murphy had deep concerns about the inherent racism in the government's program but was persuaded to join the majority for the sake of a unanimous vote. Nonetheless, in a powerful concurring opinion he wrote, "Today is the first time that we have sustained a substantial restriction of the personal liberty of citizens of the United States based upon the accident of race or ancestry." He noted the obvious parallel with Nazi racism, arguing that the government's action "bears a melancholy resemblance to the treatment accorded to members of the Jewish race in Germany and in other parts of Europe ... [and] goes to the very brink of constitutional power."[26] In the second major case, the Court in December 1944 rejected Fred Korematsu's challenge to the order excluding him from the military zone and requiring him to report to a detention center. For the majority, Hugo Black, another renowned civil libertarian, conceded that "compulsory exclusion of large groups of citizens from their homes, except under circumstances of direst emergency and peril, is inconsistent with our basic governmental institutions." Nonetheless, he concluded that "our shores are threatened by hostile forces, [and] the power to protect must be commensurate with the threatened danger." He took particular offense at the reference to "concentration camps with all the ugly connotations that term implies" but did not explain how the American Relocation Centers differed from Nazi Germany's camps.[27]

No longer persuaded of the need for unanimity, Justice Murphy issued a blistering dissent, arguing that the exclusion "falls into the ugly abyss of racism." Justice Robert Jackson wrote a notably prophetic dissent, warning that "the Court for all time has validated the principle of racial discrimination in criminal procedure and of transplanting American citizens." The long-term implications of the decision were ominous: Having "validated the principle of racial discrimination ... the principle then lies about like a loaded weapon ready for the hand of any authority that can bring forward a plausible claim of an urgent need."[28]

On the same day as the *Korematsu* decision, however, the Court invalidated the internment program by unanimously ruling in *Ex parte Endo* that the government could not detain concededly loyal Japanese Americans. Finally addressing the human element of the entire government program, Justice Douglas wrote, "Loyalty is a matter of the heart and mind not of race, creed or color. He who is loyal is by definition not a spy or a saboteur." Quoting Roosevelt, he added that fair treatment of "this minority as of all other minorities" represents "the very ideal for which we are fighting this war." The administration had evidently been tipped off and on December 17, the day before the *Endo* decision, informed detainees they could leave the camps. The program was completely closed by late 1945.[29]

25 *Hirabayashi v. United States*, 320 U.S. 81 (1943). Douglas, concurring, ibid. at 105–9. Concealment of the Ringle report: Irons, *Justice at War*, pp. 202–06.

26 Justice Murphy, Concurring Opinion, *Hirabayashi v. United States*, 320 U.S. 81, 111 (1943).

27 *Korematsu v United States*, 323 U.S. 214 (1944).

28 Justice Murphy, Dissenting Opinion, *Korematsu v. United States*, 323 U.S. 214, 233 (1943). Justice Jackson, Dissenting Opinion, ibid., 246. See the discussion of Jackson's *Korematsu* dissent in Jack Goldsmith, "Justice Jackson's Unpublished Opinion in Ex Parte Quirin," *The Green Bag* 9 (Spring 2006): 222–41.

29 *Ex part Endo*, 323 U.S. 283, 302 (1944). Robinson, *By Order of the President*, Ch. 5, "Covering a Retreat," pp. 177–206.

When the war ended, Americans began to awake to the racism and terrible violation of rights in what the government had done. The shift in public opinion was swift and nearly total. In a September 1945 article in *Harper's Magazine* by the Yale Law professor Eugene V. Rostow condemned the entire process as "Our Worst Wartime Mistake." The revelations of the Nazi Holocaust, meanwhile, heightened public sensitivity to American racism. Congress paid $38 million for lost property under a 1948 reparations law and, after a long campaign for redress, passed the 1988 Civil Liberties Act awarding individual evacuees twenty thousand dollars in compensation. The historian and legal scholar Peter Irons uncovered evidence of government lying in the original court cases, and in 1984 a federal court invalidated Fred Korematsu's conviction through a rarely used *coram nobis* action.[30]

The treatment of the Japanese Americans is a shameful chapter in American history. President Roosevelt bears direct responsibility for it, and his indifference to both the fate of the victims and the profound constitutional issues involved haunts his legacy. Did he have a realistic alternative to evacuation and internment? Probably. The FBI and Naval Intelligence assessments could have given him political cover to argue that only a small group of people posed any real threat. Individual hearings for those with reasonable suspicion of being threats would have been difficult but feasible, even in wartime. His attorney general and FBI director both had told him evacuation was unnecessary. Perhaps most important, he could have claimed the moral high ground by restating the principles in his 1941 Four Freedoms speech and his January 1942 speech on tolerance to argue that America stood for individual liberty in a world of totalitarianism. It would have been a difficult challenge, to be sure, testing his legendary persuasive skills. Instead of taking the hard way, however, FDR chose the easy course and sacrificed individual liberties.

THE RIGHTS OF WORKING PEOPLE: A CASUAL INDIFFERENCE

President Roosevelt "declined to state his position" on a major bill before Congress in summer 1935. The bill in question soon became the Wagner Act, which has been hailed as "labor's magna carta," guaranteeing working people the right to organize labor unions of their own choosing. The law ended the long era of sweeping violations of workers' rights of freedom of speech, assembly, and association. In terms of its direct impact on the lives of ordinary Americans and broader impact on American society, the Wagner Act is rivaled only by the Social Security Act, the 1964 Civil Rights Act, and the 1965 Voting Rights Act. It is ironic that while FDR had legendary rapport with the "common man," he refused to support until the last minute the federal law that most directly benefited working people.[31]

Roosevelt's indifference to labor's rights was clear from his first year in office. His first economic recovery program, the 1933 National Recovery Administration (NRA),

[30] Eugene V. Rostow, "Our Worst Wartime Mistake," *Harper's Magazine* 191 (September 1945): 193–201. Peter Irons, ed., *Justice Delayed: The Record of the Japanese American Internment Cases* (Middletown, CT: Wesleyan University Press, 1989). McWilliams, *The Education of Carey McWilliams*, p. 106. Irons, *Justice at War*, p. 371.

[31] Irving Bernstein, *Turbulent Years: A History of the American Worker, 1933–1941* (Boston: Houghton, Mifflin, 1969). Free speech and labor in the 1920s: Paul L. Murphy, *The Meaning of Freedom of Speech: First Amendment Freedoms from Wilson to FDR* (Westport, CT: Greenwood Publishing, 1972).

nominally guaranteed workers the right to organize but achieved little in practice. When Senator Robert Wagner of New York drafted a bill with stronger guarantees in 1934, FDR engineered a deal to prevent a Senate vote on it. Wagner introduced an even stronger bill in 1935, buoyed by the large Democratic gains in the 1934 elections. FDR remained silent, however, and instructed Secretary of Labor Francis Perkins to give it only lukewarm support. Perkins later wrote that FDR "did not take part in developing" the Wagner Act; "it was not part of [his] program [and] ... it did not particularly appeal to him."[32]

Several factors explain the contradiction between FDR's image as the great friend of working people and his indifference to the Wagner Act. His patrician background insulated him from the experiences of ordinary Americans. First Lady Eleanor Roosevelt had the same background but transcended it through her activities with social settlements in the New York slums, which began in 1902 when she was eighteen years old (but ended three years later when she married FDR). Similarly, he had no direct experience with African Americans, while she gained it through her reform efforts. In this respect, his life experience was worlds apart from those of Harry Truman and Lyndon Johnson. Truman had a very modest background, served as an infantry captain in World War I commanding many Irish-American troops from Kansas City, and had run-ins with the Ku Klux Klan in his early political career. Lyndon B. Johnson (LBJ), meanwhile, spoke many times about his first job as the principal of an elementary school serving Mexican-American children and how he was moved by their hunger and lack of opportunities for advancement in America. Roosevelt had no equivalent experiences with ordinary people, much less ordinary working people or poor people, and that lack affected his responses to both labor and civil rights issues as president.[33]

As it happened, the Wagner Act was the occasion for a historic Supreme Court reversal on the constitutionality of New Deal economic measures. The Court had provoked a national crisis by striking down the NRA and the Agricultural Adjustment Act as violations of the liberty of contract under the Fourteenth Amendment. The decisions left the federal government paralyzed in the face of the economic catastrophe, despite overwhelming popular demands for federal action. The crisis ended suddenly and unexpectedly when the Court reversed itself in the spring of 1937. The *Jones and Laughlin v. NLRB* case was seen as so consequential that 1,000 people tried to cram into the Court's chambers, which could only hold 250 people, on April 12 to hear the decision.[34] The Court upheld constitutionality of the NLRB, and in subsequent decisions withdrew from its earlier judicial activism on where it struck down economic regulation as a violation of the Fourteenth Amendment and launched a new activism on behalf of individual rights. Led by Roosevelt's appointees, this development marked the beginning of the civil liberties and civil rights revolution in American constitutional law.

32 J. Joseph Huthmacher, *Senator Robert F. Wagner and the Rise of Urban Liberalism* (New York: Atheneum, 1968), pp. 161–71, 190–8. Francis Perkins, *The Roosevelt I Knew* (New York: Viking 1946), p. 239. "Labor's Pet Bills Run into Trouble," *NYT*, May 1, 1935; "President to Hold Labor Bill Parley," ibid., May 18, 1935; "President Orders Speed on NRA and Wagner Bills," ibid., May 24, 1935.

33 Brigid O'Farrell, *She Was One of Us: Eleanor Roosevelt and the American Worker* (Ithaca, NY: ILR Press, 2010), pp. 7–10. On President Truman, see Chapter 5 of this book; on Lyndon Johnson, see Chapter 7.

34 *Jones and Laughlin v. National Labor Relations Board*, 301 U.S. 1 (1937). Drama of the Court's decision: Joseph P. Lash, *Dealers and Dreamers: A New Look at the New Deal* (New York: Doubleday, 1988), p. 431.

Boss Hague and the First Amendment in Jersey City

Ignoring his bad leg, the ACLU general counsel Arthur Garfield Hays climbed atop a car in Jersey City, New Jersey, on May 19, 1938, and gave an impromptu speech defying Mayor Frank Hague's ban on union organizing. Two weeks earlier, Hague's police had evicted the Socialist Party leader, Norman Thomas, from the city, throwing him down the steps to the subway to New York City. The Wagner Act may have guaranteed workers the right to organize on paper, but many employers and local officials ignored it and fiercely fought union organizing with lawless tactics. The Jersey City struggle ultimately led to a landmark Supreme Court decision (*Hague v. CIO*, 1939) affirming a broad constitutional freedom of assembly. Throughout the Jersey City controversy, however, President Roosevelt remained aloof, never intervening on behalf of the rights of the unions.[35]

The colorful Mayor Hague ruled Jersey City with a ruthless hand, once declaring, "I am the law," and earning the label "Dictator - American style," with its obvious reference to Hitler and Mussolini. Although the leader of a blue collar–based Democratic Party political machine, he attacked unions in the hope of attracting employers to the city. On his orders, the city denied all requests for union meeting permits, while the police routinely broke up meetings, seized handbills, and rousted Thomas, Hays, and other speakers from the city. President Roosevelt never tried to rein in Mayor Hague. At a May 10, 1938, press conference, he dismissed the controversy as "a local police matter." A week later, in response to ACLU demands for a federal investigation, he referred the matter to the Justice Department. Four months later, however, Attorney General Homer Cummings, a reliable FDR political ally with no civil liberties commitments, ruled that there was no evidence of any denial of civil rights.[36]

Political pragmatism dictated FDR's response. Early in his career he made peace with the New York City political machine, and he maintained that policy as president. The big city bosses were a vital part of his New Deal coalition, and Boss Hague was head of the New Jersey Democratic Party and vice chairman of the Democratic National Committee. FDR "showered the New Jersey boss with favors," according to one historian, giving him control over seventy-six thousand to ninety-seven thousand Works Progress Administration (WPA) jobs in the state each year, $500,000 a month in emergency relief for families, and $17 million in Public Works Administration projects in Hudson County alone between 1933 and 1938. With the exception of Tom Pendergast, the corrupt head of the Kansas City Democratic Party machine, who was convicted of federal income tax charges in 1939, Roosevelt did not challenge local Democratic Party bosses. If that meant sacrificing both the workers in Jersey City and an important constitutional principle, it did not bother him.[37]

By the time a challenge to Boss Hague reached the Supreme Court, it was already fashioning a new body of civil liberties law. In the 1939 *Hague* decision it invalidated

35 "Hague Speech Ban Is Defied by Hays," *NYT*, May 20, 1938. "Hague Police Oust Thomas from City," ibid., May 1, 1938.

36 "Thomas is Routed as Riot Halts Speech in Newark," NYT, June 5, 1938. Lyle W. Dorsett, *Franklin D. Roosevelt and the City Bosses* (Port Washington, NY: Kennikat Press, 1977), pp. 83–111. "Roosevelt Avoids Comment on Hague," *NYT*, May 11, 1938. "Protest on Hague Given to Cummings," ibid., May 18, 1938. "Hague Cleared in Federal Inquiry," ibid., September 8, 1938. ACLU, *Annual Report*, 1938, p. 36.

37 Dorsett, *Franklin D. Roosevelt and the City Bosses*, pp. 83–111.

the Jersey City permit ordinance and enunciated a broad freedom of assembly under the First Amendment. Jersey City had turned its permit requirement into an unconstitutional "instrument of arbitrary suppression of free expression." The case reflected growing American awareness of international developments. In his district court opinion, Judge William Clark referred specifically to the international context, writing that "Russia will not be judged by how much bread it has given its people," but by how much freedom "it has brought into the world." In a world of totalitarianism, Americans began to discover that First Amendment freedoms represented the essence of Americanism. FDR paid rhetorical tribute to those values on occasion but ignored them in politically tinged cases such as *Hague*.[38]

FEDERAL PROTECTION FOR CIVIL RIGHTS: ORIGINS OF THE CIVIL RIGHTS DIVISION

"In a democracy," the newly appointed attorney general Frank Murphy announced, "the aggressive protection of fundamental rights" is "an important function" of the federal government. No previous attorney general had ever pledged to defend the rights of American citizens. Murphy, responding in part to the international context and the new understanding of the Bill of Rights, honored his promise just one month after his appointment by establishing the Civil Liberties Unit within the Justice Department on February 2, 1939. Renamed the Civil Rights Unit in 1941 and elevated as the Civil Rights Division in 1957, it represented for the first time since Reconstruction the federal government's active defense of the rights of individual citizens.[39]

President Roosevelt played no evident role in creating the Civil Liberties Unit. Murphy was already committed to the idea and corresponded with the ACLU director Roger Baldwin, the ACLU general counsel Arthur Garfield Hays, and the Congress of Industrial Organizations (CIO) general counsel Lee Pressman about how to proceed. In one subsequent letter to FDR, Murphy mentioned establishing the unit "at your order," but no other evidence supports this assertion, and it may have been Murphy's attempt to flatter his boss. FDR did not mention it at the press conference the day it was created. A month later, addressing Congress on its 150th anniversary, FDR talked extensively about the Constitution and the Bill of Rights but did not mention his administration's historic initiative to enforce the rights those documents guaranteed.[40]

Launched with grand aspirations, the Civil Liberties Unit immediately ran into the simple fact that it had almost no federal civil rights laws to enforce. The 1964 Civil Rights Act lay a quarter of a century in the future. In an eighteen-page memo to Murphy, Assistant Attorney General Brien McMahon explained the "severe limitations" involved in using

38 Clark: *Hague v C.I.O., 25 F. Supp. 127, 152 (1938). Hague v. C.I.O.*, 307 U.S. 496 (1939). Impact of the international context: Walker, *In Defense of American Liberties*, pp. 112–14.

39 Office of the Attorney General, Order No. 3204, February 3, 1939, FMP, Box 57, Reel 112. "'Civil Rights' Unit Set Up by Murphy," *NYT*, February 4, 1939. Robert K. Carr, *Federal Protection of Civil Rights: Quest for a Sword* (Ithaca, NY: Cornell University Press, 1947). Richard W. Steele, *Free Speech in the "Good War"* (New York: St. Martin's, 1999), pp. 20, 23.

40 J. Woodford Howard, Jr., *Mr. Justice Murphy: A Political Biography* (Princeton, NJ: Princeton University Press, 1968), pp. 203–4, citing correspondence between Murphy and Baldwin, Ernst, and Pressman in January 1939 in Murphy Papers, Boxes 60, 61, University of Michigan. Murphy to Roosevelt, July 7, 1939; cited in Kevin J. McMahon, *Reconsidering Roosevelt on Race: How the Presidency Paved the Road to Brown* (Chicago: University of Chicago Press, 2004), p. 145, n. 4. Murphy interview: Carr, *Federal Protection of Civil Rights*, p. 25.

even the existing Reconstruction era statutes, one making it a crime for public officials to deprive citizens of their rights "under color of law," and another covering private citizens who conspire to deprive people of their civil rights. The Justice Department had begun bringing cases under the 1867 Anti-Peonage Act in 1936 and scored one victory by convicting the town marshal of Earl, Louisiana, for "holding seven negroes as slaves" during a sharecroppers' strike. Altogether, however, McMahon could cite only a handful of convictions. Existing laws did not guarantee the right to participate in primary elections, to assemble peaceably unless specifically petitioning the federal government, or to be free of forcible deportation from a state. Unless the Supreme Court takes "a broader and more liberal view," he concluded, existing laws "provide no adequate remedy" for fully protecting Americans' rights.[41]

Strong opposition from southerners in Congress and from some members of the Roosevelt administration also hindered an aggressive litigation program by the Civil Liberties Unit. Negotiating these political pressures was "tricky business," according to Eleanor Bontecu, one of the unit's first attorneys. During World War II, for example, the War Department resisted its attempt to defend African-American soldiers facing discrimination within the military or near southern military bases. In fact, Bontecu recalled, military officials "wanted us to bring cases not in the favor of civil rights but against the victims." Secretary of War Stimson labeled civil rights leaders "foolish" and contemptuously dismissed their "radical" demands for equality."[42]

Perhaps the greatest failure of the new Civil Liberties Unit was its weak response to the wave of attacks on Jehovah's Witnesses in 1940. The plight of the Witnesses is now long forgotten by Americans, but at the time they were the most hated group in America. Their aggressive proselytizing tactics and deliberately anti-Catholic rhetoric - calling the Roman Catholic Church a "whore" and a "harlot" - offended many Americans, some of whom responded with vigilante violence. The April 1940 Supreme Court decision upholding a Pennsylvania law compelling Witness schoolchildren to salute the American flag (*Minersville School District v. Gobitis*) unleashed a massive wave of violent attacks. A 1941 ACLU report cited attacks on fifteen hundred Witnesses in 335 separate incidents. In one typical incident a Huntsville, Arkansas, mob in October 1941 led by the acting mayor attacked Witnesses distributing their literature. A mob burned down the Witnesses' Kingdom Hall in Kennebunk, Maine, in June, while the police did nothing. Local law enforcement officials either stood by passively or actually participated in many of these incidents - thereby giving the Civil Liberties Unit a cause of action.[43]

Attorney General Biddle condemned the mob violence in a nationwide radio broadcast on June 16 and ordered an "immediate investigation." With both Europe and the World War I experience in America clearly on his mind, he declared, "We shall not defeat the Nazi evil by emulating its methods." FDR never spoke out in defense of the Witnesses and said nothing about the wave of lawlessness. The ACLU demanded the Justice Department prosecute local law enforcement officials, but Henry Schweinhunt,

41 Brien McMahon, assistant attorney general, Memorandum for the Attorney General, February 3, 1939, FMP, Box 57, Reel 112. Eleanor Bontecu, OH, p. 4, HSTPL.

42 Bontecu, OH, p. 8, HSTPL. Henry L. Stimson, Diary, January 17, 1942, January 24, 1942.

43 Shawn Francis Peters, *Judging Jehovah's Witnesses: Religious Persecution and the Dawn of the Rights Revolution* (Lawrence: University of Kansas Press, 2000). ACLU, *The Persecution of the Jehovah's Witnesses* (New York: ACLU, 1941). Walker, *In Defense of American Liberties*, pp. 107–10.

director of the Civil Liberties Unit, replied that prosecution in such cases was "cumbersome and generally unsatisfactory." As with race discrimination cases in the Deep South, obtaining witnesses and getting convictions before local judges and juries were virtually impossible.[44]

In the end, although the Civil Liberties Unit accomplished little in the 1940s, its very creation was an important symbolic step in federal protection of individual rights, and a foundation for more effective actions in the future. The credit, however, all goes to Attorney General Murphy and not President Roosevelt.

UNLEASHING FBI SPYING: THE PERMANENT NATIONAL SECURITY STATE

It began very quietly on August 24, 1936. Meeting at the White House, President Roosevelt told the FBI director J. Edgar Hoover he wanted information on "subversive activities in the United States, particularly Fascism and Communism." The request gave Hoover the green light to reactivate the political spying Attorney General Harlan Fiske Stone had ended in 1924. Hoover had changed dramatically in the intervening twelve years. The once dutiful bureaucrat had mastered bureaucratic politics and now seeing an opportunity took Roosevelt's request, launched a secret spying program that continued until his death in 1972, and was responsible for the longest running violation of civil liberties in American history.[45]

Apart from among FBI history specialists, Roosevelt's role in reopening FBI spying is not well known and is rarely mentioned in biographies of him. Even many FBI critics mistakenly see an unbroken record of FBI political surveillance from World War I through the 1970s. The FBI files on the ACLU, W. E. B. Dubois, and A. Philip Randolph, for example, reveal few if any items between 1924 and the late 1930s, after which the files become massive. In short, Hoover complied with Stone's 1924 ban on spying, and Roosevelt was responsible for authorizing him to reactivate it.[46]

Although FDR's responsibility is clear, exactly what he authorized or thought he did is less certain. The only surviving document of the August 1936 meeting is a memo by Hoover, and it may well misrepresent FDR's words and intentions. A follow-up meeting the next day of FDR, Hoover, and Secretary of State Cordell Hull led to a deliberately vague proposal for an FBI "survey" of "conditions." Roosevelt had legitimate cause for concern about possible illegal activity by groups with foreign allegiances. After Hitler's rise to power in 1933, domestic fascist groups proliferated in the United States, including paramilitary groups like the White Shirts, the Grey Shirts, and the largest of them all, William Dudley Pelley's Silver Shirts. Roosevelt and many others, meanwhile, also worried about possible spying by the Soviet Union. A "survey," however, did not include creating files on individuals or groups because of their political beliefs. Hoover, however,

44 *Minersville School District v. Gobitis*, 310 U.S. 586 (1940). Letter, Barry to Clifford Forster, ACLU, November 25, 1941, ACLUP, MF ED (1996), Reel 197. Biddle: "Bars Nazi Methods in U.S. Spy Hunts," *NYT*, June 17, 1940. Peters, *Judging Jehovah's Witnesses*, pp. 117–18.

45 The 1936 memo: Athan Theoharis, *From the Secret Files of J. Edgar Hoover* (Chicago: Ivan Dee, 1991), pp. 180–3. Athan Theoharis, *Spying on Americans: Political Surveillance from Hoover to the Huston Plan* (Philadelphia: Temple University Press, 1978), p. 68.

46 FBI files on the ACLU, Mudd Library, Princeton. Federal Bureau of Investigation, FBI File on A. Philip Randolph, MF ED (Wilmington, DE: Scholarly Resources, 1990).

simply stretched Roosevelt's request, and neither FDR nor subsequent presidents or attorneys general questioned him carefully about it.[47]

The transformation of the FBI was fully consistent with the New Deal expansion of government activity. A wave of bank robberies and the sensational 1932 kidnapping of the son of Anne and Charles Lindbergh fueled fears of a national crime wave, which Hoover cleverly manipulated. He developed a slick publicity machine that transformed small-time criminals such as John Dillinger into national celebrities and cast the FBI as the defender of law and order. A package of new laws in 1934 gave the FBI authority over bank robbery, kidnapping, and other crimes. Expanded FBI crime fighting paralleled other New Deal initiatives to address social problems through federal action. A "war on crime" was a natural counterpart to FDR's rhetoric about a war on the economic collapse. In early 1939 Hoover launched a national campaign to have all Americans fingerprinted; FDR enthusiastically said he was "all in favor of everyone submitting" to the program.[48]

Hoover expanded his mandate again in 1939, and a crucial FDR statement on September 6, 1939, illustrated his devious methods. Issued in an atmosphere of high alarm immediately after Nazi Germany invaded Poland and launched World War II, the memo's first paragraph gave the FBI authority over espionage, treason, and sabotage – three specific federal crimes. Hoover, however, inserted the phrase "subversive activities" into the third paragraph, an elastic term that he used to investigate political activities. Hoover's maneuver was no secret. The ACLU noticed and protested the reference to subversive activities. With the world plunging into war, however, few others cared. Roosevelt declared a limited national emergency on September 8, and concern about foreign enemies was running high. Hoover made some token investigations of fascist and other right-wing groups but directed the full force of the bureau's new spying program against leftists and liberals. Even by 1938 the FBI claimed to have more than twenty-five hundred names of alleged subversives in its files. Hoover sought to shield his new initiatives from close scrutiny, and in 1938 he counseled FDR against asking Congress for legislation authorizing intelligence gathering. This would only provoke criticisms by "ill-informed persons or individuals with some ulterior motive," he advised, and FDR evidently agreed.[49]

An important question is how much Attorneys General Frank Murphy, Robert Jackson, and Francis Biddle knew about Hoover's activities. All three had excellent civil liberties credentials, but their actions were not always consistent with their reputations. Murphy is widely regarded as the most committed civil libertarian of the three. He was an ACLU member, spoke at an ACLU conference on the national emergency in October 1939, and became a solid civil libertarian on the Supreme Court. The historian Richard W. Steele, however, argues that as attorney general, Murphy regarded Hoover as an important asset and did not question his activities. Murphy, in fact, authorized several Justice Department actions that violated First Amendment rights, including the arrest of Detroit leftists who had been volunteers in the Spanish Civil War on the antifascist side supported by the

47 Travis Hoke, *Shirts!* (New York: ACLU, 1934). Leo P. Ribuffo, *The Old Christian Right: The Protestant Far Right from the Great Depression to the Cold War* (Philadelphia: Temple University Press, 1983), pp. 25–79. That Hoover "stretched" authorizations: Athan Theoharis, "The FBI's Stretching of Presidential Directives, 1936–1953," *Political Science Quarterly* 91 (Winter 1976): 649–72.

48 "President Hopes to See All of Us Fingerprinted," *NYT*, March 11, 1939. Samuel Walker, *Popular Justice: A History of American Criminal Justice*, 2nd ed. (New York: Oxford University Press, 1998), pp. 159–62.

49 Statement Placing the Federal Bureau of Investigation in Charge of Espionage Investigation, September 6, 1939, APP. ACLU, *Annual Report, 1940*, pp. 16–18. Figure of 2,500: Theoharis, *Spying on Americans*, p. 71.

communists. Robert Jackson was actually better on many civil liberties issues, dismissed the Detroit cases, and privately expressed disgust at Murphy's wayward commitment to civil liberties. In the heated atmosphere of June 1940 Jackson counseled that "we must permit no tampering with our civil rights" (by which he meant First Amendment freedoms), because they are the "bulwark" of "our democratic system." Biddle's record is very ambiguous. He had handled cases for the ACLU and in 1943 ordered J. Edgar Hoover to end the FBI's program of listing people for custodial detention in the event of a national emergency. But as did Murphy, he felt he had to trust and work with the bureau. In a speech to the American Bar Association he praised the bureau for working effectively against spies and saboteurs "without resorting to the 'Gestapo's persecution and official brutality.'" He capitulated on evacuating the Japanese Americans, however, and as we shall see did the same on several high-profile First Amendment cases.[50]

The memory of the World War I violations of free speech by the Wilson administration weighed heavily on the minds of the three attorneys general. The Palmer Raids were only twenty years in the past, and all three were determined not to repeat the abuses. Jackson, for example, was particularly worried that a proposed "intelligence gathering" effort by the American Legion could spin out of control into private vigilantism. Hoover again saw an opportunity and convinced Jackson to centralize all such efforts in the FBI and have American Legion members report suspicious activity to the bureau. His central role in the Palmer Raids had vanished from public memory, and he convinced Jackson and others that he was the responsible alternative to private lawlessness. The FBI's aggressive public relations campaign had already projected an image of the bureau as the epitome of professionalism, especially in comparison to the generally corrupt and inefficient local police.[51]

On several occasions, moreover, Roosevelt used the FBI to spy on his political opponents, including both citizens who criticized him and members of his own administration. In 1940 he asked Hoover to gather information on the GOP presidential candidate Wendell Willkie's extramarital affair (which was no secret among political insiders). In May of that year, after the swift German conquest of France, he requested the FBI to investigate people who sent letters and telegrams protesting his May speech calling for a significant increase in defense spending. Previously, in June 1939 he sent a note to Hoover asking, "Will you look into this man? It may be all right but I would like to have a check." There was no national security question or other legitimate reason for the FBI to investigate this person. Learning to cover itself, the bureau in its reports pointedly noted that they were done "at the President's suggestion." FDR's secretary, Steven Early, thanked the bureau for "the many interesting and valuable reports that you have made to me." Hoover's experience with Roosevelt taught him a lesson that proved invaluable with subsequent presidents: He could curry favor and immunity by running political errands for them.[52]

50 "Jackson Counsels Calm in Nation," *NYT*, June 30, 1940. Richard W. Steele, *Free Speech in the "Good War* (New York: St. Martin's, 1999), p. 33. "Biddle Reports 5th Column Curb," *NYT*, March 3, 1942.

51 Steele, *Free Speech in the Good War*, p. 80.

52 Memoranda, circa May, 1940 in Senate Select Committee to Study Governmental Operations with Respect to Intelligence Activities, Hearings, V. 6, Federal Bureau of Investigation, 94th Cong., 1st Sess., pp. 452–4. The memos were found in Official File 10-B, Box 14, FDRPL. Willke: Michael R. Beschloss, *Presidential Courage: Brave Leaders and How They Changed America, 1789–1989* (New York: Simon & Schuster, 2007), p. 176. FDR to J. Edgar Hoover, October 5, 1939, PSF, Justice, 1939, Box 56, FDRPL.

One day after Germany invaded Poland on September 1, 1939, Hoover directed FBI agents to prepare reports on "persons of German, Italian, and communist sympathies." This soon evolved into a semisecret plan for the emergency detention of people he deemed threats to national security. Hoover's notion of threats swept very broadly, and in 1940 the ACLU director, Roger Baldwin, was just one of many political activists marked for detention. The program was not completely secret. Hoover mentioned it publicly on a few occasions but always implied that it was simply a contingency plan. Recalling the World War I Palmer Raids, the ACLU condemned the "resurrection of an index," not knowing that its own director was on it. Attorney General Jackson endorsed the Custodial Detention Index in May 1940. There is no record of whether Jackson or Hoover briefed FDR about the program or received the president's approval. Jackson's successor, Francis Biddle, objected to the plan, however, and on July 16, 1943, ordered Hoover to cancel it because it served "no useful purpose" and the designations were "inherently unreliable." The devious Hoover simply directed FBI field offices to drop the term "Custodial Detention" and substitute "Security Matter" instead. Thus, the program survived.[53]

Whatever FDR may have known about the full scope of Hoover's intelligence gathering – and it is most likely that he knew very little given the demands of the depression and then the war – he had no objections to national security-related investigations. As his 1937 speech on the Constitution indicated, he had no patience with lawyerly objections to actions he thought necessary for national security. In his only known statement on the subject, he tartly replied to an ACLU protest about alleged military spying on pacifist groups in March 1936, "As the head of the government, I cannot for the safety of the nation, agree never to look into the affairs of any organization." This included groups who distribute "false information" and engage in "false teaching." Neither of those two activities was a federal crime, but he clearly thought they were enough to warrant government inquiry. Roosevelt's 1919 experience of having his own house in Washington bombed by anarchists may well have influenced his thinking about the dangers of political radicals.[54]

Building the national security state

The revival of FBI spying was only one part of the creation of the national security state. The entire New Deal was a watershed in American history, expanding the role of government activity and regulation in all phases of American life, and national security was no exception. Temporarily interrupted in the 1920s, it became a permanent set of institutions and assumptions under Roosevelt. Several events precipitated the change. The Great Depression revived political radicalism and consequent public fears of communism,

[53] Baldwin: J. Edgar Hoover, Memorandum for Mr. L. M. C. Smith, Chief, Special Defense Unit, April 3, 1941, Roger Baldwin FBI Files, Mudd Library, Princeton University. ACLU, *Annual Report*, 1940, p. 16. Walker, *In Defense of American Liberties*, p. 161. This author obtained Baldwin's FBI file under the Freedom of Information Act and donated it to the Mudd Library, Princeton University. Biddle to Hugh B. Cox and J. Edgar Hoover, July 16, 1943 (ordering program terminated); FBI, Memorandum, August 14, 1943 (changing the name of the program), in Church Committee, *Federal Bureau of Investigation*, V. 6, pp. 412–14.

[54] Steele, *Free Speech in the "Good War,"* p. 30, observes that this letter is probably the only document regarding FDR's views on the subject; FDR "head of government" quote, ibid., p. 30. ACLU, Board of Directors, Minutes, March 9, 1936, March 30, 1936, ACLUP-MF (1977), Reel 6. Harry F. Ward to FDR, March 7, 1936; FDR to Ward, March 23, 1936, ACLUP-MF (1996), Reel 128. "Palmer and Family Safe," *NYT*, June 3, 1919. Blanche Wiesen Cook, *Eleanor Roosevelt* (New York: Viking, 1992), V. 1, pp. 244–5.

while Hitler aroused fears of domestic Nazi groups. The outbreak of war, first in Asia and then in Europe, convinced many people that it was necessary to guard American security and that civil liberties could be limited for that purpose.[55]

Events related to national security moved quickly in the late 1930s and early 1940s. FDR reauthorized FBI spying in 1936, and two years later the House of Representatives created the House Un-American Activities Committee (HUAC), which began a thirty-eight-year campaign of pillorying people for their political beliefs and associations. Being "named" by HUAC became tantamount to being found guilty of subversion. After FDR authorized the FBI to investigate subversive activities in late 1939, the bureau ballooned from 650 to 4,000 agents. Attorney General Robert Jackson banned all wiretapping in March 1940, but FDR told him in a May 21, 1940 memo that the 1939 Supreme Court decision *Nardone v. United States* limiting federal wiretapping was "never intended" to "apply to grave matters involving the defense of the nation." He then explicitly "authorized and directed" the use of "listening devices" against "subversive activities" or spies, as necessary.[56] In June 1940 Congress passed the Smith Act (officially the Alien Registration Act) making it a crime to advocate the overthrow of the government – the first federal law in American history to proscribe specific political ideas. Hearings on the bill occurred in the charged atmosphere following Germany's stunning conquest of France, and it passed with little opposition or debate over its First Amendment implications. FDR made no public comment about it. Attorney General Biddle, setting a precedent for later cold war "listing" practices, created a list of alleged subversives in 1942. Roosevelt created the Office of Strategic Services, forerunner of the CIA, in June 1942, launching a new era of secret and unaccountable overseas activities. In short, within just a few years, the entire apparatus of national security developed.[57]

Steady HUAC allegations that his administration employed communists and their sympathizers put Roosevelt on the defensive. In early 1942 the Justice Department attorney James Rowe warned Attorney General Biddle that the public believed the entire Justice Department "are 'civil liberties boys' and 'softies.'" Biddle advised FDR to create an Interdepartmental Committee to review and recommend action on federal employees suspected of disloyalty, both to provide "uniform treatment" for all cases and to "take 'the heat' off the government." The cabinet and FDR rejected the idea, at least for the moment. Nonetheless, in another compromise of his civil liberties principles, Biddle created the first official Justice Department list of subversive organizations later that year, anticipating President Truman's more famous Attorney General's List of Subversive Organizations

[55] Alan Brinkley, *Voices of Protest: Huey Long, Father Coughlin, and the Great Depression* (New York: Knopf, 1982) on the radical social movements in 1933–5.

[56] F. D. R., Memorandum for the Attorney General, May 21, 1940, PSF, Robert Jackson, Box 57, FDRPL. *Nardone v. United States*, 302 U.S. 379 (1939). U.S. Senate, Select Committee to Study Governmental Operations with Respect to the Intelligence Activities, *Final Report, Book III, Supplementary Detailed Staff Reports on Intelligence Activities and the Rights of Americans* (April 23, 1976). p. 6.

[57] Proclamation 2352 – Proclaiming a National Emergency in Connection with the Observance, Safeguarding, and Enforcement of Neutrality and the Strengthening of the National Defense within the Limits of Peace-Time Authorizations September 8, 1939, APP. FDR, Signing Statement, June 29, 1940, APP. Steele, *Free Speech in the Good War*, p. 81. Documents on Bethune: Biddle to Mrs. Roosevelt, September 26, 1942, ERP, Box 365, FDRPL. Extremely valuable is Douglas M. Charles, *J. Edgar Hoover and the Anti-Interventionists: FBI Political Surveillance and the Rise of the Domestic Security State, 1939 to 1945* (Columbus: Ohio State University Press, 2007). History of HUAC: Walter Goodman, *The Committee* (New York: Farrar, Straus & Giroux, 1968).

by five years. Although it was intended to be secret, a conservative congressman placed the list in the *Congressional Record.*[58]

FDR finally yielded to the anti-communist attacks and in February 1943 created the first federal loyalty program. Executive Order 9300 established an Interdepartmental Committee that would review employees in the executive branch suspected of "subversive activity." The program was far more limited in scope and impact on civil liberties than President Truman's 1947 program, which was a sweeping assault on freedom of speech and association. It did not require the review of all federal employees, as Truman's would; was invoked only when there were allegations about a specific employee; and did not use the principle of guilt by association.[59]

The dirty business of penalizing people who had been "named" or "listed" exploded into a controversy in 1943 when Congress passed an amendment denying compensation to thirty-nine government employees identified by HUAC as "subversives." Most were no longer with the government, but Robert Morss Lovett, assistant to the governor of the Virgin Islands, and Goodwin Watson and William E. Dodd, at the Federal Communications Commission, lost their salaries. They sued, alleging the law was an unconstitutional bill of attainder (a law naming and penalizing a specific individual). In 1946, the Supreme Court unanimously agreed and in *United States v. Lovett* (1946) ordered them paid. The controversy also brought up the issue of presidential signing statements. Signing the original appropriations bill, FDR issued a statement declaring Section 304 an unconstitutional bill of attainder. Sixty years later, President George W. Bush's extensive use of signing statements created enormous controversy as an effort to thwart the will of Congress. Roosevelt's statement in 1943, however, indicates that other presidents used them quite properly in some instances to denounce unconstitutional laws. He did not say he would ignore the law (in fact he did not have the power to pay the salaries), whereas Bush announced his intention to ignore Congress and not to enforce many laws.[60]

The shameful case of the German saboteurs

In June 1942 eight German saboteurs landed in the United States, setting in motion a travesty of justice by the administration. The affair was a comic opera, as two saboteurs immediately turned themselves in to the FBI, which initially refused to believe their seemingly ludicrous story. All eight were soon arrested, however. Roosevelt's response reflected a high disregard for legal principles, as he immediately decided that "the death penalty is almost obligatory" and began designing a process that would achieve that

58 James Rowe to Biddle, "Personal and Confidential," March 23, 1942, FPBP, "Propaganda Domestic," Box 2, FDRPL. Biddle, Cabinet Minutes, FPBP, Box 1, FDRPL. Origins of the list and the 1947 Federal Loyalty and Security Program: Elizabeth Bontecu, *The Federal Loyalty-Security Program* (Ithaca, NY: Cornell University Press, 1953), Ch. 1, "Genesis of the Program," pp. 1–34. Robert Justin Goldstein, "Prelude to McCarthyism: The Making of a Blacklist," *Prologue* 38 (Fall 2006): 22–33.

59 Executive Order 9300 on Subversive Activities by Federal Employees, February 5, 1943, APP.

60 *United States v. Lovett*, 328 U.S. 303 (1946). Original list of "subversives": "Dies Denounces New List of 'Reds,'" *NYT*, February 2, 1941. Robert Morss Lovett, *All Our Years: The Autobiography of Robert Morss Lovett* (New York: Viking Press, 1948), pp. 297–309, and Appendix. Statement against a Rider Prohibiting Federal Employment of Three Individuals.September 14, 1943, APP. Signing statements and other mechanisms of presidential power: Philip J. Cooper, *By Order of the President: The Use and Abuse of Executive Direct Action* (Lawrence: University Press of Kansas, 2002), pp. 199–230.

result. After improperly consulting the Supreme Court justice Felix Frankfurter about its constitutionality, he issued an executive order creating a special Military Commission to try the saboteurs. All eight were quickly tried and found guilty. In an extraordinary summer session after the trial, on July 29 and 30, the Supreme Court in *Ex parte Quirin* upheld the constitutionality of the Military Commission and the guilty verdicts. The two saboteurs who had cooperated with the prosecution received prison terms while the other six were executed a week later, exactly six weeks after they had landed.[61]

The *Quirin* case was filled with miscarriages of justice. FDR created the Military Commission even though civilian courts were still functioning, thereby violating the Supreme Court's opinion in *Ex parte Milligan*, where President Abraham Lincoln suspended the right of habeas corpus during the Civil War. Commission procedures, moreover, allowed hearsay evidence and changed the review process in the Articles of War for death penalty cases. Justice Felix Frankfurter's advice to Roosevelt on designing a commission that would pass muster with the Court was a violation of judicial ethics. At one point Frankfurter even said the defendants "have no procedural rights." (The Supreme Court justice James Byrnes, meanwhile, spent so much time advising FDR that Attorney General Biddle actually thought he was on leave from the Court.) Through Biddle, FDR sent a clear message to the Court that he would execute the saboteurs no matter how it ruled, telling Biddle, "I won't give them up.... I won't hand them over to any United States Marshall armed with a writ of habeas corpus. Understand?" Finally, the Court acted with undue haste, issuing its decision the day after the hearing and without a written opinion. It then spent three months trying to fashion an opinion to support its decision and the executions that had already occurred.[62]

Sixty years later the *Quirin* case provided a rationale for George W. Bush's military commissions for terrorist suspects held at Guantanamo Bay. Several historians, however, filed an amicus brief with the Supreme Court in the critical 2006 *Hamdan v. Rumsfeld* case, arguing that the *Quirin* case was so "tainted by improper bias, conflicts of interest, undue executive influence, judicial haste, and lack of authority" that it should not serve as a valid precedent for the Bush commissions. Earlier, in the 2004 *Hamdi* case, even the very conservative Justice Antonin Scalia dismissed *Quirin* as "not this Court's finest hour."[63]

TROUBLING CLAIMS OF PRESIDENTIAL POWER

In his first inaugural, as we have seen, Roosevelt warned that he would exercise executive authority in a "temporary departure" from normal procedures if Congress failed to act on the economic collapse. He never acted on that threat, but it was a clear indication of his

61 Roosevelt, Memorandum for the Attorney General, June 30, 1942, PSF, Justice 1940–4, Box 56, FDRPL. Order Establishing a Military Commission to Try Eight Captured German Saboteurs, July 2, 1942, APP. Proclamation 2561 Denying Certain Enemies Access to the Courts, July 2, 1942, APP. *Ex parte Quirin*, 317 U.S. 1 (1942). Louis Fisher, *Nazi Saboteurs on Trial: A Military Tribunal and American Law*, 2nd ed. (Lawrence: University Press of Kansas, 2005).

62 Biddle, *In Brief Authority*, p. 331. James F. Byrnes, *All in One Lifetime* (New York: Harper and Brothers, 1958), Ch. 10, "Extracurricular Activities," pp. 147–57. Pierce O'Donnell, *In Time of War: Hitler's Terrorist Attack on America* (New York: New Press, 2005).

63 Brief of Legal Scholars and Historians as Amici Curiae in Support of Petitioner, *Hamdan v. Rumsfeld*, 548 U.S. 557 (2006). Scalia: *Hamdi v. Rumsfeld*, 542 U.S. 507 (2004).

belief that presidents had unlimited power to act in a national emergency.[64] Long celebrated by historians and the public for his strong executive leadership in the face of the depression and then World War II, Roosevelt made assertions of presidential power that are deeply troubling today.

The most serious problems involved foreign policy in the late 1930s when Roosevelt skirted the law and clear congressional intent. As Europe headed for war, isolationist sentiment dominated Congress, which enacted several neutrality laws to keep the United States out of foreign conflicts. The 1935 Neutrality Act, for example, prohibited military aid to belligerents in a foreign war. FDR at that time enthusiastically called the law "wholly excellent." In January 1938 the House of Representatives fell just twenty-one votes short of approving the Ludlow Amendment to the Constitution, which would have required a popular referendum for a declaration of war. By then, however, FDR had decided that aid to England was crucial for U.S. national security and saw the various neutrality acts as an unjustified limitation on his power to direct foreign policy. Despite his great popularity, however, he did not feel he could convince the nation about aiding England. He remembered well Woodrow Wilson's failure to persuade Congress to ratify the League of Nations in 1919 and was determined not to repeat that mistake. Thus, he opted for unilateral action.[65]

The issue first came to a head on October 5, 1937, with FDR's famous "quarantine" speech. The world situation, he warned, "has been growing progressively worse," and "there is no escape through mere isolation or neutrality." In a medical epidemic, he argued, we use a "a quarantine of the patients." He concluded with a strong but vague promise to take "positive endeavors to preserve the peace." It was not clear what this meant and whether any actions might violate the neutrality acts. The next day, in an off-the-record press conference, reporters pressed the issue. He tried to finesse it by saying that his speech expressed "an attitude" rather than a specific policy. The reporter Ernest K. Lindley pointedly asked him whether there were "any conflict between what you outline and the Neutrality Act." FDR chided him, "Put your thinking cap on, Ernest," without answering the question. Lindley was right on the mark, however, as subsequent events would prove.[66]

To get around the neutrality acts, FDR on July 1, 1939, sent Attorney General Frank Murphy a "Confidential" note, asking, "how far do you think I can go in ignoring the existing [Neutrality] act – even though I did sign it?!" Murphy's response is not clear, but Secretary of the Interior Ickes argued forcefully that as president FDR was "amply justified" in maintaining that "the Constitution gives the Executive power to conduct foreign affairs." He added that he should not seek congressional authorization since that would concede to Congress "power that it does not have." President Harry Truman received and acted on exactly the same advice at the outset of the Korean War, and other presidents would make similar claims of unilateral authority over foreign affairs and war.[67]

64 Inaugural Address. March 4, 1933, APP. Cooper, *By Order of the President*, p. 40. Address on Constitution Day, Washington, DC, September 17, 1937, APP.

65 Peter Beinart, *The Icarus Syndrome: A History of American Hubris* (New York: Harper, 2010), pp. 73–5.

66 Address at Chicago, October 5, 1937, APP. Press Conference, October 6, 1937, APP. Refusal to elaborate: "Roosevelt Keeps Silent," *NYT*, October 7, 1937.

67 FDR, "Confidential" Memorandum for the Attorney General, July 1, 1939; Ickes to "My Dear Mr. President," July 1, 1939, Box 58, FMP. In 1950, President Harry Truman was similarly advised not to seek a congressional

The critical event was FDR's "destroyers for bases" deal on September 2, 1940, through which the United States gave Britain fifty aged navy destroyers (suddenly declared "surplus" for this purpose) in return for ninety-nine-year leases for British naval bases, including Newfoundland and Jamaica. England was besieged and alone and legitimately worried about its survival. Germany had captured France in May and began bombing London and other cities (the "Blitz") on September 7. An invasion seemed very possible.[68]

The destroyers for bases deal outraged isolationists, who saw it as a clear violation of the neutrality laws. Edward S. Corwin, Yale Law professor and the foremost scholar on the Constitution, wrote an extraordinary letter to the *New York Times* that was virtually a law review article. Arranging the deal as an executive agreement rather than a treaty, he argued, bypassed the constitutional requirement of congressional approval for treaties. It also violated Article 4 of the Constitution, which gives Congress the power to dispose of American territory or property. Even worse, he continued, Attorney General Robert Jackson's memo justifying the deal made broad claims about the president's power as commander in chief and declared that it is "beyond doubt that present world conditions forbid him to risk any delay" in acting, an argument that future presidents would also make. In words that would resonate sixty years later under President George W. Bush, Corwin condemned Jackson's memo as "an endorsement of unrestrained autocracy in the field of foreign relations" and concluded that "no such dangerous opinion was ever before penned by an Attorney General of the United States."[69]

Historians have generally approved FDR's aid to England in the 1940–1 crisis. World War II is celebrated as "the good war," justified by the moral imperative of both responding to the Pearl Harbor attack and defeating Nazi Germany. (The Lend Lease program, which provided material aid to England, Russia, and other counties in early 1941, was authorized by Congress and thus did not raise questions of presidential power.) Many Americans have argued that the United States should have been more aggressive in standing up to Hitler in the late 1930s, but Congress had spoken clearly through the neutrality laws. Rather than undertake a very difficult political effort to change public opinion, FDR chose to act unilaterally, setting a dangerous precedent for subsequent presidents.

Everything changed with Pearl Harbor and the declaration of war on December 8, 1941. Roosevelt exercised enormous executive authority during the war, but within the bounds of powers Congress granted him. In fact, Congress gave him virtually anything he wanted. Attorney General Biddle prepared a seventeen-page memo in late 1941 on "The Powers of the President in Time of War," concluding that special powers had been "given freely" but carefully noting that "they were given only temporarily, for use in emergency situations." Roosevelt did not, however, hesitate to bully Congress when he felt it necessary, just as he did the Supreme Court in the German saboteurs case. In fall

resolution on sending troops to Korea. Garry Wills, *Bomb Power: The Modern Presidency and the National Security State* (New York: Penguin Press, 2010), pp. 105–13.

68 Pre-World War II events: Warren F. Kimball, "Franklin D. Roosevelt and World War II," *Presidential Studies Quarterly* 34 (March 2004): 83–99. Beinart, *The Icarus Syndrome*, pp. 72–7. Peter Irons, *War Powers: How The Imperial Presidency Hijacked the Constitution* (New York: Metropolitan Books, 2005).

69 Edward S. Corwin, "Executive Authority Held Exceeded in Destroyer Deal," *NYT*, October 13, 1940. Corwin developed his argument at greater length in *The President – Office and Powers, 1787–1957*. 4th ed. (New York: New York University Press, 1957), pp. 238–9. Robert H. Jackson, "Opinion on Exchange of Over-Age Destroyers for Naval and Air Bases, *American Journal of International Law* 34 (1940): 728; available at www.roberthjackson.org/documents/.

1942, in response to a "runaway cost of living," he demanded Congress revise the existing wage-price controls. "In the event that the Congress should fail to act," he warned bluntly, "I shall accept the responsibility, and I will act." The president, he explained in a reprise of his first inaugural address and his 1937 speech, "has the powers under the Constitution ... to take measures necessary to avert a disaster which would interfere with the winning of the war." He did not specify where those powers were to be found in the Constitution, but Congress got the message and revised the law. There seems little question, however, that if it had not acted, Roosevelt would have followed through on his threat, with consequences we can only imagine.[70]

Roosevelt's record on war and national security issues left an ominous legacy for later presidents. Many of his successors claimed similar power to act unilaterally in foreign affairs. In the wake of the Vietnam War disaster, this habit was labeled the "Imperial Presidency." Roosevelt's actions are not strictly comparable to those of his successors, however. Jack Goldsmith, who served briefly as head of the Office of Legal Counsel under George W. Bush and courageously revoked the infamous "torture memos," argues persuasively that Roosevelt acted in a legally innocent era. The major constraints on presidential power – the Geneva Conventions, the Convention against Torture, the 1952 Supreme Court decision in the steel seizure case, the Foreign Intelligence Surveillance Act, among other developments all lay in the future. Nor were there any federal civil rights laws that would have applied to the Japanese-American evacuation. In strictly legal terms, FDR had a much freer hand than subsequent presidents.[71]

A MARCH ON WASHINGTON? FDR CONFRONTS THE CIVIL RIGHTS MOVEMENT

The tall, stately, and utterly determined civil rights leader stared down the president. A. Philip Randolph, head of the Brotherhood of Sleeping Car Porters, issued a call in early 1941 for a March on Washington of possibly 100,000 African Americans to demand equal employment opportunity in the booming defense industries. A very worried President Roosevelt invited him to the White House for a meeting on June 18 to talk him out of it. Randolph bluntly told him he wanted an executive order creating a committee on fair employment practice. When Roosevelt said he could not issue one, Randolph without flinching told him, in that case, the march would go forward. Faced with someone who would not compromise, FDR blinked. Seven days later he issued Executive Order 8802 creating an FEPC.[72]

70 Memorandum, The Powers of the President in Time of War, Biddle Papers, Box 7, GU. The memorandum is unsigned, but undoubtedly written or approved by Biddle. Saboteurs: Biddle, *In Brief Authority*, pp. 325–43. Wages-price controls: Message to Congress on Stabilizing the Economy, September 7, 1942. Corwin, *The President – Office and Powers, 1787–1957*, pp. 250–2. John Yoo, author of the controversial "torture memos" for President George W. Bush, argues that Bush was more restrained with regard to presidential powers than was Roosevelt: "FDR, Civil Liberties, and the War on Terrorism," in Daniel Farber, ed., *Security v. Liberty: Conflicts between Civil Liberties and National Security in American History* (New York: Russell Sage Foundation, 2008), pp. 42–66.

71 Jack L. Goldsmith, *The Terror Presidency: Law and Judgment inside the Bush Administration* (New York: W. W. Norton, 2007), pp. 192–205.

72 Executive Order 8802 – Reaffirming Policy of Full Participation in the Defense Program by All Persons, Regardless of Race, Creed, Color, or National Origin, and Directing Certain Action in Furtherance of Said Policy, June 25, 1941, APP. Herbert Garfinkel, *When Negroes March* (Glencoe: Free Press, 1959). Lucy G. Barber,

Randolph's proposed March on Washington was a milestone in the emerging civil rights movement. The Scottsboro case, involving eight young African-American men accused of raping a white woman in Alabama in 1931, was the first civil rights case to became a national cause celebre. Letters poured into the White House demanding federal action, but FDR said nothing. The Supreme Court, meanwhile, signaled a new opposition to racial segregation in *Missouri ex rel. Gaines v. Canada* (1938), holding that Missouri was required to provide an African American, Lloyd Gaines, an in-state legal education. Sensing a new opportunity for civil rights litigation, the NAACP promptly established the Legal Defense Fund (LDF) as a tax exempt arm, with Thurgood Marshall as its director. The case launched the long campaign that culminated in the historic 1954 *Brown v. Board of Education* decision declaring segregated public schools unconstitutional. The Carnegie Corporation, meanwhile, hired the Swedish economist Gunnar Myrdal in 1938 for a comprehensive study of American race relations, and his 1944 report, *An American Dilemma,* became the classic statement of America's failure to honor its commitment to equality. Finally, the specter of Nazi racism in Germany awakened many Americans to the shame of race discrimination the United States.[73]

In this context of rapidly rising expectations about racial equality, Randolph decided to press forward on employment discrimination. The war in Europe created full employment and ended the depression almost overnight. Race discrimination pervaded the defense industries, however. Lockheed Aircraft employed not a single African American among its forty-two thousand workers in the 1940s. The president of North American Aviation declared, "No matter what their qualifications, they will only be used as janitors." Randolph found tremendous enthusiasm for a campaign among ordinary African Americans on a trip through the South in late 1940, and in January 1941 he issued a "Call to Negro America to March on Washington for Jobs and Equal Participation in National Defense on July 1, 1941." Promising to bring "power and pressure to bear" on the government, he skillfully linked the demand for equality with national defense: "We loyal Negro American citizens demand the right to work and fight for our country." It was a brilliant stroke that appealed to white Americans and put Roosevelt in a bind. The very idea of a march was an electrifying sign of a new African-American militancy. Only sixteen years earlier, in 1925, thirty-five thousand Ku Klux Klan members had marched in the nation's capital. And in 1934 the NAACP had been talked out of a silent march to support federal antilynching legislation because of fears of an adverse reaction. The political climate had changed dramatically by 1941, however, and Randolph fully understood that he had new leverage. The official call for the march stated, "It will shake up official Washington."[74]

Marching on Washington: The Forging of an American Political Tradition (Berkeley: University of California Press, 2002), Ch. 4.

73 Letters to FDR re Scottsboro: OF 532, Box 1, FDRPL. Dan T. Carter, *Scottsboro: A Tragedy of the American South* (Baton Rouge: Louisiana State University Press, 1969). Mark V. Tushnet, *Making Civil Rights Law: Thurgood Marshall and the Supreme Court, 1936–1961* (New York: Oxford, 1994). Gunnar Myrdal, *An American Dilemma: The Negro Problem and Modern Democracy* (New York: Harper and Brothers, 1944).

74 Garfinkel, *When Negroes March.* Jervis Anderson, *A. Philip Randolph: A Biographical Portrait* (Berkeley: University of California Press, 1973), pp. 324–30. Defense industry employment: McWilliams, *The Education of Carey McWilliams*, p. 99. *The Call to Negro America to March on Washington* (1941) in *Reporting Civil Rights*, V. 1 (New York: Library of America, 2003), pp. 1–4. Robert L. Zangrando, *The NAACP Crusade against Lynching, 1909–1950* (Philadelphia: Temple University Press, 1980), p. 119.

Indeed it did. The White House panicked, and FDR told an aide he was "much upset" about it and could imagine "nothing that will stir up race hatred and slow up progress more than a march of that kind." He was particularly afraid the march would anger powerful southern Democrats in Congress whom he needed for his national defense program. He initially asked the first lady, Eleanor Roosevelt, to talk Randolph out of it. Although a prominent racial justice advocate, on this occasion she did his bidding and wrote to Randolph on June 10 that the march was "a very grave mistake [that] will set back the progress which is being made" on racial equality. Violence, she warned, would discredit civil rights efforts. Not having seen much racial progress, Randolph rejected her advice and even invited her to speak at the march. The New York City mayor, Fiorello LaGuardia, a Randolph friend, also tried and failed to dissuade him. With the march only two weeks away, LaGuardia said the only solution left was to invite Randolph to the White House to "thresh it out right then and there." He and others fully expected FDR's legendary powers of persuasion to work. FDR also sought to preempt Randolph by issuing a memo to the Office of Production Management a few days before the meeting, directing them to take "immediate steps" to end the "grave" problem of race discrimination in defense industries.[75]

They should have known that Randolph would be in no mood for sweet talk. He had been to the White House nine months earlier to challenge racial segregation in the new military draft and was badly mistreated. By 1940 FDR was under mounting pressure to ensure equal treatment of African Americans. Both the Republican and the Democratic Party platforms that summer included planks on racial justice (a first for the Democrats), and both specifically opposed discrimination in the military. Section 4 of the 1940 Selective Training and Service Act explicitly prohibited "discrimination against any person on account of race or color." (Although rarely cited as such, it was the first federal antidiscrimination law of modern times.) Roosevelt himself promised "equal rights, equal privileges, and equal opportunities" in military service. It was a false promise. The law also granted the military full discretion in applying the policy, and it proceeded largely to maintain the traditional system of racial segregation.[76]

When Randolph arrived in the Oval Office on September 27, 1940, to discuss the draft, FDR launched into one of his well-practiced monologues to avoid a difficult issue. Finally getting around to the draft issue, he said that desegregation was already in process. This was true only for a few specialty units, however. After the meeting, the presidential aide Steven Early played a dirty trick on Randolph by releasing a statement implying that he supported the administration's policy. Feeling betrayed, Randolph issued an angry rebuttal, and the White House had to apologize publicly. Shortly after this unpleasant White House experience, Randolph embarked on his tour of Sleeping Car Porter local unions in the South. At one point, he said to his aide Milton Webster, "You know, Web, calling

75 Panic: Doris Kearns Goodwin, *No Ordinary Time: Franklin and Eleanor Roosevelt: The Home Front in World War II* (New York: Simon & Schuster, 1994), pp. 248–51. FDR, Memo for Mac, June 7, 1941, OF 93, Colored Matters, Box 4, FDRPL. Eleanor Roosevelt to Randolph, June 10, 1941; Randolph to Eleanor Roosevelt, June 23, 1941, ERP, Box 748, FDRPL. "Thresh it out": Edwin M. Watson to The President, June 14, OF 391, Box 1, FDRPL. OPM Memo: Roosevelt to Knudsen and Hillman, Memorandum Condemning Discrimination in Defense Work June 12, 1941. APP. "President Assails Racial Job Barrier," *NYT*, June 16, 1941.

76 Democratic and Republican Party platforms, 1940, APP. Roosevelt, Statement on Peace Time Universal Selective Service, September 16, 1940, APP.

on the President and holding those conferences are not going to get us anywhere.... We are going to have to do something about it." That something became the March on Washington.[77]

His 1940 experience left Randolph very suspicious of his host at the June 1941 White House meeting. FDR began another of his monologues, but Randolph saw the ruse and interrupted him, bluntly saying, "Mr. President, time is running on." Finally getting down to business, Roosevelt asked, "Well, what do you want done, Phil?" Randolph said he wanted an executive order creating a fair employment practices committee. FDR said, "Well Phil, you know I can't do that," which of course was not true. He then repeated his concerns about violence and made it clear he wanted the march "called off." As a compromise, he offered to "call up the heads of the various defense plants" and ask them personally to guarantee fair employment for African Americans. Randolph cooly rejected this proposal and said he would go ahead with the march. At that tense moment, Mayor LaGuardia jumped in and suggested a compromise.[78]

Roosevelt agreed to create a Committee on Fair Employment Practice by executive order, and Randolph would cancel the march. When Randolph rejected the initial draft of the executive order because it excluded federal agencies, an exasperated FDR said, "Put it in." Executive Order 8802, signed on June 25, declared "there shall be no discrimination in the employment of workers in defense industries or government because of race, creed, color, or national origin." It was the first declaration by a president on equal employment opportunity, and it set the nation on the road to the 1964 Civil Rights Act. Keeping his half of the bargain, Randolph cancelled the march because its goal "was secured." Not done, however, he suggested FDR hold an "appropriate ceremony" to announce the executive order. FDR declined without comment. Some militant African Americans criticized Randolph for cancelling the march, but he understood that he had scored an unprecedented victory. For the first time, a civil rights leader had faced down a president and extracted a major concession.[79]

Randolph's daring was truly breathtaking. He was possibly the only person ever to force FDR to back down in a face-to-face confrontation. Joe Rauh, who became a powerful civil rights lawyer after World War II, was assigned to draft the order. When FDR capitulated to Randolph's demands, he exclaimed, "Who the hell is this guy Randolph?" and "What the hell has *he* got over the President of the United States?" Randolph's audacity is highlighted by Harry Truman's account of his first meeting with FDR in 1935. Even though he was a U.S. senator, he recalled that "it was quite an event for a country boy to go calling on the President of the United States" and confessed that he was almost completely tongue-tied in his presence. Robert Jackson, who served as attorney general between 1940 and 1941, wrote that "there was no one to whom he would surrender his

77 Anderson, *A. Philip Randolph*, pp. 243–8. Apology: Statement by President Roosevelt, October 1940, Niles Papers, HSTPL. "Negro Air Force Planned," *NYT*, October 16, 1940. Nancy J. Weiss, *Farewell to the Party of Lincoln*, pp. 274–7. Philip McGuire, "Desegregation of the Armed Forces: Black Leadership, Protest and World War II," *Journal of Negro History* 68 (Spring 1983): 147–58.

78 Anderson, *A. Philip Randolph*, pp. 256–7. Randolph, OH, pp. 4–5, LBJPL. Randolph was interviewed several times about this meeting, and gave slightly different versions of the exact words spoken, although with no variation in either the tone or outcome of the meeting. Two days after the meeting, J. Edgar Hoover alleged to Roosevelt that Randolph had radical political associations. Merl E. Reed, "The FBI, MOWM, and CORE, 1941–46," *Journal of Black Studies* 21 (June 1991): 465–79.

79 Anderson, *A. Philip Randolph*, pp. 256–7

own judgment. No one could overbear him and he never abdicated." Randolph, it would seem, succeeded where others feared even to try.[80]

Although a historic step, the Committee on Fair Employment Practice was only moderately effective. Its powers were limited, many private employers and federal agencies refused to cooperate, and it faced severe hostility from segregationists in Congress. Attorney General Biddle pointed out the political dilemma in a January 29, 1943, memo to FDR. On the one hand, "The South is in a state of emotional alarm" over possible federal intervention in "every phase of race relationship," while on the other, "there is widespread discontent among Negroes." He advised FDR to strengthen the Committee, convene a national conference on race relations, and make a public statement on the issue. FDR declined. Consumed by the war effort and not wanting to offend southerners in Congress, he gave the FEPC little support. A history of the Committee's work concludes that the administration "gave it lip service instead of support, used it callously to defuse black protest, and blocked it when political expediency so dictated." Nonetheless, it was a historic step, the first official government program on behalf of equal opportunity in employment.[81]

The proposed march had another significant consequence. Two days after the 1941 White House meeting the FBI began monitoring Randolph and sent its reports to the White House. The deeply racist J. Edgar Hoover was alarmed about militant civil rights action. A year later as racial conflicts began to spread (major riots broke out in summer 1943) he ordered every FBI field office to compile information on "racial conditions" in their area. The subsequent 730-page report in September 1943, with nearly 50 pages on Randolph's completely lawful activities, was classified secret. Only six copies were ever distributed, and even Attorney General Biddle had to make a specific request to get one.[82]

FDR – and the first lady – on race

Roosevelt's reluctance to create the CFEP was part of his general indifference to racial justice. He publicly remained almost completely silent on the issue for several reasons. Personally, he had no experience with African Americans and harbored traditional racist attitudes about both African Americans and Japanese Americans. As president, he was preoccupied first by the depression and then by the war and was dependent on the powerful southern bloc in Congress. He never mentioned civil rights in any of his famous Fireside Chats, when a statement on racial justice would have had a major impact on

[80] The White House aide Frank Walker remembered the budget director Lewis Douglas as "the only man I ever heard" openly express "disrespectful opposition to the president's personally expressed views." Robert H. Ferrell, ed., *FDR's Quiet Confidant: The Autobiography of Frank C. Walker* (Boulder: University of Colorado Press, 1997), p. 104. David McCullough, *Truman* (New York: Simon & Schuster, 1992), p. 215. Margaret Truman, *Harry S. Truman* (New York: Morrow, 1973), p. 91. Jackson, *That Man*, p. 15. Rauh: Anderson, *A. Philip Randolph*, pp. 258–9. Randolph, Telegram to Eleanor Roosevelt, June 24, 1941, ERP, Box 748, FDRPL.

[81] Executive Order 8802 – Reaffirming Policy of Full Participation in the Defense Program by All Persons, Regardless of Race, Creed, Color, or National Origin, and Directing Certain Action in Furtherance of Said Policy, June 25, 1941, APP. Biddle to The President, January 29, 1943, FPBP, "Civil Rights – Employment," FDRPL. Merl E. Reed, *Seedtime for the Modern Civil Rights Movement: The President's Committee on Fair Employment Practice, 1941–1946* (Baton Rouge: Louisiana State University Press, 1991), p. 345.

[82] Robert A. Hill, comp. and ed., *The FBI's RACON: Racial Conditions in the United States during World War II* (Boston: New England Press, 1995), pp. xvii, 459–97, 29, 58, n. 73. Hoover to Harry Hopkins [circa late 1941 or 1942], OF 10b, Box 17, FDRPL.

public opinion. He never supported the NAACP's antilynching bill, which had gained considerable support in Congress in the 1930s. He candidly told the NAACP's Walter White in 1934, "I've got to get legislation passed by Congress to save America." Southerners, he explained, "will block every bill I ask Congress to pass to keep America from collapsing. I just can't take that risk." As an alternative, he privately suggested either a Senate or FBI investigation of lynchings, but the NAACP rejected both ideas. FDR did condemn lynching in a nationally broadcast 1933 speech to the Federal Council of Churches, but he still did not support the antilynching law. (Interestingly, the speech was prompted by the lynching of a white man in San Jose, California.)[83]

Lobbying for the antilynching bill, NAACP leaders experienced FDR's tactic of "filibustering." Joel Spingarn, president of the NAACP in the 1930s, explained to his son Stephen (later a top aide to President Truman) how Roosevelt "would always change the subject with some story." After fifteen minutes his secretary would walk in to say his next appointment was waiting. Walter White recalled that "when he wished to avoid discussing a subject, he told many gay and amusing anecdotes to postpone the anticipated ordeal." The elder Spingarn concluded acidly that "Roosevelt is sometimes described as a lion and a fox," but on civil rights "he was pretty much of a weasel."[84]

On a few isolated occasions, FDR privately expressed some concern for civil rights. In 1942 he suggested to Attorney General Biddle that he had a "fundamental duty" to challenge restrictions on voting rights and asked about a possible challenge to the Mississippi poll tax. A year later, he again wrote to Biddle about the "good deal of a howl" from liberals because the Justice Department did not file an amicus brief in the Supreme Court case challenging the white primary elections in Texas (which in 1944 the Court declared unconstitutional in *Smith v. Allwright*). Biddle objected, however, arguing that the white primary was a "purely political" and not a constitutional issue. These two inquiries were isolated incidents, not matched by other actions, much less public statements or a program on civil rights.[85]

The most significant steps on behalf of racial equality in the New Deal were taken by Secretary of the Interior Harold Ickes. He dismantled racial segregation in his department, abruptly ending the ban on African Americans' eating in the main cafeteria, telling the staff, "it's just a matter of fundamental justice." In 1935, he ended a ban on appointing African Americans as supervisors in Negro units of the Civilian Conservation Corps, declaring, "I don't think that they should be discriminated against merely on account of their color" (although evidently segregated units continued).[86]

The advocate of racial justice in the White House was Eleanor Roosevelt. From the minute she became first lady she spoke out on race and involved herself in several controversies.

[83] Fireside chats: Russell D. Buhite and David W. Levy, *FDR's Fireside Chats* (Norman: University of Oklahoma Press, 1992). Roosevelt to White, cited in Weiss, *Farewell to the Party of Lincoln*, p. 106. Walter White, *A Man Called White* (New York: Viking Press, 1948), pp. 169–70.

[84] Stephen Spingarn, OH, p. 222, HSTPL. White, *A Man Called White*, pp. 169–70. White House aide James H. Rowe said, "He was noted as a filibusterer.... You had 15 minutes; he took 14 and a half." Katie Louchheim, ed., *The Making of the New Deal: The Insiders Speak* (Cambridge, MA: Harvard University Press, 1983), pp. 286–7.

[85] FDR to Attorney General, November 17, 1942; Biddle to The President, October 30, 1943; FDR to Attorney General, October 25, 1943, FBP, Box 3, GU. *Smith v. Allwright*, 321 U.S. 649 (1944).

[86] Cafeteria: Clark Foreman, OH, p. 24, SOHC. Ickes to Fechner, September 26, 1935, Ickes Papers, Box 213, LOC. John B. Kirby, *Black Americans in the Roosevelt Era: Liberalism and Race* (Knoxville: University of Tennessee Press, 1980).

She told the National Conference on the Education of Negroes in May 1934 that "the same opportunities should be accorded to every child regardless of race." In a time when few white leaders in Washington supported racial equality this was a strong message, especially from the wife of the president. She learned about racial justice on her own, overcoming her elite social insularity through the same social work activity that gave her an understanding of poor people.[87]

Eleanor also helped create the so-called Black Cabinet, an informal group of African Americans in federal agencies led by Mary McLeod Bethune, who lobbied hard for creating the National Youth Administration and was hired as its staff assistant in 1936. Another member was Robert C. Weaver, who began his career as an adviser to Secretary of the Interior Ickes and in 1966 became the first African-American cabinet member. The Black Cabinet was a major leap forward in the political status of African Americans, the first time a group held nonmenial positions and met as a group to plan strategies for advancing their interests.[88]

Nonetheless, Eleanor was at times ambivalent about how hard to press racial justice and some other civil liberties issues. She tried to talk A. Philip Randolph out of the 1941 March on Washington and two years later said that if she were a Negro, she would be bitter but "would not do too much demanding." She pointedly told her African-American friend Pauli Murray in 1944 that she did not support a broad interpretation of "social equality" and was reluctant to make a strong public statement against segregation because "I do not think it wise to add any antagonisms that we do not have to have." She was then already under heavy attack by southerners for her civil rights activity. She defended the Japanese-American evacuation in 1942, and while she made a highly publicized visit to the Gila River, Arizona, internment camp in April 1943, she carefully said nothing about the injustice of the evacuation and internment.[89]

In her most famous gesture on behalf of racial justice, Eleanor facilitated a concert by the noted African-American singer Marian Anderson at the Lincoln Memorial in April 1939. The Howard University School of Music had sponsored her concerts since 1936 and because of their growing popularity needed a larger venue. The Daughters of the American Revolution (DAR) denied permission to use their Constitution Hall.

[87] Eleanor Roosevelt, "Speech to The National Conference on the Education of Negroes, *Journal of Negro Education*," 3 (October, 1934): 573–5; in *What I Hope to Leave Behind*, p. 141. Eleanor Roosevelt's activities on civil rights and her relationship with her husband on this issue: Weiss, *Farewell to the Party of Lincoln*, Ch. VI, pp. 120–35. Her writings: Allida M. Black, ed., *Courage in a Dangerous World: The Political Writings of Eleanor Roosevelt* (New York: Columbia University Press, 1999). Allida M. Black, "Defining Eleanor, Defining Power: World War II, Racism, and a Preoccupied White House," in Mark J. Rozell and William D. Pederson, eds., *FDR and the Modern Presidency: Leadership and Legacy* (Westport, CT: Praeger, 1997), pp. 209–27.

[88] Bethune and HUAC: Biddle to Mrs. Roosevelt, September 26, 1942, ERP, Box 365, FDRPL. Bethune Papers, MF ED (Bethesda: University Publications of America, 1996). Weiss, *Farewell to the Party of Lincoln*, Ch. VII, pp, 136–56.

[89] Buck letter: Eleanor Roosevelt to Pearl Buck, May 29, 1942, in Eleanor Roosevelt, *It Seems to Me: Selected Letters of Eleanor Roosevelt* (Lexington: University of Kentucky Press, 2001), pp. 39–40. Internment camp visit: Kearns Goodwin, *No Ordinary Time*, pp. 427–31. Eleanor Roosevelt, "Freedom: Promise or Fact," *Negro Digest* 1 (October 1943): 8–9; in *What I Leave Behind*, p. 165. Eleanor Roosevelt, "A Challenge to American Sportsmanship," *Collier's*, October 16, 1943, in Black, ed., *Courage in a Dangerous World*, pp. 140–4. "Social Equality: Eleanor Roosevelt to Pauli Murray, October 3, 1944, FDRPL, ERP, MF ED, Reel 14. Eleanor's conflicts with the president over civil rights: Black, "Defining Eleanor, Defining Power," pp. 209–27. "Too much demanding:" Eleanor Roosevelt, "Freedom: Promise or Fact," *Negro Digest*, 1 (October 1943): 8–9; reprinted in *What I Leave Behind: The Essential Essays of Eleanor Roosevelt* (New York: Carlson, 1995), p. 165.

(Some African-American entertainers had performed there in earlier years, but the DAR imposed a racial ban in 1933.) The Washington, D.C., School Board, meanwhile, denied permission to use the auditorium at the white-only Central High School. The DAR's refusal created a public uproar, and Eleanor publicly resigned from the organization. The concert promoter S. Hurok then suggested a large outdoor concert, and at Eleanor's prompting Interior Secretary Ickes took "literally one minute" to approve using the Lincoln Memorial. FDR gave his consent, and on Easter Sunday, April 9, 1939, more than seventy-five thousand people attended the fully integrated and nationally broadcast concert. Hurok described Anderson as "the voice of a race." Ickes introduced her, while the Supreme Court justice Hugo Black, still scarred by the revelations of his former KKK membership, attended, the only justice to do so. The now famous concert was one of several events in those years (especially the Scottsboro case) that both reflected rising public concern about racial justice and encouraged civil rights activism.[90]

Far more controversial was Eleanor Roosevelt's role in integrating a Detroit public housing project. As war-related production in the automobile plants boomed, tens of thousands of new white and African-American residents poured into Detroit, many arriving from the segregated South. As both races had to learn new rules of social interaction, on the job, on streetcars, and in public parks, conflict inevitably resulted. The White House was drawn into Detroit's problems because a New Deal housing program raised the issue of federal funding of segregated facilities. A public housing project was scheduled to open in 1942 for whites only. Eleanor intervened and forced it to be integrated, over the objections of Charles Palmer, coordinator of federal housing programs. A mob of seven hundred whites with burning crosses met the first two dozen African-American families attempting to move in during February 1942. The confrontation deeply alarmed the administration. Archibald MacLeish, director of the wartime Office of Facts and Figures, reported that shortwave radio broadcasts covered the incident around the world, and that "our actions belie our words" about the wartime fight for democracy. African-American men, moreover, were reportedly "tearing up their draft cards and the blow to morale is serious." He recommended FDR make a strong public statement, but the president declined. Worried federal officials backed off and postponed opening the integrated housing project for a year.[91]

The African-American families finally moved into their homes in April 1943, guarded by eight hundred armed Michigan state troopers. Tensions in the city continued to mount, and on June 21 a minor incident at Belle Isle park sparked a race riot that affected the city for a full week. Disrupting production in critical defense plants, the riot threatened the

90 Raymond Arsenault, *The Sound of Freedom: Marian Anderson, The Lincoln Memorial, and the Concert That Awakened America* (New York: Bloomsbury Press, 2010). S. Hurok, *Impresario: A Memoir by S. Hurok* (New York: Random House, 1946), pp. 251–61. Peggy Anderson, *The Daughters: An Unconventional Look at America's Fan Club – the DAR* (New York: St. Martin's, 1974), pp. 109–54. Black: Ickes, Diary, April 15, 1939, p. 615. Ickes, however, denied A. Philip Randolph permission to hold a rally at the Lincoln Memorial in 1942 to protest racial discrimination, arguing that the president did not "look with favor upon meetings of this sort during war time," and adding the dubious argument that it would diminish the historic Anderson concert and that only equally "historic" events should be held there. Ickes to Randolph, April 13, 1942, Ickes Papers, Box 213, LOC.

91 Black, "Defining Eleanor, Defining Power." The 1943 Detroit riot: Alfred McClung Lee and Norman D. Humphrey, *Race Riot* (New York: Dryden Press, 1943). MacLeish: Biddle, Cabinet Meeting Minutes, March 6, 1942, FPBP, Box 1, FDRPL. R. Allen Hays, *The Federal Government and Urban Housing: Ideology and Change in Public Policy*. 2nd ed. (Albany: SUNY Press, 1995).

war effort. Thirty-four people died, half of them African Americans shot by the police. Racial disturbances also broke out in New York City and Los Angeles (the famous "Zoot Suit" riot) and nearly erupted in the nation's capital. Fears that Germany and Japan might exploit America's race problem gripped the administration. Ickes unsuccessfully urged FDR to create a National Committee on Race Relations, forwarding a list of possible members. Attorney General Biddle, however, advised him that a public address on the racial crisis would be "unwise." Order was finally restored in Detroit by the intervention of six thousand federal troops.[92]

The first lady's prominent role in the housing controversy provoked harsh attacks from segregationists in Congress. Hoping to defuse the situation, FDR dispatched her to New Zealand, allegedly to boost the morale of U.S. troops. This was patently not true, as she had previously requested and been denied permission to visit troops overseas. The trip was designed to get her out of the country and cool off the racial controversy. As two New Deal officials later recalled, she was "ordered to go" because "the Negro situation was too hot."[93]

The issue of racial segregation in the armed services did not end with Randolph's 1940 White House confrontation. Three years later, an African-American gardener named Winfred Lynn challenged the segregated draft, arguing that it violated the guarantee of "no discrimination" in the 1940 Selective Training and Service Act. The case was potentially an even bigger bombshell that the challenges to the Japanese-American evacuation, since if successful it would require a major reorganization of the military in the midst of war. The NAACP thought it was too hot to touch, but A. Philip Randolph took it up, and the ACLU's Arthur Garfield Hays wrote the brief. The appellate court found a legal pretext to dismiss the case, however, and the case died.[94] Nonetheless, the case set in motion events that came to fruition in 1948. Immediately after the war, the Lynn defense committee evolved into the National Committee to Abolish Segregation in the Armed Services, and on July 26, 1948, President Harry Truman took the historic step of ordering the end of racial segregation in the U.S. military.

FREEDOM OF SPEECH IN PEACE AND WAR

Norman Rockwell's poster *Save Freedom of Speech,* is an American icon, reprinted in books, magazines, coffee mugs, and other artifacts of popular culture. Relatively few people, however, know that it originated with President Roosevelt's Four Freedoms speech, a part of his 1941 State of the Union Address (the other three freedoms are freedom of religion, freedom from fear, and freedom from want).[95]

92 Biddle, Memorandum for the President, July 15, 1943, FPBP, "Detroit Riots," Box 2, FDRPL. Ickes to FDR, July 1, 1943, Ickes Papers, Box 213, LOC. Lee and Humphrey, *Race Riot.*

93 "Eleanor Roosevelt and Wartime Campaign," *Social Education* 60 (September 1996): 284–6. Vice President Henry Wallace and the New Deal official Gardner Jackson, quoted in Black, "Defining Eleanor, Defining Power," 215. Weiss, *Farewell to the Party of Lincoln,* argues that Eleanor shied away from urging challenges to segregation. The Detroit affair suggests otherwise. Roosevelt, *The Autobiography of Eleanor Roosevelt* (New York: Da Capo Press, 1992), p. 253.

94 Materials on the Lynn case in APRP, Box 19, 26, LOC.

95 Cultural artifacts in the author's possession The Rockwell illustrations: *Norman Rockwell's Four Freedoms: Images That Inspire a Nation* (Stockbridge, MA: Berkshire House, 1993).

If the presidency is a bully pulpit that can be used to educate and lead the country, then FDR deserves credit for the most prominent and eloquent statement on behalf of freedom of speech and religious liberty ever made by a president. (John F. Kennedy's 1960 campaign speech on church and state is a far more detailed discussion of that subject, but he was still a candidate for the office at the time.) Addressing Congress in early January 1941, he painted a grim picture of a world engulfed in war in both Europe and Asia, solemnly advising that much sacrifice would be required of Americans in the years ahead. In this world crisis, America had a high responsibility to affirm the core values of American democracy once victory was won: "we look forward to a world founded upon four essential human freedoms. The first is freedom of speech and expression - everywhere in the world. The second is freedom of every person to worship God in his own way - everywhere in the world." According to his speechwriter Samuel Rosenman, FDR personally added the Four Freedoms to the original draft. No previous president had used such a prominent occasion to extol First Amendment freedoms. As we shall see, however, on some key issues FDR's actions contradicted his words.[96]

A second Bill of Rights?

Three years after his Four Freedoms speech, FDR offered an even broader vision of the rights of Americans in his 1944 State of the Union Address. The eminent constitutional law scholar Cass R. Sunstein regards the speech as a call for a "Second Bill of Rights" that included economic and social rights. Americans, FDR told Congress, were entitled to "a useful and remunerative job," food and clothing, "a decent home," medical care, "a good education," and more. "After this war is won," he pledged, "we must be prepared to move forward in the implementation of these rights." No other president - not even Lyndon Johnson with his idea of a Great Society - ever expressed such a grand vision of social justice, much less one that reached far beyond the specific provisions of the Bill of Rights. A year later, he repeated the call in his 1945 State of the Union Address.[97]

Sunstein argues that the speech was one of the great lost opportunities in American history, a brief moment when the scope of freedom in America might have been enormously enlarged. Despite his eminence as a legal scholar, however, Sunstein fails as a historian in this instance. There is simply no persuasive evidence that Roosevelt was seriously committed to a radical program of social and economic equality. He did not mention this idea on other occasions and offered no specific programs to implement it. As we have seen, he was ambivalent about the Wagner Act, which gave a new measure of justice to working people. New Deal reforms had stalled almost completely by 1938, and FDR essentially abandoned domestic reform when the United States entered the war. If historians agree on anything, it is that the New Deal was always an ad hoc, experimental, and pragmatic approach to social and economic reform. FDR was famously not an ideologue, and it is impossible to find any consistent vision of social and economic equality over his

96 State of the Union Address, January 6, 1941, APP. Significance of the speech, see Eric Foner, *The Story of American Freedom* (New York: W. W. Norton, 1998), p. 223. Later that year, FDR proclaimed December 15 Bill of Rights Day. Proclamation 2524 on Bill of Rights Day. November 27, 1941, APP.

97 Cass R. Sunstein, *The Second Bill of Rights: FDR's Unfinished Revolution and Why We Need It More Than Ever* (New York: Basic Books, 2004). State of the Union Address, January 11, 1944, APP. Preparation of the speech: Rosenman, *Working with Roosevelt*, 419–25; State of the Union Address, January 6, 1945, APP.

twelve years in office. Most historians today argue that the New Deal preserved the free enterprise system by reforming it, creating a stable economic system that endured for half a century until it was undone by neoconservative deregulation beginning in the 1980s.

Sunstein says FDR's call for a Second Bill of Rights was later completely forgotten, but the truth is it was little noticed even at the time. Public attention focused on another part of the speech, where he proposed a national service law subjecting all adults – men and women – to conscription for work in any assignment the government deemed necessary. The government had the power to "draft capital and property," FDR argued, and so why not people? "When the very life of the Nation is in peril the responsibility for service is common to all men and women," he argued, adding that this would be "the most democratic way to wage a war." He blandly claimed that millions of Americans really wanted to "do their share" and would derive great "inner satisfaction" from "making the fullest contribution to victory." It is far more likely that most Americans would strenuously object to being conscripted for whatever purpose a president wanted. In fact, FDR anticipated a hostile reaction to his proposal and kept that section of the speech secret, having it typed separately from the main body of the text. Additionally, he candidly admitted that the proposed law was designed to eliminate strikes, which were plaguing the war effort. If strikes occurred in critical industries, the government would draft the workers and assign them to their current jobs.[98]

FDR's national service idea was greeted by loud protests from Congress and labor leaders. Labor correctly saw it as a strikebreaking measure. R. J. Thomas, president of the United Automobile Workers (UAW), said it "smacks of slave labor." Only one of the eighteen members of the Senate Military Committee endorsed it, even after Secretary of War Stimson spent three hours defending it. One vigorous opponent was the Missouri senator Harry Truman, who in just fourteen months would himself be president and ironically in 1952 would seize the American steel industry on the basis of a similar assertion of government power in wartime (although FDR called for a statute, while Truman acted unilaterally on claims of presidential power). Faced with strong opposition and no support, FDR dropped the idea.[99]

The significance of the conscription proposal is that in the same speech where he talked about expanding the rights of Americans, FDR also proposed the most drastic limitation on individual rights ever made by any president, including a direct attack on the rights of organized labor, his most loyal political supporters. Commentators at the time did not emphasize the obvious parallels with the totalitarian idea that the rights of private citizens were subordinate to the needs to the state (which Roosevelt blithely defined as "responsibilities"). FDR does not seem to have thought through the implications of his extraordinary proposal.

To Roosevelt's great credit, his administration did not repeat during World War II the massive suppression of dissent that occurred in the First World War. In his history of free speech in wartime, Geoffrey Stone observes that all three of FDR's attorneys general in this critical period – Murphy, Jackson, and Biddle – "had learned the lessons of World

98 State of the Union Address, January 11, 1944, APP.

99 "Service Act Urged," *NYT*, January 12, 1944. "Thomas, UAW Head, Assails Plan," ibid., January 12, 1944. "Senate Group Cool to Job Draft Bill," ibid., January 24, 1944.

War I" and were determined not to repeat those mistakes. Biddle in June 1940 advised the nation that what people called "propaganda" was "legal" and protected by "Constitutional sanction." In June 1941 a pleased ACLU commented, "On the whole, the federal agencies at Washington have not only kept their heads in confronting pressure to restrict civil liberties, but have made efforts to protect them." It did not know the full story of the FBI's secret activities at that point, and the Japanese-American tragedy was months away, but on free speech it maintained a generally optimistic view throughout the war.[100]

When pressured by critics or his own political allies, however, Roosevelt on several occasions cast aside the First Amendment. On November 17, 1941, as Americans hotly debated the issue of intervention into the European war, he asked Attorney General Biddle for a grand jury investigation of the "money sources" behind the America First Committee, the leading opponent of U.S. entry into the war. "It certainly ought to be looked into," he argued, complaining that he could not get Congress to investigate. Isolationism ran strong in America at that time (witness the Neutrality Acts), and America First was a legitimate expression of political opposition to America's going to war.[101]

A year later with the country at war, the administration suppressed the reactionary Catholic priest Father Charles E. Coughlin. He had developed a large populist following in the 1930s through his radio broadcasts and eventually became bitterly anti-Roosevelt, calling for his impeachment in October 1940. FDR raised the issue of doing something about "subversive sheets" at a 1942 cabinet meeting, and Biddle, bowing to the pressure, had the Post Office revoke the second-class mailing privilege of Coughlin's magazine, *Social Justice.* Also responding to White House pressure, prominent Catholic laymen persuaded the Detroit archbishop to silence Coughlin, and by late 1942 the rebellious priest was completely "out of circulation." Roosevelt was reportedly "delighted" at this. The suppression of *Social Justice* and the Socialist Worker's Party magazine, the *Militant*, was among the few exceptions to the tolerant policies of the administration during the war.[102]

Invoking the Smith Act: The Minneapolis Trotskyists

The 1940 Smith Act making it a crime to advocate the violent overthrow of the government raised serious First Amendment questions about what kinds of political speech, if any, the government could prohibit. With the direct support of FDR, the Justice Department first invoked the law in a shabby politically motivated case. In late June 1941 the FBI raided the offices of the Minneapolis Teamsters Union, and the Justice Department then

[100] "Biddle for Adding Executive Power," *NYT*, June 25, 1940. Biddle assisted the ACLU with *Lovell v. Griffin, 303 U.S. 444 (1938)*. ACLU, *Annual Report, 1938*, p. 17. Geoffrey Stone, *Perilous Times: Free Speech in Wartime from the Sedition Act of 1798 to the War on Terrorism* (New York: W. W. Norton, 2004), p. 249. Murphy: Sidney Fine, *Frank Murphy*, 2 Vols. (Ann Arbor: University of Michigan Press, 1975–9). Steele, *Free Speech in the Good War.* See his discussion of Attorney General Robert Jackson on this issue. ACLU, *Annual Report, 1941*, p. 5.

[101] America First: FDR to Attorney General, "Confidential," November 17, 1941, PSF, Justice, 1940–4, Box 56, FDRPL. Roosevelt to Biddle, October 1, 1942, in Elliott Roosevelt, ed., *FDR: His Personal Letters, 1928–1945, II* (New York: Duell, Sloan, Pearce, 1947–50), p. 1241.

[102] Coughlin: Biddle, Cabinet Meeting Minutes, March 20, 1942, May 1, 1942, May 7, 1942, FPBP, Box 1, FDRPL. "Coughlin Admits Magazine Control," *NYT*, April 21, 1942. Douglas M. *Charles, J. Edgar Hoover and the Anti-Interventionists: FBI Political Surveillance and the Rise of the Domestic Security State, 1939 to 1945* (Columbus: Ohio State University Press, 2007). Charles J. Tull, *Father Coughlin and the New Deal* (Syracuse, NY: Syracuse University Press, 1965), pp. 225–36.

indicted the union leader Vincent Dunne and twenty-eight colleagues under the Smith Act. Labor union rivalries prompted the case. Dunne and his group were a dissident faction in the Teamsters Union and also members of the Trotskyist Socialist Workers Party. Dan Tobin, national president of the Teamsters and a member of the Democratic Party National Committee, wanted to be rid of this troublesome group. He warned the White House that the "subversive, communistic, socialistic, and radical" elements within his union planned strikes that would hamper defense production. FDR was eager to do his political ally a favor while also averting harmful strikes. Always contemptuous of legalisms, he was not worried about the First Amendment implications of the Smith Act. He also had a cynical ally in the Communist Party (then aggressively supporting action against Nazi Germany which had invaded the Soviet Union), which enthusiastically supported the prosecution of its leading rival on the Left. While Trotskyists advocated revolution in theory, the Minneapolis group hardly posed a threat to national security. The FBI raid found some weapons, but they were more related to the violent Minneapolis labor wars than any plot to overthrow the government.[103]

The Dunne case presented the first opportunity for a constitutional test of the Smith Act. The Minneapolis Teamsters were convicted and sentenced to sixteen months in prison. The ACLU assisted on their appeal, but the Eighth Circuit Court of Appeals upheld the law and the Supreme Court declined to hear the case. Thus, the Smith Act survived and became available for the assault on civil liberties during the cold war. The principal victim would be the very Communist Party that had cheered the prosecution of the Trotskyists. (Another dubious legacy of the case was that by removing the Dunne group, the government cleared the way for a young Jimmy Hoffa's rise to power within the Teamsters Union.)[104]

A shameful prosecution: "The Great Sedition Trial" of 1944

There was no massive suppression of dissent in World War II mainly because with Pearl Harbor and Hitler it was the "good war," with no significant opposition. The only vocal critics were a mixed bag of die-hard isolationists, right-wing cranks, bitter-end Roosevelt haters, and anti-semites. Some liberals and leftists, nonetheless, demanded Roosevelt prosecute the most prominent critics. FDR took offense at the more extreme personal attacks and decided to placate his political allies. At cabinet meetings he badgered Attorney General Biddle to do something about the "subversive sheets." After one meeting, he asked Biddle to stay and presented him with right-wing pamphlets and newspapers denouncing him as a "warmonger." "What are you going to do about this?" he demanded. Biddle knew the material would not support a prosecution and replied that "nothing can be done." Unsatisfied, FDR continued to pressure him "every week." Eventually worn down, Biddle authorized an indictment in July 1942 charging conspiracy to violate both the Espionage Act and the Smith Act. FDR "commended me on the drive against the seditious papers," he wrote in his cabinet notes, "and seemed pleased."[105] As

103 Tobin: Stephen T. Early to The President, "Confidential," June 11, 1941, Early Papers, Box 214, FDRPL. Stone, *Perilous Times*, pp. 236–79.

104 *Dunne v. United States*, 138 F.2d 137 (8th Cir. 1943).

105 Biddle, Cabinet Minutes, March 20, 1942, April 24, 1942, FPBP, Box 1, FDRPL. Biddle, *In Brief Authority*, pp. 151–2. *U.S. v. McWilliams*, 54 F. Supp. 791 (1944).

he had with the Japanese Americans, Biddle yielded to the pressure and compromised his own principles. Apparently, he thought a small concession would get the president off his back and insulate the administration from political attacks.

The thirty defendants in what was called "the Great Sedition Trial" were a bizarre collection of eccentrics. Elizabeth Dilling was a wealthy and flamboyant Roosevelt hater who had published *The Roosevelt Red Record,* purporting to show communist influence in the New Deal. The most substantial defendant was Lawrence Dennis, the foremost American fascist intellectual and author of several serious books on political theory. William Dudley Pelley led the Silver Shirts, the largest of the many crypto-Nazi paramilitary groups.[106] The government's case was as embarrassingly weak as Biddle knew it would be and was widely denounced. Biddle himself later called the trial "a dreary farce." Prosecutors had no evidence of an actual conspiracy among the defendants and no evidence of direct links with the German government. Difficulties in assembling a credible case delayed the trial until April 1944. The defendants promptly turned the trial into a circus, while the chief prosecutor, O. John Rogge, spent nearly seven months mainly reading from their writings. The *Washington Post* acidly editorialized that it was a "travesty," causing "serious impairment of our judicial system." Fate brought the case to an abrupt end when Judge Edward C. Eicher died, and a mistrial was declared.[107]

The Great Sedition Trial is today almost completely forgotten, apart from Far Right and anti-semitic Web sites. Nonetheless, it stands as a melancholy testimony of the willingness of President Roosevelt to cast aside First Amendment principles and pressure his attorney general into a political show trial. Once again, the tragic figure was Attorney General Biddle, who knew better but caved in to pressure from his boss, as he had with both the Minneapolis Smith Act case and the Japanese-American evacuation.[108]

CREATING THE ROOSEVELT COURT

Without any question, President Roosevelt's appointments to the Supreme Court represented his greatest contribution to civil liberties. Hugo Black and William O. Douglas rank among the greatest civil libertarians ever to sit on the Court. Both were instrumental in forging the revolution in constitutional law, beginning in the late 1930s, that for the first time established broad protection of individual rights. They also became key members of the famously rights-oriented Warren Court in the 1950s and 1960s. Two other Roosevelt appointments were also strong civil libertarians. Although never regarded as great jurist, Frank Murphy was a consistent libertarian, and the less well-known Wiley Rutledge was also a solid pro-civil liberties vote. These four were joined in a number of crucial instances by Robert Jackson, who in several important cases wrote eloquent

[106] Elizabeth Dilling, *The Roosevelt Red Record and Its Background* (Kenilworth, IL: Author, 1936). Elizabeth Dilling, *The Red Network: A "Who's Who" and Handbook of Radicalism for Patriots* [1934] (New York: Arno Press, 1977). Lawrence Dennis, *The Coming American Fascism* (New York: Harper, 1936); *The Dynamics of War and Revolution* (New York: Weekly Foreign Letter, 1940). Leo P. Ribuffo, *The Old Christian Right* (Philadelphia: Temple University Press, 1983). Rebuttal by a defendant and his lawyer: Maximilian St. George and Lawrence Dennis, *A Trial on Trial: The Great Sedition Trial of 1944* (n.p.: National Civil Rights Committee, 1946). The case is rarely mentioned in biographies of Roosevelt, and is today mainly discussed on contemporary right-wing and anti-semitic Web sites: e.g., www.antiwar.com.

[107] Biddle, *In Brief Authority,* p. 242. *U.S. v. McWilliams,* 54 F. Supp. 791 (1944).

[108] Biddle, *In Brief Authority,* pp. 151–2.

statements of civil liberties principles. His concurring opinion in the 1952 steel industry seizure case, for example, established the framework that continues to shape discussions of presidential powers. With eight appointments (two to the same seat because of James Byrnes's quick resignation) and his choice for chief justice, Roosevelt transformed the Supreme Court.[109]

The irony of Roosevelt's Court appointments is that civil liberties was never a consideration in his selection process. Loyalty to the New Deal was always his paramount criterion. He told both Hugo Black and James Byrnes, for example, that he had been reluctant to choose them because he needed them in the Senate. A prominent New Dealer described Byrnes as FDR's "primary lieutenant" in Congress. No one, including FDR, imagined that Black and Douglas would emerge as great civil libertarians. Hugo Black's nomination, in fact, was almost derailed by the revelation that he had once been a member of the Ku Klux Klan. The ACLU, meanwhile, fired off a telegram asking the Senate to examine the issue and to look closely at some overzealous Senate investigations Black had directed in which he subpoened letters and telegrams critical of FDR. No one knew where he stood on issues of race or the First Amendment. Once on the Court, however, the former Klansman became an unswerving supporter of racial equality.[110]

William O. Douglas was a paradox throughout his life, and his emergence as a civil libertarian on the Court was a complete surprise. He idolized Justice Louis Brandeis, but primarily for his views on economic justice. As with Black, Roosevelt chose him because he supported New Deal economic policies and because he wanted to appoint someone from "the West" (even though Douglas had spent his entire postcollege career in elite institutions in the East). Once on the Court, Douglas surprised everyone by his passionate commitment to civil liberties.[111]

Felix Frankfurter, by contrast, had the strongest civil liberties record of anyone appointed to the Court to that time. He had been a founding member of the ACLU in 1920, wrote a 1927 book critical of the Sacco and Vanzetti prosecution, and in the 1920s was the foremost academic expert on labor injunctions. When he was nominated in 1939, friends were very concerned that his views and associations might block his confirmation. These fears proved groundless, and he was easily confirmed. On the Court, however, Frankfurter often disappointed civil libertarians, frequently siding with the government and becoming the leading advocate of judicial restraint, arguing that the Court should defer to the judgment of legislatures. He wrote a long dissent in *West Virginia v. Barnette,* where the majority upheld the right of Jehovah's Witnesses

109 Melvin I. Urofsky, "The Roosevelt Court," in William H. Chafe, ed., *The Achievement of American Liberalism: The New Deal and Its Legacies* (New York: Columbia University Press, 2003), pp. 63–98. C. Herman Pritchett, *The Roosevelt Court: A Study in Judicial Politics and Values, 1937–1947* (Chicago: Quadrangle Books, 1948). Sidney Fine, *Frank Murphy: The Detroit Years* V. 1 (Ann Arbor: University of Michigan Press, 1975); V. 2 (Chicago: University of Chicago Press, 1979). Fowler Harper, *Justice Rutledge and the Bright Constellation* (Indianapolis: Bobbs, Merrill, 1965).

110 Henry J. Abraham, *Justices, Presidents, and Senators: A History of the U.S. Supreme Court Appointments from Washington to Bush II*, 5th ed. (Lanham, MD: Rowman & Littlefield, 2008), pp. 130 (Byrnes), 166 (criteria), p. 166 (Black). Byrnes: Leon Keyserling in Katie Louchheim, ed., *The Making of the New Deal: The Insiders Speak* (Cambridge, MA: Harvard University Press, 1983), p. 200. ACLU, Letter to Senator Black, March 10, 1936, ACLUP-MF (1996), Reel 130. Telegram, ACLU, Ward, Baldwin, Hays to Senator Robert LaFollette, August 16, 1937, ibid., Reel 144. Roger K. Newman, *Hugo Black: A Biography* (New York: Pantheon, 1994).

111 *Skinner v. Oklahoma*, 316 U.S. 535 (1942). Bruce Allen Murphy, *Wild Bill: The Legend and Life of William O. Douglas* (New York: Random House, 2003).

children not to be compelled to salute the flag that is notable for its aggressive emphasis on the need for national unity. A study of the Roosevelt Court found that, apart from racial justice cases, he had the worst record of any of the Roosevelt appointees on civil liberties, voting to support individual rights in only 29 percent of the cases. The Court historian Melvin I. Urofsky labels him "one of the great disappointments in modern times."[112]

The Roosevelt Court and civil liberties

It was an odd place to announce a revolution in constitutional law: a footnote in an otherwise obscure 1938 case. Justice Harlan Fiske Stone explained in Footnote Four of *Carolene Products* that in future cases it would closely examine "statutes directed at particular religious, or national, or racial minorities: whether prejudice against discrete and insular minorities may be a special condition" that may call for "searching judicial inquiry." Stone's dictum became the guiding principle of a revolution in constitutional law that would underpin today's vast body of civil rights and civil liberties law. This legal revolution transformed the country, shaping everyday habits and people's values on everything from free speech to church and state, civil rights, police practices, and individual privacy. The Warren Court (1953–69) is justly famous for its expansion of civil liberties, but the Roosevelt Court laid the groundwork. The historian William M. Wiecek characterizes the work of the Roosevelt Court as "The Birth of the Modern Constitution." In this respect, Roosevelt, however unintentionally, had a more profound impact on civil liberties in America than any other president.[113]

The Court's new role regarding civil liberties was one-half of a jurisprudential revolution in the late 1930s that included withdrawing from scrutiny of economic regulation. Until 1937, the conservative Court struck down New Deal measures on the grounds that they interfered with the liberty of contract guaranteed by the Fourteenth Amendment. The decisions paralyzed efforts to deal with the depression and provoked an angry and frustrated FDR into his unsuccessful and politically disastrous "court-packing" plan in 1937.[114]

FDR lost the court-packing battle, but he had already won the war over the Court. As the debate over the plan raged in spring 1937, the Court did an unexpected about-face and upheld two New Deal measures. *West Coast Hotel v. Parrish* on March 29 sustained the constitutionality of a Washington state wages and hours law – precisely the

[112] Felix Frankfurter and Nathan Greene, *The Labor Injunction* (New York: Macmillan, 1930). Frankfurter, *The Case of Sacco and Vanzetti* (Boston: Little, Brown, 1927). Frankfurter's writings in the 1920s clearly reveal both his belief in judicial restraint and his passionate patriotism. Writing about the Scopes case in 1925, he questioned whether the courts could bring about greater toleration for differences in American society. Felix Frankfurter, "Can The Supreme Court Guarantee Toleration?" *The New Republic*, June 17, 1925; reprinted in Frankfurter, *Law and Politics: Occasional Papers of Felix Frankfurter, 1913–1938* (New York: Capricorn Books, 1962), pp. 195–7. Pritchett, *The Roosevelt Court*, Table XVI, p. 131. Urofsky, "The Roosevelt Court," p. 67.

[113] *United States v. Carolene Products*, 304 U.S. 144 (1938). Urofsky, "The Roosevelt Court," pp. 73–4. C. Herman Pritchett, *Civil Liberties and the Vinson Court* (Chicago: University of Chicago Press, 1954). Truman appointments: Chapter 5 of this book. William M Wiecek, *The Birth of the Modern Constitution: The United States Supreme Court, 1941–1953* (New York: Cambridge University Press, 2006).

[114] Message to Congress on the Reorganization of the Judicial Branch of the Government, February 5, 1937, APP. The atmosphere of the crisis: Drew Pearson and Robert S. Allen, *The Nine Old Men* (Garden City, NY: Doubleday, Doran, 1937)."A Full Surrender," *NYT*, July 23, 1937. Leuchtenburg, *Supreme Court Reborn*.

kind of government economic regulation it had previously invalidated. Two weeks later it upheld the constitutionality of the Wagner Act in *NLRB v. Jones and Laughlin*, giving the New Deal another great victory. The turnabout was actually the result of Justice Owen Roberts's reversing himself and turning the previous four-vote minority into a majority. As if by magic, the constitutional crisis over the Court and national economic policy evaporated. The aged conservative justices, evidently recognizing they had lost the battle, began retiring, giving Roosevelt his opportunity to change the Court.[115]

As it withdrew from scrutinizing economic regulation, the Court developed a new activism on civil liberties, following the principles laid out by Justice Stone in *United States v. Carolene Products*. The Court first signaled its shift in January 1937, when it overturned the conviction of the Communist Party organizer Dirk DeJonge under the state criminal syndicalism law. DeJonge had done nothing more than organize a meeting to support a longshoreman's strike. In a major First Amendment victory, the Court held that "peaceable assembly for lawful discussion cannot be made a crime." Other civil liberties victories quickly followed. The Court overturned the conviction of Angelo Herndon, an African-American Communist Party organizer, sentenced to death under an old Georgia law for inciting insurrection. Herndon was indeed a Communist Party member, but his actions consisted of distributing pamphlets advocating unemployment insurance, relief for farmers, and racial equality. The Court ruled that "to make membership in the party ... a criminal offense, punishable by death ... is an unwarranted invasion of the right of freedom of speech."[116]

The greatest advances in First Amendment law were prompted by the small, troublesome, and hated religious sect the Jehovah's Witnesses. The national crisis over religious tolerance involving the group in the late 1930s and 1940s is now long forgotten by most Americans, but the group brought nineteen cases to the Supreme Court, winning fourteen and giving the Court the opportunity to refashion First Amendment law. The Court overturned a law directed at the sect making it illegal to distribute literature without a permit (*Lovell v. Griffin*, 1938), an antilittering law that was used to restrict advocacy (*Schneider v. New Jersey*, 1939), and a prohibition on door-to-door canvassing (*Martin v. Struthers*, 1943). In *Cantwell v. Connecticut* (1940), the Court incorporated the free exercise clause of the First Amendment into the Fourteenth Amendment, holding that it restricted the religious liberty of the Witnesses.[117]

The Witness cases did not reach the Court by happenstance. The historian Jennifer Jacobs Henderson argues that the Witnesses' legal director Hayden Covington developed a "nationally orchestrated, aggressive campaign" to secure constitutional protection for their group. Both the NAACP and the ACLU quickly adopted similar strategies and began winning important victories before the newly receptive Court. Covington carefully selected towns where a restrictive law existed or where he anticipated public hostility. The *Cantwell* case, for example, originated in a New Haven, Connecticut, neighborhood that was 90 percent Roman Catholic. Potential plaintiffs were screened to prevent any complicating factors. African Americans were excluded so as to avoid racial issues and

[115] *West Coast Hotel v. Parrish*, 300 U.S. 379 (1937). *NLRB v. Jones and Laughlin*. 301 U.S. 1 (1937).

[116] *DeJonge v. Oregon*, 299 U.S. 353 (1937). *Herndon v. Georgia*, 295 U.S. 441 (1937).

[117] Witness legal strategy: Jennifer Jacobs Henderson, "The Jehovah's Witnesses and Their Plan to Expand First Amendment Freedoms," *Journal of Church and State* 46, no. 4 (2004): 811–32. *Cantwell v. Connecticut*, 310 U.S. 296 (1940).

focus only on the First Amendment issues. Covington fully understood that they were embarking on a "long-term struggle" that would not be won easily or quickly. His strategy was enormously successful, and it became the model for rights advocacy in the decades ahead.[118]

The most explosive and best-remembered controversy involved the refusal of Witness schoolchildren to participate in compulsory flag salute exercises because of religious scruples. In the heightened atmosphere of nationalism resulting from the world war, millions of Americans were outraged at this seeming lack of patriotism. The first Supreme Court decision, upholding compulsory flag salutes in 1940 (*Minersville v. Gobitis*), provoked a wave of vigilante attacks against the group. The three leading civil libertarians on the bench (Black, Douglas, and Murphy) voted with the majority but soon had second thoughts and reversed themselves in a second case. In *West Virginia v. Barnette* (1943)the Court upheld an individual's right to obey his or her conscience in the face of a government regulation. In one of the most eloquent statements of the meaning of the Bill of Rights, and with obvious reference to the totalitarian regimes around the world, Justice Robert Jackson wrote, "If there is any fixed star in our constitutional constellation, it is that no official, high or petty, can prescribe what is orthodox in politics, nationalism, religion, or other matters of opinion or force citizens to confess by word or act their faith therein."[119]

Although the Roosevelt Court transformed American law and life, FDR seemed not to notice. He never expressed his approval or disapproval of the major cases affirming new constitutional rights. The legacy of his appointees continued for years after his death. In the historic *Brown v. Board of Education* (1954) decision outlawing the principle of "separate but equal," five of the nine justices were his appointees.

America transformed: The emerging rights culture

The Supreme Court's new sympathy for political and civil rights did not arise in a social and political vacuum. The Roosevelt years witnessed the first appearance of a "rights culture" in America, the pervasive if often only vaguely understood sense of entitlement to certain freedoms. In the 1960s and 1970s, that culture became deeply embedded in American society.[120]

The rise of totalitarianism in the late 1930s and 1940s, as we have already seen, profoundly heightened public consciousness about the importance of constitutional rights in protecting powerless groups and unpopular ideas. The rise of Nazi anti-semitism forced Americans to confront the ugly reality of race discrimination at home. Many liberals and leftists were profoundly disillusioned by the Stalinist repression in the Soviet Union, and particularly the bizarre spectacle of the Moscow trials (1936–8), where former Bolshevik leaders "confessed" their crimes and were executed. These frightening events fostered the concept of totalitarianism and the recognition that repressive regimes could

118 Covington quoted in Henderson, "The Jehovah's Witnesses and Their Plan to Expand First Amendment Freedoms," 818. Walker, *In Defense of American Liberties*, pp. 111–12.

119 *Minersville v. Gobitis*, 310 U.S. 586 (1940). The courts consistently misspelled the family name of Gobitas as Gobitis. Peters, *Judging Jehovah's Witnesses. West Virginia v. Barnette*, 319 U.S. 624 (1943).

120 Critique of the rights culture and its impact on American society: Mary Ann Glendon, *Rights Talk: The Impoverishment of Political Discourse* (New York: Free Press, 1991). A rebuttal is Samuel Walker, *The Rights Revolution: Rights and Community in Modern America* (New York: Oxford University Press, 1998).

be ideologically left-wing or right-wing. This in turn led many Americans to discover a new appreciation of the unique strengths of American constitutional democracy, and in particular the protections the Bill of Rights provided for political dissidents and racial and ethnic minorities. Many American leftists who had previously sneered at constitutional rights as a "bourgeoise" sham now saw that they had real meaning. Some conservatives, meanwhile, came to understand that the American way included constitutional protection of individual rights as well as the free enterprise system.[121]

The dramatic contrast between the 150th anniversaries of the Constitution in 1937 and the Bill of Rights in 1941 signaled the change in public attitudes. The Sesquicentennial of the Constitution was a very muted event. The political crisis over the Supreme Court and the New Deal left many Americans uncertain about what exactly they should celebrate. (The historian Eric Foner points out that the 50th and 100th anniversaries in 1841 and 1891 passed with almost no public recognition.)[122] FDR marked the 1937 anniversary with a major address on the Constitution that gave only passing mention to individual rights and emphasized the power of the presidency.

Conditions changed quickly over the next four years. Across the country, established organizations took new steps to give meaning to the Bill of Rights. The American Bar Association, until then indifferent to civil liberties, established a Committee on the Bill of Rights in 1938 and joined with the ACLU in filing amicus briefs in the *Hague* case and the Jehovah's Witness flag salute case. The American Library Association, in direct response to Nazi exclusion of Jews from German libraries, drafted a Library Bill of Rights in 1939 affirming the right of all people to use libraries and of libraries to provide books without regard to their content. The American Association of University Professors (AAUP), after a struggle that had begun in 1915, finally won acceptance of its Statement on Academic Freedom, a document that remains the basic charter of academic freedom in the United States in 1940.[123]

The new rights culture included an about-face by civil libertarians on the role of government in protecting individual rights. World War I and the ensuing decade and a half taught Roger Baldwin and other ACLU leaders that government was a threat to civil liberties. Consequently, they initially regarded with great suspicion "the enormous increase of the power of the federal government under New Deal policies" and organized a December 1934 conference to express their concerns about the Roosevelt administration. By the late 1930s, however, they saw federal agencies protecting individual rights, notably the National Labor Relations Board and the Civil Liberties Unit, and found friends in key positions in the Roosevelt administration, particularly Harold Ickes and Frank Murphy. The ACLU's Roger Baldwin and others shed their traditional hostility to government and developed a new appreciation for the strengths of American political and legal institutions, particularly the Bill of Rights and the courts.[124]

121 This theme is developed in Walker, *In Defense of American Liberties*, pp. 127–34. The classic study of the change in American culture: Alfred Kazin, *On Native Grounds: An Interpretation of Modern American Prose Literature* (New York: Reynal and Hitchcock, 1942).

122 Eric Foner, *The Story of American Freedom* (New York: W. W. Norton, 1998), p. 163.

123 ABA Committee: Gerald T. Dunne, *Grenville Clark: Public Citizen* (New York: Farrar, Straus and Giroux, 1986), pp. 105–18.

124 ACLU, *Annual Report, 1934*, pp. 3–4. Conference on Civil Liberties under the New Deal, Minutes, ACLUP-MF (1996), Reel 107. Walker, *In Defense of American Liberties*, pp. 95–6, 111–12, 133–4.

PRESIDENT ROOSEVELT VERSUS THE ROOSEVELT YEARS

With the perspective of seventy decades it is clear that the Roosevelt years marked a watershed in the history of American civil liberties in innumerable ways. The role of President Franklin D. Roosevelt in this historic transformation was both complex and contradictory. Overshadowing everything else in his presidency was the Japanese-American tragedy. It is arguably the worst single violation of civil liberties in American history, and he bears personal responsibility for it. It is, of course, true that the Congress endorsed it, as did the Supreme Court (until very late, with *Endo*), and only a few Americans or organizations objected. But it could only have happened because FDR signed the order. No other president ever put American citizens in concentration camps. That episode alone calls into question his traditional ranking by historians as one of only three "great" presidents in American history. Roosevelt was indifferent to civil liberties in other areas. He did not to support the rights of working people with regard to the historic Wagner Act or in the epic battle over freedom of assembly in the *Hague* case. He remained indifferent to the cause of racial justice, in the face of a rising national civil rights movement. In several notable instances he directed serious violations of the First Amendment, and he made a number of troubling assertions of presidential power.

At the same time, however, FDR was directly or indirectly responsible for the first meaningful protections of individual rights. Most important, his appointments to the Supreme Court launched a revolution in constitutional law with a host of decisions protecting freedom of speech and assembly, religious liberty, and - tentatively - racial justice. This revolution remains an enduring part of American law and the rights of American people. While FDR deserves credit for his appointments, it is also true that he did not choose his nominees with civil liberties in mind. The credit he certainly deserves is, therefore, tinged with ambiguity. FDR and his administration also made significant contributions to civil liberties in other ways. Attorney General Frank Murphy created the forerunner of the modern Civil Rights Division in the Justice Department and launched the first efforts by the federal government to defend the rights of Americans affirmatively. FDR (albeit under duress) also established the first Committee on Fair Employment Practice to combat race discrimination in employment. His Four Freedoms speech was the first and one of the most eloquent statements about freedom of speech and religious liberty ever given by a president. It occurred at a critical moment in world history, and the images of the Four Freedoms continue to educate and inspire Americans. Finally, during World War II his administration despite some lapses did not repeat the massive suppression of freedom of speech and press that Woodrow Wilson perpetrated during the First World War.

The most ominous developments, for which Roosevelt was almost always directly responsible, lay in the broad area of national security. He personally reauthorized FBI spying in 1936, and in 1942 he personally created the Office of Strategic Services, forerunner of the CIA, introducing an era of secret and unaccountable foreign adventurism. A habit of government secrecy, born in the conditions of World War II, endured after the war and became almost reflexive. In the late 1930s he flouted the clear will of Congress expressed in the various Neutrality Acts, advancing an argument of presidential autonomy that set a dangerous precedent for future generations. What in the Vietnam War years became known as the Imperial Presidency began with FDR. Underpinning his assertions of presidential power was a view of the Constitution as a pragmatic, "flexible" document granting the president essentially unlimited authority to act in the event of a national emergency.

The ambiguities of the Roosevelt years – the growth of individual rights and the counterclaims arising from the growth of government regulation and the national security pressures in a global world environment – define the place of civil liberties in America even today.

PART II

Civil Liberties in the Cold War and Civil Rights Eras

President Harry Truman awards the Distinguish Service Medal to General Douglas MacArthur, commander in chief of United Nations forces during the Korean War, October 15, 1950, Wake Island. In April 1951 Truman would remove MacArthur from his position for statements that threatened civilian control of the armed forces.
Source: Truman Presidential Library.

5 Harry Truman

Courage and Contradictions

COLD WAR CONTRADICTIONS

This law "would put the Government of the United States in the thought control business." In uncompromising language, President Harry Truman vetoed the 1950 Internal Security Act (popularly known as the McCarran Act), which imposed severe restrictions on the Communist Party and "communist-front" organizations. Affirming a strong commitment to freedom of speech and association for unpopular views, Truman explained that parts of the law "move in the direction of suppressing opinion and belief. This would be a very dangerous course to take, and would be "a long step toward totalitarianism."[1]

Truman's September 22, 1950, veto message is the strongest defense of protecting unpopular speech by any American president. FDR's brief 1941 Four Freedoms comments, by contrast, did not touch on the difficult issues of unpopular speech. As did many members of his generation, Truman remembered the suppression of free speech during World War I. Max Lowenthal recalled that when Truman returned from World War I duty, "he was disgusted with the hysteria that prevailed in some quarters in 1919 and 1920, and I think he never forgot that."[2] Three years before the veto message, however, Truman instituted the Federal Loyalty Program, which required an investigation of all federal employees and held that mere membership in an allegedly "subversive" organization was grounds for questioning a person's loyalty. The loyalty program was a sweeping assault on freedom of belief and association and set the stage for Senator Joe McCarthy's reckless anti-communist crusade that began in 1950. President Truman never acknowledged the contradiction between the brave words in the veto message and his loyalty program's assault on civil liberties.

TRUMAN AND CIVIL LIBERTIES

A fundamental contradiction is the hallmark of President Truman's entire civil liberties record. On the one hand, he had genuine, gut-level civil libertarian instincts and often spoke passionately about the Bill of Rights. Although he never attended college (the first president not to since the nineteenth century), he had read American history extensively and revered the Constitution and the Bill of Rights. His executive order desegregating the military in 1948 is one of several bold actions that form his reputation for strong

1 Truman Veto of Internal Security Act, September 22, 1950, APP.
2 Lowenthal, OH, p. 37, HSTPL.

presidential leadership. Truman is also the only sitting president ever to pay public tribute to the ACLU, marking its twenty-fifth anniversary celebration in 1945, with a telegram praising its "outstanding service to the cause of true freedom." In addition to the loyalty program, however, his decision not to seek congressional approval for sending troops to Korea in 1950 and his seizure of the steel mills in 1952 were excessive exercises of presidential power.[3]

The contradictions in Truman's record on civil liberties reflected mainstream liberalism during the cold war. The historian Arthur Schlesinger, Jr., an adviser to Truman and later to President John F. Kennedy, defined it in his book *The Vital Center* in terms of a fighting faith ("Free society will survive ... only if enough people believe in it deeply enough to die for it.") that required vigorous support for civil rights and vigilant anti-communism at home and abroad. Both policies were designed to extend democracy in their respective spheres. As we shall see, however, Truman's domestic cold war measures involved serious breaches of constitutional principles.[4] Truman adopted both halves of the equation, and his leadership on civil rights, which jeopardized his reelection in 1948, is unmatched by other presidents in terms of political courage. Truman is today highly regarded for his strong presidential leadership and largely for that reason is now ranked among the seven or eight "near-great" presidents. That strong leadership, however, involved a very mixed record on civil liberties.

ANTI-COMMUNISM AT HOME AND ABROAD

Nine fateful days in March 1947

Truman launched the cold war at home and abroad in the space of nine fateful days in March 1947. On March 12, asking Congress for emergency aid to fight communist efforts in Greece and Turkey, he announced the Truman Doctrine, the commitment to contain communist expansion around the world. That doctrine guided American foreign policy for the next half-century. In terms that echoed Woodrow Wilson's pledge to make the world safe for democracy, Truman told Congress the United States had a solemn obligation to "help free peoples to maintain their free institutions and their national integrity" against totalitarian movements.[5] The Truman Doctrine and domestic anti-communist measures arose in response to rising tensions between the United States and the Soviet Union. On May 6, 1946, the British prime minister, Winston Churchill, announced the opening of the cold war in his famous "Iron Curtain" speech, as the Soviet Union appeared to be imposing control over Eastern European countries. A 1946 Canadian

[3] Truman's Cold War contradictions: Ellen Schrecker "'A Very Dangerous Course': Harry S. Truman and the Red Scare," in Richard S. Kirkendall, ed., *Harry's Farewell: Interpreting and Teaching the Truman Presidency* (Columbia: University of Missouri Press, 2004), pp. 227–56. Truman to ACLU: ACLU, *Annual Report 1946* (New York: Arno Press, 1970), p. 63.

[4] Arthur M. Schlesinger, Jr., *The Vital Center: The Politics of Freedom* (Boston: Houghton Mifflin, 1949), p. 245.

[5] Address of the President of the United States: Recommendation for Assistance to Greece and Turkey, March 12, 1947, APP. Haynes Johnson, *The Age of Anxiety: McCarthyism to Terrorism*. Pbk. ed. (Orlando, FL: Harcourt Books, 2006), p. 117. David Caute, *The Great Fear: The Anti-Communist Purge under Truman and Eisenhower* (New York: Touchstone Books, 1979). Stanley I. Kutler, *The American Inquisition: Justice and Injustice in the Cold War* (New York: Hill & Wang, 1982). A conservative defense of domestic anti-Communism: Richard Gid Powers, *Not without Honor: The History of American Anti-Communism* (New York: Free Press, 1995).

report on communist espionage, meanwhile, included allegations by the Russian informant Igor Gouzenko of a Soviet spy operation in the United States.

Fighting communism around the world led to another fateful step in summer 1947 when Congress passed the National Security Act establishing the Central Intelligence Agency. A cloak of secrecy, justified by the rubric of national security that went unchallenged, kept the CIA free of any scrutiny by the news media until the 1960s or meaningful congressional oversight until the 1970s. The result was a shameful record of dubious secret activities, including subverting elections and overthrowing governments in other countries. Under Truman, the agency immediately spent an estimated $1 million secretly supporting non-communist political parties in the 1948 Italian elections.

The Truman Doctrine set the United States on a path that led to innumerable civil liberties violations over the following decades: a reflexive habit of secrecy, questionable and often illegal actions overseas, unwarranted claims of presidential power, and violations of freedom of speech and association at home. And this list does not include many dubious foreign policy adventures. It all began in earnest with President Truman, and with complete justification his secretary of state, Dean Acheson, titled his memoirs *Present at the Creation*.[6]

Domestic politics were a major factor behind Truman's aggressive anti-communist polices. Republicans captured control of both houses of Congress in 1946, for the first time since 1928. After being out of power for eighteen long years, the GOP was eager to roll back the New Deal and found a powerful weapon in charging communist influence in Truman's administration. With his approval rating down to 32 percent, Truman moved to preempt the communist issue. Just two weeks after the disastrous 1946 elections, he created the Temporary Commission on Employee Loyalty, and its report became the basis for the Federal Loyalty Program four months later. In the run-up to the 1948 campaign, the White House adviser Clark Clifford noted that Truman "adroitly" stole the Republicans' "thunder" on the communist issue through the loyalty program.[7]

The loyalty program: Guilt by association as national policy

Nine days after announcing the Truman Doctrine, President Truman turned to the issue of communism at home and declared that the presence of any disloyal or subversive person in government employment "constitutes a threat to our democratic processes." For that reason, he announced on March 21 that he was issuing Executive Order 9835 creating the Federal Loyalty Program, which required "complete and unswerving loyalty" to the United States.[8]

The fatal civil liberties flaw in the Federal Loyalty Program was the principle of guilt by association. Truman's executive order specified that "sympathetic association" with alleged subversive groups or individuals was cause for doubt about a federal employee's loyalty. This included "membership in, affiliation with or sympathetic association"

6 Dean Acheson, *Present at the Creation: My Years in the State Department* (New York: W. W. Norton, 1969).

7 Executive Order 9806, Establishing the President's Temporary Commission on Employee Loyalty, November 25, 1946, APP. "President Urges Purge of Disloyal from U.S. Posts," *NYT*, November 26, 1946. Schrecker, "'A Very Dangerous Course,'" p. 232. Clifford to Truman, November 19, 1947, Clifford Papers, Political File, HSTPL.

8 Executive Order 9835 – Prescribing Procedures for the Administration of an Employees Loyalty Program in the Executive Branch of the Government, March 21, 1947, APP. "FBI Will Aid Study," *NYT*, March 23, 1947.

with any group "designated by the Attorney General as totalitarian, fascist, communist, or subversive," or advocating the violent overthrow of the government.[9] Guilt by association with alleged radicals was nothing new in American politics. It had been the basis of the assaults on freedom of speech and press during World War I, was a staple of anti-communist movements in the 1920s, and was the operating principle of the House Un-American Activities Committee, created in 1938. The FBI director, J. Edgar Hoover, also regarded association with radicalism -including civil rights - as a pretext for suspicion about a person's loyalty. Truman, however, made it the official policy of the federal government.

In practice, the loyalty program allowed questioning the loyalty of someone who had supported the anti-Fascist Republican side in the Spanish Civil War (1936–9), because communists also supported it, or had signed a petition by a left-wing group aiding the Scottsboro defendants in 1935 (which is to say, supported racial justice through the "wrong" organization). It made no difference how brief or how far in the past such activities occurred, or what the person's political views were in 1947. The taint was permanent.[10]

Sensitive to criticisms from civil libertarians, Truman claimed his loyalty program had sufficient due process protections to prevent any violations of individual rights. Employees charged with being disloyal had a right to appear before a loyalty board in each federal agency, to have a lawyer or representative, and to present evidence in the form of witnesses or affidavits. In practice these procedures were meaningless. The FBI conducted background investigations of government employees but did not have to disclose the names of its confidential informants, thereby preventing an accused employee from cross-examining his or her accusers. The process fostered the development of informants with bad motives: former communists eager to prove their loyalty and people with old personal and political grudges.

Executive Order 9835 also directed the attorney general to create a list of subversive organizations, which immediately became an official blacklist. The initial Attorney General's List of ninety-three organizations included assurances about freedom of association, stating that membership in a listed organization was to be "simply one piece of evidence" to be considered, and that " 'guilt by association' has never been one of the principles of our American jurisprudence." In the fevered atmosphere of the cold war, however, these were empty promises. If the Communist Party advocated a federal fair employment practices committee (as it did), someone who also advocated one could be suspect for following the Communist Party "line." Segregationists cited the Communist Party's strong position on racial justice to discredit all civil rights activists. Earlier precedents, such as Attorney General Francis Biddle's 1942 list of subversive organizations

9 Executive Order 9835, APP.

10 Eleanor Bontecou, *The Federal Loyalty-Security Program* (Ithaca, NY: Cornell University Press, 1953). Bontecou was one of the first staff members of the Justice Department's Civil Liberties Unit in 1939 (see Chapter 4 of this book). Robert Justin Goldstein, "Prelude to McCarthyism: The Making of a Blacklist," *Prologue* 38 (Fall 2006). Online at www.archives.gov/publications/prologue/fall/. Truman's loyalty program: Ralph S. Brown, *Loyalty and Security: Employment Tests in the United States* (New Haven, CT: Yale University Press, 1958). Alan L. Harper, *The Politics of Loyalty: The White House and the Communist Issue, 1946–1952* (Westport, CT: Greenwood, 1969). Francis H. Thompson, *The Frustration of Politics: Truman, Congress, and the Loyalty Issue, 1945–1953* (Rutherford, NJ: Fairleigh Dickinson University Press, 1979). Selma R. Williams, *Red-listed: Haunted by the Washington Witch Hunt* (Reading, MA: Addison-Wesley, 1993).

and President Roosevelt's 1943 loyalty review committee, were far more limited than Truman's program, which mandated a review of every federal employee.[11]

The Attorney General's List, moreover, encouraged other "lists," and the process of guilt by association ballooned. HUAC published its own *Guide to Subversive Organizations* in 1957, naming far more organizations than the Attorney General's List, and the California Legislature's Tenney Committee published several lists of its own. Private communist hunters also got into the business. The most aggressive group was American Business Consultants, Inc., led by former FBI agents, who successfully blacklisted alleged communists from the news and entertainment media. Its 1950 report, *Red Channels*, listed 151 actors, writers, musicians, and journalists, including the composer and conductor Leonard Bernstein (for signing a Progressive Party petition opposing HUAC in 1949), the jazz singer Lena Horne (for supporting the left-wing Civil Rights Congress), and the film director Orson Welles (for speaking at a conference sponsored by the National Council of American-Soviet Friendship).[12]

THE LOYALTY PROGRAM IN OPERATION

The ACLU immediately expressed "grave concern" about Truman's loyalty program, finding it "lacking in sufficient safeguards necessary to the protection of individuals," and thus "a menace to civil liberties." Conceding the government's "proper interest" in ensuring the loyalty of its employees, it argued that "the decisive test should be activity in a blacklisted organization, and not mere membership." The ACLU wrote to Attorney General Tom Clark demanding a right to confront and cross-examine accusers, a statute of limitations on past political activity, and clear definitions of "subversion," "disloyalty," and "totalitarian." ACLU leaders met with him in Washington, but he rejected their recommendations. (Later, as a Truman appointee to the Supreme Court, Justice Clark upheld all anti-communist measures.)[13]

The Loyalty Program had a devastating impact, creating an atmosphere of suspicion and fear among federal employees. By 1958, a total of 4,756,705 employees had been reviewed, 26,236 referred to departmental loyalty boards for review, and 560 removed or denied employment. Meanwhile, 6,828 had resigned or retired, many realizing they would never keep their jobs because of past associations. The ACLU offered to represent accused employees, but only a few chose to contest the allegations. Invoking the process only called attention to yourself, hindering your chances of finding another job.

11 Original Attorney General's List: *F. Reg, 13*, no. 56 (March 20, 1948): 1471–3. Robert Justin Goldstein, *American Blacklist: The Attorney General's List of Subversive Organizations* (Lawrence: University of Kansas Press, 2008). Executive Order 9300 on Subversive Activities by Federal Employees, February 5, 1943, APP. *Cong. Rec.*, 77th Cong., 2nd Sess., V. 88 - Part 6, September 24, 1942, pp. 7441–58.

12 U.S. House of Representatives, Committee on Un-American Activities, *Guide to Subversive Organizations* (Washington, DC: Government Printing Office, 1961). Edward L. Barrett, *The California Tenney Committee: Legislative Investigation of Subversive Activities in California* (Ithaca, NY: Cornell University Press, 1951). American Business Consultants, *Red Channels: The Report of Communist Influence in Radio and Television* (New York: Counterattack, 1950), pp. 3–4. Excerpts at: www.authentichistory.com/images/1950s/red_channels/redchannels.html. Two reports highly critical of Red Channels are Merle Miller, *The Judges and the Judged* (Garden City, NY: Doubleday, 1952), sponsored by the ACLU, and a broader examination of blacklisting, John Cogley, *Report on Blacklisting*, 2 Vols. (New York: Fund for the Republic, 1956).

13 ACLU Board, Minutes, March 24, 1947, April 7, 1947, April 14, 1947, ACLUP-MF (1977), Reel 10. ACLU, *Post-War Hysteria* (New York: ACLU, June 1947), ibid., Reel 93. Tom Clark and the Supreme Court "Red Monday" decisions: Chapter 6 of this book.

Eleanor Roosevelt was so depressed about the program that in her August 31, 1948, newspaper column she wrote that she would advise young men against taking jobs with the government.[14]

The fear of subversion expanded in many different areas. Civil rights advocacy was smeared by segregationists because leftists were involved. In 1950, moreover, a panic over homosexuals in government swept Washington, in what one historian has called the "lavender panic." The Nebraska senator Kenneth Wherry, one of Senator Joe McCarthy's most passionate followers, told the Senate in 1950 there were thirty-five homosexuals in the federal government. Even worse, he claimed, the Soviet premier, Joseph Stalin, had a complete list of every homosexual in the world (which he allegedly had received from Hitler!) and could blackmail federal employees into betraying their country. The figure of thirty-five hundred was actually a wild guess by a vice officer in the Washington, D.C., Police Department. President Eisenhower formalized the purge of homosexuals in April 1953 when he revised the loyalty program to include the more inclusive criterion of "any criminal, infamous, dishonest, immoral, or notoriously disgraceful conduct... [or] sexual perversion."[15]

Believing himself a strong civil libertarian, Truman was acutely sensitive to criticisms about the loyalty program. Eight months after launching it, he declared that agency loyalty boards "are definitely not 'kangaroo' courts." Ignoring the facts, he claimed that people were not being judged disloyal simply because they "at any time happened to belong to one these organizations" on the attorney general's list. In fact, he did not know how the program operated. The civil liberties attorney Joseph Rauh confronted him in 1951 and gave him "case after case" in which there were violations of due process. Truman did not know that people could not confront FBI informants who were their accusers. At one point he turned to two aides and asked, incredulously, "is this stuff going on?" To the end of his life, he remained unrepentant. In his *Memoirs* he acknowledged some procedural problems, but he never conceded the fundamental flaws in the program, particularly that it sanctioned guilt by association. Nor did he ever reflect on how the program contradicted the principles he expressed so forcefully in his veto of the McCarran Act.[16]

Creating the loyalty program undoubtedly helped Truman win reelection in 1948 by deflecting Republican attacks about communists in government. The White House adviser Clark Clifford pointed out in late 1947 that the program "adroitly stole" the Republicans' "thunder." In truth, many factors contributed to Truman's stunning upset victory. The GOP candidate Tom Dewey did not make communists in government a major issue in the campaign, and many overconfident Republicans stayed home on election day.[17] At the same time, however, the program hoisted Truman on his own petard. Once he conceded that there were disloyal employees in the government, rabid anti-communists

[14] Brown, *Loyalty and Security: Employment Tests in America.* Bontecou, *The Federal Loyalty-Security Program.* Eleanor Roosevelt, *My Day*, August 31, 1948, in Allida M. Black, ed. *The Papers of Eleanor Roosevelt,* V. 1 (Detroit: Thomson Gale, 2007), p. 895.

[15] Anne Braden, *HUAC: Bulwark of Segregation* (New York: National Committee to Abolish the House UnAmerican Activities Committee, 1963). "Inquiry by Senate on Perverts Asked," *NYT*, May 20, 1950. Executive Order 10450 - Security Requirements for Government Employment, April 277, 1953, APP.

[16] Statement by the President on the Government's Employee Loyalty Program, November 14, 1947, APP. "Federal Loyalty Check a Continuing Operation," *NYT*, July 29, 1951. Rauh, OH, HSTPL. Harry S. Truman, *Memoirs*, V. 2, *Years of Trial and Hope, 1946–1952.* Pbk. ed. (New York: Signet, 1965); on the loyalty program, pp, 309–35.

[17] Clifford to Truman, November 19, 1947, Clifford Papers, Political File, HSTPL. Zachary Karabell, *The Last Campaign: How Harry Truman Won the 1948 Election* (New York: Knopf, 2000).

relentlessly attacked him for failing to remove them. Rumor, innuendo, and reckless charges about "loyalty" soon dominated American politics. Senator Joe McCarthy was simply the most aggressive practitioner of what by then had become the standard anti-communist game.

As with Roosevelt's evacuation and internment of the Japanese Americans, it is fair to ask whether an alternative approach was possible, one that would have reasonably protected national security while respecting individual rights. An alternative based on individual suspicion about illegal conduct, particularly espionage, was certainly possible. Truman could have justified it with the same affirmation of civil liberties that he used in his 1950 veto of the McCarran Act. Would it have worked? We can never know. We do know, however, that he did not try. We do know that he failed at a critical moment, just as Roosevelt failed with the Japanese Americans, to use the bully pulpit of the presidency to establish a more limited loyalty program that respected civil liberties values. We also know that Truman's program failed to satisfy rabid anti-communists and only encouraged the cold war witch hunt. Some historians argue that his program set the stage for McCarthy, who simply took the principle of guilt by association to utterly unreasonable extremes.[18]

ATTACKING THE COMMUNIST PARTY AND "DANGEROUS" IDEAS

On July 20, 1948, just a week after the Democrats renominated Truman for president, the Justice Department arrested Eugene Dennis and eleven other leaders of the American Communist Party for violating the Smith Act. Although Attorney General Tom Clark denied any political motive, the timing seems hardly accidental. It represented one-half of Truman's election strategy of vigorous anti-communism and strong support for civil rights. A week after the Communist arrests, he issued Executive Order 9981 ending racial segregation in the armed services. The events of July 1948 epitomized the civil liberties contradictions in Truman's commitment to the "vital center" of civil rights and anti-communism.[19]

The arrest of the top Communists set the stage for a historic confrontation over the constitutionality of the 1940 Smith Act. The trial began on January 17, 1949, and became a stormy nine-month affair, with confrontations that distracted attention from the First Amendment issues at stake. A huge detail of four hundred New York City police officers surrounded the Foley Square courthouse in lower Manhattan that morning, and most remained throughout the trial. The Communist Party, then in one of its militant phases, organized noisy pickets outside. Inside, the party's attorneys engaged in belligerent courtroom tactics challenging both the prosecution's case and the judge on numerous points. Judge Harold Medina took it personally and ruled against virtually every objection, in some instances displaying clear bias against the defendants. President Truman, meanwhile, stoked national prejudice by referring to the defendants as "traitors" at a March press conference.[20]

18 Robert J. Donovan, *Tumultuous Years: The Presidency of Harry S. Truman, 1949–1953* (New York: W. W. Norton, 1982), pp. 163, 170. That Truman set the stage for McCarthyism: Athan Theoharis, *Seeds of Repression* (Chicago: Quadrangle Books, 1971).

19 "Bail Set at $5,000," *NYT*, July 21, 1948. Clark, OH, pp. 187–8, HSTPL. Schlesinger, Jr., *The Vital Center*.

20 Peter L. Steinberg, *The Great 'Red Menace': United States Prosecution of American Communists, 1947–1952* (Westport, CT: Greenwood Press, 1984). Samuel Walker, *In Defense of American Liberties: A History of the ACLU* (New York: Oxford, 1990), pp. 185–8. The President's News Conference of March 3, 1949, APP.

The government's case was very tenuous, relying heavily on Marxist literature rather than the defendants' actions. Prosecutors cited no specific acts of espionage or treason, and the heart of its case involved the defendants' ideas and associations. The jury took little more than eight hours to convict, and Judge Medina sentenced the Communist Party leaders to five years in prison and ten thousand dollars in fines. In a historic decision (*Dennis v. United States*, 1951), the Supreme Court upheld the constitutionality of the Smith Act by a 6–2 vote. Writing for the majority, Chief Justice Fred M. Vinson rejected the idea that the Smith Act punished the discussion of ideas, holding that the defendants had gone beyond mere discussion of Marxism and revolution. The heart of the Court's opinion was an interpretation of the clear and present danger test formulated by Judge Learned Hand of the Second Circuit Court of Appeals. "In each case," Hand wrote, courts "must ask whether the gravity of the 'evil,' discounted by its improbability, justifies such invasion of free speech as is necessary to avoid the danger." Hand's opinion was filled with irony. In the early months of World War I, he affirmed the First Amendment rights of the *Masses* magazine, in an eloquent and lonely defense of freedom of the press. In the intervening three decades, however, the man regarded as one of the greatest judges in American history had moved in a conservative direction, and he now delivered a terrible blow to First Amendment freedoms.[21] Truman's appointees to the Supreme Court, all of whom are regarded as among the weakest ever to serve on the Court, comprised three of the six majority votes in *Dennis*.

Hugo Black and William O. Douglas, the two remaining strong civil libertarians on the Court, issued passionate dissents. Black saw a pure violation of the First Amendment, finding no overt acts related to any "attempt to overthrow the Government." The entire case was "a virulent form of prior censorship of speech and press, which I believe the First Amendment forbids." Douglas added, "we deal here with speech alone, not with speech plus acts of sabotage or unlawful conduct." Black looked to the future: "There is hope, however, that, in calmer times, when present pressures, passions and fears subside, this or some later Court will restore the First Amendment liberties to the high preferred place where they belong in a free society." The hope of "calmer times" ahead proved to be prophetic. The furies of the cold war eventually waned, and on June 17, 1957, famously labeled "Red Monday," the Supreme Court began to curtail anti-communist measures.[22]

The State Department issued an emergency "stop notice" to all American ports in July 1950 to prevent the noted African-American singer Paul Robeson from leaving the country. The FBI sent out an "urgent" cable directing agents to locate him. The Korean War had just begun, and as a prominent left-wing critic of American foreign policy, Robeson was now persona non grata in his own country. When his lawyer asked Secretary of State Dean Acheson for an explanation, Acheson replied that Robeson's travel abroad would be "contrary to the best interests of the United States."[23]

The Truman administration's anti-communist campaign included a more aggressive effort to restrict the flow of ideas in and out of the country than had been the case in the 1920s. Robeson was only one of many prominent people to be denied a passport or

21 *Dennis v. United States*, 341 U.S. 494 (1951). *Masses v. Patten*, 244 F. 535 (S.D. N.Y., 1917).

22 *Dennis v. United States*, 341 U.S. 494 (1951).

23 FBI Teletype, From Director, "Urgent," July [not clear], 1950, Robeson File, FBI ERR. Martin Bauml Duberman, *Paul Robeson*. Pbk. ed. (London: Pan Books, 1991), p. 389. "U.S. Cancels Robeson's Passport after He Refuses to Surrender It," *NYT*, August 4, 1950.

visa. His leftist sympathies were well known. At a November 1949 banquet he greeted Soviet Foreign Minister Andrei Vishinsky and denounced President Truman as an "imperialist wolf." His scheduled performance in Peekskill, New York, on August 27, 1949 was cancelled because of a riot by anti-communist vigilantes who pelted twenty thousand concert goers with rocks and clubs. Blacklisted at home and unable to travel overseas to perform, Robeson saw his once flourishing career ruined.[24]

For fifty years, two women directed the Passport Division's repressive policies regarding passports (at least until the Supreme Court began to rein in the office in the late 1950s). Ruth Shipley headed the division from 1927 to 1955 and was succeeded by Frances G. Knight, who served until 1977. So complete and arbitrary was their half-century of rule that the historian Stanley Kutler labeled it "the Queendom of Passports." President Roosevelt had given the State Department full discretion over passports in 1938, and the 1950 McCarran Act formally barred issuing of passports to communists or members of communist-front organizations.[25]

The ACLU challenged the Passport Division's practices, arguing that in the absence of special circumstances "all American citizens should enjoy freedom to travel." State Department policies had "no clearly defined criteria for the denial of passports," and the ACLU recommended new and clearer procedures.[26] The demand fell on deaf ears in the Truman administration, and reform did not occur until the Supreme Court intervened in the late 1950s.

TRUMAN, J. EDGAR HOOVER, AND THE FBI

Just eleven days after Truman took office in April 1945, the FBI director, J. Edgar Hoover, sent him a memo detailing discussions among some Democrats who were unhappy with him as president. Truman read the material "with much interest," and said he would be interested in "future communications." He later asked the bureau to check White House staff he suspected of being disloyal - to him, that is, not to the nation. The FBI willingly complied and began spying on Thomas Corcoran, a former FDR adviser, and some other administration officials Truman distrusted. Transcripts of the recorded conversations between 1945 and 1946, filled with meaningless political talk, are now in the Truman Library and fill an astonishing five archival boxes. Truman never acted on them, but they represent the longest sustained misuse of the FBI against a single target for political purposes by any president. In short, Truman used the FBI for political chores, just as many other presidents did.[27] Hoover complied because he had learned under Roosevelt that he could win favor with presidents through such errands.

[24] Peekskill: Howard Fast, *Being Red* (Boston: Houghton Mifflin, 1990).

[25] Kutler, *The American Inquisition: Justice and Injustice in the Cold War*, Ch. 4, "Government by Discretion: The Queendom of Passports," pp. 89–117.

[26] ACLU, *Report by the American Civil Liberties Union on the Issuance of Passports* (New York: ACLU, 1952), ACLUP-MF (1977), Reel 94. Executive Order 7856 - Rules Governing the Granting and Issuing of Passports in the United States, March 31, 1938, APP.

[27] Corcoran materials: Summaries of Conversations Files, President's Secretary's Files, HSTPL. Selection in *The Official and Confidential File of J. Edgar Hoover*. MF ed. (Wilmington, DE: Scholarly Resources, 1988), Reel 3. Kai Bird and Max Holland, "The Tapping of 'Tommy the Cork,'" *The Nation*, February 8, 1986. Memos and commentary on Truman's abuses of the FBI: Athan Theoharis, *From the Secret Files of J. Edgar Hoover* (Chicago: Ivan R. Dee, 1991), pp. 202–15.

Truman's relationship with Hoover began well. He approved FBI wiretapping in July 1946, writing, "I concur" on a memo from Attorney General Clark requesting continuation of President Roosevelt's authorization of "listening devices" to investigate "subversive activities." It is not clear whether he understood that "listening devices" included "bugs" in homes and offices that were far more intrusive that wiretaps. In February 1952, however, Attorney General J. Howard McGrath informed Hoover that while he approved of wiretapping generally, he "cannot authorize" it where it involves "*a trespass*" (italics in original). Relations between Truman and the FBI soon soured, however, and in late 1946 Hoover concluded that the president would not root out communists in his administration. The break occurred in testimony before HUAC on March 26, 1947, where Hoover presented an alarmist picture of communist subversion, without once commenting favorably on Truman's new loyalty program. He then stepped up the bureau's "educational" program, which included leaking to HUAC and others confidential FBI information unfavorable to the administration.[28]

Illegal FBI wiretapping erupted into an embarrassing public controversy in the 1949–50 trials of Judith Coplon, a State Department official charged with spying for the Soviet Union. Her case became a national soap opera, livened by a mix of espionage, a mysterious love affair, and revelations of FBI misconduct. Coplon's first conviction was overturned when it was disclosed that the FBI had listened to her conversations with her attorney, Leonard Boudin. A second conviction was also overturned because of bureau misconduct. The case provided a glimpse into the hidden world of FBI eavesdropping, momentarily tarnishing the bureau's reputation and creating rumors of Hoover's possible removal.[29]

President Truman was reportedly furious over the Coplon revelations, but only because they allowed Coplon to go free and not because FBI actions were illegal. The crisis passed, however, and Truman neither fired Hoover nor imposed tighter controls over FBI investigations. Attorney General Tom Clark was an ardent anti-communist, and not about to question the bureau. Truman himself, under relentless attack for allegedly harboring communists, did not have the political capital to take on the now solidly entrenched FBI director.

An incident involving Attorney General Clark revealed a blind spot about FBI misconduct shared by almost all officials in the cold war. A Senate staff member inadvertently discovered a secret FBI file with derogatory information about Clark. When he saw the file, Clark found it "really outrageous," including gossip from his years in private practice that had nothing to do with possible criminal activity. When he confronted Hoover about it, the FBI director blandly claimed ignorance and said that someone else must have been responsible. Clark accepted this explanation at face value, later saying, "I don't think that he would deliberately keep a file like that."[30] Until the post-Watergate revelations about FBI misconduct (discussed in Chapter Ten), top government officials

[28] Clark to Truman, July 17, 1946; McGrath to Hoover, February 26, 1952, in Theoharis, ed., *From the Secret Files*, pp. 135, 137. "FBI Head Brands Communist Party a 'Fifth Column,'" *NYT*, March 27, 1947.

[29] Marcia Mitchell and Thomas Mitchell, *The Spy Who Seduced America: Lies and Betrayal in the Heat of the Cold War – the Judith Coplon Story* (Montpelier, VT: Invisible Cities Press, 2002). Mickie Edwardson, "James Lawrence Fly, the FBI, and Wiretappings," *The Historian 61* (Winter 1999): 361–81.

[30] The Clark material had been accidentally included in materials the Bureau let the staff member examine. Clark, OH, pp. 68–9, 112–20, HSTPL.

refused to question Hoover and his methods, even when evidence of misconduct came to their attention.

The loyalty program also introduced a collateral problem of executive privilege, in this initial instance involving FBI files. Anti-communists in Congress, hoping to embarrass Truman, demanded to see bureau files on certain federal employees. Properly sensitive to the fact that the so-called raw FBI files included unverified allegations, Truman denied their requests. The Justice Department drafted a ninety-five-page memo, citing historical precedent and case law, making the extreme argument that the president has "exclusive and illimitable power" to control subordinates, a power that could not be contravened by either Congress or the courts. Three days later, on March 18, 1948, Truman sent the heads of all federal agencies a memo declaring that FBI investigative files were strictly "confidential." The refusal to turn over files inevitably inflamed his critics, who now accused the administration of a cover-up. The White House aide Stephen Spingarn told Congress the administration would readily cooperate with any "responsible" committee, a comment that was seen as a direct slap at HUAC. This episode proved to be the beginning of a long struggle over what came to be called executive privilege. (Interestingly, a young congressman named Richard Nixon sharply criticized Truman for his refusal to turn over the information in question to Congress. When he was president, Nixon's own refusal led to the first Supreme Court decision on executive privilege, and his own resignation as president.)[31]

THE RISE OF GOVERNMENT SECRECY – AND CHALLENGES

In perhaps the single most astonishing incident of censorship by the federal government in American history, the Atomic Energy Commission (AEC) in March 1950 seized and burned all three thousand copies of the April issue of *Scientific American*, which contained an article by the noted physicist Hans Bethe on the hydrogen bomb. The AEC regarded some of the information as classified and asked the editor, Gerard Piel, to delete those sections. The 1946 Atomic Energy Act gave the AEC almost unlimited control over information related to nuclear energy, with the result that much scientific information was "born secret." The contested material in the *Scientific American* represented about half of the article, however, and the issue had already gone to the printer. Federal agents then seized all copies and burned them.[32]

Remarkably, the incident generated little outrage. The editor Piel, the ACLU, and the Federation of American Scientists protested, but few others cared, and it was quickly forgotten. Such was the political climate in 1950, with Joe McCarthy riding high, news of a Soviet H-bomb, and continued allegations of Soviet spying, that few were willing to question burning a prestigious scientific magazine in the name of national security.[33]

[31] Directive on the Need for Maintaining the Confidential Status of Employee Loyalty Records March 15, 1948 [Signed on March 13; issued on March 15], APP. Department of Justice, Is a Congressional Committee Entitled to Demand and Receive Information and Papers from the President and the Heads of Departments Which They Deem Confidential, In the Public Interest? Elsey Papers, Box 90, HSTPL. Truman, *Memoirs*, V. 2, pp. 322–3. Truman, Memorandum to All Officers and Employees in the Executive Branch of Government, March 18, 1948, Elsey Papers, Box 68. Thompson, *The Frustration of Politics*, pp. 69–102. Nixon: Rozell, *Executive Privilege*. 3rd ed., pp. 55–6.

[32] "U.S. Censors H-Bomb Data: 3,000 Magazine Copies Burnt," *NYT*, April 1, 1950. Walker, *In Defense of American Liberties*, pp. 197–8.

[33] "Scientists Assail Ban on Discussion," *NYT*, May 1, 1950.

The *Scientific American* episode highlighted the ominous growth of government secrecy. In 1948, Basil Walters of the Knight newspaper chain and chair of the Freedom of World Information Committee of the American Society of Newspaper Editors (ASNE) warned that the public's right to know was disappearing, almost by default. During World War II, the federal government understandably enveloped many activities in secrecy, but the practice became routine after the war. The 1946 Administrative Procedure Act required federal agencies to publish their rules and regulations, but Section 3 exempted policies related to military or foreign affairs.[34] In the cold war, national security became a convenient and unchallenged rationale for declaring innumerable documents secret.

The first thorough report on the growing secrecy was Harold L. Cross's 1953 book *The People's Right to Know*, which immediately became the "bible" on the subject. Two years later the ACLU published a report with the same title by Allen Raymond. The leaders of this nascent movement had not at this point formulated a legal rationale for challenging government secrecy, however. The battle took a new and important turn on November 7, 1955, when Representative John E. Moss, a liberal Democrat from Southern California, convened the first hearings on government secrecy. Moss's dogged efforts over the next eleven years finally culminated in the historic 1966 Freedom of Information Act.[35]

MCCARTHYISM ARRIVES

American politics changed the night of February 9, 1950. The Wisconsin senator Joe McCarthy, hitherto an undistinguished member of Congress, gave a speech to the Republican Women's Club in Wheeling, West Virginia, claiming to have in his hand a list of 205 "known Communists" in the federal government. The number of names kept changing in the weeks ahead, from 205 to 57 to 81, but McCarthy had hit a raw nerve and proceeded to dominate American politics over the next four and a half years with reckless charges about the communist threat.[36]

In the tense atmosphere of early 1950, McCarthy played on the growing fears of communism. On September 23, 1949, the Soviet Union revealed it had successfully tested an atomic bomb, catching American experts by surprise. communist forces seized control of China a week later. The second sensational trial of Alger Hiss, a former State Department official accused of spying for the Soviet Union, ended with a perjury conviction on January 21, 1950. The Hiss case catapulted Richard Nixon to national prominence as a fierce anti-communist. Finally, on June 25, 1950, North Korea invaded South Korea, launching the first armed conflict of the cold war.[37]

34 Daniel Patrick Moynihan, *Secrecy: The American Experience* (New Haven, CT: Yale University Press, 1998), pp. 154, 156–8.

35 Kiyul Ulm, "The Cold War Communication Crisis: The Right to Know Movement," *J&MC Quarterly* 82 (Spring 2005): 131–47. Harold L. Cross, *The People's Right to Know: Legal Access to Public Records and Proceedings* (New York: Columbia University Press, 1953). Allen Raymond, *The People's Right to Know: A Report on Government News Suppression* (New York: ACLU, 1955), ACLUP-MF (1977), Reel 94. Herbert N. Foerstel, *Freedom of Information and the Right to Know: The Origins and Applications of the Freedom of Information Act* (Westport, CT: Greenwood Press, 1999).

36 A copy of the speech is in the *Congressional Record*, February 20, 1950. It is not clear, however, whether this and other versions represent the speech originally delivered. Several historians argue that an unprepared McCarthy borrowed the "Communists in government" theme from a speech by Congressman Richard Nixon just two weeks earlier. Nixon: *Congressional Record*, January 26, 1950, pp. 1006–8.

37 "Atom Bomb Blast in Russia Disclosed," *NYT*, September 24, 1949. McCarthy and the atmosphere of the period: David M. Oshinsky, *A Conspiracy So Immense: The World of Joe McCarthy* (New York: Free Press, 1983).

The media generally accepted McCarthy's allegations at face value, with subsequent fact checking having little impact. Under pressure to produce actual names, McCarthy on March 8 finally offered Dorothy Kenyon. She was a New York City liberal activist: a former judge, member of many liberal groups, a recent member of the United Nations Commission on the Status of Women, and a current member of the ACLU Board of Directors. There was nothing in her record that even remotely suggested subversive activities, and McCarthy's naming her was a classic case of cold war guilt by association. A March 29 *Washington Post* cartoon by Herblock contained the word "McCarthyism," introducing a new term into the American political lexicon.[38]

Two days after his Wheeling speech, McCarthy released a letter to President Truman alleging that there were fifty-seven communists working in the State Department and demanding he turn over the loyalty investigation files on all alleged security risks in the government. Truman reiterated his refusal to turn over investigative files, and McCarthy accused him of a cover-up. Truman angrily denounced McCarthy as "the best asset the Kremlin has." When asked by a reporter at his April 13 press conference whether he might have libeled McCarthy, Truman replied with a question of his own: "Do you think that is possible?" Throughout the remainder of his presidency, Truman was a fierce and unyielding critic of the Wisconsin senator. McCarthy's reckless tactics did incalculable damage to American politics, but many historians argue that Truman had sown the seeds of anti-communist hysteria with his loyalty program, which conceded the possibility of disloyal government employees. Robert J. Donovan observes that "McCarthy caught Truman partly in a trap of his own making" and simply upped the ante.[39]

The fate of Senator Margaret Chase Smith's challenge to him in spring 1950 dramatized McCarthy's enormous power in American politics. A moderate Maine Republican, Smith rose on the Senate floor on June 1 to rebuke his tactics in a declaration of conscience. Word had spread, and the gallery was crowded for the event. "Certain elements" in the Republican Party, she declared, were using "fear, bigotry, ignorance and intolerance" for "selfish political exploitation." She never mentioned McCarthy by name, but her target was nonetheless clear. Only six other Republican senators signed her declaration. McCarthy sat silently through the speech and then quickly left. The next day he dismissed Smith and her allies as "Snow White and the Six Dwarfs." Such was his power that GOP leaders promptly stripped her of two committee assignments, and four of her cosigners recanted and abandoned her. Smith's principled and courageous protest proved to be a lonely act and had no noticeable impact other than to convince people that Joe McCarthy was untouchable.[40]

38 "McCarthy Says Miss Kenyon Helped 28 Red Front Groups," *NYT*, March 9, 1950. "Dorothy Kenyon," Barbara Sicherman and Carol Hurd Green, eds., *Notable American Women: The Modern Period: A Biographical Dictionary* (Cambridge, MA: Harvard University Press, 1980), pp. 395–7. The original cartoon is in Herbert Block, *Herblock: A Cartoonist's Life* (New York: Times Books, 1998), pp. 132–5. William Safire, *The New Language of Politics: An Anecdotal Dictionary of Catchwords, Slogans, and Political Usage* (New York: Random House, 1968), pp. 253–4.

39 The President's News Conference of April 13, 1950, APP. "McCarthy Insists Truman Oust Reds," *NYT*, February 12, 1950. Robert J. Donovan, *Tumultuous Years: The Presidency of Harry S. Truman, 1949–1953* (New York: W. W. Norton, 1982), pp. 163, 170. Theoharis, *Seeds of Repression*.

40 "Seven GOP Senators Decry 'Smear' Tactics of McCarthy," *NYT*, June 2, 1950. Margaret Chase Smith, *Declaration of Conscience* (New York: Doubleday, 1972); the Declaration is on pp. 17–18. Frank Graham, Jr., *Margaret Chase Smith: Woman of Courage* (New York: John Day, 1964), pp. 78–80. Janann Sherman, *No Place for a Woman: A Life of Senator Margaret Chase Smith* (New Brunswick, NJ: Rutgers University Press, 2000), pp. 111–14.

During McCarthy's heyday from February 1950 through December 1954, five people who served as president had the opportunity to speak out about him. Dwight Eisenhower loathed the man and his tactics but refused to criticize him by name. Senator John F. Kennedy kept quiet and did not vote on the Senate's censure resolution. Senator Lyndon Johnson, Democratic Party minority leader in 1954, freely told people that taking on McCarthy was a losing battle for Democrats and kept quiet. Vice President Richard Nixon thought McCarthy's tactics ill advised but never publicly criticized him. There is no record that Gerald Ford, elected to Congress in 1948, ever criticized McCarthy or his tactics. In short, among those political figures in the early 1950s who served as president, only Harry Truman publicly stood up against Joe McCarthy.[41]

Truman vetoes the 1950 McCarran Act

McCarthy's dramatic rise to prominence, along with the Korean War, fueled the drive for more anti-communist legislation, and in fall 1950 Congress passed the Internal Security Act (popularly known as the McCarran Act). The law imposed a series of penalties on communist, communist-action, and communist-front organizations. A communist-front organization was one whose leaders were also "active in any Communist-action organization," or more consequentially in which its official positions "do not deviate from those of any Communist-action organization." This inevitably included some civil rights and peace groups. Organizations and their members were required to register with the new Subversive Activities Control Board (SACB). Organizations were denied tax-exempt status, while individual members were ineligible for passports and were barred from holding nonelective public office. Liberal Democrats in the Senate, led by Hubert Humphrey, sponsored Title II of the law, the Emergency Detention Act, authorizing the government to detain anyone suspected of espionage or sabotage or conspiring to commit those acts when the president had declared a national emergency.[42]

Truman courageously vetoed the McCarran Act, delivering the strongest statement ever made by a president on protecting unpopular speech. The White House aide George Elsey quoted him as declaring in private in his characteristic blunt style, "We've got to protect the Bill of Rights.... Jesus Christ, that's what we're fighting for." Congress, however, immediately overrode the veto by overwhelming majorities of 57–10 in the Senate and 286–48 in the House. The *New York Times* reported that the FBI stood ready to arrest as many as twelve thousand subversives, and fear of a mass roundup spread throughout the American Left.[43]

A public opinion poll on the Fourth of July 1951 revealed the state of fear among ordinary Americans. An enterprising reporter in Madison, Wisconsin, asked 112 people to sign a petition that contained, without identifying the source, excerpts from the Declaration of Independence and the Bill of Rights. Only one person in the famously liberal university

41 See the chapters on each of the presidents in this book. Johnson: Robert A. Caro, *The Years of Lyndon Johnson. V. 3, Master of the Senate.* Pbk ed. (New York: Random House, 2003, p. 547.

42 Michael J. Ybarra, *Washington Gone Crazy: Senator Pat McCarran and the Great American Communist Hunt* (Hanover, NH: Steerforth Press, 2004). ACLU, The Internal Security Act of 1950, November 27, 1950, ACLUP-MF (1977), Reel 93. Louis Fisher, *Detention of U.S. Citizens* (Washington, DC: Congressional Reference Service, April 28, 2005).

43 Truman Veto of Internal Security Act, September 22, 1950, APP. George McKee Elsey, *An Unplanned Life: A Memoir* (Columbia: University of Missouri Press, 2005), p. 192. FBI Roundup: "Truman Won't Sign Subversive Curb; Red Roundup Ready," *NYT*, September 8, 1950.

town was willing to sign. Truman mentioned the survey in a speech later that month, decrying the fact that so many Americans were afraid of being associated with even the founding documents of American democracy.[44]

UNMATCHED POLITICAL COURAGE: TRUMAN AND CIVIL RIGHTS

A commitment to civil rights

From the steps of the Lincoln Memorial, President Truman addressed the annual meeting of the NAACP on June 29, 1947. Speaking to a crowd of ten thousand people and a national radio audience, he delivered an uncompromising message on racial justice, declaring, "It is my deep conviction that we have reached a turning point in the long history of our country's efforts to guarantee freedom and equality to all our citizens." Then, in words that thrilled his audience, he added, "When I say all Americans I mean all Americans." Adding political weight to his message, he had Chief Justice Fred M. Vinson, Attorney General Tom Clark, and Eleanor Roosevelt with him on the podium.[45]

The speech was a historic first, as he was the first president to speak to the nation on civil rights. Breaking sharply with President Roosevelt, he pledged an active civil rights role for the federal government, asserting that he would make it "a friendly, vigilant defender of the rights and equalities of all Americans." Fully aware of the NAACP's long-standing goal of having a federal antilynching law, he condemned the brutal crime: "Many of our people still suffer the indignity of insult, the harrowing fear of intimidation, and, I regret to say, the threat of physical injury and mob violence." Everyone in the crowd knew about the enormous power of southern segregationists in Congress and the fact that the nation's capital was a segregated city, but Truman concluded on a hopeful note, advising that "the way ahead is not easy," but "we can reach the goal."

Truman's commitment to civil rights was both political and personal. Politically, he knew that African-American voters in the big cities outside the South were critical to the Democratic Party and that he did not command the enormous personal magnetism of Roosevelt. In a famous November 1947 memo, the White House aide Clark Clifford advised him to "go as far as he feels he possibly could" on civil rights to prevent African Americans from defecting to the GOP. American attitudes on civil rights, meanwhile, were changing. The horrors of the Holocaust caused an increasing number of whites to challenge racism and segregation at home. The fight against Nazism had also raised the expectations of African Americans. As the NAACP director Walter White phrased it in the title of his 1945 book, there was *A Rising Wind* of justice in the United States and among colonized people around the world.[46]

44 "Text of Truman Speech at Detroit's 250th Anniversary Celebration," *NYT*, July 29, 1951. Address in Detroit at the Celebration of the City's 250th Anniversary. July 28, 1951, APP.

45 "Truman Demands We Fight Harder to Spur Equality," *NYT*, June 30, 1947. On the historic importance of the speech: Michael R. Gardner, *Harry Truman and Civil Rights: Moral Courage and Political Risks* (Carbondale: Southern Illinois University Press, 2002), Ch. 3. Text available at APP. New Left criticism of Truman and civil rights: Barton J. Bernstein, "The Ambiguous Legacy: The Truman Administration and Civil Rights," in Barton J. Bernstein, ed., *Politics and Policies of the Truman Administration* (Chicago: Quadrangle Books, 1970), pp. 269–314.

46 Clifford to Truman, November 19, 1947, p. 41, Clifford Papers, Political File, HSTPL. Walter White, *A Rising Wind* (Garden City, NY: Doubleday, Doran, 1945). Materials on lynchings: Nash Papers, Box 29, HSTPL.

On the personal level, Truman's commitment to racial justice was deeply felt. The turning point was a September 19, 1946, White House meeting with NAACP leaders over an upsurge in lynchings. Southern racists sought to quash the rising expectations of African Americans, particularly among returning veterans, with a wave of terror. In June 1946 the Mississippi senator Theodore Bilbo publicly encouraged racist violence, calling on "red-blooded Anglo-Saxon men to resort to any means" to prevent African Americans from voting. It was not so much the number of lynchings - six in 1946 - as their grisly quality. A South Carolina mob seized the African-American veteran Isaac Woodard, discharged from the military only hours before and still wearing his uniform; pulled him out of a bus; and gouged out his eyes. The town mayor later bragged about the attack. (In 2008 the FBI reopened the investigation into one of the 1946 lynchings.) When Walter White told him about this atrocity, an outraged Truman exclaimed, "My God, I had no idea it was as terrible as that! We've got to do something." He was not just posturing for his guests. "A few days later," NAACP records note, a White House official called to say the president would create a civil rights commission by executive order.[47]

Truman's background was filled with contradictory influences about race. Many members of his Missouri family shared the traditional southern racism. Privately in 1947, he conceded he knew his mother would not like his speech to the NAACP. Friends and family members heard him using offensive racist language in private, including the "N word." The White House aide George Elsey recalled that at his regular poker games, "the language was unguarded. The use of nigger was common, as were a variety of barnyard vulgarities."[48]

Truman's first try for elective office in 1922 taught him a lesson about bigotry. Running for judge in Jackson County, Missouri (the position was an administrative office that managed county affairs), he was attacked by the Ku Klux Klan because of his association with the Catholic-dominated Pendergast political machine in Kansas City. The Klan was then a growing force in Missouri politics, as it was Indiana, Ohio, and Oregon. Although Truman won, he was defeated in 1924, in part because of Klan opposition. Yet, in another curious incident, he attempted to join the Klan and even paid the ten-dollar membership fee. He soon demanded the money back, however, and ended his flirtation with the racist organization. (Republicans mentioned the incident in both the 1944 and 1952 elections, but Truman hotly denied he had ever actually joined.) Tom Clark, his attorney general, traced Truman's commitment to equality to his Jackson County days, recalling Truman's saying that African Americans "couldn't get to first base," and that "he was going to try to do something about it." Judge William H. Hastie, whom Truman appointed to the Third Circuit Court of Appeals as the first African-American federal appeals judge, agreed, saying, "there's no question in my mind that this was a deep personal commitment as distinguished from a political maneuver."[49]

47 NAACP, "Secretary's Report for the 1946 October Meeting," October 1946. NAACPP-MF (1977), Reel 7, Part 1. Walter White, *A Man Called White: The Autobiography of Walter White* (New York: Viking Press, 1948), pp. 330–1. "End Mob Violence, Truman Is Urged," *NYT*, September 20, 1946. NAACP Board of Directors, Minutes, April 8, 1946. NAACPP-MF (1977), Reel 3. Bilbo: "Bilbo Urges Mississippi Men to Employ 'any Means' to Bar Negroes from Voting," *NYT*, June 23, 1946. 2008 FBI investigation: "GA. Authorities Probe 1946 Unsolved Lynchings," *ABC News*, July 2, 2008.

48 Elsey, *An Unplanned Life*, p. 145.

49 Nash Papers, Box 72, HSTPL. Alonzo L. Hamby, *Man of the People: A Life of Harry S. Truman*. Pbk. ed. (New York: Oxford University Press, 1998), pp. 113–14. Clark, OH, p. 141, HSTPL. Hastie, OH, p. 52, HSTPL.

Although Truman believed strongly in equal opportunity in the public sphere – employment, housing, and education – he did not believe in social equality. Writing in 1948 to Ernest W. Roberts, an old southern friend and army colleague from World War I who objected to his civil rights program, Truman explained, "I am not asking for social equality, because no such thing exists, but I am asking for equality of opportunity for all human beings." (In the 1960s, Truman steadfastly opposed interracial marriage.) The problem was that the South was "living eight years behind the times." The times now called for eliminating all barriers to opportunity, and on that point Truman stood firm.[50]

Truman's experience in World War I also reinforced his sympathy for the common person and the victims of prejudice. As commander of Battery D of the Missouri National Guard in combat, he developed a lasting bond with his men, many of whom were Irish Catholics from Kansas City. In January 1949, for example, he made a special point of inviting the surviving members of his unit to his inaugural, where they had breakfast with him that morning and served as an honor guard in the parade. Interestingly, Dwight D. Eisenhower's experience commanding racially integrated units on an emergency basis during the Battle of the Bulge crisis did not convert him to supporting integration of the military.[51]

The President's Committee on Civil Rights: A presidential first

Following up on his promise to the NAACP, Truman created the President's Committee on Civil Rights in December 1946, directing it to determine how the powers of "Federal, State, and local governments may be strengthened and improved to safeguard the civil rights of the people." Notably, he ordered all federal agencies "to cooperate with the Committee," clearly signaling that he would tolerate no stalling or obstructionism.[52]

Truman's civil rights committee was the first modern presidential initiative on civil rights. Later generations, accustomed to innumerable commissions on race, cannot readily appreciate its historic significance. Roosevelt had studiously avoided civil rights and had created the Committee on Fair Employment Practice in 1941 only in response to A. Philip Randolph's plan to organize a march on Washington. To chair the committee, Truman selected Charles E. Wilson, president of the General Electric Corporation. He not only was one of the most powerful business executives in the country, but shared the belief of other business leaders that racial strife could impede the American economy. Membership on the committee was carefully balanced with, as one observer put it, two of everything: two African Americans, two women, two business leaders, two labor leaders, two southerners, Christians and Jews, and so on. Franklin D. Roosevelt, Jr., added the luster of the late president.

The committee's report, *To Secure These Rights*, released on October 29, 1947, was described by the *Washington Post* as "social dynamite." In uncompromising language it

50 Truman, Letter to EWR, August 18, 1948, in Robert H. Ferrell, ed., *Off the Record: The Private Papers of Harry S. Truman* (New York: Harper & Row, 1980), pp. 146–7. In 1963, Truman opposed interracial marriage: Peter Wallenstein, *Tell the Court I Love My Wife: Race, Marriage, and Law: An American History* (New York: Palgrave, 2002), pp. 185–6.

51 Press Release, Battery D Association, January, 1949, HSTPL, Digital Documents, "Harry Truman's World War I." Eisenhower: see Chapter 6 of this book.

52 Executive Order 9808, Establishing The President's Committee on Civil Rights, December 5, 1946, APP. The Report with introductory essay: Steven F. Lawson, ed., *To Secure These Rights: The Report of President Harry S Truman's Committee on Civil Rights* (Boston: Bedford/St. Martin's, 2004).

declared, "We need to guarantee the same rights to every person regardless of who he is, where he lives, or what his racial, religious or national origins are."[53] It condemned "The Crime of Lynching" and the fact that perpetrators enjoyed "almost complete immunity from punishment." The report went on to catalog the major areas of discrimination, including "the denial of the suffrage on account of race" and racial segregation in the armed services, which it found "particularly repugnant" since racial minorities had been "fighting and dying for the survival of the nation." On the explosive issue of segregated schools, it declared that "it is the South's segregated school system which most directly discriminates against the Negro." A long separate section, "Segregation Reconsidered," said that racial segregation "contravenes the equalitarian spirit of the American heritage." (That same year, Truman's Commission on Higher Education recommended ending all barriers based on "economic status, race, creed, color, sex, national origin, or ancestry.") Reflecting Truman's personal commitment, the report declared that the federal government had a special responsibility to "take the lead in safeguarding the civil rights of all Americans." In conclusion, it said bluntly, "The time for action is now."[54]

The report's thirty-five-point "Program of Action" included strengthening the Justice Department's Civil Rights Section, adding a civil rights unit in the FBI, and creating both a permanent White House Commission and a Congressional Standing Committee on Civil Rights. State and local police forces should be professionalized to help end police brutality and discrimination. Congress should pass the long-proposed antilynching law, eliminate the poll tax, and pass a law "to end immediately all discrimination and segregation based on race, color, creed, or national origin" in the armed services. A federal Fair Employment Practice Act should prohibit discrimination in private employment, while the states should pass laws "guaranteeing equal access to places of public accommodation." Congress should also condition all federal financial assistance on nondiscrimination. Although divided on how to end segregated schools, with some members opposed to federal sanctions, the report unequivocally condemned the system as violating the "equalitarian spirit of the American heritage."[55]

The report also addressed issues related to other racial groups, calling on New Mexico and Arizona to grant the vote "to their Indian citizens" and asking for a full review of the Japanese-American evacuation and internment during World War II. In short, the committee report outlined most of the agenda of the post–World War II civil rights movement. Latino Americans, however, were not mentioned in the report.

Looming over the report was concern about how racial segregation harmed America's image around the world in the fight against communism. Truman's 1947 address to the NAACP, for example, was broadcast overseas by shortwave radio. Secretary of State Dean Acheson had urged a permanent fair employment practices committee in 1946 because "the existence of discrimination against minority groups in this country has an adverse effect upon our relations with other countries." The Justice Department, meanwhile, made the same point in briefs in civil rights cases before the Supreme Court.[56]

[53] *Post* quote: Gardner, *Harry Truman and Civil Rights*, p. 50. Lawson, ed., *To Secure These Rights.*

[54] Lawson, *To Secure These Rights*, pp. 111–18. Philo E. Hutcheson, "The Truman Commission's Vision of the Future," *Thought and Action* (Fall 2007): 107–15.

[55] Lawson, *To Secure These Rights*, pp. 117, 179–81.

[56] John David Skrentny, "The Effect of the Cold War on African-American Civil Rights: America and the World Audience, 1945–1968," *Theory and Society* 27 (1998): 237–85.

The FBI's J. Edgar Hoover had very different ideas about civil rights, however. Opposed to racial equality, he stepped up his allegations of communist influence in the civil rights movement. In early 1946, for example, he sent to Truman's aide Harry Vaughan a "Personal and Confidential" message warning of communist involvement in the campaign for a federal employment discrimination committee.[57]

Truman wasted no time translating the Civil Rights Commission's report into a legislative program. In his January 7, 1948, State of the Union Address, he declared, "Our first goal is to secure fully the essential human rights of our citizens." Situating civil rights in a broad context of civil liberties, he said that "religious freedom, free speech, and freedom of thought are cherished realities in our land. Any denial of human rights is a denial of the basic beliefs of democracy and of our regard for the worth of each individual." A month later he sent Congress a ten-point legislative program that included an antilynching law, an end to the poll tax in federal elections, a permanent employment discrimination committee, and a national Civil Rights Commission. "We know the way," he concluded; "we need only the will." That night he confided in his diary, "I sent the Congress a Civil Rights message. They will no doubt receive it as coldly as they did my State of the Union message. But it needs to be said." His program, however, went nowhere in the Congress effectively dominated by southern segregationists.[58]

Truman fully understood that he risked dividing the Democratic Party and losing his bid for reelection in November. An April Gallup Poll found that a mere 6 percent of Americans favored his civil rights program, while 56 percent opposed it. Even among whites outside the South, only 15 percent supported it. Predictably, the powerful southern bloc, who represented 40 percent of the Democrats in Congress and controlled about half of the committees, dug in to fight his program. In the Senate they could kill any bill with a filibuster. The Mississippi senator James O. Eastland said that southern states should deny Truman their electoral votes in November and vote for "a distinguished southerner" as president. Truman fully understood the political risks and the likelihood of congressional defeat, and it is to his great credit that he pushed his civil rights program nevertheless.[59]

Truman's civil rights stand led to a historic fight at the 1948 Democratic Party convention in mid-July. He helped draft a civil rights platform that honored his commitment but he considered vague enough to avoid driving out the southerners. It only provoked a southern alternative affirming states' rights, however, which in turn caused the liberals to offer an even stronger civil rights plank. Truman thought the liberal alternative too strong and twice dismissed it as "crackpot" in his diary. He completely failed to understand how his own strong stand on civil rights had raised the hopes of civil rights forces. Hubert Humphrey, then mayor of Minneapolis, electrified the convention and established his national reputation with a passionate speech on behalf of civil rights. "The time has arrived in America," he declared, "for the Democratic Party to get out of the shadow of states' rights and walk forthrightly into the bright sunshine of human rights." Inspired

57 Hoover to Harry Vaughan, January 16, 1946, OF 391, Box 1203, HSTPL.

58 Harry Truman, Diary, February 2, 1948, in Ferrell, ed., *Off the Record*, p. 122.

59 Message to Congress, January 7, 1948, APP. "Anti-Lynching Law, Civil Liberties Unit Sought by Truman," *NYT*, February 3, 1948. Ira Katznelson, Kim Geiger, and Daniel Kryder, "Limiting Liberalism: The Southern Veto in Congress, 1933–1950," *Political Science Quarterly*, 108, no. 2 (1993): 283–306. Gardner, *Harry Truman and Civil Rights*, Ch. 6, pp. 71–86. The Gallup Organization, *The Gallup Poll, 1935–1990* (Wilmington, DE: Scholarly Resources, 1991), April 5, 1948, p. 722.

by his soaring rhetoric, the convention adopted the stronger plank, which specifically referred to "the right of full and equal political participation," "the right to equal opportunity of employment," and "the right of equal treatment in the service and defense of our nation."[60]

As they had threatened, the southern Democrats walked out of the convention and formed the independent States Rights Party, with Strom Thurmond as its presidential candidate. Their stand on race was unyielding: "We stand for the segregation of the races and the racial integrity of each race." The Republicans, meanwhile, adopted a strong civil rights platform calling for a federal antilynching law, an end to the poll tax, equal employment opportunity, and the desegregation of the army.[61] The GOP candidate Tom Dewey, the congressman and future president Richard Nixon, and many other Republicans were strong civil rights supporters, and they envisioned winning African-American votes in the big cities.

A historic step: Truman desegregates the military

The southern walkout from the Democratic Party convention only caused Truman to reaffirm his commitment to civil rights with one of the decisive actions for which he is famous. Exactly two weeks after the Democratic Party Convention, he issued Executive Order 9981 ending racial segregation in the armed services. The order stated simply, "there shall be equality of treatment and opportunity for all persons in the armed services without regard to race, color, religion or national origin." Moreover, "This policy shall be put into effect as rapidly as possible." It was a politically bold move that was not supported by the majority of white Americans and strongly opposed by the military. Army Chief of Staff General Dwight D. Eisenhower in 1946 had ordered a report on Negroes in the military that made some limited concessions to equality but maintained an overall 10 percent quota on African Americans. When the quota was reached in 1946, the army halted their enlistment, provoking the NAACP to protest and threaten to sue.[62]

While Truman was committed to desegregating the military, he was initially hesitant about when to act and had not included it in his 1948 legislative program. His proposal for a peacetime draft in early 1948, a major part of his cold war program, altered the politics of the issue, however, as African Americans objected to the prospect of a segregated draft. The key event was another dramatic White House confrontation between A. Philip Randolph and a president. Tensions were high when Truman met with him, the NAACP's Walter White, Mary McLeod Bethune, and others on March 22, 1948. Randolph arrived buoyed by the heady experience of having forced the formidable President Roosevelt to create an FEPC in 1941. He showed Truman even less deference and boldly threatened to advise young African-American men not to comply with a segregated draft. An

60 "The Crackpots Hope the South Will Bolt," Truman, Diary, July 14, 1948, in Ferrell, ed., *Off the Record*, p. 143. Democratic Party platform, APP. "South Beaten on Race Issue as Rights Plank Is Widened," *NYT*, July 15, 1948. Clifford, Oral History, p. 233, HSTPL. The 1948 Democratic Party convention: Robert Caro, *The Years of Lyndon Johnson: Master of the Senate*. Pbk. ed. (New York: Vintage Books, 2003), pp. 439–45.

61 States Rights Democratic Party platform, August 14, 1948, APP. Republican Party platform: June 21st, 1948, APP.

62 Executive Order 9981, July 26, 1948, APP. NAACP, Report of the Secretary for the September [1946] Meeting, NAACPP-MF, Reel 3. "Negro Suit Charges Segregation in the Army," *NYT*, December 19, 1948.

offended and angry Truman replied, "I wish you hadn't made that statement. I don't like it at all." Nine days later, Randolph repeated his threat before a congressional committee, embarrassing the NAACP and other moderate civil rights leaders. (Directly advising men to break the law was certainly a crime for which Randolph would probably have been indicted.) Randolph persisted and in late June wrote to Truman telling him he was "morally obligated" to end segregation immediately. One month later Truman issued Executive Order 9981.[63]

Racial integration in the military proceeded erratically. The army dragged its feet, initially desegregating support units and services but not combat units. An October 1949 army policy statement, in fact, implied that the president's order did not really mean desegregation. This prompted public outrage, and a confrontation between the army and Truman's Committee on Equality of Treatment and Opportunity in the Armed Services. E. W. Kenworthy, director of the committee, recalled, "They were impossible! You had to cram it down their throat." The army finally backed down and began integrating combat units. The Korean War, beginning in 1950, had the first racially integrated army units in American history.[64]

A stunning upset – and retreat

By late summer 1948, Truman's chances for reelection appeared doomed. With the southern Democrats defecting to Strom Thurmond and leftist Democrats supporting the Progressive Party candidate Henry Wallace, he faced what he described as a presidential campaign "without a comparable precedent in American political history." Nonetheless, he pulled out one of the greatest upsets in presidential election history, successfully hanging a "do nothing" label on the Republican-controlled Congress and conducting a railroad "whistle-stop" campaign trip that is a legend in American political history. His two bold moves played major roles in his upset win. The loyalty program blunted Republican charges of weakness on domestic communism, while the GOP candidate Thomas Dewey did not make the charge of communists in government a major issue. Truman's strong civil rights stance, meanwhile, won African-American voters and prevented many liberals from defecting to Henry Wallace. The Truman campaign followed Clark Clifford's advice and indulged in its own red-baiting, pointing out that "the core of the Wallace backing is made up of Communists and the fellow-travelers."[65]

Despite his stunning upset victory, however, Truman backed away from civil rights, realizing that the southerners in Congress were an insurmountable obstacle. He dutifully

63 "Negro Defense View Told," *NYT*, March 23, 1948. "Congress Told UMT Racial Bars Would Unleash Civil Disobedience," ibid., April 1, 1948. Randolph to Matthew Connelly, President's Secretary, March 18, 1948; Randolph and Grant Reynolds to President Truman, June 29, 1948, Official File, HSTPL, Digital Documents. Jervis Anderson, *A. Philip Randolph: A Biographical Portrait* (New York: Harcourt, Brace, Jovanovich, 1973), p. 276. Richard M. Dalfiume, *Desegregation of the U.S. Armed Forces: Fighting on Two Fronts, 1939–1953* (Columbia: University of Missouri Press, 1969), pp. 163–5.

64 E. W. Kenworthy, OH, p. 23, HSTPL. Dalfiume, *Desegregation of the U.S. Armed Forces*, pp. 175–6, 193–5.

65 Truman, *Memoirs*, V. 2, p. 215. Clifford to Truman, November 19, 1947, p. 23, Clifford Papers, Political File, HSTPL. Steven R. Goldzwig, *Truman's Whistle-Stop Campaign* (College Station: Texas A&M Press, 2008). "Communists Guide Wallace's Party, Truman Declares," *NYT*, September 24, 1948. Dewey: Richard M. Fried, "'Operation Polecat': Thomas E. Dewey, the 1948 Election, and the Origins of McCarthyism," *Journal of Policy History* 22, no. 1 (2010): 1–22.

proposed legislation in his 1949 State of the Union Address but put little energy behind it. With one notable exception, he pursued racial justice when he could. Most important, the Justice Department filed briefs attacking discrimination in all of the major civil rights cases, most notably in the early proceedings in *Brown v. Board of Education*. In a series of decisions, the Court laid the foundation for its landmark decision in *Brown*, and the Truman administration's briefs unequivocally put the federal government on the side of racial justice. Truman also issued a 1951 executive order strengthening equal opportunity in federal contracts and briefly considered creating a federal commission on the right to vote. The glaring and embarrassing exception, however, was Truman's failure to take any meaningful steps to desegregate Washington, D.C., even though it was a federal enclave. It was a segregated southern city the day he left office in January 1953, and President Dwight Eisenhower, despite his weak position on other aspects of civil rights, moved quickly to end official segregation in the city.[66]

In the end, Truman's courage on civil rights is unmatched by any other president. Lyndon Johnson certainly achieved more, notably the 1964 Civil Rights Act and the 1965 Voting Rights Act, but he had the advantage of the pressure of civil rights demonstrations and much stronger support among white Americans. Truman was the only president who ever risked his political career for any issue of individual rights and for that reason occupies a special place among his peers in the White House.

Sadly, in retirement, Truman undermined his public image on civil rights. In February 1960, he denounced the sit-ins that were sweeping the South and transforming the civil rights movement. If anyone sat in at a business he owned, he declared, he would "throw them out." Worse, he said the sit-ins were inspired by communists. His former secretary of state, Dean Acheson, tried to rescue him, with a long letter bluntly telling him to be quiet and not to embrace J. Edgar Hoover's view on civil rights. With great insight and considerable concern, Acheson advised, "Your views, as reported, are wholly out of keeping with your public record." He was right, and Truman apparently took the lesson to heart and made no further remarks.[67]

KOREA: THREE CRUCIAL DECISIONS ON PRESIDENTIAL POWER

President Truman was home in Independence, Missouri, late Saturday night, June 25, 1950, when Secretary of State Dean Acheson called to tell him that North Korea had just invaded South Korea. The first armed conflict of the cold war presented Truman with a series of challenges as commander in chief, and he made three crucial decisions involving presidential power with important civil liberties implications. One is justly celebrated as a courageous act of presidential leadership. The other two, however, raised troubling questions about presidential war powers that also embroiled several later presidents.

66 Annual Message to the Congress on the State of the Union. January 5, 1949, APP. Executive Order 10308, December 3, 1951, APP. Other civil rights actions: see Nash Papers, Box 68, HSTPL. Eisenhower administration actions in desegregating Washington, DC, see Chapter 6 of this book.

67 Sit-ins: Materials in Post-Presidential Papers, Box 241, HSTPL. "Truman Believes Reds Lead Sit-ins," *NYT*, April 19, 1960. The Acheson correspondence is in David McCullough, Introduction, *Affection and Trust: The Personal Correspondence of Harry S. Truman and Dean Acheson, 1953–1971* (New York: Alfred A. Knopf, 2010), pp. 232–5, 238–9. David A. Nichols, A *Matter of Justice: Eisenhower and the Beginning of the Civil Rights Revolution* (New York: Simon & Schuster, 2007), p. 251. Hamby, *Man of the People*, p. 624. Criticisms of the Freedom Rides: Post-Presidential Papers, Box 731, HSTPL.

War powers: The decision to intervene in Korea

In the hours and days immediately following the North Korean invasion, the key question was whether the United States would commit troops to the conflict. After intense discussions, Truman ordered naval and army units into combat, acting under United Nations Resolution 83, passed on June 27. To his credit, Truman kept top congressional leaders informed and sought their advice. A crucial moment occurred at a June 30 White House meeting. The Republican senator Alexander Smith from New Jersey suggested a congressional resolution authorizing military action. Truman said he would think about it. Later, however, Secretary of State Acheson advised that he "should not ask for a resolution of approval, but rest on his constitutional authority as Commander in Chief." A congressional resolution, he argued, would require hearings, lead to a long debate with an uncertain outcome, and prevent immediate and necessary action. Most important, he also argued that as commander in chief Truman did not need congressional approval. Congressional leaders accepted this argument and did not want to press the point that article 1 of the Constitution explicitly gives Congress the power to declare war. Not everyone at the June 30 meeting was happy, however. The Nebraska senator Kenneth Wherry, GOP minority leader and one of Joe McCarthy's most ardent supporters, repeatedly insisted that Congress be consulted before the president commit American ground troops. Twice he rose to his feet to make his point. Truman evaded the issue, telling Wherry that ground troops were already committed. When Wherry again insisted on consultation, the president said he would "inform" the Senate should any congressional action be needed. Rep. Dewey Short, a Republican from Missouri, promptly defended Truman, saying the Congress was "practically unanimous in its appreciation of the President's leadership." [68]

Interestingly, a relatively new senator from Texas named Lyndon Johnson had already made a special effort to be the first to write to Truman expressing his "deep gratitude and admiration of your courageous response" to the Korean crisis. Even then, Johnson was evidently concerned about protecting presidential prerogatives regarding war powers.[69] Truman had twice before asserted his inherent powers as commander in chief. At an April 1948 press conference he claimed the power to send troops to the new state of Israel as part of a possible United Nations mission under his constitutional authority as commander in chief. "Read the history" of past U.S. military ventures, he told the reporters in his characteristically testy style. Then, in 1949, he claimed "implied power" as commander in chief to enjoin labor union strikes that created a national emergency. He said his attorney general had informed him of this power but conceded that he could not cite any legal authority outside the Constitution itself.[70]

Truman and the Congress were not finished with the question of presidential war powers in late June 1950, however, and debated it in briefings over the next six months. Some experts argued that a Proclamation of a National Emergency would give the

[68] George M. Elsey, Draft of Notes, Meeting June 30, 1950, Elsey Papers, HSTPL, Digital Documents. At a meeting on June 27, congressional leaders repeatedly pressed for assurance that he was acting pursuant to the UN resolution. Elsey, Notes, Meeting of June 27, 1950, Elsey Papers, HSTPL, Digital Documents. Acheson, *Present at the Creation*, pp. 413–15. Arthur M. Schlesinger, Jr., *War and the American Presidency* (New York: W. W. Norton, 2004), p. 14.

[69] Johnson letter to Truman, June 28, 1950, White House Famous Name file, Box 10, LBJPL.

[70] Israel: President's News Conference, April 22, 1948, APP. "Truman Sees Right to Dispatch Troops," *NYT*, April 23, 1948. Strikes: President's News Conference, February 3, 1949, APP.

president whatever powers he needed. At a December 13 meeting, Rep. Carl Vinson of Georgia and others endorsed this course, while the GOP leader, Senator Robert Taft, had strong doubts. To his credit, Truman went around the room, directly asking members of Congress for their opinions. Three days later, he officially declared a national emergency. Pursuant to the proclamation, he explained in a nationally broadcast speech, he had begun to impose price and wage controls in certain industries and had requested the railroad unions to end their current strike. Two months later, the Justice Department produced a forty-one-page memo, Powers of the President to Send the Armed Forces Outside the United States. It was a thoughtful review of the relevant issues and precedents concluding that the Constitution was ambiguous and that Truman was justified in sending troops to Korea.[71]

The Korean War decision was a fateful moment. Truman's decision not to seek a congressional resolution set an important precedent on the question of war powers. The historian Arthur M. Schlesinger, Jr., long a strong supporter of both strong presidential leadership and Democrats in particular, had second thoughts after the Vietnam War, and concluded that the decision on Korea "persuaded several successors that presidents possess the inherent power to go to war whenever they choose." And as subsequent events proved, they used that power on numerous occasions over the next half-century. American involvement remained officially part of a United Nations (UN) "police action," a phrase that actually originated with a reporter's question at a Truman press conference. The historian Garry Wills, however, argues that Truman violated the terms of U.S. participation in UN military actions, which required congressional ratification of any use of troops. The Proclamation of a National Emergency, meanwhile, was another significant step in the direction of transferring power to the executive branch under the rubric of national security.[72]

Acheson's opposition to congressional authorization reflected a deeply antidemocratic strain of thinking within the foreign policy establishment during the Cold war. In his 1957 book, *A Citizen Looks at Congress*, he explained that in a complex and dangerous world difficult decisions had to be made quickly. Such matters were beyond the capacity of Congress as an institution and of individual members of Congress, who he thought were essentially "amateurs" in this area. Today's world problems, he solemnly advised, "are different in their very nature from those of the heyday of democratic theory, the eighteenth century." Congress could advise, modify, or veto a policy, but the president alone had the capacity to lead. Fifteen years later, he went even further in a diatribe against democracy itself: "I say the Congress is too damn representative. It's just as stupid as the people are; just as uneducated, just as dumb, just as selfish." Democracy?, he asked rhetorically, "I don't think it's worth a damn." Acheson's contempt for a congressional role in critical national security matters and his celebration of presidential power became deeply ingrained among the bipartisan foreign policy elite in the cold war and guided

[71] Notes of meeting, December 13, 1950, Elsey Papers, Box 73, HSTPL. Truman, Radio and Television Report to the American People on the National Emergency, December 15, 1950, APP. Proclamation 2914, Proclaiming the Existence of a National Emergency, December 16, 1950, APP. David Lloyd, Memo for Mr. Murphy, Powers of the President to Send the Armed Forces Outside the United States, February 16, 1951, Elsey Papers, Box 73, HSTPL.

[72] President's Press Conference, June 29, 1950, APP. Schlesinger, Jr., *War and the American Presidency*, p. 14. Garry Wills, *Bomb Power: The Modern Presidency and the National Security State* (New York: Penguin, 2010), pp. 113–19.

American policy for decades. The end result was what the historian Schlesinger in 1973 labeled *The Imperial Presidency*, which underpinned both the tragic American involvement in Vietnam and President George W. Bush's war on terrorism.[73]

Courageous presidential leadership: Firing General MacArthur

In one of his most courageous acts as president, Truman fired General Douglas MacArthur as allied commander of the United Nations forces in Korea on April 11, 1951. China suddenly entered the war with 100,000 troops in late October 1950, catching MacArthur by surprise and dramatically transforming the conflict. The arrogant and always independent-minded general began creating political and diplomatic problems with public statements about expanding the war, grand rhetoric about "victory," and vague hints about using atomic weapons. The final straw was a letter he sent to Rep. Joseph Martin, Republican leader in the House of Representatives, praising his views on the war and declaring, "There is no substitute for victory." Truman called the letter "[r]ank insubordination." After consulting the Joint Chiefs of Staff, who unanimously supported him, he fired MacArthur. (Dwight D. Eisenhower, who had seen MacArthur's arrogance firsthand in the 1932 Bonus Army fiasco, fully agreed with Truman's action.)[74]

In relieving MacArthur of his command, Truman asserted the basic principle of civilian control of the military. Under the U.S. Constitution, he explained in a nationwide speech, "it is fundamental" that the military leader be subordinate to civilian leaders, adding pointedly that "in time of crisis," the principle of civilian control of the military "is particularly compelling." The decision is one of several that form the basis of Truman's reputation for strong presidential leadership. MacArthur, of course, was the great hero of the Pacific campaign in World War II, and his rhetoric about "victory" over communism in Asia roused conservatives. His dismissal touched off a political firestorm of criticism of Truman, and MacArthur returned to the United States to extraordinary adulation. The Los Angeles City Council adjourned in "sorrowful contemplation of the political assassination" of the general. Two thousand longshoremen in Brooklyn walked off their jobs in protest, and MacArthur was hailed in a massive tickertape parade in New York City on April 20. The day before, he delivered a speech to Congress that immediately became one of the most famous in American history, entitled "Old Soldiers Never Die." Conservative Republicans touted him for the GOP presidential nomination in 1952. Truman weathered the storm, however, and Senate Democrats held hearings that exposed MacArthur's utter lack of understanding of international relations and the implications of expanding the war in Korea. Over time, Truman's reputation for leadership steadily rose.[75]

73 Dean Acheson, *A Citizen Looks at Congress* (New York: Harper and Bros., 1957), pp. 88, 117. Acheson, OH, pp. 10–11, HSTPL.

74 Statement and Order by the President on Relieving General MacArthur of His Commands, April 11, 1951, APP. MacArthur to Martin, March 20, 1951, PSF, MacArthur Dismissal, HSTPL. Truman, Diary, April 6, 1951, in Ferrell, ed., *Off the Record*, p. 210; original in PSF, Diaries, April 6–7, 1951, HSTPL.

75 "President Truman's Statement of Regret in Announcing the Relieving of MacArthur," *NYT*, April 11, 1951. Stanley Weintraub, *MacArthur's War: Korea and the Undoing of an American Hero* (New York: Free Press, 2000). Geoffrey Perret, *Old Soldiers Never Die: The Life of Douglas MacArthur* (New York: Random House, 1996)."Dismissal Angers South California," *NYT* April 12, 1951; "Two-Hour Protest by Dock Workers," ibid., April 13, 1951; "Michigan Censures President," ibid., April 14, 1951. Robert Caro argues that Lyndon Johnson artfully stage-managed the hearings that deflated MacArthur: Caro, *The Years of Lyndon Johnson: Master of the Senate*, pp. 370–82.

Truman seizes the steel mills – and the Supreme Court says no

The case was virtually forgotten for half a century, except among historians specializing in Truman and some legal scholars, but it suddenly reappeared with enormous legal and political significance during the presidency of George W. Bush. In the spring of 1952, with the Korean War dragging on inconclusively, a nationwide steel strike threatened to shut down the steel industry. Convinced that a strike would cripple the war effort, President Truman seized control of the entire steel industry, claiming inherent presidential war powers. "These are not normal times," he told the nation; "our national security and our chances for peace depend on our defense production." With a war on, the president had both the responsibility and the power to act.[76]

Seizing the steel mills provoked a political uproar over presidential power that matched the negative reaction to Roosevelt's court-packing plan in 1937. The criticisms reflected a mixture of constitutional principle and Republican partisanship. The ACLU asked that the country "emphatically repudiate" the president's claims of "unlimited executive authority." Even many loyal Democrats were troubled, particularly when the Taft-Hartley Act "cooling-off" provision and other remedies were available. The steel industry and its allies in Congress launched an aggressive publicity campaign framing the issue in terms of the president's constitutional powers. This strategy successfully moved the public debate away from the purely economic matters Truman had emphasized.[77]

Truman fueled fears about presidential powers with an offhand remark about his power to seize newspapers if necessary. At his April 17 press conference a reporter asked, "if you can seize the steel mills under your inherent powers, can you in your opinion also seize the newspapers and/or the radio stations?" Truman replied, "Under similar circumstances the President of the United States has to act for whatever is for the best of the country." Alarm bells went off around the country. Truman tried to fudge the issue at his next press conference a week later. Saying there had been a lot of "hooey" about his previous statement, he now asserted that "the thought of seizing press and radio has never occurred to me," and he could not imagine the government's "taking over and running those industries." Nonetheless, he stuck by his claim that the president "has very great inherent powers to meet great national emergencies," although he could not say what "he would do or would not do" in a particular crisis. This was not the first time he had made such a claim. In February 1949, with regard to possible legislation granting the president power to issue injunctions to end strikes, Truman claimed he had "implied powers" under the Constitution to do so as both president and commander in chief. When a reporter asked where he could find these powers in the Constitution, Truman replied, "No, I can't" tell you, but the attorney general had assured him they existed.[78] As

[76] Radio and Television Address to the American People on the Need for Government Operation of the Steel Mills. April 8, 1952, APP. Executive Order 10340 – Directing the Secretary of Commerce to Take Possession of and Operate the Plants and Facilities of Certain Steel Companies, April 8, 1952, APP. Alan F. Westin, *The Anatomy of a Constitutional Law Case: Youngstown Sheet and Tube Co. v. Sawyer: The Steel Seizure Decision* (New York: Macmillan, 1958). Maeva Marcus, *Truman and the Steel Seizure Case: The Limits of Presidential Power* (New York: Columbia University Press, 1977).

[77] ACLU, News Release, May 4, 1952, ACLUP-MF (1977), Reel 12. Marcus, *Truman and the Steel Seizure Case*, p. 83.

[78] The President's News Conference of April 17, 1952, APP. The President's News Conference of April 24, 1952, APP. ACLU, News Release, May 4, 1952, ACLUP-MF (1977), Reel 12. The 1949 incident: President's Press Conference, February 3, 1949, APP. "President Claims Powers," *NYT*, February 4, 1949.

with Roosevelt before him, he did not believe the Constitution placed limits on presidential power in national emergencies.

Through an expedited process, the Supreme Court ruled on a steel industry suit in two months and soundly rejected Truman's claims of presidential emergency powers in a 6–3 decision. Reflecting the seriousness and complexity of the issues at stake, seven justices wrote opinions in *Youngstown Sheet and Tube v. Sawyer*. For the majority, Justice Hugo Black wrote that "the President's power, if any, to issue the order must stem either from an act of Congress or from the Constitution itself," finding "no statute that expressly authorizes the President to take possession of property as he did here." Nor could Black find a statute that implied such power.[79]

The most important opinion was Justice Robert Jackson's concurrence, which developed a three-part analysis of the scope of presidential authority. Truman's action was "an exercise of authority without law," and in words that would resonate fifty years later, he wrote, "No one, perhaps not even the President, knows the limits of the power he may seek to exert in this instance." This observation echoed his prophetic dissent in *Korematsu* eight years earlier, where he had warned about the danger of granting the government seemingly unlimited power. Jackson's *Youngstown* opinion structured the debate over presidential power in the decades ahead and became a central point of reference in the controversies over President George W. Bush's sweeping claims of presidential power after 2001.[80]

Two of President Truman's Supreme Court appointees, Harold Burton and Tom Clark, voted with the majority (Truman regarded Clark's vote as a personal betrayal), while two others, Chief Justice Fred Vinson and Sherman Minton, dissented. After the decision, the wage dispute was quickly settled, steel production resumed, and the case was largely forgotten by the public. Despite the rebuke from the Supreme Court, Truman remained unrepentant on the question of presidential power. In his memoirs he argued that a president "must be able to act at all times to meet any sudden threat to the nation's security."

Forgotten precedents

The seizure of the steel industry was not Truman's only assertion of broad presidential war powers in labor disputes. In 1946, as the economy experienced a wrenching reconversion to peacetime, strikes erupted in virtually all of the major industries – steel, automobiles, coal, and among telephone and electrical workers – and on May 23, a railroad workers' strike shut down the national rail system. In the old smokestack economy, steel, automobiles, coal, and railroads were the backbone of American economic life.[81]

Although only a year in office and still feeling his way as president, Truman nonetheless acted decisively. Concluding that he faced a national emergency, he proposed an emergency law authorizing him to draft workers and compel them to continue working at their jobs. Roosevelt had made a similar proposal two years before in 1944, and so the

[79] *Youngstown Sheet and Tube v. Sawyer*, 343 U.S. 579 (1952).

[80] Jackson, Dissent, ibid. Robert Jackson, Dissenting Opinion, *Korematsu v. United States*, 323 U.S. 214, 246 (1944). "President Truman and the Steel Seizure Case: A Symposium," *Duquesne Law Review* 41 (Summer 2003). Critics of John Yoo, who wrote critical memos justifying crucial claims of presidential power for President Bush, note that in virtually all his writings he almost completely ignores Jackson's *Youngstown* opinion.

[81] Barton J. Bernstein, "The Truman Administration and the Steel Strike of 1946," *Journal of American History* 52 (March 1966): 791–803.

idea was not new. "Farmers cannot move food to markets," Truman told the nation over the radio on May 24; "all of you will see your food supplies dwindle, your health and safety endangered, your streets darkened, your transportation facilities broken down." Then he announced that "if sufficient workers to operate the trains have not returned by 4 p.m. tomorrow ... I shall call upon the Army to assist the Office of Defense Transportation in operating the trains." Echoing FDR's first inaugural address, he said, "The Government is challenged as seldom before in our history. It must meet the challenge or confess its impotence." Despite his deep political debt to organized labor, Truman regarded the two railroad union leaders' intransigence as a direct challenge to presidential authority, and he reacted angrily and with a firmness the nation had not seen before. His aide Clark Clifford thought the tone of the initial draft of his message to Congress was "intemperate," and likely to backfire. Others intervened and toned it down. Press accounts described the president as "grim," and the *New York Times* ran a story about his health and the strains of the job.[82]

When Truman presented his cabinet with the proposed law to draft strikebreakers on May 24, he faced a stunned silence. Attorney General Tom Clark finally spoke and told him he was overstepping the bounds of the Constitution. Truman reportedly fired back, "We'll draft 'em first and think about the law later." The next day Clark put his thoughts in writing and advised the president that "it is doubtful whether constitutional powers of the President would include the right to draft individuals for national purposes." Six years later, as a Supreme Court justice, Clark ruled against Truman's seizure of the steel mills, for essentially the same reasons.[83]

While speaking to Congress on the bill on May 25, an aide dramatically handed Truman a note saying the two railroad union leaders had conceded and agreed to a settlement. (Some thought the event was staged.) The bill went to Congress, nonetheless. It would allow the president to draft into the army any worker who did not return to work within twenty-four hours after a business had been seized by presidential order. The ACLU denounced it as "involuntary servitude" and questioned whether a president has the sole authority to declare national emergencies. The House quickly passed the bill by an overwhelming majority, but a backlash developed almost overnight in the Senate, apparently after some had time to think about the bill's implications. The GOP Senate leader Robert A. Taft echoed the ACLU in denouncing it as the "most extreme proposal ever made," an "unconstitutional" form of "involuntary servitude," representing an "unlimited seizure of presidential power." Some Senate Democrats had similar doubts and deserted Truman in droves. The full Senate deleted the offending section 70–13. Three years later, in a 1949 labor controversy, Truman repeated his view that the president had "inherent" or "implied" power to end strikes unilaterally. Although defeated, Truman's proposal indicated that the seizure of the steel mills six years later was no aberration but was part of a general inclination to make sweeping claims of presidential authority under the rubric of national security.[84]

[82] Radio Address to the American People on the Railroad Strike Emergency. May 24, 1946, APP. A vivid firsthand account is in Clark Clifford, *Counsel to the President: A Memoir* (New York: Random House, 1991), "The Labor Wars of 1946," pp. 87–96. "Portrait of a President in a Time of Crisis," *NYT*, May 26, 1946.

[83] Clark, OH, p. 96, HSTPL. McCullough, *Truman*, pp. 501, 504.

[84] Special Message to the Congress Urging Legislation for Industrial Peace, May 25, 1946, APP. ACLU Board, Minutes, May 27, 1946; ACLU, Press Release, May 27, 1946, ACLUP-MF (1977), Reel 10. "Senate Ire Rises on Truman Draft Plan," *NYT*, May 27, 1946; "Senate, 70–13, Kills Labor Draft Plan," ibid., May 30, 1946.

Another aspect of unrestricted presidential power with major long-term implications emerged in an obscure 1952 Supreme Court case. A group of widows sued the government for negligence over their husbands' deaths in the crash of an experimental B-29 flight in Georgia. The Court rejected their suit, accepting the government's argument that it could withhold an air force report on the accident because it would reveal "state secrets" and jeopardize national security. Few people noticed *Reynolds v. United States* at the time, but beginning in 1977 government use of the state secrets doctrine exploded. That development also was largely unnoticed until President George W. Bush used it as one of several extraordinary claims of presidential power in his war on terrorism.[85]

On questions of presidential power, then, President Truman left a very ambiguous legacy. Firing General MacArthur was constitutionally correct and has properly been celebrated as a courageous decision. But on sending troops to Korea, seizing the steel mills, suggesting that he could also seize the media, proposing to draft striking workers, and advancing the doctrine of state secrets, Truman played a pivotal role in setting the country on the road to the Imperial Presidency.

A DIVISIVE CHURCH-STATE CONTROVERSY

In July 1949 Francis Cardinal Spellman of New York released a strongly worded letter accusing Eleanor Roosevelt of anti-Catholic prejudice and of "discrimination unworthy of an American mother," because of her opposition to federal aid for parochial schools. The issue of separation of church and state had been simmering for years, but a nasty dispute between Spellman and Roosevelt moved it to the fore and posed a serious problem for President Truman. At issue was a $300 million federal aid to education bill and whether private and parochial schools would be eligible. Spellman framed the issue in terms of a constitutional right to equal treatment for Catholic schoolchildren. Shocked at Spellman's accusation, Roosevelt denied any anti-Catholic bias and pointed to her support for Al Smith, a Catholic, "in every campaign that he made," including the 1928 presidential election when he had faced a vicious anti-Catholic smear campaign. Roosevelt insisted she wanted "freedom of religion to prevail in this country," but without compromising the principle of separation of church and state. [86]

The exchange disappeared after a few weeks, but it exposed a much deeper social, political, and legal controversy over the place of religion in American life. Politically it threatened to split the Democratic Party right down the middle, with Roosevelt and Spellman representing two major factions within the party. She was the symbolic leader of the liberal wing, which included Protestants and Jews opposed to government aid to religious

The 1949 incident: President's Press Conference, February 3, 1949, APP. "President Claims Powers," *NYT*, February 4, 1949.

85 Louis Fisher, *In the Name of National Security: Unchecked Presidential Power and the Reynolds Case* (Lawrence: University Press of Kansas, 2006). Barry Siegel, *Claim of Privilege: A Mysterious Plane Crash: A Landmark Supreme Court Case, and the Rise of State Secrets* (New York: Harper, 2008). President Barack Obama use of the state secrets doctrine: Chapter 15.

86 "Cardinal Calls Mrs. Roosevelt Anti-Catholic on School Bill," *NYT*, July 23, 1949. Text of Spellman's Letter in ibid. Roosevelt's reply in ERP, Box 4671, FDRPL. "Mrs. Roosevelt Denies Bias," *NYT*, July 26, 1949. "Schools Bill Dead, Chairman Admits," ibid., July 29, 1949. Seymour P. Lachman, "The Cardinal, the Congressman, and the First Lady," *Journal of Church and State* 7 (1965): 35–66. On the traditional handling of this issue by historians, see Donovan, *Turbulent Years*, pp. 124–5; Hamby, *Man of the People*, pp. 495–6, appreciates the divisive aspect of the school aid controversy.

schools. Spellman, meanwhile, wielded considerable political influence as a spokesperson for the large and socially conservative Catholic wing of the party. Roosevelt and many others feared the issue would inflame religious conflict in America. The aid to education bill, with considerable Republican support, passed the House of Representatives with a ban on funds for private and parochial schools. Nonetheless, the church-state dispute eventually killed it in the Senate and blocked similar bills for the next twenty years. Only an adroit compromise fashioned under Lyndon Johnson secured passage of the historic federal aid to education bill in 1965.

In the White House, President Truman tried to avoid what he called the "crippling controversy" over church and state. It was his fate, however, to be president when the Supreme Court thrust it into the national spotlight in 1947. The decision in *Everson v. Board of Education* upheld a New Jersey law allowing local school districts to contract for transporting students to and from school. By a narrow 5–4 margin the Court ruled the policy constitutional, but Justice Hugo Black's majority opinion framed the issue in terms of a "wall of separation" between church and state that shaped debate over the issue of religion in American public life from that time forward.[87]

The *Everson* decision galvanized the advocates of separation of church and state, and in late 1947 they organized Protestants and Other Americans United for Separation of Church and State (POAU, later renamed Americans United for Separation of Church and State), the first national public interest group on the issue. It joined forces with the ACLU, the American Jewish Congress, and some other groups to form what became an influential separationist lobby in Congress and local communities. A particularly powerful voice in this coalition were the southern Baptists who had traditionally been staunchly opposed to any government entanglement in religion. (That all changed in the late 1970s when they joined the New Right political coalition and reversed their position on church and state.)[88]

For their part, Catholics continued to press for public aid to parochial schools. Catholic schools represented the largest single group of nonpublic schools in the country, educating about three million children by the late 1940s, or about 10 percent of all elementary and secondary students. The cost of this system of education was increasing, and Catholics argued that since they relieved local school systems of so many students, they were entitled to government funds. They also argued, as Cardinal Spellman did in his exchange with Eleanore Roosevelt, that denying them funds violated their right to equal treatment under the Constitution.

Federal aid to schools also raised the issue of government support for racially segregated schools. Beginning in 1950, Rep. Adam Clayton Powell, now the leading African American in Congress, introduced an amendment (which became known as the "Powell Amendment") to school aid bills barring federal funds for segregated schools. Both political parties were deeply divided on the issue. Democrats were split among southern segregationists who opposed both integration and federal social programs, liberals who felt aid to education was so important they were willing to defer the issue of segregation, and

[87] "Crippling": Donovan, *Turbulent Years*, p. 125 *Everson v. Board of Education of Ewing Township*, 330 U.S. 1 (1947).

[88] Lawrence P. Creedon and William D. Falcon, *United for Separation: An Analysis of POAU Assaults on Catholicism* (Milwaukee: Bruce Publishing, 1959). Paul Blanshard, *American Freedom and Catholic Power* (Boston: Beacon Press, 1949).

other liberals determined to fight for integration even at the cost of blocking federal aid. As the national party leader, President Truman was in a politically impossible situation and remained silent. Adlai Stevenson, Democratic Party candidate in 1952, was in the middle group and was generally weak on federal civil rights enforcement. Republicans, meanwhile, were divided among hard-line conservatives who opposed all government social programs and moderates, led by Tom Dewey, who regarded education as an important national priority. The combination of church and state and segregated schools issues blocked federal aid to education until 1965, after the Supreme Court had ruled on both issues.[89]

The school aid controversy was intertwined with the Catholic Church's positions on censorship and birth control. The church joined conservative Protestant forces in supporting federal censorship of books and movies with sexual or religious themes. The Post Office had exercised a heavy hand over sexually oriented materials since the 1873 Comstock Act, and no president, including Truman, was willing to reverse federal policy and appear to support freer discussions of sexuality in any form. Thus, it remained for civil libertarians to challenge censorship through the courts, and gradually the Supreme Court began chipping away at the web of censorship across the country, including the power of the postmaster general. A clear signal of things to come was the Court's decision in *Burstyn v. Wilson* holding that movies were a form of expression protected by the First Amendment.[90] The Catholic Church also maintained its opposition to birth control. It was virtually an unmentionable topic in national politics, and Truman, along with other political figures, remained silent on the issue.

LAST GASP (FOR A WHILE) FOR THE ERA

Scheduled to meet with a group of women advocating the Equal Rights Amendment to the Constitution on September 21, 1945, President Truman noted in his appointment sheet that it involved "a lot of hooey about equal rights." The comment expressed his true feelings about women's issues. Although he gave nominal support to the ERA, he invested no effort in it and was extremely weak on other women's rights issues.

The campaign for the ERA resurfaced after World War II in a changed cultural and political environment. Women's participation in the war affected public attitudes, and in 1946 the Senate approved the ERA 38–35. Although well short of the necessary two-thirds of the Senate, the vote was a dramatic change from the past. Alice Paul, still fighting after introducing the ERA in 1923, now expressed optimism about its prospects. Both the 1948 Democratic and Republican Party platforms endorsed it, with Republicans generally more supportive than Democrats, as they had been in the past. Richard Nixon, elected to Congress in 1946, consistently supported the ERA, as he did when president in the early 1970s. Among Democrats, southern conservatives opposed the very idea of women's rights, while most liberals fought the ERA out of fear that it would wipe out protective legislation for women workers. Eleanor Roosevelt lent her influential voice to the opposition. The split among Democrats on the issue gave President Truman fits. In 1946 his aide

[89] Powell Amendment: Stevenson, Telegrams and letters, January-February, 1956, Walter Johnson, ed., *The Papers of Adlai E. Stevenson*, VI (Boston: Little, Brown, 1972–9), pp. 51–3.

[90] National Council on Freedom from Censorship, *National Council on Freedom from Censorship* (New York: ACLU, June 1946), ACLUP-MF (1977), Reel 93. *Burstyn v. Wilson* 343 U.S. 495 (1952).

David Niles declared, "This Equal Rights thing is dynamite which ever way you place it," and Truman made no further public statements on it.[91]

The ERA's prospects reached a high point in 1950 when the Senate approved it by the impressive margin of 63–19. The vote was particularly notable considering the absence of strong support from the president. The Senate resolution, however, contained an ambiguous rider stating that it was not intended to invalidate special protective legislation for women. The proposed amendment, it held, "shall not be construed to impair any rights, benefits, or exemptions, now or hereafter conferred by law upon persons of the female sex." We will never know how the Supreme Court would have resolved the two contradictory parts of the amendment, had it ever been adopted. The issue was moot in any event, as Rep. Emanuel Celler kept the ERA bottled up in the House Judiciary Committee. Celler was typical of most congressional liberals at this time: very strong on racial justice but opposed to women's rights.[92]

The 1950 Senate vote proved to be the last gasp of the ERA for two decades. Support simply evaporated in the political culture of the 1950s, and President Eisenhower gave it no support whatsoever. The ERA did not resurface until 1970, in an entirely new political climate that included a revived women's movement and was passed overwhelmingly by Congress in 1972.

Appointing women to top positions was another weak spot for Truman. He was deeply conservative on women's issues and is alleged to have said that he would not have a woman in the cabinet. In fact, he never appointed one, in contrast to both Presidents Roosevelt and Eisenhower. (Adlai Stevenson, the Democratic Party presidential candidate in 1952 and 1956, was equally insensitive on women's issues. In 1955 he spoke at Smith College emphasizing women's role in civilizing men, without any reference to careers or engagement in public affairs. It was not just Truman; it was the fifties.) Truman appointed exactly one woman as federal judge. Burnita Shelton Matthews had been a suffragist and picketed the White House with Alice Paul and done research on employment discrimination for Paul as background for the ERA. Truman interviewed her briefly and then named her a federal judge in the District of Columbia in 1949, the first female district court judge ever and the first woman named to any federal judicial post since 1934.[93]

Congress in June 1948 passed the Women's Armed Services Integration Act greatly expanding opportunities for women in the military (although maintaining some limits on opportunities). This occurred two months before Truman's order ending racial

[91] "Equal Rights Fails to Get Two-Thirds in Vote in Senate," *NYT*, July 20, 1946. Party platforms at APP. Truman: Cynthia Harrison, *On Account of Sex: The Politics of Women's Issues, 1945–1968* (Berkeley: University of California Press, 1988), p. 21.

[92] "Senate Votes Equal Rights, But Retains Women's Laws," *NYT*, January 26, 1950. "Mrs. Roosevelt against Change," ibid., January 26, 1950.

[93] Susan M. Hartmann, "Behind the Silences: Challenges to the Gender Status Quo During the Truman Years," in Kirkendall, ed., *Harry's Farewell*, pp. 257–75. Matthews, OH, ROHO. Stevenson, "Women, Husbands, and History," in Johnson, ed., *The Papers of Adlai Stevenson*, V. IV (Boston: Little, Brown, 1972–9), pp. 495–502. Sheldon Goldman, *Picking Federal Judges: Lower Court Selection from Roosevelt through Reagan* (New Haven, CT: Yale University Press, 1997), pp. 92–7. Women in the Cabinet: Ayers, *Truman in the White House: The Diary of Eban A. Ayers* (Columbia: University of Missouri Press, 1991), p. 78. Matthews: Ruth Bader Ginsburg and Laura W. Brill, "Women in the Federal Judiciary: Three Way Pavers and the Exhilarating Change President Carter Wrought," *Fordham Law Review* LXIV (November 1995): 284–6.

segregation in the military, but he made no public statement on the expansion of women's opportunities in the armed forces.[94]

MEDIOCRITY ON THE SUPREME COURT

Truman's is the most embarrassing record in the history of presidential Supreme Court appointments. A 1970 poll of scholars rated eight justices "failures"; three were Truman appointments: Harold Burton, Fred Vinson, and Sherman Minton. Vinson, moreover, has the distinction of being the only chief justice rated a failure. Truman's fourth appointment, Tom Clark, was rated only "average."[95] In addition to the overall poor quality of his choices, Truman's appointments were a disaster for civil liberties.

When Justice Owen Roberts resigned in 1945, Truman appointed an old Senate colleague, Harold Burton, to replace him. Burton was a Republican, and Truman took the advice that a gesture of bipartisanship would be politically wise. Burton's appointment established the Truman pattern of consistently choosing people he knew personally and had come to trust, with no serious consideration of judicial qualifications. Critics soon charged him with "cronyism" in all appointments, and the judgment stuck. Burton proved to be a very undistinguished justice and except in civil rights cases rarely supported civil liberties.[96]

The following year, Chief Justice Harlan Fiske Stone died. Truman again selected a loyal Democrat, Fred M. Vinson, who had served in Congress from 1924 to 1937 (except for a brief interruption), had been a judge on the U.S. Court of Appeals, and had held several positions under both Presidents Roosevelt and Truman. Perhaps most important, he was a regular member of Truman's poker parties. In short, he was another crony, a person Truman knew well, with no evident qualifications for the crucial chief justice position.[97]

Three years later, in summer 1949, the deaths of Justices Frank Murphy and Wiley Rutledge decimated the civil libertarian bloc on the Court, leaving only Hugo Black and William O. Douglas. To replace them, Truman selected Tom C. Clark and Sherman Minton. Clark was yet another loyal Democrat, having served in the Justice Department since 1937, and as attorney general since 1945. In those positions he became one of Truman's most-trusted political advisers on domestic issues, and a regular participant at the president's poker parties. Clark had a strong commitment to civil rights, almost always voting in favor of racial justice, but on cold war issues he consistently favored the government. Having been Truman's attorney general in 1947, he naturally thought the loyalty program "worked surprisingly well." In the famous "Red Monday" decisions in June 1957, when the Court struck down several anti-communist measures, Clark was the

94 "Women Get Place in U.S. Military," *NYT*, June 13, 1948. Truman issued no official statement or signing statement.

95 Henry J. Abraham, *Justice, Presidents, And Senators*. 5th ed. (Lanham, MD: Rowman & Littlefield, 2008), pp. 187–96, Appendix A, pp. 373–76.

96 Mary Frances Berry, *Stability, Security, and Continuity: Mr. Justice Burton and Decision-making in the Supreme Court, 1945–1958* (Westport, CT: Greenwood Press, 1978). "Cronyism:" Henry J. Abraham, *Justices, Presidents, and Senators*, p. 188. Truman "primarily treated judgeships as patronage": Goldman, *Picking Federal Judges*, p. 76. The cronyism issue raised in 1946: Arthur Krock, "'Government by Crony': A Lively Capital Issue," *NYT*, February 10, 1946.

97 The poker parties: Clark, OH, p. 56, HSTPL. James E. St. Clair and Linda C. Gugin, *Chief Justice Fred M. Vinson of Kentucky: A Political Biography* (Lexington: University Press of Kentucky, 2002).

lone dissenter in each case. He angered his old friend and patron Truman, however, by joining the majority in declaring unconstitutional the seizure of the steel mills.[98]

Sherman Minton had been a fervent New Deal Democrat in the Senate from 1935 to 1941, when he worked with Truman and won the personal friendship that Truman valued in his Court appointments. He had served on the Seventh Circuit Court of Appeals from 1941 until appointed to the Supreme Court. There, he quickly joined its conservative wing, giving no support to civil liberties.[99]

In his 1954 analysis *Civil Liberties and the Vinson Court*, the political scientist C. Herman Pritchett found that the four Truman appointees consistently had the worst records on civil liberties among all sitting justices, particularly on the rights of criminal defendants and federal free speech cases. Tom Clark and Harold Burton had good voting records on civil rights cases, but Chief Justice Vinson had the worst record of the group, not once voting in favor of African-American plaintiffs. Sherman Minton, meanwhile, had a very weak record, supporting civil rights in only 33 percent of the cases (where he was joined by Robert Jackson and Stanley Reed).[100]

Truman's appointments had a powerful effect on the Court's position on civil liberties for many years. Had only one of his four been as strong as Justices Murphy and Rutledge on civil liberties, a number of crucial 5–4 decisions adverse to civil liberties in the 1950s might well have gone the other way. Perhaps most important was *Adamson v. California* in 1947 in which the Court narrowly (5–4) rejected Justice Hugo Black's argument that the due process clause of the Fourteenth Amendment incorporated all of the first eight amendments in the Bill of Rights. Justices Vinson and Burton, the two Truman appointees on the Court at that time, voted with the majority. It is a remote possibility that the *Dennis* decision upholding the constitutionality of the Smith Act could have been 5–3 to invalidate the law had Truman's three appointees who voted in the case (Clark recused himself) been civil libertarians equal to the three Roosevelt appointees his choices replaced. The course of constitutional law and the domestic cold war might have been very different had Truman chosen more distinguished and pro–civil liberties justices. Instead, however, the Supreme Court did not emerge until the late 1950s, under the leadership of the new Chief Justice Earl Warren, appointed by President Eisenhower.

THE AMBIGUITY OF STRONG PRESIDENTIAL LEADERSHIP

Harry Truman more than deserves his high reputation for strong presidential leadership. On four occasions – using the atomic bomb, developing the containment doctrine, championing civil rights (especially desegregating the military), and firing General MacArthur) – he was decisive and courageous in tackling monumentally difficult issues. With respect to civil liberties, however, presidential leadership was adulterated. If he was

[98] Merle Miller, *Plain Speaking: An Oral Biography of Harry S. Truman*. Pbk. ed. (New York: Berkley Medallion Books, 1974). The authenticity of some of the material in *Plain Speaking* is challenged in Robert H. Ferrell and Francis H. Heller, "Plain Faking?" *American Heritage*, 46 (May/June, 1995): 14–15. The authors compared the book with the original tape recordings in the Truman Presidential Library. Red Monday: Arthur J. Sabin, *In Calmer Times: The Supreme Court and Red Monday* (Philadelphia: University of Pennsylvania Press, 1999).

[99] Linda C. Gugin and James E. St. Clair, *Sherman Minton: New Deal Senator, Cold War Justice* (Indianapolis: Indiana Historical Society, 1997).

[100] Pritchett, *Civil Liberties and the Vinson Court*, Table 9, p. 190. Sabin, *In Calmer Times: The Supreme Court and Red Monday*.

a pioneer on racial justice, he left a very dangerous legacy on freedom of speech and association and on presidential power. Indeed, he fashioned the anti-communist agenda at home and abroad that continued for decades and involved some of the worst assaults on civil liberties in American history.

Without any question, Truman stands as the only president who risked his political future in defense of individual rights. His early and strong support for racial equality was a courageous stand that was far in advance of public opinion and could have cost him reelection in 1948. Nor was it confined to a single act. He created the first presidential Civil Rights Commission, was the first president to address the nation's largest civil rights group, submitted the first comprehensive civil rights legislative package to Congress, and most notably ended racial segregation in the military by executive order. Lyndon Johnson achieved far more in the 1960s, but only because the politics of race had changed so dramatically in the interim and LBJ enjoyed the tide of public opinion and the courts on his side.

At the same time, however, Truman's loyalty program was a sweeping assault on freedom of belief and association. It penalized opinion, sanctioned the principle of guilt by association, and disastrously set the stage for McCarthyism. Truman also embraced a dangerously broad view of presidential power: his threat to draft strikers in 1946, his refusal to seek a congressional resolution on the Korean War, and his seizure of the steel industry in 1952. Although the Supreme Court rebuffed him in the steel industry case, his view of the president's power as commander in chief set a dangerous precedent for the future. With regard to the Supreme Court, Truman's appointments were embarrassingly mediocre, and with the exception of civil rights cases, tilted the Court in an anti–civil liberties direction for more than a decade.

In the end, President Harry Truman's record was a tangle of contradictions: outstanding on civil rights, but terrible on freedom of speech and association with regard to the cold war. He is most famous today for his courageous presidential leadership on major decision. Here, too, he was contradictory where those decisions implicated civil liberties: firing General Douglas MacArthur to preserve civilian control of the military, but seizing the steel mills in a serious overreach of presidential power. On the latter issue, his legacy is more heavily weighted on the negative side.

President Dwight D. Eisenhower, center, with Earl Warren, right, and Richard Nixon, left, 1950s. Eisenhower appointed Warren chief justice of the Supreme Court, later calling it his "biggest mistake" as president. Nixon served as vice president under Eisenhower and was elected president in 1968. He resigned in disgrace in 1974.
Source: California State Archives.

6 Dwight D. Eisenhower

A Failure of Presidential Leadership

"MY BIGGEST MISTAKE"

In an oft-told story, Dwight D. Eisenhower said his biggest mistake as president was appointing Earl Warren to the Supreme Court.[1] Even if apocryphal, the statement has metaphoric truth. Two issues dominated domestic politics during Eisenhower's presidency: McCarthyism and civil rights. Eisenhower was an abject failure on both, consistently refusing to denounce Senator Joe McCarthy by name and failing to endorse the Supreme Court's historic 1954 decision in *Brown v. Board of Education*. On both issues he refused to see the their importance to civil liberties and to American democracy. It is a sad commentary on his presidency that the person he regarded as his biggest mistake became a civil liberties icon in American history.

President Eisenhower is often regarded as the symbol of the 1950s, an allegedly tranquil period of peace, prosperity, conformity, and conservatism. The popular image of the decade, however, is utterly misleading. The Eisenhower years were filled with conflict: the hysteria of McCarthyism and the dramatic emergence of the civil rights movement, which included the electrifying *Brown* decision, the Montgomery bus boycott, and federal troops in Little Rock, Arkansas, to enforce school integration. Artistic and popular culture developments - exemplified by the Beat generation, Elvis Presley, and James Dean- challenged the norms of mainstream American culture and presaged social upheavals in the 1960s.[2]

SILENCE ON JOE MCCARTHY

Meeting with Senator Joe McCarthy in a Peoria, Illinois, hotel room on October 2, 1952, the Republican presidential candidate Eisenhower turned purple with rage. McCarthy had earlier made outrageous charges that General George C. Marshall served the cause of international communism. In addition to being Eisenhower's longtime colleague and friend, Marshall was an American hero, as army chief of staff during World War II

1 Stephen Ambrose, *Eisenhower the President*, V. 2 (New York: Simon & Schuster, 1984), p. 190, based on the author's interview with Eisenhower. The former Supreme Court justice Tom Clark recalled Eisenhower's saying he was "disappointed" and "very much disturbed" with both Warren and Justice William J. Brennan. Clark, OH, HSTPL, p. 214. Brownell doubted the story. Herbert Brownell, *Advising Ike: The Memoirs of Attorney General Herbert Brownell* (Lawrence: University of Kansas Press, 1993), p. 173, 197, n. 5. President Harry Truman is alleged to have made similar criticisms of his appointee Tom Clark, but the authenticity of the source for this statement has been questioned. Comment: Merle Miller, *Plain Speaking: An Oral Biography of Harry S. Truman* (New York: Berkeley, 1974), pp. 225-6.

2 I. F. Stone, *The Haunted Fifties* (New York: Random House, 1963).

and author of the 1947 Marshall Plan to rescue a devastated Europe. In a seventy-two-thousand-word Senate speech on June 14, 1951, however, McCarthy attacked him as part of a "great conspiracy" to allow the United States to "fall victim" to Soviet aggression abroad. Furious, Eisenhower planned to support his friend publicly during a campaign swing through Wisconsin. GOP strategists and his own aides, however, told him he simply could not rebuke McCarthy, then a fearsome political power, on his home turf. Eisenhower defended Marshall with what aides described as "red hot anger." The argument continued through several campaign stops. Angry at McCarthy, his advisers, and ultimately himself, Eisenhower caved in and deleted the reference to Marshall in a major speech in Milwaukee. Much to his embarrassment, the press reported the capitulation. McCarthy blandly denied he had pressured Ike, but it is unlikely that many believed him.[3]

Not criticizing McCarthy by name stands as Eisenhower's first great failure as president. By 1952 McCarthy's reckless and irresponsible attacks had poisoned American politics, ruined the lives of loyal public servants, and demoralized the State Department and other federal agencies. "McCarthyism" introduced an irrational and vicious incivility into American politics and cowed political leaders into silence. Criticizing McCarthy or his tactics only earned you an accusation that you too were a part of the alleged great communist conspiracy.[4]

McCarthy's critics believed that only Eisenhower, as an enormously popular president, a Republican, and a great war hero, could rebuke McCarthy and survive. The Democratic Party leader Lyndon Johnson candidly told people that attacking McCarthy was a losing proposition for a Democrat: "We will all lose and he will win." Despite repeated pleas to speak out, however, Ike kept silent. In June 1952, even before winning the GOP nomination, he was asked whether he supported McCarthy's reelection to the Senate and replied that he would not "indulge in personalities." He did deliver an indirect slap, however, by declaring that rooting communists out of government "can be done without besmirching the reputation of any innocent man or condemning by loose association or anything else."[5] It was clear whom he was referring to, but Ike refused to mention McCarthy by name throughout his presidency.

[3] Confrontation: Sherman Adams, *First-Hand Report: The Story of the Eisenhower Administration* (New York: Harper and Brothers, 1961), pp. 30–2. Stephen E. Ambrose, *Eisenhower*, V. 1, *Soldier, General of the Army, President-Elect, 1890–1952* (New York: Touchstone Books, 1985), pp. 563–6. "Marshall U.S. Foe, McCarthy Charges," *NYT*, June 15, 1951. At an August 1952 press conference an angry Eisenhower "rose from his chair" to defend Marshall, ibid., August 23, 1952. Joseph McCarthy, *America's Retreat from Victory: The Story of George Catlett Marshall* (New York: Devin-Adair, 1951). A draft of original speech: Draft page, "Sixth Draft" of Eisenhower speech given on October 3, 1952, in Milwaukee, Wisconsin on "Communism and Freedom." DDEPL, Digital Documents. The deleted paragraph refers to General George C. Marshall. Reeves, *The Life and Times of Joe McCarthy*, pp. 436–40. "McCarthy Denies Swaying General," *NYT*, October 5, 1952. Eisenhower's temper vividly described: Kay Summersby Morgan, *Past Forgetting: My Love Affair with Dwight D. Eisenhower.* Pbk. ed. (New York: Bantam Books, 1977), p. 150.

[4] Haynes Johnson, *The Age of Anxiety: McCarthyism to Terrorism* (Orlando, FL: Harcourt, Inc., 2005). Thomas C. Reeves, *The Life and Times of Joe McCarthy: A Biography* (New York: Stein and Day, 1982). Robert Griffith, *The Politics of Fear: Joseph R. McCarthy and the Senate* (Amherst: University of Massachusetts Press, 1987). Richard H. Rovere, *Senator Joe McCarthy* (New York: Harcourt, Brace, 1959). David M. Oshinsky, *A Conspiracy So Immense: The World of Joe McCarthy* (New York: Free Press 1983). Defense of McCarthy: Roy Cohn, *McCarthy* (New York: New American Library, 1968). William F. Buckley, Jr. and Brent Bozell, *McCarthy and His Enemies: The Record and Its Meaning* (Washington, DC: Regnery, 1995).

[5] Robert A. Caro, *The Years of Lyndon Johnson: Master of the Senate.* Pbk. ed. (New York: Vintage Books, 2003), p. 547. Transcript, Eisenhower Press Conference. *NYT*, June 6, 1952.

The speechwriter Arthur Larson observed that Ike had "a sense of loathing and contempt [for McCarthy] that had to be seen to be believed." Why, then, was he so reluctant to criticize the man by name? Most important, he thought it would only give McCarthy more publicity. Ten weeks into his presidency, he confided to his diary that "nothing will be so effective in combating his particular kind of troublemaking as to ignore him." He bluntly told his aide C. D. Jackson, "I will not get in the gutter with that guy." GOP leaders, meanwhile, strongly advised him that criticizing McCarthy could wreck the Republican Party.[6] The strategy of ignoring McCarthy failed, and in March 1954 the broadcaster Edward R. Murrow finally deflated the demagogue in a famous direct attack on national television.

"Don't Join the Book Burners"

On two occasions in his first year as president, Eisenhower made strong public criticisms of McCarthy-style tactics. In both cases, however, he quickly undermined his own statements. In a passionate impromptu remark at the Dartmouth College commencement on June 14, 1953, Ike warned against the dangers of hysteria and censorship, counseling the audience, "Don't Join the Book Burners." ... "Don't be afraid to go in your library and read every book, as long as that document does not offend your ideas of decency. That should be the only censorship." It was one of the most forceful statements about freedom to read by any president.[7]

There was no mystery about Ike's real target in his Dartmouth speech. His call for tolerance was prompted by the recent outrageous antics of the McCarthy aides Roy Cohn and G. David Schine. In a whirlwind tour of U.S. Information Agency (USIA) libraries in Europe, they forced the removal of allegedly subversive books by more than forty authors. The books included Dashiell Hammett's *The Thin Man* and *The Maltese Falcon* and one by the noted African-American poet Langston Hughes. Both authors were known to have leftist sympathies. USIA officials actually burned eleven books at libraries in Singapore and Sydney, Australia. This embarrassing reminder of Nazi Germany prompted a May 15 State Department order that books removed from library shelves "not be destroyed but stored pending further instructions."[8]

Ike's Dartmouth remarks gained favorable press coverage, but just three days later he undercut their impact. A reporter asked whether his comments should be interpreted "as being critical of a school of thought represented by Senator McCarthy." Ike repeated his now familiar refrain, "I never discuss personalities." He then added that he did not endorse books advocating the violent overthrow of the government and favored the

6 Arthur Larson, *Eisenhower: The President Nobody Knew* (New York: Scribner's, 1968), p. 13. Quoted in Haynes Johnson, *Age of Anxiety: McCarthyism to Terrorism* (Orlando, FL: Harcourt, 2005), p. 266. "Gutter": Robert J. Donovan, *Eisenhower: The Inside Story* (New York: Harper and Brothers, 1956), p. 249. McCarthy attacked Milton Eisenhower in an effort to provoke the president. Milton Eisenhower, *The President Is Calling* (New York: Doubleday, 1974), pp. 317–18.

7 Remarks at the Dartmouth College Commencement Exercises, Hanover, New Hampshire.June 14, 1953, APP. This version contains the "book burners" passage, which was reportedly not in his prepared speech.

8 Roy Cohn's account: Roy Cohn, *McCarthy: The Answer to 'Tailgunner Joe'* (New York: Manor Books, 1977), Ch. 6, "The Book Burners," pp. 75–92. "Books of 40 Authors Banned By U.S. in Overseas Library," *NYT*, June 22, 1953. A firsthand account of the episode by the famed cook Julia Child, whose husband was with the State Department: Child, FAOH.

destruction of such books that might be in U.S. libraries overseas. Two weeks later, he partially backtracked from these remarks, saying he did not think that Hammett's novels should have been removed. The damage was done, however, and his position on censorship of controversial authors remained completely muddled in the public eye.[9]

In the midst of this controversy, another incident prompted Eisenhower to speak out against anti-communist hysteria. McCarthy had just hired J. B. Matthews as a Senate committee staff member. Matthews was one of many former leftists who became professional anti-communists during the cold war. In the July 1953 issue of the *American Mercury* (H. L. Mencken's old magazine, which was now passionately anti-communist), he made the outrageous charge that seven thousand Protestant clergy served "the Kremlin's conspiracy." The opening sentence accused them of being "the largest single group supporting the communist apparatus" in the United States.[10] This typical McCarthy-style slur provoked a national uproar, particularly among prominent religious leaders. Many Americans willing to tolerate attacks on left-wing labor leaders or college professors were outraged at this attack on mainstream Protestant churches.

Several White House staff members schemed to maneuver their boss into a public statement by quietly inviting the National Conference of Christians and Jews to send Eisenhower a letter of protest, thereby giving him the opportunity to reply. Ike replied with a telegram, drafted by the same aides, saying that Matthews's attack represented "contempt for the principles of freedom and decency." He did not, however, denounce the man who hired Matthews and in this case was manipulated by his staff. In the face of public outrage, Matthews quickly resigned his position with McCarthy.[11]

Eisenhower finally moved against McCarthy in November 1953, but only after the senator crossed a political rubicon by attacking his administration in a national radio and television speech. White House aides regarded the speech as "a declaration of war against the president." Ike's press secretary, James C. Hagerty, noted in his diary on March 8, 1954, that Ike had "really made up his mind to fight Joe from now on in." But it was very late in the game. Even the political scientist Fred Greenstein, who argues that Ike was actually a strong leader, concluded that "he held his fire until McCarthy became open to attack by any right-thinking American."[12]

The real credit for lancing the boil of McCarthyism belongs to the CBS newsperson Edward R. Murrow for his now-famous *See It Now* program on the senator on March 9, 1954. In a mere thirty minutes, Murrow demolished McCarthy, largely by letting him speak for himself. A month later, McCarthy sealed his doom by attacking the U.S. Army (accusing it of promoting a dentist with alleged left-wing associations), in the famous

[9] The President's News Conference of June 17, 1953, APP. "Eisenhower Backs Ban on Some Books by U.S. Overseas," *NYT*, June 18, 1953. Hammett had just taken the Fifth Amendment before McCarthy's Committee on March 26.

[10] "Uncheckable Charge," *Time*, July 13, 1953. J. B. Matthews, "Reds and the Churches," *American Mercury* 77 (July 1953): 3–13. Reverend Oxnam was a good friend of the Virginia senator Harry Byrd, an influential conservative. Caro, *Master of the Senate*, pp. 548–9.

[11] "Eisenhower Scores Attack on Clergy; McCarthy Aide Out," *NYT*, July 10, 1953. Sherman Adams, *First-Hand Report*, pp. 141–2. NCCJ: Emmet John Hughes, *Ordeal of Power: A Political Memoir of the Eisenhower Years* (New York: Dell, 1964), p. 84. Donovan, *Eisenhower: The Inside Story*, p. 95. Brownell, *Advising Ike*, p. 256.

[12] "Eisenhower Staff Interprets McCarthy Speech as Attack," *NYT*, November 26, 1953. Chester J. Pach and Elmo R. Richardson, *The Presidency of Dwight D. Eisenhower* (Lawrence: University Press of Kansas, 1991), p. 67. Fred I. Greenstein, *The Hidden-Hand Presidency: Eisenhower as Leader*. Pbk. ed. (New York: Basic Books, 1984), p. 182.

Army-McCarthy hearings that exposed his reckless and cruel attacks on national television. Senate Republican leaders finally turned on him, but even then Eisenhower took no public stand. On August 4, with the Senate moving to censure McCarthy, Ike declined to "interfere" with the debate. The Senate resolution "condemning" McCarthy passed on December 2, 1954. With astonishing speed, his influence in American life collapsed (although the anti-communist crusade continued for many years).[13]

Two future presidents were in the Senate at the time of the condemnation. Lyndon Johnson, who had previously held off criticizing McCarthy, voted for the resolution. Much controversy surrounds the failure of Senator John F. Kennedy even to vote on the resolution. He was convalescing from major back surgery at the time, but as many critics have pointed out, he did not use the standard Senate practice of "pairing" his vote with someone on the other side (as four other senators did) nor make any public statement. Thus, Kennedy was the only Democrat not to vote against McCarthy. McCarthy was a friend of Kennedy's father, and, more consequentially for the man who would follow Eisenhower in the White House, Jack Kennedy accepted the basic premise of domestic anti-communism.[14]

CIVIL RIGHTS: A LEADERSHIP FAILURE

Waffling on *Brown v. Board of Education*

The night Eisenhower was elected president on November 4, 1952, his top aides knew that a momentous Supreme Court hearing on race discrimination was exactly a month away. The Court had scheduled oral arguments on *Brown v. Board of Education,* a challenge to racially segregated schools, for December 9th, bringing it face-to-face with its 1896 *Plessy v. Ferguson* decision upholding the doctrine of "separate but equal." Despite the Court's increasing hostility to race discrimination, no one in 1952 was certain how it would rule on the explosive issue of segregated public schools. Chief Justice Fred M. Vinson, for example, had a particularly weak record on civil rights, the worst among all his colleagues, in fact.[15]

The outgoing Truman administration had filed an amicus brief urging the Court to overturn the 1896 *Plessy v. Ferguson* decision, and the Court now wanted to know the new administration's views. At a Justice Department event on January 26, 1953, Chief Justice Vinson took aside the new assistant attorney general, Warren Burger (the future chief

13 Thomas Rosteck, *See it Now Confronts McCarthyism: Television Documentary and the Politics of Representation* (Tucaloosa: University of Alabama Press, 1994). Joseph E. Persico, *Murrow: An American Original* (New York: McGraw-Hill, 1988). *Good Night and Good Luck* [videorecording]: *The Edward R. Murrow Television Collection/* CBS Broadcast International (New York: Ambrose Video Publishing, Inc., 1991). See also the film *Good Night and Good Luck* (2005). Hagerty, Diary, March 8, 1954, DDEPL, Digital Documents. "President Implies McCarthy Is Peril to Unity of G.O.P.," *NYT*, March 11, 1954; "President Agrees He Should Combat Any Split in G.O.P.," ibid., August 5, 1954; Four alternative Senate resolutions are in ibid., August 1, 1954; "Republicans Split," ibid., December 3, 1954.

14 Herbert S. Parmet, *Jack: The Struggles of John F. Kennedy* (New York: Dial Press, 1980), pp. 300–11.

15 Robert Fredrick Bark, *The Eisenhower Administration and Black Civil Rights* (Knoxville: University of Tennessee Press, 1984). Irving J. Spitzberg, Jr., *Racial Politics in Little Rock, 1954–1964* (New York: Garland, 1987). George R. Metcalf, *From Little Rock to Boston: The History of School Desegregation* (Westport, CT: Greenwood Press, 1983). Daisy Bates, *The Long Shadow of Little Rock: A Memoir* (New York: David McKay, 1962). David A. Nichols, *A Matter of Justice: Eisenhower and the Beginnings of the Civil Rights Revolution* (New York: Simon & Schuster, 2007) argues unpersuasively that Eisenhower provided strong leadership on civil rights.

justice), and said it would be "very important" for the administration to file an amicus brief and "lend its support" to the case. The request forced the Eisenhower administration's hand.[16]

President Eisenhower did not want to get involved in the case, believing that a "rendering of 'opinion' by the Attorney General ... would invade the duties, responsibilities and authority of the Supreme Court." Ike was well read on American history and the Constitution and concluded that the separation of powers precluded an administration statement on the case. Attorney General Herbert Brownell, however, was committed to a strong civil rights position. A leader of the moderate wing of the Republican Party, he had fought for civil rights during ten years as a New York state legislator.[17] He not only believed in racial justice as a matter of principle, but saw political advantage in the case. Republicans had won 42 percent of the African-American vote in urban precincts outside the South in 1952, and he and other GOP moderates envisioned greater gains in 1956. Taking Vinson's request to the White House, he skillfully outmaneuvered his boss. Completely unintimidated by Eisenhower's status as president and war hero, he cleverly appealed to Ike's military background. The Court's request, he explained, was virtually a command, which the executive branch had a "duty" to honor. Brownell knew very well that the word "duty" had special meaning for a career military officer. Ignoring it, he added, might even antagonize the Court. This argument carried the day, and Eisenhower authorized a brief.[18]

Then came the question of what position to take on *Plessy*. The Truman administration's brief forthrightly declared segregation unconstitutional and urged the Court to overturn *Plessy*. Brownell opted for filing a supplement to the Truman administration brief that did not explicitly call for overturning *Plessy*, later explaining that this approach implied overturning *Plessy* without actually saying so. The oral argument was another matter, however, and Brownell again outwitted the president. He very sensibly pointed out that some justice would probably ask the solicitor general a direct question about the constitutionality of *Plessy*, and that it would be embarrassing and possibly damaging not to give a clear answer. Eisenhower asked him what he personally believed, and Brownell, choosing his words "carefully," as he later recalled, said he thought segregation was unconstitutional as a matter of law. Eisenhower, again the career military leader who believed firmly in delegating responsibility, replied that if that was his "professional opinion," he should "so state" to the Court. At the oral argument Justice William O. Douglas did ask about *Plessy*, noting that the administration's brief appeared to equivocate on the issue. "No, your honor, no," Solicitor General J. Lee Rankin insisted; the "pervading purpose of the Fourteenth Amendment" was that all men "are entitled to equal protection of

16 Firsthand account of Vinson's comments: Warren Burger, OH, pp. 24–30, ROHO.

17 Eisenhower, Memorandum for the Record, August 19, 1953. ACW Files, Administration Series, Brownell File, DDEPL. Greenstein, *The Hidden Hand Presidency*, does not discuss civil rights in his defense of Eisenhower. Michael S. Mayer, "With Much Deliberation and Some Speed: Eisenhower and the Brown Decision," *Journal of Southern History* LII (February 1986): 44 is an unpersuasive defense of Eisenhower.

18 Brownell, *Advising Ike*, Ch. 11, "Building the Foundations of Equality," pp. 186–201, is an important firsthand account of Brownell's manipulation of Eisenhower. Ike-Brownell conversation: Eisenhower Memorandum for the Record, August 19, 1953, ACW Files, Administration Series, Brownell File, DDEPL. The Truman administration claimed Democrats did well among African Americans in northern cities. Philleo Nash, Memorandum for the President, November 7, 1952, Nash Papers, Box 63, HSTPL. Kay Summersby explains his abrupt and heartbreaking termination of their affair in terms of his sense of duty: Summersby, *Past Forgetting*, pp. 279, 287.

the law." Thus, over Eisenhower's personal reservations, Brownell put the administration clearly on record favoring reversal of *Plessy*.[19]

As the Court's 1953–4 term approached, a completely unexpected event added more drama to the *Brown* case, with a result that had profound and lasting implications for civil rights and civil liberties in America. On September 8, one month before the Court's term was to begin, Chief Justice Vinson died of a heart attack. With an early opportunity to put his stamp on the Court, Eisenhower selected the California governor, Earl Warren, a popular Republican with a reputation for integrity. Many believed Vinson, a conservative Kentuckian with a very weak record on civil rights, had been reluctant to overturn *Plessy*. Warren, on the other hand, is almost universally credited with forging the unanimous opinion in *Brown* that greatly strengthened the force of the highly controversial decision. Warren, of course, went on to lead the greatest civil liberties Supreme Court in American history.[20]

The Supreme Court delivered its landmark decision in *Brown* on May 17, 1954, holding racially segregated schools unconstitutional. The unanimous 9–0 decision, and the forceful opinion by Warren, surprised even the most hopeful civil rights advocates and gave the movement for racial equality energy and optimism it had not before had.

Ike did not like the decision. In an unguarded moment, he told his speechwriter Arthur Larson, "As a matter of fact, I personally think the decision was wrong." Shocked, Larson understood this was a "bombshell" statement. Years later, he agonized over whether to mention it in his memoirs. He finally opted for candor, and his account is the only record of Ike's clear hostility to the decision. In another incident immediately after the decision, Ike told Brownell about President Andrew Jackson's famous but apocryphal remark "The Supreme Court has made its decision, let them enforce it." Alarmed, Brownell scurried back to his office and wrote Ike a memo explaining that while Jackson may have said that, he faithfully carried out the order, adding for emphasis, "just as any other good president would do." Once again, Brownell countered his boss by skillfully playing to his strong sense of duty under the law.[21]

In the wake of the momentous ruling, the country inevitably looked to the president for guidance on how to respond. At a press conference two days after the decision, a South Carolina reporter asked Ike the expected question. His answer firmly established his vacillation on *Brown*, which has haunted his reputation ever since. After counseling the country to "be calm and be reasonable," he explained that "the Supreme Court has spoken and I am sworn to uphold the constitutional processes in this country; and I will obey." Virtually everyone noticed that he did not explicitly endorse *Brown* and said nothing about the larger principle of racial equality and the nation's historic commitment to equality.[22]

The *Brown* decision arrived right in the middle of the televised Army-McCarthy hearings where Senator McCarthy effectively destroyed himself. The famous attack on him by the attorney Joseph N. Welch ("Have you no sense of decency, sir? At long last,have you

[19] Brownell, *Advising Ike*, p. 193. Mayer, "With Much Deliberation and Some Speed," p. 48.

[20] Ed Cray, *Chief Justice: A Biography of Earl Warren* (New York: Simon & Schuster, 1997, pp. 247–53. Jim Newton, *Justice for All: Earl Warren and the Nation He Made* (New York: Riverhead Books, 2006), pp. 1–11.

[21] Larson, *Eisenhower: The President Nobody Knew*, pp. 124–33. The incident occurred on October 1, 1957, one week after Eisenhower ordered troops to Little Rock, Arkansas, to enforce the school integration. Brownell, OH, pp. 29–30, DDEPL. Brownell, OH, pp. 73–4, ROHO.

[22] The President's News Conference of May 19, 1954, APP.

left no sense of decency?") that delivered the coup de grace occurred on June 9, three weeks after the decision. The two events that spring marked the beginning of the end of the era of McCarthyism in American politics and the dawn of the new era of civil rights.

Eisenhower, race, and presidential leadership

Several influences shaped Eisenhower's tepid response to *Brown* and to civil rights in general. Personally, he did not believe in racial equality or integration. He had spent forty years in a segregated army, had lived in the South, and counted several southerners among his best friends. One was the South Carolina governor James F. Byrnes, who pressed his segregationist views on the new president by letter and in person.[23] Ike repeatedly expressed his concern for white southerners' having to change their way of life, without once expressing empathy for the plight of African Americans in a segregated society. Unlike Harry Truman and Lyndon Johnson, Eisenhower was not able to transcend his background and see segregation as a violation of American ideals.

Equally important, Eisenhower did not believe that courts or government at any level should use the law to bring about racial equality. He had regarded integrating the armed services as a "social experiment," and he saw *Brown* as equally ill advised. Discussing the 1956 GOP platform, Ike told the Connecticut senator Prescott Bush that "civil rights will not be achieved by law," and that "reversals of progress" had occurred because of the *Brown* decision. The Reverend Billy Graham, on his way to becoming the unofficial religious adviser to several presidents, reinforced this view, telling Ike in 1956 that the "tensions" arising from *Brown* had set back civil rights progress. Ike believed his main responsibility as president was to maintain order, and he saw court-ordered integration as only creating disorder. As it happened, his passivity on *Brown* may well have encouraged the very lawlessness he sought to prevent, including the famous 1957 confrontation over school integration in Little Rock, Arkansas, which as we shall see forced him to dispatch federal troops to enforce a lawful court order.[24]

Eisenhower's understanding of American history and the Constitution further reinforced his passive approach to *Brown* and civil rights. As Brownell explained, Ike had a "deep respect for the Constitution, its separation of powers, and the duties it placed on the presidency." He had supported Truman's firing of General MacArthur in 1951, because he believed strongly in civilian control of the military. On civil rights, however, he interpreted the separation of powers principle to mean that the president should not intrude into the Court's business.[25]

Personal character and his view of the presidency also influenced his thinking on civil rights. In a very insightful memoir, the speechwriter Emmet John Hughes argues that despite being a great military hero and enormously popular president, "there was in him a profound humility," "a refusal to *use* the full force of his personal authority or

[23] Byrnes-Eisenhower correspondence, 1953, ACW Files, DDEPL.

[24] Wilton B. Persons, Memorandum for the Record, August 1, 1956, ACW File, DDE Diary, Box 17, DDEPL. Graham: Sherman Adams, *First Hand Report*, p. 337. Nancy Gibbs and Michael Duffy, *The Preacher and the Presidents* (New York: Center Street, 2007), pp. 41–53. Lewis Gould, *The Modern American Presidency* (Lawrence: University Press of Kansas, 2003), p. 121, argues that Eisenhower's failure to give *Brown* a strong endorsement "helped lead to the Little Rock crisis of 1957."

[25] Brownell, *Advising Ike*, pp. 190, 289.

political position." He saw himself as "a man of military affairs, a stranger to political affairs," and as a consequence was reluctant to take strong public positions on domestic issues. Additionally, he deeply respected George Washington's abhorrence of the "man on horseback," the strong leader who would impose his will on the country. As president, he saw himself as a "member of the team" and delegated great responsibility to his cabinet. In this regard, he was the antithesis of all the strong presidents of the twentieth century: Wilson, Roosevelt, Truman, Johnson, and Reagan.[26]

Ike also ignored one significant part of his military experience. Alone among the presidents of the civil rights era, he had a direct experience with racial integration. In the critical Battle of the Bulge in late 1944, a German counterattack threatened to inflict a major setback to allied forces. Desperate for troops, Eisenhower authorized two extraordinary steps: a pardon to any soldier currently detained on criminal charges who would return to combat and an opportunity for African Americans in noncombat units to serve in regular units "without regard to race or color." An estimated twenty-four hundred African Americans volunteered and served with distinction. Ike in fact told Congress in 1948 that "it worked out very well." Nonetheless, he urged Congress to maintain a segregated military. When men of different races are placed in "the most intimate circumstances," he explained, "we sometimes have trouble." He simply refused to accept the success of the improvised "experiment" of integration in the Battle of the Bulge and recognize that it was directly relevant to public school integration.[27]

In fairness, it should be noted that Eisenhower's views on race and court-ordered social change were consistent with those of many other prominent Americans. At a January 1957 meeting in the Oval Office, the *New York Times* publisher Arthur Hays Sulzberger heartily agreed with him that "the use of law or force only increased [civil rights] problems." Sulzberger then "shamefacedly admitted, for private use only, that even he would not want his 7 or 8 year old granddaughter to go to school with Negro boys just older than she is."[28]

Ike's Democratic Party opponent in 1952 and 1956, Adlai Stevenson, it is important to note, was also no crusader on civil rights. "As to the civil rights business," he wrote in early 1952, "the sledge hammer approach has been all wrong, both in the Negroes' interests as well as others." He opposed a "compulsory" federal fair employment practices commission (even though he had fought for a state commission while governor), thereby abandoning one of President Truman's major commitments. In an August 1952 speech to the New York State Democratic Convention, a center of strong civil rights support, he argued that progress on civil rights would not result from "government interference with free men, free markets, free ideas." The criticism of government activism sounded like standard conservative Republican rhetoric and owed nothing to the Democratic Party heritage of Roosevelt and Truman. To be sure, Stevenson fully supported *Brown* after it was decided but was hesitant about how to respond to southern resistance. Sounding exactly like Eisenhower, he said you cannot change long-standing customs "at the stroke of a pen." Among leading Democrats, Senators Hubert Humphrey, Paul Douglas, and Joseph

26 Hughes, *Ordeal of Power*, pp. 40, 114.

27 U.S. Senate, Committee on Armed Services, 80th Cong., 2nd Sess., Hearings, "Universal Military Training," (1948), pp. 995–96. Stephen E. Ambrose, *Eisenhower: The President*, V. 2. Pbk. ed. (New York: Simon & Schuster, 1985), pp. 364–72.

28 ACW Diary, January 3, 1957, ACW Files, Box 8, DDEPL.

Clark were the champions of civil rights, but in those years they were a minority even among northern members of the party. Stevenson's image among African Americans was so weak, in fact, that in the 1956 campaign he postponed a planned speech in Harlem because local party leaders advised him that "he might get booed." And on election day, Eisenhower scored significant gains among African-American voters, even carrying some normally Democratic big cities in the North because of African-American defections.[29]

The attitudes of Sulzberger and Stevenson remind us of the social and political context of the 1950s. Today, the history of the civil rights movement is told in triumphalist terms, with steady progress from *Brown* to the 1965 Voting Rights Act. In fact, it was a period of strong southern resistance, much conflict, and some serious setbacks. Polls indicated that a majority of white Americans outside the South did not support aggressive action against race discrimination. Although a weak president on the issue, Eisenhower was not out of step with mainstream thinking.

Implementing *Brown:* Protest and massive resistance

The Supreme Court itself was acutely aware of the practical problems involved in implementing *Brown* and scheduled oral arguments for the fall 1954 term in what became known as *Brown II*. Again forced to take a position, Eisenhower intervened directly to weaken support for integration. Brownell and Solicitor General Simon Sobeloff drafted a fairly strong brief advocating an integration plan that was both "orderly" and "as prompt as possible." When Sobeloff met with Eisenhower on Saturday, November 20, 1954, however, Ike deleted a section citing the peaceful desegregation of the armed services. He then inserted a new passage expressing sympathy for the white southern point of view, explaining that segregation was "a social institution that had existed for a long time" and was "fervently supported" by many people. Noting that *Brown* took into account psychological factors related to black children, he added a short lecture on the need to meet, "with understanding and good will," the psychological needs of white southerners wedded to the old system of segregated schools.[30] On this occasion, Ike again sympathized with white southerners while ignoring African Americans. Brownell and Sobeloff, however, outmaneuvered him, in an act of virtual insubordination. In the oral argument, Sobeloff argued that desegregation should not wait for changes in public attitudes.

Southerners responded to *Brown* with an aggressive campaign of "massive resistance" to school integration. In March 1956 nineteen U.S. senators and seventy-seven members of the House signed a Southern Manifesto that denounced the decision as an "unconstitutional" "encroachment" on states' rights and praised "the motives of those States which have declared the intention to resist forced integration by any lawful means."

[29] Stevenson to John S. Battle [Governor of Virginia], August 23, 1952, pp. 47–8; "Equal Rights," speech to NY State Democratic Convention, August 28, 1952, pp. 54–60; Press Conference, November 18, 1955, p. 605, Walter E. Johnson, ed., *The Papers of Adlai E. Stevenson*, V. IV, "Let's Talk Sense to the American People, 1952–1955 (Boston: Little, Brown, 1974). Speech on Integration, Portland, OR, February 12, 1956, ibid., VI, "Toward a New America, 1955–1957," pp. 64–7. "Harlem Opposes Stevenson Talk," *NYT*, September 7, 1956. "Negro Vote Shift Heaviest in South," ibid., November 11, 1956.

[30] Arthur Larson found Eisenhower uncomfortable using the word "racial," which he deleted, and even the word "discrimination," which remained in, for his acceptance speech at the 1956 Republican Convention. Larson astutely observes that there is "No more penetrating way of identifying the exact shades of a man's opinions" than by tracking changes in drafts of speeches. Larson, *Eisenhower: The President Nobody Knew*, pp. 126–28.

Notably, three southern senators did not sign it: Estes Kefauver and Albert Gore, Sr., of Tennessee, and, most important, Lyndon Johnson of Texas. Johnson's refusal is generally regarded as a pivotal moment in his career. Ambitious for greatness and with an eye on the White House, he began shifting his identity from southerner to national Democratic Party leader. Whatever his political motivations, however, he hated segregation and began a long campaign to end it. A year later he would engineer passage of the first civil rights law in eighty-two years.[31]

When a reporter asked Eisenhower about the Southern Manifesto he pointed out that it did not explicitly call for illegal action and affirmed his duty to uphold the Constitution. Once again, he empathized with southerners and believed that it was "going to take time for them to adjust their thinking and their progress" on this momentous change. In words that increasingly infuriated civil rights leaders, Ike counseled "patience and ... understanding" and deplored "any great extreme action on either side." It was a morally and legally obtuse remark that equated resistance to a Supreme Court ruling with demands that it be enforced.[32]

The Southern Manifesto appeared exactly three and a half months after African Americans in Montgomery, Alabama, started a boycott of the city's segregated bus system. Begun on December 1, 1955, the boycott was a pivotal moment in American history, launching a vital decade in which civil rights progress would be driven not by the courts or presidents but by ordinary people engaged in direct action. J. Edgar Hoover responded by stepping up FBI surveillance of civil rights leaders, including the young and little-known Reverend Martin Luther King, Jr., directing Alabama FBI agents to send him "derogatory information" "about KING." At a March 1956 cabinet meeting, he gave a long lecture about communist support for civil rights, and in October he sent to the White House a confidential report, "The Communist and the Negro." His campaign to discredit King would eventually escalate into grotesque abuses.[33]

As part of the massive resistance effort, Virginia denied state funds to integrated schools, provided tuition grants for private schools, and created a state Pupil Placement Board that in practice maintained segregated schools. Several states sought to restrict the activities of the NAACP (a challenge to one Alabama law resulted in a historic 1958 Supreme Court ruling affirming a freedom of association). Arkansas, meanwhile, set the stage for a historic confrontation in Little Rock with a state constitutional amendment directing the legislature to oppose "in every Constitutional manner the un-constitutional desegregation decisions" of the U. S. Supreme Court.[34] When schools opened in fall

[31] *Congressional Record*, 84th Congress Second Session, V. 102, Part 4, March 12, 1956 (Washington, DC: Government Printing Office, 1956), pp., 4459–60. Robert Dallek, *Lone Star Rising: Lyndon Johnson and His Times, 1908–1960* (New York: Oxford University Press, 1991), p. 496. Fulbright: Skrentny, "The Effect of the Cold War on African-American Rights," p. 240. Some historians believe that signing the Manifesto cost Arkansas Senator William Fulbright appointment as Secretary of State by President Kennedy in 1961.

[32] The President's News Conference of March 14, 1956, APP.

[33] Memo, Special Agent in Charge, Mobile, AL, to Director, FBI, January 4, 1956, Clayborne Carson, ed., *The Papers of Martin Luther King, Jr.* (Berkeley, University of California Press, 1992), V. III, p. 96. Hoover to William H. Jackson, Special Assistant to the President, October 24, 1956, Personal and Confidential. Enclosed: The Communist Party and the Negro, 1953–1956. Secret. Available: www.eisenhower.archives.gov/Dl/Civil_Rights_Eisenhower _Administration/EisenhowerCivilRightsfiles.html

[34] Another Arkansas law required public school teachers to disclose all organizations they belonged to in an attempt to expose and harass NAACP members. Freedom of association: *NAACP v. Alabama*, 357 U.S. 449 (1958).

1956, violence erupted over integration in Mansfield, Texas; Clinton, Tennessee; Sturgis, Kentucky; and other communities. The Texas governor, Allan Shivers, a conservative Democrat and Eisenhower supporter, mobilized the Texas Rangers, who took no action against white vigilantes while denouncing NAACP leaders as "agitators." When asked about Governor Shivers's actions, Eisenhower flatly stated that the federal government would not intervene, and at a September 6, 1956 press conference he again said, "It is difficult through law and through force to change a man's heart." And in response to a direct question, he again declined to endorse *Brown* "personally." A year later, events in Little Rock would force him to reverse his position on federal intervention.[35]

In 1956, just two years after *Brown*, civil rights leaders saw many ominous signs. There had been little progress on school integration; southern states were mounting a campaign of massive resistance, including removing African Americans from voting rolls; the president of the United States provided no political, legal, or moral leadership on civil rights; and the leader of the Democratic Party had none of the former president Truman's strong convictions.

Federal troops to Little Rock

Eisenhower was finally forced to act in a historic confrontation over the authority of the federal courts that occurred in Little Rock, Arkansas, in the fall of 1957. Although he won much praise for eventually sending federal troops to enforce integration, most analysts then and now argue that he brought on the crisis by his earlier dithering. As the school year approached in the summer of 1957, die-hard segregationists vowed to fight integration, and it was not certain that the Little Rock police and the Arkansas National Guard would or could maintain order when African-American students arrived at the previously all-white Central High School. Asked what he would do in the event of disorder, President Eisenhower said he could not "imagine any set of circumstances that would ever induce me to send Federal troops" to enforce integration. He again counseled patience, saying it was a "mistake" to "try to go too far too fast in laws in this delicate field." His words undoubtedly emboldened segregationists, and the day before school opened on September 4 the Arkansas governor, Orval Faubus, mobilized the National Guard to place Central High School "off limits" to the nine African-American students scheduled to enroll. The Little Rock School Board, fearing violence, asked the students not to attend "until the legal dilemma was solved," but their parents refused to back down. And so on the first day of school a phalanx of Arkansas National Guard soldiers, standing shoulder to shoulder, blocked the nine students. The conflict returned to federal court and a three-week standoff ensued.[36]

Against the advice of Attorney General Brownell, Eisenhower decided to negotiate personally with Governor Faubus and invited him to meet in Newport, Rhode Island, where he was vacationing. *Time* magazine described the two-hour meeting on September 14 as "a momentous confrontation" between the president of the United States and a

[35] "President Bars U.S. Move in South at Present Time," *NYT*, September 6, 1956. President's News Conference, September 5, 1956, APP. Eisenhower's view closely resembled those of the highly esteemed Justice Learned Hand, whose comments on the role of law are often quoted admiringly. Learned Hand, *The Spirit of Liberty: Papers and Addresses of Learned Hand*. 3rd ed. (New York: Knopf, 1963), pp. 189–91.

[36] Eisenhower, Press Conference, July 17, 1957, APP.

"rebellious governor" who was actively "defying U.S. Courts and U.S. law." Eisenhower thought he reached an agreement that Faubus would not obstruct integration, and the White House released a statement saying it was pleased with the governor's "intention to respect the decisions" of the court.[37]

Eisenhower quickly discovered he had been duped. Faubus went back on his word and withdrew the National Guard. And so on Monday, September 23, an angry mob of one thousand whites gathered outside Central High. Officials snuck the nine students into the school through a back entrance, and the mob turned its fury on the press, attacking reporters from the *New York Times* and *Life* magazine, whom they saw as the living embodiment of northern interference in their affairs. As the violence escalated, school officials removed the students from the school. With a lawful court order thwarted, Eisenhower finally asserted himself and ordered the Army's 101st Airborne Division to Little Rock. On Wednesday morning, the troops escorted the students into the school. They were later replaced by federalized National Guard units, who stayed at Central High until the following May. (Federal court supervision of the Little Rock schools continued for fifty years, finally ending in February 2007).[38]

The Little Rock crisis was an international embarrassment. Newspapers around the world ran pictures of the helmeted soldiers with bayonets at Central High, and "Little Rock" became a code word for American hypocrisy on racial equality. The Vatican deplored racism in the United States, while the *New York Times* reported that in communist countries the "Red Press Gloats over Little Rock." Secretary of State John Foster Dulles was "sick at heart" and told Brownell that it was "ruining our foreign policy." Eisenhower himself lamented that the crisis had "gravely harmed" America's prestige around the world.[39] Fifty miles away from Little Rock, in Hot Springs, Arkansas, an eleven-year-old white boy named Bill Clinton followed the dramatic events with unusual interest for someone his age. "I supported integration and was pulling for those kids," he recalled years later. "So were my mother and grandparents.... Seeing the Little Rock Nine face down the angry mob fascinated me, and inspired an emotional bond that has lasted a lifetime." Thirty years later as governor of Arkansas, and forty years later as president of the United States, Clinton would invite the Little Rock Nine to official ceremonies marking their heroic stand.[40]

37 Notes Dictated by the President on October 8, 1957 concerning visit of Governor Orval Faubus of Arkansas to Newport on September 14, 1957, ACW Files, ACW Diary, DDEPL. "2 Talk in Newport," *NYT*, September 12, 1957. "Rendezvous at Newport," ibid. Brownell's position: Hughes, *Ordeal of Power*, p. 212; Brownell, *Advising Ike*, pp. 209–11. Statement by the President, September 14, 1957, DDEPL, Digital Documents. See also Diary Entry Dictated by the President, DDEPL, Digital Documents.

38 Executive Order 10730, Providing Assistance for the Removal of an Obstruction of Justice within the State of Arkansas, DDEPL, Digital Documents. "Retreat from Newport," *Time*, September 23, 1957. "Little Rock Police, Deployed at Sunrise, Press Mob Back as School Barricades," *NYT*, September 24, 1957. "President Orders Troops Out of Little Rock May 29," ibid., May 9, 1958. "Federal Supervision of Race in Little Rock Schools Ends," ibid., February 24, 2007.

39 "Vatican Decries Racial Bias in U.S.," *NYT*, September 7, 1957. The Vatican statement was prompted by a request from some conservative American Catholics that the pope not endorse school integration in New Orleans. "Red Press Gloats over Little Rock," ibid., September 26, 1957. "Eisenhower on Air; Says School Defiance Has Gravely Harmed Prestige of U.S.," ibid., September 25, 1957. Dulles: Cary Fraser, "Crossing the Color Line in Little Rock: The Eisenhower Administration and the Dilemma of Race for U.S. Foreign Policy," *Diplomatic History* 24 (Spring 2000): 233–64; Penny M. Von Eschen, *Satchmo Blows Up the World: Jazz Ambassadors Play the Cold War* (Cambridge, MA: Harvard University Press, 2004), p. 64.

40 Carlotta Walls LaNier, *A Mighty Long Way: My Journey to Justice at Little Rock Central High School* (New York: Ballantine Books, 2009), p. vii.

After the fact, Eisenhower was widely praised for sending in troops and upholding the federal courts, but the historian Louis Gould argues that his earlier vacillation on *Brown* "helped lead to the Little Rock crisis of 1957." Another historian called his silence on *Brown* "destructive." The Reverend Martin Luther King, Jr., told a *New York Herald Tribune* reporter that "much of the tension in the South and many of the reverses that we are now facing could have been avoided if President Eisenhower had taken a strong positive stand … as soon as [*Brown*] was rendered in 1954." He added that "Nixon, I believe, would have done that." Forgotten today is the fact that Nixon had a very good civil rights record at that time, and that King initially favored him for president in 1960.[41]

Ike's motives for sending troops, moreover, were quite narrow. In the Eisenhower Library a hand-scribbled note on the president's stationary reads, "Troops – not to enforce integration but to prevent opposition by violence to orders of a court." His chief of staff, Sherman Adams, later wrote that sending troops had been "a constitutional duty which was the most repugnant to him of all the acts in his eight years at the White House." Louis Armstrong, the great jazz trumpeter, who normally avoided politics, publicly rebuked Eisenhower, abruptly cancelling a planned State Department tour of the Soviet Union "because of the way they are treating my people in the South." And in a statement that traveled around the world, he added, "The government can go to hell" and accused Eisenhower of having "no guts."[42]

There was also considerable political irony in Eisenhower's dispatch of federal troops to Little Rock to uphold a Supreme Court decision. Five years earlier, almost to the day, on September 2, 1952, he was wildly cheered at a campaign stop for praising the Court's decision overturning Truman's seizure of the steel mills. "Thank goodness for a Supreme Court," he told this southern audience, which would come to revile the Court in just two years. To his credit, Eisenhower also told his audience that the South needed to respect the rights of Negroes, and he repeated that point in campaign stops in Tampa and Birmingham the same day.[43]

Positive action on civil rights: Desegregating the nation's capital

The day after the *Brown* decision, Eisenhower summoned the commissioners of the Washington, D.C., schools to the White House, told them he hoped the district schools would be a "model" for other communities, and asked for regular reports on their desegregation efforts. Despite his failure to support *Brown* publicly, Eisenhower firmly believed he had both the responsibility and the power to end racial segregation in areas under the president's control. He said so in his first State of the Union Address in 1953 and in a

[41] Pach and Richardson, *The Presidency of Dwight D. Eisenhower*, p. 142. King to Earl Mazo, *New York Herald Tribune*, September 2, 1958, Carson, ed., *The Papers of Martin Luther King, Jr.* V. IV, pp. 481–3. Gould, *The Modern American Presidency*, p. 121.

[42] Note [no date], DDEPL, Digital Documents. "Louis Armstrong, Barring Soviet Tour, Denounces Eisenhower and Governor Faubus," *NYT*, September 19, 1957. On the reporter who interviewed Armstrong: David Margolick, "The Day Louis Armstrong Made Noise," ibid., September 23, 2007. The role of jazz in the cold war: Von Eschen, *Satchmo Blows Up the World: Jazz Ambassadors Play the Cold War*.

[43] Annual Message to the Congress on the State of the Union. February 2, 1953, APP. Remarks at Conference of the National Association for the Advancement of Colored People, March 10, 1954, APP. The 1952 campaign: "Eisenhower Urges South to Protect Rights of Negroes," *NYT*, September 3, 1952.

speech to the NAACP in March 1954 two months before the *Brown* decision. The problem was his very narrow conception of his responsibilities as president.[44]

Ike's narrow definition of his responsibilities reflected his very strict – critics argued, crabbed – reading of the Constitution. He felt he could act only where he had clear responsibility, including Washington, D.C., a federal enclave, the military, and federal agencies. On March 25, 1953, just two months after being sworn in, he sent a memo to the secretary of defense directing that in the next school year the army operate all of its schools "on a completely integrated basis." To his friend the segregationist Jimmy Byrnes he explained in August 1953, "I have been thinking of the whole field of equality of opportunity." It was "incumbent" on political leaders, he explained, "to show constant progress in the direction of complete justice." Racial progress in Washington and federal agencies would "prove ... mistaken" those who wanted "overriding federal legislation and federal police methods." He seemingly envisioned a painless path toward racial justice. The years ahead proved him very wrong, and the path was one of the most tumultuous chapters in American history.[45]

In the context of international affairs, racially segregated Washington, D.C., was an embarrassment in the 1950s. Ike's steps to integrate Washington, which are almost completely forgotten today, put President Truman's record to shame. Despite his strong position on civil rights, Truman took no action to desegregate the city. With Eisenhower's full support, Attorney General Brownell moved quickly on several fronts. The Supreme Court, supported by a Justice Department brief, ordered the integration of restaurants in June 1953, citing an old Reconstruction ordinance. The district's public housing authority adopted an integration policy that same month, and movie theaters voluntarily desegregated that year. The District Board of Commissioners, meanwhile, adopted a policy of equal employment opportunity in November. All in all, the Eisenhower administration generated more progress in just a few months than the Truman administration had in the previous seven years.[46]

One incident illustrates the extent to which Eisenhower was serious about desegregation within his narrowly defined scope of authority. In late 1958 the new U.S. Civil Rights Commission set out to investigate voting discrimination in Alabama. The racially integrated commission could not secure a hotel in Montgomery, however, and decided to stay at Maxwell Air Force Base. When Eisenhower heard that the base commander told them that accommodating a racially mixed group would be disruptive, he "blew a fuse," according to the commission member Father Theodore Hesburgh, and ordered the base integrated.[47]

44 "Eisenhower Spurs Capital's Schools to End Race Bars," *NYT*, May 19, 1954.

45 Eisenhower, Memorandum for the Secretary of Defense, March 25, 1953, DDEPL, Digital Documents. Eisenhower to Byrnes, August 14, 1953, ACW Files, DDE Diary, DDEPL. Annual Message to the Congress on the State of the Union, February 2, 1953, APP. Remarks at Conference of the National Association for the Advancement of Colored People, March 10, 1954, APP. "Eisenhower Renews Pledge to Strive for Racial Equality," *NYT*, March 11, 1954.

46 Report by the Attorney General on the Administration's Efforts in the Field of Racial Segregation and Discrimination, January 26, 1955, DDEPL. *District of Columbia v. John R. Thompson Co.*, 344 U.S. 102 (1953). A useful collection of documents is in Robert L. Branyan and Lawrence H. Larsen, "Desegregation of Washington, DC," in *The Eisenhower Administration, 1953–1961: A Documentary History*, 2 Vols. (New York: Random House, 1971), pp. 1057–72. Brownell, *Advising Ike*, p. 197. "Washington Acts to End Job Bias," *NYT*, November 26, 1953.

47 Theodore M. Hesburgh, *God, Country, Notre Dame: The Autobiography of Theodore M. Hesburgh* (New York: Doubleday, 1990), pp. 192–3. See also Harris Wofford [commission staff member], *Of Kennedys and*

Ike strongly opposed federal action on civil rights in other areas, however. Notably, he opposed creating a federal fair employment practices commission because it would be ineffective and "set back the cause of progress by a good many years." Vice President Nixon, however, supported an employment commission, joining several other liberal Republicans (Senators Jacob Javits and Wayne Morse, for example) in having a good record on civil rights. Eisenhower instead created a presidential committee on federal contract compliance, and Nixon earned considerable credit among African Americans for his efforts as chair.[48]

Lyndon Johnson takes the lead: The 1957 Civil Rights Act

"One thing became absolutely certain," Lyndon Johnson recalled for his biographer Doris Kearns. "The Senate simply had to act, the Democratic Party simply had to act, and I simply had to act; the issue could wait no longer."[49] The issue was a civil rights law, and as Senate majority leader Johnson engineered passage of the 1957 Civil Rights Act, the first federal civil rights law in eighty-two years. Johnson's reputation as the "Master of the Senate" originated in part because of his extraordinary role in the fight over the law. It was also a clear indication of his commitment to racial justice, and a preview of his role as president in securing passage of the 1964 Civil Rights Act and the 1965 Voting Rights Act. Although sharply criticized as weak by civil rights leaders at the time, and pathetically inadequate by later standards, the 1957 law was nonetheless a historic breakthrough.[50]

The civil rights bill originated in late 1955 when the ever-canny Attorney General Brownell, sensing an opportunity, took advantage of Eisenhower's heart attack. With Ike convalescing, Brownell obtained cabinet approval to draft a civil rights bill. Eisenhower accepted this decision as a fait accompli when he returned to work in December, as Brownell suspected he would. Ike noted in his 1956 State of the Union Address that it was "disturbing" that Negroes were "being deprived of their right to vote" in certain parts of the country and recommended the problem be "thoroughly examined by a Bipartisan Commission created by the Congress." He directed Brownell to drop the two strongest sections of the bill, however, and to introduce it as a Justice Department and not a White House bill. In an act of insubordination, Brownell arranged for the Republican representative Kenneth Keating to ask at a hearing about other possible sections to the bill, allowing Brownell to mention the sections Ike told him to drop. After long and divisive fights in both the House and the Senate, however, the bill died.[51]

Kings: Making Sense of the Sixties (Pittsburgh: University of Pittsburgh Press, 1992), pp. 468–77. A Louisiana judge barred the commission from even meeting in Shreveport, and Father Hesburgh arranged for them to meet at his Catholic order's retreat in Land o' Lakes, Wisconsin.

48 Eisenhower to Nixon ["Dear Dick"], September 4, 1953, ACW Files, DDE Diary, DDEPL. See the favorable 1960 view of Nixon in the African-American magazine *Ebony*: Simeon Booker, "What Blacks Can Expect from Nixon," *Ebony* XXIV (January 1969): pp. 27ff.

49 Doris Kearns, *Lyndon Johnson and the American Dream*. Pbk. ed. (New York: New American Library, 1977), p. 153.

50 The 1957 Civil Rights Law is widely covered. Absolutely essential is Robert Caro, who devotes 12 chapters and 327 pages to it: *The Years of Lyndon Johnson: Master of the Senate*, pp. 685–1012. Also: Robert Mann, *The Walls of Jericho: Lyndon Johnson, Hubert Humphrey, Richard Russell, and the Struggle for Civil Rights* (New York: Harcourt, Brace, 1996), pp. 191–224. Dwight D. Eisenhower, *Waging Peace, 1955–1961: The White House Years* (Garden City, NY: Doubleday, 1965), pp. 154–61.

51 Rights Program: Memorandum, The Civil Rights Letter and Statement by the Attorney General, April 10, 1956. DDEPL, Digital Documents. Brownell, *Advising Ike*, pp. 218–20. State of the Union Address, January 5, 1956,

Brownell refused to give up and reintroduced his bill in early 1957. Once again he drafted four separate sections: creating a permanent Civil Rights Commission, strengthening the Justice Department's Civil Rights Section, authorizing the Justice Department to file injunctions to prevent the denial of individuals' civil rights (what became the controversial Section 3), and authorizing the Department to seek injunctive relief against violations of the right to vote. Testifying before the Senate, Brownell tried to downplay the significance of the law, saying that it would not "enlarge" on existing "Constitutional limitations" on federal civil rights action. Nonetheless, everyone knew that it was indeed a dramatic new initiative with enormous social and political implications. Section 3 in particular terrified southerners, who imagined hordes of injunction-filing U.S. attorneys invading the South in a replay of Reconstruction.[52]

Unlike the previous effort, the 1957 bill had powerful new support in the Democratic majority leader Lyndon Johnson, who brought to bear the full force of his legendary capacity to cajole, manipulate, call in IOUs, exaggerate, and even lie. His aide Harry McPherson described his strategy on the bill: "He warned [southerners] that much worse would come unless they would pass this modest bill, and he would tell some of the Northerners that if they would only let this modest bill go through, they would get a better bill later. So he was playing it out of both sides." Among southerners he freely used the word "nigra," but he spoke of "negroes" with liberals. LBJ had several motives. African-American voters had defected to the GOP in large numbers in both the 1952 and 1956 presidential elections, and he felt Democrats needed a civil rights bill to shore up this increasingly important constituency. He also dreamed of being president and knew that he had to distance himself from southern segregationists. But he also genuinely hated segregation and believed it stood in the way of fulfilling America's greatness. It was an immodest ambition, fully characteristic of the man.[53]

Eisenhower remained disengaged from the congressional fight over the bill, publicly supporting it but providing no real leadership. One historian characterizes his position as a "fog of apparent ignorance." In the climactic weeks of summer 1957, just as the crisis in Little Rock was developing, Ike appeared not to understand some important parts of the bill. At a July press conference, he admitted that he was "reading part of that bill this morning, and there were certain phrases I didn't completely understand." It was another embarrassing incident that contributed to his image of being disengaged from civil rights.[54]

Hoping to derail the bill, the southerners seized on the part of section 4 that denied defendants the right to a jury trial in federal contempt proceedings. Civil rights leaders thought it essential because everyone knew that no southern jury would convict a white defendant in a civil rights case. The ACLU and some others, however, saw this as a dangerous compromise on the constitutional right to a jury trial. The ACLU was so divided

APP. A detailed account of Brownell's commitment to a civil rights bill and his insubordination is in J. W. Anderson, *Eisenhower, Brownell, and the Congress: The Tangled Origins of the Civil Rights Bill of 1956–1957* (University: University of Alabama Press, 1964). Mann, *The Walls of Jericho.*

52 Statement of the Attorney General on the Proposed Civil Rights Legislation, February 14, 1957, p. 12, DDEPL, Digital Documents.

53 McPherson, OH, p. 12, LBJPL. Caro, *Master of the Senate*. Mann, *The Walls of Jericho*. Caro argues that Senator Richard Russell supported Johnson because he dreamed of having a southerner as president and thought he was the best possibility (pp. 853, 865–6). See also LBJ aide Busby, OH, p, 5, JFKPL.

54 "Fog of Ignorance:" Mann, *Walls of Jericho*, p. 203. Eisenhower, Press Conference, July 3, 1957, APP. Hughes, *Ordeal of Power*, p. 211. "President Bars Ballot on Rights," *NYT*, July 4, 1957.

that it convened an emergency Board of Directors meeting to debate it and ended almost perfectly divided. In the end, some legal scholars fashioned a fine-grained compromise that maintained the right to a jury in criminal cases, but not in the civil cases envisioned in the bill, and the bill moved forward.[55]

The ultimate hurdle was a southern filibuster in the Senate. To prevent it, Johnson made a controversial deal that earned him both praise and condemnation. He warned southerners that the liberals might pass a bill over their opposition ("we have to give them *something*"). This was very unlikely, but LBJ evidently managed to convince them. Then he persuaded his friend and mentor Senator Richard Russell of Georgia that he would kill the dreaded Section 3 in return for no filibuster. Fulfilling the deal was no easy task, as the archsegregationist Strom Thurmond threatened to filibuster and even to march on the White House personally. The North Carolina senator Sam Ervin, sixteen years later a liberal hero in the Watergate scandal, denounced the bill as "a rape upon the Constitutional and legal systems" of the country. Russell accepted Johnson's deal, and Section 3 disappeared. Liberals were outraged and threatened to vote against the bill. Southerners were also unhappy but unwilling to challenge Russell and Johnson. Thurmond remained defiant, however, and conducted a personal filibuster lasting twenty-four hours and eighteen minutes. Some historians speculate that Russell agreed to the deal because he dreamed of having a southerner as president some day, and that Johnson was the best and possibly the only hope.[56]

With the possible exception of Johnson, no one was happy with the final bill. Liberals thought it was almost worthless. The Oregon senator Wayne Morse called it a "corpse," and a deeply disappointed Roy Wilkins of the NAACP thought seriously about opposing it. In the end, however, he agreed with Martin Luther King that "the present bill is better than no bill at all." That had been Johnson's strategy all along. Even President Eisenhower seriously considered vetoing the bill, but Vice President Nixon persuaded him that Republicans would be hurt in the 1960 elections if he did. Ike's loyal secretary, Ann Whitman wrote in her White House diary, that if Ike signs the bill, "there will be no forward civil rights legislation for the next decade or so." She was wrong, but many others at the time shared her view. That same day, Frederic Morrow, Eisenhower's African-American adviser, wrote in his diary that "an emasculated Civil Rights Bill is worse than none at all" and hoped Ike would veto it. In the end, however, no one wanted to be responsible for killing the first civil rights bill in almost a century.[57] Eisenhower signed it into law on September 9, in the midst of the Little Rock crisis. Ignoring a perfect opportunity to speak to the nation about civil rights, he made no public statement.

Lyndon Johnson basked in the nearly universal recognition that it was really his law ("Johnson's Masterpiece," headlined the *Washington Post*). Civil rights leaders, however, blamed him for killing Section 3, and their suspicions dogged him in his quest for the 1960 Democratic presidential nomination. To the day he died, he was fiercely proud of

[55] ACLU, Statement on Jury Trial Amendment to Civil Rights Legislation (May 1957), ACLUP-MF (1977), Reel 94; ACLU Board, Minutes, Special Meeting, April 3, 1957, ibid., Reel 14. The ACLU affiliates ended split on the issue.

[56] Caro, *Master of the Senate*, pp. 787, 853, 865; Ervin, p. 933; "something," p. 954.

[57] Caro, *Master of the Senate*, pp. 993–7. ACW Diary, August 7, 1957, ACW Files, DDEPL. See also Robert J. Donovan, *Confidential Secretary: Ann Whitman's 20 Years with Eisenhower and Rockefeller* (New York: E. P. Dutton, 1988), pp. 114–15. Morrow, Diary, August 7, 1957, Morrow Papers, Box 2, DDEPL. Mann, *The Walls of Jericho*, pp. 189–224.

his role in winning passage of the law, and he was never shy about claiming "with full justification" that only he could have done it. He understood what few others did, that even a weak law would break the spell of segregationist power in Congress. In time, other more effective laws would follow – the two most important of which he steered through Congress and signed as president.[58]

Voting rights and school desegregation enforcement

Weak though it was, the 1957 law gave the Justice Department new authority to protect voting rights, and William P. Rogers, who succeeded Brownell as attorney general in fall 1957, immediately sought to use it. Serious obstacles limited enforcement efforts, however. The Justice Department relied on complaints brought to it by citizens. With Klan violence rising as part of the massive resistance campaign, only a few brave African Americans in the South were willing to risk stepping forward. Between 1957 and late 1959, the Justice Department received complaints from only twenty-two voting districts. The head of the Civil Rights Division, W. Wilson White, moreover, opted for a strategy of conciliation, which was doomed to failure in the Deep South, and the department filed only three voting rights suits in the first two years.[59] When Eisenhower left office in January 1961, African Americans were still heavily disenfranchised in the Deep South and only slightly less so in the border states.

Local officials went to extraordinary lengths to fight inquiries into voter discrimination. When the new U.S. Civil Rights Commission undertook an investigation in Alabama in late 1958, a politically ambitious circuit court judge named George C. Wallace had a friend file a bogus voter fraud suit so he could sequester all the voting records. The Justice Department sued to get them, and Wallace thought jail on a contempt charge for fighting Washington on civil rights would be politically advantageous. In a late night conversation at the home of the federal judge Frank M. Johnson, a law school classmate and friend, Wallace said, "my ass is in a crack." Judge Johnson replied, "George, if you don't send those records over, I'm going to send your ass to jail." Wallace asked whether he could be jailed for "just a little while," possibly for only ten or fifteen days. They finally reached a compromise through which Wallace gave the files to a grand jury so it rather than he could formally turn them over to the Justice Department. Judge Johnson was already emerging as a hero of civil rights law. One of several pro-civil rights judges appointed by Eisenhower in the South, he had already ordered the Montgomery buses desegregated, would end segregation in Alabama juries and prisons, and would issue an order permitting the famous 1965 Selma to Montgomery march for voting rights. The 1958 imbroglio with Judge Wallace over federal access to voting records was only one small chapter in a larger pattern of massive southern resistance, and Wallace's first step in a career of defying racial integration.[60]

[58] Caro, *Lyndon Johnson: Master of the Senate*, pp. 998–1001.

[59] Allan Lichtman, "The Federal Assault against Voting Discrimination in the Deep South 1957–1967," *Journal of Negro History* 54 (October 1969): 346–67.

[60] Dan T. Carter, *The Politics of Rage: George Wallace, The Origins of the New Conservatism, and the Transformation of American Politics*. 2nd ed. Pbk. ed. (Baton Rouge: Louisiana State University Press, 2000), pp. 98–103. Jack Bass, *Taming the Storm: The Life and Times of Judge Frank M. Johnson and the South's Fight over Civil Rights*. Pbk. ed. (New York: Anchor Books, 1994), pp. 186–9. U.S. Civil Rights Commission, *1959 Report* (Washington, DC: Government Printing Office, 1959), pp. 70–1.

The first "black man in the White House"

E. Frederic Morrow titled his autobiography *Black Man in the White House,* and President Eisenhower deserves credit for appointing him as the first African American to serve as a presidential adviser. The appointment seems pathetically inconsequential by today's standards, but in 1955 it had enormous symbolic importance.

Morrow's experience was frustrating and often painful, however. His diary and 1963 autobiography provide vivid firsthand accounts of Eisenhower's failures on civil rights. He had solid civil rights credentials, having been a staff member with the NAACP in the 1930's, and had met Eisenhower in Europe during World War II.[61] The greatest indignity involved his hiring. An Eisenhower aide persuaded him to quit his job with CBS and join the administration in early 1953. After his farewell party at CBS, however, he did not hear from the White House. Three or four months later the presidential counsel Bernard Shanley told him there was no position in the White House, "period!" "This was a stunning blow," Morrow recalled. In limbo, he lived on his savings until they finally found him a position in the Commerce Department. When he moved to the White House on July 10, 1955, some staff members reportedly threatened to walk out en masse, and all but two stenographers refused to work with him. At a 1956 GOP reception in Kansas, someone called him "boy."[62]

Morrow's most difficult challenge, however, was the almost impossible job of explaining Ike's performance to African Americans. Although initially not given specific responsibility for civil rights, he inevitably fell into that role. White House officials repeatedly ignored his advice, however. In late 1955, for example, when the nation was shocked by the brutal murder of Emmit Till in Mississippi, Morrow told the presidential aide Maxwell Rabb that his mail was "heavy and angry" over the case, and the "time has come" to invite some Negro leaders to the White House. "I am sitting in the middle of this," he added, "and I have been accused of being cowardly." Rabb, possibly the strongest civil rights advocate in the White House, berated him, saying civil rights leaders did not appreciate the administration's efforts on their behalf. The White House was "completely disgusted," Rabb added, and no longer regarded civil rights leaders as an "asset politically." Morrow gloomily noted these "discouraging words" in his diary.[63]

When Eisenhower did speak to a May 1958 Negro Summit of 350 business and professional leaders, he proved to be tone deaf on racial issues. The usually nonpolitical (and Republican) baseball pioneer Jackie Robinson was offended by the lecture about "patience and forbearance" on civil rights. He fired off an angry letter to Ike saying, "On hearing you

[61] Kansas incident: Frederic Morrow, Diary, February 1, 1956; quote: Diary, December 8, 1955, Morrow Papers, Box 2, DDEPL. E. Frederic Morrow, *Black Man in the White House: A Diary of the Eisenhower Years by the Administrative Officer for Special Projects, the White House, 1955–1961* (New York: Macfadden Books, 1963). NAACP Papers, Part 2, 1919–39, Personal Correspondence of Selected NAACP Officials, MF ED, Reel 5. Milton S. Katz, "E. Frederick [sic] Morrow and Civil Rights In The Eisenhower Administration," *Phylon* 42, no. 2 (1981): 133–44.

[62] Morrow Diary, February 8, 1954, DDEPL. Assistant Secretary of Labor J. Ernest Wilkins was the first African American official ever to attend a Cabinet meeting. Larson, *Eisenhower: The President Nobody Knew,* pp. 130–1.

[63] Morrow Diary, February 28, 1956, DDEPL. Morrow, Memorandum to Sherman Adams, July 12, 1957, DDEPL, Digital Documents. Morrow, letter to Rabb, November 29, 1955, DDEPL, Digital Documents. Branyan and Larsen, *A Documentary History,* pp. 1079–81. Morrow's perspective: Morrow, OH, p. 9. The Raab incident, ibid., p. 33, DDEPL, and Morrow, *Black Man in the White House.*

say this, I felt like standing up and saying, Oh no! Not again." "We have been the most patient of all people," and you have just "unwittingly crush[ed] the spirit of freedom in Negroes" and given "hope to those pro-segregation leaders like Governor Faubus."[64]

Finally, on June 23, 1958, Eisenhower acceded to Morrow's pleas and met with four top civil rights leaders in the White House: the NAACP's Roy Wilkins, the rising leader Martin Luther King, the venerable A. Philip Randolph, and the National Urban League's Lester B. Granger. Eisenhower was stiff and awkward, but he listened, and the scheduled thirty-minute meeting stretched out to an hour. They presented him with a nine-point program that included a strong presidential pronouncement that he would uphold the law "with the total resources at his command," a White House civil rights conference, and more vigorous civil rights enforcement efforts. Eisenhower did not act on these specific proposals but did support what became the very weak 1960 Civil Rights Act.[65]

Early in Eisenhower's last year in office, the sit-in movement challenged segregated facilities in the South, dramatically escalating the tone and tempo of the civil rights movement. Surprisingly, he spoke favorably about them, although incorrectly saying that the Supreme Court had ruled against discrimination in private businesses. The former president Truman denounced the sit-ins, while the presidential candidate John F. Kennedy praised them.[66]

Ike's secretary, Ann Whitman, offered a final commentary on his leadership failure on civil rights. Thirty years after leaving the White House she was asked, "If you could talk to President Eisenhower one more time, what would you say to him?" She replied that she would ask, "Don't you think you were wrong about civil rights?"[67] It was a fitting comment. Ike's weak position on civil rights bears comparing with President Franklin D. Roosevelt's weak performance. The difference was the change in the political context. During FDR's time, civil rights was still a fairly radical idea, one that politically he could safely ignore. *Brown* and the Montgomery bus boycott changed everything, however, and racial equality now had powerful legal and growing public support. Thus, Eisenhower can be held to a higher standard of performance.

IKE, COMMUNISM, AND DOMESTIC SECURITY

While Joe McCarthy dominated the headlines, the loyalty program continued to strike fear among government employees, ruining many people's careers. Eisenhower was of two minds about the issue of communists in government. Although appalled by McCarthy's methods, he was nonetheless a staunch anti-communist, who firmly believed that

64 Memorandum, Morrow to Sherman Adams, June 4, 1957, DDEPL, Digital Documents. "Eisenhower Bids Negroes Be Patient about Rights," *NYT*, May 13, 1958. Jackie Robinson, letter to Eisenhower, May 13, 1958, DDEPL, Digital Documents.

65 Memorandum for the Record, Meeting of Negro Leaders with the President – June 23, 1958, June 24, 1958, DDEPL, Digital Documents. "Negro Leaders Confer with President and Rogers at White House," *NYT*, June 24, 1958. Frederic Morrow urged Eisenhower to hold the meeting: Morrow Diary, Diary, June 23, 1958, DDEPL. Morrow, *Black Man in the White House*, pp. 165–70. Late in life Morrow was in complete despair about American race relations, writing in his 1973 memoir, "It is almost a repudiation of my whole life's work and efforts, but it must be stated. **I do not believe we are any nearer a solution to the black white controversy than we were in 1870"** [boldface in original]. Frederic Morrow, *Way Down South Up North* (Philadelphia: Pilgrim Press, 1973), p. 120.

66 Nichols, *A Matter of Justice*, p. 251.

67 Whitman, OH, p. 20, DDEPL.

security risks should be removed from federal employment. He assured the correspondent Daniel Schorr in November 1953, "there is no more active opponent of communism as an ideology in the world than I am." At the same time, however, Ike thought far more seriously about the loyalty program than President Truman ever did. Parts of it, he concluded, violated the standards of procedural regularity that were a part of his military ethos. At a November 1953 press conference, he explained that he did not want to do "injustice to any individual because I don't believe we can afford to destroy inside what we think we are protecting from the outside."[68]

To his credit, and unlike many leading Republicans, Eisenhower firmly opposed using the communist issue for partisan purposes. Joe McCarthy notoriously accused Presidents Roosevelt and Truman of giving the country "Twenty Years of Treason." Ike stipulated, however, that if any Democrat were removed from his job because of a loyalty issue, he was to be replaced by another Democrat, and vice versa. "In other words," he explained, " I do not intend to use the issue of communism to build up one party and tear down the other."[69]

In private, Ike understood the problem of guilt by association, especially regarding people who had been leftists in the 1930s or during World War II when the Soviet Union was a vital U.S. ally. "Let us remember this," he told Brownell in November 1953. "Many prominent officials of the Allied Governments <u>were at that time talking in terms of support of the Soviets; witness Winston Churchill's comment when the Soviets came into the war on the allied side</u> [underlined in original]." Moreover, "it was a policy of our government to foster friendship with the Soviets," and people could be excused for sympathy with the Soviet Union "even as late as 1948." Ruminating on the matter, he sketched out a better approach that would "have the FBI 'run a check' on suspected Communists to determine the exact date when they "deserted their Communist affiliations and habits." He conceded that this approach might be "too much of a chore" but thought it would be fair.[70]

Despite this very sound analysis, which implicated other anti-communist measures as well, Eisenhower never acted on it. Throughout his presidency he delegated responsibility for the communist issue to Attorney General Brownell. Although the administration's forceful advocate on civil rights, Brownell was a classic cold war liberal, in the manner of President Truman, equally strong on both racial justice and anti-communism. The result was a anti-communist measures that went even further than Truman's in undermining civil liberties.[71]

Soon after taking office, Eisenhower directed Brownell to revise the loyalty program and to emphasize "security" rather than "loyalty." Security, however, was a far broader

[68] Brownell, *Advising Ike*, p. 247. Jeff Broadwater, *Eisenhower and the Anti-Communist Crusade* (Chapel Hill: University of North Carolina Press, 1992), Ch. 4, "Securing the Federal Work Force," pp. 85–111. Eisenhower, Press Conference, November 18, 1953, APP.

[69] "Suggested Statement" [no date]. ACW Files, Administration Series, Brownell File, DDEPL.

[70] Eisenhower to the Attorney General, November 4, 1953. ACW Files, Administration Series, Brownell File, DDEPL. Eisenhower to Attorney General, July 2, 1953, ACW Files, Administration Series, Brownell File, DDEPL.

[71] "Brownell Seeks New Laws to End Communist Party," *NYT*, April 10, 1954. Brownell's vigorous defense of aggressive actions against Communists: Brownell to The President, October 6, 1956. ACW Files, Administration Series, Brownell File, DDEPL. Arthur M. Schlesinger, Jr., *The Vital Center: The Politics of Freedom* (Boston: Houghton Mifflin, 1949). Brownell's views on the two issues are clearly explained in *Advising Ike*.

standard than was loyalty. Eisenhower's April 1953 Executive Order 10450, based on Brownell's recommendation, included the new criterion of "any criminal, infamous, dishonest, immoral, or notoriously disgraceful conduct ... [or] sexual perversion." A homophobic panic had already swept Washington and much of the country in 1950, and the new policy gave it official sanction. Senator McCarthy called the new policy an "improvement," while the 1956 Democratic Party platform condemned the "heartless and unjustified confusing of 'security' and 'loyalty.'"[72]

Brownell then proposed three laws in 1954 designed to "destroy" the Communist Party. Many witnesses before the House Un-American Activities Committee invoked the Fifth Amendment when asked whether they were members of the Communist Party. In the poisoned atmosphere of the cold war, invoking the historic privilege against self-incrimination was regarded as a virtual admission of guilt, and anti-communists invented the new category of "Fifth Amendment Communists." "Taking the Fifth" cost some witnesses their jobs. (Only a few courageous individuals, including playwright Arthur Miller, refused to testify on the then-untested First Amendment grounds that the government had no right to inquire into the beliefs and associations.) Brownell told Congress that subversives were having a "field day" with the Fifth Amendment, and the resulting 1954 Immunity Act authorized congressional committees to compel testimony in return for immunity from prosecution. The law remains today a major blow to the protection against self-incrimination.[73] In the end, Eisenhower was privately far more thoughtful about anti-communist measures than Truman, but he never acted on his reservations. He delegated responsibility for this issue to Attorney General Brownell, with unfortunate results for civil liberties.

Eisenhower, Brownell, and the FBI

To Eisenhower's credit, he appears not to have indulged in FBI political gossip as did every other president from Roosevelth through Nixon. The bureau did send him political items from time to time, and some administration aides requested information about public figures, but it is not clear that Ike knew about this. It is very likely that Hoover understood that Eisenhower's military sense of procedural regularity would be offended by any such activity. Nonetheless, Ike and his attorney general were responsible for authorizing expansions of some of the worst FBI abuses of individual rights.[74]

Ike delegated responsibility for the FBI to Attorney General Brownell, whose record proved to be very mixed. Brownell claimed that he ended such practices as the bureau's

72 Executive Order 10450 Security Requirements for Government Employment. April 27, 1953, APP. David K. Johnson, *The Lavender Scare: The Cold War Persecution of Gays and Lesbians in the Federal Government* (Chicago: University of Chicago, 2004). Democratic Party platform of 1956, August 13, 1956, APP.

73 "Brownell Seeks New Laws to End Communist Party," *NYT*, April 10, 1954. "Brownell Urged Immunity Power," ibid., June 9, 1954. *Ullman v. United States*, 352 U.S. 422 (1956) upheld the constitutionality of the immunity law. At a November 18, 1953, press conference, Eisenhower did not seem to be aware of Brownell's planned immunity legislation: "That particular point has not been discussed with me," APP. Brownell's aggressive anti-Communism: Brownell to The President, October 6, 1956, ACW Files, Administration Series, Brownell File, DDEPL. Brownell, *Advising Ike*, pp. 230–50. Arthur Miller, *Timebends: A Life* (New York: Grove Press, 1987), pp. 403–12, 449–56.

74 U.S. Senate, Select Committee to Study Governmental Operations, *Final Report*, Book II, *Intelligence Activities and the Rights of Americans*, pp. 51–2.

giving local school board officials information from FBI files about alleged subversive activities by teachers (which usually led to their firing). On wiretapping, however, Hoover misled him about the exact nature of the approval granted by previous presidents. By 1953, Hoover simply knew more about the subject than any of his superiors. He cited President Roosevelt's May 21, 1940, letter approving wiretapping, and a July 17, 1946, memo from Attorney General Tom Clark extending it, which included the elastic phrase "subversive activities." Hoover did not attach the actual documents, however, and managed to convince Brownell that a break-in to install a surveillance microphone was not a search and seizure. Brownell concluded that it was not necessary "to reopen the matter" of surveillance and went a step further in easing restrictions on microphone surveillance imposed by the Truman Justice Department. In response to the 1954 Supreme Court decision in *Irvine v. California* throwing out a conviction based on a bedroom listening device, installed through an unauthorized break-in, Brownell advised Hoover that the Court was particularly outraged by the bedroom snooping, and that the FBI could continue to eavesdrop in such intimate locations if it was the "only" way to get information essential to the "national interest." "Whether a trespass is actually involved" in placing listening devices and whether it compromised the admissibility of any evidence gathered, he continued, would depend on the "circumstances of each case." In effect, Brownell gave the FBI virtual carte blanche on intrusive snooping through the use of "bugs."[75]

In a closely related departure from legal procedures, Eisenhower and Brownell approved the FBI's COINTELPRO (Counter Intelligence Program) program, which eventually became the locus of its most notorious abuses. Hoover described the program to Ike, Vice President Nixon, Attorney General Brownell, and other top officials at a March 8, 1956, National Security Council meeting. Exaggerating "the Present Menace of Communist Espionage and Subversion," as he always did, he asked for authority to use whatever methods were necessary to infiltrate and destroy the Communist Party. Ike pointedly asked him what techniques he planned to use, and Hoover candidly described a program of "surreptitious entry," safecracking, mail opening, wiretapping, surveillance bugs, and other methods. Apparently, neither Eisenhower, Brownell, nor anyone else raised any questions about the legality of these methods, and Ike gave his approval. Although it was originally approved for use against the Communist Party, the bureau eventually used COINTELPRO to attack the KKK, the Socialist Workers Party, and the Black Panther Party before it was finally terminated in 1971.[76] Officially approving blatantly illegal actions is certainly the worst blot on the records of Eisenhower and his attorney general, but it was symptomatic of the cold war atmosphere, where a claim of national security could justify virtually anything.

[75] Brownell to FBI Director, May 20, 1954, in Theoharis, *From the Secret Files of J. Edgar Hoover*, p. 141. Theoharis, *Spying on Americans*, pp. 94–111. Brownell, *Advising Ike*, pp. 233–5.

[76] Minutes, National Security Council, March 8, 1956, *Minutes of Meetings of the National Security Council*, First Supplement, MF ED (Frederick, MD: University Publications of America, 1988). James Kirkpatrick Davis, *Assault on the Left: The FBI and the Sixties Antiwar Movement* (Westport, CT: Praeger, 1997), pp. 1–20. Report on first sixty says of COINTELPRO: FBI, A. H. Belmont to L. V. Boardman, Communist Party, USA, Counterintelligence Program, November 9, 1956, available at www.icdc.com. Brownell, *Advising Ike*, pp. 233–5. The Church Committee investigation does not report this approval: U.S. Senate. Select Committee to Study Governmental Operations with Respect to Intelligence Activities, *Book III, Supplementary Detailed Staff Reports on Intelligence Activities and the Rights of Americans*, pp. 15–66.

SECRECY, EXECUTIVE PRIVILEGE, AND THE CIA

The hearings on government secrecy began the morning of November 7, 1955, before the House Committee on Government Operations, launching the chairperson, Rep. John E. Moss's, eleven-year campaign, which would culminate in the historic 1966 Freedom of Information Act. (Over the course of his long career in Congress, Moss would badger six presidents – from Eisenhower to Jimmy Carter – over secrecy.)[77] In the ensuing struggle over access to government information, the Eisenhower administration articulated a new doctrine of executive privilege to justify withholding information from Congress. That doctrine would embroil several subsequent presidents and contribute directly to the resignation of one.

Not surprisingly, a cold war issue launched Rep. Moss's inquiry on secrecy. In 1953, as a member of a different committee, he asked the Civil Service Commission for details about the reported twenty-eight hundred federal employees terminated under the loyalty program. He particularly wanted to know how many had been terminated specifically for disloyalty. The commission flatly rejected his request. Upset and intrigued, Moss convinced the House to create a Special Subcommittee on Government Operations, which became his vehicle. (The FBI responded by opening a file on Moss in 1957, and it was two inches thick by the time he died.)[78]

Moss quickly uncovered a pervasive and now ingrained culture of secrecy in Washington. The Civil Service Commission told him it had "inherent power" to withhold information from Congress, a claim that had no legal basis. A Defense Department official refused to provide him an unclassified army manual because "there is no reason why he should have it." The general counsel to the Defense Department interrupted a Moss subcommittee hearing three times in 1957 with belligerent tirades against the proceedings and had to be gaveled into silence. By 1958 Moss concluded that "under the prevailing attitude in the Pentagon, an employee must justify the release of even the most innocuous nonsecurity information," warning that Congress should consider "suitable legislation to guarantee the public's right to know – a right so obviously fundamental to our form of government."[79]

Congress had willingly contributed to the growing culture of secrecy. The 1946 Atomic Energy Act declared all information related to atomic weapons classified ("born secret," in the words of critics). Section 3c of the 1946 Administrative Procedure Act, meanwhile, exempted from public disclosure "any function of the United States requiring secrecy in

[77] Kiyul Uhm, "The Cold War Communication Crisis: The Right to Know Movement," *Journalism and Mass Communication Quarterly* 82 (Spring 2005): 131–47. U.S. House of Representatives, Committee on Governmental Operations, *Availability of Information from Federal Departments and Agencies, Hearings*, 84th Cong., 1st Sess., November 7, 1955. Moss: Mark Rozell, *Executive Privilege*. 3rd ed., pp. 56–7, 74–5, 80–1.

[78] Moss inquiry: Daniel P. Moynihan, *Secrecy: The American Experience* (New Haven, CT: Yale University Press, 1998), p. 172. U.S. Senate, Select Committee to Study Governmental Activities, Book VI, *Supplementary Reports on Intelligence Activities* (1976), pp. 327–44. FBI File: Michael Doyle, "Right to Know Crusader Moss Was FBI's Thorn," *Sacramento Bee*, September 2, 2001.

[79] House of Representatives, Government Operations Committee, Special Subcommittee on Government Information, Availability of Information from Federal Departments and Agencies, *Twenty-Fifth Intermediate Report of the Committee On Government Operations*, July 27, 1956. House Report No. 2947, 84th Cong., 2nd. Sess., pp. 13. House of Representatives, Committee on Government Operations. Special Subcommittee on Government Information, *Availability of Information from Federal Departments and Agencies (Scientific Information and National Defense)*, April 22, 1958, House Report No. 1619, 85th Cong., 2nd Sess., pp. 13, 89, 153. "2 Pentagon Aides Balked at Inquiry," *NYT*, November 19, 1957.

the public interest." Moss charged that "slowly, almost imperceptibly, a paper curtain has descended over the Federal Government." Two years later he blasted secrecy as "the first refuge of incompetents."[80]

Moss's efforts were aided by rising concern among a then-small number of journalists increasingly skeptical of claims of national security. Leading this movement was the American Society of Newspaper Editors's Freedom of Information Committee. Two 1955 reports, *The People's Right to Know* by Harold L. Cross and a similar ACLU report by Allen Raymond, raised public awareness of the issue. The very concept of a legal "right to know" was new and had not yet been established as a matter of law.[81]

The combined efforts of Moss, Cross, and the ACLU slowly bore fruit. The Defense Department's 1956 Coolidge Report on Classified Information concluded that as a matter of principle in a democracy "the government cannot cloak its operations in secrecy," and "there is a tendency to use the classification system to protect information which is not related to the national security." Moss discussed the issue with Senator John F. Kennedy, and the 1956 and 1960 Democratic Party platforms included strong attacks on government secrecy. (Kennedy's record on secrecy as president, however, suggests that these were partisan attacks on the Eisenhower administration rather than a principled commitment to openness in government.) Then, in 1958 Congress passed a one-sentence law directing federal agencies to make information public. Moss saw it as a "modest first step," but like the 1957 Civil Rights Act it was just a beginning. President Eisenhower signed the law but explained that government officials could keep "appropriate information or papers confidential in the public interest." Then, reiterating his view of executive privilege, he argued, "This power in the executive branch is inherent under the Constitution."[82]

Joe McCarthy, the CIA, and executive privilege

Senator Joe McCarthy did much damage in his five-year assault on reason, civil liberties, and American political discourse, but two often overlooked parts of his legacy were strengthening of the cloak of secrecy around the CIA and the development of the concept of executive privilege.

Created in 1947, the CIA escaped serious legislative oversight because members of Congress eagerly accepted the idea that keeping its activities secret was necessary to protect national security. As a political maverick, however, McCarthy rejected the conventional wisdom and pursued his certainty that the CIA employed both former communists

80 Laws cited by agency officials: U.S. House of Representatives. Government Operations Committee, Special Subcommittee on Government Information, Availability of Information from Federal Departments and Agencies, *Twenty-Fifth Intermediate Report*, July 27, 1956. House Report No. 2947, 84th Cong., 2nd. Sess., pp. 50–3; Moss quote, p. 81. "Pentagon to Cut Secrecy of Files," *NYT*, July 3, 1960.

81 Harold L. Cross, *The People's Right to Know: Legal Access to Public Records and Proceedings* (New York: Columbia University Press, 1953). Allen Raymond, *The Peoples' Right to Know: A Report on Government News Suppression* (New York: ACLU, 1955), ACLUP, MF ed. (1977), Reel 94.

82 Moss, OH, pp. 7–9, JFKPL. 1956 Democratic Party platform, APP. Department of Defense, Report to the Secretary of Defense by the Committee on Classified Information (December 8, 1956), available at www.thememoryhole.org. "Eisenhower Signs Information Bill," *NYT*, August 13, 1958. Statement by the President upon Signing Bill Relating to the Authority of Federal Agencies to Withhold Information and Records, August 12, 1958, APP. Two years later the Pentagon declassified "tons" of documents, although it conceded that a major factor was the cost of maintaining so many secret documents. Despite reforms requiring greater openness, the habit of secrecy continues: *Pseudo-Secrets: A Freedom of Information Audit of the U.S. Government's Policies on Sensitive Unclassified Information* (March 14, 2006), at the National Security Archive.

and homosexuals. In the strange politics of the 1950s, the CIA's shield of secrecy protected it from congressional or media scrutiny and thereby allowed it to be the only federal agency able to hire members of both groups. A small controversy arose in 1953 when McCarthy learned that the CIA staffer William Bundy had contributed four hundred dollars to the legal defense fund of Alger Hiss, an old college friend, and he demanded both public testimony and documents. (Richard Nixon first made his national reputation over Hiss, an accused Soviet agent who was eventually convicted of perjury in one of the most celebrated cold war controversies.)[83]

The bipartisan foreign policy establishment was terrified that a McCarthy inquiry would destroy the CIA, as it might well have, and closed ranks, fully supporting President Eisenhower's refusal to provide any information about the agency. Seeing McCarthy as a "challenge" "to our political system itself," Attorney General Brownell drafted a memo for Eisenhower citing the actions of earlier presidents to justify rejecting McCarthy's demands. When McCarthy then attacked the CIA director, Allen Dulles, in July 1953, Dulles threatened to resign. Vice President Nixon was delegated to talk with McCarthy and, according to press reports, successfully "encouraged" him to redirect his efforts elsewhere. The CIA was spared, but McCarthy embarked on his ultimately self-destructive crusade against alleged communists in the army.[84]

The immediate threat from McCarthy passed, but Brownell saw a broader issue at stake and set to work on a legal rationale for withholding information from Congress. He prepared a memo citing precedents reaching back to Presidents George Washington and Thomas Jefferson and including ten instances when President Truman had either withheld documents from Congress or refused to let administration officials testify. The memo became the basis for a formal Eisenhower statement in the form of a memo to the secretary of defense on May 17, 1954 (the very day of the momentous *Brown* decision). A president has always withheld information, he argued, "whenever he found that what was sought was confidential or its disclosure would be incompatible with the public interest or jeopardize the safety of the Nation." Legal scholars and members of Congress alike attacked the new doctrine of executive privilege. Joe McCarthy called it an "iron curtain." The conservative Republican Michigan representative George Meader denounced it as a "nonexistent, imaginary" theory, "nowhere recognized in the Constitution, in statutes, or in court decisions." Technically, he was correct; the privilege had no legal basis other than the precedents cited by Brownell. Eisenhower eventually invoked executive privilege more than forty times. Interestingly, Brownell titled the chapter on this issue in his memoirs "Protecting the Presidency." Elevated to a full-blown doctrine, executive privilege eventually provoked a constitutional crisis and President Richard Nixon's resignation in 1974 and reappeared as a controversy with several subsequent presidents.[85]

83 Tim Weiner, *Legacy of Ashes: The History of the CIA* (New York: Doubleday, 2007). L. Britt Snider, *The Agency and the Hill: CIA's Relationship with Congress, 1946–2004* (Washington, DC: Center for the Study of Intelligence, 2008), pp. 11, 313–15. The CIA arranged for the alleged homosexual in this instance to resign quietly. Evan Thomas, *The Very Best Men: The Early Years of the CIA* (New York: Simon & Schuster, 1995), p. 100.

84 "McCarthy Strikes at Allen Dulles," *NYT*, July 10, 1953. "C.I.A. Plays Vital Role in National Security," ibid., July 19, 1953. "McCarthy Planning Shift in Inquiries," ibid., July 26, 1953. Church Committee, Book 6, *Supplementary Reports on Intelligence Activities*, p. 257. Brownell, *Advising Ike*, pp. 251, 257–8. CIA spying on McCarthy: Thomas, *The Very Best Men*, p. 100.

85 Letter to the Secretary of Defense Directing Him To Withhold Certain Information from the Senate Committee on Government Operations. May 17, 1954, APP. "Text of Eisenhower Letter and Brownell Memorandum on

The administration's concern about maintaining presidential prerogatives was reinforced in those years by the controversy over the Bricker Amendment. Named for the conservative Ohio senator John W. Bricker, it would have placed significant limits on a president's power to sign treaties and executive agreements, requiring among other things specific authorizing legislation for any treaty provision that "conflicted" with the Constitution. It was prompted primarily by the conservatives' memory of President Roosevelt's actions in violation of the 1930s neutrality acts. Eisenhower successfully fought it, aided by Senator Lyndon Johnson, who devised a clever strategy to divide the amendment's supporters. As he had in supporting President Truman's decision to go to war in Korea, LBJ was concerned to preserve presidential authority in foreign affairs, a power he would use to escalate American involvement in the Vietnam War.[86]

Protecting the CIA

The CIA dodged a McCarthy attack, but some members of Congress began to express concern about the lack of oversight of the agency. Senator Mike Mansfield of Montana began a fight for more information in 1954 and, frustrated by a wall of uncooperativeness, in 1956 introduced a resolution to create a joint Senate-House CIA oversight committee. A surprising thirty-four other senators signed on. Predictably, President Eisenhower objected, and in a revealing statement of his attitude about the CIA he told a press conference that intelligence activities were "a military matter, largely," beyond the authority of Congress. Senator Leverett Saltonstall, Republican of Massachusetts, warned that such a committee "might destroy the agency." White House lobbying succeeded, and on April 11 the Senate rejected Mansfield's resolution 59–27.[87]

Mansfield's bill was the first real challenge to the secrecy surrounding the CIA. William Colby, CIA director from 1973 to 1976, later explained that intelligence "was the sovereign's business," beyond the purview of Congress, the media, and the general public alike. The CIA duly briefed the heads of the Armed Services and Appropriations Committees of both houses of Congress, but mainly over budget matters, with no questions about operations. The briefings often occurred on Sundays, when few people were around congressional offices. Richard Helms, also later a CIA director, recalled senators' saying they "are not wild to know about some types of things that go on," and "Look, forget it and don't bother to tell us." Senator Saltonstall, chair of one of the Senate committees, said, "It's better for gentlemen not to know what's going on." [88]

Testimony in Senate Inquiry," *NYT*, May 18, 1954. Acting Attorney General William P. Rogers to Mr. President, March 2, 1954, "Power and Authority of the President of the United States to Withhold Information Relating to the Executive Branch of Government from Congressional Committees," ACW Files, Administration Series, Brownell File, DDEPL. "'Privilege' Is Scored," *NYT*, March 11, 1958. "Senate Rejects C.I.A. 'Watchdog,'" ibid., April 12, 1956. Weiner, *Legacy of Ashes*, pp. 105–7. Brownell, *Advising Ike*, p. 251. McCarthy and the pivotal role of Brownell's memo: Rozell, *Executive Privilege*. 3rd ed., pp. 40–1.

86 Duane Tannanbaum, *The Bricker Amendment Controversy: A Test of Eisenhower's Political Leadership* (Ithaca, NY: Cornell University Press, 1988). Johnson role: Caro, *The Years of Lyndon Johnson: Master of the Senate*, pp. 527–41.

87 'Showdown Near on C.I.A. Policy," *NYT*, April 6, 1956. "Senators Assail Secrecy of C.I.A., ibid., April 10, 1956; "Senate Rejects C.I.A. 'Watchdog,'" ibid., April 12, 1956. Don Oberdorfer, *Senator Mansfield: The Extraordinary Life of a Great American Statesman and Diplomat* (Washington, DC: Smithsonian Books, 2003), pp. 144–5. The President's News Conference of March 7, 1956, APP.

88 "Oral History: Reflections of DCI Colby and Helms on the CIA's 'Time of Troubles,'" Center for the Study of Intelligence, pp. 3,15. LeRoy Ashby and Rod Gramer, *Fighting the Odds: The Life of Senator Frank Church*

The antidemocratic norms surrounding the CIA reflected a now-well-established worldview about national security. The 1954 Doolittle Commission, which Ike appointed to head off congressional scrutiny of the CIA, explained that "we are facing an implacable enemy whose avowed objective is world domination by whatever means.... There are no rules in such a game.... Hitherto acceptable norms of human conduct do not apply ... [and] long-standing American concepts of 'fair play' must be reconsidered." Such thinking, shocking to many Americans in later years, became deeply ingrained among intelligence professionals and was shared by most members of Congress, the media, and all presidents until the post-Watergate period. (Fifty years later, the George W. Bush administration used a similar rationale that the war on terrorism was "a different kind of war," while Vice President Dick Cheney immediately after the September 11, 2001, terrorist attacks said the country would have to go over to "the dark side" in that war.)[89]

Eisenhower became enthusiastic about CIA covert actions as an instrument of American foreign policy for two reasons. First, he saw how the Korean War had ended in military stalemate and had seriously damaged President Truman politically. Second, covert actions were an inexpensive way to fight communism, allowing him to honor his commitment to reducing government spending, including the defense budget. Thus, covert action greatly expanded under Eisenhower and included the 1953 CIA-engineered coup in Iran and the 1954 coup in Guatemala. The two coups appeared to be huge successes at the time but only fueled a disastrous hubris in the CIA and among other foreign policy experts. Additionally, at an April 1954 press conference, Eisenhower coined the so-called domino theory, which became the rationale for American policy in much of the world and underpinned the tragic Vietnam War.[90]

Shielded from scrutiny, the CIA undertook illegal spying operations in the United States, in violation of its charter. In Eisenhower's first year as president, it began an illegal "mail cover" program, eventually opening 215,000 letters to Americans from overseas and photographing the covers of 2.7 million pieces of mail before the program was terminated in 1973. On February 18, 1954, meanwhile, the Justice Department agreed that the CIA would have full discretion over whether to report any criminal conduct by agency people. Deputy Attorney General William P. Rogers, moreover, agreed not to put the agreement in a formal document. Twenty-two years later to the day, on February 18, 1976, President Gerald Ford ended this practice with Executive Order 11905 requiring the CIA to report all "possible violations of law by any person" associated with the agency.[91]

(Pullman: Washington State University Press, 1994), p. 471. [Church interview]. Snider, *The Agency and the Hill*, pp. 5, 9, 11, 17.

89 Doolittle Commission: *Report on the Covert Activities of the Central Intelligence Agency* (September 30, 1954); released to the Church Committee, U.S. Senate, 1975, and available at www.foia.cia.gov/helms/pdf/doolittle_report.pdf. Snider, *The Agency and the Hill: CIA's Relationship with Congress, 1946–2004*, p. 7.

90 Press Conference, April 7, 1954, APP. Iran coup: William J. Daugherty, *Executive Secrets: Covert Action and the Presidency*. Pbk. ed. (Lexington: University of Kentucky, 2006), pp. 131–49. The conspiracy-minded might notice that the husband of Eisenhower's personal secretary, Ann Whitman, was the publicity director for the United Fruit Company, which had major interests in Guatemala. Thomas, *The Very Best Men*, p. 111.

91 U.S. Senate, Senate Select Committee on Governmental Operations, V. 4, *Mail Opening*, Hearings, October 21, 22, 24, 1975. Criminal conduct: Central Intelligence Agency, Office of the Inspector General Investigations Staff, *Allegations of Connections Between CIA and the Contras in Cocaine Trafficking to the United States*. V. II, The Contra Story, "Reporting Potential Crimes to Department of Justice." Executive Order 11905, February 18, 1976, APP.

The media, including the *New York Times* and CBS television, actively cooperated with the CIA. Years later, the veteran *Times* reporter Harrison Salisbury recalled this "special relationship," a bond based on shared Ivy League backgrounds, a resulting social "intimacy," and "a common view of the world in which you simply served your country when asked by top officials." In 1946, Lt. General Hoyt Vandenberg, head of the Central Intelligence Group (predecessor to the CIA), wrote to the *Times*'s Arthur Hays Sulzberger asking for the paper's "assistance in accomplishing our assigned task." Sulzberger promptly assured him he would "always meet with the fullest cooperation from all of us here at the *New York Times*." The *Times* began forwarding overseas reporters' background communications to the CIA, which even had a case officer assigned to the paper. CBS News, meanwhile, shared unused film of news events. The special relationship eventually collapsed when the Vietnam War shattered the bond of trust.[92]

Eisenhower acquired the image of a passive chief executive who failed to provide leadership on critical social issues. Democrats promoted this image for their own partisan purposes. John F. Kennedy, for example, promised to "get this country moving again" in the 1960 election campaign. With regard to national security, however, the public image is quite misleading. Ike's special assistant for national security affairs, Gordon Gray, recalled that he was "perhaps more security conscious or as security conscious as any President we've had in history." He took an active role in national security issues, establishing clear procedures for National Security Council (NSC) meetings, requiring a written record of all decisions (but not of the debates), and was deeply engaged in covert operations decisions. He personally approved, for example, the initial planning for what became the 1961 Bay of Pigs invasion of Cuba.[93]

The CIA director, A. Dulles, met with Eisenhower in March 1960 and proposed a program of harassing the new Fidel Castro regime in Cuba, which then appeared to be leaning toward communism. His plan called for anti-Castro propaganda and sabotage of sugar refineries. Ike responded, "Allen, this is fine, but if you're going to make any move against Castro, don't just fool around with sugar refineries. Let's get a program that will really do something about Castro." Seeing his opportunity, Dulles immediately replied, "Yes, Sir." In his memoirs, Ike recalled ordering the CIA "to begin to organize the training of Cuban exiles ... against a possible day when they might return to their homeland."[94]

In the revelations of CIA misdeeds that poured forth in 1975, many people saw the agency as a "rogue elephant," completely free of presidential or congressional control. Eisenhower's enthusiasm for covert action and his direct involvement in NSC deliberations tell a different story, however. On major initiatives, the CIA had presidential

[92] Harrison E. Salisbury, *Without Fear or Favor: An Uncompromising Look at The New York Times and Its Times* (New York: Times Books, 1980), pp. 566, 576; "The Special Relationship," Ch. 49, pp. 576–91. The special relationship was first exposed by Carl Bernstein in "The CIA and the Media," *Rolling Stone* (October 20, 1977). *The New York Times*, to its credit, then published a three-part review by the reporter John Crewdson and Joseph B. Treaster, "The C.I.A.'s 3-Decade Effort to Mold the World's Views: Agency Network Using News Organs, Books and Other Methods Is Detailed," *NYT*, December 25, 1977, and following stories on December 26, 1977 and December 27, 1977.

[93] Gray, OH, DDEPL; on Ike's security consciousness, p. 26.

[94] Ike-Dulles meeting: Gordon Gray, OH, p. 28, DDEPL; cited by John Prados, *Presidents' Secret Wars: CIA and Pentagon Covert Operations from World War II through Iranscam*. Rev. ed. (New York: William Morrow, 1988), p. 177. Generally: Prados, Ch. X, "Cuba I: 'Another Black Hole of Calcutta,'" pp. 171–93. Eisenhower, *Waging Peace*, p. 533.

approval. Gordon Gray recalls that Ike managed the NSC, and by extension the CIA, very closely: He "wanted to be involved and he was involved."[95]

A WEAK RECORD ON WOMEN'S ISSUES

While Eisenhower appointed a woman to his cabinet, Secretary of Health, Education, and Welfare Oveta Culp Hobby, his record on women's issues was only slightly better than President Truman's very weak performance. He appointed two women as federal judges, doubling the total ever appointed. In 1959, with an apparent eye on Nixon's run for the presidency in 1960, the White House issued a series of reports on women in various federal positions. (It employed a very generous interpretation of "top" level appointments, however, and mainly listed appointments to advisory commissions.)[96] Eisenhower's record lends credence to the standard cliches about the role of women in the 1950s. The Equal Rights Amendment, for example, almost completely disappeared from view in Congress.

CREATING THE WARREN COURT

Eisenhower later called it his greatest mistake as President, but his appointment of Earl Warren as chief justice of the Supreme Court stands as his greatest contribution to civil liberties. It was a momentous choice for the history of the Court and the entire nation. The Warren Court (1953–69) expanded civil liberties in ways few could have imagined in the early 1950s and transformed the daily lives of Americans across the country – establishing a new freedom to read previously banned books, greater protection against coercive police practices, a guarantee of a lawyer at trial, a new right to privacy, more representative legislatures, and more.[97]

Just eight months into Eisenhower's presidency, on September 8, 1953, with a new Court term only a month away, Chief Justice Fred Vinson died of a heart attack. Ike had thought seriously about the Court and believed that Presidents Roosevelt and Truman's choices had lacked the proper qualifications for this high office. Consequently, he pledged that all federal judicial appointees would be people of "known and recognized integrity," with "wide experience in government" and "competence in the law"; people who would "restore the Court to the high position of prestige that it once enjoyed." He then pointedly added, "This prestige, I think, was lost in the appointment of such men as Murphy, Rutledge, and a few others." He and Brownell were equally determined to clean up the aura of politics and corruption that surrounded Truman's Justice Department. Brownell ended the practice of allowing local U.S. attorneys to work part-time while maintaining a private law practice.[98]

95 Gray, OH, p. 14, DDEPL.

96 *List of Top Women Appointments in the Eisenhower Administration (1959)*, Bertha Adkins Papers, Box 20 DDEPL, Digital Documents.

97 Jim Newton, *Justice for All: Earl Warren and the Nation He Made* (New York: Riverhead Books, 2006). G. Edward White, *Earl Warren: A Public Life* (New York: Oxford University Press, 1982). Ed Cray, *Chief Justice: A Biography of Earl Warren* (New York: Simon & Schuster, 1997). Bernard Schwartz, *Super Chief: Earl Warren and His Supreme Court* (New York: New York University Press, 1983).

98 Supreme Court: Eisenhower to Milton Eisenhower, September 11, 1953, ACW Files, Diary, Box 3, DDEPL. Justice Department: Brownell, *Advising Ike*, pp. 147–51.

Earl Warren, the popular Republican governor of California, was Ike's first choice, in return for his crucial support for the 1952 GOP nomination, because Eisenhower had promised Warren the first vacancy on the Court. Given Warren's lack of judicial experience and deep involvement in Republican Party politics, however, he did not really meet Eisenhower's stated criteria for the most important judicial position in the land.[99] The question of exactly when Warren would take his seat posed a problem, however, and the eventual solution had critical implications for *Brown v. Board of Education.* With no time for confirmation hearings before the new Court term, and with a rehearing of *Brown* on the docket, there was much concern about not having nine justices. The result was an interim appointment that allowed Warren to serve pending his confirmation hearings, which finally occurred in early March 1954.

Warren's appointment was a momentous event in the history of American life, and the term "Warren Court" is shorthand for the dramatic growth of civil liberties. The legal scholar Henry J. Abraham offers the widely held view that Warren was "not a great lawyer ... not a great legal scholar ... [and] not a judicial philosopher.... But he was the Chief Justice par excellence," second only to John Marshall.[100] As chief justice, he is credited with fashioning the unanimous opinion in *Brown*, a result that added enormously to the credibility of the very controversial decision. The Court's decisions on freedom of expression (*Jacobellis v. Ohio*, 1964), which ended most censorship in the arts; due process rights of criminal suspects (*Miranda v. Arizona*, 1966); reapportionment of legislative districts (*Baker v. Carr*, 1962); and privacy (*Griswold v. Connecticut*, 1965) completely refashioned the meaning of individual rights in America. The subtitle of a recent biography, *Earl Warren and the Nation He Made*, overstates the case, but even if Warren did not do it all himself, he certainly played a pivotal role as chief justice.[101]

The great irony is that nothing in Warren's prior career suggested he would became a great civil libertarian, and some of the most controversial events suggested just the opposite. As district attorney in Alameda County (Oakland), California, he had been a tough "law and order" prosecutor. His prosecution of labor activists in the 1936 King-Ramsay-Conner murder case raised questions about his tactics that dogged his early political career. Most famously, as California attorney general in 1942 he had vigorously urged the federal government to remove the Japanese Americans from the West Coast, voicing particularly offensive racist views. It was highly ironic, then, that he would write the Supreme Court's opinions in both *Brown v. Board of Education* and *Miranda v. Arizona* in 1966 affirming the rights of people in custody of the police.[102] Brownell recalled that in 1953 Warren was known primarily as "a very tough prosecutor," with "not much" of a record on civil rights. The journalist I. F. Stone wrote at the time of his appointment that "the law as interpreted by the Court under Warren is unlikely to differ sharply from the

[99] Henry J. Abraham, *Justices, Presidents, and Senators: A History of the U.S. Supreme Court Appointments from Washington to Bush II.* 5th ed. (Lanham, MD: Rowman & Littlefield, 2008), pp. 199–202.

[100] Abraham, *Justices and Presidents*, p. 203.

[101] Newton, *Justice for All: Earl Warren and the Nation He Made.*

[102] No Warren biographer has adequately explained his dramatic transformation on civil liberties. Edward G. White, *Earl Warren: A Public Life* (New York: Oxford University Press, 1982). Ed Cray, *Chief Justice: A Biography of Earl Warren* (New York: Simon & Schuster, 1997). Bernard Schwartz, *Super Chief: Earl Warren and His Supreme Court* (New York: NYU Press, 1983). Warren's memoirs say little: Earl Warren, *The Memoirs of Earl Warren* (Garden City, NY: Doubleday, 1977).

law as dispensed under Vinson."[103] He was not the only person to misjudge the new chief justice completely.

Eisenhower's second appointment, to fill Justice Robert Jackson's seat in October 1955, was imbued with powerful symbolism. Everyone knew that John Marshall Harlan II was the grandson and namesake of the Supreme Court justice now celebrated for his lonely dissent in *Plessy v. Ferguson* upholding segregation, and whom the Court had vindicated in *Brown* the year before. Harlan proved to be a classic conservative civil libertarian, siding with the government on many issues but with a strong commitment to civil rights and certain First Amendment rights. Notably, his dissent in a 1961 birth control case, *Poe v. Ullman*, expressed a pioneering view of a constitutional right to privacy (that the Connecticut law prohibiting birth control devices "is an intolerable and unjustifiable invasion of privacy in the conduct of the most intimate concerns of an individual's private life"). His opinion laid the foundation for both the landmark *Griswold v. Connecticut* case of 1965 affirming a right to privacy and then the historic *Roe v. Wade* decision on abortion rights.[104]

The appointment of William J. Brennan was also filled with surprises and ironies. When Sherman Minton retired in 1956, Republican Party strategists decided that appointing a Catholic would help the GOP in the upcoming presidential election. No Catholic had served on the Court since Justice Frank Murphy died in 1949, and there was talk of "restoring" the Catholic seat. The administration's pandering to the Catholic vote, of course, made a mockery of Eisenhower's grand statement about basing appointments strictly on judicial qualifications. The politically powerful Francis Cardinal Spellman of New York City had spoken to Eisenhower two years before about appointing a Catholic but was initially unhappy about Brennan because he had never met him and therefore the nominee did not owe him any favors. Spellman checked with Brennan's parish priest to make sure he was a good Catholic. The priest reported that he attended mass every week. Once on the Court, however, Brennan proceeded to outrage Catholic leaders with his libertarian positions on censorship, separation of church and state, birth control, and abortion.[105]

At his confirmation hearings, Brennan was subject to "persistent questioning" by Senator Joe McCarthy. Although not even a member of the Judiciary Committee and fading in power, he was granted the special privilege of participating. McCarthy objected to speeches in which Brennan had referred to "witch hunts" and "inquisitions." Brennan replied that he approved of congressional investigations and the exposure of communism. Four months later, however, he joined a 7–1 majority in *Watkins v. United States*

103 Brownell, OH, pp. 71–2, ROHO. I. F. Stone, *The Haunted Fifties* (Column, October 3, 1953), p. 59. Ike to Hunt, September 24, 1953, Official File 100-A, DDEPL.

104 "Eisenhower Names U.S. Judge Harlan to Supreme Court," *NYT*, November 9, 1954. The symbolic aspect is noted by the historian Michael Mayer, "With Much Deliberation and Some Speed: Eisenhower and the Brown Decision," *Journal of Southern History*, LII (February 1986): 62–3. Tinsley E. Yarborough, *John Marshall Harlan: Great Dissenter of the Warren Court*. New York: Oxford University Press, 1992). Norman Dorsen and Amelia Ames Newcomb, "John Marshall Harlan II, Associate Justice of the Supreme Court 1955–1971: Remembrances by his Law Clerks," *Journal of Supreme Court History*, 27 (July 2002): 138–75. *Poe v. Ullman*, 367 U.S. 497 (1961).

105 Stephen J. Wermeil, "The Nomination of Justice Brennan: Eisenhower's Mistake? A Look at the Historical Record," *Constitutional Commentary* 11 (1994): 515. Kim Isaac Eisler, *A Justice for All: William J. Brennan, Jr., and the Decisions That Transformed America* (New York: Simon & Schuster, 1993); on Spellman's role and his unhappiness, pp. 68–96. Roger Goldman with David Gallen, *Justice William J. Brennan, Jr.: Freedom First* (New York: Graf, 1994).

ruling that the power of Congress to investigate "is not unlimited," and he joined in several other cases striking down anti-communist measures.[106]

Brennan is now generally recognized as the intellectual leader of the Warren Court, fashioning a jurisprudence that endured long after the Supreme Court became dominated by conservatives. He wrote some of the most important Court opinions (notably in *New York Times v. Sullivan*, 1964, arguable the most important decision on the First Amendment) and was particularly skilled at fashioning compromises to secure a majority. (He reportedly once told his clerks that the most important word in American jurisprudence is "five.") Legend has it that Eisenhower regarded appointing Brennan as his second greatest mistake as president, after appointing Warren, although there is no written record of this comment.[107]

Eisenhower' fourth appointment, Charles Whittaker, joined the Court in 1957 and proved to be an embarrassing failure as a Supreme Court Justice. He had no coherent philosophy and reportedly had a nervous breakdown under the strain of wrestling with a major case in 1962. Chief Justice Warren then persuaded him to resign

"Red Monday:" The Warren Court arrives

"Red Monday," June 17, 1957, announced the arrival of the Warren Court as an activist guarantor of individual rights, and the impact of Eisenhower's Supreme Court appointments. The Court decided four cases involving anti-communist measures that day, all in favor of the plaintiffs. Eisenhower's appointees voted with the majority in each case.[108]

Two decisions placed limits on legislative investigations. In *Watkins,* the Court overturned a HUAC contempt citation against the leftist labor leader John Watkins, holding that the scope of HUAC's enabling authority was too broad and had no clear legislative purpose. In a rebuke to a long history of legislative investigations, the Court held that Congress has no authority "to expose for the sake of exposure." The Court also overturned a contempt citation against Professor Paul Sweezy because the questions posed by a New Hampshire state investigating committee were unrelated to any clear legislative purpose.[109]

In *Yates v. United States*, the Court reversed by a 6–1 margin the convictions of fourteen Communist Party member in one of the "second-tier" Smith Act cases. In the Court's first attempt to clarify its original 1951 *Dennis* decision upholding the Smith Act, it now held that the law did not bar advocacy and teaching of the overthrow of the government and that the government had presented no evidence of acts related to overthrowing the government. Many observers wondered whether the government would be able to obtain any further convictions under the Smith Act. In the least significant case that day, the Court overturned (8–0) the dismissal of a former State Department official,

106 "Brennan Favors Inquiries on Reds," *NYT*, February 27, 1957. *Watkins v. United States,* 354 U.S. 178 (1957).

107 Eisler, *A Justice for All*. Goldman and Gallen, *Justice William J. Brennan*. Disparaging remark about Brennan: Hunter R. Clark, *Justice Brennan: The Great Conciliator* (Secaucus, NJ: Carol Publishing Group, 1995), pp. 79–80. "Five" stories are in Henry J. Abraham, *Justices, Presidents, and Senators: A History of the U.S. Supreme Court Appointments from Washington to Bush II*. 5th ed. (Lanham, MD: Rowman & Littlefield, 2008), p. 211.

108 Arthur J. Sabin, *In Calmer Times: The Supreme Court and Red Monday* (Philadelphia: University of Pennsylvania Press, 1999).

109 *Watkins v. United States*, 354 U.S. 178 (1957). *Sweezy v. New Hampshire*, 354 U.S. 234 (1957).

John W. Service, because Secretary of State John Foster Dulles had violated department procedures regarding dismissals.[110]

The four Red Monday cases were not wholly unexpected to close Court watchers. Just two weeks earlier it dealt a serious blow to the FBI's system of confidential informants. It overturned the conviction of the labor union official Clinton Jencks, convicted of falsely stating that he was not a member of the Communist Party, because he had been denied permission to examine the reports of FBI confidential informants stating that he was a communist.[111] In two other cases, the Court ruled that left-wing lawyers had been unfairly denied admission to state bars because of their political associations.

The Red Monday decisions outraged anti-communist hard-liners. FBI Director Hoover denounced them as "the greatest victory the Communist Party in America has ever received." President Eisenhower was reportedly "livid," particularly over the fact that his appointees all voted with the majority. (Charles Whittaker, who joined the Court in March, participated in only one decision.) At a party he was reportedly "mad as hell," but when word leaked out, he wrote a conciliatory letter to Warren to smooth the waters.[112]

Inevitably, Ike was asked about the decisions. At his press conference two days later a reporter posed the question on many peoples' minds: Did the president think "the Court has gone too far in protecting these rights at the expense of the law enforcement?" Eisenhower's answer was evasive and embarrassing. After first declining "to answer that question in the specific way you seem to expect," he said that he had his own "fixed convictions about these things," which were "very strong." But he did not explain what those convictions were.[113] As with *Brown*, the president of the United States failed to take a stand on the most urgent question of the day.

The day after Red Monday, both HUAC and the Senate Internal Security Committee postponed hearings when attorneys for witnesses argued that *Watkins* meant their clients did not have to answer the expected questions. The journalist I. F. Stone, by now undoubtedly rethinking his opinion of Warren, commented that June 17 "will go down in the history books as the day on which the Supreme Court irreparably crippled the witch hunt." *Time* magazine summed it up in its July 1 issue, with Chief Justice Warren on the cover and the prophetic headline "U.S. Supreme Court: The New Direction."[114]

Ensuring integration: Ike's southern judges

Eisenhower's appointment of several key judges to southern federal courts made an incalculable contribution to the civil rights and civil liberties in America. In what became known as *Brown II*, the Supreme Court in 1955 handed responsibility for implementation of desegregation to the federal district courts. With Attorney General Brownell

110 *Yates v. United States*, 354 U.S. 298 (1957). *Service v. Dulles*, 354 U.S. 363 (1957).

111 *Jencks v. United States*, 353 U.S. 657 (1957).

112 "President Declines to Give Court View," *NYT*, June 20, 1957. Jim Newton, *Justice for All: Earl Warren and the Nation He Made* (New York: Riverhead Books, 2006), pp. 354–5. President's News Conference, June 26, 1957, APP.

113 The President's News Conference of June 19, 1957, APP."President Declines to Give Court View," *NYT*, June 20, 1957. Despite his reaction at the time, Eisenhower did not mention the Red Monday decisions or his reaction in his memoirs, *Waging Peace*.

114 Stone, *The Haunted Fifties*, pp. 199–200. *Time Magazine*, July 1, 1957.

again managing events, Eisenhower appointed several judges in the South who are now famous for their roles in implementing school desegregation.

The most celebrated Eisenhower appointments in the South were Elbert Tuttle and John Brown (Fifth Circuit Court of Appeals, 1955), John Minor Wisdom (Fifth Circuit, 1957), and Frank M. Johnson (District Court, Alabama, 1955). As Republicans they were independent of the patronage system that allowed segregationist Seators to control appointments by Democratic presidents. (The first federal judge appointed by President John F. Kennedy in 1961, for example, was the racist Harold Cox, former college roommate of Mississippi's die-hard segregationist senator James Eastland.)[115]

The work of this remarkable group of judges extended beyond school desegregation. Frank Johnson became one of the great civil libertarian judges of his time. His 1956 decision in *Browder v. Gale* ordered the desegregation of the buses in Montgomery, Alabama, which was still the target of the boycott initiated by Rosa Parks. In a case that eventually went to the Supreme Court, Johnson struck down a twenty-eight-sided voting district that excluded almost all African-American voters from the city of Tuskegee, Alabama (*Gomillion v. Lightfoot,* 1960). In other cases, he struck down literacy tests and the poll tax in Alabama, integrated the University of Alabama, outlawed discrimination in Alabama libraries, and ended discrimination against both African Americans and women in Alabama jury service. In 1961 he enjoined local officials from violence against the Freedom Riders, and in 1965 he made possible the famous Selma to Montgomery march by ruling that the marchers had a First Amendment right of freedom of assembly (*Williams v. Wallace*, 1965). In *Wyatt v. Stickney* (1971) he defined a right to treatment for patients in the state mental hospital. For his efforts, he was called "the most hated man in Alabama," his mother's house was bombed, two crosses were burned on his lawn in 1957, and he endured many threats on his life. The Alabama governor, George Wallace, whom Johnson threatened to jail in 1958, once said he should be given a "barbed wire enema." President Jimmy Carter elevated him to the Fifth Circuit Court of Appeals in 1977 and would have appointed him director of the FBI if not for an unexpected medical condition.[116]

John Lewis, savagely beaten in the 1965 Selma march and later a long-term member of Congress, paid Johnson a fitting tribute upon his death in 1990: "Frank Johnson was the best example of what this country can be." His decision in the Montgomery bus case "may have changed my life more than any other event before or since." Because his decisions transformed local bus systems, state election systems, the university, juries across the state, the prisons, and mental hospitals, Lewis said people appropriately called him "the real Governor of Alabama."[117] His appointment to the federal bench was one of Eisenhower's greatest decisions. Although rarely mentioned in assessments of his presidency, Eisenhower's appointment of Frank Johnson was one of his greatest contributions to civil liberties and to American life.

[115] Jack Bass, *Unlikely Heroes: The Dramatic Story of the Southern Judges of the Fifth Circuit Who Translated the Supreme Court's Brown Decision into a Revolution for Equality* (New York: Simon & Schuster, 1981). Bass, *Taming the Storm*. Joel W. Friedman, "Desegregating the South: John Minor Wisdom's Role in Enforcing Brown's Mandate," *Tulane Law Review* 78, no. 6 (2004): 2207–78. Tinsley E. Yarbrough, *Judge Frank Johnson and Human Rights in Alabama* (University: University of Alabama Press, 1981). Robert Francis. Kennedy, Jr., *Judge Frank M. Johnson, Jr.: A Biography* (New York: Putnam, 1978). Arthur Selwyn Miller, *"A Capacity for Outrage": The Judicial Odyssey of J. Skelly Wright* (Westport, CT: Greenwood Press, 1984).

[116] Bass, *Taming the Storm*. Kennedy, Jr., *Judge Frank M. Johnson*.

[117] John Lewis, "Reflections on Judge Frank M. Johnson, Jr.," *Yale Law Journal* 109 (April 2000): 1253–6.

THE END OF THE FIFTIES

The year 1954 was a watershed in American history. On March 9, Edward R. Murrow's television show on Senator Joe McCarthy marked the beginning of the end of the scourge of McCarthyism. And on May 17 the Supreme Court decision in *Brown v. Board of Education* ushered in a new era in civil rights, which would dominate American society over the next turbulent decade and put an end to the ugly scar of legal racial discrimination. Both issues cried out for presidential leadership, and on both President Eisenhower failed. Not once did he denounce Senator McCarthy by name or lead a fight for a reasonable approach to domestic threats to national security. Nor did he endorse the *Brown* decision or express support for the aspirations of the civil rights movement (even though his administration quietly desegregated Washington, D.C.). His vacillation, in fact, probably encouraged the very resistance to integration and the disorder he wanted to prevent.

Had Eisenhower provided leadership on these two issues, the course of American history might well have been very different. And his reputation today would also be completely different. While president he was mocked for playing golf so frequently. But golf was only a convenient symbol for his leadership failures. It is a fair guess that had he taken a strong public stand on McCarthy or *Brown,* his golfing never would have been an issue. Some revisionist historians argue that Eisenhower actually provided quiet, effective leadership behind the scenes. The chief proponent of this view, the Princeton University political scientist Fred Greenstein, titled his book *The Hidden-Hand Presidency.* Unfortunately, Greenstein's own evidence persuasively undermines his own case, with no mention of civil rights whatsoever, and a special chapter on McCarthy that actually disproves his thesis.[118]

Eisenhower had some good criticisms of the Federal Loyalty Program and the anti-communist crusade but never acted on them. Instead, he allowed Attorney General Herbert Brownell to pursue aggressive anti-communist measures. On the national security issues, Eisenhower left a troubling legacy. He enthusiastically embraced CIA covert actions, protected the CIA and other government secrets with a full-blown doctrine of executive privilege, broadened the scope of the Federal Loyalty Program, and personally approved the FBI's COINTELPRO program, which included illegal FBI conduct. On the positive side, his administration ended the embarrassing racial segregation in the nation's capital, and he appointed several outstanding federal judges in the South, who enforced school integration and made other important contributions to civil liberties.

The great irony of Eisenhower's presidency, of course, was his appointment of Earl Warren and William Brennan to the Supreme Court. With Warren providing the political leadership and Brennan much of the jurisprudential theory, they were the key figures in the great expansion of individual rights in the 1960s. The Warren Court's constitutional revolution transformed the daily lives of American citizens – on racial justice, freedom of expression, the place of religion in American life, legislative representation, criminal justice, and the right to privacy – and it endured long after Warren and Brennan had left the bench. Eisenhower, however, not only did not appoint these towering justices

[118] Greenstein, *The Hidden Hand Presidency*, pp. 155–227 on McCarthy. See also the recent revisionist and unpersuasive view of Eisenhower and civil rights: Nichols, *A Matter of Justice*.

because of their views on civil liberties, but regarded his choice for chief justice as his greatest mistake.

Buried in the Eisenhower papers in Abilene, Kansas, is a fall 1953 memo analyzing a public opinion poll commissioned by the White House. Only partway through Ike's first term, the report was harshly critical of Ike's failure to lead. "Mr. President," the author wrote, "your play is still on in the most important theater in the world.... You are on the stage, but the lights are out. Please go on with the play - talk to your audience - be the leader of the United States and the world!" The anguished plea stands today as a prescient assessment of Eisenhower's failures on the crucial civil liberties issues of his time.[119]

[119] "Grass Roots" Report. Highlights of Second Public Opinion Poll in California, September 30, 1953 ACW Files, DDE Diary Series, Box 3, DDEPL.

Senator John F. Kennedy, then a candidate for president, speaks to the Ministers' Association of Greater Houston, September 12, 1960, about the place of religion in American life. The speech was in response to anti-Catholic prejudice among some Americans.
Source: Associated Press.

7 John F. Kennedy

The Failed Promise of the New Frontier

A WALK IN THE ROSE GARDEN

President John F. Kennedy took the Reverend Martin Luther King, Jr., aside for a private conversation in the White House Rose Garden on June 22, 1963. Placing his hand on the civil rights leader's shoulder, he told him to fire his two closest aides, Stanley Levison and Jack O'Dell: "They're Communists, you've got to get rid of them," he said, ominously adding, "I assume you know you are under very close surveillance."[1]

The incident marked the intersection of three civil liberties issues in Kennedy's presidency. First, the president's warning was based on FBI surveillance, which Kennedy never challenged and soon expanded. Second, ordering King to fire his assistants represented his uncritical embrace of guilt by association. Finally, in several instances, the Kennedy administration pressured civil rights leaders to accommodate the administration's priorities.

President Kennedy is widely viewed as a great champion of civil rights, an image largely based on his nationally televised speech on June 11, 1963, when he proposed what eventually became the historic 1964 Civil Rights Act. In fact, however, Kennedy dragged his feet on civil rights, failed to grasp the moral urgency of the issue, and introduced a civil rights bill only when pressured to act by the massive civil rights demonstrations in Birmingham, Alabama.

Kennedy and civil liberties

Kennedy's record on all civil liberties issues was decidedly mixed. On some, he had a very commendable record. His 1960 election campaign speech is the greatest on the subject of religious liberty by any president or candidate in American history. He also advanced women's rights through his President's Commission on the Status of Women 1961, although not in ways he expected. As attorney general, his brother, Robert F. Kennedy (RFK), promoted important criminal justice reforms, notably bail reform. Bobby Kennedy, in fact, was responsible for some of the best and the worst of the administration's actions. His role raises the question of whether the president deserves credit or blame for what he really did. In truth, despite their very different temperaments, the two were so close as to be virtually one in terms of policy making. RFK said as much.

[1] Taylor Branch, *Parting the Waters: America in the King Years, 1954–1963* (New York: Simon & Schuster, 1988), 835–7. Edwin O. Guthman and Jeffrey Shulman, eds., *Robert F. Kennedy in His Own Words: The Unpublished Recollections of the Kennedy Years* (New York: Bantam Books, 1988), pp. 143–6.

Asked whether he checked with his brother about important actions, he replied, "I never would have to call him."[2]

On other issues, however, Kennedy's record was very disturbing. The administration authorized FBI wiretaps of Reverenc Martin Luther King, and used the FBI improperly in other ways. On national security, President Kennedy made an outrageous proposal for press self-censorship and was entranced by the CIA as a flexible, action-oriented instrument of foreign policy. Robert Kennedy was the driving force behind the CIA plots to assassinate Fidel Castro.[3] John F. Kennedy's civil liberties record, in short, is as contradictory as that of many other presidents.

A VOICE FOR RELIGIOUS TOLERANCE

"I believe in an America where the separation of church and state is absolute." The Democratic Party candidate for president added, "I believe in an America where religious intolerance will someday end." Two months away from election day in 1960, John F. Kennedy delivered a powerful defense of religious tolerance and separation of church and state.[4]

Indirectly, Kennedy made his greatest contribution to civil liberties simply by being elected. The ugly anti-Catholic attacks on the Democratic Party candidate Al Smith in 1928 had created the conventional wisdom that no one of that faith could ever be elected president. Kennedy's emergence as a serious contender put the issue at the fore again. Acutely sensitive to the threat anti-Catholic prejudice posed to his candidacy, Kennedy early on began distancing himself from his religion. He clearly stated his opposition to federal aid for parochial schools in 1959 and, to the dismay of many Catholics, made it clear he did not favor establishing diplomatic relations with the Vatican. To help him navigate the treacherous waters of religion and politics, he hired James Wine as a special adviser on religious issues. Wine was a lawyer, a Presbyterian, and a former official with the Protestant National Council of Churches.[5]

Kennedy's Catholicism finally erupted into a public controversy in early September 1960, just as the campaign was moving into high gear, with attacks from a new organization called the National Conference of Citizens for Religious Freedom. Head of the conference was the Reverend Norman Vincent Peale, a prominent Protestant leader, and a friend of the GOP candidate Richard Nixon. After a closed all-day meeting, the conference released a set of clearly hostile questions for Kennedy about his religion. It

2 Ronald Steel, *In Love with Night: The American Romance with Robert Kennedy* (New York: Simon & Schuster, 2000), pp. 83–4. Similar questions of assigning proper responsibility arise with regard to Attorney General Frank Murphy's creation of the Civil Rights Division in 1939 (see Chapter 4) and Attorney General Herbert Brownell's leadership on civil rights in the Eisenhower administration (see Chapter 6). Guthman and Shulman, *Robert F. Kennedy in His Own Words*, p. 104.

3 Semi-official accounts by his former staff members are Arthur M. Schlesinger, Jr., *A Thousand Days: John F. Kennedy in the White House*. Pbk. ed. (New York: Fawcett Crest, 1967) and Theodore C. Sorensen, *Kennedy*. Pbk. ed. (New York: Bantam Books, 1966). Garry Wills, *The Kennedy Imprisonment: A Meditation on Power* (Boston: Little, Brown, 1982) provides valuable insights into President Kennedy's character and public life.

4 The text and an audio recording of the speech are available at APP.

5 "Kennedy Opposes Church-State Tie," *NYT*, February 17, 1959. "Catholic Censure of Kennedy Rises," ibid., March 1, 1959. Vatican: Kennedy to Robert Dasher, February 4, 1958, Sorensen Papers, Box 15, JFKPL. There are twenty-one boxes of material on the religious issue in the Pre-Presidential Papers, Boxes 1002–22, JFKPL. Wine, OH, JFKPL. Wine, FAOH, LOC.

implicitly accused Kennedy of failing to repudiate the teachings of his church – a truly insulting expectation. It asked Nixon no questions about his religion. (It might have asked whether, as a Quaker, he had renounced pacifism.) Peale declared, "Our American culture is at stake" with Kennedy's candidacy. The attack provoked a political uproar, and an embarrassed Peale resigned from the conference. Wine said the conference "pretty well shot their own bird down," but the Catholic issue was now out in the open. After worried deliberations with his advisers, Kennedy decided to confront it head on by addressing the Greater Houston Ministerial Association, a hostile audience in the heart of conservative Protestant territory. It was a huge gamble, and Wine recalled, "There was no doubt in my mind that [the speech] would make or break us."[6]

"Tension and hostility hung in the air" in the Rice Hotel on the night of September 12, as Kennedy rose to speak. In a calculated appeal to his conservative audience, he opened by emphasizing the worldwide struggle against communism. The real issue in the campaign was "not what kind of church I believe in, but what kind of America I believe in." The most important issue was "the spread of Communist influence," he said, pointing to Castro's Cuba only ninety miles from Florida. Other "real issues," which the religious controversy had obscured, included child hunger, health care for the elderly, and inadequate schools. Turning to religion, Kennedy declared that separation of church and state meant a country "where no Catholic prelate would tell the President (should he be a Catholic) how to act and no Protestant minister would tell his parishioners for whom to vote." On federal aid to schools, moreover, "no church or church school" should be granted any public funds. The America he sought was a country "where no man is denied public office" because of his religion or takes "instructions on public policy from the Pope, the National Council of Churches or any other ecclesiastical source." Kennedy ended on a high note, saying, "Finally, I believe in an America where religious intolerance will someday end." Questions followed his speech, and he handled them with the ease that would later characterize his presidential press conferences.[7]

Virtually everyone immediately sensed the speech was a huge success. His aide Ted Sorensen, who had written much of it, called it "the best speech of his campaign and one of the most important in his life." He was certainly correct, as the speech laid to rest the Catholic issue and helped JFK win the election. Speaker of the House Sam Rayburn offered earthier praise: "As we say in my part of Texas, he ate 'em blood raw." In truth, politics drove Kennedy to his strong stand on separation of church and state, as he had to make a special effort to thwart allegations that he would advance Catholic policies. As his commissioner of education described it, his Catholicism made him "more Protestant."[8]

6 "Protestant Unit Wary on Kennedy," *NYT*, September 8, 1960. "Protestant Groups' Statements," ibid., September 8, 1960. Kennedy's initial response: "His Speeches Quoted," ibid., September 9, 1960. Wine, OH, pp. 36, 65, JFKPL.

7 "Protestant Group Applauds Kennedy for Houston Speech," *NYT*, September 13, 1960. Theodore H. White, *The Making of the President 1960*. Pbk. ed. (New York: Signet Books, 1967), pp. 296–8. Views of the speech's principal author: Sorensen, *Kennedy*, pp. 212–20, and Theodore C. Sorensen, *Counselor: A Life at the Edge of History* (New York: Harper, 2008), pp. 156–66. Johnson's use of the event: Jack Valenti, OH, pp. 4–5, JFKPL. Speech material: Pre-Presidential Papers, Boxes 911, 1016, JFKPL. The speech is available at APP.

8 Sorensen, *Kennedy*, p. 215. In December 2007, Mitt Romney speech, "Faith in America," modeled after Kennedy's 1960 speech: "Romney's 'Faith in America' Address," *NYT*, December 6, 2007. Francis Keppel, OH, p. 11, JFKPL.

FDR had mentioned Freedom of Worship in his 1941 Four Freedoms speech, but did not elaborate on any of the specifics, as Kennedy did. The presidency is a bully pulpit, and Kennedy used that forum to greater effect on the place of religion in American life than any other president. So successful was his speech in laying to rest the religious issue that it did not became a controversy again until 2008, when Mitt Romney, a Mormon, ran for the GOP presidential nomination, and some conservatives believed that Barack Obama was a Muslim.

"BYSTANDER": KENNEDY'S FAILURE ON CIVIL RIGHTS

The president and the attorney general were furious. Pictures of a burning Greyhound bus in Anniston, Alabama, on May 14 flashed around the world. The Freedom Riders, an interracial group seeking to test the right to travel through the South, had been viciously attacked in Birmingham and then Anniston. Local police stood by and let KKK-led vigilantes attack them. Kennedy was angry at both the damage to America's international reputation and for being placed in a difficult political position between the demands by civil rights activists that he provide them federal protection and the power of southern segregationists in Congress. At one point he shouted at Harris Wofford, his chief aide on civil rights, "Stop them." "Tell them [the Freedom Riders] to call it off!"[9]

In this moment of crisis, one of the iconic events of the civil rights movement, President Kennedy wanted civil rights activists to back off, avoid public confrontations, and let him concentrate on his top priority of confronting international communism. The Freedom Rides coincided with his planning for a June summit meeting with the Soviet premier Nikita Khrushchev in Vienna, Austria. Throughout his presidency, civil rights took a back seat to other issues he deemed more urgent: the Bay of Pigs debacle, the Vienna Summit, the Berlin Wall, the Cuban missile crisis, his tax cut bill, and other legislative priorities. Again and again, he asked civil rights leaders to back off. The historian of the Freedom Rides Raymond Arsenault concludes that Kennedy "was first and foremost a Cold Warrior," for whom civil rights took a back seat.[10]

Kennedy's record on civil rights before being elected president was very mixed. Announcing his candidacy for president on January 2, 1960, he outlined his goals of helping the new nations of Africa, preventing "the collapse of our farm economy and the decay of our cities," and expanding economic growth, among other issues. Civil rights was not on his list of "the real issues of 1960." The first sit-ins, in Greensboro, North Carolina, exactly one month later, however, propelled the civil rights movement into a new era of confrontation. Civil rights leaders in early 1960 much preferred Hubert Humphrey among Democratic contenders. Martin Luther King initially saw little difference between Kennedy and the GOP candidate, Richard Nixon. Nixon had a good record on civil rights as vice president, heading up the administration's equal employment opportunity efforts; he was a member of the NAACP, while Kennedy was not; and Kennedy had actively courted southern senators in his pursuit of the nomination.

[9] Harris Wofford, *Of Kennedys and Kings: Making Sense of the Sixties* (1980, reprint, Pittsburgh: University of Pittsburgh Press, 1992), p. 153.

[10] Raymond Arsenault, *Freedom Riders: 1961 and the Struggle for Racial Justice* (New York: Oxford, 2006), p. 164.

The baseball great Jackie Robinson thought Kennedy had a "very bleak record" on civil rights.[11]

Events immediately overtook the Kennedy administration, as militant actions in the streets, over which he had no control, made racial justice the most urgent national crisis. In important respects, Kennedy himself had raised the expectations of civil rights leaders and other young activists with his youth and his campaign promised to get America "moving again." In June 1960 he praised the sit-ins as a sign that "the American spirit is coming alive again." The 1960 Democratic Party platform, meanwhile, praised recent "peaceful demonstrations." John Lewis, sit-in leader and later a member of Congress, recalled that Kennedy's election "ushered in a sense to optimism – of great expectation.... There was something about the Kennedy presidency – about the man – that touched the black people immediately."[12]

Kennedy gave civil rights leaders particular hope with a now-famous telephone call to the wife of Martin Luther King in October 1960. King was arrested and jailed in Atlanta, Georgia, for a sit-in. Ominously, he was transferred to the Reidsville, Georgia, state prison to serve a four-month sentence on a previous charge of driving with an out of state license plate. His wife, Coretta Scott King, pregnant at the time, was alarmed that he might be lynched, fear that was understandably heightened when King was transferred in the dead of night, at 3:00 a.m. At the suggestion of his brother-in-law Sergeant Shriver, Kennedy called Mrs. King to express his concern. He did not promise any action, but the call itself made a strong impression, and reports circulated widely among civil rights leaders and then in the media. Some observers believed (probably incorrectly) that gesture swung enough African-American votes to give Kennedy the election. Frederic Morrow, Eisenhower's African-American adviser, then on loan to the Nixon campaign, "begged the Nixon managers" for a statement, but to no avail.[13]

The first months in office: Two crises

Kennedy faced two civil rights crises in his first months in office. In several embarrassing incidents, African diplomats were denied service at segregated restaurants in the Washington area. They represented many of the eighteen African nations that gained their independence in 1960 alone. The State Department's chief of protocol, Angier Biddle Duke, recalled, "The colonial world was exploding into independence." Most of the incidents occurred on Route 40 outside Washington, in parts of Maryland where segregation

[11] "The Kennedy Statement," *NYT*, January 3, 1960. Statement, Pre-Presidential Papers, Box 905, JFKPL. King to Chester Bowles, June 24, 1960, Clayborne Carson, ed., *The Papers of Martin Luther King, Jr.* (Berkeley: University of California, 1992), V. V, p. 480. Jackie Robinson, *I Never Had It Made* (New York: G. P. Putnam's Sons, 1972), p. 150. Race in the 1960 campaign: Jeremy D. Mayer, *Running on Race: Racial Politics in Presidential Campaigns, 1960–2000* (New York: Random House, 2002), pp. 9–39.

[12] Arthur M. Schlesinger, Jr., *Journals, 1952–2000* (New York: Penguin, 2007), p. 194. Sit-in comment: "Kennedy Salutes Negroes' Sit Ins," *NYT*, June 25, 1960. 1960 Democratic Party platform, APP. Lewis: Deborah Hart Strober and Gerald S. Strober, eds., *"Let Us Begin Anew": The Kennedy Presidency: An Oral History of the Era* (New York: Harper Perennial, 1994), p. 273.

[13] King, OH, pp. 7–12, JFKPL. Insider's account of the phone call: Wofford, *Of Kennedys and Kings*, Ch 1. "Calling Mrs. Martin Luther King," pp. 11–28. Shriver's firsthand account is in Strober and Strober, *"Let Us Begin Anew,"* pp. 35–6. Nixon's version: Richard M. Nixon, *Six Crises* (New York: Pocket Books, 1962), pp. 390–1. White, *The Making of the President 1960*, pp. 361–3. Morrow's recommendation to Nixon: Morrow, OH, pp. 7–8, DDEPL.

still prevailed. The ambassador from Chad was turned away at a Maryland restaurant, prompting embarrassing headlines around the world. Attorney General Robert Kennedy persuaded the governor of Maryland to apologize to the ambassador. Duke worked almost full-time talking with local business owners and others in a desperate effort to minimize the damage to America's reputation in Third World countries.[14]

In one private White House moment, an exasperated JFK exploded at staff members: "Can't you tell them not to do it?" One aide misunderstood and tried to explain that, with no state or federal public accommodations laws, they could only try to persuade business owners to accept African-American patrons. "That's not what I'm talking about," JFK exclaimed. "Can't you tell these African ambassadors not to drive on Route 40?"[15]

Violence and embarrassment: The Freedom Rides

John F. Kennedy's forty-fourth birthday on May 29, 1961, occurred in the midst of the crisis over the Freedom Rides. The savage beatings and the pictures of the burning Greyhound bus in Anniston two weeks earlier outraged the nation and spread around the world. Kennedy chose to mark his birthday with a "Special Message to the Congress on Urgent National Needs," covering economic growth, national defense, increased foreign aid, and landing a man on the moon. With a civil rights crisis gripping the nation, he said not a word about racial justice.[16]

The Freedom Rides began on May 4, when a racially integrated group left Washington planning to travel through the Deep South and reach New Orleans on May 17, the seventh anniversary of *Brown v. Board of Education*. The ride was organized by James Farmer of the Congress on Racial Equality (CORE), which had cosponsored a similar Journey of Reconciliation through the Upper South in 1947. His strategy was clear: provoke a crisis to force the administration to act on civil rights. Only a few months earlier, on December 5, 1960, the Supreme Court had ruled that bus terminal restaurants were an "integral part" of interstate travel and could not engage in racial discrimination.[17]

As it passed through the Upper South, the Freedom Ride was relatively uneventful, but violence struck when it reached Alabama. On May 14 a violent mob in Anniston, Alabama, stoned one of the buses, slashed its tires, and then firebombed it. The second bus was met by a mob in Birmingham, Alabama, that attacked and beat the Riders. Jim Peck, a veteran of the 1947 Journey to Reconciliation, required fifty stitches. The Birmingham public safety commissioner, Bull Connor, who would become world famous two years later for his brutal tactics, kept his officers away. Faced with the near-certainty of more violence, the Freedom Riders abandoned their original plan and flew to New Orleans. The crisis,

14 Duke, OH, FAOH, LOC. "Maryland Apologizes to Four African Envoys," *NYT*, July 12, 1961. State Department lobbying: Stanley B. Frosh [Montgomery Country, Maryland], to Hon. Angier Biddle Duke, Chief of Protocol, State Department, September, 1961, Wofford Papers, Box 1, JFKLP. A similar incident occurred under Eisenhower in October, 1957. Eisenhower was "incensed" and promptly invited the Ghanaian finance minister to breakfast at the White House the next day. Frederic Morrow, Diary, Morrow Papers, Box 2 Diary October 9, 1957, DDEPL.

15 Wofford, *Of Kennedys and Kings*, p. 127.

16 Special Message to the Congress on Urgent National Needs, May 25, 1961, APP. Bryant, *The Bystander*, 279.

17 Bryant, *The Bystander*, p. 262. CORE and the Freedom Rides: Arseneault, *Freedom Riders*; 1947 Journey of Reconciliation, pp. 22–57. David Niven, *The Politics of Injustice: The Kennedys: The Freedom Rides, and the Electoral Consequences of a Moral Compromise* (Knoxville: University of Tennessee Press, 2003). *Boynton v. Virginia*, 346 U.S. 454 (1960), which was decided on December 5, 1960.

however, only inspired African-American college students in Nashville, battle-tested from the sit-ins, to carry on. Descending on Birmingham by bus, they were promptly arrested, driven to the Tennessee state line, and dumped. Undaunted, some returned to Birmingham and took buses to Montgomery, where they were attacked by a mob shouting, "Get them Niggers." The mob also beat into unconsciousness the Justice Department official John Siegenthaler, present as an observer for Attorney General Kennedy.[18]

In the midst of the crisis, Kennedy berated his aide Harris Wofford: "Can't you get your goddamned friends off those buses? … Stop them." Wofford pleaded unsuccessfully for a strong public statement from the president, pointing out that Eisenhower had never given a "clear moral expression to the issues involved" on civil rights. Kennedy was preoccupied with his upcoming summit meeting in Vienna and regarded the crisis in the South as a distraction. Attorney General Bobby Kennedy, however, was drawn into the crisis by virtue of his job, and he soon became deeply and personally involved. Even before the violence erupted, on May 6, he gave a Law Day address at the University of Georgia, where he forthrightly told his southern audience that his administration would enforce civil rights laws. Observers widely praised him for his candor and commitment. Once the Freedom Rides crises erupted, he and his aides Burke Marshall, John Doar, and John Siegenthaler spent long and difficult hours trying to negotiate a deal with Alabama officials. Bobby's main goal was to prevent violence and, as he put it, "to close the episode out." This meant asking civil rights forces to back off. Martin Luther King recalled that Bobby "strongly urged" calling off the Freedom Rides until after the president's summit meeting. When King threatened to send students to Alabama "by the hundreds – by the hundreds of thousands," Bobby snapped back, "Don't make statements that sound like a threat." He then disparaged one of the Freedom Riders for being a pacifist who had protested the atomic bomb (it was undoubtedly Albert Bigelow, who had in 1958 sailed into an atomic bomb test zone in the Pacific Ocean; some believe RFK asked the FBI for unflattering information about any of the Riders). In Bobby's mind, civil rights militants were just unreasonable people who had no sense of the really important business of the administration – dealing with the Soviet Union.[19] Nonetheless, most historians believe that Bobby Kennedy's personal involvement in this and later civil rights crises transformed him, giving him a sense of urgency about America's racial problem that his brother the president never had.

One week after the Anniston violence, President Kennedy finally made his first public statement about the Freedom Rides. He began by saying the crisis was a "source of deepest concern" and urging restraint on all sides. Incredibly and inexcusably, he equated racist mob violence with the lawful exercise of a constitutional right by the Freedom Riders. His "hope that any persons, whether a citizen of Alabama or a visitor there, would refrain from any action which would in any way tend to provoke further outbreaks" defined the two sides as morally and legally equivalent. Four days later, Bobby Kennedy called for a "cooling off" period. Privately, he felt the Freedom Riders were just seeking "publicity." For their part, civil rights leaders were rapidly learning that militant action could shape

18 Arseneault, *Freedom Riders*, pp. 140–76.

19 Wofford, Memorandum for the President, May 29, 1961, President's Office Files, Staff Memos, Box 67, JFKPL. King, OH, p. 24, JFKPL. Arsenault, *Freedom Riders*, p. 164, 274–5. Bryant, *The Bystander*, pp. 269, 278 (RFK "threat" comment). Schlesinger, Jr., *A Thousand Days*, pp. 316–23, confirms the actions of both JFK and RFK in this crisis.

the agenda and the tempo of racial justice, and they rejected the cooling off idea. The CORE leader James Farmer said, "we've been cooling off for 350 years." Bobby's request was no different from the former president Eisenhower's counsel of patience.[20]

When it was clear that Alabama Governor John Patterson and local officials would not control lawlessness, the administration finally dispatched four hundred U.S. marshals to preserve order. (Both Kennedys thought President Eisenhower's use of troops in Little Rock in 1957 was a mistake because it so offended southerners. Consequently, as attorney general Bobby developed a special force of U.S. marshals for civil rights enforcement efforts.) On Sunday night, May 21, a tense confrontation lasting several hours outside the First Baptist Church in Montgomery came close to mass violence and possible deaths. Freedom Rides leaders, Martin Luther King, and about fifteen hundred other African Americans huddled inside the church, while a howling, rock-throwing mob assembled outside. The outnumbered marshals barely managed to keep order with batons and tear gas. On an open phone line from Washington, Bobby Kennedy directed Deputy Attorney General Byron White and other federal officials throughout the crisis. Governor Patterson finally declared martial law in the city, and the church was evacuated the next morning in what was essentially a military operation.

Governor Patterson then arranged for law enforcement officers to escort buses with the new Freedom Riders to the Mississippi line. In Jackson, Mississippi, there was no violence, but only because of a cynical deal secretly negotiated between Attorney General Kennedy and the Mississippi senator James Eastland. Kennedy promised not to send federal marshals or troops to Mississippi if Eastland would guarantee there would be no violence. Eastland was just as fearful people would be killed as Kennedy.. In a 1964 interview with Anthony Lewis, RFK was unembarrassed and unapologetic about the deal, candidly explaining, "What we finally decided," was "they'd lock them all up"; he added, "my primary interest was that they weren't beaten up." Constitutional rights took a back seat to keeping the peace and avoiding embarrassing headlines. Burke Marshall, assistant attorney general for civil rights, also later conceded that the arrests were "unconstitutional ... without any question." Police arrested all the Freedom Riders the minute they stepped off the buses in Jackson. The arrests only inspired more activists, and eventually more than three hundred descended on Jackson. Most served sixty days in Mississippi's notorious Parchman prison farm.[21]

Determined to avoid future confrontations, the Kennedys tried to redirect the southern civil rights movement into voter registration and helped secure private foundation funding for the Voter Education Project, which began a major voter registration drive in southern states. The voter registration strategy had a compelling political logic, as African-American voting could be the key to broad social change. Only 7 percent of eligible African Americans in Mississippi were registered, for example. The addition of black voters would transform southern politics, as in fact happened after passage of the 1965

[20] Statement by the President Concerning Interference with the "Freedom Riders" in Alabama. May 20th, 1961, APP. "Cooling Off": "Attorney General's Pleas," *NYT*, May 25, 1961. Bryant, *The Bystander*, p. 270. RFK's recollections: Guthman and Shulman, eds., *Robert F. Kennedy in His Own Words*, pp. 97–8.

[21] RFK, the Army, and U.S. Marshals: Nicholas deB. Katzenbach, *Some of It Was Fun: Working with RFK and LBJ* (New York: W. W. Norton, 2008), pp. 42–3, 47, 83. RFK's deal with Eastland: Guthman and Shulman, eds., *Robert Kennedy in His Own Words*, pp. 96–8. Bryant, *The Bystander*, pp. 275–6. Marshall, OH, p. 41, JFKPL.

Voting Rights Law. At a June 16 meeting at the Justice Department, Bobby Kennedy personally urged Diane Nash and other young African-American activists to shift to voter registration. Some saw the political logic of the idea, but Nash, a leader of both the sit-ins and the Freedom Rides, and others thought it sounded like a bribe. She recalled Justice Department officials talking about "thousands and thousands" of dollars that would become available to them. The Kennedys' attempt to limit confrontational tactics misfired, however. No person or organizations controlled the civil rights movement, and militant protests continued. Additionally, the failure to take strong action and the attempts to persuade civil rights groups to moderate their demands only infuriated and alienated young African American activists. The leaders of the Student Nonviolent Coordinating Committee (SNCC), which had emerged from the sit-ins, became convinced they could not trust the administration, and in 1966, SNCC's Stokely Carmichael was the first to raise the cry of "black power."[22]

A "stroke of a pen": Two years late

In the last weeks of the 1960 presidential election campaign, Kennedy told the National Conference on Constitutional Rights and American Freedom, "Many things can be done by a stroke of the Presidential pen" and mentioned "an executive order for equal opportunity in housing." (The conference title was an evasive ploy. Although the program was almost entirely devoted to racial issues, Kennedy strategists wanted to downplay that fact, out of fear of alienating southern voters.) Civil rights leaders took Kennedy at his word and criticized him for failing to sign an executive order once he was president. The CORE leader James Farmer complained that "he didn't move on the stroke-of-a-pen promise ... for two years." At one point, some activists began sending the White House hundreds of ball point pens bearing the label "stroke of a pen."[23]

Inside the White House, Harris Wofford was deeply frustrated by the president's inaction. As he was leaving for a trip to Africa in August 1962, Kennedy tried to reassure him, saying, "You will see, with time I will do them all." In his book on Kennedy, Ted Sorensen, without apparently realizing what he was revealing, described in detail each of the delays, and the reasons why some other issue always took priority. Bobby Kennedy later candidly conceded that his brother just "didn't want to do it."[24]

Finally, on November 20, 1962, nearly two years after taking office, Kennedy issued Executive Order 11063 barring discrimination in federal housing assistance. Even then, he buried the story by issuing it two days before Thanksgiving when most of the country was preoccupied with the holiday.[25]

[22] DOJ meeting: Raymond Arsenault, *Freedom Riders*, pp. 328–30; Nash, comments, Freedom Riders 50th Anniversary Conference, Chicago, May 1, 2011. Branch, *Parting the Waters*, pp. 480–2. Bryant, *The Bystander*, pp. 283–6. VEP: Pat Watters and Reese Cleghorn, *Climbing Jacob's Ladder: The Arrival of Negroes in Southern Politics* (New York: Harcourt, Brace, 1967).

[23] JFK, Remarks, National Conference on Constitutional Rights and American Freedom, New York City, October 12, 1960, Presidential Papers, Box 913, JFKPL. "Kennedy Pledges Wide Rights Plan," *NYT*, October 13, 1960. Farmer: Strober and Strober, *"Let Us Begin Anew,"* p. 278.

[24] Wofford, *Of Kennedys and Kings*, p. 125. Sorensen, *Kennedy*, pp. 531–42. RFK: Guthman and Shulman, eds., *Robert F. Kennedy in His Own Words*, pp. 154–6.

[25] Executive Order 1106, "Equal Opportunity in Housing," November 20, 1962, APP. Kennedy, Press Conference, November 20, 1962, APP. Wofford, *Of Kennedys and Kings*, pp. 124–77.

Birmingham, the Civil Rights Bill, and the March on Washington

Martin Luther King's "I Have a Dream" speech and the historic August 28, 1963, March on Washington where he delivered it are now icons of the post–World War II civil rights movement. They were preceded by President Kennedy's June 11 television address when he proposed a federal civil rights bill, which transformed his public image as a civil rights advocate. What few Americans realize is that Kennedy was forced to give the speech only by the demonstrations in Birmingham that spring and the rapid spread of civil rights protests all across the country and that he tried to block the March on Washington.

The Birmingham demonstrations were part of a carefully calculated plan by Martin Luther King to provoke a crisis that would force the administration to act on civil rights. The plan was prompted by King's failed campaign the year before in Albany, Georgia, where Police Chief Laurie Pritchett skillfully avoided any confrontations that would generate national headlines. (Pritchett later explained that he had studied King's philosophy of nonviolence and prepared an elaborate plan to defuse the demonstrations.) Deeply frustrated, King convened a staff retreat in Dorchester, Georgia, in January 1963 to assess the failure and devise a new strategy. The result was "Plan C" (for Confrontation) calling for aggressive tactics in a different city. Although King publicly claimed that Albany had confirmed the effectiveness of nonviolent tactics, the author Diane McWhorter in her book on the Birmingham struggle was closer to the truth: "The real lesson of Albany was that nonviolence could not succeed without violence – segregationist violence."[26]

The Albany campaign was the source of tremendous disillusionment with the Kennedy administration for SNCC and Dr. King. When they repeatedly asked the administration to intervene, they were rebuffed. At one six-hour meeting, Leslie Dunbar, head of the Southern Regional Council, recalled Burke Marshall's saying, "I cannot do it. I cannot do it." Dunbar finally rebuked him: "Stop trying to be a private person. You're the Assistant Attorney General.... Go down there and act like an official." But the Justice Department refused to intervene.[27]

The Birmingham campaign began on "B Day" (for Birmingham), April 3, with King's demand for an end to segregation at lunch counters and hotels, and a fair employment policy for businesses and city agencies. Initially, the marches and demonstrations had little impact. Behind the scenes, Attorney General Kennedy and his aides desperately worked to negotiate an agreement with Birmingham business leaders, but they were caught between the intransigence of local officials and King's escalating militancy. King's hoped-for confrontation finally occurred when he mobilized thousands of schoolchildren as demonstrators, a tactic that even some civil rights activists questioned, promising to "fill the jails." On "D Day," May 2, one thousand children skipped school to demonstrate, and soon most were in jail. Another three thousand children were said to be planning to march. Twelve-year-old-Anita Woods, held in the Jefferson County Detention Home with

[26] Pritchett, OH, OHAS. Hugh Davis Graham, *The Civil Rights Era: Origins and Development of National Policy, 1960–1972* (New York: Oxford University Press, 1990), p. 74. Howard Zinn, *Albany: A Study in National Responsibility* (Atlanta: Southern Regional Council, 1962), pp. 26–34, is a sharp criticism of the administration. King's version: Martin Luther King, Jr., *Why We Can't Wait* [1963]. (New York: Signet Books, 1964), pp. 43–4. Diane McWhorter, *Carry Me Home: Birmingham, Alabama: The Climactic Battle of the Civil Rights Revolution* (New York: Simon & Schuster, 2001), p. 308.

[27] Dunbar, OH, FAOH, LOC.

legendary Master of the Senate then berated the White House for not doing its legislative "homework." They needed to win over senators from the west, where race was not a major issue, he lectured, and most important gain the support of the Senate Republican minority leader Everett Dirksen, who could bring along Republican votes. In a matter of a few minutes, speaking off the top of his head, Johnson outlined the very strategy that would win passage of the bill a year later. By then, of course, Kennedy would be dead and Johnson himself would be president.[39]

Throughout spring and summer 1963, meanwhile, the administration desperately sought to control events. An August Justice Department memo listed 978 civil rights demonstrations across the country between late May and early August. The White House was terrified that Birmingham-style conflicts would erupt all across the country, and Justice Department staff frantically talked with local officials about preventing ugly confrontations. The administration also launched an intensive lobbying effort for the civil rights bill, holding White House meetings with groups of businessmen (June 4), labor leaders (June 13), religious leaders (June 17), lawyers (June 21), and women's groups (July 9). Incredibly, civil rights leaders were not invited to the White House until the next to last meeting on June 22.[40]

Behind the scenes, J. Edgar Hoover continued his vendetta against Martin Luther King and the entire civil rights movement. The Mississippi governor, Ross Barnett, told a Senate committee that summer that communists influenced the civil rights movement and implied that the FBI knew this. Hoover publicly denied it but privately circulated a vicious report on King. Attorney General Kennedy read it and ordered all copies immediately returned to the bureau. In October 1963, however, Bobby authorized the FBI to place wiretaps on King. At the critical June 22 meeting, first Burke Marshall, then Bobby Kennedy, and then JFK, uncritically accepting Hoover's allegations, told King to get rid of his alleged communist-associated aides, in what King regarded as a triple "ambush."[41]

"I Have a Dream": The March on Washington

While the White House haggled over the civil rights bill, civil rights leaders announced a march on Washington for August. A. Philip Randolph saw it as the fulfillment of his planned 1941 march. The idea upset the Kennedys, much as Randolph's proposal had alarmed FDR, and they tried to talk civil rights leaders into cancelling it. At the June 22 White House meeting, the Kennedys warned that a demonstration could lead to violence and kill all chances for the civil rights bill. The president asked that they "consider carefully the negative impact of a march on Congress," which he claimed did not like pressure

39 Steven F. Lawson, "'I Got It From *The New York Times*': Lyndon Johnson and the Kennedy Civil Rights Program," *The Journal of Negro History* 67 (Summer 1982): 159–73 contains the transcript of the conversation. Bryant, *The Bystander*, pp. 409–10.

40 "Robert Kennedy Warns of Increasing Turmoil," *NYT*, May 4, 1963. Local officials: Attorney General's Statement, June 30, 1965, Katzenbach Papers, Box 8, JFKPL. Guthman to Attorney General, August 13, 1963, President's Office Files, Subject Files, Box 97, JFKPL. Louis F. Oberdorfer to RFK, July 9, 1963, RFK Papers, General Correspondence, Box 9, JFKPL. Material on the various meetings: White House Central File, Subject Files, Box 374, JFKPL. Material on the Lawyers' Committee for Civil Rights: Burke Marshall Papers, Box 28, 76, JFKPL.

41 Attorney General to Senator Monroney, July 22, 1963, Marshall Papers, Box 10, JFKPL. "U.S. Denies Reds Lead Integrationists," *NYT*, July 26, 1963. FBI report on King: Guthman, Memo for the Files, May 18, 1964, Marshall Papers, Box 10, JFKPL. "Ambush": Branch, *Parting the Waters*, pp. 835–8

tactics. Randolph had heard exactly the same arguments in his 1941 White House meeting, and he would not yield. "Mr. President," he said, speaking as bluntly as he had to Presidents Roosevelt in 1941 and Truman in 1948, "the Negroes are already in the street. It is very likely impossible to get them off." The NAACP was uncertain about a march, but Martin Luther King sided with Randolph. Feeling empowered by his experience in forcing the president to act through the Birmingham demonstrations, King was in no mood to back off. To the argument that the march was "ill timed," he pointedly rebuked the Kennedys, replying, "Some people thought Birmingham was ill-timed." The president's mind was on his upcoming trip to Germany and on leaving the meeting immediately boarded a helicopter to Andrews Air Force Base and flew to Germany that evening.[42]

Unable to prevent the August march, the Kennedys proceeded to take control of it. Bobby Kennedy felt it "was very, very badly organized" and assigned the Justice Department lawyer John Douglas to work on it full-time. Administration officials eventually dictated the day of the week, the location (shifting it from the Capitol building to the Lincoln Memorial), and other details. Wednesday might seem an odd day for a march designed to draw thousands of people from around the country, but White House officials calculated (or hoped) that on a weekday people would come and leave quickly, thereby reducing the chance for any spontaneous sit-ins or demonstrations. They also arranged for twenty-five thousand troops to be on standby in case of trouble. Under a very tight schedule the day of the march, the hundreds of out of town buses all left town by 7:00 p.m.[43]

As the day of the march approached, a furious battle erupted behind the scenes over the SNCC leader John Lewis's planned speech, which included some incendiary rhetoric that expressed the anger of the young generation of activists. He used the word "revolution" eight times and threatened to "march through the south, through the Heart of Dixie, the way Sherman did ... [to] burn Jim Crow to the ground – nonviolently." The White House was especially offended by his bitter question "I want to know: which side is the federal government on?" which was prompted by the administration's failure to protect civil rights protesters in Albany, Georgia, the year before and the fact that just two weeks before the march, in a sop to segregationists, the Justice Department indicted nine Albany civil rights figures on flimsy criminal charges. Lewis's planned speech was too much for the both the administration and march leaders. The Catholic archbishop of Washington, Patrick O'Boyle, threatened to withdraw, a defection that would likely cause the march coalition to collapse. Bobby Kennedy called it "a bad speech. There was an attack on the country. It attacked the President." Facing a potential disaster, the older civil rights leaders asked Lewis to remove the offending passages. A. Philip Randolph, now seventy-four years old and weary, told Lewis, "I have waited twenty-two years for this. I've waited all

[42] Preparations for the meeting: Lee White, Memorandum for the President, June 22, 1963, President's Office Files, Subject Files, Box 97, JFKPL. Press accounts omitted the most important parts of the meeting: "Negroes Inform Kennedy of Plan for New Protests," *NYT*, June 23, 1963. Guthman, and Shulman, eds., *Robert F. Kennedy in His Own Words*, pp. 143–6; Marshall memo to Hoover, September 20, 1963, Federal Bureau of Investigation, *Official and Confidential File of FBI Director J. Edgar Hoover*. Microfilm ed. (Wilmington, DE: Scholarly Resources, Inc., 1988), Folder 24. Branch, *Parting the Waters*, pp. 835–7; Garrow, *Bearing the Cross*, pp. 272–3.

[43] RFK: Guthman and Shulman, eds., *Robert F. Kennedy in His Own Words*, p. 227. The buses: Louis Martin, in Strober and Strober, eds., *"Let Us Begin Anew,"* pp. 310–11. Douglass role in the planning: "John W. Douglass, Champion of Civil and Human Rights, Dies at 88," *NYT*, June 5, 2010.

my life for this opportunity. Please don't ruin it." Lewis could not refuse this giant figure and complied.[44]

In the end, the August 28 march, highlighted by King's soaring "I Have a Dream" speech, was a huge success that exceeded everyone's expectations. Afterward, President Kennedy invited civil rights leaders to the White House for a celebration. Randolph, having finally realized his dream, recalled that "the President was all smiles." Beneath the surface, however, the militant young activists were angry about the administration's heavy-handed tactics over the march, and this set the stage for future discord.[45]

The march and the civil rights crises preceding it in the early 1960s are among the most dramatic events in modern American history. The deeply entrenched institutions of racial segregation were challenged by the militant actions of ordinary people. Between the first sit-ins in 1960 and the passage of the 1965 Voting Rights Act, the United States became a very different country. In this epic struggle, however, President Kennedy provided no real leadership until the last half year of his presidency and even then acted only when pressured to act. Kennedy's most loyal aides unconsciously revealed the administration's policy priorities. The historian Taylor Branch sardonically points out that Arthur M. Schlesinger, Jr.'s, monumental history of the administration, *A Thousand Days*, covers civil rights in the next to last two chapters of a thirty-seven-chapter book. Ted Sorensen also put civil rights in the back of the bus of his memoir, *Kennedy*. The delays and broken promises, however, are amply documented in the memoirs of Harris Wofford, Kennedy's civil rights aide.[46]

ROBERT KENNEDY'S JUSTICE DEPARTMENT

Wiretapping and bugging Martin Luther King

When President Kennedy took Martin Luther King aside on June 22, 1963, to tell him to fire his two aides because of their alleged Communist Party ties and warn him that he was under "close surveillance," he obviously knew about the FBI's spying campaign, or at least some of it. Four months later, in fact, Robert Kennedy formally authorized FBI wiretaps on King's Atlanta home and Southern Christian Leadership Conference (SCLC) offices. In January 1964 the bureau also began installing what became an estimated fifteen microphones in hotel rooms used by King. (These were the kinds of bugs authorized by Attorney General Herbert Brownell in May 1954.) The Church Committee in the 1970s could not determine whether Bobby Kennedy was aware of the bugs which he had not explicitly authorized. The Church Committee also reported that under Kennedy the IRS established a Special Service Staff that investigated twenty-five "extremist" political groups between 1961 and 1963. Some conservatives have alleged that the list included primarily right-wing groups, while Richard Nixon long charged that he was the target of a politically motivated IRS investigation.[47]

[44] John Lewis, *Walking with the Wind: A Memoir of the Movement* (New York: Simon & Schuster, 1998), pp. 214–27. Zinn, *Albany: A Study in National Responsibility*. Indictments: Branch, *Parting the Waters*, pp. 866–8. Guthman and Shulman, eds., *Robert F. Kennedy in His Own Words*, p. 129.

[45] The "Dream" speech is widely available on the Web. "All smiles": Randolph, OH, p. I-4, LBJPL.

[46] Branch, *Parting the Waters*, p. 919. Schlesinger, Jr., *A Thousand Days*. Sorensen, *Kennedy*.

[47] RFK: "I gave them also permission to put a tap on his telephone [in October, 1963]; Guthman and Shulman, eds., *Robert F. Kennedy in His Own Words*, p. 140. FBI's vendetta: U.S. Senate, Select Committee to Study Governmental Operations with Respect to Intelligence Activities [hereinafter Church Committee], Book III,

RFK was concerned about the FBI's allegations of King's communist ties as early as 1961 and told Burke Marshall and Harris Wofford to warn King about it. When King ignored them, he talked with King himself. Both Kennedys accepted Hoover's view that King's key aide Stanley Levison was still working with the Communist Party. Bobby believed this was "damaging to the civil rights movement," and that it potentially "damaged us" as well. Levison had quit the Communist Party in the 1950s. The administration aide Arthur M. Schlesinger, Jr., defended the wiretaps as an effort to "protect" King, because they might refute the FBI's allegations. In the poisonous cold war guilt-by-association game, a person could never escape past communist associations. Levison became one of King's closest confidants, advising him on strategy and doing much of his writing. The FBI's allegations are mainly refuted by the fact that absolutely nothing in these efforts even remotely reflected communist ideology. Indeed, King's genius and the basis of his stature in history was his capacity to frame civil rights as a moral crusade and the fulfillment of the American dream. His "I Have a Dream" speech was pure Americana, and as remote from Marxism as could be.[48]

Hoover circulated a critical report on King's alleged communist ties to a number of federal agencies in October 1963, but an alarmed RFK ordered it withdrawn, fearing it would embarrass the administration if it were leaked. Harris Wofford recalls Hoover's sending over "vile, vile material" on King, and shortly after Kennedy's assassination, the LBJ aide Walter Jenkins refused at least two FBI offers to listen to tape recordings of King's private behavior. In late 1964 (with President Kennedy now dead), Hoover escalated his campaign into a public attack. In an extraordinary three-hour press briefing, on November 18, Hoover accused King of being "the most notorious liar in the country." The crudeness of the attack shocked almost everyone. (Throughout this period, moreover, the NAACP's Roy Wilkins tried to undermine King by talking with the FBI about the need for a "responsible" alternative to King as a civil rights leader.) On the defensive, King requested a private meeting with Hoover. When they met, Hoover launched into detailed accusations, citing information about King's private life that King knew could only have been gained by bugs and wiretaps. Stunned, King emerged from the meeting evidently cowed, expressing "appreciation" for the FBI's civil rights enforcement.[49]

The King surveillance has long been a matter of controversy regarding the Kennedys, and it is important to pinpoint responsibility for various actions. The FBI launched its vendetta against King long before either of the Kennedys knew about it. In addition to the wiretaps and the far more intrusive bugs, the bureau bribed an SCLC accountant to provide information, leaked unflattering allegations to sympathetic reporters, and tried to block several speaking engagements. Motivated by a combination of racism and fear

Supplemental Detailed Staff Reports on Intelligence Activities and the Rights of Americans (Washington, DC, 1976), pp. 79–184. IRS: Church Committee, V. 3, *Internal Revenue Service*, p. 105.

48 Guthman and Shulman, eds., *Robert F. Kennedy in His Own Words*, pp. 141–3. Marshall and King: Church Committee, Book III, *Supplemental Detailed Staff Reports on Intelligence Activities and the Rights of Americans*, pp. 95–7. Schlesinger, Jr., *A Thousand Days*, pp. 356–61. Schlesinger's belief that Hoover would be convinced by evidence that Levison was not a Communist reveals his utter naivete about Hoover and the dynamics of the anti-Communist hysteria.

49 Wofford, OH, pp. 140–1, JFKPL. Jenkins: Church Committee, Book III, *Supplemental Detailed Staff Reports on Intelligence Activities and the Rights of Americans*, p. 151. "Hoover Assails Warren Findings," *NYT*, November 19, 1964. "Hoover and King Discuss Dispute," ibid., December 2, 1964. RFK in Guthman and Shulman, eds., *Robert Kennedy in His Own Words*, p. 140. Wilkins correspondence with the FBI: Kenneth O'Reilly, *Black Americans: The FBI Files* (New York: Carroll & Graf, 1994), pp. 424–1.

of social change, Hoover explicitly stated his goal of destroying King's influence as a civil rights leader. At a December 23, 1963, strategy meeting, the bureau developed a plan for "neutralizing Martin Luther King, Jr., as an effective Negro leader." The most notorious action was a blackmail attempt involving a tape recording of King's alleged extramarital sexual activities, which in October 1964 it mailed to both King and his wife. King's copy included a letter suggesting he commit suicide. (President Kennedy was dead and Bobby had resigned as attorney general by then.) It is a telling commentary on the political climate of the times and the power of the FBI that no reporter or member of Congress who received the tape blew the whistle on the bureau.[50]

There is no question that President Kennedy and his brother knew about some, but not necessarily all, of the FBI's improper activity. They knew about the 1963 report on King, but possibly not about the blackmail tape. In fact, they were deeply implicated in some of the FBI's other illegal activities, even benefiting from them on occasion. The Kennedy confidant Benjamin Bradlee, then a *Newsweek* reporter and later famous as editor of the *Washington Post* during the Watergate scandal, recalled JFK's commenting after a lunch with Hoover, "Boy, the dirt he has on those Senators. You wouldn't believe it." Bradley also described an episode when the FBI secretly allowed the Kennedys to see FBI files regarding a spurious allegation that Kennedy had previously been married. None of the Kennedys ever questioned these or other improper and illegal practices, much less ordered them stopped. A contributing factor was J. Edgar Hoover's personal relationship with the president's father, Joe Kennedy. Bobby Kennedy recalled, "My father was a good friend of his."[51]

As attorney general, Robert Kennedy was an enthusiastic believer in wiretapping. Ramsey Clark, an assistant attorney general at the time, could not recall his ever turning down a wiretap request. Clark recalled bureau agents' presenting the attorney general with wiretap requests without explanation and standing by silently until he signed them. Edward Levi, whom President Gerald Ford appointed attorney general in 1975, encountered this practice on his first day on the job (but declined to go along with it). Nicholas Katzenbach later said that it was not just RFK. There had been no record of approved wiretaps, and no attorney general knew how many wiretaps were active at any given time. Additionally, Hoover believed approved taps had no time limit and could be reactivated years later without notifying the Justice Department. Both Katzenbach and Clark claim to have instituted a systematic file of approved wiretaps when each became attorney general. Bobby believed wiretaps were a necessary crime-fighting tool, especially against organized crime, which was one of his obsessions. In 1961 he proposed what would have been the first federal law authorizing wiretapping.[52]

50 FBI, Memorandum, F. J. Baumgardner to W. C. Sullivan, January 8, 1964, excerpt in Michael Friendly and David Gallen, *Martin Luther King, Jr.: The FBI File* (New York: Carroll & Graf, 1993), p. 199. Mailed tape recording: Church Committee, Book III, *Supplemental Detailed Staff Reports on Intelligence Activities and the Rights of Americans*, pp. 158–61. David J. Garrow, *The FBI and Martin Luther King: From 'Solo' to Memphis* (New York: W. W. Norton, 1981), pp. 102–4. Branch, *Pillar of Fire*, pp. 195–7. Federal Bureau of Investigation, *Official and Confidential File of FBI Director J. Edgar Hoover*. Microfilm ed. (Wilmington, DE: Scholarly Resources, Inc., 1988), Folders 24, 100.

51 Kennedy FBI Files: FBI, *Official and Confidential File of FBI Director J. Edgar Hoover*, Folders 4, 7, 13. 96. Benjamin C. Bradlee, *Conversations with Kennedy*. Pbk. ed. (New York: Pocket Books, 1976), p. 225. In one episode the Kennedys arranged for Bradlee to see FBI files for a story offsetting damaging rumors about the president (ibid., p. 109). RFK in Guthman and Shulman, eds., *Robert F. Kennedy in His Own Words*, p. 119.

52 Katzenbach, *Some of It Was Fun*, pp. 182–3. Katzenbach, OH, p. 58, JFKPL. Ramsey Clark, OH, p. 43, JFKPL. Levi: John T. Elliff, *The Reform of FBI Intelligence Operations* (Princeton, NJ: Princeton University Press, 1979), pp. 55–64; Appendix 1, pp. 196–202.

JFK was also highly vulnerable to potential blackmail by the bureau. His sexual escapades, both before and during his presidency, are now the stuff of legend.[53] The most potentially damaging episode was his steamy affair with Inga Arvad in 1941 and 1942. A journalist and former Miss Denmark, Arvad had been to Nazi Germany, interviewed Hitler, and apparently gotten along very well with Nazi leaders. Hitler allegedly described her as "a perfect Nordic beauty." Consequently, the FBI placed her under surveillance as a possible spy when she arrived in the United States (in the end, they never found any suspicious behavior). Working as a reporter she met Kathleen Kennedy, who in turn introduced her to her brother John, then a lieutenant in the navy. The FBI's surveillance uncovered intimate details of their sexual activities. Word of the affair eventually reached Kennedy's father, who intervened with the navy to prevent him from being discharged; instead he was transferred to South Carolina. The affair continued, and the FBI captured their intimate activities in Charleston.[54]

Later, as a member of Congress, Kennedy was a well-known womanizer, and some of this activity entered the FBI files when enemies or aggrieved spouses sent damaging information to the bureau. In one incident, someone photographed Kennedy leaving a woman's house at 1:00 a.m. As president he had an affair with Judith Exner, who was simultaneously a lover of the Chicago Mafia boss Sam Giancana. Revelation of this relationship would have destroyed Kennedy as president and possibly even forced his resignation.[55]

J. Edgar Hoover, in short, had a trove of dirt on President Kennedy. Cartha DeLoach, Hoover's assistant director, staunchly denies that the director ever tried to blackmail the president, but he misses the point. Hoover did not actually have to say anything, because Kennedy knew he had the damaging information. Hoover had lunch regularly with JFK and used these occasions to impress him with gossip about Washington officials. Bobby also received regular briefings from a bureau official, and his recollections are a damning indictment of the Kennedys' attitude about the FBI. "Every month or so," he recalled in 1964, "he'd send somebody around to give information on somebody I knew or a member of my family or allegations in connection with myself. So that it would be clear … that he was on top of all these things." The interviewer, the *New York Times*'s Anthony Lewis, was shocked and asked about the possibility of blackmail. Bobby conceded that, yes, "it's very tough," but then justified Hoover's practices: "This information has to be there, I suppose. You have to accumulate it." When Lewis then asked whether he thought Hoover was dangerous, Bobby answered, yes, "I think he's dangerous," but quickly added that "it was a danger we could control.… He served our interests." The

[53] Potential blackmail: Steel, *In Love with Night*, pp. 65–8. Kennedy's sexual escapades are covered in many books. FBI documents: FBI, *Official and Confidential File*, Folders 4, 7, 13, 96. Denial of blackmail allegations: Deborah Hart Strober and Gerald S. Strober, eds., *The Kennedy Presidency: An Oral History of the Era* (Washington, DC: Brassey's, 2003), Cartha DeLoach, p. 267; Courtney Evans, p. 269; Bobby Baker believes Hoover virtually blackmailed Robert Kennedy (p. 268). Theoharis doubts any overt blackmail attempts: Athan Theoharis, *The FBI and American Democracy: A Brief Critical History* (Lawrence: University of Kansas Press, 2004), p. 103.

[54] Arvad materials: Memorandum for the Director, December 12, 1941; interview with Arvad; "heatedly denied" accusations re Nazis, FBI, *Official and Confidential File*, Folder 7. Joan and Clay Blair, Jr., *The Search for J.F.K.* (New York: Berkeley Medallion Books, 1976), pp. 122–54.

[55] Memorandum, L. B. Nichols to Tolson, May 14, 1957, FBI, *Official and Confidential File*, Folder 13. Judith Exner, *My Story* (New York: Grove Press, 1978). Exposure of the Campbell affair: Church Committee, *Interim Report: Alleged Assassination Plots Involving Foreign Leaders*, p. 129.

comment was a classic expression of the Kennedy arrogance: the belief that they were smart and tough enough to control Hoover. Most important, neither Kennedy ever indicated that spying on people's private lives was wrong or that he as attorney general had a responsibility to stop it.[56]

The Kennedys were not alone in deferring to Hoover. Every president from Roosevelt through Nixon found it politically impossible to replace him, such were his popular reputation and influence in Congress (many members were also vulnerable because of their own misdeeds). Hoover could always allege that a president was "soft" on communism in some respect. Kennedy was simply more vulnerable because of his private behavior than were other presidents. Kennedy's sexual activities raise the question, later a public issue during President Bill Clinton's affair with Monica Lewinsky, of whether private behavior affects the ability of a president to serve effectively. In the case of Kennedy, the answer is an unequivocal yes.

At the same time, however, Victor Navasky, in a thorough study of Bobby Kennedy's Justice Department, argues that Bobby did exert some control over the FBI, arguably more than any previous attorney general (a low standard, to be sure). Most important, he limited direct contact between the bureau and the president and sought to require it to go through his office. Significantly, immediately after JFK's assassination Hoover restored the old pattern of direct contact. Bobby also required all FBI press releases to be cleared by the attorney general and directed Hoover to hire more African-American agents. RFK's greatest success was in forcing Hoover to take on organized crime, which Hoover had denied even existed. When Kennedy asked for all FBI files on the mob, he found they had "not even the slightest piece of information." Under pressure, the FBI finally began investigating the mob.[57]

While all of these steps were progress in the direction of controlling the FBI, Navasky concedes that the bureau may have exercised more influence over the Kennedys. They did not challenge bureau wiretapping or other illegitimate practices. Bobby himself later recalled, "I really deferred to him.... I was young." Kennedy always went to Hoover's office and later conceded, "I'd never ask him to come to my office." He and his brother were in thrall to the image of the bureau, calling it "a helluva good investigative agency."[58] It took the post-Watergate revelations of FBI misconduct in the mid-1970s to create a political climate that permitted a critical view of the bureau.

Robert Kennedy's reputation for ruthlessness was based in part on his celebrated pursuit of the Teamsters Union leader Jimmy Hoffa, a crusade that raises troubling questions about his priorities. He hated Hoffa from the moment they first met in 1957, when Kennedy was staff counsel to Senator John McClellan's committee investigating labor union racketeering. (In a disturbing side note, Nicholas Katzenbach observes that Kennedy and the McClellan Committee freely imitated Senator Joe McCarthy's technique of using hearings to pillory witnesses and force them to invoke the Fifth Amendment repeatedly.) As attorney general, he established a special unit, known informally as the

56 RFK in Guthman and Shulman, eds., *Robert F. Kennedy in His Own Words*, pp. 125, 128–9, 133–4. DeLoach, in Strober and Strober, eds., *"Let Us Begin Anew,"* p. 267.

57 Navasky, *Kennedy Justice*, pp. 8–12, 44–95. Schlesinger, Jr., *Journals, 1952–2000*, p. 212. Ronald Steel finds Robert Kennedy "strikingly passive" toward Hoover: *In Love with Night*, p. 65, in large part to protect his brother.

58 Navasky, *Kennedy Justice*, p. 9. Guthman and Shulman, eds., *Robert Kennedy in His Own Words*, pp. 120, 124–5, 135.

"Get Hoffa Squad." This unprecedented operation was directed toward a person rather than a crime category and was run by Walter Sheridan, who was not a lawyer. The unit eventually indicted 190 people and convicted 115, an incredible record, including Hoffa himself in May 1964.[59]

In a scrupulous examination of the Hoffa episode, Victor Navasky concludes there was no illegal wiretapping or bugging. The problem involved enforcement priorities. Criminal charges would probably never have been brought in many cases without the Hoffa connection. The "pursuit of justice," Navasky argues, looked "like the pursuit of Hoffa" (as it really was). In the end, it was not an abuse of law, but an abuse of discretion by the attorney general. Most seriously, the Kennedy administration never committed the same kind of resources to civil rights enforcement, despite bombings, murders, attacks on civil rights activists, and other efforts to prevent people from registering to vote, in clear violation of federal law. The contrast between the Hoffa pursuit and the neglect of civil rights was a revealing index of Robert Kennedy's priorities.[60]

Reforming the criminal justice system

As the keynote speaker at the National Conference on Bail in 1964, Attorney General Kennedy opened with passionate words about the plight of poor criminal defendants: "There is a special responsibility on all of us here" have, he declared, "a special responsibility to represent those who can not be here, those who are poor, those who are the unfortunate – the 1,500,000 persons in the United States who are accused of crime, who haven't yet been found guilty, who are yet unable to make bail." If Robert Kennedy was utterly ruthless in pursuing Jimmy Hoffa, he also showed extraordinary compassion for the poor in some important criminal justice reforms. This side of his political commitments moved to the fore after his brother's assassination, but it was evident earlier in his deep concern about bail reform and the larger problem of poverty in America.[61]

Bobby's initiative on bail reform stimulated changes in law and practice at both the federal and state levels that resulted in greater justice for poor defendants. The traditional American money bail system often meant that poor people accused of crime sat in jail awaiting trial simply because they could not raise bail money. Most important was the 1966 federal Bail Reform Act, which created a presumption of pretrial release. Virtually every state passed a similar law, and "release on recognizance" or 10 percent bail plans drastically reduced the number of defendants in jail awaiting trial. In the early 1960s, more than half of all people in jail were there awaiting trial; by 2002 the figure was down to 28 percent. It was an achievement that improved the justice system for poor people.[62]

59 On RFK as his brother's protector and troubleshooter: Steel, *In Love with Night*, pp. 70, 72. Kennedy's views on Hoffa and their initial clashes: Robert F. Kennedy, *The Enemy Within* (New York: Harper, 1960). Committee hearings tactics: Katzenbach, *Some of It Was Fun*, p. 24. (The tactic of pillorying witnesses included both HUAC and some liberal-oriented committees in the 1930s.) Navasky, *Kennedy Justice*, Ch. 9, "Civil Liberties: Hoffa and the General," pp. 392–439. Walter Sheridan, *The Fall and Rise of Jimmy Hoffa* (New York: Saturday Review Press, 1972).

60 Navasky, *Kennedy Justice*, pp. 392–439 (quote p. 436).

61 Robert Kennedy, "Welcome," *National Conference on Bail and Criminal Justice, Proceedings of May 27–29, 1964 and Interim Report, May 1964–April 1965* (New York: Arno Press, 1974), p. 5. Warren: ibid., p. 11. Robert Kennedy's image and transformation after 1963: Steel, *In Love with Night*. Michael Harrington, *The Other America: Poverty in the United States* (New York: Macmillan, 1962).

62 Wayne Thomas, *Bail Reform in America* (Berkeley: University of California Press, 1976).

Bail reform represented Robert Kennedy at his best. His legendary passion and tireless work inspired others to similar efforts. It also dramatized the wide gulf that separated him from his brother, the president, who was famously cool and aloof from civil rights and other issues that aroused the passions of many people. There is no record of President Kennedy's having an interest in the problem of the poor in jail.

Although the prisoners' rights movement would not blossom until the early 1970s, Robert Kennedy took a small but important step in that direction by closing the famous (or infamous) federal penitentiary on Alcatraz Island. On a visit to the Bay Area, he looked at the aging and decrepit prison and ordered it shut down. It officially closed on March 21, 1963. The closing was part of a larger program of correctional reform that included an expansion of halfway houses and other community-based facilities designed to enhance rehabilitation. Director J. Edgar Hoover, meanwhile, worried that the Kennedys were "soft" on crime. Kennedy's views on imprisonment and treatment were carried forward by President Lyndon Johnson and embraced by his President's Crime Commission in 1967.[63]

Surprisingly, both President Kennedy and the attorney general were silent on the national controversy over Supreme Court rulings on police practices. The 1961 Court decision in *Mapp v. Ohio,* establishing the exclusionary rule for local police, provoked an angry outcry from the police and their conservative political allies, who accused the Court of "handcuffing" the police. President Kennedy escaped the controversy and was not asked about the *Mapp* decision at his next press conference in June 1961. The controversy and its attendant political impact would become even more intense after the famous 1966 *Miranda v. Arizona* decision requiring the police to advise suspects of their rights.[64]

A brother as attorney general

Robert Kennedy's role as attorney general raises a larger question about the kind of person who should hold that critical position. At the time, critics questioned the propriety of an attorney general's having such close ties to the president as well as the fact that he had never practiced law in any form. Even Nicholas Katzenbach, who worked for him and deeply admired him, later wrote that in 1961 he was "too young, too inexperienced, too political, too brash, [and] too immature in every way." Bobby got the job, nonetheless, and received generally high marks during his tenure.[65]

The question of the independence of attorneys general finally exploded in the Watergate scandal under President Nixon. Many observers argued that because Attorney General John Mitchell had been Nixon's campaign manager in 1968 he was incapable of giving independent legal advice regarding White House actions. (Mitchell resigned in early 1972 to head up Nixon's reelection campaign and was later convicted of Watergate-related criminal charges. The Watergate scandal is covered in Chapter 9 on President Richard Nixon.) Similar questions arose years later when Edwin Meese moved from

63 "Alcatraz Closing Urged at Hearing," *NYT*, July 3, 1962.

64 Fred P. Graham, *The Self-Inflicted Wound* (New York: Hayden Book Co., 1970). Samuel Walker, *Popular Justice: A History of American Criminal Justice*, 2nd ed. (New York: Oxford University Press, 1998), pp. 180–5.

65 Katzenbach, *Some of It Was Fun*, p. 22.

the White House to become President Ronald Reagan's attorney general, as did Alberto Gonzales under President George W. Bush.[66]

Robert Kennedy was more than just the president's brother. He was his closest adviser and soon became more directly involved in matters outside his jurisdiction as attorney general. Particularly troubling, as we shall see, was his deep involvement in the effort to remove Fidel Castro as Cuba's leader, as considerable evidence indicates that he relentlessly pushed for action. Nonetheless, the point is that Attorney General Robert Kennedy was not going to give the president independent advice about actions that are now regarded as highly questionable.[67]

THE PRESS, SECRECY, AND THE CIA

"Managing" the press

Speaking to the nation's newspaper publishers, President Kennedy advised them to consider whether a story was in the national interest and suggested they not publish some information about American foreign policy that might compromise national security. The speech to the American Newspaper Publishers Association on April 27, 1961, was the worst he ever gave as president, and a disturbing threat to freedom of the press. Suggested by his press secretary, Pierre Salinger, it was a response to the disastrous Bay of Pigs invasion of Cuba.[68]

The April 17, 1961, invasion of Cuba by CIA-trained forces was a complete fiasco. To his great credit, President Kennedy took full responsibility for it, but the operation exposed the cozy relationship between the news media and the government on national security matters in the cold war. The press willingly downplayed or did not publish stories about the planning for the Cuban invasion. Kennedy personally pressured the *New York Times* into moving one important story off the front page and talked the *The New Republic* into killing a story altogether. (Gilbert Harrison, publisher of the magazine, said he felt it was his duty to do so.) In fact, the invasion planning was no secret at all, except to most Americans. Anti-Castro Cubans in Miami openly bragged about it in advance, and stories appeared in several U.S. and Latin American newspapers. Because of the refusal of major American news media to pursue the story, Americans remained largely ignorant of it, as they were about the CIA generally. President Kennedy later mused that the disaster might have been averted if the media had covered the planning thoroughly, but his actions before and afterward indicate that he fully accepted the culture of secrecy surrounding the CIA.[69]

[66] The best discussion is in Cornell W. Clayton, *The Politics of Justice: The Attorney General and the Making of Legal Policy* (Armonk, NY: M. E. Sharpe, 1992), Ch. 4, "The Political Role of the Attorney General," pp. 48–88. Clayton notes that at least three highly regarded attorneys general also had close ties to their presidents: Herbert Brownell was Eisenhower's campaign adviser; Robert Jackson was a loyal political ally of Franklin D. Roosevelt; Griffin Bell was close to Jimmy Carter personally and politically.

[67] A very insightful analysis of Robert Kennedy's increasing role as the President's advisor is in Steel, *In Love with Night*.

[68] Kennedy, "The President and the Press," Before the American Newspaper Publishers Association, New York City. April 27, 1961, APP. Pierre Salinger, *With Kennedy* (New York: Avon Books, 1967), pp. 201–8.

[69] Peter Wyden, *Bay of Pigs: The Untold Story* (New York: Simon & Schuster, 1979). James G. Blight and Peter Kornbluh, eds., *Politics of Illusion: The Bay of Pigs Invasion Reexamined* (Boulder, CO: Lynne Reinner, 1998).

In his speech to the newspaper publishers, Kennedy delivered a stern lecture about deferring to the government's priorities. "You bear heavy responsibilities these days," he told them. The threat of international communism meant that "the danger has never been more clear and its presence has never been more imminent." America's enemies had "boasted" about obtaining important defense information from American newspapers. Getting to his real point, Kennedy explained that the press "recognized only the tests of journalism and not the tests of national security." The press today only asks, "'Is it news?' All I suggest is that you add the question: 'Is it in the interest of national security?'" Fully aware of their concerns about censorship, he quickly assured them that he opposed formal government restraints on the media, of the kind wielded by the World War II Office of War Information. Nonetheless, his point was clear: they should withhold news the administration thought implicated national security.

The speech was a complete disaster. Press Secretary Salinger recalled, "The reaction was violent." Publishers and editors saw it as a call for self-censorship, and dismissed Kennedy's suggestion out of hand. Everyone agreed he or she would never publish anything clearly damaging to the national interest, but most also agreed with the editor of the *Washington Star*, who asked, rhetorically, "What is it that is damaging to the interests of the country?" as opposed to what an administration regarded as merely politically embarrassing.[70]

The speech focused attention on the issue of "managed news" that had been simmering from the first days of the Kennedy administration. Salinger set it off when he told the National Press Club on January 25 that the administration would have "an open information policy *within the confines of national security*" [italics in Salinger's memoirs]. Five hours later a reporter asked JFK about this exception. He replied by complaining that the nation's enemies had "very ample information" about national defense matters, and that he was eager to discuss a reasonable accommodation about not publishing sensitive national security matters. His statement provoked Eugene Pulliam, chair of the American Society of Newspaper Editors Freedom of Information Committee, to write a letter charging that the White House had not "lived up to [its] promise" about freedom of information. The issue of "managing" the news thus arose months before the Cuban invasion, and it continued to dog the administration afterward. Kennedy also tried to bully the *New York Times* over its coverage of the Vietnam War, and in an October 22, 1963, meeting with its publisher, Arthur Ochs Sulzberger, suggested that the reporter David Halberstam, whose stories indicated a failing American effort in Vietnam, be transferred to Rome or Paris.[71]

After the disastrous April speech, Kennedy met with seven of the nation's top editors and publishers at the White House on May 9. According to Salinger, the two sides were on completely different wavelengths. As a compromise, Kennedy suggested the publishers choose someone from their ranks who would serve as a liaison for stories with national security implications. The administration would provide him with a confidential briefing on a story, and he would then recommend whether or not the material should be

John Prados, *Presidents' Secret Wars: CIA and Pentagon Secret Operations from World War II through the Persian Gulf* (Chicago: Ivan R. Dee, 1996).

70 Salinger, *With Kennedy*, pp. 206–8.

71 The President's News Conference of January 25, 1961, APP. Kennedy pressure: David Halberstam, *The Powers That Be* (New York: Knopf, 1979), pp. 445–6.

published. Although strictly voluntary, the process was seen by the press leaders as a subtle and manipulative way of co-opting them, and they rejected it.[72]

In truth Kennedy simply expressed in public the assumptions that had guided every administration throughout the cold war, when major media willingly and secretly cooperated with the CIA and accepted government rationales regarding national security. The winds of change were rising through American society by 1961, however, and they included a new skepticism about government. Kennedy faced the first stirrings of this dramatic development, but in just a few years the Vietnam War would completely shatter trust in government, as the gap between official statements and the reality on the ground became too obvious to ignore. The famous "credibility gap" pushed some (but by no means all) of the media into an adversarial posture, which later culminated in the Watergate scandal and the resignation of President Nixon.[73]

The Bay of Pigs fiasco led Kennedy to fire the CIA director, Allen W. Dulles, as a sacrificial lamb, but it did not prompt a broader reexamination of the CIA or of American policy toward Cuba. Richard Bissell, who led the CIA's planning of the Cuban invasion and resigned after its failure, recalled that Kennedy questioned the *process* by which the invasion decision was made but not the wisdom of the invasion itself, the lack of controls over CIA covert actions, or the secrecy surrounding the agency. Many historians argue that the Bay of Pigs fiasco only drove the Kennedys to pursue more aggressively other means of removing Castro. Congress, meanwhile, saw no reason to increase its oversight of the CIA, while the media refused to look critically at the agency. After the Bay of Pigs disaster, President Kennedy faced exactly one question about it at his next press conference, and the reporters willingly accepted his statement that "I do not think that any useful national purpose would be served by my going further into the Cuban question this morning."[74]

Rising concerns about government secrecy

The news management controversy encouraged the concerns about government secrecy, in particular the inquiries that Rep. John Moss had begun in the mid-1950s. By 1961 the tide of public opinion was turning in his favor. The anti-communist hysteria was losing its grip on the public, and more people felt free to ask probing questions about what the government was doing. Moss sent queries about secrecy policies to all federal agencies and the White House in February 1961. All of the agencies responded, but not the White House. This response contradicted both Kennedy's conversations with Moss in the 1950s and the 1956 and 1960 Democratic Party platforms which had criticized the Eisenhower administration over the issue of government secrecy. Moss's probe uncovered an array of secrecy practices that had no connection whatsoever to national security. The Commerce

[72] "Salinger Replies to Critic on News," *NYT*, April 20, 1961; "Press Is Cautious on Kennedy Plea," ibid., April 28, 1961; "Kennedy Pledges Free News Access," ibid., May 10, 1961.

[73] Salinger's account: Salinger, *With Kennedy*, pp. 204–8. Kennedy persuaded both *The New Republic* and the *New York Times* not to publish articles immediately before the invasion. Arthur M. Schlesinger, Jr., defended both publications for their "patriotic" actions, but also thought that more coverage might have averted the disaster: Schlesinger, Jr., *A Thousand Days*, pp. 244–5.

[74] The best history of the subject calls these years "A Period of Quiescence": L. Britt Snider, *The Agency and the Hill: CIA's Relationship with Congress, 1946–2004* (Washington, DC: Center for the Study of Intelligence [CIA], 2008), p. 23. The failure to reexamine the CIA or Cuba policy: Lawrence Freedman, *Kennedy's Wars: Berlin, Cuba, Laos, and Vietnam*. Pbk. ed. (New York: Oxford University Press, 2002), especially p. 147. Bissell, OH, Tape 2, p. 49, JFKPL. The President's News Conference of April 21, 1961, APP.

Department kept secret the details of export licenses (largely at the behest of business interests); Labor Department reports about wages and hours violations were closed; and in perhaps the most ludicrous case, the Migratory Bird Conservation Commission labeled its reports "confidential." While some issues undoubtedly had national security implications, agency policies were excessive, inconsistent and often irrational. Moss found instances when certain journalists were granted special access to documents that were denied to others.[75]

Moss's inquiries provoked an intense White House debate over executive privilege, but the administration never developed a definitive policy on it. The Justice Department spokesperson Ed Guthman explained in April 1961 that despite "numerous conferences" with the White House, they had concluded that "it would be very difficult to draft a formal policy beyond saying that it will be exercised only in the interest of national security." That statement, of course, only begged the key questions: What standard would determine when national security was involved, and who had the authority to make such determinations? The administration made very limited use of executive privilege and avoided the sweeping assertions made by President Eisenhower. President Lyndon Johnson was equally circumspect about the privilege, never officially invoking it. Under President Richard Nixon it finally exploded into a constitutional crisis and helped drive him from office.[76]

CIA assassination plots and other abuses

Only in 1975 did the country learn the full story of the CIA's plots to assassinate the Cuban leader Fidel Castro and other foreign officials. The idea of assassinating Castro was a direct outgrowth of the Bay of Pigs fiasco. Embarrassed and humiliated, the Kennedys resolved to remove Castro by some other means. The president gave his brother direct responsibility for coordinating the effort, and he put together the Special Group Augmented to direct it. In a January 19, 1962, memo, "The Cuba Project," Bobby Kennedy called it "the top priority in the United States Government - all else is secondary," and the president was reported as saying "it's got to be done, and will be done." Getting rid of Castro became an obsession for Bobby, as had been the case with Jimmy Hoffa. Richard Helms, in charge of CIA covert actions, later recalled "relentless pressure from Bob Kennedy" and said that he always spoke "for his brother." Other memos indicate that the president was regularly briefed and approved or disapproved of particular items. The CIA was not a "rogue elephant," as some suggested in the 1970s, but acted at the specific direction of the president and his brother with regard to removing Castro.[77]

It is not clear how much either of the Kennedys actually knew about the CIA assassination plans, as opposed to other actions to remove him. No existing document directly

[75] Moss letters to Agencies, February 23, 1961; Secretary of the Interior to Moss, April 4, 1961; Samuel Archbald to Salinger, May 26, 1961, Salinger Papers, Box 143, JFKPL. Moss, OH, pp. 7–9, JFKPL. The administration's position on the "news management" issue is defended in Sorensen, *Kennedy*, pp. 356–61. 1960 Democratic Party platform, APP.

[76] Guthman to Salinger, April 8, 1961, Salinger Papers, Box 143, JFKPL.

[77] Memorandum From the Chief of Operations in the Deputy Directorate for Plans (Helms) to Director of Central Intelligence McCone, January 19, 1962, *Foreign Relations of the United States, 1961–1963*, V. X, *Cuba* (Washington, DC: Government Printing Office, 1997), pp. 719–20. Richard Helms, *A Look over My Shoulder: A Life in the Central Intelligence Agency* (New York: Random House, 2003), pp. 202, 205. The "rogue elephant" metaphor regarding the CIA is discussed in Chapter 10.

links either of them. Most likely, the president was kept uninformed, to preserve "plausible deniability," but it is very probable that Bobby Kennedy knew and approved. At times, the attempt to maintain plausible deniability for the president was simply ludicrous. A July 25, 1962, memo, for example, describes the objectives "desired by higher authority" and asserts that this same "higher authority has been kept informed of progress" on the project. Everyone knew who that authority was.[78]

The CIA's actual plans for assassinating Castro were often comical, including an exploding cigar and a depilatory designed to make Castro's beard fall out (which presumably would cause him to lose respect among the Cuban people). On the day Kennedy was assassinated in Dallas, a CIA operative in Paris handed a bribed Cuban official a poison pen designed to kill Castro. The CIA anti-Castro effort led to an unholy alliance with the Mafia, which had an interest in restoring its gambling enterprises in Cuba and still had connections on the island. The arrangement, of course, would have been politically embarrassing if exposed at the time but even more seriously it compromised Attorney General Kennedy's campaign against organized crime. The plots, moreover, had disastrous consequences. Steel argues that they convinced Castro he was indeed under attack by the United States, and this led him to the fateful decision to accept the presence of Russian missiles in Cuba, which in turn led to the 1962 Cuban missile crisis, when the United States and the Soviet Union went to the brink of nuclear war.[79]

In evident response to the Kennedys' goal of removing Castro, meanwhile, the Joint Chiefs of Staff on March 13, 1962, approved an incredible proposal to create a pretext for a full-scale military invasion of Cuba. It suggested possible provocations such as sinking an American ship and blaming it on Castro, in what the memo described as a "Remember the Maine" incident; a "terror campaign" of bombs in Miami, Washington, D.C., and other cities, where they believed no one would be killed; and sinking "a boatload of Cubans en route to Florida." The proposal went to Secretary of Defense Robert McNamara and then to President Kennedy. A memo reports that he "expressed skepticism" that under "foreseen circumstances" it would be justifiable or desirable to "use American forces for overt military action." Notably, he did not say it was wrong for the U.S. government to set off bombs in American cities or to kill Cuban refugees by sinking their boats.[80]

The obsession with Castro was part of President Kennedy's fervent anti-communism, which was evident when he entered Congress in 1946. His historic speech to the Houston ministers in 1960, for example, began with a warning about Castro's communist government only ninety miles from U.S. shores. He never criticized Senator Joe McCarthy, and although hospitalized at the time the Senate censured McCarthy, he did not take

[78] Memorandum From the Chief of Operations, Operation Mongoose (Lansdale) to the Special Group (Augmented), July 25, 1962, *Foreign Relations of the United States, 1961–1963*, V. X, *Cuba*, pp. 878–9.

[79] United States Senate, *Alleged Assassination Plots Involving Foreign Leaders: An Interim Report of the Select Committee to Study Governmental Operations with Respect to Intelligence Activities* (New York: W. W. Norton, 1976), plausible deniability, pp. 11–12; Castro, pp. 71–190; organized crime, pp. 259–60. The CIA's "Family Jewels": CIA, FOIA Electronic Reading Room, www.foia.cia.gov. Steel, *In Love with Night*, pp. 72–97. CIA plots: Evan Thomas, *The Very Best Men: The Early History of the CIA* (New York: Simon & Schuster, 1995). Impact of plots: Steel, *In Love with Night*, pp. 72–97.

[80] Lyman L. Lemnitzer, Chairman, Joint Chiefs of Staff to Secretary of Defense, Justification for US Military Intervention in Cuba, March 13, 1962; copy at National Security Archive, www.gwu.edu/~nsarchiv/. *Bay of Pigs 40 Years Later, March 23–24, 2001*, www.gwu.edu/~nsarchiv/. The Kennedy quotes are from a memo by Deputy Under Secretary of State U. Alexis Johnson, published as a footnote in *Foreign Relations of the United States, 1961–1963*, V. X, *Cuba* (Washington, DC: Government Printing Office, 1997), p. 771.

advantage of the established Senate practice of "pairing" his vote with that of someone on the other side. Once he was in the White House, Kennedy's anti-communism expressed itself in a preference for action and unconventional military tactics that became part of the celebrated Kennedy "style" of energy and action. He shared with the CIA a disdain for the formal bureaucratic procedures that characterized both the State and Defense Departments. He became infatuated with the Green Berets as a flexible, low-cost way to fight unconventional wars in places such as Vietnam. The famous internal CIA report known as the "Family Jewels," released in 2007, revealed that under Project Mockingbird the administration in 1963 ordered "telephone intercepts" on two reporters who had published articles based in part on classified information. The documents state that the surveillance was conducted "in coordination with the Attorney General." This episode, however, was a rare lapse by the Kennedy administration with regard to surveillance of the news media and pales in comparison with the abuses by President Nixon.[81]

Despite his generally strong anti-communist outlook, however, Kennedy took pro-civil liberties positions on some domestic cold war programs. While in the Senate, for example, he sponsored a bill to eliminate the loyalty oath for college student loans under the National Defense Education Act. This took some political courage in the middle of the cold war and certainly offered no political benefit for an aspiring presidential candidate. Additionally, in perhaps his only rejection of McCarthyite tactics, he spoke out against a proposed Senate investigation of alleged communist subversion in colleges and universities in 1953. In his first months as president, meanwhile, he ended the interception of communist "propaganda" by the Post Office and the Customs Bureau. In a program begun under President Truman in 1948 and extended in 1951, officials destroyed periodicals without notifying their intended recipients. (Libraries and universities were exempt, and the program did not extend to first-class mail.) The National Security Council had recommended ending the program in 1960, and Attorney General Bobby Kennedy concurred in May 1961. His decision, however, was heavily influenced by the four pending lawsuits against the program and the belief that the Supreme Court would probably strike it down.[82]

STANDING FIRM ON CHURCH AND STATE: THE SCHOOL PRAYER DECISION

In his greatest contribution to civil liberties, the candidate John F. Kennedy gave a ringing endorsement of the two religion clauses of the First Amendment, in his 1960 speech to the Houston ministers. Once in office he faced a politically charged test of that commitment in June 1962, when the Warren Court declared officially sponsored prayers in public schools unconstitutional.

The Court's decision in *Engel v. Vitale* ranks with *Brown v. Board of Education*, *Miranda v. Arizona*, and *Roe v. Wade* in the public outrage it provoked. The day after the decision,

[81] The Kennedy "style": Wills, *The Kennedy Imprisonment*. Affinity with the CIA: Thomas, *The Very Best Men*, pp. 237–8. Navasky, *Kennedy Justice*. CIA, Family Jewels, www.foia.cia.gov. The revelations about the CIA: Chapter 10 of this book.

[82] Oaths: JFK, Remarks, Mills College, Oakland, CA, October 30, 1959, JFK Pre-Presidential Papers, Box 905, JFKPL. Colleges: Kennedy to Charles A. Compton, February 27, 1953, JFK Pre-Presidential Papers, Box 482, JFKPL. Attorney General to the President, May 17, 1961, WHCF, Subject Files, Box 375, JFKPL.

both the House and the Senate were flooded with proposals to amend the Constitution to permit prayer in public schools. One irate southern member of Congress charged, "The Supreme Court put Niggers in the schools and now they kicked Christ out," and the South Carolina representative L. Mendel Rivers said the Court always had "one eye on the Kremlin and the other on the NAACP." Northerners were also outraged. Rep. Frank J. Becker, a Republican from Long Island, where the case originated, called *Engel* "the most tragic in the history of the United States." A week after the decision, the annual Governor's Conference passed a resolution calling for a constitutional amendment to permit prayer. Only the New York governor, Nelson Rockefeller, abstained. A few elected officials supported the decision. Rep. Emanuel Celler, the powerful chair of the House Judiciary Committee, said the Court did not have "any other choice" under the First Amendment. The Republican senator Everett Dirksen proved to be a prophet, suggesting that the idea of separation of church and state "is so ingrained into our people" that he did not think a constitutional amendment would be adopted. And in fact, over the course of the next half century years, despite pressure from a powerful religious political movement, no constitutional amendment on school prayer ever received serious consideration in Congress.[83]

The press inevitably wanted to know what the president of the United States thought about the decision, and it was the subject of the very first question at Kennedy's June 27 press conference. His response was everything a civil libertarian could wish for: "we have in this case a very easy remedy and that is to pray ourselves;" Americans "can pray a good deal more at home ... attend our churches with a good deal more fidelity ...[and] make the true meaning of prayer much more important in the lives of all of our children." He not only refused to criticize the decision or the Supreme Court, but stressed the importance of respecting the role of the Court in American life: "it is important for us if we are going to maintain our constitutional principle that we support the Supreme Court decisions even when we may not agree with them."[84]

Given his celebrated 1960 speech in Houston, Kennedy's support for the controversial decision was not surprising. Nonetheless, it would have been politically expedient for him to have criticized the decision on some limited grounds in order to win conservative votes in Congress, but to his great credit he did not. Nor did he support any of the hundreds of proposals to permit prayer.

The media thought the prayer decision so consequential they queried three former presidents and a former vice president about their views on it. Herbert Hoover called for a constitutional amendment to permit prayer. Harry Truman acknowledged the authority of the Supreme Court as the "interpreter of the Constitution" but did not take a position on a constitutional amendment. Eisenhower issued a characteristically muddled statement saying he "always thought this nation was essentially a religious one," but expressing no opinion about an amendment. The future president Richard Nixon, then running for governor of California, criticized the decision but hedged on important details. The decision was consistent with the intent of the framers of the Constitution, he said, but he welcomed the "very healthy debate" on the issue. While suggesting an amendment to "clarify" the status of prayer in schools, he did not say exactly what that clarification might involve.[85]

83 *Engel v. Vitale*, 370 U.S. 421 (1962). "Both Houses Get Bills to Lift Ban on School Prayer," *NYT*, June 27, 1962. "Governors Seek Prayer Measure," *NYT*, July 4, 1962. "Court's Decision Stirs Conflicts," ibid., June 27, 1962.

84 Kennedy, Press Conference, June 27, 1962, APP. "President Urges Court Be Backed on Prayer Issue," *NYT*, June 28, 1962.

85 "Amendment for School Prayers Suggested by Nixon at Stop Here," ibid., July 1, 1962.

A FORGOTTEN INITIATIVE ON WOMEN'S RIGHTS

"[T]he Fifth and Fourteenth Amendments do embody the principle of equality for women," and judicial clarification of this issue by the courts is "urgently needed." To that end, "interested groups should give high priority" to filing suits challenging discriminatory laws and practices. The recommendation is probably the only time a presidential commission encouraged people to sue the government, but that is exactly what President Kennedy's Commission on the Status of Women did in October 1963. Rarely mentioned among President Kennedy's achievements, the commission gave an important boost to the women's movement at a critical turning point in history. One historian argues that the commission's work represented "a fundamental shift in federal policy." Its creation was all the more remarkable because in 1961 there was no pressure from a strong women's movement.[86]

The moving force on women's issues in the Kennedy administration was Esther Peterson, head of the Women's Bureau in the Department of Labor and the administration's highest-ranking woman. A former lobbyist for the American Federation of Labor–Congress of Industrial Organizations (AFL-CIO), she was politically savvy and committed to the interests of working women. She was a major force behind the 1963 Equal Pay Act, for example. The campaign for the Equal Rights Amendment was nearly dead in 1961, but not completely. Its author, Alice Paul was still alive and active. Peterson recalled administration officials' saying, "Oh, Esther … the tennis shoe ladies are back. Esther, what are we going to do?" As did most liberals, she believed an ERA would wipe out hard won protective legislation for working women and advised President Kennedy to "do a substantive study" that would develop constructive alternatives. "And he liked the idea," she recalled. JFK had no strong feelings about women's issues, but he evidently thought a commission might be helpful politically and created it in December 1961. He gave it special status by first making it a presidential rather than a Department of Labor commission, and then appointing his brother to it and naming the formidable Eleanor Roosevelt as chair.[87]

The commission debated the ERA but after much internal debate took no firm position on it. Leaving the door slightly open, it concluded that a constitutional amendment "need not *now* be sought" [emphasis added]. The qualifying word was a clear indication of changing attitudes among mainstream women's advocates. Then, in a radical departure from previous discussions, it argued that the Fifth and Fourteenth Amendments guaranteed equality for women. Acknowledging that the issue was still unresolved, it called for a "definitive court pronouncement" and explicitly encouraged groups to file test cases. This was no casual recommendation. The attorney general was on the commission, and he certainly had ample opportunity to kill it.

The commission's position on the Fourteenth Amendment was based on a paper it had commissioned from Pauli Murray, then a Yale Law School student. Despite many potential obstacles, she optimistically noted that "the genius of the American Constitution is

[86] Margaret Mead and Frances Balgley Kaplan, eds., *American Women: The Report of the President's Commission on the Status of Women and other Publications of the Commission* (New York, Scribner's, 1965), pp. 149, 213. "U.S. Panel Urges Women to Sue for Equal Rights," *NYT*, October 12, 1963. Jo Freeman, "How 'Sex' got into Title VII: Persistent Opportunism as a Maker of Public Policy," *Law and Inequality: A Journal of Theory and Practice* 9 (March 1991): 163–84. Cynthia E. Harrison, "A 'New Frontier' for Women: The Public Policy of the Kennedy Administration," *Journal of American History* 67 (December 1980): 630–46; quote on p. 630.

[87] Peterson, OH, FAOH, LOC. Peterson to The Secretary [of Labor], June 2, 1961, White House Central Files, Subject Files, Box 206, JFKPL. See also Peterson Papers, JFKPL; materials on the commission in ERP, Box 4644, FDRPL. Harrison, "A 'New Frontier' For Women," 630–4.

its capacity through judicial interpretation for growth and adaptation to changing conditions and human values." What the Supreme Court had done for racial equality in *Brown v. Board of Education*, it could also do for women's rights. Murray had a fascinating career as an African-American lawyer, poet, Episcopalian minister, member of the ACLU board, and in 1966 cofounder of the National Organization for Women (NOW) with Betty Friedan. In 1943 she and fellow Howard University students staged one of the first sit-ins challenging segregated restaurants in Washington, D.C. Her paper for the commission is generally regarded as the seminal work on the question of women and the Fourteenth Amendment. Murray later called the commission "the most exciting and important development affecting women in decades."[88]

The commission's report also recommended that "equal opportunity for women ... should be the governing principle in private employment." It called for repealing the laws in the three states that barred women from serving on juries and the twenty-six other states that allowed women but not men an exemption from jury duty. It also recommend paid maternity leave for working women and tax deductions for child care. From the perspective of almost half a century, the commission's report is particularly notable for what it does not discuss. It contains only one passing reference to birth control, no mention of abortion, and no reference to "pregnancy" in the index. Despite extensive discussion of marriage and marriage laws, it does not mention the miscegenation laws forbidding interracial marriage in sixteen states at that time. Even with rising public consciousness about racial equality, it is likely the commissioners feared a call to end miscegenation laws would provoke vicious attacks and distract attention from all other recommendations.[89]

Although President Kennedy's assassination a month after it was released blunted the report's impact, it had a significant influence nonetheless. Betty Friedan, author of *The Feminine Mystique* and founder of NOW, believes it created a "climate" favorable to women's rights at a time when there was little support. Most important, it spurred the creation of state commissions on the status of women. At the third annual conference of these commissions in 1966, Friedan and her friends became so angry with the lack of substantive action they decided to form NOW. Thus, if only inadvertently, President Kennedy helped give birth to the modern feminist movement.[90]

A mixed record on other women's issues

Although probably better than any previous president's, Kennedy's overall record on women's issues was very mixed. In addition to the commission, he ordered the Civil

88 Mead and Kaplan, *American Women*, pp. 149–51, 212–13. Pauli Murray, "A Proposal to Reexamine the Applicability of the Fourteenth Amendment to State Laws and Practices Which Discriminate on the Basis of Sex per Se" (December, 1962), p. 23. Murray Papers, Subseries II.C, "Work," Doc. 887. Schlesinger Library, Harvard University. Pauli Murray, *Song in a Weary Throat: An American Pilgrimage* (New York: Harper & Row, 1987), pp. 347–57. 1943 Sit-in: "H.U. Student Pickets Force Restaurant to Drop Color Bar," *Afro-American*, April 23, 1943, and other related material, FDRPL, ERP, MF ED, Reel 14. Susan M. Hartmann, "Pauli Murray and the 'Juncture of Women's Liberation and Black Liberation,'" *Journal of Women's History* 14 (Summer 2002). Online at muse.http://jhu.edu. Betty Friedan, *The Feminine Mystique*. Pbk. ed. (New York: Dell, 1963), p. 347. Pauli Murray, OH, OHAS.

89 Mead and Kaplan, *American Women*, pp. 151, 211–13. On the Loving case that ended state miscegenation laws: Peter Wallenstein, *Tell the Court I Love My Wife: Race, Marriage and Law: An American History* (New York: Palgrave, 2002).

90 Friedan, *The Feminine Mystique*, p. 361. Harrison, "A 'New Frontier' for Women," 645. The Commission is not mentioned in either Schlesinger, Jr., *A Thousand Days* or Sorensen, *Kennedy*. President Johnson's and the creation of NOW: Chapter 7 of this book.

Service Commission in 1962 to end the practice of designating some jobs for men or women only, which almost always worked to the disadvantage of women, and ordered that all appointments be made "without regard to sex, except in unusual situations." Previously, an estimated 94 percent of all Civil Service Commission job announcements in grades 13 to 15 explicitly excluded women. With Peterson's effective lobbying, Kennedy also supported the 1963 Equal Pay Act, along with legislation funding day care facilities for working women. Secretary of Defense Robert McNamara, meanwhile, abolished the quota on women in the military.[91]

The administration's record on appointing women to top positions, however, was poor and received increasing criticism from women's advocates. One administration insider pointed out that only one woman had been appointed a federal judge in nearly a decade, and there had been no high-ranking Justice Department official since Mabel Walker Willebrandt had been assistant attorney general under President Hoover. Nor had there ever been a woman adviser to the president. Whereas both FDR and Eisenhower appointed women to their cabinets, Kennedy's, like Truman's, was all male. Esther Peterson at the midlevel Women's Bureau was the most influential woman in the administration.[92]

Signing into law a bill creating seventy-three new federal judgeships on May 19, 1961, Kennedy pledged to "choose men and women of unquestioned ability." This was the first explicit promise by any president to appoint women as federal judges. He failed, however, to honor that promise fully, appointing only one woman, Sarah T. Hughes, to a district court in Texas. In a strange twist of fate, she administered the oath of office to Lyndon Johnson after Kennedy's assassination. Rep. Emanuel Celler, chair of the House Judiciary Committee, urged him to nominate more women judges, but no nominations were forthcoming. (Nicholas Katzenbach, however, did include Soia Mentschikoff of the University of Chicago Law School on an early list of possible Supreme Court nominees in 1962, in probably the first such consideration in history.) In a study of presidential judicial appointments, Sheldon Goldman concludes that "there is no evidence that women were given serious consideration either by Democratic senators or by the president's men in the administration," adding that his record was as poor in this regard as those of the three previous presidents.[93]

INITIATING IMMIGRATION REFORM

Existing law embodied "an indefensible racial preference," the president declared, and it needed to be reformed. In July 1963 President Kennedy proposed an overhaul of the nation's immigration law, which still embodied the national origins quota established in 1924, which he pointed out was "strongly weighted toward so-called Anglo-Saxons." On this issue, Kennedy was running with the tide of public opinion, as the civil rights movement fostered a broadly egalitarian spirit. The political power of Italian Americans, Polish Americans, and Jews, offended by the old law, also helped, as did the Kennedy family

[91] Memorandum on Equal Opportunity for Women in the Federal Service, July 24, 1962, APP. Harrison, "A 'New Frontier' for Women," 631–5.

[92] Clayton Fritchey, U.S. Mission to the United Nations, Memorandum, July 22, 1963, WHCF, Subject Files, Box 374, JFKPL. Celler to The President, September 12, 1961, WHCF, Subject Files, Box 374, JFKPL.

[93] Statement by the President upon Signing Bill Providing for an Increase in the Federal Judiciary.May 19, 1961, APP. Sheldon Goldman, *Picking Federal Judges: Lower Court Selection from Roosevelt Through Reagan* (New Haven, CT: Yale University Press, 1997), p. 180. Mentschikoff: Katzenbach, *Some of It Was Fun*, p. 57.

memory of anti-Irish prejudice. Immigration reform was "a compelling need." Kennedy did not live to see his proposal come to fruition. Lyndon Johnson signed the historic 1965 Immigration Reform Act, but JFK deserves credit for initiating it.[94]

A MIXED RECORD ON JUDICIAL APPOINTMENTS

President Kennedy's two appointments to the Supreme Court balanced each other out in terms of civil liberties. Byron ("Whizzer") White, his first appointment, proved to be a conservative justice. While he was certainly a far more distinguished jurist than Charles Whittaker, whom he replaced, his record on civil liberties was very mixed. He generally supported civil rights and voted with the majority in the pivotal early cases affirming women's rights. On the other hand, he joined a dissent in *Miranda v. Arizona*, defending existing police practices. And while he voted with the majority in the *Griswold* v. Connecticut decision affirming a right to privacy, he later dissented in the *Roe v. Wade* abortion decision.[95]

Arthur Goldberg's appointment in 1962 was an entirely different matter. Replacing Felix Frankfurter, the strongest advocate of judicial restraint on the Court, he shifted the complexion of the Court substantially, creating a solid activist civil libertarian majority. One Goldberg biographer hyperbolically calls his appointment "one of the most consequential in history." That is an exaggeration, but Warren Court activism on civil liberties escalated with Goldberg's appointment. He wrote a concurring opinion in *Griswold* arguing that privacy was among the liberties protected by the Ninth Amendment. Particularly notable, he wrote a dissent in a 1963 death penalty case that essentially invited attorneys to challenge capital punishment on the grounds that it violated the Eighth Amendment prohibition of cruel and unusual punishment.[96]

Kennedy's appointments to the federal judiciary in the South, however, were a disaster for racial justice. He was the prisoner of Senate segregationists, and his very first appointment was Harold Cox, a bitter-end segregationist who just happened to have been a college roommate of Senator James Eastland, chair of the Senate Judiciary Committee. As a district court judge in Mississippi, Cox obstructed racial justice at every turn, particularly in voting rights cases It must be noted, however, that Cox received a high rating from the American Bar Association and gave proper answers in interviews before being confirmed. Whereas President Eisenhower's appointees became famous for their courage in implementing *Brown v. Board of Education*, Kennedy's were often obstructive on civil rights.[97]

A PRESIDENCY CUT SHORT

John F. Kennedy's life was cut short before he completed even three years as president. It is impossible to speculate on what his overall record might have been had he finished

[94] John F. Kennedy, *A Nation of Immigrants*. Pbk. ed. (New York: Popular Library, 1964), p. 114 [published posthumously].

[95] Dennis J. Hutchinson, *The Man Who Once Was Whizzer White: A Portrait of Justice Byron R. White* (New York: Free Press, 1998).

[96] David L. Stebenne, *Arthur J. Goldberg: New Deal Liberal* (New York: Oxford University Press, 1996), p. 316.

[97] Bryant, *The Bystander*, pp. 286–8.

his first term and possibly a second. Overall, his civil liberties record as president was mixed, with some positive contributions offsetting several very disturbing actions on important issues.

The most disappointing aspect of Kennedy's record was his leadership failure on civil rights. The quest for racial justice was simply the most significant domestic issue of the early 1960s, transforming America in ways no one could have imagined on the day Kennedy took the oath of office. Yet, he was indifferent to the moral and political dimensions of the struggle, proposed a federal civil rights law only when forced to by the crisis in the streets. Again and again, he expressed irritation at civil rights militancy – the force that really brought about change in America – and asked civil rights leaders to postpone their demands. At no time did he exercise the kind of presidential leadership that Presidents Harry Truman earlier and Lyndon Johnson later displayed. The historian Nick Bryant titles his book on Kennedy's civil rights record *The Bystander*. The judgment is harsh but appropriate.

Kennedy's greatest contribution to civil liberties was his strong public stand on separation of church and state, including his justly famous speech to the Houston ministers in the 1960 presidential campaign and his firm defense of the Supreme Court's 1962 decision on prayer in public schools. His President's Commission on the Status of Women made a significant early contribution to women's rights, and his initiative on immigration reform set in motion a historic reform he would not live to see fulfilled.

On national security, secrecy, and the intelligence agencies, however, Kennedy's record is very troubling. He and his brother authorized FBI spying and never once objected to questionable and illegal bureau practices of which they were fully aware. The administration encouraged the CIA to remove Castro, and Robert Kennedy probably knew about the assassination plots. President Kennedy issued an alarming call for media self-censorship on national security issues. Kennedy's real priority as president was to fight international communism, and this left him tone deaf on both civil rights activism and openness on national security.

Finally, and in a more fundamental sense, Kennedy was disconnected from the dramatic changes sweeping through American society: the rising demands for rights and freedom of individual expression. It is ironic that the president most remembered for exemplifying youth, vigor, and activism was aloof from the outburst of youthful activism that characterizes the decade of the sixties. And on civil rights, he was hostile to demands that arose from common people in the streets.[98] The Supreme Court under Chief Justice Earl Warren was both engine and facilitator of much of the rising tide of individual rights and is justly famous for its major role in curbing police abuse, requiring the separation of church and state, limiting cold war anti-communist measures, striking down censorship in the arts, enunciating the principle of one-man, one-vote, and eventually establishing a constitutional right to privacy. In short, President John F. Kennedy was a bystander on these issues as well as civil rights.

[98] Samuel Walker, *The Rights Revolution: Rights and Community in Modern America* (New York: Oxford, 1998).

President Lyndon Johnson discusses strategy with civil rights leaders in the White House, c. 1964. James Farmer, head of CORE, is on the right. John Lewis, SNCC leader and future member of Congress, is next to Farmer. Johnson engineered passage of both the 1964 Civil Rights Act and the 1965 Voting Rights Act.
Source: White House Photo Office.

8 The Glory and the Tragedy of Lyndon Johnson

"WE ... SHALL ... OVERCOME"

The president paused and very slowly and deliberately told the nation, "And ...we ... shall ... overcome." On national television the night of March 15, 1965, President Lyndon B. Johnson spoke to Congress and the nation about the urgent need for a federal voting rights law. Leaving no doubt about the depth of his commitment, he embraced the slogan of the civil rights movement. One of the greatest presidential speeches in American history, "The American Promise" was a sweeping affirmation of the right to vote and a statement of the meaning of American democracy.[1]

Lyndon Johnson is a towering figure in American political history: an oversized personality, ambitious beyond reason, domineering, manipulative, occasionally lying, and the legendary Master of the Senate. His vision of an inclusive American society with opportunity for all and his commitment to the Bill of Rights were unmatched by any other modern president. Only Franklin D. Roosevelt rivals him for his legislative achievements. Johnson's aide Larry O'Brien summed up the achievements of 1965 and 1966: "two hundred administration measures advocated, a hundred and eighty-one passed.... So the batting average was .905." His speechwriter Richard Goodwin said, "He wanted to out-Roosevelt Roosevelt." And he came very close. LBJ was passionately committed to social justice. He alone was responsible for steering the 1957 Civil Rights Act through Congress. As president he won passage of the 1964 Civil Rights Act and the 1965 Voting Rights Act, two of the most important pieces of legislation in all of American history. The 1965 Education Act gave federal aid to public schools, Medicare provided health insurance to the elderly, and his ambitious War on Poverty was a noble effort whose purposes and impact are still matters of great controversy.[2]

[1] Special Message to the Congress: The American Promise, March 15, 1965, APP. Garth E. Pauley, *LBJ's American Promise: The 1965 Voting Rights Address* (College Station: Texas A&M University Press, 2007).

[2] O'Brien, Oral History, XVII, p. 24, LBJPL. Richard N. Goodwin, *Remembering America: A Voice from the Sixties*. Pbk. ed. (New York: Harper & Row, 1989), p. 259. Indispensable is Robert Caro's three-volume biography: *The Years of Lyndon Johnson: The Path to Power* (New York: Knopf, 1982); *Means of Ascent* (New York: Knopf, 1990); and *Master of the Senate* (New York: Random House, 2002). Robert Dallek, *Flawed Giant: Lyndon Johnson and His Times 1961–1973* (New York: Oxford University Press, 1998). Irwin Unger and Debi Unger, *LBJ: A Life* (New York: Wiley, 1999). Robert Dallek, *Lone Star Rising: Lyndon Johnson and His Times, 1908–1960* (New York: Oxford University Press, 1991). Mitchell B. Lerner, ed., *Looking Back at LBJ: White House Politics in a New Light* (Lawrence: University Press of Kansas, 2005). Doris Kearns, *Lyndon Johnson and the American Dream*, Pbk. ed. (New York: Signet, 1977) is more of a portrait than a full biography, but it is filled with valuable insights. Johnson's memoirs are not insightful: *Lyndon Johnson, The Vantage Point: Perspectives of the Presidency, 1963–1969* (New York, Holt, Rinehart & Winston 1971).

"What the hell's the presidency for?"

Johnson met with advisers, both his own and the late President Kennedy's, in the late afternoon of November 26, 1963, to prepare for his address to Congress the next day and told them he wanted to make Kennedy's civil rights bill his top priority. Several of the pragmatic-minded warned about risking his political capital on a bill that might not pass. (They included some of the same JFK advisers who had counseled him against a televised speech on civil rights.) Johnson sat silently for a minute and then said, "Well, what the hell's the presidency for?" LBJ understood the special power of the presidency and was naked in his ambition to use it to build a better America. In his voting rights speech he candidly explained that when he taught poor Mexican-American children in 1928 he never imagined he would ever have a chance to "help people like them," but "now I do have that chance – and I'll let you in on a secret, I mean to use it."[3]

This incredibly complex man could tell outlandish tales and blatant lies. To round up votes for the 1957 Civil Rights Act he gave southern segregationists and ardent liberals completely different warnings about what might happen if they did not support his compromise bill. During the Vietnam War he told American troops his great-great grandfather died at the Alamo. When challenged with the story's falsity, he compounded it with the equally untrue claim that his ancestor had died at the more important Battle of San Jacinto. His longtime aide George Reedy saw in him "a combination of complexities and simplicities that bewildered all observers."[4]

Harry McPherson, another aide, said that Johnson had "the most acute sense of civil liberties of any modern president."[5] In addition to the two great civil rights laws, he signed into law the historic Freedom of Information Act, championed a nondiscriminatory immigration law, supported the constitutional rights of criminal suspects, introduced federal support for family planning, and passionately opposed wiretapping. Nonetheless, his record on civil liberties was far from perfect. Women's rights were a blind spot, he directed the FBI to spy on civil rights activists, he personally ordered the CIA to spy on domestic antiwar activists, and he retreated on school integration and crime policy when faced with adverse political pressures. The Vietnam War overshadows all of Johnson's great achievements. It bitterly divided the country, destroyed his plans for domestic reform, and eventually drove him from the White House. He had lied in August 1964 to get Congress to approve a resolution escalating American involvement in Vietnam. His sudden fall from grace between the triumphs of 1965–6 and his humiliating decision not to seek reelection in 1968 encapsulates the glory and the tragedy of this giant figure.

The pivotal moment in Johnson's presidency occurred in early March 1965. Sunday, March 7, is remembered as "Bloody Sunday," when state and local police savagely beat six hundred civil rights marchers on the Edmund Pettus Bridge in Selma, Alabama. Outrage swept the country and led to the historic Voting Rights Act. The day after the Selma beatings, meanwhile, a contingent of U.S. marines stormed ashore near Da Nang, Vietnam.

3 Edwin O. Guthman and Jeffrey Shulman, eds., *Robert F. Kennedy in His Own Words: Unpublished Recollections of the Kennedy Years* (New York: Bantam Books, 1988), pp. 175–6.

4 George Reedy, *Lyndon B. Johnson: A Memoir* (New York: Andrews and McMeel, 1982), p. 9. Reedy argues that LBJ "never told a deliberate lie. But he had fantastic capacity to persuade himself that the 'truth' which was convenient for the present was *the truth*" (p. 3). Kearns tells an illustrative and amusing story of Johnson's false boast about his great-great grandfather's dying at the Alamo: *Lyndon Johnson and the American Dream*, p. 15.

5 McPherson, OH, p. 21, LBJPL.

Officials described it as a "strictly defensive" operation, but it marked a fateful turning point in American involvement in Vietnam. It was the beginning of what for a time was the longest war in American history, in which fifty thousand Americans would die. The conjunction of events that weekend in March 1965 symbolizes the stark contradictions in Johnson's presidency.[6]

PRESIDENTIAL LEADERSHIP: THE 1964 CIVIL RIGHTS ACT

Assuming the presidency in an atmosphere of national crisis following the assassination of President Kennedy on November 22, 1963, Lyndon Johnson wasted no time proving his commitment to civil rights. Passage of Kennedy's civil rights bill was still uncertain, and civil rights leaders distrusted him as a southerner who they believed had weakened the 1957 Civil Rights Bill. At the 1960 Democratic Party convention, civil rights forces booed a mention of his name. Now president, Johnson immediately set out to win their trust.[7] Despite the crushing demands of his first days in the White House, LBJ immediately began phoning top civil rights leaders. James Farmer, leader of the 1961 Freedom Rides, picked up the phone the night just after the assassination and heard a long-distance telephone operator say "the president" was calling. He almost asked, "the president of what?" and was astonished when Lyndon Johnson came on the line. LBJ told him he needed his support on the civil rights bill and said to "stop by" when he was in Washington. "And I was astounded," Farmer recalled. "I'd never been called by a president before!" He called the White House the next day and arranged a meeting. Later, in a handwritten note, he wrote, "After talking with the President I am convinced of his complete sincerity and firm convictions." LBJ also phoned Martin Luther King, A. Philip Randolph, and others in his first days on the job.[8]

In another move designed to demonstrate his commitment to racial justice, Johnson reached into the White House secretarial pool and hired Geri Whittington, a tall, attractive African-American woman, as his personal secretary. She was the first of her race to hold that position. He then took her to Austin, Texas, for a New Year's Eve ball. The town was abuzz over a Texan as the new president, and the University of Texas's football game in the Cotton Bowl the next day. To the astonishment of all present, LBJ entered the then-segregated Faculty Club, not with his wife, Lady Bird, but with Geri Whittington on his arm. One amazed person in the audience whispered to Bill Moyers, "Does he know what he is doing?" Moyers replied, "He always knows what he is doing."[9]

6 "Alabama Police Use Gas and Clubs to Rout Negroes," *NYT*, March 8, 1965. "Force 'Strictly Defensive,' Arrival Is Protested by Hanoi and Peking," ibid., March 8, 1965. The conjunction of the two events, together with the assassination of Malcolm X: Taylor Branch, *Pillar of Fire: America in the King Years, 1963–1965* (New York: Simon & Schuster, 1998), pp. 571–601.

7 Robert Caro's treatment of LBJ and race extends over twelve chapter and 327 pages in *Master of the Senate: The Years of Lyndon Johnson*, pp. 685–1012. Monroe Billington, "Lyndon B. Johnson and Blacks: The Early Years," *The Journal of Negro History* 62 (January 1977): 26–42, and Joe B. Frantz, "Opening a Curtain: the Metamorphosis of Lyndon B. Johnson," *Journal of Southern History* 45 (February 1979): 3–26. 1960 Convention: "Texan Is Absent as 6,000 Rally," *NYT*, July 11, 1960.

8 James Farmer, OH, p. I-8, LBJPL. Farmer, Notes, Lyndon Johnson File, CORE Papers, MF ED, Reel 2. A Philip Randolph, OH, p. I-9, LBJPL. Johnson to King, Telephone call, November 23, 1963, Audio, LBJPL. Transcripts of Johnson's calls: Jonathan Rosenberg and Zachary Karabell, eds., *Kennedy and Johnson, and the Quest for Justice: The Civil Rights Tapes* (New York: W. W. Norton, 2003), pp. 199–207.

9 Merle Miller, *Lyndon: An Oral Biography* (New York: Putnam, 1980), p. 366. LBJ hiring Whittington: Michael R. Beschloss, *Taking Charge: The Johnson White House Tapes, 1963-1964* (New York: Simon and Schuster, 1998),

Johnson's early commitment to civil rights

Johnson's support for civil rights was not a politically expedient response to the protests in the streets, but an expression of his lifelong commitment, reaching back to 1935, when President Roosevelt appointed him Texas state director of the National Youth Administration (NYA). The NYA was a federal work-study program to help high school and college students stay in school. Although the youngest state director at age twenty-seven, he quickly gained a national reputation for his energy and for doing more to help African Americans than any other NYA administrator. In one of his first memos he lectured the NYA director, Aubrey Williams, about the need to get moving because of the huge task they faced. Eleanor Roosevelt visited Austin, Texas, reportedly to meet this hardworking young man. Working quietly behind the scenes, he formed an unofficial Colored Advisory Committee, met privately with African-American leaders, and worked closely with African-American college presidents. When some white programs had funds left over, he transferred them to African-American programs. Word got around, and Robert Weaver, whom Johnson would appoint as the first African-American cabinet member in 1966, recalled hearing from friends about "this guy in Texas who was really something." When LBJ ran for the Senate in 1948, some state African Americans touted him as "a new day in Texas politics."[10]

One NYA episode illustrated Johnson's concern with getting results even if it required sacrificing a principle. Washington NYA officials wanted him to appoint an African American to his state advisory committee. Johnson told them such a highly visible step would only provoke local racists and jeopardize the entire program. He convinced them he should continue his low-visibility efforts and get tangible results. The NYA experience had a profound impact on him, giving him a firsthand taste of government programs opening the doors of opportunity for poor people. Thirty years later as president, he often reminisced about those days.[11]

In another early and artful compromise, he launched his 1948 campaign for the Senate by criticizing Truman's civil rights program. In another speech he said he "voted against all of it because I believed the Federal government was overstepping its functions." Few apparently noticed that he did not actually say he opposed racial justice per se. Most important, he never mentioned the subject again. He threw segregationists a bone to get elected, but he never once descended into racist rhetoric or explicitly supported segregation.[12]

Johnson's concern for racial justice sprang from his populist background and his direct contact with both the very poor and ordinary middle-class people struggling to

pp. 126–30. Obituary: "LBJ's Executive Secretary Dies," *Jet Magazine*, February 15, 1993. Whittington died on January 24, 1993, the same day as the Supreme Court justice Thurgood Marshall.

10 Johnson to Aubrey Williams, August 8, 1935, NYA Papers, Box 8, LBJL. Mitchell Lerner, "'To Be Shot At by the Whites and Dodged by the Negroes': Lyndon Johnson and the Texas NYA," *Presidential Studies Quarterly* 39 (June 2009): 245–74. Dallek, *Lone Star Rising*, pp. 125–39. Caro, *The Master of the Senate*, pp. 723–34. "New day" quote: Clarence Mitchell, OH, p. 1, LBJPL. Lobbying: Kearns, *Lyndon Johnson and the American Dream*, pp. 88–9. Weaver: Miller, *Lyndon*, p. 56.

11 Richard R. Brown to Johnson, December 2, 1935; John J. Corson to Aubrey Williams, September, 25, 1935, and accompanying letters, NYA Papers, Box 8, LBJPL. Johnson to Sergeant Shriver, Telephone Conversation, August 9, 1964; Johnson to Senator Thomas J. Dodd [Dodd also worked in the NYA] November 3, 1964, LBJPL.

12 Johnson's 1948 campaign: Statements File, Box 6, LBJPL. In his first Senate speech Johnson endorsed the southern filibuster blocking a fair employment practices commission: Kearns, *Lyndon Johnson and the American Dream*, p. 111. He soon began distancing himself from the southern bloc, however.

avoid falling into the ranks of the poor. In this respect, he had much in common with Harry Truman, who also had a humble background. Truman never went to college, while Johnson graduated from the low-status Southwest Texas State Teachers College. Both used the "N" word in private but did not let it affect their positions on public policy. Johnson repeatedly talked about the poor Mexican-American children he saw in his first job, as principal of Welhausen Ward Elementary School in Cotulla, Texas, and how moved he was by their hunger and sense of exclusion from America. He may have embellished this story for effect, but there is no doubt the experience was real and his feelings genuine. His biographer Robert Dallek writes that Johnson had a "strong commitment to opening the doors of opportunity." Even FBI Deputy Director Deke DeLoach, hardly known for his compassion for the downtrodden, believed that "the compassion of Lyndon Johnson stemmed from his days as a poor boy in the hills of Texas."[13] By contrast, his fellow Democratic presidents Franklin D. Roosevelt and John F. Kennedy attended Harvard and had virtually no contact with poor people or African Americans. Lawrence O'Brien, who served both JFK and LBJ, commented tartly that Johnson "knew the Depression," whereas "Jack Kennedy never worked for the NYA or anyone else." Roosevelt did nothing to support civil rights, while Kennedy was coolly indifferent until forced to act by massive demonstrations in the street in 1963.[14]

Addressing Congress and the nation just five days after Kennedy's assassination, Johnson skillfully framed the civil rights bill as a memorial to his slain predecessor: "no memorial or eulogy could more fittingly continue the work of President Kennedy." Johnson brought to bear his ferocious determination and unparalleled legislative skills, using the very strategy he had outlined in his June 1963 phone conversation with Ted Sorensen. He virtually ordered civil rights leaders around, calling the NAACP head Roy Wilkins in early January to demand, "When are you going to get down here and start civil righting?" "What I want you to do," he explained, is to help round up GOP votes. The strategy worked, and the bill passed with support from a coalition of nonsouthern Democrats and moderate Republicans. Even then, it required a heroic effort to end a three-month southern filibuster (the longest "debate" in the history of the Senate) with a difficult and rarely used vote on cloture on June 10. LBJ signed the historic bill into law on July 2. After the cloture vote, Anthony Lewis in the *New York Times* observed that President Johnson "made it all possible by his outspoken commitment to civil rights."[15]

13 Dallek, *Flawed Giant*, p. 139. DeLoach, OH, p. 27, LBJPL. O'Brien, OH, Part VI, p. 10; Part V, p. 43, LBJPL. Kearns calls LBJ a "true believer" on civil rights from his earliest days: *Lyndon Johnson and the American Dream*, p. 241.

14 John Morton Blum, *The Progressive Presidents. Roosevelt, Wilson, Roosevelt, Johnson* (New York: W. W. Norton, 1980), p. 165. A. Philip Randolph recalled that Roosevelt asked him what class he was at Harvard, suggesting that FDR could not imagine anyone in a position of leadership who had not graduated from his own alma mater. Jervis Anderson, *A. Philip Randolph: A Biographical Portrait* (New York: Harcourt Brace Jovanovich, 1973), p. 256. Address before a Joint Session of the Congress. November 27, 1963, APP. Preparations: Lyndon Johnson, Daily Diary, November 26, 1963, LBJPL, available on-line. Miller, *Lyndon*, p. 337. But see the critical examination of Miller's oral biography of Harry Truman by Robert H. Ferrell and Francis H. Heller, "Plain Faking," *American Heritage* 46 (May/June 1995): 14–15, which found that Miller fabricated some quotes.

15 Johnson mapped out a legislative strategy for the Kennedy administration in a phone conversation with Theodore Sorensen on June 3, 1963. Transcript with analysis: Steven F. Lawson, "I Got It from *The New York Times*": Lyndon Johnson and the Kennedy Civil Rights Program," *Journal of Negro History* 67 (Summer 1982): 159–73. Wilkins call: Goodwin, *Remembering America*, p. 313. Anthony Lewis, "The Strategy of Closure," *NYT*, June 11, 1964.

The 1964 Civil Rights Act was far stronger than Kennedy's original bill and included a ban on employment discrimination, thought to be politically impossible in 1963. The political context had changed dramatically in just twelve months. "The world had turned around," Harry McPherson explained. The August 1963 March on Washington was a huge success, with Martin Luther King's "I Have a Dream" speech brilliantly framing civil rights in terms of the highest American ideals.[16] At a stroke, the 1964 Civil Rights Act ended the scar of official segregation in public accommodations and established equal opportunity in employment as national policy. It remains one of the most important laws in American history. Although it ignored the vital issue of voter disenfranchisement, it nonetheless marked the end of a shameful era in American life. Civil rights leaders barely had time to celebrate the historic achievement, however. Two weeks after the bill became law, a racial disturbance broke out in Harlem, the heart of the African-American ghetto in New York City, and was soon followed by similar disturbances in other cities. At the very moment of a great civil rights triumph, the country faced a dramatic turn in racial politics in America.

SELMA AND THE VOTING RIGHTS ACT: LBJ SEIZES THE MOMENT

It was a truly remarkable phone conversation. The president and the nation's top civil rights leader quietly plotted a strategy to get a voting rights bill through a reluctant Congress. President Johnson phoned Martin Luther King on January 15, 1965, ostensibly to congratulate him on his thirty-sixth birthday. King had just won the Nobel Peace Prize, and was in Selma, Alabama, to launch a major voting rights campaign. After an exchange of pleasantries, Johnson got to his real agenda: the "dire need" for a voting rights law. Oddly, only a month earlier, he had privately told King that voting rights might have to wait because "I need the votes of the southern bloc to get these other things through." LBJ had soaring ambitions for his Great Society, and it appeared that voting rights would have to wait. For some unknown reason, however, he changed his mind and now told King that African-American voting power would "answer 70 percent of your problems." King immediately understood Johnson's game and played to it by pointing out that African Americans were most heavily disenfranchised in the five Deep South states he did not carry in the 1964 election. Black voting power "would really make the New South," he told the president. "That is exactly right!" exclaimed Johnson. One historian wrote that the conversation sounded like a pair of old politicos plotting campaign strategy.[17]

Johnson then explained that to win over Senate and House members from outside the South, King should find "simple examples of discrimination" in voting that would dramatize systemic disenfranchisement. He suggested highlighting the requirement that applicants interpret a complex clause in the Constitution or memorize a passage from the poet Longfellow. As a southerner, Johnson knew all about such devices. Take the worst

[16] The 1964 Civil Rights Act: Robert Mann, *The Walls of Jericho: Lyndon Johnson, Hubert Humphrey, Richard Russell, and the Struggle for Civil Rights* (New York: Harcourt Brace, 1996). Nick Kotz, *Judgment Days Lyndon Baines Johnson, Martin Luther King, Jr., and the Laws That Changed America* (Boston: Houghton Mifflin, 2005). Harry McPherson, *A Political Education* (Boston: Little, Brown, 1972), p. 195.

[17] Text of conversation: Michael Beschloss, ed., *Reaching for Glory: Lyndon Johnson's Secret White House Tapes, 1964–1965* (New York: Simon & Schuster, 2001), pp. 159–63. Nick Kotz, *Judgment Days*, pp. 250–77. LBJ-King December conversation: Clayborne Carson, "1965: A Decisive Turning Point in the Long Struggle for Voting Rights, *Crisis* 112, no. 4 (2005): 16–20. Politicos: Kotz, *Judgment Days*, p. 252.

example you can find, he advised, and "get it on the radio, get it on television, get it in the pulpits." King flattered LBJ by saying, "Yes, you're exactly right about that." Johnson said a voting rights law would be an even greater accomplishment than the 1964 Civil Rights Act. The conversation ended with King understanding that his voting rights campaign suddenly had a powerful new ally.

If the story of this extraordinary phone conversation was based only on second-hand accounts, most people would dismiss it as another Johnson tall tale. But LBJ had installed a secret tape recording system in the White House (as had Roosevelt, Truman, Eisenhower, and Kennedy for brief periods), and a recording of the call exists. It is an ironic footnote to history that Richard Nixon's taping system provided the evidence that drove him from office, while Johnson's confirms for posterity his deep commitment to civil rights.

Selma: Crisis and opportunity

At the time of the phone conversation, the systematic disenfranchisement of African Americans was appalling. Only 6.7 percent of eligible African-American voters in Mississippi were registered in 1964; in Alabama it was only 23 percent. The 1957 and 1960 Civil Rights Acts had proven to be almost worthless, as southern officials used every legal device to thwart Justice Department efforts. Nicholas Katzenbach, Johnson's attorney general, later conceded that the government's strategy of county-by-county litigation "was just an impossible system." Burke Marshall, head of the Civil Rights Division in 1964, also conceded the "seeming inability to make significant advances in making the right to vote real for Negroes in Mississippi" and other Deep South states.[18]

King and his staff had already decided that the time was ripe for a full-bore assault on disenfranchisement and in late 1964 decided to repeat the Birmingham strategy of rousing national public opinion through confrontational tactics. (An informant provided the FBI with details of the plan.) King chose Selma because it was the "symbol of bitter-end resistance" to civil rights. African Americans were half the population, but only 156 of 15,000 eligible adults were registered to vote. Employment discrimination remained pervasive. King counted on the Dallas County sheriff, Jim Clark, to replay the scenario that had worked in Birmingham two years earlier, by responding with arrests and brutality that would create a national crisis. Clark played his assigned role perfectly. On Tuesday, January 19, after some relatively peaceful demonstrations, he ordered the arrest of African Americans attempting to register to vote. Six days later, newspapers around the country published a shocking photograph of him kneeling over Mrs. Annie Lee Cooper, an African American, with his billy club raised over her head. The confrontations escalated, and in early February, Clark arrested dozens of schoolchildren whom King had mobilized. King himself was arrested, and SCLC published a letter from him in a full-page ad in the *New York Times* declaring, "There are more Negroes in jail with me than there are on the voting rolls."[19]

[18] Voting Data: Chandler Davidson and Bernard Grofman, eds., *Quiet Revolution in the South: The Impact of the Voting Rights Act, 1965–1990* (Princeton, NJ: Princeton University Press, 1994). Katzenbach, OH, I, p. 21, LBJPL. Burke Marshall, *Federalism and Civil Rights* (New York: Columbia University Press, 1964), p. 37.

[19] FBI informant: "Re: Southern Christian Leadership Conference," January 6, 1965, *Communist Infiltration of the SCLC: FBI Investigation File*, MF ED (Wilmington, DE: Scholarly Resources, 1983), Reel 2. Selma

The climax occurred on "Bloody Sunday," March 7, in an attempted march from Selma to the state capital in Montgomery, fifty-five miles away. The Selma mayor Joe Smitherman and the public safety director Wilson Baker had desperately tried to negotiate a peaceful settlement that would include promises of job opportunities and warned Kennedy administration officials about the danger of violence. That fateful Sunday afternoon, 525 marchers led by SNCC's John Lewis and SCLC's Hosea Williams, set out for Montgomery. (King was in Atlanta, preaching). After passing three dozen sheriff's posse members on the Selma side of the Edmund Pettus Bridge, they were met on the other side by fifty helmeted state troopers and several dozen sheriff's deputies and ordered to turn back: "This is an unlawful assembly.... You are ordered to disperse and go back to your church or to your homes."[20]

At about 4:15 p.m., the order "Troopers, advance," rang out, and the officers charged, viciously attacking marchers with tear gas and billy clubs. "Get the Niggers," some cried, and white bystanders joined in the assault. A beaten John Lewis fell to the ground, thinking, "I am going to die here." Televised film of the brutal assault provoked national outrage. Thousands of sympathizers flocked to Selma to lend their support. An injunction held up the march for two weeks, but Judge Frank M. Johnson (one of the great Eisenhower appointees, who had ordered the Montgomery buses integrated in 1956) finally ruled the march could proceed, and on Sunday, March 21, thirty-two hundred people, guarded by federal troops, set out for Montgomery. They numbered twenty-five thousand by the time they reached Montgomery on March 25. The last great moment of the civil rights movement, the march succeeded in rousing the political support for a voting rights bill that Johnson told King he needed in their January phone conversation.[21]

In a sad footnote, the former president Harry Truman criticized militant civil rights action. He dismissed the march as "silly" and said it "can't accomplish a darned thing" and was only designed to "attract attention." What he did not understand but LBJ and Martin Luther King both did was that demonstrations were indeed designed to attract "attention," and that is what made the landmark law possible.[22]

A presidential civics lecture: "The American Promise"

A week after "Bloody Sunday" and before Judge Johnson let the march proceed, President Johnson went on national television to call for a federal voting rights law. His "The American Promise" speech to Congress on March 15 is one of the greatest speeches ever given by an American president. He embraced the slogan of the civil rights movement and framed voting rights in terms of the highest American ideals: "I speak tonight for the dignity of man and the destiny of democracy." The country had an opportunity now "to right wrong, to do justice, to serve man." The issue transcended race and region: "There is no Negro problem. There is no Southern problem.... There is only an American problem."

campaign: David J. Garrow, *Protest at Selma: Martin Luther King, Jr., and the Voting Rights Act of 1965* (New Haven, CT: Yale University Press, 1978), pp. 6–77. "Alabama Vote Drive Opened by Dr. King," *NYT*, January 3, 1965. "Woman Punches Alabama Sheriff," ibid., January 26, 1965; "A Letter from Martin Luther King from a Selma, Alabama Jail," ibid., February 5, 1965.

20 "Unlawful assembly": John Lewis, *Walking with the Wind: A Memoir of the Movement* (New York: Simon & Schuster, 1998), pp. 326–32.

21 Garrow, *Protest at Selma*, pp. 31–76.

22 "Truman Doubts March Accomplishes Anything," *NYT*, March 23, 1965.

Johnson promised to send Congress a voting rights law in a few days and advised the members of Congress seated before him that "we waited a hundred years and more, and the time for waiting is gone." The high point of the speech occurred when Johnson solemnly told the country, "These are the enemies: poverty, ignorance, disease. They are the enemies." Then, pausing for emphasis, he declared, "And these enemies too, poverty, disease and ignorance, we ... shall ... overcome."[23]

In the midst of the speech, moreover, Johnson gave the nation a short civics lesson on the First Amendment. The issue was more than voting rights: "We must preserve the right of free speech and the right of free assembly." Assuming the role of schoolmaster to the nation, he explained that freedom of speech was vital but not unlimited and did not include, for example, "the right to holler fire in a crowded theater." Additionally, "We must preserve the right of free assembly." It too had certain limits and did not include "the right to block public thoroughfares to traffic." (This was a reference to a threatened "stall-in" at the 1964 World's Fair in New York City.) "We do have a right to protest," but not in ways that "infringe the constitutional rights of our neighbors. And I intend to protect all those rights as long as I am permitted to serve in this office." No other president of the United States ever gave the people of America such an informed discussion of freedom of speech and assembly, however brief. President Roosevelt's 1941 Four Freedoms speech was an inspiring statement but offered no details about difficult First Amendment issues.

Johnson also explained how he learned about injustice in his first job and openly revealed his ambitions as president. Even before graduating from college he was the principal of a predominantly Mexican-American school in Cotulla, Texas. He movingly described how "few of them could speak English," and how they "were poor and they often came to class without breakfast, hungry." "I saw it in their eyes," he continued, and "somehow you never forget what poverty and hatred can do when you see its scars on the hopeful face of a young child." He then candidly explained his plans as president: "It never even occurred to me in my fondest dreams that I might have the chance to help the sons and daughters of those students and to help people like them all over this country. But now I do have that chance – and I'll let you in on a secret – I mean to use it." In Selma, Martin Luther King watched the speech with tears in his eyes.[24]

The Voting Rights Bill moved through Congress fairly quickly, considering its enormous implications for American politics, and passed with huge majorities in both houses of Congress (328–74 in the House). Johnson signed it on August 6, regarding it the crowning achievement of his career. Joseph Califano recalled, "I would rarely see him happier," while "joyous pandemonium" prevailed in the Capitol Rotunda.[25]

The law ended the use of literacy, good character, and other tests for registering to vote. Section 5 required local jurisdictions to "preclear" any changes in voting election procedures, such as the composition of districts, that potentially discriminated against minorities. This requirement was extremely important in preventing redistricting plans designed to dilute the African-American vote. In just a few short years, the

[23] Special Message to the Congress, The American Promise, March 15, 1965, APP. Pauley, *LBJ's American Promise*, provides an excellent analysis of the speech and the political context. The speech is ranked tenth among the 100 greatest American speeches by www.americanrhetoric.com.

[24] Goodwin, *Remembering America*, p. 310.

[25] Joseph A. Califano, Jr., *The Triumph and Tragedy of Lyndon Johnson: The White House Years* (New York: Simon & Schuster, 1991), p. 57.

law transformed southern politics. Registration of African Americans across the South jumped from 43 percent in 1964 to 62 percent four years later; in Mississippi registration leapt from a mere 7 percent to 59 percent. Registration was already relatively high (57.7 percent) in Texas, and it reached 83 percent by 1968. The law resulted in the election of African-American officials across the South, particularly in small towns and rural counties. John Lewis, severely beaten on "Bloody Sunday," was elected to the House of Representatives from Atlanta in 1987. By the mid-1980s Mississippi had more African-American elected officials than any other state. Richard Goodwin, who wrote Johnson's voting rights speech, proudly and appropriately called the law "the single largest and most enduring liberal accomplishment of the sixties."[26]

The Voting Rights Law did not, of course, end all attempts to limit African-American voting power. White southerners employed a number of strategies over the next forty years to dilute that power, including establishing at-large districts that favored white majorities. Southerners in Congress made repeated attempts to weaken key provisions, and Justice Department enforcement under several presidents was so uneven that Laughlin McDonald, director of the ACLU's Voting Rights Project, brought far more suits to enforce the law than did the government.[27]

LBJ confronts the new era of civil rights

The Civil Rights Act and the Voting Rights Act swept aside de jure discrimination but hardly ended America's racial problem. They only introduced a new era when the central question was how to achieve equality. The result was a historic shift from color-blind to race-conscious policies, a reversal that shattered the post–World War II civil rights coalition. President Johnson was one of the few public figures who understood the new challenge and certainly the only one willing to discuss it openly. Only three months after his Voting Rights speech, he gave the nation another civics lesson, telling his speechwriter Goodwin, "We've got the biggest pulpit in the world up here, and we ought to use it to do a little preaching."[28]

LBJ chose historically African-American Howard University for a speech entitled "To Fulfill These Rights" on June 4, 1965. After noting the historic new civil rights laws, he explained that "freedom is not enough. You do not wipe away the scars of centuries by saying: Now you are free to go where you want, and do as you desire." More was needed to achieve true equality. "Thus, it is not enough just to open the gates of opportunity. All our citizens must have the ability to walk through those gates." And in a passage far more prophetic than he imagined, he explained, "This is the next and the more profound stage in the battle for civil rights." Over the next several decades, that battle involved

26 Laughlin McDonald, *A Voting Rights Odyssey: Black Enfranchisement in Georgia* (New York: Cambridge University Press, 2003). McDonald was the longtime director of the ACLU Voting Rights Project and deeply involved in Voting Rights Act litigation. Chandler Davidson and Bernard Grofman, eds., *Quiet Revolution in the South: The Impact of the Voting Rights Act, 1965–1990* (Princeton, NJ: Princeton University Press, 1994), p. 374, table 12.1; impact of the law: pp. 378–87. Steven F. Lawson, *Black Ballots: Voting Rights in the South, 1944–1969* (New York: Columbia University Press, 1976). Black elected officials: U.S. Bureau of the Census, *2011 Statistical Abstract of the United States* (Washington, DC: Bureau of the Census, 2011), Table 413.

27 McDonald, *A Voting Rights Odyssey*, p. 128. Goodwin, *Remembering America*, p. 339.

28 Commencement Address at Howard University: "To Fulfill These Rights," June 4, 1965, APP. Goodwin, *Remembering America*, pp. 342–8; (quote: p. 343).

race-conscious and results-oriented remedies, on jobs, public school enrollments, and college admissions. In a historic first step, he issued Executive Order 11246, establishing affirmative action as official federal policy.[29]

The issue of racial preferences, however, would shatter the black and white coalition of the civil rights movement and generate conflict for the next half-century. Looking back, the sociologist John David Skrentny observes critically that Johnson never discussed the difficult details of goals, timetables, or quotas. In fact, they became embedded in federal policies with hardly any public debate at the outset. Thus, Skrentny argues, the country was left unprepared for race preferential policies until they erupted into controversy in the 1970s. Johnson did fail to initiate that debate, but he at least deserves credit for understanding and telling the nation that a new and more difficult civil rights era had dawned.[30]

The Howard speech also opened a bitter racial divide on another issue. Johnson addressed the "special nature of Negro poverty," drawing primarily on the still-unreleased report *The Negro Family* by a then-little-known Labor Department official named Daniel P. Moynihan. The Moynihan report, characterized in 2011 as "probably the most famous piece of social scientific analysis ever published," described a "tangle of pathologies" contributing to systematic "family breakdown" among African Americans: unemployment, single-parent families, absent fathers, and out-of-wedlock births. Copies were leaked and immediately provoked outrage from African Americans, who thought it shifted the blame for America's race problem from discrimination to the black community. Moynihan anticipated this reaction and warned some friends in advance that he had "opened a Pandora's Box." [31]

Acrimonious debate over the Moynihan report poisoned the White House Conference on Civil Rights in mid-November (actually a planning meeting for a full conference the following June). Instead of a grand celebration of the historic gains of the last two years, it was a bitterly divisive affair. Moynihan himself was "treated as an untouchable, unspeakable object," according to LBJ aide Harry McPherson.[32] Rather than thanking Johnson for his historic achievements, civil rights leaders attacked his administration for not doing enough. The recent gains only fostered the proverbial revolution of rising expectations, and they now demanded both freedom and equality, "Now." The escalating Vietnam War only added to the angry mood, as some delegates opposed the war outright and others feared the war's guns would crowd out the domestic policy butter they sought. Always independent, A. Philip Randolph proposed a Freedom Budget calling for a massive federal public works program that would increase the federal budget by 35 percent in three

[29] Executive Order 11246, Equal Employment Opportunity, September 24, 1965, APP.

[30] John David Skrentny, *The Ironies of Affirmative Action: Politics, Culture and Justice in America* (Chicago: University of Chicago Press, 1996).

[31] U.S. Department of Labor, *The Negro Family: The Case for National Action* (March 1965). The controversy: Lee Rainwater and William L. Yancey, *The Moynihan Report and the Politics of Controversy* (Cambridge, MA: M.I.T. Press, 1967), pp. 246–70. "Slum Plea Made at Rights Parley," *NYT*, November 18, 1965. Godfrey Hodgson, *The Gentleman from New York: Daniel Patrick Moynihan: A Biography* (Boston: Houghton Mifflin, 2000), pp. 90–8, 113–19, 126–9. "Most famous piece": Douglas Massey and Robert J. Sampson, "Moynihan Redux: Legacies and Lessons," *The Annals of the American Academy of Political and Social Science* 621 (January 2009): 6–27.

[32] McPherson, OH, IV, pp. 2–10, LBJPL. Some sociologists argue that the Moynihan Report unfairly singled out African-American family problems, and that they were essentially "in the vanguard of change in marriage practices" among white teenagers and older women: Frank F. Furstenberg, *Destinies of the Disadvantaged: The Politics of Teen Childbearing* (New York: Russell Sage Foundation, 2007), pp. 12–17.

years and 50 percent in eight years. LBJ reportedly "went through the roof" over the cost. Interestingly, it was a race neutral program for all the poor and unemployed. It is a matter of debate even today whether Randolph's far more radical and expensive proposal would have addressed poverty more effectively than LBJ's more limited War on Poverty.[33]

Bitter conflict continued into the main conference in June 1966. Administration loyalists worked hard to kill a resolution condemning the Vietnam War, and moderates of both races were alienated by the angry rhetoric of militants, particularly the attacks on America as a racist society. James Meredith, who had integrated the University of Mississippi in 1962, attended but found little support for his "Freedom from Fear" march in Mississippi the following week. At that march, Meredith was shot and wounded, and the SNCC leader Stokely Carmichael first raised the cry of "Black Power," a slogan than alienated many whites. The great days of "black and white together" evaporated, replaced by an acrimonious debate over affirmative action and a white backlash fueled by the urban riots of 1964–8. Lyndon Johnson's instrumental role in ending historical racial segregation in America was an achievement unmatched by any other American president. But like so many other white Americans, he was confused and hurt by the tone and substance of the new racial politics. For the first time in his life, he had no legislative response to propose. His War on Poverty seemed increasingly irrelevant to the deeply entrenched and interrelated problems of race and poverty, and both he and the nation were increasingly preoccupied by the Vietnam War.[34]

Retreat from principle: Title VI and the Chicago schools

As his insightful Howard speech indicated, Johnson understood intellectually the challenge of fulfilling the promise of equality. When confronted with the political realities of that challenge, however, he drew back. The first big test arose, interestingly enough, not in the South but in a northern city, Chicago.[35]

The world of race and education in America was completely transformed in the space of nine months between the Civil Rights Act (signed on July 2, 1964) and the Elementary and Secondary Education Act (April 11, 1965). Together, they gave the federal government a powerful new tool to fight segregated schools. Title VI of the 1964 law authorized withholding federal funds from any organization practicing racial discrimination, while the Education Act provided vast federal funds for local schools ($1.3 billion the first year). Chicago became the first test of how the federal government would use these tools.

A coalition of Chicago community groups, which had been fighting de facto racial segregation in the city's schools, quickly filed a discrimination complaint with the Department of Health, Education and Welfare (HEW), submitting it on July 4, in fact. HEW officials were caught off guard because they had not considered de facto segregation

[33] A. Philip Randolph Institute, *A Freedom Budget for All Americans* (October 1966), in U.S. Senate, Subcommittee on Employment, Manpower, and Poverty, Committee on Public Welfare, 90th Cong., 1st Sess., Hearings, *Examining the War on Poverty*, March 13, 15, 16, 1967. Morris Abram, OH, Part II-3, 12, LBJPL. *Report of the White House Conference "To Fulfill These Rights"* (Washington, DC: Government Printing Office, 1966).

[34] "Mississippi Story," *NYT*, June 12, 1966. "Mississippi Reduces Police Protection for Marchers," ibid., June 17, 1966. Divisions over civil rights policy: Morris Abram, OH, Part I, pp. 10–11, LBJPL. Goodwin, *Remembering America*, pp. 424, 543.

[35] See the indispensable analysis in Dean J. Kotlowski, "With All Deliberate Delay: Kennedy, Johnson, and School Desegregation," *Journal of Policy History* 17, no. 2 (2005): 155–92.

when developing Title VI guidelines. The Chicago complaint, according to one scholar, was well documented, and on October 1, Commissioner of Education Francis Keppel announced he would "defer" $32 million in federal aid to Chicago's schools until the city presented a plan to end de facto segregation. The political reaction was immediate and predictable. The Chicago mayor, Richard M. Daley, probably the most powerful figure in the Democratic Party aside from the president, raised hell with LBJ on October 3 at the Statue of Liberty, where LBJ signed the historic immigration reform law. Johnson was furious at HEW for not giving him advance warning. (The HUD secretary, Robert C. Weaver, meanwhile, was considering withholding federal housing funds for Chicago.) Back in Washington, Johnson called an emergency meeting with HEW officials and then dispatched the HEW secretary Wilbur Cohen to Chicago to negotiate a settlement. Cohen was not a strong civil rights advocate and emerged from an all-day meeting with an agreement that the Chicago school system would make a series of changes (e.g., reviewing school attendance boundaries, ending discriminatory patterns in vocational training programs). HEW then released the Chicago school funds.[36]

The agreement was worthless, and Attorney General Katzenbach wrote to the White House several weeks later to say that Chicago's progress report was "not very good," and that the School District had made "no meaningful program proposals." Nonetheless, politics prevailed and the administration refused to cut off the funds. The Johnson aide Douglass Cater later said the entire episode "was a real embarrassment." The case shaped future events. While it is true, as Cater pointed out, that Johnson never again intervened to block Title VI enforcement, it is nonetheless also true that HEW shied away from using the powerful weapon of cutting off funds. Gary Orfield, the leading scholar on school desegregation, argues that the Chicago episode showed southern school districts that HEW "could be beaten politically." This only encouraged them to delay integration efforts, while northern school districts drew the same lesson.[37]

HEW desegregation guidelines became a continuing controversy. The first set in early 1965 was greeted with protests from both southern school districts who objected to any federal enforcement and civil rights leaders who felt they had no real teeth. In practice, school districts could accept the guidelines and then do almost nothing. Leon Panetta, an HEW staff member under President Richard Nixon, characterized 1965 as "the year of paper compliance." LBJ's new HEW secretary, John W. Gardner, proposed a goal of having 20 percent African-American students in previously all-white schools, but Attorney General Katzenbach advised against a numerical formula. President Johnson supported Gardner, but the battle over "goals," "timetables," and "quotas" was just beginning, and not just in education. Southern school districts devised "freedom of choice" plans that put the burden on African-American parents to enroll their children in all-white schools

[36] "Chicago Schools May Lose Federal Aid over Race Issue," *NYT*, October 2, 1965. "$6 Million Released to Chicago Schools," ibid., October 28, 1965. Agreement: Califano to Lee White, October 11, 1965, White Files, Box 5, LBJPL. Gary Orfield, *The Reconstruction of Southern Education: The Schools and the 1964 Civil Rights Act* (New York: Wiley, 1969), pp. 151–207. U.S. Commission on Civil Rights, *Racial Isolation in the Public Schools*, V. 1. (Washington, DC: Government Printing Office, 1967), p. 4. Dionne Danns, *Something Better for Our Children: Black Organizing in Chicago Public Schools, 1963–1971* (New York: Routledge, 2003), pp. 50–5. Housing funds: Johnson to Daley, Telephone Conversation, September 15, 1965, LBJPL.

[37] Attorney General to Lee White, Douglass Cater, The Chicago School Situation, December 17, 1965, WHCF, Subject Files, Federal Aid, Box 6, LBJPL. Orfield, *The Reconstruction of Southern Education*, p. 206. Douglass Cater, OH, I-14, LBJPL. Califano, Jr., *The Triumph and Tragedy of Lyndon Johnson*, pp. 70–3.

and produced few results. Panetta explained that integration typically involved "only the smallest handful, frequently children from only one brave black family in town." The Supreme Court, frustrated over the lack of progress in integration, ruled freedom of choice plans invalid in 1968.[38]

Johnson never formally signed the HEW guidelines, and after much debate the administration kept them as "guidelines" rather than "regulations," which would have had more legal force. The historian Dean Kotlowski and the political scientist Stephen C. Halpern both argue that this sleight of hand was a deliberate effort to insulate LBJ from the political controversy over school desegregation. Compelling integration through the blunt instrument of federal funds had political consequences in both the North and the South. Kotlowski points out that for all his genuine commitment to civil rights, Johnson said almost nothing publicly about school desegregation after 1965. Leaving office in early 1969, he essentially dumped the problem in the lap of his successor, Richard Nixon.[39]

Once Mayor Daley had shown the way, local communities in both the North and the South fought integration and found considerable support in Congress. Dominated by Democrats in those years, Congress on three occasions sought to limit the use of busing to achieve racial integration. Preserving "neighborhood schools" became a political code for opposing busing. Increasingly consumed by the Vietnam War, urban riots, and growing hostility from both white liberals and militant civil rights leaders, President Johnson by 1966 had neither the time, the energy, nor the political capital to push hard on school integration. Nor did any subsequent president use Title VI for school desegregation. President Nixon devised the strategy of shifting primary responsibility for enforcing integration to the Justice Department. Not only did this require a long legal process, filled with all the inevitable appeals, but, most important, a federal judge rather than a presidential administration was the villain who ordered integration. Halpern concludes, more in sadness than in anger, that Title VI was simply too powerful a weapon, and both Democratic and Republican presidents shied away from it.[40]

LBJ'S VISION OF A TRULY EGALITARIAN SOCIETY

"Most Americans enjoy a good life," LBJ explained in his 1965 State of the Union Address, but many are excluded from its opportunities. "Let a just nation throw open to them the city of promise ... the elderly ... the poor ... Negro Americans ... [and] "those in other lands that are seeking the promise of America."[41] Johnson's vision of a Great Society was far more egalitarian than that of any other president, including FDR. With huge majorities in Congress after the 1964 elections, he set out to fulfill the promise of equality for all Americans.

[38] An excellent account is Leon E. Panetta and Peter Gall, *Bring Us Together: The Nixon Team and the Civil Rights Retreat* (Philadelphia: J. B. Lippincott, 1971); quote on p. 40. Guidelines: U.S. House of Representatives, Committee on the Judiciary, Special Subcommittee on Civil Rights, "Guidelines for School Desegregation," Hearings, December 14, 15, 16, 1966, 89th Cong, 2nd Sess. *Green v. County School Board of New Kent County*, 391 U.S. 430 (1968).

[39] Stephen C. Halpern, *On the Limits of the Law: The Ironic Legacy of Title VI of the 1964 Civil Rights Act* (Baltimore: Johns Hopkins University Press, 1995), Ch. 3; on Johnson not signing the Guidelines: pp. 49–50. Kotlowski, "With All Deliberate Delay," 171–3.

[40] Kotlowski, "With All Deliberate Delay." Halpern, *On the Limits of the Law*, pp. 283–321.

[41] Annual Message to the Congress on the State of the Union, January 4, 1965, APP.

A secularized religious faith underpinned LBJ's egalitarianism. When he quoted the book of Isaiah in his remarks a the 1964 National Prayer Breakfast, he was in familiar territory. He never made an issue of his religious faith, as did so many later presidents, but he was in fact guided by religious principles. (He did make a grand display of his faith in private meetings with the Reverend Billy Graham, in what appears to have been an effort to manipulate a gullible Graham.) As had most southerners, he had attended church since he was a child and was conversant with the Bible. Faith shaped his politics, and he was the last great embodiment of the old Protestant Social Gospel, the belief that we are on this earth to serve humankind. Politics was not a shameful activity but a civic duty. President Jimmy Carter had a deeper religious faith, but he lacked Johnson's egalitarian vision. LBJ hated religious intolerance, and he despised the KKK as much for its religious bigotry as for its racism. Kennedy's 1960 speech to the Houston ministers on religious freedom had thrilled him, and he frequently told audiences that when American soldiers died in battle, "nobody wanted to know whether they were Catholic, Jewish or Muslim."[42]

Johnson invoked the Social Gospel when he lobbied for the 1964 Civil Rights Bill. On March 25, 1964, with the bill struggling in Congress, he invited a group of Southern Baptist leaders to the White House Rose Garden and gave them a lecture on their responsibilities as Christians. Acting like what the historian Taylor Branch characterized as a "brimstone preacher," he told them, "no group of Christians has a greater responsibility in civil rights than Southern Baptists," reminding them they were among the most respected and influential members of their communities. In three decades of public service he said he had seen "first-hand how basic spiritual beliefs and deeds can shatter barriers of politics and bigotry," adding, "I have seen those social barriers crumble in the presence of faith and hope."[43]

Johnson's faith also underpinned his commitment to the traditional Southern Baptist belief in separation of church and state. At the 1964 National Prayer Breakfast he forthrightly told them that "the separation of church and state has served our freedom well." In the midst of the 1965 debate over the federal aid to education bill, he wrote to a Texas Baptist minister, "By my office – and by personal conviction, "I am sworn to uphold [the] tradition" of separation of church and state. President Jimmy Carter, also a Southern Baptist, took the same position. (The Southern Baptists overthrew their long-standing position in the late 1970s, however, rejecting Carter, embracing Ronald Reagan, and supporting government-sponsored prayer in school.)[44]

American all: Immigrants, the elderly, and the mentally retarded

Reform of the nation's immigration laws was another of LBJ's legislative efforts. The notorious "national origins" quota system in the 1924 law, which favored Northern and

[42] Graham, OH, LBJPL. Valenti, OH, pp. 4–5, JFKPL.

[43] Remarks to Members of the Southern Baptist Christian Leadership Seminar, March 25, 1964, APP. Rev. Roy W. Fields, Pastor, Sterling Baptist Church, East St. Louis, MO to Billy Moyer [*sic*], December 9, 1963, Subject Files, Religious Matters, Box 2, LBJPL. Branch, *Pillar of Fire*, p. 266.

[44] Johnson to Dr. E. S. James, The Baptist Standard, Dallas, Texas, WHCF, Subject Files, Religious Matters, Box 2, LBJL. Remarks at the 12th Annual Presidential Prayer Breakfast, February 5, 1964, APP. Jimmy Carter, *Our Endangered Values* (New York: Simon & Schuster, 2005).

Western Europeans, he believed contradicted the ideals engraved on the Statue of Liberty. President Kennedy deserves credit for launching immigration law reform in 1961, and Johnson simply brought it to fruition. In a special message to Congress on January 13, 1965, he denounced the quota system as "incompatible with our basic American tradition" and quoted Walt Whitman on America as "A Nation of Nations." "We have no right to disparage the ancestors of millions of our fellow Americans in this way," he added. In the egalitarianism mood of the 1960s, the bill sailed through Congress by the huge margins of 326–69 in the House and 76–18 in the Senate. He signed the bill at the foot of the Statue of Liberty.[45]

Johnson's populist background also gave him strong empathy for the plight of the elderly, especially poor older Americans. In his 1967 State of the Union Address, he declared, "We must eliminate by law unjust discrimination in employment because of age." He quickly followed up with a special message to the Congress calling for "meaningful retirement for each senior citizen," an increase in social security benefits, and finally a federal law "prohibiting arbitrary and unjust discrimination in employment because of a person's age." Congress promptly passed the Age Discrimination in Employment Act. Signing the bill into law, Johnson could not resist pointing out that "this measure joins more than 50 other humane legislative proposals written into law during the first session of the 90th Congress."[46]

The mentally retarded were another historically excluded group, and in 1964 Johnson launched a program to hire mentally retarded people in the federal service that could serve as a national model. On March 26, 1965, he proudly explained that 361 people had been hired under the program, and only 21 (or 5.5 percent) had been separated from federal employment. President Kennedy deserves credit for initiating this effort, and Johnson for completing it. These new federal programs reflected broader currents of new thinking about the mentally retarded, and the beginnings of a disabilities rights movement.[47]

Finally, a fair housing law, 1968

The 1964 Civil Rights Act did not address housing discrimination, and the reasons are not hard to discern. Housing integration is a particularly sensitive social and political issue because it challenges all-white neighborhood schools, and for that reason it was historically a more explosive issue in the North than in the South. President Kennedy, after all, delayed for two years honoring his campaign pledge to sign a limited executive order ending discrimination in federally assisted housing. Housing discrimination, moreover, is a particularly elusive problem, as it is maintained through a set of covert practices by real estate agents and lending institutions.

Johnson was committed to ending housing discrimination and called for legislation in his 1966 State of the Union Address. A bitter fight erupted in Congress, and in 1966 the spokesperson for American real estate agents warned that the pending bill was a threat to

[45] Special Message to the Congress on Immigration, January 13, 1965, APP. John F. Kennedy, *A Nation of Immigrants* (New York: Harper & Row, 1964).

[46] Annual Message to the Congress on the State of the Union, January 10, 1967, APP. Special Message to the Congress Proposing Programs for Older Americans, January 23, 1967, APP. Statement by the President after Signing the Age Discrimination in Employment Act of 1967, December 16, 1967, APP.

[47] Statement by the President on Federal Employment of Mentally Retarded Persons, March 28, 1965, APP.

the traditional "right of property ownership." Fair housing bills died in Congress in 1966 and 1967. By then Johnson was losing support in Congress because of the Vietnam War and Republican gains in the 1966 elections. The assassination of Martin Luther King on April 4, 1968, however, transformed the issue politically, shaming a reluctant Congress into passing the Fair Housing Act on April 11, 1968, exactly one week after King's death. In a sad commentary on the times, federal troops guarded the Capital building because of the post-King assassination riots in the city.[48]

Lyndon Johnson's first job in 1928 was as a teacher and principal at an elementary school where the students were largely Mexican Americans, and, partly as a result, Johnson was sensitive to the problems of non-English-speaking Americans. The Bilingual Education Act of 1968 was the first federal law designed to help minority language speakers. It encouraged instruction in English and multicultural awareness and gave school districts the option of offering bilingual education programs without violating segregation laws. Despite his formative experience of teaching Mexican-American children, Johnson's efforts on behalf of Latino Americans were late and rather modest. In 1967 he announced, "The time has come to focus our efforts more intensely on the Mexican Americans of our nation." He ordered a Report on Social and Economic Conditions of Mexican Americans and in 1968 appointed the first Latino to the U.S. Civil Rights Commission. Later presidents would do more for Latino Americans, mainly because the Latino rights movement was only beginning to forming during Johnson's presidency.[49]

BLIND SPOT: LBJ AND WOMEN'S RIGHTS

Betty Friedan and her friends were so disgusted by the lack of action plans at the June 1966 National Conference of State Commissions on the Status of Women that they resolved to found a national feminist organization. Thus was born the National Organization for Women (NOW), which became the leading group in the reborn women's rights movement.

Certainly one of the factors fueling Friedan's anger at the conference was the June 28, 1966 speech in the East Room of the White House by President Lyndon Johnson. Although sex discrimination was forbidden by Title VII of the 1964 Civil Rights Act, LBJ had deliberately omitted women from his 1965 Executive Order 11246 on affirmative action. The Equal Employment Opportunity Commission, moreover, had decided that sex segregated want ads (e.g., "Help Wanted, Male") were not illegal. Johnson's speech cited some recent gains in women's rights, but his vision of the Great Society where Americans would have "the right to live their lives without discrimination.... the right to a decent job .... the right to a fair wage," among other rights, was couched in terms

[48] "Realtors' Lobby Calls for Fight on Open Housing," *NYT*, July 29, 1966. Annual Message to the Congress on the State of the Union, January 12, 1966, APP. "President Signs Civil Rights Bill; Pleas for Calm," *NYT*, April 12, 1968.

[49] Congressional Relations Service, *Bilingual Education: An Overview*, 98-501 (Washington, DC: CRS, Updated June 7, 2001). Johnson to Cabinet Members, June 9, 1967, McPherson Papers, Box 11. LBJPL. "Johnson Maps Aid for U.S. Mexicans," *NYT*, June 9, 1967. Report: Ben Wattenberg to McPherson et al., December 29, 1967, McPherson Papers, Box 11, LBJPL. Civil Rights Commission: Califano to Ramsey Clark, September 4, 1968, Califano Papers, Box 40, LBJPL. Julie Leininger Pycior, *LBJ and Mexican Americans: The Paradox of Power* (Austin: University of Texas Press, 1997).

that applied to all Americans, with no specific reference to problems facing women. (His State of the Union Addresses also contained references to every imaginable interest group except women.)[50] Johnson's speech on older Americans a few months later, by comparison, referred to the specific problems of "job discrimination, inadequate incomes, inadequate medical care" facing the elderly and offered concrete proposals to address each of them. With respect to appointing women to positions of responsibility, he complained, "My problem ... is in finding these women." An equivalent statement about not being able to find "qualified" African Americans would have provoked howls of protest. Friedan was also undoubtedly infuriated by his affectionate but paternalistic references to his wife, Lady Bird Johnson, including her interest in getting the grass to grow in the Rose Garden. [51]

Johnson's record on women's rights to that point was very poor. When the category of sex was added to Title VII on employment discrimination of the 1964 Civil Rights Act, LBJ maintained a discreet silence and had the Labor Department send Congress a letter opposing it. Racial equality was the urgent issue of the day, and he saw the Civil Rights Bill as the fulfillment of a lifelong commitment. He and many other liberals believed that the Virginia representative Howard Smith, a conservative segregationist, introduced the sex amendment to derail the entire bill. The brief House floor debate on sex discrimination, which fills but seven pages in the *Congressional Record* and was the only debate on the issue, was replete with jokes and dismissive remarks about women's rights. Emanuel Celler, chair of the House Judiciary Committee and an opponent of the amendment, asked several questions he evidently thought were far-fetched – about equality in child custody, alimony, and military service, for example – clearly unaware they involved real issues for women. After a relatively short debate, the House added sex discrimination to Title VII by a vote of 168–133. Revealingly, only one of the men voting for the sex amendment voted for the final civil Rights Bill, suggesting that their motives were cynical. Neither the Senate nor LBJ wanted any further trouble on the bill, and so there was no effort to rescind the addition of women. Thus was launched a revolution in the legal status of women.[52]

Johnson's 1965 Executive Order 11246 on affirmative action, however, blatantly omitted women. Most of the staff and board members of the new Equal Employment Opportunity Commission (EEOC) considered the addition of sex discrimination illegitimate because of Rep. Smith's motives. In one of its first actions, the EEOC approved separate male/female categories in employment advertisements. And in an act of judicial misconduct, the Supreme Court justice Abe Fortas, evidently doing an errand for his friend the president, reportedly passed word that the Court would strike down a ban

50 Remarks to Delegates to the Conference of State Commissions on the Status of Women, June 28, 1966, APP. Betty Friedan, *Life So Far* (New York: Simon & Schuster, 2000), pp. 172–5. There is some ambiguity regarding Johnson's actual remarks, involving conflict between the text cited here and the printed text in the Johnson Presidential Library. Statements File, Box 193, LBJPL.

51 Special Message to the Congress Proposing Programs for Older Americans, January 23, 1967, APP. Julia Kirk Blackwelder, "President Lyndon Johnson and the Gendered World of National Politics," in Mitchell B. Lerner, ed., *Looking Back at LBJ: White House Politics in a New Light* (Lawrence: University of Kansas Press, 2005), pp. 218–49. Janet M. Martin, *The Presidency and Women: Promise, Performance and Illusion* (College Station: Texas A&M University Press, 2003), pp. 87–122.

52 U.S. House of Representatives, *Congressional Record*, 88 Congress, 2nd Sess., V. 110, Part 2, January 8, 1964, pp. 2577–84. Cynthia Harrison, *On Account of Sex: The Politics of Women's Issues, 1945-1968* (Berkeley: University of California Press, 1988), pp. 176–81; one vote, p. 179.

on separate categories on grounds of freedom of the press. LBJ then threw more fuel on the fire in 1966 by not reappointing the EEOC commissioner Richard Graham, a white Republican who had supported women's issues. The EEOC's failure to take sex discrimination seriously was another factor behind the creation of NOW.[53]

Protests by NOW and others, including a blistering attack by Rep. Martha Grifiths (who would soon reintroduce the moribund ERA), finally forced Johnson to act on women's rights. In 1967, the year-old NOW sharply criticized the "failure of the administration to obtain true equality for women, and the lack of recent appointments of women." There were so few women in high places in the administration in 1966 that they were only two of the twelve top people on LBJ's Interdepartmental Committee on the Status of Women, and both were in subordinate positions. Under pressure, Johnson amended his 1965 executive order and in October 1967 issued Executive Order 11375 adding sex discrimination to affirmative action policy. A month later he signed a law ending barriers to promotion of women in the military. And as we shall see shortly, he had already become the most vigorous supporter of family planning services among all the presidents.[54]

Johnson passed up one high-profile opportunity to act on women's rights. For the annual Presidential Prayer Breakfast at the Mayflower Hotel, the president traditionally spoke first to men in the Presidential Ballroom and then to women gathered in the East Room. (In these years, it should be remembered, the National Press Club forced women reporters to sit in the balcony.) In his initial appearance in February 1964, Johnson evidently found this arrangement odd and commented that "when the prophet Isaiah said, Come, let us reason together, he did not have in mind that the men and women should assemble in separate rooms." As president, he could have ended the practice with just a word but did not. President Richard Nixon spoke to the first integrated breakfast in 1969.[55]

The glaring blind spot regarding women was the one exception in Johnson's vision of an egalitarian society. This failure is all the more striking because with the birth of the modern feminist movement the moment was there for him to seize. LBJ, however, simply had no feeling for women's rights. Although he overcame his southern background with regard to race, he was unable to do likewise with regard to gender. In a devastating portrait, his longtime aide George Reedy wrote that LBJ saw women as "bed mates, cooks, housekeepers, mothers, and secretaries," but not as equals in the worlds of public affairs.[56]

53 Executive Order 11246, Equal Employment Opportunity, September 24, 1965, APP. Harrison, *On Account of Sex*, pp. 187–96; Fortas, p. 188. David M. O'Brien does not mention Fortas in this episode: *Storm Center: The Supreme Court in American Politics*. 8th ed. (New York: W. W. Norton, 2008), "Off the Bench Activities," pp. 89–98.

54 NOW: Unsigned Memorandum to The President, January 29, 1967, Confidential Files, Box 57, LBJPL. Interdepartmental Committee: Confidential File, Box 57, LBJPL. Blackwelder, "President Lyndon Johnson and the Gendered World of National Politics," 225. Executive Order 11375 – Amending Executive Order No. 11246, Relating to Equal Employment Opportunity, October 13, 1967, APP. Remarks upon Signing Bill Providing Equal Opportunity in Promotions for Women in the Armed Forces, November 8, 1967, APP.

55 Remarks at the 12th Annual Presidential Prayer Breakfast, February 5, 1964, APP. Job Corps: O'Brien, OH, LBJPL, VIII, p. 49. Copy of speeches in Statements File, Box 6, LBJPL. On the National Press Club: Nan Robertson, *The Girls in the Balcony: Women, Men, and the New York Times* (New York: Random House, 1992), pp. 99–101.

56 Johnson and women: George Reedy, *Lyndon B. Johnson: A Memoir* (New York: Andrews and McMeel, 1982), pp. 31–8; quote on p. 32. Johnson briefly discussed the idea of appointing a woman to the Supreme Court in 1965 but then dismissed it as "gimmicky." Phone conversation, Johnson-Ramsey Clark, July 23, 1965, Recording 88381, WH6507.07; transcript at MCPA.

The family planning president

Lyndon Johnson risked a serious confrontation with the hierarchy of the Catholic Church. A prelate with the National Catholic Welfare Conference spotted a reference to international population control efforts in Johnson's 1965 State of the Union Address and publicly objected. LBJ "spoke so often and so forcefully about birth control," his aide Joseph Califano recalled, "the Catholic Bishops denounced him publicly." To "cool them off," LBJ dispatched Califano, a Catholic, to negotiate a deal. The bishops eventually agreed not to criticize him if he would avoid the term "birth control" and refer to the "population problem," which allowed for different policy alternatives. The church was further mollified by LBJ's antipoverty efforts which it supported. Johnson changed his rhetoric and continued pursuing family planning as federal policy.[57]

Forgotten today, Johnson's efforts on family planning are among the most important initiatives of his presidency. In his 1965 State of the Union Address, he promised to "help deal with the explosion in world population and the growing scarcity in world resources." Later that year he sponsored two White House conferences recommending federal support for birth control in domestic policies. The November White House Conference on Health urged the federal government to help provide birth control services – including both devices and information – to all Americans. In a time when many Americans regarded birth control as a subject not suitable for public discussion, the report was described as "the first public discussion of family planning every held under the auspices of the Federal Government." (President Kennedy's Commission on the Status of Women just two years earlier had not mentioned it.) Only three days before, the first federally assisted birth control program began, in a rural area in York, Pennsylvania, funded by the Office of Economic Opportunity, Johnson's War on Poverty agency. The White House Conference on International Cooperation recommended then $300 million in U.S. aid to family planning in foreign countries. At the end of the year, a *New York Times* reporter noted the dramatic change in U.S. policy. President Johnson, he noted, had "dared to mention the once politically taboo subject of birth control four times in public speeches."[58]

LBJ genuinely believed in family planning. He told Congress in March 1966, "It is essential that all families have access to information and services" giving them the freedom to plan "the number and spacing of their children within the dictates of individual conscience." His views might seem surprising, given his Southern Baptist background, and they were more characteristic of the eastern elite, which regarded overpopulation as a worldwide crisis that threatened economic development in poor countries. The cold war reinforced this view, as economic development was seen as crucial to undercutting the appeal of communism in the Third World. In his 1967 State of the Union Address, LBJ argued that countries with food shortages "must put more of their resources into voluntary family planning programs." In one international crisis, in fact, he refused to send emergency food aid to famine-stricken India, unless they agreed to adopt family planning programs. Notably absent from the debates over family planning was the bitter

[57] "Catholics Reaffirm Birth-Control Bans in Reply to Johnson," *NYT*, January 9, 1965. Califano, Jr., *The Triumph and Tragedy of Lyndon Johnson*, p. 52.

[58] Annual Message to the Congress on the State of the Union, January 4, 1965, APP. Califano to Harry McPherson, August 4, 1965, Confidential Files, Box 37, LBJPL. "Birth Control Now a Major Part of U.S. Aid," *NYT*, December 26, 1965.

religious polarization that characterized controversies over abortion and sexuality from the late 1970s onward. It is a curious aspect of Johnson's personality and political agenda that women's rights per se and family planning remained separate.[59]

Sex and censorship

A potentially explosive issue involving sexuality arose as the Supreme Court steadily striking down state and federal censorship laws. The growing flood of sexually explicit books and movies in the marketplace roused social conservatives to mobilize, and antipornography groups called for federal action. The Republican senator Karl Mundt of South Dakota pushed for a congressional investigation. Although he never spoke directly on the issue, Johnson was evidently opposed to censorship and mainly wanted to avoid the issue altogether. The result was a classic political maneuver: creating a presidential study commission whose work would delay action. Thus, Congress created the Presidential Commission on Obscenity and Pornography in 1967. Its 1970 report, which turned out to be quite libertarian, opposing censorship and advocating sex education, dropped into the lap of President Richard Nixon.[60]

FINESSING THE WALL OF SEPARATION

For the occasion, President Johnson invited his first teacher, Katherine Dietrich Loney ("Miss Kate," to him), to sit beside him while he signed into law the 1965 Elementary and Secondary Education Act. LBJ loved to give symbolic meaning to signing important new laws (he chose the Statue of Liberty for signing the 1965 immigration reform law), and for the federal education law he chose the abandoned schoolhouse a mile and a half from his Texas ranch where he had first attended school.[61]

The Education Act was a historic event, marking the first significant federal aid to public education in American history. It passed only because Johnson and his aides fashioned a compromise resolving the impasse over church and state that had blocked education bills since the 1940s. The advocates of aid to parochial schools, led by the National Catholic Welfare Conference, argued that denying them federal aid constituted religious discrimination. They had been effectively opposed by a coalition that included the ACLU, Americans United for Separation of Church and State, the American Jewish Congress, and southern Protestants. President Kennedy's commissioner of education Francis Keppel, education task force chair John W. Gardner, and Johnson HEW Secretary Wilber Cohen began fashioning an ingenious two-pronged rationale that finessed the church-state controversy. First, they proposed extending the existing practice of federal aid to local schools "impacted" by military bases to cover school districts impacted by poverty, as well. This idea dovetailed perfectly with Johnson's War on Poverty. Second, they proposed extending the "child benefit" theory to poor schoolchildren. In the pivotal

59 Special Message to the Congress on Domestic Health and Education, March 1st, 1966, APP. Califano, Jr., *Governing America*, p. 52. President's Committee on Population and Family Planning, *Population and Family Planning: The Transition from Concern to Action* (Washington, DC: Government Printing Office, November 1968).

60 Ducking the issue: Jim Gaither to Califano, April 24, 1967, Subject Files, Federal Government, Box 373, LBJPL.

61 Johnson, *The Vantage Point*, p. 212.

1947 *Emerson* decision articulating the wall of separation, the Supreme Court approved public funds for transporting students to and from nonpublic schools on the grounds that they benefited students and not the schools. Thus, federal aid could be premised on assistance to poor children. The compromise won Catholic support by allowing federal aid for federally-supported services, books and materials to students in religious schools, and satisfied some separationists by not permitting direct aid to the schools themselves.[62]

Johnson strongly opposed public funds for parochial schools. In his January 12, 1965, Message to Congress on Education, he skirted the church-state issue by making only the vaguest reference to nonpublic schools. Bombarded with mail from Southern Baptists protesting any compromise on aid to parochial schools, he reiterated his commitment to the separation of church and state. He liked the proposed compromise, incorporated it into his education bill, and put all of his prodigious legislative skills into getting it passed. Federal aid to education tapped into his belief that government programs could benefit ordinary people, and that education was the path to opportunity for all, especially the poor. He gave congressional leaders the extraordinary order that no amendments would be permitted and was certainly the only president who would make such an order stick. With huge Democratic majorities the bill bulldozed through Congress in an astonishing eighty-five days, and with no amendments. To ensure Catholic support, he had Keppel meet with the bishops and Jack Valenti talk with the U.S. representative from the Vatican. Another aide lobbied Jewish leaders, who were mostly separationists. The National Education Association (NEA) put aside its opposition to any help for parochial schools, while the National Catholic Welfare Conference abandoned its demand for general aid to Catholic schools. The ACLU and its allies lobbied hard against what they called the "Johnson compromise," but to no avail.[63] Thus, the law broke a two-decades-long impasse over federal aid to education. And in another example of his willingness to yield on a principle in order to get results, he allowed a small compromise on the separation of church and state while still barring any direct aid to parochial schools.

WIRETAPPING, THE FBI, AND CRIME

"I'm against wiretapping, period," Johnson exclaimed to his attorney general, Nicholas Katzenbach, on March 29, 1965. He was not posturing. LBJ genuinely hated wiretapping and other invasions of privacy. Ironically, his strong feelings on the matter are well documented by his secret White House tape recording system, in conversations the other people had no idea were being recorded.[64]

Johnson asked Katzenbach, rhetorically, "Nick, have I ever asked you or suggested to you that you tap a line?" Katzenbach replied, "No, Mr. President." A highly publicized

[62] Goldman, *The Tragedy of Lyndon Johnson*, pp. 350–65.

[63] Special Message to the Congress: "Toward Full Educational Opportunity," January 12, 1965, APP. Goldman, *The Tragedy of Lyndon Johnson*, pp. 352–64. "Issue of Church Is Skirted in President's School Plan," *NYT*, January 2, 1965. Johnson's version: Johnson, *The Vantage Point*, pp. 209–12. The LBJ Papers contain many strongly worded letters from southerners insisting on separation of church and state: Subject Files, Religious Matters, Box 2, LBJP. "School Aid Funds Fought by ACLU," *NYT*, February 3, 1965. "Jewish Unit Maps Suit on School Aid," ibid., April 12, 1965. ACLU, *46th Annual Report*, July 1, 1965 to January 1, 1967 (New York: ACLU, 1967), pp. 47–52.

[64] Johnson-Katzenbach telephone conversation: Beschloss, *Reaching for Glory*, pp. 252–3.

investigation by the Missouri senator Edward V. Long had exposed extensive snooping by the Internal Revenue Service, and LBJ declared, "Well, I want them brought to an irreducible *minimum*. And only in the gravest cases ... and then by God, I want to know about them." With characteristic emotion, he declared, "I'm against wiretapping, period." He directed Katzenbach "to get you up the strongest letter you can to the [the heads of all federal agencies], and say that none of them [is] to be tapped, except by signature of the Attorney General." Then, in a hyperbolic outburst, he proclaimed, "I'm a red-hot one-million-two percent civil liberties man, and I'm just *against* them."[65]

The day before, Johnson directed his friend Abe Fortas to tell the IRS, "I want anybody fired that even proposes a wiretap." He then sent the IRS commissioner, Sheldon Cohen, a blistering note: "Sheldon, Stop it all at once, and this is final - no microphones, taps or any other hidden devices, legal or illegal if you are going to work for me. - L." Johnson certainly must have long known that government wiretapping was widespread, but he had never before publicly protested. (The Supreme Court justice William O. Douglas claimed in 1973 that LBJ had once said he thought "even his phone was tapped.") Also reflecting his concern for privacy, LBJ in early 1967 signed a memo banning the use of polygraphs for federal employees, except in three very limited situations.[66] LBJ was nothing if not contradictory, on wiretapping as on other issues. As we shall see, he had been aware of FBI wiretaps on Reverend Martin Luther King in 1964, ordered FBI spying on civil rights activists at the 1964 Democratic Party convention, and in 1967 ordered the CIA to spy on Americans.

Although Katzenbach personally believed that properly controlled wiretapping was both necessary and proper for effective law enforcement, he faithfully carried out his boss's order and "got up" the memo. Issued on June 30, 1965, it embodied LBJ's strong opposition to "the interception of telephone conversations as a general investigative technique," and ordered no wiretapping without the approval of the attorney general. And in an obvious message to the FBI and the IRS, it ordered that all federal agencies "immediately conform" to the policy.[67]

Johnson's feelings about privacy were undoubtedly heightened by the tragedy of his chief White House aide, Walter Jenkins. In October 1964, just weeks before the presidential election, Washington, D.C., police caught Jenkins in a homosexual encounter in the YMCA just blocks from the White House. He paid a fine and was quietly released, but within a week the police leaked the story to the press. A stunned LBJ had absolutely no idea about this hidden side of Jenkins's life. He briefly thought it was a Republican plot to embarrass him and cynically discussed tying Jenkins to the GOP candidate Barry Goldwater through a connection in their National Guard service. The destruction of a

65 Ibid. Edward V. Long, *The Intruders: The Invasion of Privacy by Government and Industry* (New York: Praeger, 1967).

66 Beschloss, *Reaching for Glory*, p. 374. Jeff, Shesol, *Mutual Contempt: Lyndon Johnson, Robert Kennedy, and the Feud That Defined a Decade* (New York: W. W. Norton, 1997), p. 353. Douglas, Dissent in *Heutsche v. U.S.*, 414 U.S. 898 (1973). There is some dispute as to whether the polygraph ban became official policy. In early 2009, based on an Office of Legal Counsel memo, the George W. Bush administration held that it was inoperative. Office of Legal Counsel, Memorandum Opinion for the General Counsel Justice Department Management Division, January 14, 2009. www.justice.gov/opinions.

67 Johnson, Memo, To Heads of All Executive Departments and Agencies, June 30, 1965, WHCF, Box 4, LBJPL; available in Athan G. Theoharis, *From the Secret Files of J. Edgar Hoover* (Chicago: Ivan Dee, 1991), pp. 146–7. Memorandum to the Heads of Executive Departments and Agencies, Re: Wiretapping and Electronic Eavesdropping, June 16, 1967, Ramsey Clark Papers, Box 139, LBJPL. Katzenbach, OH, Part I, p. 37, LBJPL.

public figure through exposure of his private life, in short, was a tragedy Johnson experienced firsthand.[68]

The 1965 memo was just the start of LBJ's campaign against snooping. Two years later, he directed his new attorney general, Ramsey Clark, to extend the 1965 guidelines and prohibit bugging (termed "Non-telephone Conversations"), emphasizing that eavesdropping "accomplished by means of a trespass into a constitutionally protected area is a violation of the Fourth Amendment." Clark's memo, however, specifically exempted national security investigations and asserted that such cases had to be "taken up directly with the Attorney General."[69]

Lyndon Johnson's 1965 and 1967 directives represented the tightest controls over wiretapping ever issued by a president, and they posed a challenge to the FBI director J. Edgar Hoover. For the moment, he decided to lie low and comply with the new policy. "[R]eading the writing on the wall," as the Senate Church Committee later put it, he halted the bureau's most intrusive actions. The number of "surreptitious entries" to place electronic surveillance equipment dropped to zero in 1966, down from 102 in 1962 and 33 in 1965, and remained there for the next two years. (There is some dispute, however, over whether the FBI's accounting of these activities is fully accurate and whether Hoover fudged the labeling and reporting as he had in earlier instances.) Hoover understood better than many others in Washington that public attitudes about privacy and wiretapping were changing rapidly. Senator Edward V. Long's hearings on snooping by the IRS, other government agencies, and private investigators were an alarm bell. He argued there was an "undeclared war on privacy," and *Life* magazine published a cover story on his exposés in May 1966 with the provocative title "The Big Snoop." Few Americans had ever worried about the FBI spying on communists, and most would have approved, but everyone feared the IRS. The Senate Church Committee in the mid-1970s found that the IRS ended its investigations of political groups by the Special Services Staff, which had begun under President Kenndy in 1961, in 1967, but that it resumed in 1969 under President Richard Nixon. The FBI's vendetta against Martin Luther King, which involved both wiretaps and bugs, meanwhile, burst into the headlines in 1966, further arousing public opinion.[70]

In early 1967, Johnson decided it was time to outlaw wiretapping. In his State of the Union Address he declared, "We should protect what Justice Brandeis called the 'right most valued by civilized men,' – the right to privacy," and a federal law to ban "all wiretapping – public and private," except in national security cases, "and only then with the strictest governmental safeguards." His comments reportedly received "hearty

[68] Al Weisel, "LBJ's Gay Sex Scandal," *Out*, December 1999, pp. 76–131. http://home.nyc.rr.com/alweisel/outwalterjenkins.htm. FBI perspective on the Jenkins affair: Cartha "Deke" DeLoach, Oral History, LBJPL, pp. 23–8; Cartha "Deke" DeLoach, *Hoover's FBI: The Inside Story by Hoover's Trusted Lieutenant* (Washington, DC: Regnery, 1995), p. 385. Johnson's conspiracy theories: Johnson to Fortas, Telephone conversation, October 15, 1964; Johnson to Katzenbach, Telephone Conversation, October 15, 1964, LBJPL.

[69] Ramsey Clark, Attorney General, Memorandum to Heads of Executive Departments and Agencies, June 16, 1967, Clark Papers, Box 139, LBJPL.

[70] Memorandum, Mr. Cleveland to R. J. McCarthy, re Surreptitious Entries, October 9, 1975, FBI ERR. "Hoover Asserts Robert Kennedy Aided Buggings," *NYT*, December 11, 1966. Washington: "The Kennedy-Hoover Controversy," ibid., December 14, 1966. Long, *The Intruders*, p. 3. "The Big Snoop," *Life Magazine*, May 20, 1966. Hoover's reaction: Church Committee, Book III, *Supplementary Detailed Staff Reports on Intelligence Activities and the Rights of Americans*, pp. 365–6, 930–1. Hoover's retreat alarmed hard-liners in the bureau; in 1970 he refused to approve the Nixon administration's Huston Plan, which led the White House to create the "Plumbers" unit. See Chapter 9 of this book. Shesol, *Mutual Contempt*, pp. 349–50. IRS: Church Committee, Volume 3, *Internal Revenue Service*, p. 105.

applause" from members of Congress, with the notable exception of Senator Bobby Kennedy, who saw a sly political attack on his having authorized the King wiretaps, and he sat silently with his arms folded.[71]

Attorney General Ramsey Clark testified before Congress, "Public safety will not be found in wiretapping. Security is to be found in excellence in law enforcement, in courts, and corrections." Congress balked at the bill, however. By 1967 the Vietnam War had eroded LBJ's support, and three summers of urban riots had aroused public fears of lawlessness. Just weeks after his speech, moreover, Johnson's own Crime Commission recommended a federal law allowing wiretapping with some administrative controls. (The commission was deeply split on the issue, with a minority opposing the recommendation.) Finally, in 1968 Congress passed the first federal law authorizing wiretapping. In response to riots, antiwar protests, and rising crime rates, Congress had no interest in protecting the rights of criminal suspects.[72]

Two aspects of the wiretap law deserve comment. First, it contained a specific exemption for presidential power in the area of national security. Nothing, it stated, shall "limit the constitutional power of the President" to act with regard to threats to overthrow the government or other dangers to the "existence of the government." The exact scope of the constitutional power of the president in these matters remained unresolved and would embroil subsequent presidents. LBJ himself believed there was a national security exception to the new Freedom of Information Act. Second, Johnson issued a signing statement declaring the wiretap provision "an unwise and dangerous step" and asking Congress to repeal it. Few people thought much about presidential signing statements in those years, but they became a major controversy a quarter of a century later under President George W. Bush. LBJ's 1968 statement, however, was not a promise not to enforce a law, but a legitimate expression of his views and a call for Congress to reexamine the new law.[73]

LBJ'S DARK SIDE: ABUSE OF THE FBI AND THE CIA

President Johnson summoned the CIA director Richard Helms to the White House in August 1967 and told him he wanted the CIA to investigate the influence of foreign governments on radical antiwar and racial protest in the United States. Helms carefully advised him that intelligence gathering within the country would be an illegal violation of the CIA's charter. LBJ immediately replied, "I am quite aware of that. What I want is for you to pursue this matter, and do what is necessary to track down the foreign communists who are behind this intolerable interference in our domestic affairs."[74] Despite his strong

[71] Annual Message to the Congress on the State of the Union, January 10, 1967, APP. "Crime Control Bill Urged on Congress," *NYT*, January 11, 1967. RFK reaction: Shesol, *Mutual Contempt*, p. 353.

[72] Clark, testimony: Senate, Committee on the Judiciary, Subcommittee on Administrative Practice and Procedure, *Right of Privacy Act of 1967*, Hearings, March 20, 1967, p. 376. President's Commission on Law Enforcement and Administration of Justice, *The Challenge of Crime in a Free Society* (Washington, DC: Government Printing Office, 1967), p. 203. Samuel Walker, *Popular Justice: A History of American Criminal Justice*. 2nd ed. (New York: Oxford University Press, 1998), pp. 202–5. Edith J. Lapidus, *Eavesdropping on Trial* (Rochelle Park, NJ: Hayden Book Co., 1974). Administration opposition: Clark to Califano, February 5, 1968; Clark to the President, May 2, 1968, Subject Files, Legislation, Box 80, LBJPL.

[73] Statement by the President upon Signing the Omnibus Crime Control and Safe Streets Act of 1968, June 19, 1968, APP. Background: Califano to the President, June 19, 1968, Subject Files, Legislation, Box 80, LBJPL.

[74] Richard Helms, *A Look over My Shoulder: A Life in the Central Intelligence Agency* (New York: Random House, 2003), pp. 279–80. Commission on CIA Activities [Rockefeller Commission], *Report to the President by the Commission on CIA Activities within the United States* (Washington, June 1975), pp. 130–3.

feelings about snooping, Johnson ordered illegal spying by the CIA. He had, in fact, previously ordered the FBI to spy on civil rights activists.

LBJ's abuse of the intelligence agencies began in summer 1964 when civil rights forces challenged the all-white prosegregation Mississippi delegation to the Democratic Party convention. The Mississippi controversy threatened to disrupt his plans for a grand, celebratory renomination. Walter Jenkins called the FBI's Deke DeLoach to express his concern about the president's safety and to ensure "that there aren't any disruptions at the convention." Possible threats to the president would be legitimate FBI business, but protests related to a political issue were not. Hoover brooded over the request, according to DeLoach, but finally said, "Tell Walter we'll give him whatever help he wants." The FBI then created a "special squad" for the job and kept the White House "fully apprised of all major developments." Hoover carefully covered himself on the spying, and one FBI memo pointedly noted that the information was developed "at the direction of the President." Bureau agents wiretapped the offices of the Student Nonviolent Coordinating Committee and the Congress of Racial Equality and, more significantly, Martin Luther King (in his case with taps that had previously been approved by the Kennedy administration). Informants infiltrated the groups, and one even became a confidant of some top leaders. Agents also used "appropriate cover as reporters," and one obtained valuable information about strategy in off-the-record interviews. In the absence of any suspected criminal activity or threat to national security or the president's safety, the operation was entirely an improper use of the FBI for political purposes. In all the race-related crises of 1964 – the murders in Mississippi, the Democratic Party convention, the urban riots – Johnson believed that communists were probably involved, a view that Hoover only encouraged. In short, the Kennedys were not the only ones to spy on Martin Luther King, and Richard Nixon not the only president to spy on political opponents.[75]

LBJ's public antiwiretapping posture was also hypocritical because he enthusiastically received sordid gossip from FBI files about the private lives of members of Congress and other prominent figures. Hoover sent an FBI agent to the White House to show files to LBJ aide Marvin Watson, who then passed the information on to LBJ. Johnson certainly understood how the FBI got this information but never objected. Memos and at least one recorded White House phone conversation clearly indicate that LBJ and his attorney general knew about the FBI's allegations of Martin Luther King's extramarital sexual activities. At the same time, however, he was disgusted by damaging stories about the secret gay lifestyle of the powerful political columnist Joseph Alsop. When Alsop complained to him, LBJ told Katzenbach, "I resent this so deeply." Harry McPherson summed up the contradictions, recalling that Johnson "despised the existence of the reports and yet like all of us, was impressed by what they revealed."[76]

[75] Memo, C. DeLoach to Walter Jenkins, August 25, 1964; Memo, C. D. DeLoach to Mr. Moore, August 29, 1964. U.S. Senate. Select Committee to Study Governmental Operations with Respect to Intelligence Activities of the United States Senate, Hearings. V. 6. Federal Bureau of Investigation, 94th Cong. 1st Sess. pp. 495–6, 714–17. DeLoach, *Hoover's FBI,* pp. 3–9. DeLoach's memoir is unreliable on several crucial points as he attempts to exonerate Hoover and place all the blame on William C. Sullivan. LBJ and communists: Bechloss, *Taking Charge,* pp. 461–2, 466–7.

[76] Beschloss, *Reaching for Glory,* pp. 252–4. Watson as the handler of FBI files: W. Marvin Watson and Sherwin Markman, *Chief of Staff: Lyndon Johnson and His Presidency* (New York: St. Martin's, 2004), p. 214. Johnson's knowledge of the FBI files on King: McPherson, OH, Part V., Tape 1, pp. 13–14, LBJPL. Hoover to Attorney General, February 20, 1968, Clark Papers, Box 67, LBJPL ("Attached is a communication setting forth information concerning an illicit love affair being carried on by Martin Luther King, Jr. . . .").

In summer 1964 after the murder of three civil rights workers, Johnson ordered the FBI to open its first field office in Mississippi. This was a virtually unprecedented act of presidential direction of the bureau. He also ordered the FBI to attack the Ku Klux Klan. "Attacking" the KKK meant different things to different people, however. Attorney General Ramsey Clark advised Congress that a proposed anti-Klan law "must at all times consider the aspects of free speech and assembly ... no matter how abhorrent the pronouncements."[77] The FBI on July 30 added the KKK to its notorious COINTELPRO program, with a plan to "expose, disrupt, and otherwise neutralize" white hate groups. The anti-Klan effort included "black-bag" jobs, the FBI term for illegal entries to place microphones or steal materials. "Neutralize," of course, was what the bureau explicitly set out to do to Martin Luther King. Although he probably did not know the details about COINTELPRO tactics, Assistant Attorney General Burke Marshall sent LBJ a memo telling him that the program had been "spectacularly efficient" against the Communist Party and should be applied to the Klan. The FBI was undoubtedly happy to have the president's approval for this initiative since it would justify earlier actions against the Communist Party. For his part, Johnson wanted results and did not inquire into the details of FBI tactics. Deke DeLoach, a top official at the FBI, later explained that "no one ever complained that COINTELPRO had violated the civil rights of klansmen."[78] He had a point. The public and politicians became outraged about FBI abuses only when the Watergate scandal alerted them to those directed at "respectable" Americans rather than communists or the Klan.

As urban riots continued through summer 1967, Johnson enlisted the military to preserve order. Federal troops were dispatched to control the 1967 riot in Detroit (National Guard troops were sent to the Newark riot that summer). To prepare for such contingencies, the Pentagon launched an intelligence gathering program that eventually expanded into a secret spying effort that violated the First Amendment rights of antiwar protesters, not unlike the FBI's program. The extent to which President Johnson ordered or was fully aware of the scope of the spying is not clear.[79]

The first cracks in the CIA's wall of secrecy

The rising opposition to the Vietnam War led to revelations that penetrated the secrecy surrounding the CIA. In March 1967 *Ramparts* magazine, which had emerged as the leading radical publication in the country, published a sensational exposé of secret CIA funding of the National Student Association. This and subsequent revelations provoked outrage and embarrassment among organizations, magazines, and journalists who were eventually identified as having received funds. The Senate majority leader Mike Mansfield, who had proposed congressional oversight of the CIA in 1956, demanded an

77 Clark to Sidney Moskow, October 14, 1965, Clark Papers, Box 67. LBJPL. Justice Department discussions of anti-Klan legislation: James T. Devine to Yeagley et al., April 21, 1965, Clark Papers, Box 67, LBJPL.

78 Senate, Select Committee to Study Governmental Operations With Respect to Intelligence Activities, *Supplementary Detailed Staff Reports on Intelligence Activities and the Rights of Americans*, Book III, pp. 12–13; in particular, FBI Memoranda of July 30, 1964, September 2, 1964; Marshall memo: p. 470. DeLoach, *Hoover's FBI*, p. 293. DeLoach, however, unconvincingly claims that the Bureau's COINTELPRO program was entirely run by William C. Sullivan, without the knowledge or approval of him or J. Edgar Hoover. FBI investigation of the KKK: Ku Klux Klan, FBI ERR. DeLoach, *Hoover's FBI*, p. 293.

79 Christopher H. Pyle, *Military Surveillance of Civilian Politics, 1967–1970* (New York: Garland, 1986).

investigation into "the full extent of this practice." In fact, the CIA had learned about the forthcoming *Ramparts* story in 1966, and Deputy Director Richard Helms ordered an investigation of the magazine and sent reports to the White House, suggesting that LBJ knew about the CIA's domestic snooping before the *Ramparts* story.[80]

LBJ denounced secret CIA funding of American groups but also did not want a congressional investigation of the CIA, undoubtedly worried about possible embarrassing revelations. Instead, he appointed Nicholas Katzenbach, by then under secretary of state, to chair a committee to explore the idea of a new public-private agency that could publicly fund programs advancing America's interests around the world. A month later the committee recommended that "No federal agency shall provide any covert financial assistance or support, direct or indirect, to any of the nation's private voluntary organizations" [underlining in original]. LBJ's aide George Reedy told the president that "the real mischief" of covert CIA funding of Americans was that "it casts doubt on America's proud boast of a free and open society."[81]

With antiwar protests steadily growing in numbers and vehemence by 1967, Johnson was convinced they were directed and supported by foreign governments. Other administration officials encouraged this conspiratorial view. Secretary of the Cabinet Robert E. Kintner suggested in May 1967 that Attorney General Clark develop a report showing "there was a common planning throughout the United States of public demonstrations, riots in colleges, and similar types of activities." He pointedly added, "The President is interested in this." Ben Bradlee of the *Washington Post* told the White House that the paper was working on a similar story and suggested they coordinate their efforts. The antiwar protests, and particularly the personal attacks on him ("Hey, Hey, LBJ, How Many Kids Did You Kill Today?"), pushed LBJ over the line, and he replied with a curt note, "I agree with this – get on that last part of it.[82]

And so in August 1967, Johnson summoned the CIA's Richard Helms to the White House and ordered him to "do what is necessary to track down the foreign communists" behind the antiwar protests. Helms was not surprised by Johnson's order. He later testified that LBJ "was after this all the time" by 1967, and it "came up almost daily and weekly." The CIA deputy counterintelligence officer Richard Ober had already begun keeping files on domestic dissidents, and LBJ's order launched what eventually became Operation

80 "A Short Account of International Student Politics and the Cold War with Particular Reference to the NSA, CIA, etc.," *Ramparts*, March 1967, pp. 29–38. Mansfield to The President, February 22, 1967, National Security File, Agency File, Box 10, LBJPL. Johnson is often quoted as saying the CIA was running a "murder incorporated" in Latin America. The quote, however, comes from an interview published in 1971 and may reflect what LBJ knew later rather than at the time of the anti-Castro assassination plots: Leo Janos, "The Last Days of the President: LBJ in Retirement," *Atlantic Monthly 232* (July 1973): 35–41. The CIA disclosed its secret activities to a number of White House officials over the years. Richard Goodwin recalled that in his first weeks as a member of the Kennedy administration, the CIA informed him about "some of our activities," and also the "seductive power" of being an insider: Goodwin, *Remembering America*, pp. 169–70).

81 Report: National Security File, Subject File, Box 44, LBJPL. Reedy to the President, February 20, 1967, Clark Papers, Box 20 (Part 2), LBJPL. Statement by the President Concerning the Report on the Relationship Between the CIA and Private Voluntary Organizations, March 29, 1967, APP. CIA use of academic and private organizations: Church Committee, *Book I: Foreign and Military Intelligence*, pp. 181–2. CIA investigation of Ramparts: Church Committee, *Book III, Supplementary Detailed Staff Reports on Intelligence Activities and the Rights of Americans*, p. 690. Frances Stonor Saunders, *The Cultural Cold War: The CIA and the World of Arts and Letters* (New York: New Press, 1999), p. 381.

82 Kintner to Mr. President, May 18, 1967; LBJ note, May 18, 1967, 6.25 p.m.; Kintner to Attorney General, "Secret," May 19, 1967, Confidential File, Box 57, LBJPL.

CHAOS, a massive illegal domestic spying operation that compiled files on about ten thousand Americans. Exposure of the program by the *New York Times* in December 1974 triggered sensational congressional investigations of abuses by the CIA, FBI, and National Security Agency and led to new laws to control the intelligence agencies. Although Nixon received the blame for CHAOS, Lyndon Johnson had initiated it. The 1975 Rockefeller Commission report on CIA abuses found that CHAOS was prompted by "continuing and insistent requests of the CIA" from both Presidents Johnson and Nixon.[83]

Richard Helms personally delivered the CIA's report on, International Connections of US Peace Groups, to LBJ in the White House on November 15, 1967. In a covering note, he prudently protected himself and the agency by noting "this is the study... you requested." The report found no evidence of foreign influence in the antiwar movement, which it described as a homegrown protest. Johnson flatly rejected this conclusion and ordered a new report. That report, "Demonstration Techniques," reached the same conclusions, and Johnson rejected it as well on December 22. A third report, "Student Dissent and Its Techniques in the United States," arrived on January 5, 1968, and met the same fate. By this point, Johnson was so bitter over the attacks on the war and on him that he refused to believe anything contradicting his views. Years later, his chief of staff, Marvin Watson, still clung to the White House belief that "both the Soviets and the Chinese distributed cash to some leaders of the antiwar protesters," with the Chinese allegedly never using anything larger that twenty-dollar bills.[84]

Oddly enough, Director Helms of the CIA offers the best explanation for Johnson's order to spy on Americans. LBJ loved America so much, he argues in his memoirs, and believed so deeply that America was a land of opportunity for all that he "simply could not believe that American youth would on their own be moved to riot in protest against U.S. foreign policy." "We can't imagine that good Americans do things like this," he and Vice President Hubert Humphrey both complained. Johnson later told his biographer Doris Kearns, "I just don't understand those young people. Don't they realize I'm really one of them?" He truly believed that, but a new generation, horrified by the Vietnam War with its napalm and relentless bombing, felt otherwise. Although his abuses of presidential power were far less systematic than President Nixon's and never involved any obstruction of justice, when confronted with militant protests against his Vietnam War policies, he responded with a similar paranoid view that sinister forces were behind them and authorized spying on protesters.[85]

Johnson also manipulated the press when he felt it politically necessary. Immediately after Walter Jenkins's arrest in October 1964, he dispatched the formidable team of Abe Fortas and Clark Clifford to the *Washington Post* and other news media to ask them not

83 DeLoach to Tolson, July 10, 1967, in Theoharis, *From the Secret Files of J. Edgar Hoover*, pp. 121–2. DeLoach, OH, p. 54, LBJPL. "Huge CIA Operation in U.S. Against Antiwar Forces, Other Dissidents during Nixon Years," *NYT*, December 22, 1974. Helms, *A Look over My Shoulder*, p. 280. CIA domestic spying: Church Committee, Book III, *Supplementary Detailed Staff Reports on Intelligence Activities and the Rights of Americans*, pp. 679–732; LBJ's 1967 order, p. 689.

84 CIA, International Connections of US Peace Groups, November 15, 1967, available, along with other related documents, on the CIA FOIA ERR: www.foia.cia.gov/. Report to the President by the Commission on CIA Activities within the United States (Washington, DC, June 1975), p. 133. Available at: www.history-matters.com. Watson and Markman, *Chief of Staff: Lyndon Johnson and His Presidency*, p. 210.

85 Helms, *A Look over My Shoulder*, p. 279. Helms, Jack Smith Interview, June 22, 1983, p. 3. CIA, FOIA Documents, Richard Helms Collection, at www.foia.cia.gov. Kearns: Goodwin, *Remembering America*, p. 425.

to report the story. Then he pressured the FBI to add a sentence to its report that muddied the question of whether Jenkins had any previous arrests the White House should have known about. Johnson also discussed trying to embarrass his presidential opponent Barry Goldwater, on the very flimsy point that Jenkins had served in Goldwater's Air Force Reserve unit. Cooler heads prevailed, however, and the idea was dropped.[86] Johnson could be extremely vindictive toward media critics of the Vietnam War. When the venerable columnist Walter Lippmann became one of the earliest critics, LBJ unleashed a full-bore attack on him. White House staffers were directed to scour Lippmann's half-century of writings for items that might now appear embarrassing. Some labeled the effort the "Lippmann Project." He also attacked the columnist in private and occasionally in public. President Nixon was later notorious for his "enemies list" of prominent individuals to be attacked. LBJ's list was far shorter, but his attacks no less vindictive.[87]

Challenging government secrecy: The Freedom of Information Act

Perhaps to make a political statement, Lyndon Johnson signed the historic Freedom of Information Act (FOIA) into law on the Fourth of July 1966. The truth of the matter is a bit more complicated, as he signed it reluctantly, at the last minute, and with deep reservations.

FOIA marked the culmination of a long campaign against government secrecy begun in the 1950s by the California congressmen John Moss. Johnson worried about a broad freedom of information law, however, believing that the release of some information could harm national security. All post–World War II presidents shared this view, differing only over the proper degree of openness. LBJ undoubtedly knew that he might be embarrassed by certain documents, for example those related to his misrepresentation of the events surrounding the 1964 Gulf of Tonkin Resolution.[88]

The freedom of information bill Moss drafted was cosponsored by a young Illinois congressman named Donald Rumsfeld, who earnestly declared that it would "secure a very important right for the people of this country." A week after Johnson signed the bill, Rumsfeld wrote to him to express his "sincere appreciation" for doing so. As he rose in power and influence over the years, however, Rumsfeld changed his views about FOIA completely. In 1974, as a top adviser to President Ford, he led the fight against amendments expanding FOIA, and as secretary of defense under President George W. Bush, he was a member of one of the most secretive administrations in American history[89]

Johnson could have easily killed the FOIA bill with a simple phone call to Congressman William Dawson of Chicago, chair of the Government Operations Committee, asking him

86 "Johnson Friends Called on Press," *NYT*, October 16, 1964. Weisel, "LBJ's Sex Scandal." Clark Clifford, OH, Part II, pp. 8–9, LBJPL. DeLoach, OH, p. 26, LBJPL. Goldwater angle: RFK in Guthman and Shulman, eds., *Robert F. Kennedy in His Own Words*, p. 131.

87 "Lippmann Project": Peter Beinart, *The Icarus Syndrome: A History of American Hubris* (New York: Harper, 2010), p. 170. Ronald Steel, *Walter Lippmann and the American Century*, Boston: Little, Brown, 1980), pp. 578–80.

88 Neil Sheehan, et al., *The Pentagon Papers* (New York: Bantam Books, 1971), pp. 234–306. The complete *Pentagon Papers* was released by the National Archives in 2011 and is available on its Web site.

89 Rumsfeld, remarks, *Congressional Record*, V. 112, p. 13007 (June 20, 1966). Rumsfeld to Johnson, July 11, 1966. WHCF, Subject Files, Federal Government, LBJPL; copy online at www.gwu.edu/~nsaarchiv.html.

to bottle it up in committee. He had certainly done that innumerable times in the Senate, and he could have thrown Dawson some patronage to ensure the deal. To his credit, he did not make that call. In signing the bill, his comments were decidedly balanced. The new law, he declared, "springs from one of our most essential principles," that "a democracy works best when the people have all the information" they need. Nonetheless, he cautioned, "the welfare of the Nation or the rights of individuals may require that some documents not be made available." Thus, he accepted a national security exception to freedom of information. Among some FOIA advocates the legend is that he kept the FOIA bill signing secret, making no official announcement. This is not true. He issued a formal statement on July 4, and it was duly reported in the press.[90]

The FOIA became one of the greatest pieces of civil liberties legislation ever passed. Over nearly a half-century it made public a flood of revelations about government misconduct, bringing to light FBI spying, CIA misdeeds, and literally tens of thousands of pages of documents on President George W. Bush's abuse of presidential power in the war on terrorism. With respect to secrecy and presidential power, Johnson made no public assertions of executive privilege as had President Eisenhower (and would President Nixon after him) and followed President Kennedy's course of never issuing a formal statement of administration policy on it while also never renouncing the idea that presidents had a broad power to withhold documents from Congress concept.[91]

THE END OF THE LIBERAL MOMENT: RIOTS AND THE WAR ON CRIME

The celebration of the 1964 Civil Rights Act was barely over before urban riots cast an ominous storm cloud over American race relations. Exactly two weeks after Johnson signed the law, a racial disturbance erupted in Harlem, the historic heart of the African-American community in New York City. The shooting of an African American by an off-duty white police officer sparked violent disturbances the night of July 18 and further disturbances on two other nights. Similar violence followed in Rochester, New York, and in several New Jersey cities and Philadelphia. American society had been warned of a potential explosion of anger in the big city ghettos, notably at the acrimonious confrontation between Attorney General Robert Kennedy and African-American leaders in May 1963 and in the author James Baldwin's best-selling book that year, *The Fire Next Time*. From summer 1964 through April 1968, it would be the fire this time.[92]

Civil rights leaders feared a backlash against the riots that would hurt President Johnson's reelection chances in November. The GOP candidate Barry Goldwater had opposed the Civil Rights Act, and they worried that recent and future gains might be

[90] Sam Archibald, "The Early Years of the Freedom of Information Act, 1955 to 1974," *PS: Political Science and Politics* 26 (December 1993): 726–31. Herbert N. Foerstel, *Freedom of Information and the Right to Know: The Origins and Applications of the Freedom of Information Act* (Westport, CT: Greenwood Press, 1999); the legend of no publicity about signing the bill is on p. 42. Statement by the President upon Signing the "Freedom of Information Act," July 4, 1966, APP. "Johnson Supports Greater Access to U.S. Data," *NYT*, July 5, 1966. National Security Archive, *Freedom of Information at 40* (July 4, 2006).

[91] "Reaffirm the principle:" Rep. John E. Moss to Johnson, March 31, 1965, www.johnemossfoundation.org/foi/to_lbj.htm. Mark Rozell, *Executive Privilege: Presidential Power, Secrecy, and Accountability*. 3rd ed. (Lawrence: University Press of Kansas, 2010), pp. 42–3.

[92] "Thousands Riot in Harlem Area; Scores Are Hurt," *NYT*, July 19, 1964. National Advisory Commission on Civil Disorders, *Report* (New York: Bantam Books, 1968). James Baldwin, *The Fire Next Time* (New York: Dial Press, 1963).

threatened. Johnson understood this as well and quietly asked them to help prevent further violence. On very short notice they convened a "summit meeting" at NAACP headquarters on July 29. Moderates, led by the NAACP's Roy Wilkins and the Urban League's Whitney Young, wanted a moratorium on demonstrations. SNCC's John Lewis and James Farmer of CORE strenuously objected, arguing they could not give up the tactic that had been their most effective weapon. Martin Luther King was deeply torn and tried to fashion a compromise. When that failed, the meeting ended with two separate statements. The moderates declared that the present situation was a "serious threat" that required "a broad curtailment, if not total moratorium, of all mass marches, mass picketing and mass demonstrations until after Election Day, next Nov. 3." The militants expressed their "concern with the recent riots" but drew "a sharp distinction" between lawlessness and legitimate protest, called for "more socially sensitive police action," and urged national leaders to seek justice as well as law and order.[93]

Johnson swept to a landslide victory in November, but the long-term effect of the riots, together with the protests against the Vietnam War that escalated in early 1965, produced the very backlash they feared, introducing an era of conservative "law and order" politics that dominated the country for the next forty years.[94]

Standing firm: Crime and the rights of suspects

Johnson was acutely sensitive to changes in the political winds and grasped the growing public concern about crime. The GOP candidate Barry Goldwater raised the law and order issue in his 1964 acceptance speech ("Tonight there is violence in our streets"). Moving quickly to preempt the issue, LBJ in March 1965 created the President's Crime Commission to conduct the first comprehensive study of the American criminal justice system since Herbert Hoover's Wickersham Commission (1929–31). These events marked the "nationalization" of crime, transforming it from its historic state and local focus into a national political issue. The Crime Commission's report two years later recommended a standard set of 1960s liberal reforms: federally funded research, model crime and delinquency programs, and federal financial assistance to state and local agencies. It ducked, however, the politically sensitive issue of the Supreme Court decisions on police practices and angered LBJ by recommending a federal wiretap law.[95]

One week before his March 1965 Voting Rights speech, Johnson delivered a message on crime that, in retrospect, is unique among presidential speeches on the subject. Again playing the role of national civics teacher, he unambiguously endorsed the constitutional rights of criminal suspects. Controversy already swirled over the 1961 Supreme Court ruling in *Mapp v. Ohio*, imposing the exclusionary rule on illegal searches by local police,

93 "Texts of Statements by Negro Leaders," *NYT*, July 30, 1964. "Key Negro Groups Call on Members to Curb Protests," ibid.

94 J. William Middendorf, II, *A Glorious Disaster: Barry Goldwater's Presidential Campaign and the Origins of the Conservative Movement* (New York: Basic Books, 2006).

95 Special Message to the Congress on Law Enforcement and the Administration of Justice, March 8, 1965, APP. Goldwater Acceptance Speech, July 16, 1964, APP. Commission's final report: President's Commission on Law Enforcement and the Administration of Justice, *The Challenge of Crime in a Free Society* (Washington, DC: Government Printing Office, 1967). Samuel Walker, *Popular Justice: A History of American Criminal Justice*. 2nd ed. (New York: Oxford University Press, 1998), p. 202. Willard M. Oliver, *The Law and Order Presidency* (Upper Saddle River, NJ: Prentice-Hall, 2003), pp. 70–2.

and it would reach a new level of intensity with *Miranda v. Arizona* in 1966, requiring the police to advise suspects of their right to remain silent. Police officials and their conservative allies accused the Court of "handcuffing" police crime fighting. (Interestingly, Johnson was not asked about *Miranda* at his next press conference.) In the face of growing attacks on the Court, Johnson reaffirmed his belief in constitutional rights of criminal suspects in his 1965 speech. Quoting the former Supreme Court justice Felix Frankfurter, he told the nation, "A democratic society, in which respect for the dignity of all men is central, naturally guards against the misuse of the law enforcement process," and he pointedly endorsed "the historic protections our Nation has accorded to the accused." The real problem, he explained, was that police officers failed to understand these principles, and, as a remedy, he called for "creat[ing] greater understanding . . . of the efforts of federal courts to ensure protection of individual rights." Federal aid for police education and training would be one of the main recommendations of his Crime Commission.[96]

Johnson's speech was the first and certainly the last by a president affirming the rights of criminal suspects. Beginning with Richard Nixon just three years later in the 1968 presidential campaign, conservative Republican candidates would attack the Supreme Court for its decisions on police practices, pornography, separation of church and state, and later abortion. Suspects were always labeled "criminals," even though they had not yet been convicted. Democrats bent to the change in the political winds as well, and their presidential candidates after Johnson sought to appear tough on crime.[97]

Before the tide of law and order politics swept the country, Johnson scored a major victory for the rights of criminal defendants. On June 22, 1966, he signed into law the landmark Bail Reform Act, creating a presumption of pretrial release for defendants awaiting trial. The law was a historic breakthrough, ending the long-standing money bail system, which kept poor defendants in jail before trial. Bail reform had been initiated by the Kennedys, and Johnson brought their efforts to fruition. Johnson used the bill signing for yet another civics lesson. The law, he explained, serves "to greatly enlarge justice in this land of ours." Better than any other president in American history, he articulated a vision of the place of civil liberties in American society. "So our task is to rise above the debate between rights of the individual and rights of the society, by securing and really protecting the rights of both." He delivered these remarks exactly nine days after the controversial *Miranda* decision.[98]

The federal Bail Reform Act affected only a small percentage of all criminal defendants in the United States. Its real impact was as a national model for the state bail reform laws incorporating the same principle that defendants have a presumptive right to bail. The result was a proliferation of state bail programs involving release on recognizance or 10 percent plans. The impact on local jails was dramatic: the percentage of persons who were in jail because they were awaiting trial, as opposed to sentenced offenders, dropped by almost half from the early 1960s to the later years. The problem was not completely solved, to be sure, but to a great extent, American jails were no longer the nation's "poorhouses."[99]

96 Special Message to the Congress on Law Enforcement and the Administration of Justice, March 8, 1965, APP.

97 Walker, *Popular Justice*, pp. 211–31.

98 Remarks at the Signing of the Bail Reform Act of 1966, June 22, 1966, APP. Crime laws: Oliver, *The Law and Order Presidency*, pp. 73–4.

99 Wayne H. Thomas, Jr., *Bail Reform in America* (Berkeley: University of California Press, 1976). Walker, *Sense and Nonsense about Crime, Drugs, and Community*, 7th ed. (Belmont, CA: Cengage, 2011), pp. 133–6.

The politics of bail changed very quickly in response to the riots and rising crime rates, however. In the 1968 presidential election, both Richard Nixon and the independent candidate George C. Wallace ran on "law and order" platforms, decrying the rise in crime and attacking the Supreme Court. Johnson was affected by the new mood, and his legislative package on crime in early 1968 was a world apart from his earlier speeches on the rights of suspects. He now proposed revising the Bail Reform Act to allow preventive detention of "dangerous" defendants, embracing what became one of conservatives' lead issues in the following decades.[100]

Johnson held the line on several crime issues, however. He maintained his staunch opposition to wiretapping, even after Congress authorized it in 1968, and both he and Attorney General Clark rejected calls for a constitutional amendment to overturn the Supreme Court's *Miranda* decision. Clark proposed working within the decision's framework to develop "effective alternatives," with proper "procedural safeguards." During the April 1968 riots in Chicago after Martin Luther King's assassination, Mayor Richard Daley told the police to "shoot to kill." Clark denounced the order, saying that "firm and effective action" against lawlessness was "not synonymous with brutal or inhumane actions." For this stand, he was loudly denounced from many quarters. Nonetheless, the riots following King's assassination forced Johnson to order federal troops to Chicago, Baltimore, and Washington, D.C., where rioting occurred just ten blocks from the White House.[101]

Johnson responded to the devastating 1967 riots in Newark and Detroit by appointing the National Commission on Civil Disorders, known as the Kerner Commission, to investigate their causes and make recommendations. Its report on March 1, 1968, included many standard Great Society recommendations regarding jobs and ending race discrimination. With the nation consumed by the Vietnam War, however, no action followed. Neither LBJ nor most Americans, moreover, were ready to accept the commission's grave warning that America was becoming "two societies, one black, one white – separate and unequal."[102] At the end of his presidency, LBJ had no meaningful response to the tangled web of race, poverty, and violence.

CIVIL LIBERTARIANS TO THE SUPREME COURT

"I believe it is the right thing to do, the right time to do it, the right man and the right place." President Johnson was correct on all four points. The occasion was his nomination of Thurgood Marshall to the U.S. Supreme Court on October 2, 1967. Appointing the first African American to the high court was certainly the right thing to do. With barriers to integration falling, it was entirely proper that an African American serve on the Court. (Only a year before, Johnson had appointed the first African American to the cabinet,

100 Legislative proposals on crime: Califano to Clark, September 4, 1968, Califano Papers, Box 40, LBJPL

101 Ibid. "Clark Criticizes Daley's Order to Shoot Looters," *NYT*, April 18, 1968. "Army Troops in Capital, as Negroes Riot; Guard Sent into Chicago, Detroit, Boston," ibid., April 6, 1968. *Miranda*: Nancy A. Thompson to Ramsey Clark, July 22, 1966, Clark Papers, Box 72, LBJPL. Shoot to Kill: Cliff Sessions, Director of Public Information, Department of Justice, to Martin Karant, May 7, 1968, Clark Papers, Box 68, LBJPL. The Clark papers at the LBJPL contain many letters denouncing him for "condoning" riots.

102 Director FBI to Attorney General, February 20, 1968, Clark Papers, Box 67, LBJPL. National Advisory Commission on Civil Disorders, *Report* (New York: Bantam Books, 1968), p. 1.

Robert C. Weaver as secretary of housing and Urban development.)[103] Johnson did not mention race in his effusive nomination remarks, but he hardly needed to. Marshall was the right person. As head of the NAACP Legal Defense Fund from the late 1930s to 1961, he led the long legal campaign that culminated in the historic 1954 *Brown v. Board of Education* decision. Johnson added that "probably only one or two other living men have argued as many cases before the Court." (He is, in fact, rivaled only by Hayden Covington of the Jehovah's Witnesses and the ACLU's Osmond Fraenkel in terms of the number and weighty impact of cases won before the Court.) Finally, the Supreme Court was definitely the right place, given its impact on society.[104]

On the Court, Marshall immediately joined the civil libertarian bloc and for twenty-four years never wavered from his earlier commitments. Replacing Tom Clark, who was conservative on many issues, he shifted the Court's balance in a more libertarian direction. He remained the advocate of civil liberties until he resigned in 1991, when that was a lonely and isolated position.

Two years before naming Marshall, Johnson appointed another great civil libertarian, his old friend and political aide Abe Fortas. Their friendship had been solidified in 1948 when Fortas represented Johnson in a crucial court case over LBJ's disputed eighty-seven-vote victory in the Democratic Party primary for the Senate. Fortas represented a number of victims of the cold war witch hunt in the 1950s and later argued and won the landmark 1963 case of *Gideon v. Wainwright* holding that felony defendants had the right to an attorney at trial. The nomination was a classic story of the legendary Johnson "treatment." Fortas had previously refused to be nominated to the Court, and so on July 28, 1965, without any warning, Johnson just told his friend he was going to a press conference to announce his nomination and that he could come along if he wished. Fortas went along and accepted this highest of honors. (Some observers dispute the story, believing the ambitious Fortas always wanted the appointment.)[105]

Fortas was a solid member of the civil libertarian majority of the Warren Court, authoring several important decisions that broke new ground on individual rights. *In re Gault* (1967) declared unconstitutional the basic procedures of juvenile courts, including the long-standing denial of the right to an attorney. *Tinker v. Des Moines* (1969) affirmed for the first time that public schools had a constitutional right to freedom of

[103] Remarks to the Press Announcing the Nomination of Thurgood Marshall as Associate Justice of the Supreme Court. June 13, 1967, APP. Howard Ball, *A Defiant Life: Thurgood Marshall and the Persistence of Racism in America* (New York: Crown Publishers, 1998). Mark V. Tushnet, *Making Civil Rights Law: Thurgood Marshall and the Supreme Court, 1936–1961* (New York: Oxford University Press, 1994). Roger Goldman and David Gallen, *Thurgood Marshall: Justice for All* (New York: Carroll & Graf, 1992). Remarks at the Swearing In of Robert C. Weaver and Robert C. Wood as Secretary and Under Secretary of Housing and Urban Development, January 18, 1966, APP. Walter B. Hill, Jr., "Finding Place for the Negro: Robert C. Weaver and the Groundwork for the Civil Rights Movement," *Prologue* 37 (Spring 2005): 1–42, 51.

[104] Remarks to the Press Announcing the Nomination of Thurgood Marshall as Associate Justice of the Supreme Court. June 13, 1967, APP. On Marshall, Covington, and the ACLU's Osmond K. Fraenkel before the Supreme Court, see Samuel Walker, *In Defense of American Liberties: A History of the ACLU* (New York: Oxford University Press, 1990).

[105] Fortas and the 1948 election: Caro, *The Years of Lyndon Johnson: Means of Ascent*, pp. 369–80. Bruce Allen Murphy, *Fortas: The Rise and Ruin of a Supreme Court Justice* (New York: William Morrow, 1988). No warning: Johnson, *The Vantage Point*, p. 545; Fortas, OH, p. 19, LBJPL. LBJ told Fortas not to act surprised when he announced the nomination: Johnson to Fortas, Telephone Conversation, July 28, 1965, LBJL. Anthony Lewis, *Gideon's Trumpet* (New York: Random House, 1964).

expression and that schools "may not be enclaves of totalitarianism." And in 1968 he wrote the majority opinion in *Epperson v. Arkansas,* declaring unconstitutional a state law forbidding the teaching of evolution. The decision occurred forty-three years after the famous 1925 Scopes "Monkey Trial."[106]

On occasion, however, Fortas was too much LBJ's friend and confidant. They regularly talked about current politics in ways that were inappropriate for a Supreme Court justice. In one case, Fortas committed a serious violation of judicial ethics, by protecting the FBI. When the lobbyist Fred Black appealed his conviction for income tax fraud, Attorney General Katzenbach felt duty-bound to disclose to the Court that FBI listening devices ("bugs") had picked up conversations between Black and his attorney. Although not relevant to the appeal, Katzenbach felt obligated to disclose the details nonetheless. Disclosure threatened to expose the broader pattern of FBI eavesdropping. Fortas recused himself from the case but provided back channel communication to both the bureau and the White House in an effort to shape the Justice Department brief so as to not expose the FBI. The effort failed, and Hoover was greatly embarrassed, but Fortas's efforts were nonetheless unethical.[107]

Fortas's Supreme Court career ended unhappily. When Johnson tried to elevate him to the chief justice position in 1968, someone leaked information that he had accepted speaking fees of fifteen thousand dollars from funds donated by friends and former clients. Johnson, now with little political clout, withdrew the nomination. The following year, Fortas's fortunes turned even worse, when his enemies made new accusations that he had received a secret twenty-thousand-dollar retainer in 1966 while on the Court. The money was from a family foundation associated with the Wall Street financier Louis Wolfson, who had legal problems. The ethical cloud was now too great, and Chief Justice Warren, in his own last months on the Court, told Fortas he would have to resign or face impeachment. Fortas resigned and President Nixon appointed the moderate conservative Harry Blackmun as his replacement. The change shifted the Court in a conservative direction on most issues.[108]

THE TRAGEDY OF VIETNAM

The Vietnam War aroused bitter opposition, divided the country, and eventually destroyed Lyndon Johnson's presidency and his dreams of a Great Society. The war drained national resources and cost Johnson support among many liberals (including, for example, Martin Luther King). Antiwar protests, as we have seen, also drove him to betray his civil liberties principles, as he ordered the CIA to spy on Americans.

While Johnson inherited a deteriorating situation in Vietnam, he only had himself to blame for introducing ground troops and extending bombing to North Vietnam. Even worse, he lied to secure congressional approval of the Gulf of Tonkin Resolution in

106 *Tinker v. Des Moines,* 393 U.S. 503 (1967). *Epperson v. Arkansas,* 393 U.S. 97 (1968).

107 Fortas – LBJ phone conversations are at the LBJPL. Alexander Charns, *Cloak and Gavel: FBI Wiretaps, Bugs, Informers, and the Supreme Court* (Urbana: University of Illinois Press, 1992), Fortas as FBI informant, Ch. 4, pp. 44–63. Charns's book details other unethical actions by Fortas and other Justices. FBI perspective: DeLoach, *Hoover's FBI,* pp. 53–9.

108 Robert Shogan, *A Question of Judgment: The Fortas Case and the Struggle for the Supreme Court* (Indianapolis, Bobbs-Merrill, 1972).

August 1964. The resolution authorized the president "to take all necessary steps, including the use of armed force," to help a member of the Southeast Asia Collective Defense Treaty requesting assistance, and it became the basis for escalating American involvement in Vietnam the following year. It passed the House unanimously, and with only two negative votes in the Senate. Immediately after it passed, a very pleased Secretary of Defense Robert McNamara told LBJ it was "generally a blank check authorization for further action." The evidence now indicates that attacks on the two naval ships did not occur as originally described. Daniel Ellsberg, who leaked the *Pentagon Papers* to the *New York Times* in 1971, was on duty at the Defense Department when the first reports of the incident arrived. He vividly recalls the ambiguity of the events in those tense hours. In requesting the resolution, Johnson falsely said, "the United States intends no rashness, and seeks no wider war." During the election campaign that fall he lied when he declared he would not send American troops to Vietnam and presented himself as the cautious and responsible alternative to the GOP candidate Barry Goldwater (who damaged his own image by suggesting he might use nuclear weapons). White House tapes, however, reveal Johnson discussing covert American military actions that probably provoked the North Vietnamese, and his anger at Hubert Humphrey, his vice presidential nominee, for publicly talking about them. The *Pentagon Papers*, moreover, revealed that Johnson and the Pentagon had begun planning to escalate military action in Vietnam six months before the Gulf of Tonkin incident.[109]

In terms of both its intent and its ultimate consequences, Johnson's lying about the Gulf of Tonkin episode matches George W. Bush's distortion of intelligence data about weapons of mass destruction to justify the invasion of Iraq in 2003. Both incidents led the United States into disastrous and divisive wars.[110]

The antiwar movement exploded in spring 1965, surprising even its organizers with its support and intensity. The signal event was a marathon twelve-hour "teach-in" at the University of Michigan on March 24 attended by three thousand people. The Students for a Democratic Society (SDS), which quickly emerged as the leading student antiwar group, organized a protest demonstration in Washington for April. Hoping for a few thousand people, they were stunned when between fifteen thousand and twenty-five thousand arrived. Pickets in front of the White House focused blame for the war squarely on President Johnson. From that point on, protests escalated along with American involvement in Vietnam.[111]

109 Special Message to the Congress on U.S. Policy in Southeast Asia, August 5, 1964, APP. Remarks before the National Convention upon Accepting the Nomination, August 27, 1964, APP. Pre-Tonkin Gulf planning: *The Pentagon Papers, New York Times Edition*, Ch. 5, The Covert War and Tonkin Gulf: February–August, 1964, pp. 234–306. That "Asian boys" should do the fighting in Vietnam: Remarks in Memorial Hall, Akron University, October 21, 1964, APP. McNamara: Telephone conversation, Johnson-McNamara, August 6, 1964, Tape WH6408.08, LBJPL, transcript at MCPA. Daniel Ellsberg, *Secrets: A Memoir of Vietnam and the Pentagon Papers* (New York: Viking, 2002), pp. 7–20. White House tapes: Beschloss, *Taking Charge*, pp. 493–510. A more recent analysis based on newly declassified documents: John Prados, *40th Anniversary of the Gulf of Tonkin Incident* (August 4, 2004), National Security Archive, www.gwu.edu/~nsarchiv.html. The history of misleading statements is in Louis Fisher, "When Wars Begin: Misleading Statements by Presidents," *Presidential Studies Quarterly* 40 (March 2010): 171–84.

110 John Prados, "Essay: 40th Anniversary of the Gulf of Tonkin Incident," Posted August 4, 2004, National Security Archive, www.gwu.edu/`nsaarciv.html.

111 "Professors Hold Vietnam Protest," *NYT*, March 25, 1965. "15,000 White House Pickets Denounce Vietnam War," ibid., April 18, 1965. Thomas Powers, *The War at Home: Vietnam and the American People, 1964–1968* (New York: Grossman, 1973).

There was no massive suppression of dissent in the Vietnam War, as had occurred in World War I. The legal scholar Geoffrey Stone notes that neither President Johnson nor Nixon ever contemplated prosecutions of pure dissent such as occurred under President Woodrow Wilson. "The change in the extent to which the United States has learned to tolerate dissent in wartime," he observes, "is quite dramatic." (The Spock case discussed later was a notable exception, however, and President Nixon's assault on dissent took on a very special character.) Nonetheless, the war provoked a host of civil liberties violations. Johnson ordered the CIA to spy on Americans, the military developed its own spying campaign, and the FBI continued its COINTELPRO program and other spying on political groups. State and local officials committed their own abuses, as police broke up demonstrations, public officials and school administrators banned speakers and demonstrations, and state and local police spied on political groups. The Selective Service System punished some political activists by reclassifying and drafting them, although it is not clear whether local draft boards were acting on their own or on orders from Director Lewis Hershey. SNCC leaders were special targets of punitive reclassification.[112]

The highest-profile attack on dissent by the Johnson administration was the prosecution of the famous pediatrician Dr. Benjamin Spock and four other antiwar activists for conspiracy to obstruct the draft. Dr. Spock was the most famous physician in America, and his best-selling 1946 book *Baby and Child Care* had influenced a generation of parents. The Spock indictment was part of a new determination by the Justice Department in late 1967 to crack down on the growing resistance to the draft. In December, for example, hundreds of people, including Dr. Spock and the poet Allen Ginsberg, were arrested in New York City for attempting to shut down the military induction center. On December 9h, Attorney General Clark and Selective Service Director Hershey jointly announced a new special unit in the Justice Department to prosecute people who "counsel, aid, or abet" resistance to the draft.[113]

The Spock case raised fundamental questions about free speech in wartime. The principal evidence against the defendants was the Call to Resist Illegitimate Authority, published in late 1967 in the *New York Review of Books* and the *Nation* and eventually signed by an estimated twenty thousand people. In uncompromising terms, the call declared the war unconstitutional and asserted that "every free man has a legal right and a moral duty to exert every effort to end this war ... and to encourage others to do the same." Signatories pledged to support "those who undertake resistance to this war" and called on others "to join us in this confrontation with immoral authority." In labeling the federal government and the war "illegitimate authority," the call summed up better than anything else the extent to which the Vietnam War had undermined the trust of millions of Americans in their government. In that respect alone, Lyndon Johnson undermined all of his previous contributions to the growth of civil liberties in America. The Spock

[112] Stone in Daniel Farber, ed., *Security v. Liberty: Conflicts between Civil Liberties and National Security in American History* (New York: Russell Sage Foundation, 2008), p. 108. The U.S. Justice Department did intervene, however, to help John Lewis win his appeal to gain conscientious objector status in 1965. Lewis, *Walking with the Wind*, p. 272.

[113] Jessica Mitford, *The Trial of Dr. Spock, the Rev. William Sloane Coffin, Jr., Michael Ferber, Mitchell Goodman, and Marcus Raskin* (New York, Knopf, 1969). "264 Seized Here in Draft Protest," *NYT*, December 6, 1967. Joint Statement by Attorney General Ramsey Clark and Director of Selective Service Lewis B. Hershey, December 9, 1967, White House Central Files, Justice-Legal Matters, Box 27, LBJPL. "Draft Violators Face Stiff Curbs," *NYT*, December 10, 1967.

prosecution proved to be a legal morass and public relations disaster for the government. It indicted the defendants for conspiracy, but there were few instances when any of the five had actually met and talked with each other. Whether the "call" for people to resist the draft represented advocacy of an idea, protected by the First Amendment, or incitement to illegal action was a difficult legal question. In Dr. Spock, meanwhile, the government could not have chosen a target more likely to generate sympathy among a broad range of Americans. Additionally, the case was filed in Boston, one of the hottest centers of antiwar activity.[114]

Spock wanted his defense "based on the Nuremberg Principles," but Judge Francis Ford refused to allow testimony on the legality of the war. Spock and three codefendants were convicted and sentenced to two years in prison (Marcus Raskin was acquitted). The First Circuit Court of Appeals overturned the convictions (two because of insufficient evidence), and the cases were ultimately dismissed on narrow legal grounds. Ramsey Clark later became a prominent radical critic of the American government, representing such unpopular clients as the Palestine Liberation Organization, but he never discussed his role in attacking dissent in the Spock case.

A PRESIDENCY RUINED, DREAMS DESTROYED

The angry protests against the Vietnam War, the worsening racial crisis, the steady erosion of his political support, and finally the recognition that the war was unwinnable ultimately drove Lyndon Johnson from the White House. In a televised speech on March 31, 1968, he stunned the nation with the surprise announcement that he would not seek reelection in November. His presidency was in ruins. No president experienced such a radical shift in popularity and power, from his enormous legislative accomplishments of 1964–5 to 1966–8 when he could no longer even meet the public because of antiwar protests. (The historian Eric Goldman, who had served in the White House, notes that even in his last two years in office, Johnson actually had a substantial legislative record: creation of the Transportation Department, the Fair Housing Act, a truth-in-packaging law, automobile safety regulation, federal support for public television, the 1968 omnibus crime bill, and a new [albeit weak] federal gun control law.) By 1968 the country was more bitterly divided than any time since the grim World War I years, and faith in the American political system at its lowest ebb ever. Lyndon Johnson left office on January 20, 1969, a broken man. His biographer Doris Kearns, who assisted him with his memoirs, found a man unable to sleep well, with no power to wield, and barely interested in his own book.[115]

[114] Michael Ferber and Staughton Lynd, *The Resistance* (Boston: Beacon Press, 1971), contains a chapter on "The Call to Resist." Benjamin Spock, "The Conspiracy to Oppose the Vietnam War," in Bud Schultz and Ruth Schultz, *It Did Happen Here* (Berkeley: University of California Press, 1989), pp. 91–100. Geoffrey R. Stone, *Perilous Times: Free Speech in Wartime* (New York: W. W. Norton, 2004), pp. 477–82. Clark mentions the case only briefly: Clark, OH, V, p. 15, LBJPL. By the post-Watergate period, Clark was a vigorous critic of the abuse of the intelligence agencies: Testimony in Church Committee, V. 6, *Federal Bureau of Investigation*, pp. 220–5. There is no biography of Clark; his recent activities are on the Web site of the International Action Center: www.iacenter.org.

[115] Robert Dallek, *Hail to the Chief: The Making and Unmaking of American Presidents*. Pbk. ed. (New York: Oxford University Press, 1996), p. 161. Goldman, *The Tragedy of Lyndon Johnson*, pp. 604–5. Kearns, *Lyndon Johnson and the American Dream*, pp. 16–19.

Lyndon Johnson was the greatest supporter of civil liberties ever to occupy the White House. No other president had such an impressive record on civil rights, the rights of criminal defendants, opposition to wiretapping, and the rights of immigrants, the elderly, family planning, and the mentally retarded. No other president used the bully pulpit of the White House to give the nation so many civics lessons on race, on freedom of speech and assembly, on equality of opportunity, or on the rights of criminal defendants, and of course on his passionate belief in the destiny of America as the land of opportunity. No other president, with the possible exception of Franklin D. Roosevelt, understood political power so well and used it so effectively. Despite the unhappy end of his presidency, and despite the conservative mood that overtook the country in the decades ahead, his two civil rights laws remained enduring accomplishments. Solidly entrenched in American law, they embody the highest values of America. With respect to the spirit of the times, Johnson stood in marked contrast to his predecessor. While JFK was cooly detached from the emerging rights revolution in America, LBJ embraced its spirit and in many important ways sped its development.

LBJ was a man of enormous contradictions, however, with regard to civil liberties as with everything else. Despite his great civil rights laws, he personally intervened to prevent a cutoff of federal funds to Chicago schools because of de facto segregation. He believed in equality of opportunity for African Americans, the elderly, the mentally retarded, and immigrants but had a blind spot with regard to women's rights. He hated wiretapping passionately, but he wiretapped Martin Luther King and other civil rights activists. He hated snooping in all its forms but ordered the CIA to break the law and spy on Americans. And he lied to Congress to get a resolution allowing him to escalate military actions in Vietnam.

Eric Goldman concludes that Johnson was a "tragic figure ... an extraordinarily gifted President who was the wrong man from the wrong place at the wrong time under the wrong circumstances." Goldman is entirely wrong. Lyndon Johnson was exactly the right person – someone with a broad vision of justice and individual rights, and who knew how to use power – at the right place – the White House – at the right time – the moment when new visions of rights were sweeping the country. George Reedy, who served him loyally for many years, got it right: LBJ was "the right man in the right place at the right time." In June 1964, Johnson asked his speechwriter Richard Goodwin to draft a statement for the public. After a long soliloquy on his great plans for the country, he told Goodwin, "then let's you and me go make a little history." Make history he did, leaving an enduring institutional legacy rivaled only by FDR. The historian Robert Dallek titled his biography *Flawed Giant*, a perfect summary of this extraordinarily complex person. Lyndon Johnson died on January 22, 1973, the same day the Supreme Court announced its historic decision in *Roe v. Wade*. Symbolically, the two events marked the end of one political era and the beginning of a new and more conservative one.[116]

[116] Goldman, *The Tragedy of Lyndon Johnson*, p. 628. George E. Reedy, *Twilight of the Presidency* (New York: World Publishing, 1970), p. 89. Goodwin, *Remembering America*, p. 317. Dallek, *Flawed Giant*.

Richard Nixon, having just resigned as president, waves farewell to people on the White House grounds before flying to California, August 9, 1974. Nixon was facing almost certain impeachment and conviction for abuses of power in the Watergate scandal and for other actions.
Source: National Archives.

9 Richard Nixon

A Singular Abuse of Presidential Power

"I AM NOT A CROOK"

The president of the United States declared at a press conference, "I am not a crook." No other president ever felt compelled to declare his innocence, but Richard Nixon needed to on the night of November 17, 1973. The expanding Watergate scandal had engulfed his presidency for seventeen months, linking him to serious misdeeds, including criminal conduct. Nine months later, the scandal drove him from office.[1]

Despite his protestation, Richard Nixon was indeed a crook. He suborned perjury, obstructed justice, and authorized spying on journalists and political opponents. These charges formed the most serious Articles of Impeachment approved by the House Judiciary Committee on July 27, 1974. Three days earlier, the Supreme Court had unanimously ordered him to turn over sixty-four tape recordings of White House conversations. In the famous June 23, 1973, "smoking gun" tape, he discussed blocking the FBI investigation of the Watergate break-in. Facing certain impeachment and likely conviction, he resigned on August 9, 1974, the only president ever to do so.[2]

Richard Nixon stands in a special category among presidents with respect to violations of civil liberties. All the other presidents who violated the rights of Americans did so in the sincere, if misguided, belief their actions were necessary to protect the nation's security: Woodrow Wilson's suppression of dissent in World War I, Franklin D. Roosevelt's evacuation of the Japanese Americans, Harry Truman's loyalty program, and George W. Bush's war on terrorism. Nixon's abuses, however, sprang from a personal and political interest in protecting himself and his administration. Some of these actions had arguable national security implications: The *Pentagon Papers* leaked by Daniel Ellsberg, for example, might have included classified information. But as the Senate Watergate Report concluded, the burglary of Ellsberg's psychiatrist by the White House "Plumbers" unit was primarily "a campaign to destroy Ellsberg's image," and the national security rationale was "an afterthought contrived to provide protection for those involved." There was some truth in Nixon's claim that other presidents had spied on their political opponents or journalists But those actions by Roosevelt, Truman, Kennedy, and Johnson were relatively isolated events that did not match Nixon's relentless efforts. Nixon is infamous for saying, "If the president does it, it can't be illegal."

1 "Nixon Declares He Didn't Profit from Public Life," *NYT*, November 18, 1973.

2 The literature on Watergate is enormous. A starting point is Stanley I. Kutler, *The Wars of Watergate: The Last Crisis of Watergate* (New York: Knopf, 1990). House of Representatives, *Impeachment of Richard M. Nixon, President of the United States: The Final Report of the Committee on the Judiciary, House of Representatives* (New York: Viking Press, 1975).

Even George W. Bush had elaborate legal memoranda justifying his most questionable actions in the war on terrorism.[3]

Nixon without Watergate; Watergate without Nixon

To understand Nixon's violations of civil liberties, it is important to view his presidency whole. In her insightful biography, the historian Joan Hoff asks whether it is possible to consider Nixon apart from the Watergate scandal. Answering her own question, she persuasively argues that it is necessary to see his presidency in all its dimensions. His election marked the advent of a new conservative era in national politics that produced major changes in racial justice, crime policy, women's rights, and abortion and dominated national politics for a generation. In fact, as we shall see, he was comparatively liberal on many issues compared with the neoconservative presidents of later years. The neoconservative firebrand Pat Buchanan criticized Nixon's liberal tendencies even while serving in his administration. Hoff then turns the question around and asks whether we can consider Watergate apart from Nixon. Again, she answers her own question affirmatively. The expansion of presidential power and the misuse of national security claims were long-term developments that implicated presidents from Roosevelt on. Demonizing Nixon, as a generation of liberals has, deflects attention away from the deeper long-term trends regarding presidential power.[4]

Nixon's election was also a watershed in American politics because the 1968 campaign marked the advent of civil liberties as central issues in presidential politics. Nixon campaigned against the Supreme Court, blaming it for decisions that had caused a breakdown in "law and order" and a decline in public morality. Accepting the GOP nomination in August 1968 he declared that some Court decisions "have gone too far in weakening the peace forces as against the criminal forces in this country." Social conservatives had campaigned for school prayer and against pornography for many years; the 1968 election yoked them with other issues and made civil liberties issues the dominant theme in national politics (where they were joined by abortion and gay rights in the 1970s). In 1980 the neoconservative movement, which Watergate temporarily interrupted, would realign American party politics in what can be called the Great Realignment, with civil liberties the central issues.[5]

THE CONSERVATIVE REACTION, 1968

The year 1968 was the most conflict-ridden year in American history since 1919, with assassinations, riots, the collapse of public support for the Vietnam War, and a pervasive loss of

[3] Ellsberg break-in: U.S. Senate, *The Senate Watergate Report* [Abridged ed.], *The Final Report of the Senate Select Committee on Presidential Campaign Activities* (New York: Carroll & Graf, 2005), pp. 67–8.

[4] Joan Hoff, *Nixon Reconsidered* (New York: Basic Books, 1994).Nixon's reputation as a liberal: David Greenberg, *Nixon's Shadow: The History of an Image*. Pbk. Ed. (New York: W. W. Norton, 2004). See also the prescient analysis of this point in Garry Wills, *Nixon Agonistes: The Crisis of the Self-Made Man* (Boston: Houghton Mifflin, 1970), pp. 534–46. Buchanan's criticisms: Annotated News Summaries, Circa February, 1969, President's Office File, Box 30, RNPL. Nixon biographies include Herbert S. Parmet, *Richard Nixon and His America* (Boston: Little, Brown, 1990). Stephen E. Ambrose, *Nixon: The Triumph of a Politician, 1962–1972* (New York: Simon & Schuster, 1989).

[5] Address Accepting the Presidential Nomination at the Republican National Convention in Miami Beach, Florida, August 8, 1968, APP.

confidence in American institutions. On January 29, seventy thousand North Vietnamese and Viet Cong forces launched the Tet Offensive, catching the Americans completely by surprise. Although the North Vietnamese suffered huge casualties, they scored a psychological victory that convinced many Americans the war was lost. On March 31, President Lyndon Johnson stunned the nation by announcing he would not run for reelection. Four days later, Martin Luther King was assassinated in Memphis, and his murder sparked riots in Chicago, Washington, D.C., and other cities. Robert Kennedy was assassinated on June 5, and at the August Democratic Party convention in Chicago, demonstrators were tear gassed and beaten in a shocking display of police abuse, all on national television. From the podium, the Connecticut senator Abraham Ribicoff denounced the "Gestapo tactics in the streets of Chicago." With good reason, one historian titled his book on 1968, *The Year the Dream Died*.[6]

The presidential election campaign was one of the ugliest in modern history. Protesters denounced Nixon as the harbinger of a cold war–style crackdown on dissent and a reversal of the nation's commitment to civil rights. The Democratic Party candidate Hubert Humphrey was attacked by antiwar activists for not breaking with President Johnson on the Vietnam War. The Independent Party candidate George Wallace was widely attacked as a racist defender of segregation, but he also attracted considerable support outside the South for his strong anti-Washington views.[7]

During the campaign, Nixon tried to have it both ways. One moment he presented himself as a statesman who would "bring us together." At the same time, however, he sent out a strong conservative message, equating his opponent with urban racial violence and radical antiwar protests, appealing to the so-called silent majority of Americans alarmed by rising crime rates, riots, militant protests, and an emerging youth counterculture. In mid-September, he exclaimed that a new television ad on crime "hits it right on the nose." The ad featured a lonely police officer, scenes of violence, and a bullet shattered window. The voice-over solemnly intoned, "We owe it to the decent and law abiding citizens of America to take the offensive against the criminal forces that threaten their peace and security.... This time vote like your whole world depended on it. Nixon." Nixon attacked the Kerner Commission report on the urban riots because it "blames everybody for the riots except the perpetrators."[8]

On civil rights, Nixon attacked busing students to achieve school integration, usually labeling it "*forced*" busing to suggest that it was coercive and unnatural. The message played well in the North and the South. Attacks on Supreme Court decisions on criminal procedure, school prayer, and pornography played to the fears and anxieties of millions of Americans. Nixon summed it all up in a September campaign speech, saying, "Something has gone terribly wrong in America." Nixon was accused of having a "southern strategy" to win over southern Democrats with an anti–civil rights message. But as the Nixon aide

6 "Police Battle Demonstrators in Streets," *NYT*, August 29, 1968. Jules Witcover, *The Year the Dream Died: Revisiting 1968 in America* (New York: Warner Books, 1997).

7 Lewis L. Gould, *1968: The Election That Changed America* (Chicago: Ivan R. Dee, 1993). Theodore H. White, *The Making of the President 1968*. Pbk. ed. (New York: Pocket Books, 1970).

8 The celebrated account of Nixon's campaign ads: Joe McGinniss, *The Selling of the President 1968*, Pbk. ed. (New York: Pocket Books, 1970). "Negroes and Rights," *NYT*, March 10, 1968. "Nixon Said to Bar Southerners' Bid," ibid., August 7, 1968. Witcover, *The Year the Dream Died*, pp. 90–1. Dan T. Carter, *The Politics of Rage: George Wallace, the Origins of the New Conservatism, and the Transformation of American Politics*, 2nd ed., Pbk. ed. (Baton Rouge: Louisiana State University Press, 2000), p. 348.

Charles Colson explained, the antibusing rhetoric was actually more a "northern strategy," directed toward northern white Democrats terrified at the prospect of inner city African Americans' being bused into their neighborhood schools. Many GOP strategists envisioned building a new majority by peeling away several segments of the long-standing Roosevelt coalition – Catholics, blue-collar workers, and the South – a transformation that in fact occurred by 1980.[9]

The real attack dog in the campaign was the vice presidential candidate, Spiro Agnew. His charge that antiwar demonstrators had "learned their trade at the feet of international Communist conspirators" raised the specter of a new McCarthyism. On NBC's *Meet the Press* he accused the Democrats of encouraging "permissiveness" and later said they were "soft on inflation, soft on communism, and soft on law and order." These attacks struck a responsive cord. A September Harris Poll found that 81 percent of Americans believed that "law and order has broken down." In a white working-class neighborhood in Chicago, Agnew promised new curbs on protests, and in Milwaukee he attacked dissidents as "elitists" and "spoiled brats." With a wave of his arm, he said the country should "cast out" those "dissidents who advocate the use of violence." His words convinced civil libertarians that a revived cold war crackdown on dissent was possible.[10]

The Nixon-Agnew message was echoed in even rougher terms by the independent candidate George Wallace, who attacked "bearded beatnik bureaucrats," a federal judiciary "infested" with "social engineers," civil rights "agitators," communists, and welfare recipients. Both the Democrats and Republicans tolerated "anarchy," he added. Early in the campaign his message helped attract crowds as large as Nixon and Humphrey drew. Although he eventually won only 13 percent of the vote, his rhetoric profoundly influenced the political discourse, in 1968 and beyond. The historian Dan T. Carter labels his impact "the Southernization of American Politics."[11]

NIXON TAKES OFFICE; THE ABUSES BEGIN

President Nixon looked at his chief aide, H. R. Haldeman, and said, "Play it tough. That's they way they play it and that's the way we are going to play it." The comment occurred in June 1972, just after the Watergate break-in, but it captured perfectly the attitude of the White House from the very beginning. Nixon took to the presidency a host of bitter resentments. Ever since a 1952 slush fund scandal and his famous "Checkers" speech, he felt the media and other powerful liberal forces were out to get him. He was absolutely convinced the media had mistreated him in the 1960 presidential election campaign, and even more so in his 1962 California governorship race. The Kennedy administration, he was convinced, had ordered a vindictive IRS audit in 1961.[12]

9 "Excerpts from the Address by Nixon on Crime and Violence," *NYT*, September 30, 1968. Witcover, *The Year the Dream Died*, p. 300. Reg Murphy and Hal Gulliver, *The Southern Strategy* (New York, Scribner, 1971), p. 2. Colson, Exit Interview, RNPL. The Nixon strategist Kevin Phillips outlined a strategy in 1968 that proved to be remarkably prophetic: *The Emerging Republican Majority* (New Rochelle, NY: Arlington House, 1969).

10 Agnew speeches: *NYT*, September 8, 1968, September 10, September 11, September 16, September 29, 1968; available in John R. Coyne, ed., *The Impudent Snobs: Agnew vs. the Intellectual Establishment* (New Rochelle, NY: Arlington House, 1972).

11 Carter, *The Politics of Rage*, Ch. 11.

12 The "play it tough" quote is on the June 23, 1972, White House "smoking gun" tape, available at Stanley I. Kutler, *Abuse of Power: The New Nixon Tapes*, Pbk. ed. (New York: Free Press, 1997), pp. 67–9, and www.watergteinfo.

Nixon's critics saw his mean streak early on. In the 1950s, the famous *Washington Post* cartoonist Herblock portrayed him with evil intent and always needing a shave. The image originated with his anti-communist stand in the Alger Hiss case and in his red-baiting his opponent in the 1950 Senate race. What is striking, however, is how many of Nixon's associates saw the same trait. Donald Segretti, a Watergate operative, said Nixon was "basically a good person with a black, dark side – and the dark side has to do with politics." Alexander Butterfield, who revealed the White House tape recording system, added that "he does have a dark side for sure."[13]

At the heart of Nixon's dark side was a bitter "us versus them" attitude. The most illuminating analysis of this trait is by William Safire, one of his speechwriters and later a noted author and columnist. In his memoir of his White House years, *Before the Fall*, Safire catalogs the various "them" who haunted Nixon: the so-called eastern establishment of Ivy League educated politicians, advisers, and journalists; the news media, and the *New York Times* and *Washington Post* in particular; Kennedy loyalists; and long-standing "Nixon haters." In 1972 Nixon told Pat Buchanan that the Democrat George McGovern and the liberal press "will lie, distort and do anything that is necessary to get into power." The list also included people who had no work ethic or were just "against" everything America stood for. Finally, on foreign policy, there were the "new isolationists," who, in reaction to the Vietnam War, objected to the use of American power around the world.[14]

The irony of Nixon's hatred for the "eastern establishment" was that by 1968 he was very much a part of it: a senior partner in a large New York City law firm, an active Republican Party leader, and a respected commentator on international affairs. Nonetheless, as his press secretary Herbert Klein concluded, despite his enormous accomplishments in life – he was, after all, now president of the United States – Nixon still harbored "the feeling of a poor boy from a small store in a small town who kind of wished he had the trappings that go with being a Yale graduate." Nixon was often oblivious to his audience with some of his attacks. He once told Henry Kissinger, "the professors are the enemy." When Kissinger pointed out that he was a professor, Nixon did not respond. He attacked Ivy League types in front of George H. W. Bush, then chair of the Republican Party. A Yale graduate, Bush was tempted to ask, "Mr. President, do you mean me?" but did not. Nixon's paranoia metastasized in late 1972 to the point where he and his chief aide Bob Haldeman believed there was a clique inside the White House out to get him. One incident illustrates how the administration brazenly threatened reprisals against the press. When the *Los Angeles Times* reporter Richard Bergholz asked Nixon aide John Ehrlichman how they were going to pay for the Family Assistance Plan, Ehrlichman snapped back, "I know you; we have a file on you; we know all about you."[15]

org. Ambrose, *Nixon*, p. 568. Nixon's bitterness about the press in the 1960 campaign: David Halberstam, *The Powers That Be* (New York: Knopf, 1979), pp. 347–51.

13 Gerald S. Strober and Deborah H. Strober, eds., *Nixon: An Oral History of His Presidency* (New York: HarperCollins, 1996), pp. 39–40.

14 William Safire, *Before the Fall: An Inside View of the Pre-Watergate White House*, Pbk. ed. (New York: Belmont Tower, 1975), "'Us" Against 'Them,'" pp. 307–15. Nixon to Buchanan, June 10, 1972, President's Personal File, Box 4, RNPL.

15 Strober and Strober, eds., *Nixon: An Oral History of His Presidency*, p. 47 (Klein), 283–4 (Bergholz). H. R. Haldeman, *The Haldeman Diaries: Inside the Nixon White House* (New York: Putnam's, 1994), July 1, 1971, p. 313. Kissinger: White House tape recording, December 14, 1972, available at www.nixontapes.org. George H. W. Bush, *All the Best, G. Bush: My Life in Letters and Other Writings* (New York: Scribner, 1999), p. 181. White House clique: Ambrose, *Nixon: The Triumph of a Politician*, p. 641.

The "us versus them" attitude, Safire explains, led Nixon to believe that it was a waste of time to appeal to his opponents, and that he could score political points by defining himself as opposed to "them." On a few occasions he staged confrontations with his critics. After a 1970 speech in San Jose, he provoked a screaming crowd of protesters by jumping on top of his limousine and waving his arms in his favorite "V" sign. Getting down, he declared with grim glee, "These kids hate this." In the same vein, when campaigning in one Democratic, labor union-dominated neighborhoods, a witness commented, "It looked like he deliberately provoked that crowd."[16]

Nixon's resentments eventually led to the famous "enemies" list. The original list of twenty people was created by his aide Charles Colson and included the CBS reporter Daniel Schorr ("a real media enemy"), the columnist Mary McGrory ("Daily hate Nixon articles"), the African-American congressmen John Conyers ("Has known weakness for white females"), and the movie star Paul Newman ("Radic-lib causes"). Subsequent lists added many more names. John Dean explained in August 1971 that the list was for using "*the available federal machinery to screw our political enemies*" [italics in original]. The "enemies list" was unique in the history of the presidency (with the possible exception of John Adams's vindictive use of the 1798 Sedition Act). All presidents have vented their anger at reporters at one time or another, and some undoubtedly had mental lists of those they particularly hated. Nixon's list was different because his administration acted on it, targeting illegal actions against some of those on it. White House aides collected personal information on Daniel Schorr, on the ludicrous pretext that he was being considered for a job with the administration, and threatened the *Los Angeles Times* editor Richard Bergholz. About Edward Bennett Williams, a Washington powerhouse lawyer, Nixon said, "I think we are going to fix the son-of-a-bitch."[17]

Previous presidents, Nixon and his closest aides always argued, had also used federal agencies for vindictive political purposes. In addition to the 1961 IRS audit Nixon believed the Kennedys had ordered, he was convinced that he had been bugged during 1962 and 1968 election campaigns. As he once put it, "everybody bugs everybody else." The White House tapes record Nixon's complaining, "We were bugged in '68 on the plane and in '62 even running for governor – [expletive deleted] thing you ever saw." On September 15, 1972, Nixon lamented to Haldeman and Dean, "We haven't used the [FBI] and we haven't used the Justice Department, but things are going to change now." In March 1973 he asked Haldeman about the idea that the IRS "run audits on all members of the Congress?" By then, however, the Watergate crisis had descended on him, and he rejected the idea because it "may stir up a lot of our friends."[18]

Polarizing the country

Despite his campaign promise to "bring us together," Nixon proceeded to do just the opposite once in office. Angry over the massive antiwar moratorium demonstrations in

16 Tom Wells, *The War Within: America's Battle over Vietnam* (New York: Henry Holt, 1996), pp. 465–6. San Jose incident: Safire, *Before the Fall*, pp. 327–34.

17 Senate, *Senate Watergate Report*, pp. 58–64; Dean memo, p. 59. Bergholz: Strober and Strober, eds., *Nixon: An Oral History of His Presidency*, pp. 283–4.

18 Washington Post, *The Presidential Transcripts*. Pbk. ed. (New York: Dell Books, 1974), pp. 34, 50, 54, 57. Nixon to Haldeman, March 12, 1973, President's Personal File, Box 4, RNPL. Ambrose, *Nixon: The Triumph of a Politician*, p. 610.

fall 1969, he unleashed Vice President Agnew, who gave a series of speeches with catchy, inflammatory phrases designed to demonize the administration's critics.

The October 15 Vietnam Moratorium moved antiwar protest to a new level, with 22,000 people marching in Washington and coordinated demonstrations across the country. A demonstration of 100,000 in Boston was no surprise, but a protest in Duluth, Minnesota, indicated the depth of opposition to the war. Agnew responded with one of his most memorable phrases, calling moratorium leaders an "effete corps of impudent snobs" and warning that "hardcore dissidents and professional anarchists" in the antiwar movement planned "wilder, more violent" protests for the November 15 Moratorium. On November 3, Nixon appealed to a "silent majority": "And so tonight – to you, the great silent majority of my fellow Americans – I ask for your support." Media response to the speech was generally favorable, but Nixon was "livid with anger" over criticisms by some television network commentators. Ten days later, in a speech written by Pat Buchanan, Agnew attacked the news media as an "unelected elite." The speech created a sensation and solidified the vice president' reputation as "Nixon's Nixon" (a reference to Nixon's role as the attack dog for President Eisenhower).[19]

The White House stepped up its attacks on the media. Two days before the November Moratorium, Agnew accused the television networks of distorting the news and called on Americans to call or write to them to protest: "The views of this fraternity do not represent the views of America." Well aware of their status as a government regulated industry, all three networks carried his speech live. Agnew then attacked the *New York Times* and the *Washington Post*, accusing the *Times* of covering the administration's critics but not the fact that three hundred Congressmen and fifty-nine senators had endorsed the president's Vietnam policy.[20] Many regarded the attacks as the most serious threat to a free press by a presidential administration in memory.

The author of Agnew's most provocative phrases, thirty-one-year-old Pat Buchanan, represented the hard-line ideological conservative faction in the administration. The White House was deeply divided, ideologically. The White House attorney Leonard Garment and the HEW secretary Robert Finch were moderately liberal, and strong civil rights advocates. Daniel P. Moynihan, meanwhile, was in rapid transition from liberal to neoconservative. Buchanan was the most aggressive conservative in pushing "wedge" issues – all of them civil liberties issues – to split the Democrats and win various groups over to the GOP. Federal aid to parochial schools, he explained, could "drive a wedge right down the middle of the Democratic Party," and "the same is true of abortion; the same is true of hard-line anti-pornography laws." Repeatedly, Buchanan and his allies vented their frustration at what they saw as Nixon's middle of the road stance. Howard Philips, a future neoconservative leader, later dismissed Nixon with contempt: "there was no principle to which Nixon was really attached."[21]

19 Address to the Nation on the War in Vietnam. November 3, 1969, APP. Coyne, ed., *The Impudent Snobs*. Haldeman indicates that Nixon at times thought Agnew's attacks were too polarizing: Haldeman, *The Haldeman Diaries*, pp. 106, 109.

20 "Agnew Says 'Effete Snobs' Incited War Moratorium," *NYT*, October 20, 1969. "Agnew Says TV Networks Are Distorting the News," ibid., November 14, 1969. "Agnew Attacks Press as Unfair: Names 2 Papers," ibid., November 21, 1969. Coyne, *The Impudent Snobs*, pp. 253–74.

21 Robert Mason, *Richard Nixon and the Quest for a New Majority* (Chapel Hill: University of North Carolina Press, 2004), p. 153. Buchanan to Ehrlichman, Haldeman, and Colson, September 23, 1971, WHSF, Buchanan Files, BOX 3, RNPL. Phillips: Strober and Strober, eds., *Nixon: An Oral History*, p. 109.

Wrong from the start: The abuse of power begins

A May 9, 1969, front page story in the *New York Times* revealed secret American bombing of Cambodia. The White House response set the four-month-old administration on the road to Watergate. National Security Advisor Henry Kissinger, outraged, persuaded Nixon to authorize wiretaps on seventeen NSC staff members, including Morton Halperin, and several reporters, to find the source of the suspected leaks. For other reasons, the White House also wiretapped the journalist Joseph Kraft, a political moderate, hiring the retired New York City police officer John Caulfield for the job. Caulfield later became one of the many colorful characters in the Watergate saga.[22] The White House also ordered IRS audits of Lawrence W. O'Brien, chair of the Democratic Party, and the Washington attorney Edward Bennett Williams, who represented the hated *Washington Post.* Audited three years in a row, Williams first took it as a badge of honor but then realized something ominous was afoot. The IRS did not bend to every White House request, however. The Nixon staffer Tom Charles Huston complained that they had "no friends" at IRS and suggested to Haldeman they "clean house" at the agency. Huston had demanded information on "unfriendly" groups and individuals, such as the Brookings Institution, the Ford Foundation, "establishment types" like the Yale University president Kingman Brewster, and the "JFK Crowd." Discussing the efforts to get information about Senator Ted Kennedy, Nixon in May 1971 told Bob Haldeman he wanted "more use of wiretapping."[23]

These abuses of power in the very first months in office clearly indicate that the Watergate break-in was not an aberration. Even more important, they were one of the main reasons for the Watergate cover-up. On the famous June 23, 1972, "smoking gun" tape, Nixon worried that an FBI investigation of the break-in would uncover earlier misdeeds: "You open that scab there's a hell of a lot of things." Secrecy soon became an administration obsession. On March 24, 1969, Nixon wrote a statement on executive privilege that followed Presidents Kennedy and Johnson's promises to cooperate with congressional requests for information while withholding some information on national security grounds. Nixon pledged that he would use the exception "only in the most compelling circumstances" and that each case would require his personal approval. In the Watergate scandal, however, he would invoke a radically expansive view of executive privilege, encompassing material with no national security connections.[24]

While the White House attacked its critics, the army and the CIA expanded their domestic spying programs. The CIA effort, now code-named Operation CHAOS, ballooned

[22] "Raids In Cambodia by U.S. Unprotested," *NYT*, May 9, 1969. House Judiciary Committee, *Impeachment Report.* Halperin sued Nixon and Kissinger, winning a $5.00 judgment against Nixon. The suit against Kissinger ended after 19 years when Kissinger gave him a formal apology. Copies of the original FBI memos (with heavy deletions), beginning on May 12, 1969, are in U.S. House of Representatives, Select Committee on Intelligence, *United States Intelligence Agencies and Activities: Domestic Intelligence Programs*, Hearings, 94th Cong., 2nd Sess., 1975, pp. 1205ff. Kraft: Senate, *Senate Watergate Report*, pp. 185–8.

[23] Huston to Haldeman, July 16, 1970, Bruce Oudes, ed., *From: The President: Richard Nixon's Secret Files* (New York: Harper & Row, 1989), pp. 147–8. Huston to George Bell, January 25, 1971, ibid., pp. 207–8. IRS: Senate, *Senate Watergate Report*, pp. 60–1, 210–28. Wiretapping: Transcript, Oval Office Conversation, May 28, 1971, MCPA.

[24] Smoking gun tape recording is widely available, at the RMNPL and at www.watergate.info. "Nixon Gives His Stand on 'Executive Privilege,'" *NYT*, March 29, 1969, Cited by Nixon in Statement About Executive Privilege. March 12, 1973, APP. Mark Rozell, *Executive Privilege.* 3rd ed. (Lawrence: University Press of Kansas, 2010), pp. 55–72.

and eventually contained files on "at least 10,000 Americans." Nixon's deputy attorney general, Richard Kleindienst, urged the army to continue the program begun in 1965 in response to the urban riots and not transfer it to the FBI, as some had proposed. The army spying program was exposed by Christopher H. Pyle, a former army intelligence officer, in January 1970, and his revelations prompted Senate hearings the following year by Senator Sam Ervin's Subcommittee on Constitutional Rights. These events indicated how radically the political climate had changed as a result of the Vietnam War. Individuals and journalists were now ready to expose government misdeeds. Their ranks included Pyle, a former military officer. The most famous dissident would be Daniel Ellsberg, a former Vietnam War hawk and Pentagon employee, who leaked the *Pentagon Papers* in 1971. Nixon's spying efforts, in short, were not simply worse than previous presidents,' but occurred in a new political climate of whistle-blowing.[25]

"LAW AND ORDER" POLITICS

"There has never been a time in this Nation's history when more Americans were more concerned about the enforcement of law and reestablishing not only respect for laws but laws that deserve respect." President Nixon's remarks to Justice Department employees just ten days after taking office expressed the "law and order" theme of his election campaign. Five years of urban racial violence, the violence accompanying some antiwar protests, the growth of a drug-centered counterculture, and what Nixon believed was a culture of permissiveness, all deeply alarmed his conservative instincts. He singled out campus radicals as "a small, irresponsible minority" who threatened "legitimately constituted authority" with "a complete disregard for the rights of others." He delegated Vice President Agnew to meet with the nation's governors to discuss how "to cope with the growing lawlessness and violence on our campuses."[26]

The Nixon administration sought to quash dissent even before taking office, when the incoming deputy attorney general, Richard Kleindienst, tried to deny parade permits to a "Counter-Inaugural" protest at Nixon's swearing in. "No permits!" he insisted. Johnson administration officials were still in office, however, and issued the permits. One new White House staff member recalled Nixon's personally ordering the arrest of some disorderly protesters.[27]

The crackdown on dissent feared by antiwar activists occurred just two months after Nixon took office. In March 1969, the Justice Department indicted eight prominent activists

[25] Military spying program exposed: Christopher H. Pyle, *Military Surveillance of Civilian Politics, 1967–1970* (New York: Garland, 1986). Pyle, "CONUS Intelligence: The Army Watches Civilian Politics," *Washington Monthly* 1 (January 1970): 3 16. U.S. Senate, Committee on the Judiciary, Subcommittee on Constitutional Rights, *Federal Data Banks, Computers, and the Bill of Rights*. Hearings 92nd Congress, 1st Session. (Washington, DC: Government Printing Office, 1971). Joan M. Jensen, *Army Surveillance in America, 1775–1980* (New Haven, CT: Yale University Press, 1991), pp. 240–7. Kutler, *Wars of Watergate*, pp. 121–5. Daniel Ellsberg's transformation from Pentagon staff member to war critic: Daniel Ellsberg, *Secrets: A Memoir of Vietnam and the Pentagon Papers* (New York: Viking, 2002).

[26] Remarks to Employees at the Department of Justice, January 30th, 1969, APP. Letter to the President of the University of Notre Dame on Student Unrest, February 24, 1969, APP.

[27] Pyle, *Military Surveillance*, pp. 195–7. The demands of the incoming administration are not mentioned in National Commission on the Causes and Prevention of Violence, *Rights in Concord: The Response to the Counter-Inaugural Protest Activities in Washington, DC, January 18–20, 1969* (Washington, DC: Government Printing Office, 1969), "Permit Negotiations," pp. 82–8. Arrests: Bud Keogh to Ehrlichman, January 24, 1969, President's Office File, President's Handwriting, Box 1, RNPL.

over the protests at the 1968 Democratic Party convention, charging them with violating the new 1968 antiriot law. The law and the indictments represented a serious threat to freedom of speech and the right to travel. The Chicago Seven (the Black Panther Party leader Bobby Seale was severed from the original case) included three prominent antiwar radicals, Tom Hayden, Abbie Hoffman, and Jerry Rubin. The trial quickly descended into a circus, marked by overt hostility and misconduct by Judge Julius Hoffman. When Bobby Seals was literally bound and gagged in the courtroom, the defense attorney, William Kunstler, declared, "This is no longer a court of order, your Honor; this is a medieval torture chamber." Hoffman promptly cited him and his fellow defense attorneys for contempt. Five of the Chicago Seven were convicted, but the Seventh Circuit overturned both the criminal convictions and the contempt citations, citing Judge Hoffman's prejudicial demeanor, exclusion of expert witnesses, and failure to question prospective jurors about pretrial publicity.[28]

In the end, the Justice Department embarrassed itself in all of the high-profile prosecutions of dissenters: Dr. Spock and his codefendants; the Chicago Seven; Daniel Ellsberg, and Anthony Russo, who released the *Pentagon Papers*; and other less well-known cases. Charges were often dismissed, or defendants either were acquitted or had the their convictions overturned on appeal. Far from restoring law and order, the Nixon Justice Department only brought the legal system into disrepute.[29]

"Lock em up": Preventive detention

Candidate Nixon had loudly promised to do something about crime in the streets, but as president he faced the simple fact that criminal justice in America is primarily a local responsibility, with the federal government playing a minor role. The exception is the District of Columbia, a federal enclave, and Nixon chose to make it a showcase for his crime-fighting initiatives: "a city where we set an example for the rest of the major cities."[30]

The White House immediately focused on bail, believing that a combination of "soft" judges and the 1966 Bail Reform Act, a symbol of Kennedy and Johnson liberalism, turned predatory criminals loose on society. Nixon embraced the idea of preventive detention, which would allow judges to deny bail to defendants they deemed dangerous. At an October 1969 event, Nixon turned the podium over to the Washington, D.C., police chief, Jerry V. Wilson, a move designed to cement his identification with the police on the front line against crime. Wilson played his part and declared that what "we need most at this time is pretrial detention." Revising the 1966 bail law "might abate our armed robberies," he advised, and locking up just "the 300 main criminals" in the District would drastically reduce crime.[31]

28 *United States v. Dellinger*, 472 F2d 340 (November 21, 1972). Jon Wiener, ed., *Conspiracy in the Streets: The Extraordinary Trial of the Chicago Eight* (New York: New Press, 2006).

29 Even Mitchell's sympathetic biographer concedes this point: James Rosen, *The Strong Man: John Mitchell and the Secrets of Watergate* (New York: Doubleday, 2008), pp. 83–5.

30 Remarks with Participants in the Bipartisan Congressional Leadership Meeting on Crime in the District of Columbia, October 9, 1969, APP.

31 Statement Outlining Actions and Recommendations for the District of Columbia,January 31, 1969, APP. "Pretrial Jailing Weighed by Nixon," *NYT*, January 30, 1969. Remarks with Participants in the Bipartisan Congressional Leadership Meeting on Crime in the District of Columbia, October 9, 1969, APP.

Preventive detention served Nixon's political goals by presenting him as a tough crime fighter, concerned about protecting the law-abiding citizen. Alarmed civil libertarians saw preventive detention as an assault on the constitutional right to bail and a precursor to other assaults on the Bill of Rights. The ACLU denounced it as a "devious euphemism" for holding people who had not been "tried and found guilty of a crime." Together with Attorney General John Mitchell's plans to use wiretaps aggressively and the indictment of the Chicago Seven, preventive detention seemed to confirm the worst fears of Nixon's hostility to civil liberties. The Nixon administration correctly read the public mood about crime, however. Pat Buchanan in 1969 saw preventive detention as a "towering legal issue of the coming decade," adding that "many urban liberals already support it." White House officials took delight in 1972 when the Democratic presidential candidate George McGovern proposed an even harsher version of preventive detention (calling for the automatic reincarceration of anyone arrested while on probation or parole, where the administration allowed judicial discretion in detention decisions). Buchanan was right, and Democrats began matching Republicans with draconian anticrime measures, including especially harsh sentencing laws.[32]

Congress passed a preventive detention law for Washington, D.C., in 1970, but it proved to be an empty promise, as it was hardly ever used. The elaborate procedural safeguards led prosecutors simply to ignore it. Like many other "get tough" crime measures, preventive detention was based on a faulty premise. Research consistently found low rates of reoffending by people out on bail, and no criminologist ever devised a formula for identifying the three hundred repeat offenders Police Chief Wilson mentioned. The D.C. law, however, was simply ahead of its time. Within a decade, every state and the entire federal criminal justice system would have preventive detention laws that judges would use.[33]

Launching the war on drugs

President Nixon also launched the so-called war on drugs. In a July 1969 message to Congress, he warned that the drug problem had grown "from essentially a local police problem into a serious national threat." In retrospect, however, Nixon's original drug program was fairly moderate and included many items consistent with President Johnson's liberal crime policies, including public education about drugs, more research, and treatment for addicts. Most criminologists agreed with Nixon's caution against the "common oversimplification" that the drug problem is "a law enforcement problem alone." Drug users were "genuinely sick people," he said, and "society has an obligation both to itself and to these people to help them break the chains of their dependency." The most influential proposal, however, was tough law enforcement to interdict the flow of drugs into the country and to suppress drug trafficking on the streets. Nixon reiterated these points in a June 17, 1971, message to Congress that many observers later regarded as the beginning

[32] "Preventive Detention Plan Scored by Liberties Union," *NYT*, April 16, 1969. Buchanan: News Analysis, Annotated News Summary, January 30, 1969, President's Office File, Box 30, RNPL. [Buchanan's job included preparing a daily summary of media coverage of the administration. These summaries often include his comments on items, or the comments of other White House staff, and are particularly valuable in that regard. Undated memo, circa 1972, WHSF, Buchanan Files, Box 10, RNPL.

[33] Preventive detention as a crime reduction measure: Samuel Walker, *Sense and Nonsense about Crime, Drugs and Community: A Policy Guide*. 7th ed. (Belmont, CA: Wadsworth, 2011), pp. 147–50.

of the "war on drugs." That speech called for a "full-scale attack" on the scourge of drugs and a new centralized federal effort, but even then he opened with the section "A New Approach to Rehabilitation."[34]

In retrospect, what sets Nixon's original program apart from subsequent antidrug crusades is the absence of harsh sentencing provisions. Mandatory sentencing and long prison sentences would soon dominate crime policy, championed by presidents from Gerald Ford to Bill Clinton. They would send the American prison population soaring, with a particularly devastating effect on African Americans. That shift did not begin until the mid-1970s, however, after Nixon had left the White House.[35]

Declaring a "war" on drugs was part of a long presidential tradition of using the war metaphor to mobilize public support for policies. Franklin D. Roosevelt famously declared in his first inaugural speech that he would attack the depression "as we would treat the emergency of a war." Lyndon Johnson declared a war on poverty, and George W. Bush launched a war on terrorism. The war metaphor has been consistently inappropriate, however, raising unrealistic public expectations about an eventual "victory" and often justifying inappropriate policies on the grounds that they address a special problem requiring extraordinary measures. Nixon's war on drugs falls squarely in this dangerous territory.

A DIFFERENT VISION OF PROGRESS ON RACE

"Certain changes are needed in the Nation's approach to school desegregation," President Nixon told the nation in a lengthy March 1970 statement on education that also addressed race.[36] Nixon's image, then and now, is one of hostility to civil rights. In the 1968 campaign he signaled that he would scale back federal enforcement of school integration and was absolutely opposed to school busing. The campaign rhetoric and his initial actions as president created a bitter conflict with civil rights leaders. Nixon's attitudes and policies on race were extremely complex, however. In fact, he pushed affirmative action in federally funded jobs far more than any other president. And while he backed off on school integration, so had Lyndon Johnson before him, notably in the 1965 Chicago case.

Nixon was not indifferent to race, as his critics alleged; he simply had a vision of racial progress that diverged from the agenda of national civil rights leaders. His approach was summed up in the phrase "black capitalism," which the historian Garry Wills argues was rooted in a sentimentalized faith in individualism, hard work, self-reliance, and upward mobility. As president he often violated the terms of that faith (supporting affirmative action and imposing wage and price controls in 1971), but his belief in it endured, particularly with regard to race. Government, he believed, should neither bar opportunity, as segregation had, nor promise it as he saw liberals doing. This explains his very good

[34] Special Message to the Congress on Control of Narcotics and Dangerous Drugs, July 14, 1969, APP. The more famous message is Special Message to the Congress on Drug Abuse Prevention and Control, June 17, 1971, APP.

[35] "Key Facts on D.C. Crime," "Key Facts on Dangerous Drugs," Ehrlichman, "Selling Our Line of Domestic Issues" circa mid-1972, WHSF, Ehrlichman Files, Box 26, RNPL. Samuel Walker, *Popular Justice: A History of American Criminal Justice*, 2nd ed. (New York: Oxford University Press, 1998), pp. 222–4.

[36] Statement about Desegregation of Elementary and Secondary Schools, March 24, 1970, APP.

civil rights record early in his career, including the public support for *Brown v. Board of Education* that President Eisenhower never gave.[37]

Personally, Nixon was not a racist. From the moment he was elected to the House of Representatives in 1946, he supported every civil rights bill, and in 1968 he supported the Fair Housing Act, which most Republicans opposed. In the 1960 presidential election, Martin Luther King initially favored him over Kennedy for president. He joined Nelson Rockefeller in having one of the best records on civil rights among leading Republicans in those years (both future presidents Ronald Reagan and George H. W. Bush, meanwhile, had opposed the 1964 Civil Rights Act).[38] In the post-1965 era of race-conscious policies such as affirmative action, however, Nixon clung to his earlier belief in color-blind policies.

The attacks on him by civil rights leaders left Nixon confused and angry, and he never understood that they involved his policies and not his personal beliefs. (Ronald Reagan had the same experience.) Jews were another matter with Nixon, however. The White House tapes contain many anti-semitic remarks. In the midst of the *Pentagon Papers* crisis, for example, he ordered a ban on all contact with the *New York Times*, including no talking with "any of those Jews." In another outburst, he announced, "The government is full of Jews.... most Jews are disloyal." Oddly, however, despite these profoundly prejudiced comments, he had many Jews as his closest advisers, notably Henry Kissinger, Leonard Garment, and William Safire, and they served him loyally.[39]

Nixon's policies on race and civil rights were a complex mixture of sincere opposition to de jure segregation, a desire to be a pragmatic national leader who achieved results, and a healthy dose of raw political calculation. His aides included an unstable mixture of civil rights advocates, such as Robert Finch and Leonard Garment, and fire-breathing conservatives such as Patrick Buchanan and Charles Colson, who were eager to court white southern votes. The result was a series of zigzags on civil rights policy that were obscured by what his own lawyer, Leonard Garment, characterized as "clouds of retrogressive rhetoric." [40]

The first crisis: Desegregation in the South

In its very first weeks, the Nixon administration faced a crisis on school integration. President Johnson had delayed the implementation of HEW guidelines on desegregation, and five southern school districts finally faced a January 29,1969 cutoff of federal funds, forcing the administration to act. At the last minute, the HEW secretary, Robert H. Finch, granted a sixty-day extension, in what was described as the "administration's first major civil rights action." Another seven hundred to eight hundred southern districts were also negotiating with HEW over their desegregation plans, and Nixon's critics believed his

37 Wills, *Nixon Agonistes*, presciently argued in 1969 that Nixon was perhaps "the last liberal" (pp. 534–46).

38 A thorough treatment of the subject: Dean J. Kotlowski, *Nixon's Civil Rights: Politics, Principle, and Policy* (Cambridge, MA: Harvard University Press, 2001). See also Hoff, *Nixon Reconsidered*, pp. 77–114.

39 Jews in the government: John Prados and Margaret Pratt Porter, eds., *Inside the Pentagon Papers* (Lawrence: University Press of Kansas, 2004), p. 81. David Gergen, *Eyewitness to Power: The Essence of Leadership, Nixon to Clinton* (New York: Simon & Schuster, 2000), p. 20. Gergen notes that Nixon's Jewish aides were among his most vigorous defenders in public. See Kenneth J. Hughes, Jr., "Nixon vs. the Imaginary 'Jewish Cabal,'" hnn.us/articles/42970.html.

40 Garment: Kotlowski, *Nixon's Civil Rights*, p. 1.

campaign statements had encouraged them to delay or resist outright. Finch, however, was committed to enforcing federal fund cutoffs in both the North and the South and incurred attacks from southern Republicans who wielded great influence in the new administration. One labeled him "a disaster in every sense of the word" in early 1970, and he was soon transferred from HEW to a lesser White House post. Southern school districts devised "freedom of choice" plans, which generally resulted in only limited integration. The five southern school districts threatened by Finch in January 1969 all received their funds in April when HEW accepted their freedom of choice plans.[41] The issue of de facto segregation in school districts outside the South was another matter altogether. Nixon understood, as had Lyndon Johnson, that the heavy weapon of even threatening to cut off federal funds under Title VI was political dynamite. Thus, while the nation's attention was focused on southern schools, the administration did not address the increasingly segregated schools in the big cities outside the South.

Suspicions about Nixon's commitment to civil rights enforcement were inflamed early in 1969 by the leak of a White House memo urging "benign neglect" of racial issues. The memo's author was Daniel P. Moynihan, a former Johnson administration official, who was now Nixon's principal adviser on urban issues. Bitter over the attacks on his 1965 report *The Negro Family* and disillusioned with liberal social reform in general, he was becoming an influential neoconservative voice on social policy issues. Inside the White House, he peppered Nixon and his staff with long and often turgid memos, filled with academic theories and historical references (one exasperated White House aide made a snide reference to "Moynihanistic philosophizing"). The idea of benign neglect reflected his belief that civil rights leaders' rhetoric raised expectations that could not be met. Nixon agreed, sharing Moynihan's distaste for radical rhetoric on civil rights or the Vietnam War, and took particular offense at charges that America was a racist society.[42] Benign neglect, however, was an inaccurate label for Nixon's race policies. In fact, he aggressively promoted black capitalism and affirmative action. The real dispute with the civil rights establishment was not the role of government per se, but very different visions about how government programs could facilitate racial progress.

Nixon's meetings with civil rights leaders were completely counterproductive. A session with Ralph Abernathy, the new head of Martin Luther King's Southern Christian Leadership Conference, and other civil rights leaders on May 13, 1969, went very badly. Afterward, H. R. Haldeman called it "pretty ridiculous" and complained that Abernathy tried to "trap" the president into endorsing certain positions. He felt that Abernathy "stabbed us" in a postmeeting press conference and concluded that "there's no use dealing honestly with these people. They obviously want confrontation, not solutions." (President Kennedy and Robert Kennedy, it should be noted, felt the same way in the face of demands for more aggressive civil rights action.) As a result, the administration refused to meet with the Congressional Black Caucus. The White House adviser on civil

41 "South Wins Delay on Desegregation," *NYT*, January 30, 1969; "3 Southern Areas Denied School Aid," ibid., February 14, 1969; "Carolina Schools Will Get U.S. Aid," ibid., April 20, 1969. Finch: Clarke Reed, Chair, Southern Association of Republican State Chairmen, to Ehrlichman, January 12, 1970, WHSF, Ehrlichman Files, Box 21, RNPL.

42 "Benign Neglect on Race Is Proposed by Moynihan," *NYT*, March 1, 1970. Typical Moynihan memo: Moynihan, Personal and Confidential Memorandum for Ehrlichman, July 24, 1970, WHSF, Ehrlichman Files, Box 21, RNPL. Comment on Moynihan: Jim Keogh to Staff Secretary, August 26, 1969, WHCF, Subject File, Human Rights, Box 21, RNPL.

rights Robert J. Brown, an African American, advised that "I don't think a meeting at this point would be very beneficial." In response, caucus members announced they would boycott Nixon's 1971 State of the Union Address.[43]

Although Nixon promised to "bring America together," and by implication avoid interest group politics, in office he aggressively cultivated constituencies based on race and religion. Pat Buchanan plotted wedge strategies to steal groups away from the Democrats. Nixon initiated what later administrations institutionalized as the Office of Public Liaison, the home of outreach to interest groups. Buchanan was the link to Catholics, Anne Armstrong handled women's issues, and Robert Armstrong reached out to African Americans.[44]

"I am opposed to busing"

The flash point of controversy on civil rights was busing students to achieve racial integration. Nixon's vocal opposition to busing included a high degree of political calculation, because it appealed to northern white voters. The prospect of African-American students' being bused into their neighborhood schools was an alarm bell for both suburbanites and traditionally Democratic blue-collar neighborhoods within big city school districts. Nixon always referred to "forced" or "court-ordered" busing to suggest that it was imposed by unelected judges. In a long March 24, 1970, statement on desegregation, he firmly declared, "We are not backing away," from the principle of *Brown* but added that "certain changes are needed in the Nation's approach to school desegregation." After a long discussion of recent court decisions, he got to his main point: "I have consistently expressed my opposition to any compulsory busing of pupils beyond normal geographic school zones for the purpose of achieving racial balance." The basic problem was "de facto racial separation, resulting from housing patterns," which should not "by itself be cause for Federal enforcement actions."[45]

Nixon had thought seriously about public education and concluded that it was "not just a matter of race," and his approach was rooted in an old-fashioned Republican ideology of individualism, economic opportunity, and upward mobility, with education playing the key role for both African Americans and whites. To build good schools that would prepare black and white students Nixon proposed $1.5 billion in federal aid to education, with one-third of it directed toward "racially impacted areas." Sounding a lot like Lyndon Johnson, he outlined an ambitious federal effort to develop data on desegregation, new programs for gifted children, and a general goal of raising the quality of education "in all schools," but particularly in "racially-impacted schools," in order to raise the poorest performing schools to a level of equality.[46]

[43] Haldeman, *The Haldeman Diaries*, p. 55. David N. Parker to Bob Brown, September 15, 1971, WHCF, Subject File, Human Rights, Box 3, RNPL. "Black Congressmen to Boycott Nixon," *Washington Post*, January 22, 1971.

[44] Joseph A. Pika, "The White House Office of Public Liaison," *Presidential Studies Quarterly* 39 (September 2009): 549–73.

[45] "Agnew Declares He's Antibusing," *NYT*, September 17, 1969. Leonard Garment recalls Agnew's antibusing speech was an unauthorized action by the hard-line conservatives within the administration to offset the White House's official position. Leonard Garment, *Crazy Rhythm: My Journey from Brooklyn, Jazz and Wall Street to Nixon's White House, Watergate, and Beyond* (New York: Times Books, 1997), pp. 205–7. Statement about Desegregation of Elementary and Secondary Schools, March 24, 1970, APP.

[46] Statement about Desegregation of Elementary and Secondary Schools, March 24, 1970, APP.

The vast majority of Americans opposed busing, and Nixon fully understood that. A fall 1970 Gallup Poll found that 78 percent of people in the Midwest and 71 percent in the East opposed school busing, compared with 82 percent in the South. The Democratically controlled Congress read the same polls and eventually passed three amendments seeking to limit busing in various ways. The Delaware senator Joe Biden, later a candidate for president and then vice president, cosponsored one of these amendments. In March 1974, for example, the House overwhelmingly (293–117) approved an amendment prohibiting federal courts from ordering busing of students to "any but the school closest or next closest to the student's home." The Senate rejected the amendment by one vote, 46–47, but would later pass a similar version. It is noteworthy that Robert Kennedy, running for the Senate in New York in 1964, said he was opposed to "long distance transportation" of students to end de facto school segregation. In a Binghamton, New York, campaign speech he said he was "strongly in favor of local control over education." Asked about a planned school boycott of an integration plan by New York City parents, he said that he "might oppose a particular plan, but would not take part in a boycott."[47]

Instead of enforcing school integration through HEW and threatening to cut off federal funds, Nixon shifted enforcement to the Justice Department. This approach embodied a devious political strategy. The legal process was inevitably lengthy, and in the case of a court order cast the federal judge and not an administration figure loomed as the villain in the eyes of opponents. (Nicholas Katzenbach, a Justice Department official under Presidents Kennedy and Johnson, later wrote that Kennedy favored the same strategy.) The Supreme Court, meanwhile, increasingly frustrated with the lack of progress on implementing *Brown*, began striking down desegregation plans that did not achieve results and ordering specific methods to achieve integration. Anticipating an adverse Supreme Court decision in 1971 (the Court held school busing constitutional in *Swann v. Mecklenberg Board of Education* on April 20), Nixon directed his staff to have a "game plan" ready, including a constitutional amendment to ban busing, if the Court went "in the wrong direction." Because southern delaying tactics began to run out in the late 1960s, far more progress on school integration occurred under Nixon than under any previous president. In 1968, 186,000 African Americans attended desegregated schools in the South; in the 1970–1 school year the figure was two million. One observer called Nixon the "greatest desegregator in American history," but this was misleading. The progress was more an accident of timing and the exhaustion of delaying tactics.[48]

The administration's policy on housing discrimination paralleled that in the school busing controversy. On the one hand, Nixon opposed overt race discrimination, and George Romney, his secretary of housing and urban development, was a strong civil

[47] Murphy and Gulliver, *The Southern Strategy*, p. 261. George Gallup, Jr., *The Gallup Poll: Public Opinion 1935–1971* (New York: Random House, 1972), p. 2271. Lawrence J. McAndrews, "Missing the Bus: Gerald Ford and School Desegregation," *Presidential Studies Quarterly* 27 (Fall 1997): 791–804. "Kennedy Says He Opposes Distant Busing of Students," *NYT*, September 9, 1964. Critical view of Kennedy's programs for African Americans: Ronald Steel, *In Love with Night: The American Romance with Robert Kennedy* (New York: Simon & Schuster, 2000), p. 165.

[48] Haldeman, *Haldeman Diaries*, p. 214. President to Ehrlichman, February 8, 1971, Oudes, ed., *From: The President*, p. 214. Also, Kotlowski, *Nixon's Civil Rights*, p. 39. *Swann v. Charlotte Mecklenberg Board of Education*, 402 U.S. 1(1971). Kennedy strategy: Katzenbach, *Some of It Was Fun*, p. 72. Kotlowski, *Nixon's Civil Rights*, p. 37.

rights advocate. In the debate over "open housing," however, Nixon opposed any program that would "force" integration.[49]

The affirmative action president

No less a figure than the civil rights leader James Farmer, who organized the 1961 Freedom Rides, called Richard Nixon was "the strongest president on affirmative action – up to that point." The conservative *Fortune* magazine agreed, observing on the occasion of Nixon's death in 1994, "It was the Nixonites who gave us employment quotas."[50]

Despite Nixon's faith in individualism and limited government, historians generally agree that Nixon established affirmative action as the official policy of the federal government. This judgment surprises most liberals, but the record is very clear, and it involves another of Nixon's contradictions. On the one hand, affirmative action served his belief that jobs would accomplish what liberal social welfare programs never would. But it also contradicted his individualistic rhetoric about freedom from government regulation. Several historians explain the contradiction in terms of Nixon's self-image as a pragmatist who could get things done. If affirmative action was necessary to ensure jobs for African Americans, he would support it. "To foster the economic status and the pride of members of our minority groups," he argued, "we must seek to involve them more fully in our private enterprise system." And so in August 1969, he issued an executive order directing federal agencies to "establish and maintain an affirmative program of equal employment opportunity for all civilian employees and applicants for employment."[51]

Race-conscious preferences in federal contracts, Nixon and his aides believed, could also advance black capitalism. In one of his long memos, Daniel Moynihan argued that "procurement is unquestionably the most powerful engine the Federal establishment has to promote minority enterprise." The Defense Department consequently created a program of preferential contracts for minority-owned businesses in cooperation with the Small Business Administration. The program, however, did not always go well. In 1969, for example, the Pentagon contracted with the Watts Manufacturing Co., an aerospace firm in Los Angeles, for five thousand tents. A subsequent White House memo, however, reported that the company suffered operating problems, and its future was uncertain. Scribbled in the margin of the memo was the comment "This shows the enormous problems in our minority enterprise program.... Good luck." They needed it. Over time, preferential contract programs had only marginal success, and absolutely no impact on hard-core poverty. The administration also developed a Minority Bank Deposit Program, in which every federal agency would deposit funds in minority-owned banks. The Commerce Department announced a goal of $100 million in 1970, with $35 million in deposits from federal agencies and $65 million from private corporations. By April 1971, however, federal deposits totaled only $5 million.[52]

49 Kotlowski, *Nixon's Civil Rights*, pp. 66–7.

50 Farmer: Strober and Strober, eds., *Nixon: An Oral History of His Presidency*, p. 114. Kotlowski, *Nixon's Civil Rights*, p. 97. Daniel Seligman, "Where Quotas Came From," *Fortune* 129 (May 30, 1994): 174–5.

51 Executive Order 11478 – Equal Employment Opportunity in the Federal Government,August 8, 1969, APP. John David Skrentny, *The Ironies of Affirmative Action: Politics, Culture, and Justice in America*, Pbk. ed. (Chicago: University of Chicago Press, 1996), pp. 177–221.

52 Moynihan to The Staff Secretary, October 17, 1969, WHCF, Subject File, Human Rights, Box 2, RNPL. Annotated News Summary, March 11, 1969, p. 2, President's Office File, Box 30, RNPL. Garment to Cole, June 11, 1971;

The historian Dean Kotlowski accurately titles a chapter of his book on Nixon and civil rights, "Jobs Are Nixon's Rights Program." The centerpiece of Nixon's affirmative action program was the Philadelphia Plan. Announced on September 23, 1969, it required "goals" for African-American employment in six skilled construction crafts in all federally assisted construction projects in the Philadelphia area. Similar plans for other cities soon followed. Some officials in the administration argued that the plan involved reverse discrimination, in violation of the 1964 Civil Rights Act, and the U.S. controller general, Elmer Staats, ruled it illegal. Attorney General John Mitchell, attentive to Nixon's economic and political goals, intervened to rule it legal because "goals" were not "quotas." The national debate over the use of racial preferences had just begun. Opposition to the Philadelphia Plan was mainly from organized labor. Some in Congress also objected, and in late 1969 amendments to ban quotas and effectively kill the Philadelphia Plan were only narrowly defeated in the House and the Senate.[53]

In the long run, the Philadelphia Plan had only limited impact. Most important, Nixon himself soon backed away from vigorous enforcement. By 1970, with opposition to his Vietnam War policy growing, he saw organized labor as a source of support for the war and another traditional Democratic Party constituency he could peel away. He clearly understood the political implications of a series of highly publicized attacks by construction union workers on antiwar demonstrators in New York City in 1970. Although he backed off from enforcement, he had nonetheless set in motion something he could not fully control. Deep within the federal bureaucracy, affirmative action acquired a life of its own and in the years ahead became deeply entrenched in federal employment, state and local governments, and the private sector. Some analysts have pointed out that preferential, race-conscious plans eventually became government policy with no endorsement from Congress and only intermittent support from various presidents. The Supreme Court would wrestle with race-conscious remedies for almost forty years.[54]

NIXON CONFRONTS THE SEXUAL REVOLUTION

It was Nixon's fate to be president when Lyndon Johnson's Commission on Pornography and Obscenity delivered its report in 1970. Personally and politically, he was not ready for the sexual revolution or the liberal policies the commission recommended. The Warren Court's First Amendment decisions had brought about a revolution in freedom of expression, dismantling the long-standing apparatus of censorship, and the result was a flood of sexually explicit materials, readily available in bookstores, magazine stands, and movie theaters. One of the many landmarks of the new sexual freedom was the 1967 Danish film

Ken Cole to Garment, June 14, 1971, WHCF, Subject File, Human Rights, Box 3, RNPL. Dean Kotlowski, "Black Power - Nixon Style: The Nixon Administration and Minority Business Enterprise," *Business History Review* 72 (Autumn 1998): 409–45.

53 Kotlowski, *Nixon's Civil Rights*, Ch. 4, 97–124. "U.S. to Start Plan to Give Minorities Jobs in Building," *NYT*, September 24, 1969. J. Larry Hood, "The Nixon Administration and the Revised Philadelphia Plan for Affirmative Action: A Study in Expanding Presidential Power and Divided Government," *Presidential Studies Quarterly* 23 (Winter 1993): 145–269. Statement Urging Senate and House Conferees to Permit Continued Implementation of the Philadelphia Plan, December 19, 1969, APP. "Congress Avoids Tie-Up on Rights," *NYT*, December 23, 1969.

54 Stephen C. Halpern, *On the Limits of the Law: The Ironic Legacy of Title VI of the 1964 Civil Rights Act* (Baltimore: Johns Hopkins University Press, 1995), Ch. 4, "The Nixon-Ford Years," pp. 81–136.

I Am Curious (Yellow), which featured nudity, staged sexual activity, and one kiss of a flaccid penis. Massachusetts banned the film and prosecuted the distributor, but federal courts later held it not obscene.[55]

To put it mildly, Nixon was appalled by the commission's recommendations that all laws restricting consenting adults access to sexually explicit materials be repealed, that exposure to such material did not cause crime, that the real problem was the inability of Americans to be open about sexuality, and that the nation should undertake a "massive sex education effort." The report epitomized the very liberal "permissiveness" he regarded as responsible for the moral decay of America. Social conservatives complained that the ACLU had captured the commission, and the Senate voted 60–5 to condemn the report. And although Nixon called it "morally bankrupt," the White House opted for a "very soft, low-key approach" that barely acknowledged it. Surprisingly, this approach was recommended by Pat Buchanan, who was rarely low-key about anything and certainly not on such a hot-button social issue as pornography. The administration emphasized the dissenting statement by the commission member Charles Keating, the nation's leading antipornography crusader, and argued that the report was deeply flawed. In Haldeman's words, they would let "the issue to be their bad report." Buchanan also recommended issuing a White House statement late on a Friday, since Saturday's was always "the smallest paper of the week."[56] Thus, despite his rhetoric about America's moral decay, Nixon passed on this opportunity to seize the issue.

PAROCHAID: ATTACKING THE WALL OF SEPARATION

"This will drive a wedge right down the middle of the Democratic Party," advised Pat Buchanan, urging the White House to push federal aid to parochial schools aggressively. Normally, he was ideologically opposed to federal aid programs, but here he cynically saw an enormous political opportunity and helped persuade Nixon that it could help win over Catholic Democrats. The compromise over the 1965 Education Act had not completely settled the issue of public funding for parochial schools, and Catholic leaders continued to press for state funds. Nixon endorsed this approach in the 1968 election campaign, and the 1968 GOP platform urged "states to present plans for federal assistance which would include state distribution of such aid to non-public school children." Several states enacted what became known as "parochaid" programs.[57]

The Supreme Court's decisions on separation between church and state posed a formidable obstacle, however. A challenge to the parochaid program in several states finally reached the Court in the 1970–1 term. The White House aide John Ehrlichman directed

55 Charles Rembar, *The End of Obscenity: The Trials of Lady Chatterley, Tropic of Cancer, and Fanny Hill* (New York: Random House, 1968). *I Am Curious Yellow* litigation: *Byrne v. Karalexis*, 396 U.S. 976 (1969) and 401 U.S. 216 (1971).

56 *Report of the Commission on Obscenity and Pornography* (New York: Random House, 1970), pp. 28–31, 53–62. Response: Leigh Ann Wheeler, *How Sex Became a Civil Liberty* (New York: Oxford University Press, 2012). Tod R. Hullin to Ehrlichman, August 25, 1970, WHCF, Subject Files, Commission on Pornography, Box 1, RNPL. Haldeman, *The Haldeman Diaries*, p. 191. Statement: Buchanan to Ehrlichman/Haldeman, October 22, 1970, WHCF, Subject File, FG 95, COP, Box 1, RNPL. "Text of Nixon's Statement Rejecting the Report of Obscenity Panel," *NYT*, October 25, 1970.

57 Buchanan to Ehrlichman, Haldeman, and Colson, September 23, 1971; quoted in Mason, *Richard Nixon and the Quest for a New Majority*, p. 153. 1968 Republican Party platform, 1968, APP.

Solicitor General Erwin Griswold to file an amicus brief supporting the Rhode Island program permitting the state to supplement the salaries of parochial school teachers up to 15 percent of their base salary. A Pennsylvania law, meanwhile, authorized state funds for salaries, textbooks, and other instructional materials. In an act of principled defiance, Griswold refused, believing the state laws unconstitutional and considering the brief Ehrlichman wanted a blatantly political maneuver unworthy of his office. Instead, his first deputy, Daniel Friedman, filed the administration's brief. Griswold was vindicated when the Supreme Court unanimously declared parochaid programs unconstitutional, calling the Rhode Island law a "significant aid to a religious enterprise."[58]

The Court's decision in *Lemon v. Kurtzman* was a major political defeat for Nixon in two respects. Not only did he lose on the parochaid issue, but it also revealed that his plan to reshape the Supreme Court was not working. His two appointees joined the decision, and Chief Justice Warren Burger wrote the opinion. Nixon refused to give up, however, and he told the National Catholic Education Association in April 1972 that "America needs her nonpublic schools," and "we must and will find ways to provide that help." The 1972 GOP platform that summer expressed the hope that "means which are consistent with the Constitution can be devised for channeling public financial aid" to public and nonpublic schools. For the moment, however, the wall of separation was stronger than before.[59]

A SURPRISING STAND ON WOMEN'S RIGHTS

"Throughout twenty-one years of public service," President Nixon wrote to the Senate Republican leader Hugh Scott, "I have not altered my belief that equal rights for women warrant a Constitutional guarantee," and that he supported the proposed Equal Rights Amendment guaranteeing equality for women.[60] Nixon supported the ERA when first elected to Congress in 1946, cosponsored it as a senator in 1951, and supported it in the 1968 presidential campaign. Despite his conflicts with African-American leaders over civil rights policies, as president he was a consistent supporter of the ERA and women's rights.

The ERA had virtually died in the late 1950s but reemerged with powerful political support during Nixon's presidency, buoyed by the new feminist movement. Representative Martha Griffiths, Democrat from Michigan, who had helped add sex discrimination to Title VII of the 1964 Civil Rights Act, reintroduced it in early 1970. The traditional opposition from prolabor Democrats simply evaporated in the new social and political climate. The AFL-CIO, the League of Women Voters, and the ACLU, all longtime opponents, reversed themselves and endorsed the amendment.[61]

58 *Lemon v. Kurtzman*, 403 U.S. 602 (1971). Erwin N. Griswold, *Ould Fields, New Corne: The Personal Memoirs of a Twentieth Century Lawyer* (St. Paul: West, 1992), pp. 290–1. The Acting Solicitor General is listed on the Court opinion. Mason, *Richard Nixon and the Quest for a New Majority*, p. 152.

59 Remarks at the Annual Convention of the National Catholic Education Association in Philadelphia, Pennsylvania, April 6, 1972, APP. Mason, *Richard Nixon and the Quest for a New Majority*, p. 152. 1972 GOP platform, APP.

60 Letter to the Senate Minority Leader about the Proposed Constitutional Amendment on Equal Rights for Men and Women, March 18, 1972, APP. Kotlowski, *Nixon's Civil Rights*, pp. 232–40. Nixon and women's issues: Janet M. Martin, *The Presidency and Women: Promise, Performance and Illusion* (College Station: Texas A&M Press, 2003), pp. 123–66.

61 Joan Hoff-Wilson, ed., *Rights of Passage: The Past and Future of the ERA* (Bloomington: Indiana University Press, 1986).

Nixon administration officials were sharply divided over the ERA, however. First Lady Pat Nixon, Secretary of Labor George Shultz, and Vice President Spiro Agnew strongly supported it. Attorney General John Mitchell was opposed, however, on the grounds that the Fifth and Fourteenth Amendments adequately protected women's rights. Leonard Garment, the most liberal member of Nixon's staff and a strong civil rights supporter, advised Nixon to oppose it on strategic grounds. Twenty-two constitutional amendments were then pending in Congress, including one that would bar busing students to achieve school integration. To head off this and other troubling amendments, Garment advised opposing all amendments. John Ehrlichman, hardly a liberal, argued that "politically this [ERA] is a golden opportunity and ... we should, whenever possible, champion female equality." Nixon did not need any convincing and maintained his support for the ERA.[62]

Notably, one of the strongest voices of opposition was that of the assistant attorney general heading the Office of Legal Counsel, William H. Rehnquist. The future Chief justice of the Supreme Court, voicing one of the main themes of the neoconservative movement, argued that the clear "implication" of the amendment "is nothing less than the sharp reduction in importance of the family unit," and that "the eventual elimination of that unit [is] by no means improbable."[63] Nixon's support for the ERA stands in sharp contrast to the opposition to feminism by President Ronald Reagan and other neoconservatives from the 1980s onward. The difference reflects the radical shift in presidential politics with the rise of neoconservativism and is another indicator of how the later generation regarded Nixon as a liberal.

Forty-seven years after Alice Paul had introduced it, the House on May 4, 1970 passed the ERA by an overwhelming 350–15 vote. The Senate also passed it, and on March 22, 1972, it went to the states for ratification. After being quickly adopted by thirty states, however, the ERA ran headlong into ferocious opposition from the rising neoconservative movement and stalled just three states short of the necessary thirty-eight. Led by Phyllis Schlafly and her Eagle Forum, ERA opponents stopped the ERA dead in its tracks.

On other women's issues, Nixon was also rather liberal. He appointed a Task Force on Women's Rights and Responsibilities in 1969 and accepted many of the recommendations in its 1970 report. *A Matter of Simple Justice* endorsed the ERA, extending the jurisdiction of the U.S. Civil Rights Commission to discrimination against women, barring sex discrimination in higher education (what later became Title IX), and removing gender inequities in Social Security. Nixon did not comment on Title IX when it was passed in 1972, mainly because he directed his fire that day at an antibusing amendment in the same bill that was not as strong as the one he wanted.[64]

Nixon also never sounded or acted more like Lyndon Johnson than in his support for family planning. After mentioning it in his first State of the Union Address, he appointed

62 Pat Nixon, Schultz, and Agnew: Ehrlichman to the President, May 25, 1970; Ehrlichman, For the President, September 29, 1969, WHCF, Subject File, Human Rights, Box 21, RNPL. Kotlowski, *Nixon's Civil Rights*, pp. 235–7.

63 Ehrlichman to the President, May 25, 1970, WHCF, Subject File, Human Rights, Box 21, RNPL. In his testimony before Congress, Rehnquist dutifully endorsed the administration's support for the ERA but made clear his "reservations." Rehnquist, Asst. AG, Office of Legal Counsel, Testimony, House Judiciary Committee, Subcommittee No. 4, April 1, 1971, [ERA], WHCF, Subject File, Human Rights, Box 21, RNPL.

64 Task Force on Women's Rights and Responsibilities, *A Matter of Simple Justice* (Washington, DC: DC: Government Printing Office, 1970). Title IX and anti-busing amendment: Statement on Signing the Education Amendments of 1972, June 23, 1972, APP. The statement was made the same day as the "smoking gun" conversation that drove Nixon from office.

a Commission on Population Growth and the American Future. His Special Message on the subject in July 1969 sounded like an LBJ Great Society speech, explaining how population affected the cities and the environment and arguing that more research and training on population control were urgently needed. The commission's 1972 report reads today like a standard liberal/feminist policy statement, recommending that states eliminate restrictions on "access to contraceptive information, procedures, and supplies" and public funding for abortion services "in states with liberalized statutes." It also endorsed the ERA and called for "fair and equal treatment to all children."[65]

Abortion, however, began rising as a volatile legal and political issue, as public attitudes about sexuality, privacy, and abortion began changing rapidly in the late 1960s. California passed the first liberalized abortion law in 1967 (with tepid support from Governor Ronald Reagan), and other states began to follow suit. Few national politicians wanted to deal with this very controversial issue, and Nixon was quite happy that the 1972 GOP platform did not mention it. The Supreme Court issued its bombshell decision in *Roe v. Wade*, declaring abortion a constitutional right, on January 22, 1973, two days after Nixon's second inauguration. Almost immediately, however, the Watergate scandal exploded, and he never seriously addressed the issue in his remaining eighteen months as president.[66]

On the appointment of women to top positions, Nixon deserves credit for naming Anne Armstrong counsel to the president in 1973. With cabinet rank, she was the first woman ever to serve a president in such a high-level position Finally, Nixon considered appointing a woman to the Supreme Court. First Lady Pat Nixon took an uncharacteristically active role on this matter, urging him to do so. White House Counsel John W. Dean in 1971 wrote to advocates of that step that "you can be sure all qualified persons, irrespective of sex, are being considered." For a brief moment that year, Nixon considered nominating the California judge Mildred Lillie, but he withdrew her name when the American Bar Association found her not qualified.[67]

THE NIXON COURT: THE CONSERVATIVE REVOLUTION DELAYED

Changing the Supreme Court in a conservative direction was one of Nixon's main themes in the 1968 election campaign. Appointing "strict constructionists" to the Court, he promised, would reverse the many decisions on crime, prayer, and pornography that had undermined the moral fabric of America.

A funny thing happened on the way to a conservative Supreme Court, however. Not only was a significant change in the Court long delayed, but judicial activism actually continued, with some of Nixon's own appointees joining the majority in some of the most

65 Special Message to the Congress on Problems of Population Growth, July 18, 1969, APP. Commission on Population Growth and the American Future, *Population and the American* Future (Washington, DC: Government Printing Office, 1972).

66 1972 GOP platform, APP. Convention: Rita E. Hauser to Ehrlichman, August 28, 1972, WHSF, Colson Files, Box 28, RNPL.

67 Republican National Committee, *Women in Public Service* (Washington, DC: Republican National Committee, n.d.). Available at *A Few Good Women*, Pennsylvania State University, afgw.libraries.psu.edu/history.html. Armstrong: Martin, *The Presidency and Women*, pp. 158–62. John W. Dean to Hon. Bess B. Stinson, Senator, State of Arizona, October 22, 1971, WHCF, Subject Files, Human Rights, Box 21, RNPL. There are several items on Lillie on the Web, but no biographical sketch in any scholarly encyclopedia. "Best Women Held Too Old for Court," *NYT*, September 25, 1971. Martin, *The Presidency and Women*, p. 144.

controversial decisions. The most famous example, of course, was *Roe v. Wade* in 1973, written by the Nixon appointee Harry Blackmun. The Burger Court also issued the first important decisions on women's rights and rights of prisoners and imposed a moratorium on the death penalty in 1972. Finally, three appointees (with one abstaining) joined the unanimous 1974 decision in the Watergate tapes case, *United States v. Nixon*, which quickly led to his resignation.[68]

The failure of Nixon to transform the Supreme Court was particularly surprising considering the opportunity he was given by four appointments, including that of chief justice. At the press conference announcing the nomination of Warren Burger to replace Earl Warren, he reiterated his belief that "the Constitution should be strictly interpreted" and cited the former justice Felix Frankfurter on judicial restraint, which respected "the right of the Congress and the right of the State legislatures to write the laws and have great leeway to write those laws." Burger, however, proved to be surprisingly activist on some issues. He wrote the opinion striking down the state parochaid laws and voted with the majority in *Roe v. Wade*.[69]

Nixon was handed an unexpected opportunity in 1969 when an exposé of improper conduct forced the resignation of the very libertarian justice Abe Fortas. He bungled it, however, with two very weak nominees who were eventually rejected by the Senate. Both Clement Haynsworth and G. Harrold Carswell were dogged by questions about their civil rights records and their competence as jurists. Haynsworth was the first Court nominee to be rejected by the Senate since 1930, and Carswell soon joined him. Nixon then nominated Harry Blackmun, a judge on the Eighth Circuit Court of Appeals. It was a fateful choice. Blackmun had a background in medical law and would write the majority opinion in *Roe v. Wade*, which made him a leading target for neoconservatives for two decades. Not only did he become very protective of *Roe* (reportedly delaying his retirement until after Bill Clinton was elected president), but he became steadily more aligned with Justice William Brennan, leader of the old liberal, civil libertarian bloc on the Court. One analysis found that in the late 1980s, Blackmun voted with Brennan more than 90 percent of the time.[70]

When the great civil libertarian Hugo Black retired in 1971, Nixon replaced him with the moderately conservative Lewis Powell. The loss of the third civil libertarian in a row significantly shifted the ideological balance of power on the Court in a more conservative direction. Finally, Nixon replaced John Marshall Harlan in 1971 with William H. Rehnquist. Harlan had been a civil libertarian on privacy rights, some free speech issues, and all civil rights matters. Rehnquist proved to be the kind of conservative Nixon had envisioned in 1968, and he faced strong opposition to his nomination in the Senate. Particular controversy

68 Vincent Blasi, ed., *The Burger Court: The Counter-Revolution That Wasn't* (New Haven, CT: Yale University Press, 1983). Francis Graham Lee, ed., *Neither Conservative nor Liberal: The Burger Court on Civil Rights and Liberties* (Malabar, Fl: R. E. Krieger Pub. Co., 1983). Early alarmist account of the Burger Court: Leonard W. Levy, *Against the Law: The Nixon Court and Criminal Justice* (New York: Harper & Row, 1974).

69 Conversation With Newsmen on the Nomination of the Chief Justice of the United States, May 22, 1969, APP. Remarks Announcing the Nomination of Judge Warren Earl Burger to Be Chief Justice of the United States, May 21st, 1969, APP. There are several books on the Burger Court, but no biography of Burger himself.

70 John P. Frank, *Clement Haynsworth, the Senate, and the Supreme Court* (Charlottesville: University Press of Virginia, 1991). In 1976 Carswell was arrested in a men's room for assault of an undercover police officer. Some believe he was the first homosexual ever nominated to the Supreme Court. Linda Greenhouse, *Becoming Justice Blackmun: Harry Blackmun's Supreme Court Journey*. Pbk. ed. (New York: Times Books, 2006), pp. 52, 122, 232, 235.

arose over a 1952 memo he had written while a clerk for Justice Robert Jackson supporting *Plessy v. Ferguson* and the separate but equal doctrine. On the Court, Rehnquist had little sympathy for individual rights, and in 1986 President Ronald Reagan elevated him to chief justice. Over time, he moved from an often lonely dissenter to a voice for the majority.[71]

Timing and chance had a profound effect on the composition of the Court. Had Black and Harlan stayed on the Court two more years, Nixon by 1973 would have been so gravely weakened by the Watergate scandal and lacking support in Congress that their replacements would either have been delayed or been more liberal than either Powell or Rehnquist.

The abortion bombshell – and other Court activism

On January 22, 1973, the same day Lyndon Johnson died, the Court announced one of the most controversial decisions in its history. Striking down state criminal abortion laws under a constitutional right to privacy, *Roe v. Wade* was a legal and political bombshell. Few people foresaw how it would transform American politics over the next generation. Oddly, given its significance, President Nixon was not asked about it at his next press conference. The cover-up of the Watergate break-in was beginning to unravel and for the moment overshadowed the significance of *Roe*. Conservatives were particularly outraged that three Nixon appointees voted with the majority: Chief Justice Burger, Lewis Powell, and the opinion's author, Harry Blackmun. Only Rehnquist voted against it. Before *Roe*, Nixon had been a somewhat moderate conservative on abortion. While personally opposed to the procedure, he never endorsed outlawing it. In 1970 he dodged the issue, arguing that it was a matter for the states. In spring 1971, however, he ordered military hospitals to reverse their liberalized policies on abortion, calling it "an unacceptable form of population control." Pressure from social conservatives within the GOP mounted, however, and in early 1972, anticipating the upcoming election, he sent the Roman Catholic cardinal Terence Cooke a strong antiabortion statement. Watergate intervened, however, and was not a factor in his last two years in office.[72]

Roe v. Wade was not entirely a surprise to close Court watchers. The Court had already continued Warren Court activism on several issues. It struck down a Massachusetts law that denied unmarried individuals access to contraceptives in 1972 (*Eisenstadt v. Baird*) and issued the first important rulings on women's rights. In *Reed v. Reed* (1971) it held that the Fourteenth Amendment to the Constitution guaranteed equal protection to women. Other decisions on women's rights followed the breakthrough in *Reed*. The major area where the Court fulfilled the hopes of conservatives was criminal procedure. Even there, however, it whittled away at the exclusionary rule and *Miranda* but never reversed them. Nixon's 1968 promise of a truly conservative Court that would undo the work of the Warren Court was not fulfilled until 2006–7, almost forty years later.[73]

[71] John Jeffries, Jr., *Justice Lewis F. Powell, Jr.: A Biography* (New York: Scribner's, 1994). Mark Tushnet, *A Court Divided: The Rehnquist Court and the Future of Constitutional Law* (New York: W. W. Norton, 2005). Sue Davis, *Justice Rehnquist and the Constitution* (Princeton, NJ: Princeton University Press, 1989).

[72] *Roe v. Wade*, 410 U.S. 113 (1973). The President's News Conference of January 31, 1973, APP. Mason, *Richard Nixon and the Quest for a New Majority*, pp. 154–5.

[73] Blasi, *The Burger Court*. Jeffrey Toobin, *The Nine: Inside the Secret World of the Supreme Court* (New York: Doubleday, 2007).

THE ROAD TO WATERGATE

The road to Watergate and President Nixon's resignation in disgrace began in the first months of his presidency, with White House wiretapping reporters and its own National Security Council staff. Protests against the war steadily drove the White House to more aggressive actions: the 1969 moratorium, the massive protests after the 1970 shooting of four students at Kent State University, and most important the publication of the *Pentagon Papers* in 1971. Nixon was convinced the collapse of law and order was a real possibility, and this belief led his administration to ever more drastic steps that finally crossed over into criminality.

On June 5, 1970, a month after the Kent State shootings, Nixon summoned the heads of the four intelligence agencies – the CIA, the FBI, the Defense Intelligence Agency, and the National Security Agency – to the White House for what his aide Haldeman labeled a "historic meeting." Nixon opened the meeting with a grave warning about thousands of young Americans "determined to destroy our society" and demanded a new action plan to end the threat. Some White House officials had believed that J. Edgar Hoover had "lost his guts years ago" and was not up to the challenge. To coordinate developing a new plan, Nixon appointed Tom Charles Huston, a conservative ideologue obsessed with intelligence gathering. The previous fall he had someone infiltrate the moratorium planning committee, and now with Nixon's support he developed what became known as the Huston Plan.[74]

The Huston Plan called for monitoring international communications of U.S. citizens, increased wiretapping of protesters and their organizations, and burglarizing ("surreptitious entry") homes and offices. Huston freely admitted that surreptitious entries were "clearly illegal." All of the intelligence officials supported the plan except the FBI director Hoover. Despite his own long history of spying and break-ins, he understood that in the new political climate illegal actions risked exposure and a public backlash. Nixon approved the plan on July 14, but after Hoover lobbied Attorney General Mitchell about the proposed illegal activities, Nixon abruptly cancelled it on July 27. Mitchell advised him that it was "inimical to the best interests of the United States," and apparently both concluded that the political risks were not worth the potential gains.[75] The plan died only in a formal sense, however, as it became the model for similar actions over the next two years run directly out of the White House.

[74] Haldeman, *Haldeman Diaries*, p. 172. Address to the Nation on the Situation in Southeast Asia, April 30, 1970, APP. Tom Charles Huston, Memorandum for the President, August 18, 1969, WHCF, Subject File, Human Rights, Box 24, RNPL. *Senate Watergate Report*, pp. 53–8. On Hoover: John Dean, March 13, 1973, Washington Post, *The Presidential Transcripts*, p. 72. Huston in 1970 warned of congressional efforts to encroach on the constitutional powers of the president as commander in chief, calling it a "historic assault," and a "constitutional revolution that would destroy the moral foundation of the Presidency." It is arguably the earliest statement of the view that became central to the presidency of George W. Bush thirty years later. Huston to Bryce Harlow, et al., May 23, 1970, WHCF, SMOF, Harlow Files, Box 10, RNPL

[75] Origins and history of the plan: Athan G. Theoharis, *Spying on Americans* (Philadelphia: Temple University Press, 1978), pp. 13–39. "Clearly illegal": Senate, *Senate Watergate Report*, p. 54. Huston Plan: *United States Senate, Final Report of the Select Committee to Study Governmental Operations with Respect to Intelligence Activities. Supplementary Detailed Staff Reports on Intelligence Activities and the Rights of Americans. Book III* (Washington, DC: April 23, 1976), pp. 951–86. Hoover: Kutler, *The Wars of Watergate*, pp. 99, 120.

Confrontation over freedom of the press: *The Pentagon Papers*

The case began with a sensational front page story in the Sunday *New York Times* on June 13, 1971, and ended with a historic Supreme Court decision on freedom of the press. The *Times* published excerpts from what were called *The Pentagon Papers*, a forty-seven-volume history of American involvement in Vietnam, commissioned in 1967 by Secretary of Defense Robert McNamara. The three thousand pages of analysis and four thousand pages of documents revealed many secrets, including Lyndon Johnson's September 1964 approval of a plan to bomb North Vietnam, at the very moment he was campaigning on a promise not to expand the war.[76]

Oddly, Nixon initially responded to the story with casual indifference. When the White House aide Alexander Haig called him that morning, he had not even read the *Times*. He was still basking in the glow of his daughter Tricia's White House wedding the day before and seemed unmoved by Haig's claim that it was a "devastating ... security breach." When he finally read it, he and some advisers relished the fact that the *Papers* reflected badly on Presidents Kennedy and Johnson. Charles Colson argued that "it nails [the] Dems," and "what we want to do is nail the Kennedy elite, Harvard, Eastern establishment." Nixon's anger rose only later in the day, largely because of National Security Advisor Henry Kissinger, who cleverly played to his fears of appearing weak: "It shows you're a weakling, Mr. President." John Ehrlichman recalled that Kissinger "fanned Richard Nixon's flame white hot." Only then did Nixon call publication of the *Papers* "criminally traitorous" and tell Kissinger they needed to "get the son-of-a-bitch" who had leaked them. Otherwise, the White House might have let the *Papers* go as "Lyndon Johnson's problem, not ours." Once Nixon decided to act, Attorney General Mitchell sent the *Times* a telegram demanding "that you publish no further information of this character." The *Times* refused, and the Justice Department immediately obtained a federal court injunction halting publication. When the *Washington Post* then began publishing excerpts from the *Papers*, the administration stopped it with a similar injunction. (Eventually, seventeen newspapers published articles based on the *Papers*.)[77]

The injunctions against the *Times* and the *Post* set in motion a historic confrontation over freedom of the press in wartime, exceeding than anything in either World War I or II. In an atmosphere of national crisis, the courts moved with unprecedented speed, and *New York Times v. United States* reached the Supreme Court on June 26. At issue was whether the *Papers* contained vital secrets, and whether there was a national security exception to the freedom of the press clause of the First Amendment. In the 1931 *Near v. Minnesota* decision, when the Court first ruled prior restraints on the press unconstitutional, the

[76] "Vietnam Archive," *NYT*, June 13, 1971; and related stories. Neil Sheehan et al., *The Pentagon Papers as Published by the New York Times* (New York: Quadrangle Books, 1971). Daniel Ellsberg, *Secrets: A Memoir of Vietnam and the Pentagon Papers*, Pbk ed. (New York: Penguin Books, 2003), pp. 299–410. On June 13, 2011, the National Archives released and put online the complete *Pentagon Papers*.

[77] June 13 transcripts are available on the Web site of the National Security Archive at George Washington University: www.gwu.edu/~nsarchiv/. Haldeman, *The Haldeman Diaries*, pp. 299–300. Colson, Memorandum, Notes on the Meeting with the President Today, June 23, 1971 WHSF, Colson Files, Box 15, RNPL; additional notes on meetings, ibid. "Weakling": John Prados and Margaret Pratt Porter, *Inside the Pentagon Papers* (Lawrence: University Press of Kansas, 2004), p. 78; (Mitchell telegram) p. 119. Kissinger: John Ehrlichman, *Witness to Power: The Nixon Years* (New York: Simon & Schuster, 1982), pp. 301–2. Sanford J. Ungar, *The Papers and the Papers: An Account of the Legal and Political Battle over the Pentagon Papers* (New York: Dutton, 1972).

Court held that publication of military information such as the movement of troops could be prohibited. Adding to the drama was the well-known hatred of the Nixon administration for both the *Times* and the *Post.* Civil libertarians saw the injunctions as proof of the administration's contempt for the First Amendment and foresaw even worse assaults on freedom of the press if the government prevailed.[78]

On the central point of sensitive information, the court proceedings were utterly bizarre. The government's lawyers never read the entire *Papers* and had no idea what the *Times* or the *Post* had not yet published. Solicitor General Erwin N. Griswold filed a secret brief (which he had to write in twenty-four hours and which was declassified only years later) conceding that "the United States does not know what materials are in the possession of the *New York Times* or the *Washington Post.*" Subsequent publication of the *Papers* revealed they contained no potentially damaging secrets. In fact, Ellsberg deliberately did not to give the *Times* the sections on the peace negotiations because they might contain more recent and potentially harmful information. Moreover, none of the dire warnings about damage to the war effort or the peace negotiations alleged by the administration was ever confirmed.[79]

Four days after accepting the case, the Court ruled the injunctions against both the *Times* and the *Post* unconstitutional prior restraint on the press in a 6–3 decision. (Two of the three dissenters were Nixon's two appointees: Chief Justice Burger and Harry Blackmun). In a brief *per curiam* opinion, Justice William Brennan noted the unprecedented nature of the case: "never before has the United States sought to enjoin a newspaper from publishing information in its possession." He then held that "the First Amendment stands as an absolute bar to the imposition of judicial restraints in circumstances of the kind presented by these cases." In dissent, Burger complained about the "unseemly haste" of the entire case with the result that "We do not know the facts of the cases."[80]

A large "what if" hangs over the *Pentagon Papers* episode. Had Nixon acted on his initial reaction, allowed the *Papers* to be published, and used them to blame the Vietnam War on Presidents Kennedy and Johnson, his ultimate fate might have been very different. The White House might not have created the Plumbers unit to find who leaked the *Papers,* and the Watergate break-in that flowed directly from its activities might not have occurred. Nixon might well have completed his second term as president and retired to great acclaim. A cynical political response to the *Papers,* in short, could have saved his presidency and reputation in history.

From the Plumbers to GEMSTONE and Watergate

The *Pentagon Papers* case had three effects that propelled the nation toward Watergate and Nixon's resignation. First, by confirming the charges of government lying about the war, it strengthened the antiwar movement. Second, it emboldened much of the media to become even more adversarial toward the administration. The CBS newsperson Fred

[78] *Near v. Minnesota*: Fred W. Friendly, *Minnesota Rag: The Dramatic Story of the Landmark Supreme Court Case That Gave New Meaning to Freedom of the Press* (New York: Random House, 1981).

[79] Prados and Porter, eds., *Inside the Pentagon Papers*, p. 156; generally: "What Was So Secret?" pp. 147–82. Griswold, *Ould Fields, New Corne*, pp. 296–314.

[80] *New York Times v. The United States*, 403 U.S. 713 (1971).

Friendly explained that the case "stiffened the spines of all journalists." Finally, it spurred the White House to more extreme actions against its critics. Leonard Garment recalled, "Thus, the White House plumbers were born." The *Times* reporter Harrison Salisbury later wrote that the case was "the embryo of almost all that was later to follow" in the White House. [81]

The Plumbers was officially the Special Investigations Unit in the White House, created to stop leaks. David Young and Egil Krogh headed it, and they were soon joined by E. Howard Hunt (a CIA veteran of the Bay of Pigs disaster) and G. Gordon Liddy, who became central figures in the Watergate break-in. Their first assignment was to get damaging information about Daniel Ellsberg, a job that had everything to do with politics and nothing at all with national security. Hunt and Liddy flew to Los Angeles and on September 9 directed a burglary of the office of Ellsberg's psychiatrist, Dr. Lewis J. Fielding. Their team ransacked the office to disguise their real purpose but found nothing useful in Fielding's files. The break-in had two important ramifications. First, when it was later exposed, the judge in Ellsberg's 1973 criminal trial for theft of the *Pentagon Papers* dismissed the case on grounds of official misconduct. Second, as the former Plumber Egil Krogh later explained, the break-in was the seminal event when White House operatives "crossed the Rubicon into the realm of lawbreakers." And in a revealing comment on the prevailing atmosphere within the White House he added that "at no time did I or anyone else ... question whether the operation was necessary, legal or moral."[82]

Gordon Liddy expanded the Plumbers' idea into a much larger and unbelievable plan he labeled Operation GEMSTONE. Thinking he had White House approval for a $1 million budget for security at the 1972 GOP convention, he developed a plan that included illegal spying, kidnappings, break-ins, and sabotage of the Democratic Party. In an incredible meeting at 11:00 a.m. on January 27, 1972, in Attorney General John Mitchell's office, he outlined GEMSTONE with six four-foot by three-foot flip charts, describing the various components code-named DIAMOND, RUBY, and so on. Operation DIAMOND called for kidnapping protest leaders at the GOP convention, drugging and transporting them to Mexico, and holding them incommunicado. Liddy was enthralled with Nazi symbols and rhetoric. (Even President Nixon once called Liddy "a little nuts.") With Attorney General Mitchell looking on silently, he described Operation DIAMOND as "*Nacht und Nebel*," German for the Nazi "Night and Fog" kidnapping operations.[83]

As the Senate Watergate report later concluded, the crucial aspect of the meeting was that "such a plan was presented in the office of the Attorney General of the United States" and that Liddy continued to be responsible for intelligence gathering for the president's reelection committee after the meeting. Mitchell rejected GEMSTONE, curtly telling Liddy to return with something more "realistic" and to "burn those charts. Do it personally." It is clear that he objected to the price tag, but not entirely clear that he objected

[81] Prados and Porter, *Inside the Pentagon Papers*, p. 183. Garment, *Crazy Rhythm*, p. 297. Emboldening the press: Kutler, *Wars of Watergate*, p. 111. Harrison E. Salisbury, *Without Fear or Favor: The New York Times and Its Times* (New York: Times Books, 1980), p. 266. Senate *Watergate Report*, pp. 64–71.

[82] G. Gordon Liddy, *Will: The Autobiography of G. Gordon Liddy* (New York: St. Martin's, 1980), pp. 161–9, is a fascinating and candid firsthand account. Senate *Watergate Report*, pp. 64–71. Egil Krogh, "The Break-in That History Forgot," *NYT*, June 30, 2007.

[83] Liddy, *Will*, pp. 196–200. As a six-year-old, Liddy listened to Hitler's speeches over a shortwave radio with the family's German-born maid. Liddy recalled that the speeches "sent an electric current through my body" (p. 11). Nixon: White House tape recording, June 23, 1972.

to the obviously illegal actions. He did not, after all, interrupt Liddy and throw him out of his office, as every other attorney general most certainly would have. A scaled down plan that included spying and disrupting the Democratic Party was later approved with a $300,000 budget, and that led directly to the Watergate break-in. There is no evidence that President Nixon had direct knowledge of GEMSTONE or its successor, but he certainly created the climate that led to them.[84]

The leap into criminality also included an apparently serious discussion of firebombing and burglarizing the Brookings Institution, the respected Washington, D.C., think tank, which some administration figures believed was a hotbed of anti-Nixon activists. Charles Colson argued that a fire would provide cover for White House operatives to enter the building and seize the files of former the NSC staff members Morton Halperin and Leslie Gelb, which they believed contained Nixon era materials. No such operation ever materialized, but the idea revealed the thinking inside the White House.[85]

THE WATERGATE BREAK-IN AND THE END OF A PRESIDENCY

From "third rate burglary" to constitutional crisis

It is the most famous burglary in American history. At about 2:30 a.m. on June 17, 1972, the security guard Frank Wills caught five men burglarizing the offices of the Democratic Party in the Watergate office complex in Washington, D.C. A small story appeared in the *Washington Post* on June 18, which at the time did not seem very important. Two days later, however, reporters linked one of the burglars to the White House. Twenty-six months later, after a steady series of shocking revelations of misuse of presidential power and a constitutional crisis over executive privilege, President Nixon resigned in disgrace.[86]

The motives behind the burglary are still not clear. The historian Joan Hoff identified six different theories that had been advanced. The most widely accepted one is that the White House wanted to see what if anything the Democrats knew about possible ties between Nixon and the reclusive billionaire Howard Hughes. Actually, the June 17 incident was not the first illegal entry or attempt by the White House crew. An unsuccessful attempt at the Watergate complex occurred on May 26, and in a successful entry two days later the Nixon operatives placed taps on Democratic Party telephones. In between, they unsuccessfully tried to break into the headquarters of the Democratic presidential hopeful George McGovern. Attorney General Mitchell, by then head of the Committee to Reelect the President (CREEP), read the material from the May 28 taps and dismissed it as "not worth the money." He wanted better information, and this led to the June 17 break-in.[87]

84 Liddy, *Will*, pp. 197 200. Similar account in Jeb Stuart Magruder, *An American Life: One Man's Road to Watergate*. Pbk. ed. (New York: Signet, 1975). Senate, *Senate Watergate Report*, pp. 75–6. The biography of John Mitchell argues unpersuasively that he was not a conservative ideologue and resisted White House pressures to politicize the Justice Department: James Rosen, *The Strong Man: John Mitchell and the Secrets of Watergate* (New York: Doubleday, 2008).

85 Kutler, *Wars of Watergate*, p. 111.

86 Liddy's firsthand account: *Will*, pp. 234–46. "5 Held in Plot to Bug Democrats' Office Here," *Washington Post*, June 18, 1972; available at www.watergateinfo.org. Contrary to popular myth, the first story was written by Alfred E. Lewis, not Bob Woodward or Carl Bernstein.

87 Hoff, *Nixon Reconsidered*, pp. 304–12. Mitchell complaint: Senate, *Senate Watergate Report*, p. 85. Kutler, *The Wars of Watergate*. The best-selling account, written before much additional information became available, is Carl Bernstein and Bob Woodward, *All the President's Men* (New York: Simon & Schuster, 1974).

The cover-up begins – and unravels

The cover-up of the Watergate burglary began immediately, with President Nixon personally involved. The famous "smoking gun" tape that forced his resignation involved a June 23 meeting between Nixon and his chief aide, H. R. Haldeman, at 10:04 a.m. in the Oval Office. Haldeman complained that the FBI was not "under control" and had already traced the Watergate burglars' money to the president's reelection committee. He added that John Dean, counsel to the president, had proposed and Attorney General John Mitchell had endorsed a plan to have the CIA deputy director Vernon Walters call the acting FBI director L. Patrick Gray and tell him, "Stay the hell out of this ... we don't want you to go any further on it." Nixon indicated his approval ("Um huh") and said an FBI investigation "will uncover a lot of things. You open that scab there's a hell of a lot of things and that we just feel that it would be very detrimental to have this thing go any further." This plan to use the CIA to prevent an FBI investigation became the cornerstone of the obstruction of justice charges against Nixon. Watergate had been discussed in the Oval Office three days earlier, but part of the recording of that June 20 meeting was somehow erased, and revelation of the "eighteen and a half minute gap" only fueled the suspicions of a White House cover-up.[88]

A number of people, including several Nixon associates, have wondered why Nixon did not cut his losses immediately, by admitting the burglary was wrong, accepting responsibility for it, and firing those directly involved. Twenty years later, Alexander Butterfield speculated there would have been a two- or three-week uproar at most, and Nixon would have survived. The June 23 tape, however, indicates that Nixon knew very well he could not risk that strategy because of the "hell of a lot of things" that might come to light. They included the 1969 wiretaps, the Plumbers' burglary of Dr. Fielding's office, and GEMSTONE, among others. As John Dean understood then and explained later, the Watergate break-in was only one part of "a pattern of activities." Leonard Garment observed that "the transition from bungled break-in to cover-up took place automatically, without discussion, debate, or even the whisper of gears shifting, because the president was involved."[89]

At a June 22 press conference, Nixon condemned the break-in, saying that it "has no place whatever in our electoral process" and that the White House had "no involvement" in it. Nonetheless, the cover-up proceeded. Dean cleaned out E. Howard Hunt's

[88] The historian Stephen Ambrose argues that the cover-up began within "minutes" of Nixon's first learning about the arrests: Ambrose, *Nixon*, p. 571. June 23 meeting transcript: Kutler, *The Abuse of Power*, pp. 67–9, and www.watergateinfo.org. The meeting is also covered in Haldeman, *The Haldeman Diaries*, pp. 474–5. Ambrose, *Nixon*, pp. 567–8. The CIA in 1971 regarded E. Howard Hunt as a dangerous loose cannon and was reluctant to give the White House certain documents for that reason. Transcript, Meeting Notes, Ehrlichman and Helms, September 24, 1971, WHSF, Ehrlichman Files, Box 28, RNPL. June 20th meeting: Haldeman, *The Haldeman Diaries*, p. 473; Ambrose, *Nixon*, pp. 563–4. Some argue that the erasure was entirely accidental, but few people outside the White House were willing to believe that in the heated atmosphere of 1973–4: Strober and Strober, *Nixon: An Oral History of His Presidency*, pp. 402–6.

[89] "Why Didn't Nixon Deal with the Problem Sooner?" Strober and Strober, *Nixon: An Oral History of His Presidency*, pp. 415–18; Helms: p. 415. Nixon told Haldeman to burn most of the White House tapes, but his aide did not follow through. Destruction of the crucial tapes would probably have saved Nixon from impeachment or resignation. Phone conversation, Nixon-Haldeman, April 18, 1973, transcript ("Why Didn't Nixon Burn the Tapes?"), MCPA. Dean: Strober and Strober, *Nixon: An Oral History of His Presidency*, p. 345. Safire, *Before the Fall*, pp. 307–15. Garment, *Crazy Rhythm*, p. 297.

White House safe and told the FBI director, L. Patrick Gray, to burn the contents (as Gray did in his home fireplace). The files reportedly included incriminating material on the Plumbers, GEMSTONE, and more. White House officials pressured the five Watergate burglars to commit perjury in return for financial assistance and possible clemency. On March 21, 1973, when John Dean told Nixon in the Oval Office that a million dollars would be needed over the next two years because of the burglars' "continued blackmail," Nixon replied, "We could get that.... I know where it could be gotten."[90]

For almost four months, the cover-up seemed to work. With the exception of the *Washington Post* reporters Bob Woodward and Carl Bernstein, who later became national celebrities for their reporting, the news media almost completely ignored Watergate. On October 3, Nixon confidently proclaimed, "Watergate is out of the news," and a Gallup Poll found that 48 percent of all Americans had not even heard of it. Nixon cruised to one of the greatest landslide victories in history in November, with 60 percent of the vote. The only problems were a few *Washington Post* stories that put the story closer to the White House.[91]

It all began to unravel in early 1973. In February, the Senate created a Select Committee on Presidential Campaign Activities, chaired – crucially, it turned out – by the North Carolina senator Sam Ervin. A conservative southerner, he had fought civil rights and women's rights but now became the darling of liberals on Watergate. A self-styled expert on the Constitution, he was troubled by violations of civil liberties and in 1970 held Senate hearings on military spying on Americans. The seven Watergate burglars were convicted in late January and sentenced to very long prison terms by Judge John ("Maximum John") Sirica. Gordon Liddy, for example, got twenty years for conspiracy, burglary, and wire-tapping. On the afternoon of March 20, as Judge Sirica was wrapping up what he thought were the final details of the case, he was "shocked" to discover the convicted burglar James McCord in his outer office talking to one of his law clerks. McCord was delivering an explosive letter alleging perjury under duress: "There was political pressure applied to the defendants to plead guilty and remain silent." The very next day, a White House tape recorded Nixon approving payments to the burglars; E. Howard Hunt received seventy-five thousand that night. On March 23, Judge Sirica read McCord's letter in open court. The allegations dwarfed all previous accusations against Nixon, with evidence of criminal obstruction of justice by the president himself.[92]

The Watergate scandal soon became a national obsession. On April 6 John Dean began cooperating with federal prosecutors, and on April 30 Nixon fired him and announced the resignation of his two top aides, H. R. Haldeman and John Ehrlichman, and that of Attorney General Richard Kleindeinst. On May 17, Senator Ervin's committee began public hearings, and the following day, Acting Attorney General Elliott Richardson appointed Archibald Cox as special prosecutor for Watergate. Through it all, Nixon in private continued to argue belligerently that other presidents had done similar things. In response

90 The President's News Conference of June 22, 1972, APP. Transcripts of the March 21 tape recording: Kutler, *Abuse of Power*, p. 254, and elsewhere.

91 Nixon quote: Ambrose, *Nixon*, p. 621.

92 Ervin's contradictions: Karl E. Campbell, *Senator Sam Ervin: Last of the Founding Fathers* (Chapel Hill: University of North Carolina Press, 2007), especially pp. 161–83. "Watergate Spy Says Defendants Were under 'Political Pressure' to Admit Guilt and Keep Silent," *NYT*, March 24, 1973. John J. Sirica, *To Set the Record Straight: The Break-In, the Tapes, the Conspirators, the Pardon*, Pbk. ed. (New York: New American Library, 1979), pp. 70–3. Copy of the letter available at www.watergate.info.

to a forthcoming *New York Times* series on the abuse of presidential power, he fired off a memo suggesting a counterseries by a sympathetic reporter to expose the misdeeds of Presidents Kennedy and Johnson. In July, he again demanded aides get out "the story on the Kennedy Administration's use of the FBI for wiretapping." (In his post resignation grand jury testimony in June 1975 he belligerently brought up the subject of previous presidents' abuses, particularly of the IRS.)[93] He had a point but never understood that his abuses were so different from those of any other president.

Matters steadily worsened for Nixon in summer 1973. The White House aide Lawrence Higby recalled, "It's hard for us today to remember the almost supercharged environment that we all lived in and acted in on a day-to-day basis." On June 25, John Dean publicly testified that President Nixon was directly involved in a cover-up. The scandal took a dramatic turn on July 13 when the White House staff member Alexander Butterfield told the Ervin committee about a White House tape recording system. Suddenly, there might be direct evidence that could prove or disprove allegations of presidential criminality. William Saxbe, who later became Nixon's last attorney general, recalled that "things were collapsing on an almost daily basis."[94]

Compounding Nixon's problems, Vice President Spiro Agnew was forced to resign on October 10, 1973, over allegations of bribery when he was governor of Maryland. In a plea bargain, he admitted to tax evasion and money laundering, becoming only the second vice president ever to resign and the first to do for misconduct. Congressman Gerald Ford was appointed vice president, having no idea that in less than a year he would become president.[95]

The Agnew resignation was immediately followed by the "Saturday Night Massacre" the evening of October 20. Special Prosecutor Archibald Cox had subpoened certain White House tapes, and when he rejected a proposed compromise. Nixon ordered Attorney General Elliott Richardson to fire him. Richardson refused and resigned in protest. Nixon then ordered Deputy Attorney General William Ruckelshaus to fire Cox; he also refused and resigned. Solicitor General Robert Bork then became acting attorney general and did the president's bidding, firing Cox. The "massacre" provoked a political uproar that further eroded Nixon's public trust. Even beforehand, a Gallup Poll found that 71 percent of Americans thought Nixon either planned the Watergate break-in, knew about it in advance, or covered it up; 44 percent favored impeachment.[96] Three days later, Nixon agreed to comply with the subpoena and turn over most, but not all of the tapes. The Texas attorney Leon Jaworski became the new special prosecutor.

These tumultuous events set the stage for Nixon's November 17 press conference where he declared, "I am not a crook." Actually, he was referring to separate allegations of

[93] Nixon to Ehrlichman, March 4, 1973; Nixon to Haig, July 7, 1973, PPF, Box 4, RNPL. The grand jury testimony was released in November 2011: Richard M. Nixon, Testimony-Motions and Stipulations, U.S.D.C., Misc. #75-104, Folder 9/16, National Archives.

[94] White House issued an edited selection of transcripts on April 30, 1974. The unreleased tapes are included in Kutler, *Abuse of Power.* Howard Ball, *No Pledge of Privacy: The Watergate Tapes Litigation* (Port Washington, NY: Kennikat Press, 1977). Strober and Strober, eds., *Nixon: An Oral History of His Presidency*, pp. 425 [Higby], 429 [Saxbe].

[95] Richard M. Cohen and Jules Witcover, *A Heartbeat Away: The Investigation and Resignation of Vice President Spiro T. Agnew* (New York: Viking Press, 1974).

[96] "Richardson Quits over Order on Cox," *NYT*, October 21, 1973, and related stories. George Gallup, *The Gallup Poll: Public Opinion, 1972–1977* (Wilmington, DE: Scholarly Resources, 1978), p. 184.

financial misdeeds, claiming in a long and mawkish statement that he had never "profited from public service." And while in the same breath he did say, "I have never obstructed justice," the media and the public thought only of Watergate. Four days later, investigators discovered the eighteen-and-a-half-minute gap in the June 20, 1972, White House tape. Although some analysts subsequently argued that it was an unintentional error, Nixon was long beyond getting a break. The gap loomed as further evidence that the president of the United States had indeed committed crimes. By late 1973, the many catastrophes had essentially destroyed Nixon's capacity to govern as president. At a December 6 meeting on important economic issues, the Federal Reserve chairperson Arthur Burns found him looking "sad, his mind elsewhere ... clearly not interested [in the topic under discussion]." Henry Kissinger told Burns and others that Nixon was a "felon."[97]

By early 1974 calls for impeachment were rising, and on February 6 the House of Representatives authorized an impeachment inquiry. (John Doar, director of the committee's inquiry, recruited staff from Yale Law School. Bill Clinton declined an offer, but Hillary Rodham accepted.) Special Prosecutor Jaworski subpoened sixty-four White House tapes in April, and Nixon's refusal to turn them over on grounds of executive privilege set the stage for a Supreme Court confrontation over presidential power. On June 6 it was publicly revealed that the Watergate grand jury had named Nixon as an unindicted coconspirator in February, representing judicial notice that he had in fact broken the law.[98]

In an interesting sidelight, the chair of the House impeachment committee, Rep. Peter Rodino, asked the distinguished Yale historian C. Vann Woodward for a report on allegations of misconduct by other presidents. Under great deadline pressure, Woodward enlisted a panel of scholars and produced a hasty review of presidential controversies. It found nothing new or important but essentially missed the point of the Watergate scandal. It reviewed well-known scandals but did not inquire into abuses of presidential power such as misuse of the FBI, CIA, and IRS, or the misuse of executive privilege. After Watergate, however, two congressional committees found evidence of misconduct in these areas by earlier presidents.[99]

Executive privilege and other presidential powers

The White House tapes catapulted the issue of executive privilege to the center of Washington politics and American law. In an August 15, 1973, speech to the nation, Nixon explained that "a much more important principle is involved in this question than what the tapes might prove about Watergate" ... the "principle of confidentiality of Presidential conversations." Nixon abandoned his 1969 statement setting forth a limited interpretation of executive privilege and now made a sweeping claim of the privilege. That change set him on the road to a confrontation before the Supreme Court. Under intense public pressure, the White House released an edited collection of White House tapes on

97 Question-and-Answer Session at the Annual Convention of the Associated Press Managing Editors Association, Orlando, Florida, November 17, 1973, APP. Burns, *Inside the White House*, p. 112.

98 Doar: David Maraniss, *First in His Class: A Biography of Bill Clinton* (New York: Simon & Schuster, 1995), p. 297. Hillary Rodham Clinton, *Living History*. Pbk. ed. (New York: Scribner, 2004), pp. 65–9. "Jury Named Nixon a Co-Conspirator but Didn't Indict," *NYT*, June 7, 1974.

99 C. Vann Woodward, ed., *Responses of the President to Charges of Misconduct* (New York: Dell Books, 1974).

April 30, 1974. Public attention focused on the White House efforts to cleanse the tapes of vulgarities, and "expletive deleted" became another Watergate catchphrase.[100]

The Watergate tapes issue coincided with two other simmering controversies over presidential power. The collapse of Nixon's popular support emboldened Congress finally to assert itself on the Vietnam War. In January 1971 it had officially repealed the 1964 Gulf of Tonkin Resolution, which President Lyndon Johnson had used to escalate the war. In a move that would resonate thirty years later in George W. Bush's presidency, Nixon said the repeal was irrelevant because as commander in chief he had full constitutional authority to commit American troops overseas at his discretion.[101] After much intense debate, Congress passed the War Powers Act in late 1973. Nixon vetoed it, but Congress overrode the veto on November 7. The resolution sought to reassert Congress's constitutional authority to declare war by requiring the president to report any commitment of troops to Congress within forty-eight hours and obtain either an authorization to use force or a declaration of war within sixty days. The next three decades, however, would prove it to be a weak and possibly even meaningless instrument.[102]

A separate issue involved presidential impounding of funds appropriated by Congress. Very early in his presidency, Nixon claimed authority to impound – that is, not spend – funds for certain programs. At one point he proposed holding back as much as 20 percent of all discretionary funding. Politically, Nixon saw impounding as a way of limiting policies enacted by the Democratic-controlled Congress, but he claimed the Constitution gave him the power to do so. Congress struck back in 1974 and with Nixon gravely wounded by Watergate passed the Budget Reform and Impoundment Control Act setting certain procedures for impoundment. The bill passed the Senate, 75–0. Nixon meekly signed it on July 12, maintaining a "jovial" attitude in the face of an impending vote on his impeachment.[103]

The final days

In the heated atmosphere of summer 1974, with a seemingly endless flow of ever more damaging revelations, and with the House Judiciary Committee holding hearings on impeachment, the Supreme Court took up the historic case of *United States v. Nixon*, over Nixon's claim of executive privilege to withhold the sixty-four White House tapes. The Court heard oral arguments on July 8 and two weeks later delivered Nixon a devastating blow in a unanimous 8–0 decision. (Justice Rehnquist abstained, but Nixon's other three appointees voted against him.) The Court conceded that some presidential matters could

100 Address to the Nation about the Watergate Investigations, August 15, 1973, APP. Nixon's changed position on the privilege: Rozell, *Executive Privilege*. 3rd ed., pp. 55–8. Hoff studied the original tapes and argues that the cleansing efforts actually made the tapes appear worse than they actually were. The "expletives" deleted were relatively mild "damns," "goddamns," "Christ," and "shit," but not one use of the "f-word." Hoff, *Nixon Reconsidered*, pp. 315–16.

101 Nixon: "Gulf of Tonkin Resolution Is Repealed without Furor," ibid., January 14, 1971.

102 Peter Irons, *War Powers: How the Imperial Presidency Hijacked the Constitution* (New York: Metropolitan Books, 2005), pp. 196–9. Garry Wills, *Bomb Power: The Modern Presidency and the National Security State* (New York: Penguin, 2010), pp. 187–96.

103 U.S. Senate, Committee on the Judiciary, Subcommittee on Separation of Powers, *Executive Impoundment of Appropriated Funds, Hearings*, 92nd Cong., 1st Sess., 1971. "Congress Gains Wide Budget Role," *NYT*, July 13, 1974.

be withheld on grounds of confidentiality, but it soundly rejected Nixon's "broad claim" of "an absolute, unqualified Presidential privilege of immunity from judicial process under all circumstances."[104] It was the first Supreme Court ruling on the long-standing issue of executive privilege. Nixon's critics were jubilant, certain that the evidence of his criminality would soon be released. Three days later, the House Judiciary Committee approved the first article of impeachment.

Nixon's critics were so busy hailing the Court's decision that most failed to notice important aspects of the opinion. In fact, the Court accepted the basic principle of executive privilege and left unresolved a host of specific questions about its use. It accepted the principle that the government could protect "military, diplomatic, or sensitive national security secrets," and cited a 1952 case that established a "state secrets" doctrine that would become enormously important over the next three decades. Endorsed by the Supreme Court, the state secrets doctrine became a powerful tool for government secrecy.[105]

Rebuked by the Supreme Court, Nixon's lawyers turned over the crucial tapes, including the June 23, 1972, "smoking gun" conversation when Nixon had clearly obstructed justice. Equally incriminating was the March 21, 1973, tape in which Nixon and Dean freely discussed paying blackmail to the Watergate defendants. Nixon's own lawyers were stunned by the transcripts. Fred Buzhardt said, "It's all over." Impeachment now seemed certain, and White House staff began discussing how to arrange a resignation. Leonard Garment recalled that "all that was left was the death watch." The entire administration was paralyzed, and Henry Kissinger told Arthur Burns on July 25, "we have no government at present." When the Watergate special prosecutor Leon Jaworski finally listened to the crucial tapes, he "was badly shaken, so shaken that I didn't want anyone to notice it.... I needed to be alone." "The gravity of the situation was almost overwhelming," he recalled; "the *President* was involved.... he appeared to be criminally involved.... It was "shattering."[106]

On July 30, the House Judiciary Committee approved the last of three articles of impeachment. The first article held that President Nixon had "prevented, obstructed, and impeded the administration of justice"; given false and misleading statements to investigators; withheld information; and engaged in a pattern of "approving, condoning, acquiescing in, and counseling witnesses" to give false or misleading statements. Nixon had interfered with investigations by the Department of Justice, the FBI, the Watergate special prosecutor, and congressional committees and had misused the CIA. He had approved the payment of hush money and led witnesses to believe they would receive favored treatment for their silence or for giving misleading testimony. The second article of impeachment alleged violations of the constitutional rights of citizens, misusing the

[104] *United States v. Nixon*, 418 U.S. 683 (1974).

[105] Louis Fisher, *In the Name of National Security: Unchecked Presidential Power and the Reynolds Case* (Lawrence: University Press of Kansas, 2006). Barry Siegel, *Claim of Privilege: A Mysterious Plane Crash, a Landmark Supreme Court Case, and the Rise of State Secrets* (New York: Harper Collins, 2008). President Barack Obama also maintained the state secrets claim. See Chapter 15 of this book.

[106] Buzhardt: Strober and Strober, *Nixon: An Oral History of His Presidency*, p. 467. Garment, *Crazy Rhythm*, p. 294. Burns, *Inside the Nixon White House*, p. 131. Leon Jaworski, *The Right and the Power: The Prosecution of Watergate*, Pbk. ed. (New York: Pocket Books, 1977), pp. 51–2. Ch. 4, "The Damning Tapes." pp. 51–73. The popular account of the period is Bob Woodward and Carl Bernstein, *The Final Days* (New York: Simon & Schuster, 1976) but historians do not regard it as reliable on all points.

IRS and the FBI, maintaining a secret investigative unit (the Plumbers), and so on. A third article charged Nixon with refusing to cooperate with the Judiciary Committee itself.[107]

Today, it is difficult to imagine the drama of impeaching a president, particularly when conviction seemed almost certain. Elizabeth Holtzman, a member of the House Judiciary Committee, vividly recalls how difficult it was even for her, a strong antiwar liberal. When called to vote on the first article, she said, "I felt jarred; at first no word would come out. Then I heard myself say, 'Yes' … "I did not want to see my president abuse power and commit crimes. I did not want to have to vote for impeachment."[108]

On August 5, the White House publicly released the incriminating tapes, and on August 8, Nixon indicated that he would resign the next day. At 9:35 a.m. eastern time on the August 9, he handed his letter of resignation to Secretary of State Henry Kissinger. In his farewell speech to the nation he said, "I have never been a quitter." But quit he did.[109]

AN ABUSE OF PRESIDENTIAL POWER UNLIKE ANY OTHER

Richard Nixon left the White House in complete disgrace, the only president ever to resign the office of president. The profound irony of his presidency was that he completely undermined his original goal of restoring law and order and respect for American institutions. Instead, he broke the law and disgraced the highest office in the land. He had campaigned in 1968 to bring America together, yet he deeply divided the country. Resignation spared him certain conviction of the impeachment charges by the Senate, and he avoided prosecution as a common criminal only because his successor pardoned him. To the end of his life, Nixon refused to admit that he did anything wrong or even appear to understand the real meaning of Watergate and the related charges. In his 1991 memoir, *In the Arena*, he grudgingly conceded that mistakes had been made but claimed that the entire Watergate affair was "a concerted political vendetta by my opponents." And in interviews with Monica Crowley published in 1998, he said that Watergate was "just an excuse" for those out to get him. If not that, it simply would have been something else.[110]

Nixon's abuses of power were singular in the history of the presidency, in that they were motivated by political and personal considerations. All of the other abuses of presidential power were done in the sincere if mistaken belief they were necessary to protect the nation's interests. Woodrow Wilson believed the suppression of criticism was necessary to prosecute the war successfully. Franklin D. Roosevelt ordered the evacuation of the Japanese Americans because he believed a Japanese invasion was likely. George W. Bush believed that extraordinary measures were necessary to protect the country against an unprecedented threat from international terrorism. Nixon had no similar justification. In his famous television interviews with David Frost, he made the astounding claim that

[107] *Impeachment of Richard M. Nixon, President of the United States: The Final report of the Committee on the Judiciary, House of Representatives* (New York: Viking Press, 1975).

[108] Elizabeth Holtzman and Cynthia L. Cooper, *The Impeachment of George W. Bush: A Handbook for Concerned Citizens* (New York: Nation Books, 2006), p. 3.

[109] Address to the Nation Announcing Decision to Resign the Office of President of the United States, August 8, 1974, APP.

[110] Richard Nixon, *In the Arena: A Memoir of Victory, Defeat and Renewal*. Pbk. ed. (New York: Pocket Books, 1991), p. 40. Monica Crowley, *Nixon in Winter* (London: I. B. Tauris, 1998), p. 290.

"if the president does it, that means it is not illegal." No other president has ever made such a claim of being above the law, and it is a statement that justifiably haunts Richard Nixon's reputation.[111]

Professor Joan Hoff offered the sound advice of considering Nixon apart from Watergate.[112] On other civil liberties issues, his record was very bad, punctuated by a few bright spots, notably women's rights, family planning, and support for the ERA. With respect to the rights of criminal defendants, he was the first prominent champion of preventive detention, granting judges the right to deny bail to allegedly "dangerous" offenders. On church and state, he advocated state funding for parochial schools but was thwarted by the Supreme Court. His civil rights record is particularly complex. He was opposed to busing students and withholding federal funds to integrate schools, but then so were most Democrats in Congress. He is remembered for having a policy of "benign neglect" on civil rights, but that is hardly accurate. Far from neglecting racial issues, he pursued the advancement of African Americans through black capitalism and affirmative action. The former was fully consistent with his traditional Republican views of hard work and personal advancement. The latter, curiously, contradicted that completely. Nonetheless, historians are unanimous in their judgment that Nixon firmly implanted affirmative action as the policy of federal agencies.

Was Richard Nixon guilty of the worst record on civil liberties of any president? Not necessarily. His actions were truly unlike any other president's, and a fair comparison is difficult. President George W. Bush did more violence to the Constitution and the Bill of Rights, and in ways likely to have a lasting impact on American life and law. But however misguided he might have been, Bush at least genuinely believed he was acting in the national interest. Richard Nixon's worst abuses were motivated entirely by politics and his personal interests. In that respect he belongs in a category by himself among presidents.

[111] Nixon quote: April 6, 1977. David Frost, *Frost/Nixon: Behind the Scenes of the Nixon Interviews* (New York: Perennial Books, 2007), p. 266. Hollywood film version is *Frost/Nixon* (2008).

[112] Hoff, *Nixon Reconsidered*.

PART III

The Post-Watergate Era

Edward H. Levi, attorney general for President Gerald Ford, introduces John Paul Stevens, whom Ford has nominated for the Supreme Court, before the Senate Judiciary Committee, December 8, 1975. Levi restored integrity to the scandal-torn attorney general's office. Stevens became a consistent supporter of civil liberties as a Supreme Court justice.
Source: Associated Press.

10 Gerald Ford

A Minor President in Very Interesting Times

THE NIXON PARDON

"I hereby grant a full, free, and absolute pardon unto Richard Nixon for all offenses against the United States which he, Richard Nixon, has committed or may have committed or taken part in during the period from January 20, 1969 through August 9, 1974."[1]

President for exactly a month, Gerald Ford sought to "heal" the nation on September 8, 1974, by pardoning Nixon, hoping to put the Watergate scandal to rest. It backfired. "All hell broke loose," and another political firestorm engulfed the country, as people were outraged that Nixon would not be prosecuted. The day after the pardon, Ford was greeted in Pittsburgh by picket signs reading, "Jail Ford." Three days later, to quell the uproar, he felt compelled to say he would not pardon any of the other forty-eight Watergate figures implicated in the scandal.[2]

Ford was motivated by a combination of sympathy for Nixon and his family and concern about the national mood. A criminal trial, he argued, would only prolong the "long national nightmare" of Watergate, "cause prolonged and divisive debate," and expose "to further punishment and degradation a man who has already paid the unprecedented penalty" of resigning the presidency. "[U]gly passions would again be aroused," he argued, and "the credibility of our free institutions of government would again be challenged at home and abroad." Nixon faced several different charges, not all related to Watergate, and the case would certainly drag out for years, with serious questions of whether Nixon could receive a fair trial. Nixon, moreover, was ill with phlebitis. Benton Becker, sent to California by Ford to negotiate the pardon, found his appearance "one of freakish grotesqueness," with a shockingly thin body, and thought he might not live to November.[3]

The pardon should have been no surprise. Only two weeks earlier, the newly appointed vice president, Nelson Rockefeller, had said Nixon should not be prosecuted, and four days later at his first press conference, Ford himself said, "I subscribe to that point of

1 Proclamation 4311 – Granting Pardon to Richard Nixon, September 8, 1974, APP.

2 "Study Is Denied," *NYT*, September 12, 1974. "All hell": Richard Reeves, *A Ford, Not a Lincoln* (New York: Harcourt Brace Jovanovich, 1975), p. 108. At his confirmation hearings as vice president Ford had said he would not pardon Nixon (p. 64). "Jail Ford": Gerald R. Ford, *A Time to Heal: The Autobiography of Gerald R. Ford*. Pbk. ed. (New York: Berkeley Books, 1980), p. 175.

3 Proclamation 4311 – Granting Pardon to Richard Nixon, September 8, 1974, APP. "No Conditions Set," *NYT*, September 9, 1974. Becker's firsthand account, written the day after the pardon, is essential: Benton L. Becker, Memorandum, "History and Background of Nixon Pardon," September 9, 1974, GFPL, Digital Library. Ford's account: Ford, *A Time to Heal*, pp. 161–8. Ford wanted to delete the phrase "long national nightmare," but its author threatened to resign if he did: Robert T. Hartmann, *Palace Politics: An Inside Account of the Ford Years* (New York: McGraw-Hill, 1980), p. 159. Pardon materials: Buchen Files, Box 32, GFPL.

view." Incredibly, Nixon regarded the pardon as an insult. Accepting it, he recalled, was the "most painful decision of my political career," as it implied admitting his guilt. The pardon controversy finally ended in March 1975 when a Wisconsin federal judge dismissed a suit challenging its constitutionality. The judge's opinion, however, was a damning indictment, writing that Nixon had been a "putative rebel leader," engaged in "an insurrection and rebellion against constitutional government itself." Nonetheless, the Constitution gives presidents unlimited discretion in granting pardons, and Ford's decision represented a "prudent public policy judgment." [4]

BETWEEN WATERGATE AND NEOCONSERVATISM

Watergate and its aftermath cast a long shadow over Gerald Ford's presidency. He stands as a minor president, a decent person but with a limited vision who accomplished little of significance in his 895 days in office. His presidency is nonetheless extremely important because of the dramatic events that swirled around him: the exposés of the intelligence agencies, efforts by Congress to curb presidential power and the intelligence agencies, and finally the surging tide of neoconservatism in national politics. Caught between his brand of traditional conservatism and the hard edge of the New Right, Ford was a transitional president.[5]

On civil liberties, Ford had a mixed record. He was genuinely appalled by Nixon's abuses of power and sought to distance himself from them. In a 1976 speech at Villanova University, for example, he pointedly criticized the idea of an "imperial White House." He named as attorney general the respected legal scholar Edward H. Levi, who established a solid record of independence, issued an executive order banning the assassination of foreign leaders, and strongly supported the Equal Rights Amendment. He also cleaned up some unfinished civil liberties business. On February 19, 1976, the thirty-fourth anniversary of President Roosevelt's Executive Order 9066, he formally rescinded the order to evacuate the Japanese Americans. The Bicentennial of the Declaration of Independence was an appropriate occasion, he said, for the country to learn from its mistakes, particularly this "setback to fundamental American principles."[6] It was a small gesture, with no practical effect, but an important statement, nonetheless.

Ford's position on most civil liberties issues, however, was either weak or hostile. He urged both the Senate and the House not to publish their reports on abuses by the

[4] "Rockefeller Asserts Nixon Should Not Be Prosecuted," *NYT*, August 24, 1974. The President's News Conference of August 28, 1974, APP. Richard Nixon, *In the Arena: A Memoir of Victory, Defeat and Renewal*, Pbk. ed. (New York: Pocket Books, 1991), p. 15. *Murphy v. Ford*, 390 F.Supp. 1372 (March 28, 1975). "Judge Upholds Pardon of Nixon under Power to Calm Rebellion," *NYT*, March 30, 1975.

[5] James Lindgren and Steven Calabresi, "Rating the Presidents of the United States, 1789–2000: A Survey of Scholars in Political Science, History, and Law," *Constitutional Commentary* 18 (Winter 2001): 583–605. Ford, *A Time to Heal*. James Cannon, *Time and Chance: Gerald Ford's Appointment with History* (New York: HarperCollins, 1994). Ford's reputation suffers unfairly from a *Saturday Night Live* routine where Chevy Chase portrayed him as a stumbling klutz. An All-American football player at University of Michigan, he was probably the most athletic person ever to serve as president. Chase later conceded that Ford had the last laugh. Chase later was a patient in the Betty Ford Clinic. Chevy Chase, "Mr. Ford Gets the Last Laugh," *NYT*, January 6, 2007.

[6] "Ford Seeking to Cut Links to Watergate," *NYT*, October 28, 1976. "Ford Again Backs Rights Proposal," ibid., August 23, 1974. Proclamation 4417 – an American Promise. February 19, 1976, APP. Ford also reinstated the citizenship of Robert E. Lee and pardoned "Tokyo Rose."

intelligence agencies and vetoed bills to strengthen the Freedom of Information Act. On civil rights, he opposed school busing even more vigorously than Nixon, while on crime he launched the drive for long mandatory prison sentences that sent the American prison population soaring. On abortion, he was a moderate conservative much like Nixon, troubled by abortion but opposed to outlawing it. Under political pressure from the New Right, however, he steadily edged toward stronger opposition.

As the only president never elected either president or vice president, he had an inherently weak mandate. A *Washington Post* obituary in December 2006 observed that he became president only "as a result of some of the most extraordinary events in U.S. history." At his first cabinet meeting on August 10, he commented, "Who knows how long the honeymoon will last?" The *Post* noted that it "lasted precisely one month." The pardon controversy was followed by catastrophic losses for the Republican Party in the November 1974 elections, with the Democrats gaining three seats in the Senate and forty-two seats in the House. Many of the new Democrats were more liberal than the mainstream of their party, and they felt a strong mandate to advance liberal social policies. Speaker of the House Tip O'Neill called them the "Watergate Babies." The result was continuing conflict with President Ford. By December 3, even before they took their seats, Ford had vetoed fifteen bills; by July 1976 the total was fifty.[7]

On three issues, Ford immediately sought to separate himself from Nixon and set a new political tone for the country. On August 21 he met with the Congressional Black Caucus, which had clashed with Nixon, and on September 6 he invited leaders of the women's movement to the White House. Both efforts, however, were undone by sharp differences on policy questions. In a courageous act, Ford granted amnesty to the estimated fifty thousand Vietnam War draft evaders or deserters, announcing it at an August 19 meeting of the Veterans of Foreign Wars, an audience he knew would not like it. He wanted to "draw a real distinction" between himself and President Nixon's insistent demand for punishment, which he thought only prolonged the divisions in America over the Vietnam War. While condemning both draft evasion and desertion, he offered one of the most humane statements by an American president, saying the exiles are all "casualties, still abroad or absent without leave from the real America. I want them to come home if they want to work their way back." This involved two years of work in a public service job. Many exiles denounced his plan, since it was not the amnesty they demanded, but it was nonetheless a bold step in the direction of reconciliation.[8]

Domestic and international crises quickly overtook Ford's presidency. In mid-September, with the pardon controversy still burning, violence erupted in Boston over court-ordered busing of schoolchildren to achieve integration. Busing remained a major controversy for the rest of his presidency. An explosive *New York Times* story on December 22 exposed massive domestic spying by the CIA and provoked a year of revelations of misdeeds by all the intelligence agencies. Ford also faced the worst economic

[7] "Gerald R. Ford, 93, Dies," *Washington Post*, December 27, 2006. Memorandum, Cabinet Meeting, August 10, 1974, National Security Memoranda of Conversations, GFPL, Digital Library. "Ford Uses 50th Veto on Bill He Regards as Curb on Office," *NYT*, July 3, 1976. A. James Reichley, *Conservatives in an Age of Change: The Nixon and Ford Administrations* (Washington, DC: Brookings Institution, 1981), pp. 317–36. Tip O'Neill, *Man of the House: The Life and Political Memoirs of Speaker Tip O'Neill* (New York: Random House, 1987), p. 283.

[8] Remarks to the Veterans of Foreign Wars Annual Convention, Chicago, Illinois, August 19, 1974, APP. Ford, *A Time to Heal*, pp. 137–8. "President Meets Blacks in House," *NYT*, August 22, 1974. "New President of NOW Prepares New Message for Another New President," ibid., September 6, 1974.

recession since the late 1950s, characterized by the new and intractable phenomenon of "stagflation," a combination of economic stagnation and inflation, for which economists had no effective remedy. Finally, in April 1975, the South Vietnamese government collapsed, and with horror and embarrassment the country watched televised images of the humiliating evacuation of Americans being rescued by helicopters in Saigon. The war had cost fifty thousand American lives and untold billions of dollars and had generated bitter social and political divisions. The images from Saigon inescapably suggested it had all been for naught.

The large Democratic majorities in Congress were only half of Ford's political problems. Neoconservatives in his own party were angry at Nixon for establishing relations with China, imposing wage and price controls, and not fighting aggressively on abortion and other social issues. They did not like Ford for many of the same reasons and felt emboldened to challenge this unelected president. In mid-February 1975, the North Carolina senator Jesse Helms announced plans to explore creating a conservative third party for the 1976 election. Some neoconservatives described Ford as "almost a hopeless case," seeing him failing to attack the budget deficit and appointing liberals such as Nelson Rockefeller, whom they regarded as the very embodiment of the eastern liberal establishment. The New Right leader Richard Viguerie said that when Ford chose Rockefeller, "I could hardly have been more upset if [he] had selected Teddy Kennedy." It was a measure of the dramatic shift to the right within the GOP when one neoconservative leader characterized Barry Goldwater, once the great conservative hero, as "10 years out of date." Bowing to neoconservative pressure, Ford made several concessions. In March 1976, in response to criticisms from Ronald Reagan, he "discarded" the word "detente" to describe American relations with the Soviet Union. This abrupt reversal embarrassed his own secretary of state, Henry Kissinger.[9]

EDWARD H. LEVI: INTEGRITY IN THE ATTORNEY GENERAL'S OFFICE

On his very first day as President Ford's new attorney general, Edward Levi made it clear that a new standard of lawfulness and integrity had arrived at the Justice Department. "I vividly recall that quite late in the afternoon on my first day ... [s]ettling into my chair and observing the handsome wood paneling," an FBI agent appeared unannounced and presented a warrantless wiretap request for his signature. As the agent silently waited, Levi recalled, "I thought it was a bit unusual that I was expected to sign it automatically." Levi asked the agent to leave so he could consult other officials about the request. As Ramsey Clark had discovered in the Kennedy Justice Department, this practice was well established by the early 1960s. Levi, however, clearly signaled that procedures would now be very different.[10]

Ford's appointment of Levi was certainly the best thing he did for civil liberties, and probably the best act of his entire presidency. Then president of the University of

[9] Richard A. Viguerie, *The New Right – We're Ready to Lead* (Falls Church, VA: Viguerie Co., 1980), p. 51. "Study of 3rd Party for 76 Approved by Conservatives," *NYT*, February 17, 1975. "What the Right Thinks of Mr. Ford," ibid., April 13, 1975. Ford, *A Time to Heal*, p. 142. "Ford Says "In Time" He Expects to Talk with Nixon on China," *NYT*, March 2, 1976.

[10] John T. Elliff, *The Reform of FBI Intelligence Operations* (Princeton, NJ: Princeton University Press, 1979), p. 64. Ramsey Clark, OH, p. 43, JFKPL.

Chicago, former dean of its Law School, and a highly respected legal scholar, Levi was a thoroughly nonpolitical appointment. Even he was surprised to be chosen. The fifth attorney general in three years, Levi inherited a Justice Department wracked by scandal and chaos. Nixon's first attorney general, John Mitchell, was convicted in early 1975 of Watergate related perjury, obstruction of justice, and conspiracy charges (and eventually served nineteen months in prison.) His successor, Richard Kleindienst, pled guilty to a misdemeanor charge of perjury for lying to Congress. Ford thought the problem was deeper than Nixon, Mitchell, and Watergate. President Truman's attorneys general in his opinion were undistinguished, and he felt that it was highly inappropriate for President Kennedy to appoint his brother to the job. The Levi appointment resembled President Calvin Coolidge's choice of Harlan Fiske Stone in 1924: a new and unelected president's seeking to revive a tarnished Justice Department by choosing a respected and nonpolitical legal scholar as attorney general.[11]

Some conservatives opposed Levi, thinking he was a liberal academic, but he was actually a moderate conservative whose legal philosophy resembled that of the former Supreme Court justice Felix Frankfurter: a stickler on procedural issues, but reluctant to extend the reach of the Bill of Rights into new areas of the law. At his confirmation hearings, Levi made it very clear he would resist political pressure, even from the president. He vowed to exercise his own "independent judgment" on sensitive issues, using the word "independent" repeatedly and declaring "I don't really care where the call comes from." Asked about wiretapping, a matter of great concern at that moment with revelations of FBI and CIA misconduct pouring forth, he offered a thoughtful and balanced opinion. Such intrusive measures, he explained, needed to be "cloaked with very important safeguards." He was not sure, however, that judicial warrants were necessary in national security cases. This did not satisfy civil libertarians, but Levi nonetheless said that even if warrants were not required by law, wiretaps needed to be governed by clear administrative procedures, and that it was his duty as attorney general to develop such guidelines in consultation with Congress. Particularly important, he explained the dangers of even small exceptions to the warrant requirement: "The erosion [of standards] is very easy because it is very easy to assume that someone is a foreign agent." Unchecked, the practice "is likely to spread over into other areas." And in a statement that acquired special resonance under President George W. Bush thirty years later, he declared that the "fundamental purpose of the Fourth Amendment cannot be served if the President or the Attorney General or somebody else at the highest level judges his own case as to whether there is or is not a foreign connection."[12]

Levi fulfilled his promise of independence, on several occasions publicly disagreeing with his boss in the White House. He disavowed Ford's suggestions about curbing the power of federal courts to order busing in school desegregation cases. He prepared and submitted a comprehensive plan for outlawing the sale of handguns, but Ford, beholden

[11] "For Top Legal Post: Edward Hirsch Levi," *NYT*, January 15, 1975. Ford, *A Time to Heal*, pp. 229–30. "Edward Levi and President Ford," in Nancy V. Baker, *Conflicting Loyalties: Law and Politics in the Attorney General's Office, 1789–1990* (Lawrence: University Press of Kansas, 1992), pp. 140–51. There is no biography of Levi.

[12] Victor Navasky, "The Attorney General as Scholar, Not Enforcer," *NYT*, September 7, 1975, pp. 13 ff. Nomination of Edward H. Levi to be Attorney General: Hearings, Judiciary Committee United States Senate, 94th Cong., 1st Sess., *Nomination of Edward H. Levi of Illinois, to be Attorney General*, January 27, 28, and 29, 1975 (Washington, DC: Government Printing Office, 1975), pp. 17–19, 23.

to conservative, progun forces, rejected it in favor of a far narrower limit on the so-called Saturday Night Specials. Levi won a hard fought debate and persuaded President Ford not to oppose what eventually became the 1978 Foreign Intelligence Surveillance Act controlling national security wiretapping. And in perhaps his most audacious exercise of independence, Levi in 1976 asked the Watergate special prosecutor, then completing his work, to look into allegations about Ford's fund-raising while in Congress. Someone leaked the story and it was a brief media controversy. There was no finding of wrongdoing, but Levi's decision was a strong statement of his independence.[13]

When CIA plots to assassinate foreign leaders were exposed in spring 1975, Levi publicly stated that not even the president could authorize assassinations. He conceded there were unresolved issues on this matter, saying the question of a president's "implied constitutional powers" was "complicated," and there were "extenuating factors" related to national security. Levi never rejected the idea that the president had special power in national security issues, but he nonetheless understood that it involved fundamental principles that needed to be carefully considered. Perhaps better than any modern attorney general, Levi recognized that both the law and government practice expressed the country's deepest values. Banning assassinations, he explained, was "important in terms of the morality of our country, our way of life and the things we believe in."[14]

Levi immediately set out to develop guidelines for FBI intelligence gathering that would prevent the kind of abuses that were coming to light almost weekly in 1975. The resulting Levi Guidelines, promulgated in March 1976, fell short of what civil libertarians wanted, and some critics charged that they were a strategy to head off a legislative charter, which the ACLU urged. Nonetheless, they were a major step forward in imposing controls over the FBI. They limited domestic security investigations to allegations of specific criminal offenses, including plotting to overthrow the government and depriving citizens of their constitutional rights, and they limited the use of informants, "mail covers," and electronic surveillance. The guidelines were also less than what Levi himself, preferring a presidential executive order that would have greater legal authority, wanted. President Ford refused, however, and the Levi Guidelines remained internal Justice Department policy. As subsequent events proved, they could be easily changed and weakened by future attorneys general.[15]

The implications of Levi's Guidelines ranged far beyond the FBI, embodying a view of the role of law in modern society that he had expounded for many years. Long before Watergate created a pervasive "crisis of legitimacy," Levi expressed grave concern about the dangers of expanding executive power and the resulting threats to the rule of law. The remedy, he argued, was for officials in the executive branch to take special steps to adhere to legal norms, emphasizing that it was a mistake to leave that function exclusively to the courts. That approach would both overwhelm the courts and absolve the

13 "The Attorney General Is Going from One Crisis to Another," *NYT*, July 20, 1975. "G.O.P. Fund-Raising in Michigan Studied," ibid., September 22, 1976. Charles A. Johnson and Yanette Brickman, *Independent Counsel: The Law and the Investigation* (Washington, DC: CQ Press, 2001), pp. 66–7.

14 "Levi Holds No President May Order Assassination," *NYT*, June 9, 1975.

15 Copy of Guidelines: Elliff, *The Reform of FBI Intelligence Operations*, pp. 196–202. ACLU criticisms of proposed charter: Jerry J. Berman to Senate Judiciary Committee, June 15, 1979, EHLP, Box 124, UC. Fate of the Levi Guidelines and subsequent developments: ACLU, *ACLU Reports: Controlling the FBI* (New York: ACLU, 1978). Criticisms of the Guidelines: Frederick A. O. Schwarz, Jr., and Aziz Z. Huq, *Unchecked and Unbalanced: Presidential Power in a Time of Terror* (New York: New Press, 2007), p. 55.

executive branch of its responsibilities. This logic underpinned his development of the FBI Guidelines.[16] In all, Levi brought credit to President Ford as a strong voice of integrity, and he was arguably the most politically independent attorney general in decades.

THE WATERGATE HANGOVER

A year of revelations

"Huge C.I.A. Operation Reported in U.S. Against Antiwar Forces, Other Dissidents in Nixon Years," headlined the *New York Times*. Seymour Hersh's front-page story on Sunday, December 22, 1974, exposed the CIA's Operation CHAOS, a "massive, illegal domestic intelligence operation" that had files on "at least 10,000 Americans."[17]

Hersh's sensational exposé launched the "year of revelations," a parade of revelations about CIA, FBI, and NSA misconduct in news stories, investigations by two congressional committees, a presidential commission on the CIA, and admissions by current and former government officials. The revelations confirmed what critics had long charged: that many of President Nixon's abuses of power had precedents that implicated several previous presidents, both Democratic and Republican.

Hersh's story deeply alarmed President Ford and other officials, who knew what else congressional investigations might uncover. Secretary of State Henry Kissinger denounced the story as "a burning match in a gasoline depot" and called the situation possibly "worse for the country than Watergate." Ford immediately ordered the CIA director, William Colby, to give him a report on the *Times*' s allegations. Two days later Colby delivered a six-page letter, with attachments, describing various questionable or illegal activities and referring cryptically to "certain other matters in the history of the Agency which are subject to question." The report summarized the so-called Family Jewels, an official 1973 CIA compilation of misdeeds. In an atmosphere of emergency on Christmas Day, Kissinger sent Ford a long response to Colby's letter, denying some allegations, admitting that some were illegal, and conceding that others "though not technically illegal – raise profound moral questions." Regarding Operation CHAOS, he argued that "some" CIA personnel "misinterpreted" the program and that "some improper actions were taken." Meeting in the Oval Office on January 3 Colby told Ford about wiretaps on journalists, "operations to assassinate foreign leaders," and a "book of skeletons."[18]

Worried that "the CIA would be destroyed" by further revelations, Kissinger blamed Colby for his public statements and argued that he "must be brought under control." The former CIA director Richard Helms warned that "a lot of dead cats will come out" if investigations are not contained. To head off Congress, the White House chief of staff, Dick Cheney, recommended a presidential commission on the CIA. Ford agreed and on

16 Ronald G. Carr, "Mr. Levi at Justice," *University of Chicago Law Review* 52 (Spring 1985): 300–23.

17 "Huge C.I.A. Operation in U.S. Reported against Antiwar Forces," *NYT*, December 22, 1974.

18 Colby to The President, Report and Cover Letter, December 24, 1974, Cheney Files, Box 7, GFPL. Kissinger to The President, Colby Report, December 25, 1974, Cheney Files, Box 6, GFPL. Colby meeting with Ford: Memorandum of Conversation, January 3, 1975, National Security Adviser's Memoranda, GFPL, Digital Library. In October 2011 the National Security Archive posted the declassified CIA internal history of Colby's career at the CIA, with particularly valuable information on his relations with Hersh. John Prados, CIA History of DCI William Colby, Electronic Briefing Book No. 362. www.gwu.edu/~nsarchivNSAEBB/NSAEBB362/ index/htm.

January 4 created the President's Commission on CIA Activities within the United States, with Vice President Nelson Rockefeller as chairperson. (One commission member was Ronald Reagan, who as president would loosen restraints on the CIA.) The ACLU immediately argued that the commission "seems designed more to avoid a full public review than to facilitate one."[19] Events, however, demolished the administration's hopes of containing investigations.

Asserting presidential power: The rise of Richard Cheney

In the Dick Cheney files in the Ford Presidential Library in Ann Arbor, Michigan, are a set of handwritten notes from late 1974 on yellow legal paper. As President Ford's chief of staff, he wrote that a top priority for the administration should be to head off "Congressional efforts to *further encroach on the Executive branch*" [emphasis added]. The notes are a revealing statement by the man who as vice president twenty-seven years later would be the driving force behind the most extreme assertions of presidential power in American history. Five months later in 1975, when Seymour Hersh revealed that U.S. submarines had been regularly spying in Soviet Union waters, Cheney vigorously urged prosecuting him. Attorney General Levi, again independent of political pressure, refused to authorize an investigation. This incident and some others, the journalist Charlie Savage notes, convinced Cheney of the need to limit competing points of view presented to a president, and as Bush's vice president he pursued that policy to extreme lengths. In 1980, he gave similar advice to James A. Baker, incoming chief of staff for the newly elected president Ronald Reagan. In short, there is a straight line from Cheney's December 1974 handwritten notes to the Bush administration abuses of power.[20]

Investigations and revelations

If Ford thought he could head off Congress's investigation of the CIA, he seriously misjudged its mood and the continuing outrage over Watergate. The CIA director Colby understood that the new Congress included "some pretty strong-minded younger people out to throw over the old, cozy system" of no meaningful oversight. Two weeks after Ford created the Rockefeller Commission, the Senate Select Committee to Study Governmental Operations with Respect to Intelligence Activities (known as the Church Committee after its chair, the Idaho senator Frank Church) launched its investigation. The House followed suit, establishing the House Select Intelligence Committee (eventually known as the Pike

19 Memorandum of Conversation, January 4, 1975 [9:40 a.m., 12:37 p.m., and 7:25 pm meetings], National Security Advisor's Memoranda of Conversations, GFPL, Digital Library. Cheney, undated handwritten notes, Cheney Files, Box 6, GFPL. This document is particularly relevant to Cheney's role as vice president twenty-seven years later. Additional relevant material: Cheney Files, Boxes 5 and 7, GFPL. Henry Kissinger, *Years of Renewal* (New York: Simon & Schuster, 1999), p. 320. Executive Order 11828 – Establishing a Commission on CIA Activities within the United States, January 4, 1975, APP. Statement Announcing Establishment of a Commission on CIA Activities within the United States, January 4, 1975, APP. ACLU: "Ford C.I.A. Panel: Departure from Tradition," *NYT*, January 8, 1975. Kenneth Kitts, *Presidential Commissions and National Security: The Politics of Damage Control* (Boulder, CO: Lynne Rienner, 2006), Ch. 3, pp. 47–71.

20 Cheney, undated handwritten notes, Cheney Files, Box 6, GFPL. Charlie Savage, *Takeover: The Return of the Imperial Presidency and the Subversion of American Democracy* (New York: Little, Brown, 2007), pp. 33–7, 43. Cheney's advice to Baker: Barton Gellman, *Angler: The Cheney Vice Presidency* (New York: Penguin Press, 2008), pp. 86, 101

Committee after the New York representative Otis Pike). A year of shocking revelations was under way.[21]

Almost alone in the CIA, Director William Colby understood the radically new political climate and its demands for openness, and he set out not to fight it but control it as best he could. He had advance word of Hersh's December story and invited the reporter to come over and discuss it. "Sy, you've got it all wrong," he told Hersh; there were "a few little things here and there ... that were over the line ... [but] there was no massive, no big [domestic] intelligence operations." The effort failed, and Colby's predecessor at the CIA, Richard Helms, was still furious years later about Colby's concessions, which he felt only confirmed the story for Hersh. Colby, however, realized that the old secrecy would no longer work; after Watergate, "you really weren't going to get away with stonewalling them. It just wasn't going to work." His critics eventually prevailed, however, and President Ford fired Colby in early 1976.[22] The Church Committee operated in an atmosphere of high drama, with a staff of 150 working in a room described as resembling a World War II "bunker." In the end, it conducted 800 interviews, held 21 public hearings and 250 executive sessions, and examined 110,000 documents. Together with the Pike Committee, it marked the end of an era of shielding the intelligence agencies. Helms recalled the old days when senators were "not wild to know about some types of things that go on" and would typically say, "don't bother to tell us." Congressional committee chairs asked about budget requests but not matters of CIA policy. The Georgia senator Richard Russell saw his role as protecting the agency he was charged with overseeing. CIA veterans later remembered the 1975–6 years as the agency's "time of troubles," and both Helms and Kissinger believed the Church and Pike Committees severely damaged the agency.[23]

The congressional investigations raised three critical issues: whether CIA actions conformed to the professed American values of democracy and legality, whether the principles embodied in the Constitution and the Bill of Rights applied to American actions oversees, what kind of oversight Congress should exert over the CIA – issues that had never been publicly and fully discussed before. The idea that national security was the exclusive domain of the executive branch was now discredited. Ford would be the first chief executive to confront the new era of active congressional oversight. The investigations also raised still unresolved questions of executive privilege and how much secrecy a presidential administration could or should maintain. In the face of a determined Democratic-controlled Congress, the Ford administration resisted many congressional requests for documents, and the result was a protracted and often bitter series of demands, refusals, accusations, and negotiations. Although a veteran of Congress, President Ford now saw matters through the prism of the presidency, and at every step Cheney and Kissinger pressed him to take the hardest line possible in resisting congressional demands.[24]

21 Colby: "Oral History: Reflections of DCI Colby and Helms on the CIA's 'Time of Troubles,'" Center for the Study of Intelligence, www.cia.gov/library/center-for-the-study-of-intelligence/index/html, p. 6. John Prados, *Lost Crusader: The Secret Wars of CIA Director William Colby* (New York: Oxford University Press, 2003), pp. 297–330.

22 "Oral History: Reflections of DCI Colby and Helms on the CIA's 'Time of Troubles,'" pp. 5, 7, 20–2.

23 LeRoy Ashby and Rod Gramer, *Fighting the Odds: The Life of Senator Frank Church* (Pullman: Washington State University Press, 1994), pp. 472–8. Excellent overview: L. Britt Snider, *The Agency and the Hill: CIA's Relationship with Congress, 1946–2004* (Washington, DC: Center for the Study of Intelligence, 2008), www.cia.gov/library/center-for-the-study-of-intelligence/index/html. Helms, OH, CSI, pp. 15, 22.

24 Materials in Cheney Files, Boxes 5, 6, 7, GFPL.

An international perspective puts the post-Watergate period in context. Similar events regarding secret intelligence agencies occurred in many other countries. In Canada, England, Australia, the Netherlands, Germany, Denmark, South Africa, and several Eastern European countries, secret operations were exposed, and in response to public outrage governments took steps to subject them to greater accountability. If Watergate prompted a new period in American history, the United States was not unique from a global perspective.[25]

"Like, what?" ... "Like, assassinations!"

In a two-minute segment on the *CBS Evening News* the night of February 28, 1975, the reporter Daniel Schorr revealed the most shocking news of all about the CIA: It had plotted to assassinate as many as eight foreign leaders, including Cuba's Fidel Castro. The strangest part of the revelation was that it originated with President Ford. On January 16, in an off-the-record White House meeting with the publisher and top editors of the *New York Times,* Ford expressed concern that the Rockefeller Commission might delve into matters that would embarrass the United States overseas. "Like, what?," asked Managing Editor A. M. Rosenthal. "Like, assassinations," Ford blurted out. Everyone in the room was stunned, and Ford quickly said, "That's off the record." The *Times* people left the meeting "in a state of shock" at the revelation and back in New York had a heated debate over whether they should publish the story. Inevitably, people gossiped and the story eventually reached Daniel Schorr. In a previously scheduled interview with William Colby, he asked whether the agency had assassinated anyone. "Not in this country," Colby replied. Schorr immediately realized he had confirmation of the rumors of overseas assassination plans and broadcast the story the following night.[26]

The assassinations story "blew the roof off," recalled Colby. Any attempt to limit investigations of the CIA was now politically impossible. Rumors of CIA plots to assassinate Castro, the Congo's Patrice Lumumba, Rafael Trujillo of the Dominican Republic, and others had been whispered about for years but never seriously investigated. The stories that now poured forth were both appalling and comical. The CIA had conspired with Mafia leaders, two of whom were on the FBI's Ten Most Wanted list, about killing Castro. This gave mob leaders leverage over presidents and the Justice Department. The CIA considered such bizarre schemes as poison pills and pens, trying to make Castro's beard fall out, and what the Church Committee delicately called "other devices that strain the imagination."[27]

[25] Ian Leigh, "More Closely Watching the Spies: Three Decades of Experience," pp. 3–11, in Hans Born, Loch K. Johnson, and Ian Leigh, *Who's Watching the Spies? Establishing Intelligence Service Accountability* (Washington, DC: Potomac Books, 2005).

[26] Daniel Schorr, *Staying Tuned: A Life in Journalism* (New York: Pocket Books, 2001), pp. 266–70. "Shock:" Harrison E. Salisbury, *Without Fear or Favor: The New York Times and Its Times* (New York: Times Books, 1980), p. 537. William Colby and Peter Forbath, *Honorable Men: My Life in the CIA* (New York: Simon & Schuster, 1978), pp. 409–10. Kathryn S. Olmsted, *Challenging the Secret Government: Post-Watergate Investigations of the CIA and FBI* (Chapel Hill: University of North Carolina, 1996), pp. 61–5.

[27] William Colby and Richard Helms, "Oral History: Reflections of DCI Colby and Helms on the CIA's 'Time of Troubles,'" p. 6. U.S. Senate, Select Committee to Study Governmental Operations with Respect to the Intelligence Activities [hereinafter the Church Committee], *Alleged Assassination Plots Involving Foreign Leaders: An Interim Report of the Select Committee to Study Governmental Operations with Respect to Intelligence Activities* (Washington, DC: Government Printing Office, 1976).

President Ford was appalled when he first learned the details and condemned assassinations. At a March 17 press conference he declared that "this Administration does not condone, under any circumstances, any assassination attempts." Attorney General Levi then publicly stated that the president had no authority to order assassinations. The Rockefeller Commission, however, avoided the subject and did not mention assassinations in its final report. The Church Committee, on the other hand, devoted an entire report to it. Rep. Bud Shuster of Pennsylvania, a conservative and former counterintelligence agent, expressed the disgust felt across the country in a letter to President Ford. "What has happened to the American dream?" he wrote. "Are we no better than the Communists or Fascists?"[28]

Neither Ford nor the national security establishment was ready for a full airing of assassinations and other secret CIA activities. As the Church Committee was about to release its reports in October 1975, Ford wrote to Senator Church asking him not to: "Public release of these official materials and information will do grievous damage to our country," would "likely be exploited" by America's enemies, and would "endanger individuals named in the report." The Church Committee ignored his pleas and published a series of reports. Public exposure had one salutary effect. In February 1976, Ford issued Executive Order 11905 directing that "no employee of the United States shall engage in, or conspire to engage in political assassination."[29]

More exposés followed the assassination revelations. In March, the CIA admitted opening the mail of the New York congresswoman Bella Abzug, the fiery feminist leader. Its "mail cover" program had begun in 1953, and by the time it ended in 1973 the CIA had opened 215,000 pieces of mail and photographed the exterior of another 2.7 million. In 1968 it had even opened mail to Richard Nixon and the Democratic senators Hubert Humphrey and Ted Kennedy. Senator Church simply described the entire file as "big."[30]

The Rockefeller Commission report in June 1975 praised the CIA but conceded that some of its activities had been "plainly unlawful" and should not be "permitted to happen again." It also acknowledged that "some of these activities were initiated or ordered by Presidents, either directly or indirectly," explicitly citing President Johnson's ordering the CIA to engage in domestic spying. President Ford advised Attorney General Levi that the commission wanted the Justice Department to determine whether any laws had been broken. Director Colby of the CIA told the Justice Department that the former director Richard Helms possibly committed perjury in his testimony on CIA activities regarding Chile. Helms subsequently pled guilty to a misdemeanor and given a two-year suspended prison sentence.[31]

28 The President's News Conference of March 17, 1975, APP. "Levi Holds No President May Order Assassination," *NYT*, June 9, 1975. Shuster to the President, July 26, 1975, WHCF, Judicial Legal-3, Box 21, GFPL.

29 Ford to Church, October 31, 1975; Rockefeller Commission: Buchen to David Belin [Commission Executive Director], March 31, 1975, WHCF, Judicial Legal -3, Box 21, GFPL. "Files Said to Link C.I.A. to Mafia in Plot on Castro," *NYT*, May 20, 1975. CIA's so-called Family Jewels, released in 2007: www.foia.cia.gov/. Church Committee, *Alleged Assassination Plots Involving Foreign Leaders*. Executive Order 11905 – United States Foreign Intelligence Activities, February 18, 1976, APP.

30 "C.I.A. 'Mail Cover' Put at 2.7 Million," *NYT*, October 22, 1975. Church Committee, Book III, *Supplementary Detailed Staff Reports on Intelligence Activities and the Rights of Americans*, pp. 559–677.

31 *Report to the President by the Commission on CIA Activities within the United States* (Washington, DC: Government Printing Office, June 1975), pp. 10, 132. "C.I.A. Panel Finds 'Plainly Unlawful' Acts That Improperly Invaded American Rights," *NYT*, June 11, 1975. "Summary of Rockefeller Panel's Report on C.I.A.," ibid., June 11, 1975. Termination of CHAOS: Ober Teletype, March 5, 1974, Cheney Files, Box 6, GFPL. Memorandum

On October 29, 1975, the American people learned about a huge federal agency few had even heard of, the National Security Agency (NSA). The NSA director, Lt. General Lew Allen's, testimony before a packed hearing room that day was the first public appearance ever by an NSA official. The NSA dwarfed the CIA in size and had secretly intercepted the telephone and cable messages of 1,680 Americans. The NSA spying had involved no search warrants and no authorizations from any president or attorney general. Generally, it supplied information to the FBI, the Secret Service, and other federal agencies. Its spying program ended in 1973.[32]

Exposing FBI abuses

The day before Daniel Schorr's exposé of CIA assassination plots in February 1975, Attorney General Levi, just three weeks on the job, revealed details of FBI spying on Americans. He also condemned J. Edgar Hoover's practice of maintaining secret files separate from official FBI files. Two weeks later, the FBI confessed to its vicious campaign to "neutralize" Martin Luther King. In addition to wiretaps and bugging, it admitted sending in late 1964 a tape recording of King's allegedly "unsavory" activities to him; his wife, Coretta Scott King; and friendly reporters. The accompanying letter to King clearly suggested he commit suicide. The bureau had also tried to prevent him from receiving honorary degrees by planting unflattering stories in local media and attempted to disrupt at least one banquet where he was to speak. A bureau "monograph" on King alleging communist ties had circulated among some government agencies in 1963 until Attorney General Bobby Kennedy ordered all copies immediately recalled.[33]

Embarrassing revelations kept occurring. On July 14, the FBI director, Clarence Kelley, admitted to FBI burglaries for "security" purposes, conceding that "such 'surreptitious entries' were illegal." The Church Committee eventually documented at least 238 FBI burglaries between 1942 and 1968, directed against fourteen separate "domestic security targets." The revelations included a July 19, 1966, memo from William C. Sullivan, chief of the Bureau's counterintelligence operations, conceding that "black bag" jobs were "clearly illegal" and explaining, "We do not obtain authorization for 'black bag' jobs outside the bureau" – that is, from the attorney general. Sullivan's memo also indicated that Hoover ended them, at least temporarily for two years, in response to increased public concern and media scrutiny. Hoover scrawled "no more" on Sullivan's memo. Other FBI documents indicated no "surreptitious entries" for three years beginning in 1966, after which they resumed, evidently because President Richard Nixon had created a more receptive climate.[34]

on the Report of the Commission on CIA Activities within the United States, June 12, 1975, APP. Ford to The Attorney General, June 11, 1975, WHCF, Judicial Legal-3, Box 21, GFPL. "Colby, in 1974, Reported Possible Perjury by Helms," *NYT*, July 25, 1975.

32 "N.S.A. Chief Tells of Broad Scope of Surveillance," *NYT*, October 30, 1975. Allen testimony: Church Committee, *The National Security Agency and Fourth Amendment Rights*, V. 5, pp. 5–84. The first book on the NSA: James Bamford, *Body of Secrets: Anatomy of the Ultra-Secret National Security Agency*. Pbk. ed. (New York: Anchor Books, 2002), pp. 435–40.

33 "Levi Details Wide Scope of Hoover's Secret Files," *NYT*, February 28, 1975. "Ex-officials Say F.B.I. Harassed Dr. King to Stop His Criticisms," ibid., March 9, 1975. FBI and King: Church Committee, *Book III, Supplementary Detailed Staff Reports on Intelligence Activities and the Rights of Americans*, pp. 131–2, 158–61. David J. Garrow, *The FBI and Martin Luther King, Jr.* (New York: W. W. Norton, 1981).

34 "Burglaries by F.B.I. Conceded by Kelley," *NYT*, July 15, 1975. "238 Break-ins Committed by FBI over 26 Years," ibid., September 26, 1975. FBI memo: R. J. McCarthy to Mr. Cleveland, "Surreptitious Entries," October 9, 1975, at FBI ERR. The memo lists 454 entries between 1960 and July 1975.

The FBI abuses included its notorious COINTELPRO program, approved by President Eisenhower in 1956 (and not ended until 1971), designed to disrupt the Communist Party and later other groups. FBI operatives secretly prevented meetings from being held, planted false information about members to disrupt organizations, and manipulated journalists with confidential FBI information. Even the COINTELPRO supervisor William Sullivan called it "rough, tough, dirty business."[35]

Protecting Democratic presidents

Senator Frank Church was "discreetly absent" from some of his committee's hearings on the FBI and assassination plots. The evidence clearly implicated the former Democratic presidents John F. Kennedy and Lyndon Johnson. Planning to seek the Democratic nomination for president the next year, Church did not want to embarrass party leaders. This was only one example of a partisan bias in the committee's investigations. The most explosive story involved President Kennedy's affair with one Judith Campbell. The Church Committee report on assassinations referred delicately to a "close friend" of Kennedy's who also had a relationship with the Chicago mobsters Sam Giancana and John Roselli. The *New York Times* columnist William Safire broke the story and alleged a Democratic cover-up. Within a day, Judith Campbell Exner admitted her relationships but denied she had passed any secrets. Senator Church rejected the cover-up allegations.[36]

Senator Church sought to shield previous presidents, both Democratic and Republican, from any direct involvement in the assassination plots, asserting they had found "no hard evidence," linking any former president to such ventures. The committee's interim report on assassinations concluded that it was unable "to make a finding" on whether former presidents had "authorized" any assassinations but conceded they might have known about them or hidden behind the ruse of plausible deniability. The evidence, including the recollections of key officials, ultimately indicated that Robert Kennedy aggressively pushed the CIA to act against Castro. Although it is likely he knew about the assassination plots, there are no documents proving that point. William Safire was one of the few to criticize the Church Committee's partisanship. On September 15, 1975, he reported the allegations that President Kennedy had ordered IRS investigations of twenty-five political organizations, nineteen of which were conservative groups. In November he chided Senator Church and his committee for "gingerly" examining the King wiretaps so as to "not unduly embarrass officials of the Kennedy or Johnson administration." Democrats dismissed Safire as a die-hard Nixon defender, but the evidence could not be denied. Even Safire's liberal colleague at the *Times*, Tom Wicker, conceded that past Democratic presidents had misused federal agencies.[37]

35 Church Committee, *Book III, Supplementary Detailed Staff Reports on Intelligence Activities and the Rights of Americans*, pp. 1–77.

36 "Friend" reference: Church Committee, *Interim Report: Alleged Assassination Plots Involving Foreign Leaders*, p. 129. William Safire, "The President's Friend," *NYT*, December 15, 1975 (noting Senator Church's "absence"); "Kennedy Friend Denies Plot Role," ibid., December 18, 1975; "Church Denies Cover-Up of a Kennedy Friendship," ibid., December 16, 1975. "Levi Holds No President May Order Assassination," *NYT*, June 9, 1975. Dean: Elliff, *The Reform of FBI Intelligence Operations*, p. 56.

37 "Church Doubts Plot Links to Presidents," *NYT*, July 19, 1975. Church Committee, *Interim Report: Alleged Assassination Plots Involving Foreign Leaders*, p. 7. Safire columns: "And Now the I.R.S.," *NYT*, September 15, 1975; "Mr. Church's Cover-Up," ibid., November 20, 1975; "Orchestrating Outrage," ibid., December 8, 1975. Grudging admission by the liberal columnist Tom Wicker, "Power and Corruption," ibid., December 5, 1975. Olmsted, *Challenging the Secret Government*, pp. 87–8, 98.

"A rogue elephant"? Metaphors and reform

The CIA, Senator Church charged in mid-July 1975, is "like a rogue elephant on a rampage." The colorful metaphor caught the popular imagination and still defines the CIA for many people. The evidence does not support it, however. Rep. Otis Pike, chair of the House investigating committee, flatly rejected it and concluded that CIA abuses were usually done at White House direction or with the knowledge and approval of top officials.[38]

The question of the proper metaphor for CIA misdeeds is not just a literary matter. It is central to understanding CIA operations, the role of various presidents, and the proper remedy for abuses. The rogue elephant metaphor suggests that presidents and the Congress were generally unaware of what the CIA was doing and that the appropriate remedies should involve greater political and administrative oversight. The evidence, however, clearly indicates direct involvement or knowledge of several presidents and that political direction was a part of the problem. The 1975 revelations about the CIA led Congress to create intelligence committees to oversee the agency and to pass several laws limiting presidential authority. As later chapters of this book discuss, however, the CIA soon learned to manipulate the congressional committees, while several presidents found that they could evade the new controls.

The Church and the Pike Committees differed significantly in terms of their emphases, working styles, and final products. Critics felt that Senator Church was using his committee to advance his presidential aspirations. Others thought he focused too much on bizarre aspects such as a CIA assassination dart gun (William Colby took some of the exotic weapons to the initial hearing) rather than fundamental issues about the agency's role and performance. The Pike Committee, meanwhile, developed a very contentious relationship ("open warfare" in one person's view) with the administration over access to certain documents. Secretary of State Kissinger and Chief of Staff Cheney fought both congressional committees, and the Pike Committee abrasiveness and leaks gave them ammunition to charge that such inquiries were inherently dangerous to national security.[39]

The Pike Committee's demand for certain documents illuminated the Ford administration's sensitivity to the post-Watergate climate and the issue of executive privilege in particular. Although administration leaders discussed executive privilege, Ford never issued a formal statement on it. Nixon had discredited the concept to the point that he did not want to invoke it. Although the congressional committee never received all the documents they sought, the administration, in the judgment of the scholar Mark Rozell, provided "unprecedented access" to previously secret material. The major sticking point was Henry Kissinger's refusal to cooperate. Ford negotiated a compromise under which the Pike Committee heard oral testimony about the matters in dispute.[40]

Even one CIA historian, however, has argued that the Pike Committee examined more substantive issues about CIA operations than the Church Committee, probing such

[38] Likely first use of "rogue elephant" metaphor: "Church Doubts Plot Links to Presidents," *NYT*, July 19, 1975. Loch K. Johnson, *A Season of Inquiry: The Senate Intelligence Investigation* (Lexington: University Press of Kentucky, 1985). pp. 57–8, 88, 224, 268.

[39] Johnson, *A Season of Inquiry*. Johnson was a former committee staff member.

[40] Mark J. Rozell, *Executive Privilege: Presidential Power, Secrecy, and Accountability*, 3rd ed. (Lawrence: University Press of Kansas, 2010, pp. 74–84; quote on p. 84.

sensitive issues as its secret budget (four times larger than what Congress thought), the agency's numerous intelligence failures (e.g., the 1968 Tet Offensive in Vietnam and the 1973 Middle East war), and the proper controls over the agency. Its final recommendations called for a permanent Committee on Intelligence, prompt notification of all covert actions (but not a ban on them), and annual disclosure of "the total single sum" of all intelligence expenditures. These recommendations were far more threatening to the CIA's traditional secrecy and autonomy than the Church Committee's focus on such bizarre aspects as poison dart guns. The Church Committee did, however, produce fourteen reports documenting the long history of abuses by presidents and the intelligence agencies which remain a valuable resource today.[41]

When the Church Committee published the first of its fourteen reports in November 1975, Church himself had disowned the "rogue elephant" metaphor, and the report concluded that the CIA was basically under control. Representative Pike also concluded that all major CIA actions had "approval from higher up the line." Although all of the sensational abuses had been reported in the media, President Ford, heavily influenced by Kissinger and Cheney, opposed the report's publication. Although appalled by the abuses, he still believed that national security required disclosing as little as possible.[42]

A stunning change in the political winds: The fate of the Pike Committee report

In a stunning development, the full House of Representatives in January 1976 voted 264–124 not to publish the Pike Committee's 338-page final report. President Ford was "pleased" with this decision, reiterating his concern about not releasing classified information to "our enemies and potential enemies." This was patently ludicrous, since the *New York Times* had already published a story based on the report on January 26. The House decision revealed that a year and a half after Nixon's resignation, public outrage about government misdeeds had faded. Aside from political activists, few protested the suppression of the Pike report. There was advance warning of this change the previous November, when the Senate almost did not release the Church Committee report on assassinations. In an extraordinary four-hour closed (that is, secret) session on November 20, the full Senate hotly debated the report. In the end, the Democratic Party leadership did not call for a vote, not entirely sure of the likely result, thereby sending the report back to the committee that released it.[43]

41 Gerald K. Haines, "Looking for a Rogue Elephant: The Pike Committee Investigations and the CIA," *Studies in Intelligence* 42 (Winter 1998–9). U.S., House, *Recommendations of the Final Report of the Select Committee on Intelligence*, 94th Cong., 2nd Sess., House Report No. 94–833 (February 11, 1976). The leaked summary of the Pike Committee Report: Judith F. Buchner, ed., *The CIA and the Security Debate: 1975–1976* (New York: Facts On File, 1977), pp. 84–7.

42 Letter to Senate Leaders Concerning the Report of the Senate Select Committee to Study Governmental Operations with Respect to Intelligence Activities, November 20th, 1975, APP. Olmsted, *Challenging the Secret Government*. Michael Warner and J. Kenneth McDonald, *US Intelligence Community Reform Studies since 1947* (Washington, DC: Center for the Study of Intelligence, April 2005), p. 29.

43 Statement Following House of Representatives Vote on the Release of the Report of the Select Committee on Intelligence, January 29, 1976, APP. *New York Times* story: "Secrecy Is Cited," *NYT*, January 26, 1976. Pike: Johnson, *A Season of Inquiry*, pp. 189–91; Church: ibid., pp. 131–7. "No Vote by Senate," *NYT*, November 21, 1975.

The event that turned the minds of many House members was the December 23, 1975, murder of Richard Welch, CIA station chief in Athens, who had been publicly identified as a CIA agent by the magazine *Counterspy*. Other agents were also soon named In France, *Liberation* published the names of thirty-two alleged CIA officials in January, and other names were published in Mexico. The CIA seized the opportunity and vociferously argued that public investigations jeopardized its agents' lives. Senator Church, however, thought the reaction to the Welch murder was "stage-managed" by the agency and the Ford administration, pointing to thirty-one previous murders of CIA officers that had not received any publicity. Moreover, Welch had been named long before by other publications, and he had ignored CIA warnings to change his daily routine in Athens.[44]

The Pike Committee report was not completely suppressed, however. The CBS News reporter Daniel Schorr obtained a leaked copy – the only copy in the "free world," as he put it. After much agonizing and some secret negotiations over alternative ways of releasing it, he gave it to the *Village Voice,* an independent weekly in New York City, which published excerpts in mid-February, with the blazing headline "The Report on the CIA President Ford Didn't Want You to Read." Such was the new public mood, however, that Schorr became the center of controversy. He partly brought it on himself by bungling the leak, initially concealing his role in the affair, and trying to arrange commercial publication for the report (which led to charges of "selling secrets"). CBS fired him, although again Schorr was publicly disingenuous about his actual status. The House, meanwhile, subpoened him for revealing secrets, and for a moment it appeared he might even be prosecuted.[45]

The Schorr affair also signaled a change in the mood of establishment media. As he ruefully but perceptively put it, "I got hit by a swinging pendulum." The *Washington Post,* the *Columbia Journalism Review,* and others attacked him with special zeal, pouncing on one of his stories, about alleged CIA "penetration" of the White House, that proved baseless. The historian Kathyrn Olmsted argues that media leaders took stock after Nixon's resignation and found themselves very uncomfortable with the adversarial role some had played in the Vietnam War and Watergate and seemed eager to return to the "objective" posture of the pre-Vietnam War years and prove they were not "irresponsible." In the past, however, being "responsible" meant accepting uncritically official government explanations about foreign affairs and national security issues in particular. Thirty years later, as the Iraq War descended into an utter debacle, many Americans wondered why the news media had so readily accepted the Bush administration's bogus claims that Iraq had weapons of mass destruction. They needed look no further than the events of early 1976.[46]

44 "Paris Paper Lists 32 as U.S. Agents," *NYT,* January 14, 1976. LeRoy Ashby and Rod Gramer, *Fighting the Odds: The Life of Senator Frank Church* (Pullman: Washington State University Press, 1994), p. 489. Prados, *Lost Crusader,* pp. 328–9. The future president G. H. W. Bush, when nominated to be CIA director in 1976, gave a distorted account of the Welch assassination, which he later retracted. Schwarz, Jr., and Huq, *Unchecked and Unbalanced,* p. 52.

45 "Schorr Is Source of Leaked Report," *NYT,* February 14, 1976. Olmsted, *Challenging the Secret Government,* pp. 161–7. Schorr, *Staying Tuned,* pp. 277–300. Leaked copy: Buchner, ed., *The CIA and the Security Debate: 1975–1976,* pp. 82–90.

46 Schorr: *Dallas Morning News,* February 27, 1976, in Buchner, ed., *The CIA and the Security Debate: 1975–1976,* p. 121. Olmsted, *Challenging the Secret Government,* pp. 161–72.

REFORM: CURBING ABUSES OF POWER

The period between 1973 and mid-1976 was a unique moment in American history. For the first time, Americans learned about long secret activities of the federal government, and many were outraged at the violations of individual rights. Never before had Americans been so alert to civil liberties as they might affect them personally or the image of the United States as a constitutional democracy. During the cold war, by contrast, most Americans accepted the suppression of communists, both real and alleged, and did not feel themselves threatened by government violations of freedom of speech and association. One indicator was a precipitous drop in public opinion about the FBI. In 1965, 84 percent of Americans rated it "highly favorable;" by 1975 only 37 percent did. The two congressional investigations helped to change public attitudes, and Congress now set out to rein in the intelligence agencies and the "Imperial Presidency." [47]

Presidential war powers: A failed reform

Even before Watergate, the tragedy of the Vietnam War fueled a movement to limit presidential war making power. Gerald Ford had the distinction of being the first president to confront the 1973 War Powers Act, requiring a president to notify Congress within forty-eight hours of any use of military forces overseas, the circumstances requiring it, the underlying legal authority, and the anticipated "scope and duration" of the engagement. The occasion was the *Mayaguez* incident in May 1975 when Cambodian Khmer Rouge forces seized a U.S. container ship, the S.S. *Mayaguez*, with its crew of forty people. Ford ordered military action to recover the ship and sent the required letters to the speaker of the house and the president pro tem of the Senate, but only after the military action began. More significantly for future controversies, he ended the letter asserting that he acted under his constitutional authority as commander in chief of the armed forces, an argument later made more aggressively by President George W. Bush's lawyers in the war on terrorism.[48]

At the time it was enacted, the War Powers Act appeared to be a watershed event, with Congress reasserting its exclusive power to declare war under article 1 of the Constitution. The former Lyndon Johnson aide George Reedy captured the temper of the country, writing that such a law on presidential power "meant that something had snapped" ... "the mystical trust in the chief executive" had broken, and "the institutionalization of the distrust in a specific piece of law meant that the office would never be the same again."[49]

Trust in government did not completely snap, however, although the Vietnam War and Watergate cover-up had strained it as never before. In retrospect it appears that the damage was only temporary and that Reedy's judgment was premature. The War Powers Act

[47] The Gallup Poll, *Public Opinion 1972–1977* (Wilmington, DE: Scholarly Resources, 1991), pp. 596–7. Achievements and subsequent fate of the post-Watergate reforms: Schwarz, Jr., and Huq, *Unchecked and Unbalanced*.

[48] Letter to the Speaker of the House and the President pro Tempore of the Senate Reporting on United States Actions in the Recovery of the *SS Mayaguez* May 15, 1975, APP. Louis Fisher, *Presidential War Power* (Lawrence: University of Kansas, 1995), pp. 136–8.

[49] George E. Reedy, *The Twilight of the Presidency: From Johnson to Reagan*. Rev. ed. (New York: New American Library, 1988), p. 143.

failed to curb presidential power to commit American military forces overseas. President Nixon's successors submitted more than one hundred reports to Congress under the law after 1973, but with little apparent effect on the actual use of troops around the world. President Ronald Reagan dispatched U.S. troops to Lebanon in 1982 and Grenada in 1983; George H. W. Bush invaded Iraq in 1991; Bill Clinton ordered military action in Kosovo in 1999. And, of course, George W. Bush invaded both Afghanistan in 2001 and Iraq in 2003. The Bush legal advisor John Yoo, who became notorious for authoring the Bush administration "torture memos," concluded that the War Powers Act and other restraints "have met with little success." Commentators from the other side of the political spectrum agreed. Garry Wills, in fact, argues that the law was a major concession in which Congress actually gave away its exclusive constitutional power to declare war, creating a shared authority with the president. As the congressional debates over the Iraq War indicated, Congress was extremely reluctant to take decisive action to limit presidential action in the midst of a crisis. In short, almost forty years after the War Powers Act was passed, presidential war making power remained largely untouched.[50]

Controlling the CIA, the FBI, and the NSA

The uproar over CIA assassination plots led President Ford in February 1976 to ban any "political assassination" by any U.S. government employee, along with other restrictions on the CIA and the FBI. These controls were limited and hedged with exceptions, but they represented an important step forward in terms of formal restrictions on the intelligence agencies. Ford also banned CIA drug experiments on unknowing subjects, some of which under the James Bond–sounding title of "Project MKULTRA" had ended disastrously. Ford refused, however, to ban covert actions by the CIA, arguing at a September 16, 1974, press conference that the government, as in other countries, takes "certain actions in the intelligence field" to "protect national security." Even Edward Levi, who arguably believed more strongly in subjecting the intelligence agencies to legal controls than any other attorney general before or after, accepted the idea that some secret intelligence activities were necessary. In a proposed revision to a President Ford speech in 1975 he suggested adding, "The United States cannot survive in the world of 1975 if it is to be the only nation which has destroyed its intelligence services. The hard fact is that a measure of secrecy is essential." [51]

The most important change involved new forms of congressional oversight of the intelligence agencies. The Senate transformed the Church Committee into the Senate Intelligence Committee. Matters in the House were more complicated. Disgusted with the controversy over the Pike Committee report, the House initially refused to create a permanent intelligence committee. This created an untenable situation, however, with no committee to handle bills passed by the Senate Intelligence Committee. For months,

[50] John Yoo, *The Powers of War and Peace: The Constitution and Foreign Affairs after 9/11* (Chicago: University of Chicago Press, 2005), p. 12. Garry Wills, *Bomb Power: The Modern Presidency and the National Security State* (New York: Penguin, 2010), pp. 187–96.

[51] Executive Order 11905 – United States Foreign Intelligence Activities, February 18, 1976, APP. Church Committee, Book I, *Foreign and Military Intelligence*, pp. 385–420. The President's News Conference of September 16, 1974, APP. Levi suggestion: Note, Dictated by Mr. Levi, September 19, 1975, EHLP, Box 118, UC.

CIA officials personally briefed Speaker of the House Tip O'Neill. Suddenly finding himself the repository of all the secrets, he called the system crazy. Finally, the newly elected president Jimmy Carter indicated he wanted a House committee, and the House complied by creating the Permanent Select Committee on Intelligence.[52]

The two congressional committees marked the dawn of a new era. For the first time since the CIA was created in 1947, Congress had a formal mechanism for meaningful oversight of the agency. In practice, however, the process was deeply flawed. Briefings were limited to the "Big Four," the Republican and Democratic leaders of the two intelligence committees, and they were not allowed to take notes or share information with their staff or other members of Congress. In short, the process stood oversight on its head, making the committee leaders complicit in CIA or NSA activities. Both the CIA and subsequent presidents soon found that they could easily persuade the congressional committees by providing only vague references to particular actions, respond only to very specific questions about them, and arguing that certain activities were essential to protect national security. The national security expert Loch Johnson, a key Church Committee staff member, argues that while the committees were intended to embody a "police patrol" model of oversight, providing continuous monitoring, in practice they became a "fire alarm" model, generally reacting only after the exposure of some wrongdoing. As early as 1983, an ACLU-sponsored report concluded that the "system is inadequate even when it works, and it does not always work." The greatest flaw was that "Congress has yet to display any willingness to actually stand in the way of an operation that the administration of the day wants to conduct." [53]

Congressional efforts to control the FBI met with little success. Congress debated a statutory charter for the bureau, but the ACLU argued that it did not go far enough. When the charter effort failed, it left in place Attorney General Levi's 1976 Domestic Security Investigation Guidelines. (In the end, no statutory charters for the FBI, the CIA, and the NSA were ever enacted.) While vast improvement over the previous lack of any meaningful regulations, the guidelines were simply administration policy and could be easily changed by a subsequent administration –as proved to be the case.[54]

The question of national security-related wiretapping prompted a sharp debate within the Ford administration. In light of the wiretapping controversies thirty years later, the debate, its participants, and the outcome are particularly illuminating. Attorney General Levi accepted the necessity of wiretaps to investigate possible espionage or sabotage but argued they needed to be limited and authorized by statute. On the other side, Secretary of State Kissinger, the CIA director and future president George H. W. Bush, and, notably, the White House aide Donald Rumsfeld argued that the president had inherent

52 Frank J. Smist, Jr., *Congress Oversees the United States Intelligence Community, 1947–1989* (Knoxville: University of Tennessee, 1990), pp. 214–17. House Select Committee on Intelligence, *Recommendations of the Final Report*, House Report 94-833, February 11, 1976, 94th Cong., 2nd Sess. Pike Committee: Olmsted, *Challenging the Secret Government*, pp. 111–43. Account by a CIA historian: Haines, "Looking for a Rogue Elephant: The Pike Committee Investigations and the CIA."

53 Loch K. Johnson, "Governing in the Absence of Angels: On the Practice of Intelligence Accountability in the United States," in Born, Johnson, and Leigh, *Who's Watching the Spies?*, pp. 59–60. ACLU-sponsored report: Jay Peterzell, "Can Congress Really Check the CIA?," *First Principles* 8 (May/June 1983): 1–4.

54 Griffin Bell to the Vice President, July 31, 1979; Jerry J. Berman, Morton H. Halperin, John H. F. Shattuck, *Controlling the FBI: ACLU Testimony on Charter Legislation before the Senate Judiciary Committee*, April 25, 1978 (New York: ACLU, 1978).

power under the Constitution to authorize such operations. It is worth noting that even President Lyndon Johnson, the only president who sought to outlaw wiretapping, also made an exception for national security cases. Ford resolved the debate in March 1976 by siding with Levi and on March 23 sent Congress a bill to authorize court orders "approving the use of electronic surveillance to obtain foreign intelligence information." The bill evolved into the 1978 Foreign Intelligence Surveillance Act, which President Jimmy Carter signed.[55]

Ford also engaged in an important and revealing battle over amendments to the 1966 Freedom of Information Act. People requesting documents ran into a host of problems: long delays, high fees, unclear agency policies regarding which documents they could withhold, and often costly and time-consuming litigation to obtain documents. Congress passed an amendment designed to correct these problems, which President Ford did not like but was reportedly willing to sign. Only a few months in office and facing an angry Democratic-controlled Congress, he knew a veto would be overridden. His White House aides, Rumsfeld and Cheney, and Antonin Scalia, head of the Office of Legal Counsel and future Supreme Court justice, persuaded him to veto the bill anyway, as he did on October 17, 1974, expressing concern that "our military or intelligence secrets or diplomatic relations could be adversely affected by this bill." Congress overrode the veto in late November by huge margins: 371–31 in the House and 65–27 in the Senate. Cheney later became the architect of the aggressive secrecy policies of the President George W. Bush administration.[56]

On domestic policy, however, Ford enthusiastically supported individual privacy rights. Signing the 1974 Privacy Act, a product of rising public concern about the issue, he called the law "an initial advance in protecting a right precious to every American – the right of individual privacy," and objected that it did not go far enough in protecting individuals against "unnecessary disclosure of personal information." The law, with some exceptions, prohibited government agencies from releasing personal information without the individual's consent and gave individuals a right of access to files about them and a right to amend any incorrect information.[57]

Ending with a whimper of indifference

The headline of a May 12, 1976, *New York Times* article captured the new mood of the country perfectly: "Spy Inquiries, Begun Amid Public Outrage, End in Indifference." Public outrage over abuses of power by presidents and the intelligence agencies collapsed almost as fast as it had arisen. By spring 1976, less than two years after Nixon's resignation and fourteen months after Seymour Hersh's exposé of CIA spying, the public, the media, and the Congress had tired of scandals about government misdeeds. Congressman Otis Pike concluded that "it all lasted too long, and the media, the Congress, and the people

[55] Letter to the Speaker of the House and the President of the Senate Transmitting Proposed Legislation on the Use of Electronic Surveillance to Obtain Foreign Intelligence Information, March 23, 1976, APP. "Spirited Wiretap Debate of '76," *Newsday*, February 5, 2006. Documents and analysis: National Security Archive.

[56] Veto of Freedom of Information Act Amendments, October 17, 1974, APP. "Veto Battle 30 Years Ago Set Freedom of Information Norms," National Security Archive, Electronic Briefing, No. 142, November 23, 2004, www.gwu.edu/~nsarchiv/NSAEBB/NSAEBB142/index.htm.

[57] Statement on Signing the Privacy Act of 1974, January 1st, 1975, APP.

lost interest." The *Times* reporter Leslie Gelb observed with great insight, "the political climate has changed. ... What began amid sensational publicity ... is ending now amid compromises."[58]

In the end, the intelligence agencies survived battered but essentially intact. The historian Kathryn Olmsted argues that they "clearly emerged the winners," subject only to oversight procedures they quickly learned to manipulate.[59] The collapse of public interest in reform helps to explain the resurgence of presidential power in later years. The public, it appears, has only a limited appetite for exposés of the abuse of government power. That appetite, moreover, requires an unpopular bogeyman, a role that Richard Nixon played only too well. Neither the public nor the Congress seems capable of sustained thinking about presidential power and the role of the intelligence agencies, and both were highly susceptible to claims of threats to national security.

CONFUSION ON CIVIL RIGHTS

The Boston school busing crisis

Two months to the day after he was sworn in, President Ford and the nation were confronted with racial violence in Boston over court-ordered busing to integrate its public schools. Violent disturbances on October 9, 1974 left twenty-four whites and fourteen African Americans injured, and Mayor Kevin White appealed for federal marshals to help restore order. The incident shocked many liberals, as it was the first serious violence over school desegregation outside the South – and in Boston, the supposed bastion of liberalism. In a tense atmosphere, the administration braced for even more serious disturbances and had fifteen hundred soldiers with the Army's 82nd Airborne Division standing by in an "increased state of readiness."[60]

President Ford immediately condemned the violence but also criticized court-ordered busing, declaring that the Court order was "not the best solution to quality education." The statement demolished the relations with civil rights leaders he had tried to develop in his August 21 meeting with the Congressional Black Caucus. Civil rights advocates promptly denounced his apparent retreat on school desegregation. In an obvious reference to Eisenhower's failure to support *Brown v. Board of Education* in the 1950s, the Massachusetts senator Ted Kennedy accused Ford of giving "aid and comfort" to those who flouted the law. As disturbances continued into December, the Black Caucus leader Rep. Charles Rangel demanded Ford send in the National Guard to assist "carrying out the lawful mandates of the courts." A year later, the U.S. Civil Rights Commission echoed Kennedy, criticizing the president's "equivocal" statements on school busing and the weak efforts by federal officials to enforce the court order.[61]

58 Gelb: "Spy Inquiries, Begun amid Public Outrage, End in Indifference," *NYT*, May 12, 1976.

59 Olmsted, *Challenging the Secret Government*, p. 169.

60 Federal troops: Ken Cole to the President, October 17, 1974, WHCF, HU 2-1, Box 7, GFPL. Administration response: WHCF, HU-2, Box 5, GFPL; Loen and Leppert Files, Box 3, GFPL. J. Anthony Lukas, *Common Ground: A Turbulent Decade in the Lives of Three American Families* (New York: Vintage Books, 1985).

61 Remarks on Boston School Desegregation Violence, October 12, 1974, APP. "Violence Is Deplored," *NYT*, October 10, 1974. Rangel to Ford, December 13, 1974, Buchen Files, Box 9, GFPL. "U.S. Study Assails Officials on Boston Integration," *NYT*, August 21, 1975. U.S. Civil Rights Commission, *School Desegregation in Boston* (Washington, DC: Government Printing Office, 1975).

In the midst of the Boston crisis, the HEW secretary, Caspar Weinberger, threw fuel on the fire by suggesting in a Memphis press conference that the administration might slow down on school desegregation efforts in the North because of fierce local opposition. The remark provoked a howl of protest from southern political leaders, notably the South Carolina senator Strom Thurmond, who justifiably saw a double standard in the idea of giving northern communities preferential treatment. The administration hastily disavowed Weinberger's remarks, and he apologized to Thurmond. The crisis passed, but not without sowing distrust of the administration among both white southern opponents of integration and civil rights activists.[62]

The public was strongly opposed to school busing. An October 1974 Gallup Poll found 65 percent of Americans against it. Ford tried to resolve the issue of school integration by redefining it, as President Nixon had tried, into one of high-quality education for everyone. It did not work, as critics saw it as an attempt to ignore the long history of segregated schools, the clear mandate of the federal courts, and the problem of de facto segregation in schools outside the South. The White House aide Richard D. Parsons (the future head of Time Warner Corporation) skewered Ford's conceptual and political problems in a blistering October 1975 memo. Desegregation and high-quality education, he pointed out, were two very different issues. If the administration opposed busing as a means of desegregation, it needed to "indicate the alternative means by which the constitutional objective (indeed requirement) of desegregation of public school systems can be achieved." Ford offered no alternatives, however. Politically, Parsons continued, Ford's remarks created expectations among busing opponents that "we cannot fulfill." The Supreme Court (notably in *Swann v. Mecklenberg*, 1971) made busing "the law of the land." The president, Parsons concluded, should exercise "positive leadership" by "encouraging people to comply with the law." The memory of President Eisenhower's waffling on *Brown* in the 1950s undoubtedly shaped his thinking, as it did for many others. Attorney General Levi echoed Parson's comments a year later, throwing cold water on several administration ideas for avoiding court-ordered busing. Voluntary plans, he pointed out, were "intensely unpopular" (among African Americans, although he did not specifically mention them) in communities where they had been tried. New legislation to reduce court-ordered busing offered only limited possibilities, and he noted that Congress's attempt to do so (with the 1974 Esch Amendment) had "accomplished little." He did suggest legislation requiring judges to specify the constitutional basis for whatever remedies they might impose.[63]

President Ford actually went further in his public opposition to school busing than President Nixon ever had, and his public statements gave his staff fits. After a September 1975 press briefing, one aide complained that under pressure from reporters' questions "we were forced into a corner of practically saying the President wants segregated, separate but equal schools." The next day, when Ford planned to "ad lib a few remarks on busing" at an upcoming speech in Oklahoma City, the same aide told Press Secretary Ron Nessen, "I strongly urge him not to do so." Ford put his foot squarely in his mouth on May

62 Clipping: "HEW Defends Go-Slow on Integration in North;" Thurmond to the President, September 10, 1974; Weinberger to Thumond, September 26, 1974, WHCF, HU 2, Box 5, GFPL.

63 George Gallup, Jr., *The Gallup Poll: Public Opinion, 1972–1977*, V. 1 (Wilmington, DE: Scholarly Resources, 1978), p. 370. Parsons to Cannon and Buchen, October 23, 1975, WHCF, HU-2, Box 5, GFPL. Levi to Cannon, March 29, 1976, EHLP, Box 122, UC. Lawrence J. McAndrews, "Missing the Bus: Gerald Ford and School Desegregation," *Presidential Studies Quarterly* 27 (Fall 1997): 791–804.

26, 1976, when he said he might ask the Justice Department to review *Brown v. Board of Education*. Nixon had never suggested touching the landmark Supreme Court decision, which now had iconic status. At a Columbus, Ohio, press conference reporters peppered him with questions about busing. One prefaced his question with "Mr. President, I think any number of people are a little confused about the status of the so-called alternatives to court-ordered busing." Ford replied with his standard position that "I fundamentally disagree with [busing] as the proper way to get quality education." Then, in what was probably a slip of the tongue, he said the attorney general was considering a possible amicus brief in the Supreme Court "to see if the Court would review its decision in the *Brown* case and the several that followed thereafter." The reaction was predictably immediate and critical. The very next morning Press Secretary Nessen hastened to explain that the president had "made a mistake" and was referring only to post-*Brown* busing cases. Ford had "consistently and firmly" supported *Brown*, he added. This was probably true, but his careless remark nonetheless reinforced the view that the president was deeply ambivalent about civil rights enforcement. Attorney General Levi wasted no time distancing himself from his boss and announced that he would not use the current Boston controversy for a test case on busing.[64]

During the 1976 presidential election campaign Ford proposed legislation to limit busing, allowing it only as a "last resort" and limiting it "in duration and in scope to correcting the effects of previous violations." Additionally, he would permit busing only in the case of "proven unlawful acts of discrimination." The reference to "acts" clearly meant de facto segregation, which was the issue in northern communities.[65] In fairness to Ford, it should be noted that in 1974, the Democratic-controlled Congress passed the Esch Amendment, and in 1977 the Eagleton-Biden Amendment, both designed to limit busing. The public opposed busing by wide margins, and both political parties responded to that opposition.

The civil rights quagmire

Busing was not the only civil rights issue on which Ford appeared ambivalent and confused. To his credit, he genuinely wanted to ease the racial divide that gripped the nation, was acutely conscious that "the Nixon Administration had closed the door to minorities, particularly to blacks," and was determined to establish himself as the "point man" they could call on with their concerns. On August 21, 1974, just twelve days after being sworn in, he invited the nineteen members of the Congressional Black Caucus to the White House. The gesture had a positive impact, and Rep. Charles Rangel called the meeting "absolutely, fantastically good." It did not last. Ford immediately destroyed his own efforts with his comments on busing. When he met again with the Black Caucus in January 1975 they presented him with an extensive legislative agenda. Almost all of their top priorities – congressional representation for the District of Columbia, gun control,

64 Jim Shuman to Bill Greener, September 17, 1975; Shuman to Nessen, September 18, 1975, WHCF, HU-2, Box 5, GFPL. The President's News Conference of May 26, 1976, APP. "White House Says Ford Erred in Remark on '54 School Case,'" *NYT*, May 28, 1976. "Levi, in Reversal, Won't Use Boston as Test on Busing," ibid., May 30, 1976.

65 Remarks upon Signing a Special Message to Congress Transmitting Proposed School Busing Legislation, June 24, 1976, APP. Special Message to the Congress Transmitting Proposed School Busing Legislation, June 24, 1976, APP.

federal support for child care – embodied liberal social policies that Ford had consistently opposed as a member of Congress and now opposed as president.[66]

Ford was also ambivalent about affirmative action in employment and college admissions. As had President Nixon, he opposed overt racial discrimination, voting for the 1964 Civil Rights Act as a member of Congress. He escaped having to make a policy decision on affirmative action, however, and his successor, Jimmy Carter, would face the legal and political dilemma of taking a position in the landmark 1978 Supreme Court case of *Bakke v. Regents of California*.

If Ford was uncertain about affirmative action when president, he emerged as a strong supporter of it twenty-two years after leaving office. The occasion was two challenges to the University of Michigan's affirmative action program that reached the Supreme Court in 1999. Appalled by much of the neoconservative movement, Ford roused himself to write an August op-ed piece for the *New York Times* entitled "Inclusive America, under Attack," defending his alma mater's programs for undergraduate and law school admissions. He recalled his experience as a Michigan football player in 1934 when the university yielded to demands by Georgia Tech University that Willis Ward, a star end and an African American, not play in the game. This painful memory now caused him to declare that the nation's "pursuit of racial justice" was still "incomplete." The university's efforts were "eminently reasonable," "thoughtful," and "fair." In conclusion he asked, "Do we really want to risk turning back the clock" to the days when someone like his former teammate was "penalized for the color of [his] skin"? For Ford, now in his sunset years, the answer was an unequivocal no.[67]

The eighty-two-year old former president did more than speak out. A month later he had dinner with the former White House aide James M. Cannon at a speech by the Supreme Court justice John Paul Stevens. He urged Cannon to organize an amicus brief for the two Michigan cases, which was eventually signed by a group of retired military leaders and civilian defense department leaders, including the hero of the first Gulf War, General Norman Schwarzkopf. At the oral argument Justice Ruth Ginsburg pointedly referred to the brief, and four other justices asked related questions. The Court declared unconstitutional the Michigan policy of automatically granting to African American applicants 20 points (of 100) but held that race was a legitimate consideration in admissions decisions and could be used in a more narrowly tailored system. The legal analyst Jeffrey Toobin argues, with some hyperbole, that the amicus brief initiated by Ford "may have been the most influential *amicus* brief in the history of the Supreme Court."[68]

IN THE CROSSFIRE ON WOMEN'S RIGHTS AND ABORTION RIGHTS

Less than two weeks after taking office, President Ford endorsed the Equal Rights Amendment to the Constitution guaranteeing equal protection for women. The occasion was the fifty-fourth anniversary of the certification of the Nineteenth Amendment guaranteeing women the right to vote. Ford declared, "The time for ratification of the Equal

66 Black Caucus meeting: Loen and Leppert Files, Box 3, GFPL; WHCF, HU-2, Box 5, GFPL. Ford, *A Time to Heal*, pp. 111, 136.

67 Gerald R. Ford, "Inclusive America, under Attack," *NYT*, August 8, 1999. Football game: Ford, *A Time to Heal*, p. 51.

68 Jeffrey Toobin, "Gerald Ford's Affirmative Action," *NYT*, December 30, 2006. *Gratz v. Bollinger*, 539 U.S. 244 (2003). *Grutter v. Bollinger*, 539 U.S. 306 (2003).

Rights Amendment has come just as surely as did the time for the 19th Amendment." His support for the ERA reflected both his well-established personal views and the position of the Republican Party at that time. The 1976 GOP platform reaffirmed the party's "support for ratification of the Equal Rights Amendment," regarding it as "essential to insure equal rights for all Americans." In another part of his effort to heal the nation, Ford met with the leaders of major women's organizations, including the NOW president Karen DeCrow, on September 6, 1974, only a month after taking office.[69]

Despite the growing opposition to women's rights within his own party, Ford remained steadfast in his commitment to the ERA. First Lady Betty Ford was an outspoken supporter. She also supported abortion rights and created a minor flap by candidly discussing premarital sex on national television. In March 1975, meanwhile, Ford signed both the Inter-American Convention on the Granting of Political Rights to Women, originally signed in Bogota in 1948, and the Convention on the Political Rights of Women, signed by the United Nations General Assembly in 1953. International human rights statements had become one of the bêtes noires of the neoconservative movement, but Ford held firm on signing these documents.[70]

Near the end of his term, Ford named Brig. Gen. (Ret.) Jeanne Holm, arguably the most distinguished woman in the history of the air force, as special assistant on women's issues. Anticipating ratification of the ERA, he directed her to prepare a report on federal laws and policies restricting women's rights that would need to be revised. He lost the election, but President Jimmy Carter's administration used Holm's report and made many of the recommended changes.[71]

The political ground was shifting rapidly under Ford by the end of his term. The ERA became the first major target of the neoconservative movement, and the anti-ERA campaign led by Phyllis Schlafly and her Eagle Forum stopped the ERA in its tracks. North Dakota was the thirty-fourth state to ratify the amendment on February 3, 1975, and the next to last to do so. By the end of that month, three states had rejected the amendment, and on March 1, Idaho became the first of five states to rescind their previous ratification votes. By the end of the year the ERA was dead. Feminists were stunned by their sudden reversal of fortune. The ERA had been quickly approved by twenty-six states in just the first nine months of 1972. "What has gone wrong?" they asked, bewildered. It was easy to blame the misinformation spread by Schlafly and her allies: that the ERA would "destroy the family," force everyone to use unisex bathrooms, and so on. The fierce hostility reflected something far deeper than these allegations, which neither logic nor evidence could overcome. It was rooted in deep-seated fears of social change, including the women's rights movement, legalized abortion, the availability of sexually explicit books and movies, the constitutional ban on school prayer, and affirmative action. The emerging neoconservative movement drew all of these issues together, with the ERA symbolizing the alleged collapse of traditional family values.[72]

69 Proclamation 4309 – Women's Equality Day, 1974, August 22, 1974, APP. 1976 Republican Party platform, APP. Meeting agenda and list of attendees: WHCF, HU-2-5, Box 9; other material in WHCF, HU-2-5, Box 6, GFPL.

70 Betty Ford, *The Times of My Life*. Pbk. ed. (New York: Ballantine, 1978), pp. 219–28. Statement on Signing Two Conventions Concerning Political Rights of Women, March 2, 1976, APP.

71 Holm Files, GFPL. Holm, OH, LOC. "Jeanne Holm Dies at 88; A Pioneer in the Air Force," *NYT*, March 2, 2010.

72 Mary Frances Berry, *Why ERA Failed: Politics, Women's Rights, and the Amending Process of the Constitution* (Bloomington: University of Indiana Press, 1986). Shock and confusion among feminists: "What Happens to E.R.A. Now?" *NYT*, November 9, 1975. Berry, *Why ERA Failed*.

Although committed to the ERA, Ford had a record on appointing women to top positions that was very weak. As election day approached in 1976 a staff member worried that the administration's record of appointing women to only 14 percent of top positions "is not going over very well," and that "Mr. Carter is getting a lot of mileage out of this with women."[73] In truth, Ford was caught in the tide of rising expectations. Presidents Kennedy, Johnson, and Nixon also had very weak records, but it was Ford's fate to face a newly energized women's political movement.

American politics changed the morning of January 22, 1973, with the Supreme Court's historic decision in *Roe v. Wade* striking down state criminal abortion laws. In *Roe,* neoconservatives found an issue far more potent than the ERA that would give their movement a moral dimension. As a representative of what increasingly stood as an older tradition of Republicanism, Gerald Ford was caught in the middle of the now bitter politics of abortion.

The shifting sands of conservative politics were evident in Republican Party platforms. The 1976 platform was a confused and uncertain document. Noting that "The question of abortion is one of the most difficult and controversial of our time," it acknowledged that "there are those in our Party who favor complete support for the Supreme Court decision which permits abortion on demand," and others who want "a constitutional amendment prohibiting all abortions." It first opposed government "intrusion into the family structure through its denial of the parents' obligation and right to guide their minor children," but then called for a constitutional amendment for "protection of the right to life for unborn children."[74]

Gerald Ford's personal views on abortion were similar to both Presidents Nixon's and Jimmy Carter's. All three regarded abortion as abhorrent but also opposed outlawing it. As the 1976 election approached, however, Ford felt pressured by neoconservative challengers to take a stronger antiabortion stand. In February 1976 he condemned *Roe v. Wade,* saying the Supreme Court "went too far" and arguing that the states should be free to develop their own laws on abortion. "I'm in a moderate position in that area," he said candidly. His ambivalence about the prolife movement was clearly evident in January 1976, when movement leaders asked to meet with him during their annual demonstration on the anniversary of *Roe v. Wade.* A White House staff memo delicately recommended he "avoid any hassle in meeting with this group" and suggested the administration "listen sympathetically and restate the P's position." Ford was not comfortable with the extreme antiabortion position, but in this election year he did not want to alienate the increasingly powerful antiabortion force within the GOP.[75]

Ford soon learned what Jimmy Carter would also learn: A middle-of-the-road position satisfied neither side in the bitterly polarized world of abortion politics. On the eve of the GOP convention in August 1976, he told a Catholic conference that he was concerned about "the rising tide of secularism across the world," including "the increased

[73] Jeanne Holm to Doug Bennett, September 24, 1976, WHCF, HU-2, Box 10, GFPL.

[74] 1976 Republican Party platform, APP.

[75] Kilberg to Cannon and Massengale, "President's Position on Abortion," November 21, 1975, Buchen Files, Box 1, GFPL. "Ford Says Court 'Went Too Far' on Abortion in 73," *NYT,* February 4, 1976. The President's News Conference of February 8, 1976, APP. Ann Higgins to Bill Nicholson, January 15, 1976, Buchen Files, Box 1, GFPL.

irreverence for life." Later in the campaign he went even further, telling the National Conference of Catholic Bishops that *Roe* was "unwise" and calling for a constitutional amendment to restore the authority of states to enact their own abortion laws.[76]

STEPPING UP THE WAR ON CRIME

Forwarding an article from the *New Republic* to the presidential adviser Donald Rumsfeld, the White House aide Robert Goldwin contemptuously dismissed it as an example of the "mush-head position on crime" they opposed.[77] Although President Nixon is generally viewed as launching the "war on crime," President Ford actively promoted the "get tough" sentencing policies that marked a dramatic turn in American criminal justice policy. Nixon's drug policy had been comparatively moderate, with significant commitments to drug treatment and drug education that were more consistent with President Johnson's crime policies than what began with Ford.

The White House was entranced with the new concept of the "career criminal." Recent research indicated that a small group of offenders was responsible for a huge proportion of serious crime. The policy implications were clear: If we could identify and incarcerate those offenders, the payoff in crime reduction would be enormous. Ford met with the Harvard political scientist James Q. Wilson, a prominent neoconservative and author of the recent and influential book *Thinking about Crime*. The president "thought his ideas made a lot of sense," and the staff circulated chapters around the administration. Drawing on Wilson, Ford said it was important to change "the way we *thought* abut crime." In fact, he pointedly criticized Nixon, commenting that "too often the Nixon Administration's response to [crime] was a lot of rhetoric about the need to maintain 'law and order.'" Ford then began using the bully pulpit of the White House to advocate sentencing laws to ensure longer sentences for offenders who had committed serious crimes or had long prior records. Disastrously for the country, he succeeded.[78]

President Ford chose the occasion of the 150th anniversary of Yale Law School in April 1975 to explain his views on crime. After distancing himself from Nixon and Watergate ("crime in high places [including] the federal government"), he turned to street crime and vowed to get tough on offenders. Referring again to the disgraced Nixon, he stressed, "I do not talk about law and order" but promised protection for crime victims and the constitutional mandate for "insuring domestic tranquility." A "relatively few, persistent criminals who cause so much misery and fear," he explained, "are really the core of the problem." Recognizing that crime is primarily a state and local responsibility, he pledged to create a federal "model" for tough and effective crime policies. In a September 1976 speech to chiefs of police, meanwhile, he attacked "the great emphasis [that] is now placed on the rights of the accused" and argued for "more attention to the rights of the victim of crime." Ford never attacked the Supreme Court

76 Remarks at the Conclusion of the International Eucharistic Congress in Philadelphia, Pennsylvania, August 8, 1976, APP. Letter to the Archbishop of Cincinnati Following a Meeting with the Executive Committee of the National Conference of Catholic Bishops, September 10, 1976, APP.

77 Robert Goldwin to Don Rumsfeld, April 15, 1975, WHCF, Judicial-Legal, Box 18, GFPL.

78 Ibid. Goldwin to Rumsfeld, March 27, 1975, WHCF, Judicial Legal, Box 18, GFPL. Ford, *A Time to Heal*, p. 261. James Q. Wilson, *Thinking about Crime* (New York: Basic Books, 1975).

with the same fervor that Nixon had, but he voiced a similar criticism of the Court's excessive concern about "rights." [79]

The idea of long prison terms for "hard-core" criminals swept not just the White House but the entire nation. The Ford administration encouraged this trend by sponsoring research supporting it but was hardly the mainspring of what proved to be a radical new direction in American crime policy. The result was a spectacular increase in the nation's prison population, from 240,593 in 1975 to 1,548,721 in 2009. In practice, federal and state authorities practiced not the *selective* incapacitation described by James Q. Wilson but *gross* incarceration that indiscriminately sent tens of thousands of felons to prison regardless of their propensity to become habitual offenders. Lawmakers across the country eagerly embraced a policy the public supported. On this issue Ford rather than Nixon launched the policies that would transform American criminal justice, which Republicans would use to great political advantage against Democrats.[80]

STEVENS TO THE SUPREME COURT

Among all the justices on the civil libertarian Warren Court, none roused the fury of conservatives more than William O. Douglas. His reading of the Bill of Rights was always the most expansive, most notably in the Court's 1966 decision in *Griswold v. Connecticut* establishing a constitutional right of privacy, which then provided the basis for *Roe v. Wade.* Douglas was a particularly vulnerable target because of ethical lapses involving payments from a private foundation. The anti-Douglas effort eventually led to calls for his impeachment in 1970, led by none other than the then-minority leader in the House, Gerald Ford.[81]

Douglas survived the impeachment campaign, but debilitated by strokes he finally resigned from the Court on November 12, 1975. Conservatives eagerly welcomed another opportunity to shift the balance of the Court in their direction but would be profoundly disappointed. Ford nominated John Paul Stevens, a member of the Seventh Circuit Court of Appeals since 1970. Not only was he a friend of Attorney General Levi, but Ford was attracted by his reputation for integrity, which he achieved as chief counsel to an investigation that eventually convicted the former Illinois governor Otto Kerner (who chaired the 1968 Kerner Commission report on the urban riots).

Stevens evolved into a very liberal justice and by the 2009–10 term was arguably the most consistent civil libertarian on the Court. With Stevens, Ford joined Eisenhower and Nixon in being surprised and profoundly disappointed by his choice for the Court. The appointment stands as his one important and enduring contribution to civil liberties.[82]

79 Address at the Yale University Law School Sesquicentennial Convocation Dinner, April 25, 1975, APP. Remarks at the Annual Conference of the International Association of Chiefs of Police in Miami Beach, Florida, September 27, 1976, APP.

80 The career criminal movement and its impact is discussed in detail in Samuel Walker, *Sense and Nonsense about Crime, Drugs and Communities: A Policy Guide*, 7th ed. (Belmont, CA: Wadsworth, 2011), pp. 76–88.

81 Bruce Allen Murphy, *Wild Bill: The Legend and Life of William O. Douglas* (New York: Random House, 2003), pp. 429–35. "Inquiry by House on Douglas Urged," *NYT*, April 14, 1970.

82 Kenneth A. Manaster, *Illinois Justice: The Scandal of 1969 and the Rise of John Paul Stevens* (Chicago: University of Chicago Press, 2001), p. 269. David M. O'Brien, "The Politics of Professionalism: President Gerald R. Ford's Appointment of Justice John Paul Stevens," *Presidential Studies Quarterly* 21, no. 1 (1991): 103–26. Jeffrey Rosen, "Majority of One: Stevens at the Supreme Court," *New York Times Magazine*, September 23, 2007. Jeffrey Toobin, *The Nine: Inside the Secret World of the Supreme Court* (New York: Doubleday, 2007).

A MINOR PRESIDENT IN VERY INTERESTING TIMES

Leaving office in January 1977, Gerald Ford claimed he had healed the country by leading it past the bitterness and distrust of government arising from the Vietnam War and the Watergate scandal. He titled his memoirs *A Time to Heal*. The passions of the past had indeed receded, although not because of his initiatives. As president he largely responded to events: the intelligence agency revelations, the economic stagnation, and the rise of neoconservatism as a political force. After his death, Peggy Noonan, an aide to President Ronald Reagan, wrote in the *Wall Street Journal* that Ford "did not understand, and so was undone by, the rise of the modern conservative movement," including the "prairie fire" of the tax revolt and the "deep national moral qualms about abortion."[83]

Ford stands as a minor president who lived in very interesting times, with great consequences for civil liberties. He presided over the greatest upsurge of public concern about civil liberties and the abuse of government power in American history, which led to several new measures to curb abuses by the intelligence agencies. Ford was a largely passive actor in this drama, in only a few instances taking the initiative, such as banning assassinations by the CIA. The public mood began to change again in 1976, however, and Congress, the media, and the public lost the appetite for exposés. The major reforms of the period – the congressional intelligence committees, Attorney General Levi's FBI intelligence gathering guidelines, and the Foreign Intelligence Surveillance Act – were historic advances, creating the first significant accountability procedures for the intelligence agencies. Although these reforms did not work as effectively had been hoped, as we shall see, they nonetheless introduced a new era in American history.

On civil rights, Ford fanned the flames of discord with several inept public statements opposing school busing. At the same time, however, in the face of a rising neoconservative tide, he held to his principles by supporting the Equal Rights Amendment. Ford did make two important contribution to civil liberties, one of which endured for more than thirty-five years. Edward Levi was a model attorney general, thoroughly versed on key legal questions and staunchly independent of political influence. On the Supreme Court, meanwhile, John Paul Stevens endured and by the time of his retirement in 2010 was the strongest civil libertarian on the Court. Ford did not appoint him with that in mind, and it is perhaps fitting that the person sometimes called "the accidental president" made his greatest contribution to civil liberties inadvertently.

[83] Peggy Noonan, "Ford without Tears," *Wall Street Journal*, December 29, 2006.

11 Jimmy Carter

Good Civil Libertarian, Failed President

A BLURRED VISION FOR AMERICA

"Why not the best?" asked the presidential candidate Jimmy Carter in 1976. It was a good question with the shadow of Watergate still hanging over the country. Once in office, however, Carter never convinced Americans he had a coherent vision of a better America. Scholars generally rank Carter below average, and he is popularly regarded as a failed president. A political outsider who surrounded himself with fellow Georgians, he never mastered Washington politics, alienated Democratic Party leaders and constituencies, and immersed himself in detail without projecting a credible message.[1]

Carter's record was far better than his reputation. On civil liberties he has one of the best records of any modern president. He was a strong supporter of women's rights and had a good record on appointing African Americans, was the first president to support lesbian and gay rights openly, defended separation of church and state in the face of strong Religious Right pressure, and defended abortion rights despite his own personal objection to the procedure. With Griffin Bell he selected an independent-minded attorney general, who followed Edward Levi in establishing a record of independence from his boss. On national security, Carter respected the new norms of accountability for the intelligence agencies and made no unjustified claims of presidential power. At the very end of his presidency, however, in response to new international crises, he took some questionable steps. Following President Ford's example, he studiously made no claims of executive privilege, which Nixon had discredited.[2] On non-civil liberties issues, he brokered the 1978 Camp David accords, which maintained stability in the Middle East for more than thirty years, an accomplishment unmatched by any other president. Had the country heeded his much maligned 1979 energy speech, it would have been far less dependent on oil and foreign oil imports than it was thirty years later. All in all, it was a very creditable record.

1 James Lindgren and Steven G. Calabresi, "Rating the Presidents of the United States, 1789–2000: A Survey of Scholars in Political Science, History, and Law," *Constitutional Commentary*, 18 (Winter 2001): 583–605. Assessments of Carter's presidency are summarized in Burton I. Kaufman, *The Presidency of James Earl Carter, Jr.* (Lawrence: University of Kansas Press, 1993). Carter immediately insulted Speaker of the House Tip O'Neill: Joseph A. Califano, Jr., *Governing America: An Insider's Report from the White House and the Cabinet* (New York: Simon & Schuster, 1981), p. 404. Carter's inability to project a persuasive image and immersion in detail: "The Strange Success of Jimmy Carter," *New York Review of Books* (October 28, 2010); Jimmy Carter, *White House Diary* (New York: Farrar, Straus & Giroux, 2010). A brief but insightful interpretation: Nicholas Dawidoff, "The Riddle of Jimmy Carter," *Rolling Stone*, no. 1123 (February 3, 2011): 50ff.

2 Mark J. Rozell, *Executive Privilege: Presidential Power, Secrecy, and Accountability*, 3rd ed. (Lawrence: University of Kansas Press, 2010), pp. 84–93.

Upon taking office, Carter raised the hopes of civil libertarians with the appointment of several civil rights and civil liberties activists to key positions. Midge Costanza, head of the Office of Public Liaison, openly supported both gay rights and abortion rights. Marilyn Haft, a former ACLU staff person, was associate director of his Office of Public Liaison. Patricia Derian became assistant secretary of state for human rights, and fellow civil rights activist Eleanor Holmes Norton was Equal Employment Opportunity Commission director. An ACLU official observed in 1977 that Carter had appointed "more civil libertarians to high office than any other President." Sadly, however, he alienated civil liberties and civil rights constituencies with a special knack for putting his foot in his mouth on some key issues. The result was often open conflict with his natural allies that obscured his actual accomplishments. After only one year, the ACLU Washington office director John Shattuck provided a long list of Carter's broken campaign promises and failed initiatives.[3]

Like Gerald Ford, Carter was a transitional president. The most conservative of all the Democratic aspirants in 1976, he was whipsawed by the fading liberal dreams of the 1960s, a stagnant economy, and the rising tide of neoconservatism. The White House aide Anne Wexler later described him as "the bridge president from an age of abundance ... to an age of limits."[4] An engineer by training, he immersed himself in the details of programs but could not set priorities or articulate a persuasive vision for the future. Perhaps unfairly, some have noted that he and Herbert Hoover were the only trained engineers to serve as president. As his speechwriter James Fallows later explained, "Carter believes 50 things but no one thing." His ambassador to the United Nations, Andrew Young, added, "Engineers will tell you exactly how to build a bridge, but they can't seem to explain why you need this bridge." Carter's 1976 book *Why Not the Best?* was filled with grand rhetoric about "new ideas to make a reality of the[se] dreams, still held by our people." He promised to outlaw gifts to politicians, minimize secrecy in government, make all appointments on the basis of merit, "abolish and consolidate hundreds of obsolete and unnecessary federal programs," and on and on. At the same time, however, he lectured the country about the need for modest expectations. In his inaugural address he solemnly advised that "we can neither answer all questions nor solve all problems." This was a long way from the soaring visions of Lyndon Johnson's Great Society only ten years earlier. (Few people noticed that his message was essentially the same as Daniel Moynihan's recommendation to President Nixon for "benign neglect," for which he was loudly criticized by Democrats.)[5] Defining himself as a political outsider, he had a profound distaste for conventional interest group politics of the kind that Presidents Franklin D. Roosevelt and Lyndon Johnson mastered. As a result, he could never effectively mobilize the core Democratic Party constituencies: organized labor, the civil rights establishment, the emerging women's movement, and environmentalists. The result was political futility.

[3] Florence Isbell, "Carter's Civil Libertarians," *Civil Liberties Review* 4 (July/August 1977): 55–8. John H. F. Shattuck, "You Can't Depend on It: The Carter Administration and Civil Liberties," *Civil Liberties Review* 4 (January/February 1978): 10–27.

[4] Wexler, OH, p. 91, MCPA.

[5] Fallows and Young quoted in Dawidoff, "The Riddle of Jimmy Carter," p. 61. Jimmy Carter, *Why Not the Best?* (New York: Bantam Books, 1976), pp. 168–71. Inaugural Address of President Jimmy Carter. January 20, 1977, APP.

Deeply religious, Carter sought to give high standards of personal integrity to the presidency. His byword in running for president was "I will never lie to you" (as one aide put it, "Well, there goes the liars vote"). He did not, however, understand that presidential leadership requires a clear policy agenda and the political skills to achieve it, and not just claims of personal morality. Even his promises of honesty and openness were quickly compromised early in the 1976 campaign, as he was accused of "fudging" on several controversial issues.[6]

AN INDEPENDENT ATTORNEY GENERAL

The attorney general told the president that he would not change the Justice Department's position in a pending church-state case, and to fire him if he wanted a different position. Carter's attorney general Griffin Bell, like his predecessor Edward Levi, was truly independent-minded and felt strongly that he should render legal opinions free of political considerations. In Carter's celebrated Law Day address at the University of Georgia in May 1974, which launched his bid for the White House, he condemned the recent practice of presidents' naming their "chief political appointee" as attorney general and declared that the office "should be removed from politics." Although Bell was a close political aide, he proved to be more independent than Carter bargained for.[7]

A moderate conservative and southerner, Bell was viewed by civil rights leaders with skepticism. His fellow Georgian Coretta Scott King said simply, "I don't trust him." The ACLU worried about his opposition to an expansive role for the federal courts. Others objected because he was Carter's friend and political ally. In fact, Bell strongly supported civil rights and proudly cited his record of ordering school integration in 140 cases as a court of appeals justice. He appointed Wade McCree as solicitor general, the second African American in that position after Thurgood Marshall, and Drew Days as the first African American to head the Civil Rights Division.[8]

On affirmative action, Bell fought Carter's political advisers by opposing quotas in the critical 1978 case of *Regents of the University of California v. Bakke* case before the Supreme Court, in which the Court first addressed affirmative action. Carter agreed with him on that issue, and the Supreme Court's decision in *Bakke* basically followed Bell's amicus brief. The most serious conflict arose in a church-state case in which Carter overruled his decision that religious institutions receiving federal job funds could not invoke religious criteria in hiring. An angry Bell wrote Carter a stern five-page letter reminding him that he had "directed me to establish an independent Department of Justice, a neutral zone … free of political interference." He did not, however, follow through on his threat to resign. (Bell eventually prevailed when the case reached the courts.) Bell also made prophetic criticisms about the independent counsel provisions of the 1978 Ethics in Government Act, warning that it had the potential for going completely out of control. Twenty years later, Kenneth Starr fulfilled that prophecy in his investigation of

6 "Carter's Candor Is Becoming an Issue in the Campaign," *NYT*, January 26, 1976. Abortion issue in the 1976 Iowa caucuses: Peter G. Bourne, *Jimmy Carter: A Comprehensive Biography from Plains to Postpresidency* (New York: Scribner, 1997), pp. 279–80.

7 Jimmy Carter, *A Government as Good as Its People* (New York: Simon & Schuster, 1977), p. 48; Law Day address, pp. 30–42.

8 "Coretta King Uneasy," *NYT*, January 13, 1977.

President Bill Clinton. Bell also asked for and received exemption from political duties such as speaking on behalf of the administration. Other cabinet members then asked for the same privilege, but Carter drew the line and told them no.[9]

FAITH AND POLITICS: A TIGER BY THE TAIL

"The most important thing in my life beyond all else," Jimmy Carter unabashedly told the country while running for president, "is Jesus Christ." Carter introduced something new to presidential politics, as the first candidate to make his religion the cornerstone of his policies. One scholar pointed out that he broke with the established tradition in which presidents would "privatize" their faith: indicate they were religious but strictly avoid discussing religion and public policies. John F. Kennedy had raised the issue of his religion in the 1960 campaign, but only because he needed to allay fears about his Catholicism. Carter genuinely saw his faith as a guide and presented himself as an alternative to the dishonesty of Presidents Johnson and Nixon.[10]

Although he was a churchgoing Baptist all his life, Carter's faith took a dramatic turn after he lost the 1966 Georgia gubernatorial election to the segregationist Lester Maddox. The defeat provoked a personal crisis, and he emerged as a "born-again" Christian. As a presidential candidate, he introduced the term into national politics and was part of a broader resurgence of fundamentalism in American political life. Secular liberals thought fundamentalists had been pushed to the margins after the 1925 Scopes cases and were caught off guard. Ironically, fundamentalists first helped elect Carter president in 1976 and then defeat him in 1980. A 1976 Gallup Poll found that 34 percent of Americans considered themselves "born again," and they favored Carter over Ford by 58 to 34 percent. In 1980, they abandoned him for Ronald Reagan. The rise of the Religious Right would transform American politics, as part of the Great Realignment, with the Republican Party embracing a "social agenda" that was aggressively anti-civil libertarian.[11]

Carter's faith sustained him on two controversial issues as president. He staunchly affirmed his belief in separation of church and state, the traditional position of the Southern Baptist Convention, to which he belonged. In 1980 he outraged the Religious Right leader Jerry Falwell by refusing to support Senator Jesse Helms's bill permitting voluntary prayer in public schools. Falwell denounced him in a letter to Moral Majority members declaring, "So as you can see, even the President of the United States is against us." Carter stood firm in his belief that "prayer is a matter between the individual and

[9] "Griffin Bell's Neutral Zone," in Nancy V. Baker, *Conflicting Loyalties: Law and Politics in the Attorney General's Office, 1789–1990* (Lawrence: University Press of Kansas, 1992), pp. 151–65. An early skeptical view: Victor Navasky, "The Greening of Griffin Bell," *New York Times Magazine*, February 27, 1977, 41–50. Griffin Bell, *Taking Care of the Law* (New York: William Morrow, 1982), [church-state case] pp. 24–7; [independent counsel law], p. 37. Bell, OH, MCPA.

[10] Quoted in D. Jason Berggren and Nicol C. Rae, "Jimmy Carter and George W. Bush: Faith, Foreign Policy, and an Evangelical Presidential Style," *Presidential Studies Quarterly* 36 (December 2006): 612. Jason Berggren, "'I Had a Different Way of Governing': The Living Faith of President Carter," *Journal of Church and State* 47 (1): 43–61.

[11] Berggren and Rae, "Jimmy Carter and George W. Bush," 606–32. James Wooten, *Dasher: The Roots and the Rising of Jimmy Carter* (New York: Warner Books, 1978), pp. 265–70. "Poll Finds 34% Share 'Born Again' Feeling," *NYT*, September 26, 1976. Evangelicals' withdrawal and return: Karen Armstrong, *The Battle for God* (New York: Knopf, 2000).

God," and that in the "diverse setting" of public schools it is "particularly appropriate that prayer be an individual matter."[12]

Carter's faith also underpinned his politically courageous stand on pardoning Vietnam War draft resisters, which went beyond Gerald Ford's policy on earned amnesty. On August 24, 1976, just as the presidential campaign was heating up, he told the American Legion convention (where Ford had announced his policy two years earlier) that he would pardon draft resisters. Predictably, the Legionnaires loudly booed him. True to his word, the day after he took the oath of office he granted the pardon in an executive order. Ultimately, 381 young men who had fled the country returned, 9,000 were released from jail, and the Defense Department upgraded 19,000 less than honorable discharges.[13]

The entry of Christian fundamentalism into American politics soon became the greatest threat to civil liberties, however. Subsequent professed Christian politicians sought to use government to advance religion. Ronald Reagan was the first to capture this movement in the 1980 election, and born-again Christians turned solidly against Jimmy Carter.

THE LONELY MIDDLE OF THE ROAD ON ABORTION

Jimmy Carter's middle-of-the road position on abortion was similar to Gerald Ford's: personal opposition to abortion and equally strong opposition to outlawing it. As had Ford, he quickly found that the middle of the road was a lonely place in the rising abortion war, and he drew sharp attacks from both sides of the issue.

As a candidate in 1976, Carter met with the Catholic bishops to explain that he was personally deeply troubled by abortion but did not support a law or constitutional amendment outlawing it. He then said the same thing in a letter to the prochoice National Abortion Rights Action League, adding that he strongly supported increased federal aid for family planning services. Along with Presidents Nixon and Ford, he believed birth control would reduce the need for abortions. His position on family planning reassured prochoice activists but alienated the Catholic bishops and other antiabortion leaders. Meanwhile, he alienated prochoice groups by supporting a federal law to limit access to abortion, while not fully satisfying the right to life movement. To his credit, Carter was completely candid with both sides and never tried to curry favor by fudging his true position.[14]

The abortion issue was defused in the 1976 campaign because Ford and Carter held essentially the same position, and because the nascent antiabortion movement had not fully mobilized politically. It would play a major role in his defeat in 1980, however.

12 Mailing: Falwell, "Special Announcement," March 7, 1980. Copy in Maddox Files, Office of Public Liaison, Box 107, JCPL. Helms bill: S. 450, Supreme Court Jurisdiction Act of 1979, 96th Cong., 1st Sess. Carter's beliefs: Form Letter, Robert Maddox to [Blank], April 25, 1980, OPL, Maddox Files, Box 107, JCPL.

13 "Legionnaires Boo Carter on Pardon for Draft Defiers," *NYT*, August 25, 1976. Executive Order Relating to Proclamation of Pardon Executive Order 11967, January 21st, 1977, APP.

14 "Abortion Stand by Carter Vexes Catholic Bishops," *NYT*, September 1, 1976. Andrew W. Flint and Joy Porter, "Jimmy Carter: The Re-emergence of Faith-Based Politics and the Abortion Rights Issue," *Presidential Studies Quarterly* 35 (March 2005): 28–51. John Dumbrell, *The Carter Presidency: A Re-evaluation* (Manchester: Manchester University Press, 1993), p. 71.

A political misstep and a White House crisis

"There are many things in life that are not fair," President Carter explained. There are things "wealthy people can afford and poor people can't." The comment referred to a Supreme Court decision on abortion three weeks earlier upholding the constitutionality of the 1976 Hyde Amendment prohibiting Medicaid funding for abortions.[15]

Carter's remark provoked outrage among feminists and liberals, who saw it as grossly insensitive to poor women. Alarmed prochoice advocates also saw the *Maher v. Roe* decision as a possible first step toward reversal of *Roe v. Wade* itself. Carter had previously made clear his opposition to Medicaid funding of abortions, but the remark about fairness seemed gratuitous. The ACLU executive director Aryeh Neier acidly called Carter "the President of the rich." Only six months after his inauguration, the controversy opened a wedge of distrust between Carter and his prochoice allies, and it anticipated similar controversies when his ill-considered comments on certain issues offended important constituencies.[16]

Angry calls poured into the White House office of Midge Costanza, head of the Office of Public Liaison and as such Carter's outreach person to liberal interest groups. Just three days after Carter's press conference, she convened a White House meeting with prochoice activists. She thought she was rallying a key constituency, but Carter saw it as a disloyal palace revolt, and he rebuked her at the next cabinet meeting. Politically tone deaf, he called Costanza's allies "nut groups" in his diary. She would leave the White House within a year.[17]

The incident was an early sign of Carter's difficulties with feminists, civil rights leaders, and gay rights activists. On all three issues his position was far better than that of either President Nixon or Ford, or any potential Republican presidential contender in 1980. His situation, however, paralleled President Kennedy's experience on civil rights in the early 1960s, when a tide of rapidly rising expectations outstripped what he was prepared to say or do.[18]

As it happened, Carter was spared one potential confrontation over abortion. No vacancy on the Supreme Court occurred during his presidency, leaving him the only elected president ever to serve a full four-year term without making a Court appointment.[19] Given the fierce battles over subsequent Court nominees focusing on abortion, a vacancy would undoubtedly have provoked deep divisions in the White House and among Democrats over whom to nominate, followed by a battle in Congress. Carter undoubtedly would have preferred a moderate on the issue, for both personal and political reasons,

15 "President Defends Court's Action Curbing Federal Aid for Abortion," *NYT*, July 13, 1977.

16 *Maher v. Roe*, 432 U.S. 464 (1977). Neier: "President Defends Court's Action Curbing Federal Aid for Abortion," *NYT*, July 13, 1977.

17 *Maher v. Roe*, 432 U.S. 464 (1977). "President Defends Court's Action Curbing Federal Aid for Abortion," *NYT*, July 13, 1977. National Abortion Rights Action League, Press Release, March 17, 1977; Memo re Meeting re Proposed Ad Hoc Committee on Women's Health and Reproduction, July 15, 1977; clipping, Rowland Evans and Robert Novak, "Quashing an In-House Revolt on Abortion," July 30, 1977; July 15 meeting, July 18 cabinet meeting; Memo, Costanza to the President, July 13, 1977, OPL Files, Box 1, JCPL. Carter, *The White House Diary*, p. 127.

18 "President Rejects Jordan's Criticism," *NYT*, July 26, 1977.

19 Henry J. Abraham, *Justices, Presidents, and Senators: A History of the U.S. Supreme Court Appointments from Washington to Bush II*, 5th ed. (Lanham, MD: Rowman & Littlefield, 2008), pp. 262–3.

and he would have been offended at the idea of making abortion or any other issue a litmus test. Feminists and prochoice activists, now powerful forces within the Democratic Party, would have insisted on a clear prochoice nominee.

Carter never altered his views on abortion, while in office or in his long postpresidential career. Twenty-five years after leaving the White House, in a 2005 interview, he again condemned abortion, saying, "I have never felt that any abortion should be committed," while remaining equally strong in his opposition to outlawing the procedure.[20]

DILEMMAS ON CIVIL RIGHTS

The "ethnic purity" flap

Speaking in Indianapolis on April 6, 1976, the candidate Jimmy Carter said the federal government should not use its power "deliberately to circumvent the natural inclination of people to live in ethnically homogenous neighborhoods."[21] The comment, reinforced with references to "alien groups" and "black intrusion," struck a raw nerve in the civil rights community, and provoked a brief but revealing controversy over Carter. To be sure, he expressed strong opposition to housing discrimination in the same press conference, but the damage was done. Andrew Young, Carter's chief African-American supporter, called the remarks "a disaster for the campaign." Revealing his inexperience in national politics, Carter seemed tone deaf to the political impact of his words and was both puzzled and annoyed when reporters pressed him to clarify his position. "I resent the effort," he responded, to "make something out of nothing." Finally facing up to the damage to his campaign, he issued an apology two days later, admitting to "an unfortunate choice of words." He repeated his support for open housing laws but then compounded his original gaffe by restating his opposition to using federal "force to move people of a different ethnic background into a neighborhood just to change its character." Carter did not realize that the term "force," popularized by President Richard Nixon and opponents of school busing, had became a code word implying that federal civil rights measures were illegitimate.[22]

In fact, Carter had opposed busing to achieve school integration while governor of Georgia. In 1972 a controversy erupted over a court-ordered desegregation plan in Augusta, Georgia, that included busing. Virtually all white students stayed home from school in a one-day boycott. Governor Carter expressed support for the boycott if the state legislature failed to approve a resolution calling for a federal constitutional convention to consider an antibusing amendment to the U.S. Constitution. The spectacle of a governor's endorsing an unlawful action evoked memories of Orval Faubus in 1957 and George C. Wallace in 1963 (when he vowed to "stand in the schoolhouse door"), but Carter's reputation somehow survived relatively unscathed. Carter campaigned against busing in 1976, disavowing even the Democratic Party platform's weak statement on "mandatory transportation."[23]

20 "Carter Condemns Abortion Culture," *Washington Times*, November 4, 2005.

21 "Carter Defends 'All-White Areas,'" *NYT*, April 7, 1976.

22 "Carter Issues an Apology on 'Ethnic Purity' Phrase," *NYT*, April 9, 1976. Carter does not mention the incident in his memoirs: Jimmy Carter, *Keeping Faith: Memoirs of a President* (New York: Bantam Books, 1982).

23 "Gov. Carter Buoys Georgia Busing Foes by Saying He May Endorse Boycott," *NYT*, February 17, 1972. "The Busing Issue Boils Over," *Time Magazine*, February 28, 1972. Elections: Lawrence J. McAndrews, "Talking

For all practical purposes, Carter shared the consensus of opinion among national political leaders on housing and busing in the post-1965 era. All, including Presidents Nixon and Ford, argued that de jure race discrimination was wrong but also opposed using federal authority, in their view, to *force* the integration of either schools or residential patterns. Lyndon Johnson, for all his great achievements on civil rights, had intervened in 1965 to block HEW's plan to withhold federal funds for Chicago schools because of de facto segregation. Robert Kennedy, despite his strong identification with racial justice, also opposed busing. He publicly opposed it in 1964, but when his comments provoked controversy he carefully avoided the issue for the next four years. In short, all presidents and leading presidential candidates responded to white fears in both North and South of racial change in their neighborhoods.[24]

A political bind on affirmative action: The *Bakke* case

"This is going to be a very tough issue," warned Carter's chief political adviser, Stuart Eizenstat, in a September 1977 memo.[25] Indeed it would be. The administration wanted to file an amicus brief in the Supreme Court case of Allen Bakke, a white applicant denied admission to the University of California at Davis Medical School who was now challenging its affirmative action plan. The case provoked a bitter conflict within the Carter administration over what position to take on quotas and exposed a deep national divide on the issue.

Even before the *Bakke* case arose, the Carter administration was caught in a political firestorm over racial quotas. The HEW secretary Joseph Califano, a former Lyndon Johnson staff member, saw himself carrying forward the Johnson legacy on civil rights and was the staunchest advocate of affirmative action in the administration. In March 1977, just two months into the Carter presidency, he endorsed quotas as a remedy for past employment discrimination. Angry protests erupted, many of them from liberals, with accusations that he favored reverse discrimination against whites. Forty-four university leaders wrote to President Carter demanding he repudiate Califano. The group included the scholar, political activist, and godfather of neoconservatism, Sidney Hook. Under pressure, Califano was forced to clarify, if not retract his statement, conceding that the word "quotas" was "obviously a nerve-jangling word." When he gave a previously scheduled speech at City College in New York City on June 5, he looked out on numerous Jewish faculty members who remembered the historic use of quotas against Jews in college admissions and who stared at him with evident hostility. In a partial retreat, he called for "goals" on racial minority college admissions but did not explain exactly how goals were different from quotas.[26]

the Talk: Bill Clinton and School Desegregation," *International Social Science Review* 79 (2004): 92. Race and presidential campaigns: Jeremy D. Mayer, *Running on Race: Racial Politics in Presidential Campaigns, 1960–2000* (New York: Random House, 2002); on Carter in 1976, pp. 128–30, 136–8.

24 On Johnson, see Chapter 8 of this book. On Robert Kennedy, see Ronald Steel, *In Love with Night: The American Romance with Robert Kennedy* (New York: Simon & Schuster, 2000), p. 165.

25 Memo, Eizenstat to Jordan, September 6, 1977, Chief of Staff Files, Box 33, JCPL.

26 "Califano Says Quotas Are Necessary," *NYT*, March 18, 1977. "Califano Admits Error in Advocating Job Quotas," ibid., April 1, 1977. "Califano Asks 'Goals' on Minority Students in Colleges," ibid., June 6, 1977. Califano, Jr., *Governing America*, pp. 232–5.

Attorney General Griffin Bell began work on the administration's amicus brief for *Bakke*. A moderately conservative Georgian, he spent fourteen years on the Fifth Circuit Court of Appeals (appointed by President Kennedy) and was extremely proud of his civil rights record, which included ordering school integration in 140 cases. Bakke argued that under its affirmative action program the University of California had admitted some racial minority applicants with lower cumulative scores (grade-point average, Medical College Admission Test [MCAT] score, etc.) than his, and that this was an unconstitutional form of reverse discrimination in violation of Title VI of the 1964 Civil Rights Act and the Fourteenth Amendment. Bell's initial amicus brief supported the general concept of affirmative action but also held that Bakke had a valid claim of reverse discrimination.[27]

Bell's draft quickly leaked out, and the White House was embarrassed by a *New York Times* headline, "Carter Said to Back Bar to Race Quotas." Protests from civil rights groups bombarded the administration. The Congressional Black Caucus urged it to "reverse its reported decision" on the case. Califano and the White House aides Stuart Eizenstat and Robert Lipshutz also demanded strong support for affirmative action. Although Califano had yielded on his language earlier that year, he was not about to yield on civil rights enforcement policy before the Supreme Court, declaring, "We're not going to have that [past civil rights] work thrown out the window by a couple of young lawyers." Eizenstat and Lipshultz were concerned about the impact of a weak civil rights stand on African-American voters. Eizenstat wrote to Carter's chief of staff Hamilton Jordan, "While I think that legally the Justice Department position against the University is correct, [I am] convinced from phone calls from blacks and liberals" that supporting Bakke would be seen as "a retreat from all affirmative action programs."[28]

Attorney General Bell was deeply offended by the political intrusion into the case. He saw himself following the example of Edward Levi, with a duty to serve the law free of any political pressures, and especially disliked Califano, who he thought had "his own agenda" within the administration. On this point he was right; Califano did have an agenda, particularly on civil rights.[29] President Carter was very clear about his position on affirmative action and quotas, and it was similar to Bell's. In the margins of a key memo from Eizenstat he scribbled, "I agree to (a) strong affirmative action (b) no rigid quotas.... – J. C." A few weeks later, he and his staff finally agreed that "rigid, inflexible racial quotas ... do not pass constitutional muster." He also told a reporter, "I hate to endorse the proposition of quotas for minority groups, for women, or for anyone else."[30] Legal considerations aside, quotas represented the kind of special interest politics he abhorred. The administration's amicus brief in *Bakke* followed Bell's original draft, supporting affirmative action but not the use of quotas.

27 Bell, *Taking Care of the Law*, pp. 28–32.

28 "Carter Said to Back Bar to Race Quotas," *NYT*, September 12, 1977. Califano, Jr., *Governing America*, p. 237. Memo, Eizenstat to Jordan, September 6, 1977, Chief of Staff Files, Box 33, JCPL. Congressional Black Caucus, Letter to the President, September 9, 1977, Jordan files, Box 33, JCPL. Carter quote: Bourne, *Jimmy Carter*, p. 425. Administration internal conflicts: See Joel Dreyfuss and Charles Lawrence III, *The Bakke Case: The Politics of Inequality* (New York: Harcourt Brace Jovanovich, 1979).

29 Bell, OH, pp. 14–16, MCPA.

30 Memo re Bakke, Eizenstat and Lipshutz to the President, September 6, 1977, Chief of Staff Hamilton Jordan Files, Box 33, JCPL. Lipshutz and Eizenstat for the President, the Vice President, Last Draft of the Bakke Brief, September 16, 1977, Chief of Staff Files, Box 33, JCPL. Califano later wrote "The president gave us no indication of where he stood," but this is not true; Califano, Jr., *Governing America*, pp. 231–43; quotes: p. 241. Bourne, *Jimmy Carter*, p. 425.

To put Carter in context, it should be noted that President Bill Clinton, who enjoys a much more favorable reputation among civil rights leaders than Carter, took exactly the same position on quotas. Clinton's better image among African Americans is due in large part to his extraordinary ability to communicate a genuine empathy for the experiences of African Americans.[31] The difference between the two presidents' reputations goes to the heart of Carter's problem on so many issues: his close attention to details of difficult issues but inability to communicate persuasively his values and commitments on race, as well as other issues.

Most seriously, the *Bakke* case split the old civil rights coalition, creating a serious political dilemma for Carter and the Democratic Party. The case drew fifty-eight amicus briefs, some opposing quotas filed by such normally unlikely allies as the American Jewish Committee and the Fraternal Order of Police. Quotas and the issue of reverse discrimination drove many former liberal civil rights activists into the arms of neoconservatives as they rethought their positions on race and many other issues.[32]

The Supreme Court's close 5–4 decision in *Regents of the University of California v. Bakke* (1978) reflected the national division and its own ambivalence on the thorny issue of affirmative action and quotas. The Court upheld Bakke's claim of discrimination and ordered him admitted to the medical school but also held that race could be used as one of several factors in making admissions decisions (four justices opposed any use of race in admission decisions). While the university's quota system violated the language and the legislative history of Title VII of the 1964 Civil Rights Act, the Court nonetheless held that "the State has a substantial interest that legitimately may be served by a properly devised admissions program involving the competitive consideration of race and ethnic origin." The opinion was, in fact, fairly close to Attorney General Bell's original brief. The decision hardly settled the matter, however, and the Court wrestled with affirmative action and race-conscious policies for the next thirty years. Carter, again politically tone deaf, refused to see the significance of the issue of quotas and complained in his diary that the media "highly exaggerated" the importance of the *Bakke* decision.[33]

The *Bakke* decision alarmed civil rights leaders, who saw it signaling a national retreat on racial equality. Unfairly, they directed their anger at President Carter (the administration's brief, after all, hardly dictated the Court's decision). The NAACP director, Benjamin Hooks, declared it "the worst of times because our President has not moved far enough or fast enough." A 1977 report by the Americans for Democratic Action more accurately targeted Congress, which had repeatedly expressed its opposition to quotas in employment and school busing. Democrats, moreover, had been among the leaders on both issues; Senators Thomas Eagleton and Joe Biden, for example, had cosponsored a successful antibusing amendment to an education bill.[34]

[31] DeWayne Wickham, *Bill Clinton and Black America* (New York: Ballantine, 2002). Clinton: see Chapter 13 of this book.

[32] "Longtime Allies on Rights Split by Bakke Case," *NYT*, September 25, 1977. Thomas D. Edsall and Mary D. Edsall, *Chain Reaction: The Impact of Race, Rights, and Taxes on American Politics* (New York: W. W. Norton, 1991).

[33] *Regents of the Univ. of Cal. v. Bakke*, 438 U.S. 265 (1978). Kaufman, *The Presidency of James Earl Carter, Jr.*, pp. 69–71. Howard Ball, *The Bakke Case: Race, Education, and Affirmative Action* (Lawrence: University Press of Kansas, 2000). The Court may have conferred finality on the issue of racial preferences in two 2007 school integration cases: *Meredith v. Jefferson County*, 551 U.S. (2007). *Parents Involved v. Seattle*, 551 U.S. (2007). Carter, *White House Diary*, p. 203.

[34] Hooks: Memo, Terrence B. Adamson to Joseph L. Powell, July 12, 1978, Domestic Policy Staff Files, Box 165, JCPL. ADA report: *NYT*, August 15, 1977.

Facing criticisms from its allies, the administration pledged to move forward on civil rights enforcement, with the HEW secretary Califano taking the lead. In a September 1978 speech at Howard University he pointed out that *Bakke* did not affect the power of either federal courts or federal agencies to order remedies in cases "when there is a finding of illegal discrimination." Civil rights enforcement at HEW efforts "will not slacken," he pledged, adding that he had already upgraded the department's efforts. Califano moved forward on the rights of other groups as well. In April 1977, thirteen years before Congress passed the Americans with Disabilities Act, for example, he issued HEW guidelines barring discrimination against disabled persons, alcoholics, and people with drug dependency problems.[35]

School integration, again

As every president had, beginning with Lyndon Johnson, Carter faced the issue of using Title VI of the Civil Rights Act to enforce school integration. Even Johnson had drawn back from using this powerful but politically explosive tool in the pivotal 1965 Chicago schools case. Carter took office promising to use Title VI, with the HEW secretary Califano the key administration figure. Despite Califano's deep civil rights commitment, however, even he declined to use this instrument. In early 1977 Califano had five Title VI orders on his desk, cutting off federal fund to local school districts. He never signed one of them. Congress then relieved the administration of its agony in December 1977 with the Eagleton-Biden Amendment prohibiting the use of federal funds to require busing. Biden was a strong supporter of civil rights, but Wilmington, Delaware, faced a school integration crisis, with strong local opposition to busing, and Biden faced a possibly tough reelection bid in 1978. His support of the anti-busing amendment testifies to the strength of antibusing feeling among even liberal Democratic members of Congress.[36]

The political scientist Stephen C. Halpern, in the best analysis of Title VI enforcement, called the amendment the "death knell" for Title VI. Courts could still order busing upon a finding of discrimination, but the most direct and quickest method of enforcing racially integrated schools was no longer available to presidential administrations. It was simply too potent a tool, and one that applied to communities in the North and the South. Democrats saw the political implications of this as well as Republicans and backed away. President Carter expressed reservations about the "vexing constitutional questions" the amendment raised but signed it anyway. Civil rights groups, led by the NAACP Legal Defense Fund, filed suit that very day challenging the act but eventually lost at every level of the federal courts.[37]

Despite the controversy over quotas and busing, Carter's overall record on civil rights was good, particularly on the appointment of African Americans. Patricia Roberts, secretary

[35] Califano 1978 speech: Louis Martin Files, Box 17, JCPL. "Califano Signs Regulations to Ban Discrimination against Disabled," *NYT*, April 29, 1977. Califano, Jr., *Governing America*, pp. 258–62.

[36] Stephen C. Halpern, *On the Limits of the Law: The Ironic Legacy of Title VI of the 1964 Civil Rights Act* (Baltimore: Johns Hopkins University Press, 1995), pp. 137–89. Jules Witcover, *Joe Biden: A Life of Trial and Redemption* (New York: William Morrow, 2010), pp. 132–42.

[37] Biden Amendment: Labor-HEW Continuing Appropriations Bill Statement on Signing H. J. Res. 662 Into Law, December 9, 1977, APP. Halpern, *On the Limits of the Law*, p. 155; see especially the thoughtful conclusions, p. 320.

of housing and urban development, was the first African-American woman in the cabinet, and the former Martin Luther King aide Andrew Young held the high-profile position of United Nations ambassador. Eleanor Holmes Norton chaired the EEOC, Wade McCree was solicitor general, and Drew Days headed the Civil Rights Division in the Justice Department. Carter appointed twenty-seven African-American judges, including eighteen to federal district courts and nine to circuit courts of appeals, integrating three judicial circuits. It was a record exceeded only by President Bill Clinton.[38]

FORWARD AND BACKWARD ON WOMEN AND FAMILY ISSUES

Although President Carter disappointed feminists on public funding of abortions, he was very supportive of other women's issues. His record on appointing women to top positions far exceeded that of any previous president, as a result of both his personal commitment and the dramatically changed legal and political context of women's rights. Carter and Gerald Ford were the first presidents to serve after the Supreme Court's breakthrough decisions in the early 1970s affirming equal protection for women under the Fourteenth Amendment (*Reed v. Reed*, 1971; *Frontiero v. Richardson*, 1973). The women's movement, moreover, developed a well-organized political effort and was now a powerful constituency within the Democratic Party. The National Women's Political Caucus, founded in 1971, organized the Coalition for Women's Appointments and forwarded candidates for Carter's consideration. Timing aside, Carter was genuinely committed to women's rights and took several positive steps to support them.[39]

The point person on Carter's commitment to women was Midge Costanza, the highest-ranking woman in the administration, with an office just down the hall from the president's. As head of Office of Public Liaison, she was only the second woman to hold a high White House position (President Nixon had appointed Anne Armstrong staff counsel in 1973). She was also the only non-Georgian among the seven with the title of assistant to the president in the initial Carter White House. With a strong record on both reproductive rights and gay and lesbian rights, she was the leading advocate of civil liberties in the administration. Costanza first met Carter when he campaigned for her in her unsuccessful 1974 bid for Congress in Rochester, New York. As the vice mayor of Rochester, she championed a city charter amendment to protect gay rights in 1976. Carter was thus well aware of her commitments and energetic style when he picked her for the White House staff. Her activism, however, quickly led to grief, and her fate symbolized better than anything else Carter's difficulties with the new rights activism.[40]

Costanza's problems began in summer 1977 in the flap over Carter's ill-chosen comment about "unfairness" after the Supreme Court's *Maher v. Roe* decision blocking federal funding for abortions. Carter regarded her White House meeting with his critics as an act

[38] Sheldon Goldman, *Picking Federal Judges: Lower Court Selection from Roosevelt through Reagan* (New Haven, CT: Yale University Press, 1997), pp. 271–4.

[39] Byron E. Shafer, *Quiet Revolution: The Struggle for the Democratic Party and the Shaping of Post-Reform Politics* (New York: Russell Sage Foundation, 1983).

[40] Costanza's early relationship with Carter and her role in the White House: Dudley Clendinen and Adam Nagourney, *Out for Good: The Struggle to Build a Gay Rights Movement in America* (New York: Simon & Schuster, 1999), pp. 285–90. Costanza and gay rights in Rochester: OPL Files, Box 4, JCPL. "Midge Costanza, A Top Aide to Carter, Dies at 77," *NYT*, March 24, 2010. Joseph A. Pika, "The White House Office of Public Liaison," *Presidential Studies Quarterly* 39 (September 2009): 553–4.

of disloyalty. Costanza could not be contained, however, and by 1978 he had finally had enough. In a public insult in May he cut her staff from fifteen people to one and moved her office into the basement. She got the message and resigned two months later.[41]

Women in Top Jobs

Costanza's fate aside, the administration had an excellent record with regard to appointing women to top positions. Women accounted for between 12 and 19 percent of all his high-level appointments, far exceeding those of any previous president. High-visibility appointments included Patricia Roberts Harris as the first African-American woman in the cabinet, as secretary of housing and urban development, and then Juanita Kreps as the first female secretary of commerce. Sarah Weddington, who had argued *Roe v. Wade* before the Supreme Court, became a White House adviser to the president. The high percentage of lower-level appointments indicated Carter's commitment to go beyond mere symbolic gestures. The U.S. Civil Rights Commission in 1983 applauded the "unprecedented levels of women and minority men" he appointed. In his final State of the Union Address four days before leaving office in 1981, Carter proudly pointed out that "I have appointed a record number of women to judgeships and to top government posts. Fully 22 percent of all my appointees are women, and I nominated 41 of the 46 women who sit on the Federal bench today." One of those judges was Ruth Bader Ginsburg, whom he named to the circuit court of appeals in 1980, paving the way for President Bill Clinton to appoint her to the Supreme Court in 1993.[42]

Patricia Derian held an especially prominent position as coordinator for Human Rights and Humanitarian Affairs in the State Department, and later assistant secretary of state for human rights. Introducing human rights considerations into foreign policy was arguably Carter's singular and lasting contribution as president. Derian, therefore, had special status as the point person on that groundbreaking issue. Her appointment raised the hopes of civil libertarians about the administration. She had an extensive civil rights and civil liberties background, including voting rights work in Mississippi in the 1960s, membership on the ACLU Board of Directors, and a leadership role in the ACLU's National Prison Project. Her effectiveness in the State Department was blunted, however, by her lack of experience on foreign affairs and the resentment of veteran diplomats over her outsider status.[43]

Civil libertarians, however, were often disappointed in Carter's record, as were feminists and civil rights leaders, in large part by his positions on federal aid for abortions and affirmative action. The disillusionment was very much a matter of expectations. In

41 Hamilton Jordan to President Carter [circa 1978], Chief of Staff files, Box 34A, JCPL. Demotion: "Midge Costanza," clipping, *Washington Post*, July 26, 1978, Office of the Counsel Files, Box 11, JCPL. "Miss Costanza Trying to Keep White House Office," *NYT*, May 20, 1978. "Miss Costanza Resigns as Assistant to Carter, Citing Problems of Style," ibid., August 2, 1978.

42 The State of the Union Annual Message to the Congress, January 16, 1981, APP. Dumbrell, *The Carter Presidency*, p. 69. Anne Wexler, Exit Interview, JCPL. Susan J. Carroll, "Women Appointed to the Carter Administration: More or Less Qualified?" *Polity* 18 (Summer 1986): 696–706. Weddington, Exit Interview, JCPL. United States Commission on Civil Rights, *Equal Opportunity in Presidential Appointments* (Washington, DC: Government Printing Office, June 1983). Goldman, *Picking Federal Judges*, Ch. 7, pp. 236–84.

43 Department of State Nomination of Patricia M. Derian to Be Coordinator for Human Rights and Humanitarian Affairs. March 5, 1977, APP. Dumbrell, *The Carter Presidency*, p. 63. Isbell, "Carter's Civil Libertarians," on the backgrounds of Carter's top women appointees.

the excitement of the post-Watergate moment, civil libertarians expected many more advances in individual rights. Those expectations, however, outstripped political realities, both because of Carter's basic moderation on some issues and because of the new conservative mood in the country.[44]

To advance women's issues, Carter in April 1978 created both a National Advisory Committee for Women and an Interdepartmental Task Force on Women. In a Father's Day interview on June 18, 1977, he endorsed several family-friendly policies: ending the so-called marriage tax, eliminating welfare rules that many argued drove fathers from their homes, and supporting women with children working outside the home, pointing out that his wife, Rosalynn, went to work before their oldest child was two years old. The administration inherited the report on federal laws restricting women's opportunities that had been prepared by President Ford's adviser Maj. Gen. (Ret.) Jeanne Holm, which Ford had ordered in anticipation of ERA ratification. The ERA failed, but the Carter administration, downplaying its origins, embraced Holm's report and its recommendations.[45]

With so many committed feminists staffing federal agencies, the administration effected a number of important policy changes. These included requiring informed consent of women before any sterilization could be done, eliminating an army requirement that female but not male recruits have high school diplomas, modifying the army's definition of "combat and combat-related" operations, which opened more opportunities for women, and a new navy policy permitting permanent assignment of women to non-combat ships not engaged in combat missions. The new federal job training program, meanwhile, included training for displaced homemakers. On reproductive rights, Title X funding for family planning services increased significantly, and Carter supported the 1978 Pregnancy Discrimination Act, prohibiting employment discrimination based on pregnancy.[46] Compared with previous presidents, and Ronald Reagan immediately after him, Carter's contributions to women's rights were unmatched. In the new civil rights era, when Title VII formally prohibited sex discrimination, the important changes occurred in administrative regulations covering a host of issues. They lacked the drama of a Supreme Court decision and were generally low visibility in Washington politics, but they had real impact on the lives of ordinary people. As a result, Carter's actions were often unappreciated by people who were not experts on particular policy issues.

At the FBI, William H. Webster, whom Carter appointed director in 1978, raised the number of female agents from ninety to eight hundred by the time he left in 1987. He also doubled the number of African-American agents and appointed the first African American to head a local bureau office. Webster had to fight the bureau's old guard, who were fond of telling him "what Hoover would have wanted," and whom he labeled the "Hoover Hard Hats." Exasperated at times, he told them it was time to "stop measuring sideburns" (a pointed reference to Hoover's obsession with personal grooming) and to

[44] Shattuck, "You Can't Always Depend on It."

[45] "Carter Says Plans of Government Should Keep Families Together," *NYT*, June 19, 1977. Executive Order 12050 – National Advisory Committee for Women, April 4, 1978, APP. Holm, OH, LOC.

[46] National Advisory Committee for Women, Executive Order 12050, April 4, 1978, APP. Office of Sarah Weddington, Intergovernmental Task Force on Women, *Honoring a Commitment to the People of the United States: The Record of President Jimmy Carter on Women's Issues* (Washington, DC: White House, January 1980).

accept "the emerging standards of decency" in American society with regard to both meaningful personnel standards and respect for the law.[47]

Despite these low-visibility advances, the Equal Rights Amendment remained the focus of public attention and created conflict between Carter and many feminist leaders. The ERA ratification drive came to an abrupt halt in 1975-6, in the face of fierce neoconservative opposition. Carter fully supported the ERA, but its advocates, fearing defeat, demanded he work more vigorously for ratification. Midge Costanza angered her boss again by publicly criticizing him for not doing more for the ERA. In August 1977 some feminists planned a protest march on the White House. Carter and his aides read the political mood of the country, however, and concluded he should not expend precious political capital on what now appeared to be a losing cause. A month earlier as if in a symbolic act, Alice Paul, who had introduced the ERA in 1923, died at age ninety-two.[48]

Feminist discontent with Carter reached is peak on January 12, 1979. In what some called the "Friday Afternoon Massacre," Carter fired Bella Abzug as cochair of his National Advisory Committee on Women after an angry confrontation in the White House. "She lit into him in front of nearly 40 people," according to one account. In advance of the meeting, the committee had issued a highly critical statement attacking an administration plan to increase defense spending and cut social programs. Carter fired Abzug immediately.[49] Firing a rebellious administration member was understandable, but Abzug was the most prominent feminist in Congress and a hero for activist women. In a serious rupture, NOW announced in November 1979 that it would not support Carter's renomination for president in 1980. The move upset many other feminists, who appreciated Carter's considerable achievements on appointments and eliminating sexism in government policies. They worried that a split among feminists might help elect a Republican president hostile to women's rights. Ted Kennedy was also disillusioned with Carter and, in challenging Carter for the nomination, promised to do more on women's issues. Kennedy's move reflected a broad disillusionment with Carter among liberals. The party insider Arthur M. Schlesinger, Jr., confided in his journal on August 12, 1980, that Carter had been a "disaster" for the party and the entire country. Carter fought back, hosting a "salute to the ERA" and a White House meeting with prominent women in December 1979. Eleanor Smeal, president of NOW, was pointedly not invited.[50]

In a nationwide address on February 8, 1980, President Carter explained that women should be required to register for the draft, as "a recognition of the reality that both women and men are working members of our society.... [W]omen are now providing all types of skills in every profession, [and] the military should be no exception."[51]

It was a bold move in a time of suddenly rising international tensions. The Iranian hostage crisis erupted in November 1979 and almost completely consumed his last year in office. In response he took stronger positions on national security, including renewing

47 Webster, OH, MCPA.

48 "E.R.A. Backers Plan White House March," *NYT*, August 11, 1977.

49 "Carter, in Angry Exchange, Ousts Bella Abzug from Women's Unit," *NYT*, January 13, 1979. Lenora Reese, "National Advisory Committee for Women and the 'Friday Afternoon Massacre,'" *Southern Changes* 1, no. 5 (1979): 18–20.

50 "NOW's Carter Stand Perplexes Feminists," *NYT*, December 12, 1979. Arthur M. Schlesinger, Jr., *Journals, 1952–2000* (New York: Penguin, 2007), p. 498; see also pp. 437, 453–4, 491.

51 Selective Service Revitalization Statement on the Registration of Americans for the Draft, February 8, 1980, APP.

draft registration (but not a draft itself). To be sure, Carter did not advocate full equality in the military, and he proposed registering women only for noncombat duty. Nonetheless, it was a controversial step toward gender equality in the military. "It is more urgent than ever," he explained, "that the women in America have full and equal rights under the Constitution. Equal obligations deserve equal rights." His speech was the strongest statement on behalf of equality for women by any American president to that time, particularly because it challenged the politically powerful military establishment. Congress rejected his proposal, however, and did not require women to register.[52]

The commitment of both the Carter administration and the Democratic Party to women's rights stood in sharp contrast to the Republican Party's retreat on the issue. Signaling the Great Realignment, the 1980 GOP platform, under pressure from the New Right, for the first time in half a century equivocated on the ERA, acknowledging "the legitimate efforts of [both] those who support or oppose ratification" of the amendment. Four years later, the GOP platform dropped the separate section on women that had been in its platforms for decades in favor of a statement on women in the section on individual rights. As the GOP backed away from women's rights, feminists became an ever more powerful force within the Democratic Party. One political scientist called the rise of organized feminism the "quiet revolution" within the party. In 1968 13 percent of the delegates to the Democratic Party were women; in 1972 the figure was 40 percent.[53]

Fiasao: The White House Conference on the Family

The New Right activist Connie Marshner led a walkout of thirty delegates at the 180 White House Conference on the Family, accusing planners of stacking the program an favor of liberal "antifamily" policies. The walkout was another expression of the rising power of the New Right and the inability of Carter, and in this case liberal feminists, to counter it effectively.[54]

The conference sprang from Carter's genuine commitment to more family-friendly policies. In fact, he was the first president to popularize the term and to see the need for a comprehensive revision of federal policies. He expressed this to the National Catholic Charities Conference a month before the 1976 election and followed up with conference planning soon after taking office. The New Right, however, seized on the opportunity to advance its own agenda, and the resulting conflict delayed the conference until Carter's last year in office and led to a disastrous event. Carter's key advisers on family issues, notably the HEW secretary Califano, were Great Society liberals who sought to solve family problems through job training, the elimination of sexist policies in federal programs, welfare reform, and so on. This traditional liberal approach clashed head on with the New Right's goals of preserving the "traditional family," which included outlawing abortion, opposing gay rights, approving parents' spanking their children, and opposing women's

52 The Supreme Court rejected a sex discrimination challenge by a group of men: *Rostker v. Goldberg*, 453 U.S. 57 (1981). Dumbrell, *The Carter Presidency*, p. 70.

53 Shafer, *Quiet Revolution: The Struggle for the Democratic Party and the Shaping of Post-Reform Politics*. Dumbrell, *The Carter Presidency*, pp. 66, 76.

54 "2d Day of Family Conference: Workshop and a Walkout," *NYT*, June 7, 1980. J. Brooks Flipper, *Jimmy Carter, The Politics of Family, and the Rise of the Religious Right* (Athens: University of Georgia Press, 2011).

working outside the home. The competing agendas represented such utterly different visions of American society there was no real room for compromise, and precious little space for civilized dialogue at the White House conference.[55]

Catching the Carter administration and its liberal allies completely off guard, New Right activists plunged into the conference delegate selection process at the state level, elected many delegates, and arrived focused and disciplined. After much acrimonious debate, the conference eventually produced a report embracing the administration's liberal agenda. Occurring near the very end of Carter's presidency, however, it had absolutely no impact on policy. In January 1981, the new Reagan administration fully embraced the New Right agenda on family issues.[56]

OPENING THE WHITE HOUSE DOOR TO LESBIAN AND GAY RIGHTS

The historic meeting occurred in the Roosevelt Room of the White House on March 26, 1977. With the administration in office for only two months, Midge Costanza, in another activist step, held a three-hour meeting with two dozen representatives of the National Gay Task Force (NGTF). Never before had a presidential administration opened its doors to lesbian and gay rights activists. The gay rights movement itself was barely eight years old. Historians generally regard the 1969 riot at the Stonewall bar in New York City, where lesbians and gays fought back against a police raid, as the birth of the modern movement.[57]

President Carter was at Camp David that day, but he had clearly stated his opposition to discrimination against homosexuals in the 1976 campaign. On May 21, for example, he said that homosexuals should not be singled out "for abuse or harassment or prosecution under existing laws," adding that "I favor the end of harassment or abuse [*sic*] or discrimination against homosexuals." His only reservation involved security clearances for federal employees who were not open about their sexual orientation and could be targets for blackmail. He appointed the lesbian activist Jean O'Leary to a campaign post but to avoid possible controversy fought to keep a gay rights plank out of the Democratic Party platform. Once in office, he hired Costanza for her high-profile White House position fully aware of her role in advocating an antidiscrimination law in Rochester, New York. Carter's position on gay rights was far in advance of that of any previous candidate for president.[58]

The White House meeting covered a broad range of issues, including the right of homosexuals to serve in the military; an end to discrimination in the FBI, the CIA, and

55 Remarks at the Opening Session of the White House Conference on Families, June 5, 1980, APP.

56 Leo P. Ribuffo, "Family Policy Past as Prologue: Jimmy Carter, the White House Conference on Families, and the Mobilization of the New Christian Right," *Review of Policy Research* 23, no. 2 (2006): 311–37. White House Conference on Families, *Listening to America's Families: Action for the 1980s* (Washington, DC: Government Printing Office, 1980). Southern Baptist Convention, Resolution on the White House Conference on the Family (June 1980). www.sbc.org.

57 Meeting in the Jimmy Carter Library: Office of Public Liaison Files, Box 5, JCPL. "Homosexual Leaders Meet at White House with Presidential Aide to Discuss Discrimination in Federal Law," *NYT*, March 27, 1977. Interview with delegation member: "Capital Man in Vanguard on Gay Rights, *Sacramento Bee*, March 27, 2007. O'Leary interview: Karen Ocamb, "O'Leary's Toughest Fight," *Liberation Publications* (2004). The National Gay Task Force later changed its name to the National Lesbian and Gay Task Force (NLGTF).

58 Clendinen and Nagourney, *Out for Good*, pp. 272–3. Letter, Marilyn Haft to John Kosanke, *Miami Herald*, June 3, 1977, OPL Files, Box 5, JCPL. "Carter Says Plans of Government Should Keep Families Together," *NYT*, June 19, 1977. Flippen, *Jimmy Carter and the Politics of Family*, pp. 84–5, 93.

other federal agencies; and tax-exempt status for lesbian and gay advocacy groups. It was a heady experience for the new political movement, and the NGTF spokesperson Jean O'Leary left the meeting "highly optimistic." She had good reason to feel excited. Soon after the meeting, Costanza arranged a series of meetings with federal agencies, beginning with the Justice Department on April 28 and eventually including the U.S. Civil Rights Commission, the Defense and State Departments, HEW, and other agencies. This effort slowly produced results similar to the changes in policies on women's rights. Most involved changes in agency regulations that generated little publicity but had direct impact on people's lives. In 1978, for example, the U.S. Civil Service Commission barred discrimination on the basis of characteristics not related to job performance, eliminating a host of traditional items that disadvantaged homosexuals. Two years later the Office of Personnel Management went a step further and explicitly interpreted this to include sexual orientation.[59]

Despite his historic initiative, Carter proceeded to damage his image among lesbian and gay activists with a casual remark just one month before his comment on federal funding for abortions that alienated feminists. His 1977 Father's Day interview in the Oval Office, which was designed to promote his family-friendly policies, went well and stretched from the planned ten minutes to half an hour. Near the end, the reporter asked about homosexuality and marriage. Carter replied that he did not see homosexuality as a "threat to the family" and repeated his campaign statement that society should not "abuse or harass the homosexual." As an aside, however, he added that he did not feel same-sex relations were "a normal interrelationship." The reporter, clearly sensing a story, asked about gays' adopting children. Carter, also sensing he had created a story - and an unfavorable one - dodged the question by saying, "That's something I'd rather not answer," throwing more fuel on the fire by saying he preferred to avoid the issue of homosexuality because "I've got enough problems without taking on another." The news stories were predictable, with headlines declaring the president thought homosexuals were "abnormal." Gay rights activists were outraged at this insult, and they justifiably interpreted his final comment to mean that gay rights were not important to him.[60]

Carter found himself in a the same politically awkward position he was in regarding public funding for abortions, caught between his personal feelings about an issue and his views on public policy. Just as he personally objected to abortion on moral grounds but opposed outlawing it, so he was uncomfortable with homosexuality while opposing discrimination based on sexual orientation. Politically, he wanted to avoid pushing gay rights too publicly. Hoping to dodge further controversy, he designated Vice President Walter Mondale the administration's spokesperson on the issue. Mondale, however, was equally uncomfortable about gay rights. The result was a number of angry protests by gay rights activists at public events. A Mondale speech in San Francisco was disrupted, and pickets greeted President Carter at the Waldorf Astoria in New York City. The protests embarrassed Carter and obscured his historic initiative on gay rights.[61]

59 Memo Haft to Costanza, April 11, 1977, OPL Files, Box 4, JCPL.

60 "Carter Says Plans of Government Should Keep Families Together," *NYT*, June 19, 1977.

61 Carter quote in *Washington Post*, June 19, 1977; similar remarks by Rosaylnn Carter in San Francisco, June 22, 1977; Letter, Thomas J. Herndon to Marilyn Haft, June 23, 1977, OPL Files, Box 5, JCPL. Protests: *Gay Community News*, July 16, 1977, clipping in OPL Files, Box 5, JCPL. Mondale response to gay rights leader:

To a certain extent, Carter was hoisted on a human rights petard of his own making. His most notable contribution as president was to make human rights a consideration in foreign policy. Gay rights and women's rights activists took him at his word and demanded he pursue that commitment at home on their issues. Anthony Lewis of the *New York Times* addressed the matter directly in a 1978 column on the administration's not compensating victims of CIA spying: "While the President and others rightly talk about the importance of human rights policy abroad, the Justice Department reacts with insensitivity and pettifoggery on issues of civil liberty at home." Carter did not honor his own rhetoric and paid a price politically.[62]

Underlying Carter's dilemma in his relations with feminists, African-American leaders, and the gay community were his strong feelings about special interest politics. When he asked *Why Not the Best?* in 1976, he envisioned transcending traditional interest group politics, hoping to base public policies on a broad public interest. Such an approach to presidential leadership was probably not realistic in the best of circumstances, and particularly so in the Democratic Party with its many powerful constituent groups. Carter's inexperience in national politics only added to the problem. He had none of Lyndon Johnson's skill in satisfying particular interest groups while rhetorically defining issues as in the best interests of all Americans. He was never able to articulate a compelling vision of a new America and develop realistic policies to implement it. The inevitable results for Carter were conflict with his own constituencies, policy stalemate, and an image of ineptness.

THE NEW WORLD OF NATIONAL SECURITY POLITICS

Jimmy Carter took office as the first president to serve in the new world of post-Watergate law and politics on national security, with its emphasis on openness, legal controls, and congressional oversight. Ford had presided over the stormy birth of this new world, and if the reforms often failed to achieve their basic goals, it was nonetheless a radically different environment from the pre–Vietnam War, pre-Watergate era. The CIA could no longer act in total secrecy; nor could the FBI expect to engage in illegal actions without scrutiny as it had during the J. Edgar Hoover era. The 1973 War Powers Act, meanwhile, limited a president's ability to send troops into combat – at least on paper.

To Carter's credit, he generally accepted the new norms, although with some reservations. In January 1978, he issued Executive Order 12036, requiring intelligence gathering procedures that "preserve[s] and respect[s] established concepts of privacy and civil liberties." Among other restrictions, "The CIA may not engage in any electronic surveillance within the United States." It was a long and detailed order, and the strongest statement by a president on civil liberties to that time. Attorney General Griffin Bell later estimated that he spent 70 percent of his time wrestling with difficult questions about the legality of various intelligence matters. Bell went over to Langley, Virginia, in 1979 and spoke to CIA staff members. A speech to a government agency by an attorney general would not

Walter F. Mondale to E. Carrington Boggan, General Counsel, Lambda Legal Defense and Education Fund, July 11, 1977, OPL Files, Box 5, JCPL.

62 Correspondence: OPL Files, Box 5, JCPL. Evasive letter to critic: Walter F. Mondale to E. Carrington Boggan, General Counsel, Lambda Legal Defense and Education Fund, July 11, 1977, OPL Files, Box 5, JCPL. Anthony Lewis, "Human Rights at Home," *NYT*, February 27, 1978.

normally be remarkable, but this was the first time an attorney general had ever spoken in person to the CIA. Bell was serious about legal controls over both the CIA and the FBI, and that same year he ended a secret twenty-five-year-old agreement between the Justice Department and the CIA that allowed the agency not to report possible criminal conduct by its personnel. On August 15 he issued separate guidelines requiring the reporting of violations of federal statutes by both CIA employees and nonemployees (mainly contract employees).[63]

One of the most contentious issues involved whether to prosecute former CIA and FBI officials for earlier misdeeds. Both agencies, including current and retired agents, lobbied furiously against prosecution. Nonetheless, Bell prosecuted the former CIA director Richard Helms for lying to Congress about the agency's role in overthrowing the Allende government in Chile. In the end, a plea bargain allowed him to plead guilty to failing to inform Congress "fully and completely," a misdemeanor that avoided a felony prosecution and allowed him to keep his pension. Helms received a two-year suspended sentence and a two-thousand-dollar fine (which former CIA agents paid). Civil libertarians and some members of Congress objected to the plea deal, arguing that it was a license to lie. Unrepentant to the end, Helms said he would "wear this conviction like a badge of honor." Bell also prosecuted FBI agents for illegal break-ins. More than three hundred FBI agents picketed the Justice Department in protest, but President Carter backed up his attorney general, saying, "if a crime is committed ... they should be punished." (One of those convicted was W. Mark Felt, who years later was revealed to be the famous "Deep Throat" in the Watergate scandal.)[64]

National security wiretapping: Creating the FISA court

President Carter happily signed the bill into law, hailing it as the "first in a long step toward the goal of establishing statutory charters for our intelligence agencies."[65] The 1978 Foreign Intelligence Surveillance Act (FISA) marked a radical break from the past as the first statutory control over national security-related wiretapping. Reflecting the mood of the country, the bill passed the Senate 95–1. Every president beginning with Franklin D. Roosevelt had claimed the authority to wiretap in this area, including Lyndon Johnson, the one president who strongly opposed wiretapping. The FISA law, the War Powers Act, and the new congressional intelligence committees were the monuments of the post-Watergate era efforts to subject national security activities to the rule of law.

63 Executive Order 12036, January 24, 1978, APP. Bell, *Taking Care of the Law*, p. 103, 138. Bell speech: cited in Loch K. Johnson, *America's Secret Power: The CIA in a Democratic Society* (New York: Oxford University Press, 1989), p. 253. New policies: CIA, Office of Inspector General, *Allegations of Connections between CIA and the Contras in Cocaine Trafficking to the United States*. V. II, *The Contra Story* (Washington, DC: Central Intelligence Agency, 1998), available at www.cia.org.

64 Richard Helms, *A Look over My Shoulder: A Life in the Central Intelligence Agency* (New York: Random House, 2003), pp. 441–6. License to lie: Shattuck, "You Can't Depend on It," p. 14. "Senator Fears Helms Accord Could Set a Precedent," *NYT*, November 15, 1977. "Carter Defends Continuing Investigation and Possible Prosecution of F.B.I. Agents," ibid., May 13, 1977.

65 Statement by the President, October 25, 1978, APP. Office of the Counsel Files, Box 14, JCPL. Foreign Intelligence Surveillance Act of 1978: Statement on Signing S. 1566 into Law, October 25, 1978, APP. Post-Watergate reforms and their fate, including FISA: Frederick A. O. Schwarz, Jr., and Aziz Z. Huq, *Unchecked and Unbalanced: Presidential Power in a Time of Terror* (New York: New Press, 2007).

Congressional debate over a law began in 1975 after the *New York Times* exposé of CIA spying. The national security establishment argued that wiretaps were necessary and that the president had the inherent authority to order them. The ACLU and other civil libertarians demanded strict controls over all intelligence gathering, not just wiretapping. The ACLU argued for a criminal conduct standard for issuing surveillance warrants that would not permit a wiretap based only on suspicious activity by alleged foreign agents. In Senate hearings, the ACLU's John Shattuck went to the heart of the matter, asking rhetorically, "Should Congress create a national security exception to the criminal standard for wiretapping?" He cited the abuses exposed by the Church and Pike Committees, the Church Committee's recommendation against an exception, and Vice President Walter Mondale's congressional testimony making the same point. Attorney General Griffin Bell also recommended a warrant for any wiretapping. Carter disagreed, however, and supported Defense Secretary Harold Brown's recommendation for statutory authority for the president to approve warrantless wiretapping whenever he felt national security required it.[66]

The eventual FISA law was a compromise that for the first time granted the federal government explicit wiretap authority in national security cases but subjected it to procedural controls. It created a secret FISA court with the authority to authorize wiretaps regarding foreign intelligence gathering. Civil libertarians objected not just to the national security exception, but also to the secrecy of the FISA court and the emergency exception allowing the attorney general to authorize a temporary (seventy-two-hour) wiretap without FISA court approval. Although a historic step toward controlling national security intelligence gathering, FISA proved to be as flawed as its critics feared. The FISA court was exceedingly compliant and granted virtually all government requests for warrants. Between 1978 and 2004, it rejected a grand total of 5 requests while granting 18,761. And perhaps four of those rejected were later granted after being modified to satisfy the court. What is unknown, of course, is the extent to which the mere existence of the FISA process deterred the government from seeking many dubious requests or forced it to do more investigation to provide a justifiable request.[67]

FISA exploded into a major controversy under President George W. Bush when it was revealed that he authorized secret wiretaps evading the law altogether. That controversy was a sobering commentary on the limits of not just FISA but all of the post-Watergate national security reforms. It proved that a determined and ideologically driven president could ignore formal legal controls in the name of a national emergency - and at least for a time succeed.

On executive privilege, Carter followed President Ford's example by vigilantly avoiding any public discussion of the discredited doctrine. The administration discussed the issue internally but ignored a 1977 congressional request for a statement of its policy and never issued one. Carter never repudiated the basic concept of executive privilege, and White House officials declined to testify on a few occasions, but none of these incidents escalated into a confrontation. In December 1977 Congress enacted a law on presidential

66 Shattuck Testimony, U.S. Senate, Select Committee on Intelligence, Subcommittee on Intelligence and the Rights of Americans, 95th Cong., 2nd Sess., Hearings, pp. 110–16. Administration position: Memo, Annie [Gutierrez] to Stu [Eizenstat], April 21, 1977, DPS Files, Box 228, JCPL. Shattuck, "You Can't Depend on It," pp. 14–15.

67 Donald J. Musch, *Civil Liberties and the Foreign Intelligence Surveillance Act* (Dobbs Ferry, NY: Oceana, 2003). Congressional Research Service, *The Foreign Intelligence Surveillance Act: A Brief Overview of Selected Issues*, Updated (Washington, DC: CRS, February 8, 2008).

powers in national emergencies, which had been a cooperative effort with the White House and most of which Carter accepted. In a signing statement, however, he expressed reservations about section 207(b) allowing Congress to terminate a national emergency declared by the president|. It raised "profound constitutional questions," and he said he would treat it as requiring only that he "notify [Congress] and wait" in any such situation. That even Jimmy Carter would cling to unfettered presidential power in this regard, even in the face of formal congressional objection, indicates how deep was the commitment to retaining that power among everyone who ever sat in the White House.[68]

A missed opportunity on the FBI?

With respect to the FBI, President Carter lost a potentially historic opportunity to give it fresh leadership committed to civil liberties. In August 1979 he named the U.S. District Court judge Frank Johnson FBI director. By then, Johnson was almost a civil rights and civil liberties legend. One of President Eisenhower's judicial appointees in the South who had been responsible for implementing *Brown v. Board of Education,* he had an outstanding record on a variety of civil liberties issues. He had ordered the desegregation of the Montgomery, Alabama, city buses, which were the subject of the famous boycott launched by Rosa Parks, in 1956; threatened to jail George Wallace two years later for contempt for refusing to give voting records to the U.S. Civil Rights Commission; issued an injunction in 1965 allowing the famous Selma to Montgomery march to proceed; and ordered Alabama to end discrimination against African Americans on juries.[69]

The day after Carter announced his choice, however, Johnson learned he had an aneurism requiring immediate surgery and withdrew. John Lewis, a hero of the civil rights movement, who had appeared before Judge Johnson as a Freedom Rider in 1961, said that he "would have set a new standard for integrity and justice in public service" had he become FBI director. We can only speculate, but Johnson's record suggests that Lewis was right and Johnson might have truly transformed the FBI. Carter's eventual pick, William H. Webster, did a creditable job on hiring women and African Americans as agents, as well as working to establish respect for the law in the bureau. When Congress failed to enact a charter for the bureau, Webster, who supported it, said, "Okay, but I'm going to pretend that we have a charter" and directed the FBI accordingly.[70]

The lingering shadow of Watergate: The independent counsel law

In May 1977 President Carter sent to Congress an ethics in government bill and asked that it incorporate pending bills regarding an independent counsel to investigate allegations of misconduct by the president, vice president, cabinet members, or White House

68 Memo, Lipshutz, For the White House Staff, February 8, 1979, Re Hearings, Committee on Interstate Commerce, House of Representatives, Office of Counsel Files, Box 15, JCPL. "White House Bars Woman Aide's Senate Appearance," *NYT*, February 1, 1979. Rozell, *Executive Privilege*, pp. 84–93. Carter: Presidential War Powers Bill Statement on Signing H.R. 7738 into Law, December 28, 1977, APP.

69 Statement on the Nomination of Frank M. Johnson, Jr., to be director of the Federal Bureau of Investigation, August 17, 1977, APP.

70 John Lewis, "Reflections on Judge Frank M. Johnson, Jr.," *Yale Law Journal* 109 (April 2000): 1253–6. Webster, OH, pp. 20–1, MCPA.

staff members. The bill was yet another aftermath of the Watergate scandal, specifically Nixon's firing of Special Prosecutor Archibald Cox in the notorious 1973 Saturday Night Massacre, which was still a vivid memory. The successful pursuit of the White House tapes by Cox's successor Leon Jaworski and Nixon's quick resignation when he obtained them, moreover, only seemed to confirm the need for a truly independent prosecutor. President Carter agreed.[71]

Independent counsel bills had been introduced even before Nixon resigned, and debate continued for five years. A major stumbling block involved constitutional questions of separation of powers. Who would appoint an independent prosecutor, the courts or the attorney general? How would a prosecutor's independence be ensured while maintaining some political accountability? Senator Sam Ervin, still basking in his celebrity status as a hero of Watergate, went the furthest and proposed making the Justice Department independent of the White House, with the attorney general appointed to a six-year term. His radical idea went nowhere, however. Congress finally passed the Ethics in Government Act in 1978. Under Title VI, the attorney general would conduct an initial investigation of alleged misconduct, and if the allegations had merit would report that to a three-judge panel of the Court of Appeals for the District of Columbia, which in turn would appoint a independent counsel. As a measure of accountability, the attorney general could fire the prosecutor, but only for "extraordinary impropriety" or other special circumstances.[72]

The law proved to be a sorcerer's apprentice. In the first twenty-two years, there were twenty investigations. Some were small and insignificant (investigating allegations of financial improprieties against one James Cicconi, for example, cost fifteen thousand dollars), but others were long and very costly. The investigation of Samuel Pierce, Reagan's HUD secretary, lasted eight years and cost $29 million. The most famous and controversial of all, of course, was Independent Counsel Kenneth W. Starr's investigation of President Bill Clinton, which eventually cost nearly $60 million and led to his impeachment. Starr's investigation strayed far from its original mandate regarding the Whitewater real estate deal in Arkansas and plunged into Clinton's sexual relations with Monica Lewinsky. Many regarded the entire investigation as a conservative political vendetta. The Starr investigation, however, only exposed the central dilemma at the heart of the independent counsel law: the potential lack of accountability for any prosecutor who was truly independent of political authority.[73]

Both President Ford's attorney general, Edward H. Levi, and Carter's attorney general, Griffin Bell, opposed the independent counsel law. Levi prophetically warned that an unaccountable prosecutor "would create opportunities for actual or apparent partisan influence," with the power to "publicize and dignify unfounded, scurrilous allegations." Bell said, "There's no oversight at all ... it's a bad law," and "The American people will come to regret this." The warnings of the two attorneys general, who more than any others fought to maintain the political independence of their own office, were prophetic indeed, and Congress let the law quietly expire in 1999.[74]

71 Carter, Ethics in Government Message to the Congress, May 3, 1977, APP. Charles A. Johnson and Danette Brickman, *Independent Counsel: The Law and the Investigations* (Washington, DC: CQ Press, 2001), 101–2.

72 Johnson and Brickman, *Independent Counsel*, pp. 80–8.

73 The Supreme Court upheld the constitutionality of the law, 7 to 1, in *Morrison v. Olson*, 487 U.S. 654 (1988).

74 Hearings, House Subcommittee on Criminal Justice, 94th Congress, 2nd Sess, July 23, 1978. Johnson and Brickman, *Independent Counsel*, p. 95. Bell, OH, p. 23, MCPA. The law has been replaced by the Office of the Special Counsel in the Department of Justice.

THE HOSTAGE CRISIS: BACKTRACKING ON NATIONAL SECURITY

The international situation worsened dramatically in late 1979, and the resulting Iranian hostage crisis dominated the last 444 days of Carter's presidency and led him to backtrack somewhat on national security. An Islamic revolution in Iran in early 1979 overthrew the shah and put militant Islamic ideology at the fore in international relations. On November 4 militants seized the American embassy in Tehran and took fifty-two American hostages. President Carter's media aide Gerald Rafshoon recalled, "After November 4, 1979, we never had a meeting with the President when he didn't have that on his mind."[75]

Prior to the hostage crisis, Carter had been notably restrained in using American power around the world. The writer Peter Beinart labels him the "post-toughness" president, who embodied the consensus of opinion after the Vietnam tragedy that the United States should be very cautious about military commitments around the world. That consensus began to collapse with the hostage crisis. In a sharp deviation from his previous restraint, Carter authorized Operation Eagle Claw, a military effort to free the hostages on April 24, 1980. He did not notify Congress in advance (although he talked with Speaker of the House Tip O'Neill the night before about possible action), and the raid ended in an embarrassing disaster.[76]

Even before the hostage crisis, however, Carter had changed his position on CIA covert operations. Shaped by the post-Watergate revelations, he arrived at the White House with what one historian called a "visceral dislike" of the agency, even calling it a "national disgrace." Yet, within months he authorized it to undertake covert action against the Soviet Union, which consisted largely of propaganda efforts over human rights issues. As part of his international human rights initiative, his major and lasting contribution to American foreign policy, he felt he had a right and an obligation to make the Soviet Union honor its international treaty agreements. This was a radical departure from past practices. Richard Nixon, despite his strong anti-communist past, did not think the United States should meddle directly in internal Soviet affairs. When the international tensions worsened in 1979, moreover, Carter authorized covert aid to rebels in Afghanistan and to the government of El Salvador, which was facing an armed left-wing opposition. The Afghanistan aid started as a small operation but was expanded by Presidents Reagan and George H. W. Bush. As many analysts have pointed out, some recipients of that aid later became Islamic militants and terrorists, threats to the United States.[77]

Carter's abrupt reversal on CIA covert operations has a larger lesson, one with relevance for other presidents. In situations when presidents find that diplomacy fails and formal military operations are not a feasible option, covert operations loom as a seemingly low-cost and – ideally – low-visibility option for achieving American goals. This

[75] Rafshoon, OH, p. 46, MCPA.

[76] Peter Beinart, *The Icarus Syndrome: A History of American Hubris* (New York: Harper Collins, 2010), p. 215, and the accompanying discussion of the "post-toughness" period (pp. 204–17). Hostage raid: Louis Fisher, *Presidential War Power* (Lawrence: University of Kansas, 1995), pp. 139–40. When asked decades later what one thing he would do differently as president, Carter adamantly said it would be to "send one more helicopter" in Operation Eagle Claw. He had no regrets about the dubious operation itself. Dawidoff, "The Riddle of Jimmy Carter," 56.

[77] William J. Daugherty, *Executive Secrets: Covert Action and the Presidency* (Lexington: University Press of Kentucky, 2004), pp. 183–92.

was the original lure of covert actions under Presidents Eisenhower and Truman, and it continues to be to this day.

Carter also shifted his attitude toward the application of the Freedom of Information Act to the CIA and the NSA in response to CIA concerns about disclosing the identity of people working for it and NSA concerns about the disclosure of technical information regarding its intelligence gathering techniques. His Executive Order 12036, issued on January 24, 1978 (well before the Iran hostage crisis), embodied a wide range of restrictions on intelligence gathering and maintained the ban on CIA assassinations), but it contained a loophole for warrantless searches if authorized by the president. President Carter signaled a dramatic shift in his attitude in his 1980 State of the Union Address. With fifty-two Americans still being held hostage in Tehran and presidential elections in November, the speech had a belligerent, almost warlike tone, emphasizing national defense. In particular, he called for strengthened intelligence gathering capabilities. While reiterating the goal of creating "a new charter to define the legal authority and accountability of our intelligence agencies," to "guarantee that abuses do not recur," he also emphasized the need to remove unwarranted restraints on America's ability to collect intelligence."[78]

Carter's actions were the first steps toward loosening the controls over the intelligence agencies. The post-Watergate era of accountability for the intelligence agencies was dying. Carter's successor, Ronald Reagan, adopted an aggressive national security program, including greater freedom for the CIA from external oversight and a mandate for more action overseas, even to the point of authorizing illegal actions. The plain fact, however, is that President Carter took the first hesitant steps in that direction, in response to the same concerns about threats to American national security.[79]

AN UNHAPPY END

Jimmy Carter's presidency grew steadily more unhappy in its last year and a half. In summer 1979 he gave a major televised address on the energy crisis that had gripped the nation. Abruptly cancelling a scheduled speech, he went to Camp David and conducted an extraordinary ten-day summit meeting with invited experts, exploring what he believed was a deeper crisis of confidence in American society. The result was his famous "Crisis of the American Spirit" speech the night of July 15. Carter outlined a set of energy policy initiatives that included importing no more oil than in 1977 and investing in alternative energy sources. The recommendations were far ahead of their time and could have saved the country much energy and economic trouble in the decades ahead had the country followed them. The journalist Nicholas Dawidoff, moreover, observes that the speech was "a presidential classic because Carter had done that rare thing: He had spoken to Americans like adults."[80]

78 Executive Order 12036, United States Foreign Intelligence Activities, January 24, 1978, APP. The State of the Union Address Delivered Before a Joint Session of the Congress, January 23, 1980, APP. John M. Oseth, *Regulating U.S. Intelligence Operations: A Study in Definition of the National Interest* (Lexington: University Press of Kentucky, 1985), p. 139.

79 Oseth, *Regulating U.S. Intelligence Operations,* Ch. 6, "The Carter Endgame, the Reagan Administration," 133–62.

80 Energy and National Goals Address to the Nation, July 15, 1979, APP. Dawidoff, "The Riddle of Jimmy Carter," 55. Robert A. Strong, "Recapturing Leadership: The Carter Administration and the Crisis of Confidence,"

The policy recommendations, however, were overshadowed by Carter's ruminations on the mood of Americans and the country's future. The nation's problems, he said, are much "deeper than gasoline lines or energy shortages, deeper even than inflation or recession." They involved "a fundamental threat to American democracy ... a crisis of confidence ... that strikes at the very heart and soul and spirit of our national will." This was an exceptionally downbeat message from a sitting president. (Although it is often referred to as the "malaise" speech, Carter never used the word in it.) Nonetheless, the speech was initially well received, according to press accounts. Carter then completely undermined the effort four days later by asking his entire cabinet to resign. He accepted five resignations, including those of Attorney General Bell and Secretary Califano of HEW. The abrupt housecleaning caught everyone by surprise, seemed to have no logic, and created an image of disorganization and ineptitude. A Democratic congressman said simply, "Everyone around here is very, very disgusted." The firings obscured his energy speech and pinned the label of futility on his administration that prevails to this day.[81]

Rejected by his own fundamentalists

In his last year Carter faced another political problem when evangelical Christians abandoned him. Sensing a problem (and the situation was far worse than he realized), Carter hired Robert Maddox as special assistant for religious liaison in May 1979. Maddox held a doctorate in theology from Emory University and had served as minister at several Baptist churches. To mend fences with the evangelical community, Carter in January 1980 held a White House breakfast with Jerry Falwell, Oral Roberts, Jim Bakker, and eleven other prominent figures in that community. Falwell was the leader of the Moral Majority and rapidly emerging as the most prominent spokesperson for the newly energized Religious Right. Carter emphasized that he was a "born again" Christian. By one account, they had a "cordial and frank discussion" but ended disagreeing on several key social issues. The meeting accomplished nothing. Six weeks later, Falwell told a false and malicious story about the breakfast. He claimed he asked Carter why he employed homosexuals in the administration. When Carter replied, "I am president of all the American people," Falwell said he fired back, "Why don't you have some murderers, and bank robbers...?" The White House had a tape of the speech, however, and Falwell was forced to concede that he had fabricated his account. That Falwell would tell such a lie about the president of the United States only indicated the depth of the breach between them.[82]

Presidential Studies Quarterly 16, no. 4 (1986): 636–50. Documents and commentary: Daniel Horowitz, *Jimmy Carter and the Energy Crisis of the 1970s: The "Crisis of Confidence" Speech of July 15, 1979: A Brief History with Documents* (Boston: Bedford/St. Martin's, 2005). Carter, *Keeping Faith*, pp. 114–21. Carter argues that the speech was initially received very well, and was given a bad reputation by the news media. Carter, OH, pp. 62–3, MCPA. Kevin Mattson, *"What the Heck Are You Up to, Mr. President?": Jimmy Carter, America's "Malaise" and the Speech That Should Have Changed the Country* (New York: Bloomsbury, 2009).

81 "Carter Replaces, Bell, Blumenthal, Califano," *NYT*, July 20, 1979. Strong, "Recapturing Leadership: The Carter Administration and the Crisis of Confidence."

82 Maddox's work: OPL Files, Maddox Files, JCPL. "Carter Sways Some Evangelicals in 2-Day Blitz to Regain Support," *NYT*, January 28, 1980. "Carter Tells Evangelists That He Is 'Born Again,'" ibid., January 22, 1980. Letter, Anne Wexler to Mr. Lester, [circa 1980], OPL Files, Robert Maddox Files, Box 107, JCPL. Falwell incident: Letter, Robert Maddox to Mr. W. B. Sanders, Smyrna, GA, October 17, 1980, OPL Files, Maddox Files, Box 107, JCPL.

Carter also met with the new president of the Southern Baptist Convention in early 1979. Meeting with the head of the largest organized group of white southern Baptists had been a regular event for him, but the political winds had changed dramatically, and this year the new Baptist leader told him, "We are praying, Mr. President, that you will abandon secular humanism as your religion." Carter was completely taken aback at this indictment by a coreligionist. When he discussed this "troubling comment" later with his own pastor, the two listed Carter's policies that had led to his rejection: women in positions of leadership, opposing federal funds for religious education, creating an independent Department of Education, opposing a constitutional amendment overturning *Roe v. Wade*, working with Mormons on certain foreign policy issues, normalizing relations with Communist China, calling for a Palestinian homeland, and negotiating with the Soviet Union on arms control.[83] Some of these issues, such as those related to China relations and arms control, had nothing to do with religion, but they indicated the extent to which the secular political Right had captured the evangelical movement. Carter was the first president to feel the full force of the neoconservative movement, which would dominate American politics for the next quarter-century.

Wrapped in his own self-righteousness, Carter never fully understood the basis for his rejection by his fellow evangelicals. Nor did he understand the criticisms from liberal Democrats. He always believed that personal integrity and religious faith were sufficient to govern and win public support. He did not understand that criticisms from friends and foes alike were based on his policies. This blind spot continued. His memoir, *Keeping Faith*, has no references to women, abortion, affirmative action (including the divisive *Bakke* case), his controversial comment on "ethnic purity" in the 1976 campaign, or his conflicts with Midge Costanza. It is not clear whether he truly did not understand the significance of these events or simply found it too difficult to examine them. To his great credit, however, he held to his own values, maintaining his support for separation of church and state and his difficult middle-of-the-road position on abortion. Finally, in a remarkable development he broke with the Southern Baptist Convention on October 19, 2000, denouncing their abandonment of historic principles and declaring himself "a traditional Baptist.[84]

A FAILED PRESIDENT, WITH A DECENT RECORD

On November 4, 1980, Jimmy Carter became the second straight incumbent president to fail to win reelection, losing to the Republican Ronald Reagan. Counting Kennedy's assassination, Johnson's withdrawal in 1968, Nixon's resignation, and Ford's defeat in 1976, no American president had served two full terms in the White House since Dwight Eisenhower, twenty years earlier. Reagan's election, moreover, marked the dawn of a new political era, driven by neoconservatism. As part of the Great Realignment, the Republican Party embraced the "social agenda" that included anti–civil libertarian policies on abortion, separation of church and state, civil rights enforcement, women's rights, national security, and other issues.

[83] Carter, *Our Endangered Values*, pp. 32–3.

[84] Carter, *Keeping Faith*. The biography by his close friend and administration staff member Peter Bourne, is almost equally silent on these issues. Bourne, *Jimmy Carter*. "Carter Sadly Turns Back on National Baptist Body," *NYT*, October 21, 2000. Carter, *Our Endangered Values*. "Jimmy Carter Slams Bush Administration," Associated Press, May 19, 2007.

Despite his reputation as a failed president, Jimmy Carter's civil liberties record was arguably the best of any modern president. To be sure, he achieved no major advances equal to Lyndon Johnson's, but he also committed no major violations of civil liberties, as did both Truman and Johnson. He made significant contributions on women's rights and gay rights and supported the post-Watergate reforms of the intelligence agencies. Given this record, together with such non-civil liberties achievements as his energy recommendations and the Camp David accords the middle east that lasted for over thirty years, the judgment by a panel of scholars that he is the tenth worst president in American history is surely unfair and unjustified.[85] Despite his generally good record on national security, on occasion he resorted to covert actions without notifying Congress, and his approach to national security issues worsened as a result of the Iranian hostage crisis. Although personally opposed to abortion, he defended *Roe v. Wade*, talking honestly to both sides of the controversy, and staunchly defended the separation of church and state in the face of fierce and politically costly pressure from the Religious Right. These were all significant achievements, but they have been completely overshadowed by his failure to provide a compelling vision of a new America and his political ineptitude.

Civil libertarians, however, were generally disappointed by Carter's performance. Part of the problem was his habit of making ill-advised statements that angered rights leaders and projecting an image of insensitivity to their issues. At the end of Carter's first year, the ACLU Washington office director John Shattuck saw no "significant advances for civil liberties" and "a lack of conviction about civil liberties." The judgment was unfair. Shattuck properly noted that the real problem was the "backward-looking mood of Congress," which was already in the grip of a conservative, anti–civil liberties tide.[86] Carter was criticized by civil libertarians and civil rights leaders for not endorsing quotas in the *Bakke* case. But no other Democratic Party president did (including Bill Clinton, who talked about fixing affirmative action but offered no specific remedies), and a Democratic-controlled Congress on three occasions voted to prohibit busing of students for purposes of school integration. Carter, in short, was not out of the Democratic Party mainstream on these issues and was in some respects better than most leaders.

Carter's most dubious legacy was introducing personal religious commitment into presidential politics. In so doing, he facilitated the surge of the Religious Right in American politics, which Republicans captured and used to their advantage. His departure from the White House and the inauguration of Ronald Reagan in January 1981 marked the dawn of a new aggressively anti–civil libertarian era in American politics. He and Gerald Ford presided over a historic transition period, and both experienced unhappy presidencies as a result. Carter's reputation as a failed president has been offset by his subsequent career. As an author, commentator on national affairs, negotiator on international issues, and social service activist, he has developed a record of selfless activism as a former president, which is rivaled only by that of John Quincy Adams. Carter saw the difference himself, admitting in 2005, "I can't deny I'm a better ex-president than I was a president."[87]

85 Lindgren and Calabresi, "Rating the Presidents."

86 Shattuck, "You Can't Depend on It," p. 26.

87 Douglas Brinkley, *The Unfinished Presidency: Jimmy Carter's Journey beyond the White House* (New York: Viking, 1998). "Carter Condemns Abortion Culture," *Washington Times*, November 4, 2005.

President Ronald Reagan, facing questions about the developing Iran-Contra scandal, abruptly leaves a press conference, turning it over to Attorney General Edwin Meese, November 25, 1986.
Source: Associated Press.

12 Ronald Reagan – and George H. W. Bush

The Neoconservative Assault on Civil Liberties

"I WEAR THEIR INDICTMENT LIKE A BADGE OF HONOR"

"I wear their indictment like a badge of honor." Speaking to a Catholic group in January 1984, President Ronald Reagan singled out the American Civil Liberties Union for attack, and the fiercely antiabortion delegates in the room cheered. The ACLU was a convenient symbol for his stance on the social issues – which is to say, civil liberties issues – that animated the neoconservative movement and propelled Reagan into the White House: abortion, prayer in school, pornography, and gay rights. Reagan's successor in the White House, George H. W. Bush, went one step further, denouncing his opponent Michael Dukakis in the 1988 presidential election as a "card-carrying member" of the ACLU.[1]

THE ADVENT OF REAGAN AND THE NEW RIGHT

The first months of the Reagan administration in early 1981 filled civil libertarians and civil rights leaders with palpable alarm. Republicans controlled the Senate for the first time since 1953–5, and many prominent liberals – Frank Church and George McGovern among them – had been swept out of office. The very conservative Orrin Hatch replaced the liberal Ted Kennedy as chair of the Judiciary Committee and immediately launched hearings on outlawing abortion. The head of the Coalition of Labor Union Women called the 1980 elections a "total disaster" for women. Twenty-five separate bills were introduced in Congress to strip federal courts of jurisdiction over school busing, school prayer, abortion, and sex discrimination. In May, the White House counsel, Edwin Meese, speaking to California police officers, attacked the ACLU as "a criminals' lobby," portending an assault on Supreme Court protections for criminal suspects.[2]

Just two weeks after the election, Reagan's incoming chief of staff, James A. Baker, spent two and a half hours with Dick Cheney, who had held the position under President Gerald Ford, for advice about the job. Baker's handwritten notes indicate that Cheney advised him to "restore power & auth to Exec Branch Need strong ldr'ship. Get rid of War Powers Act.... Central theme we ought to push." Cheney had given Ford the very same recommendations in December 1974 and later would aggressively pursue them as George W. Bush's vice president. The Reagan administration immediately began

1 "Reagan Appeal on Abortion Is Made to Fundamentalists," *NYT*, January 31, 1984. "Bush Turns Heat on 'Liberal Rival,'" ibid., August 27, 1988.

2 "Feminists Dismayed by the Election and Unsure of What Future Holds," *NYT*, November 7, 1980. Zillah Eisenstein, "Antifeminism in the Politics and Election of 1980," *Feminist Studies* 7 (Summer 1981): 187–205. "Charges by 2 Associates of Reagan Challenged by Civil Liberties Union," *NYT*, May 18, 1981.

loosening the new restrictions on the CIA and presidential power. Reagan's CIA director, William J. Casey, immediately asked Congress for authority to conduct surprise (i.e., warrantless) raids on the news media but backed off in the face of public outrage.[3]

The future of the Supreme Court, and *Roe v. Wade* in particular, loomed as an urgent issue. Candidate Reagan had pledged to transformthe Court and roll back many advances in civil liberties. In February 1980 he hyperbolically accused the Court of "an abuse of power as bad as the transgressions of Watergate. The 1980 GOP platform called for judges "who respect traditional family values and the sanctity of innocent human life."[4] The conservative revolution on the Court that President Richard Nixon had promised in 1968 now seemed at hand. Reagan filled the White House with New Right hard-liners. Gary Bauer, the main link to the Christian evangelical community, served in the Department of Education before taking over the Office of Policy Development in 1987. William Bennett headed the National Endowment for the Humanities and then became secretary of education. The White House aide John Roberts, the future chief justice, was a very conservative voice on policy issues. The hard-liners in the administration fulminated against both liberal policies and established law. Bauer argued that a ten-point proposal on the human immunodeficiency virus (HIV) epidemic would allow "activist courts" to create a "civil rights crusade based on sexual preferences." The White House aide Morton Blackwell warned that extending the 1965 Voting Rights Act would create a "national quota system." Another aide charged that a bill to strengthen Title IX enforcement would "widen bureaucratic meddling" in higher education. An unsigned memo claimed that the idea of comparable worth (to rectify unequal pay for women) would lead to the government's setting "salaries for all jobs in the country." Before joining the Court, John Roberts argued that Congress could constitutionally strip the federal courts of jurisdiction over school busing.[5]

There were no moderate liberals in the Reagan White House, equivalent to Robert Finch and Leonard Garment in the Nixon administration. The New Right zealots were offset by several moderate conservative pragmatists, notably Reagan's chief of staff, James A. Baker; Deputy Chief of Staff Michael Deaver; and the treasury secretary, Donald Regan, who had considerable personal influence with Reagan and were most interested in traditional Republican tax and government spending issues.

Caught off guard by the conservative tide, liberals and civil libertarians scrambled to respond. The Leadership Conference on Civil Rights convened its 150 constituent groups in early March 1981, warning of "radical changes" ahead. The NAACP director, Benjamin Hooks, claimed, "They want to roll us back." And in an observation far more prescient than he ever imagined, the ACLU's John Shattuck predicted that "terrorism" could become

[3] Charlie Savage, *Takeover: The Return of the Imperial Presidency and the Subversion of American Democracy* (Boston: Little, Brown, 2007), p. 43. "Cheney's advice to Baker," Barton Gellman, *Angler: The Cheney Vice Presidency* (New York: Penguin Press, 2008), pp. 86, 101; Stephen F. Hayes, *Cheney: The Untold Story of America's Most Powerful and Controversial Vice President* (New York: HarperCollins, 2007), pp. 161–3. "Intelligence Groups Seek Power to Gain Data on U.S. Citizens," *NYT*, March 10, 1981; "C.I.A. Seeks Law for Surprise Searches of Newsrooms," ibid., May 9, 1981.

[4] "Reagan Assails Court," *NYT*, February 22, 1980. Republican Party platform of 1980,July 15, 1980, APP.

[5] Bauer to Rhett Dawson, August 2, 1988, Bauer Files, Box 2, RRPL. Blackwell to Ken Crib, June 29, 1982, Meese Files, Box 31, RRPL. J. Douglas Holladay to Faith Ryan Whittlesey, April 20, 1984, Meese Files, Box 44, RRPL. Comparable worth: Untitled Memo, October 19, 1984, Meese Files, Box 44, RRPL. Roberts to Fred Fielding, Proposed Justice Report on S. 139, February 15, 1984, Roberts Files, Box 10, RRPL.

"a new talisman" for assaults on civil liberties. Even the conservative columnist William Safire chided the Reagan administration for considering the Freedom of Information Act an "annoyance" and called the law "a blessing for those who value a check on Government snooping."[6] The wealthy television producer Norman Lear, creator of the popular *All in the Family* show, organized a new advocacy group, People for the American Way (PAW), enlisting the African-American congresswoman Barbara Jordan and the former Notre Dame University president Theodore Hesburgh in the effort. A PAW television ad featured a man in a hard had voicing his alarm that some religious leaders were dividing Americans into "good Christians" and "bad Christians." "That's not the American way," he declared. PAW immediately signed up almost 250,000 members, while the ACLU enjoyed a membership surge because of fears about the Reagan administration.[7]

Reagan's anti-communist past also worried civil libertarians. As president of the Screen Actors Guild in the 1940s and 1950s he helped blacklist real and alleged communists. He testified to the House Un-American Activities Committee in 1947 about communist influence in Hollywood and was long rumored to have been an undercover FBI informant (rumors that were later confirmed). In 1966, the FBI director, J. Edgar Hoover, broke with his long practice of nonpartisanship and publicly endorsed Reagan for governor. In short, Reagan loomed as a fierce anti-communist politician with no regard for freedom of speech and association.[8]

THE POWERFUL NEW RELIGIOUS RIGHT

A *New York Times* headline in mid-1980 noted, "Ultraconservative Evangelicals a Surging New Force in Politics." The political power of the Religious Right was a new feature of American life in that presidential election year. The movement was born in Lynchburg, Virginia, in summer 1979 when the Reverend Jerry Falwell, encouraged by other evangelical leaders, organized the Moral Majority, which became the most prominent voice of the Religious Right. Falwell made innumerable offensive statements ("God does not hear the prayers of Jews"; "AIDS is the wrath of a just God"), but they did not diminish his influence among conservative Christians. Civil libertarians thought Christian fundamentalism had been defeated politically during the 1925 Scopes trial. Fundamentalists withdrew from political life but in retreat created a counterculture of churches, colleges, and media. These institutions provided an organizational base for an aggressive return to politics in the late 1970s, and Reagan was the first presidential candidate to benefit. In the 1980 election, he won an estimated 62 percent of the Christian evangelical vote, even though he was not a regular churchgoer and Jimmy Carter was a genuinely "born again" Christian.[9]

6 "Liberal Groups Are Joining Forces to Defend Their Goals and Gains," *NYT*, March 9, 1981. William Safire, "Reagan's Wrong Moves," ibid., May 25, 1981.

7 "Lear Assails Religious New Right, as a Threat to 'Spirit of Liberty,'" *NYT*, March 27, 1981.

8 Marc Eliot, *Reagan: The Hollywood Years* (New York: Harmony Books, 2008), pp. 190 (FBI), 216–17 (blacklisting), 296–300 (Screen Actors Guild). Hoover: "The Governor's Race," *San Francisco Chronicle*, June 9, 2002. The *Chronicle* published letters documenting Reagan's cooperation with the FBI in the 1960s regarding protests at the University of California.

9 "Ultraconservative Evangelicals a Surging New Force in Politics," *NYT*, August 17, 1980. "Evangelist Reverses Position on God's Hearing Jews," *Washington Post*, October 11, 1980. Withdrawal and return of fundamentalists: Karen Armstrong, *The Battle for God* (New York: Knopf, 2000). "Baptist Meeting Backs School Prayer

A growing "electronic church" was a crucial part of the fundamentalist political muscle. By 1980 there were four all-religion television cable networks and an estimated thirty-five hundred local cable systems and fourteen hundred radio stations broadcasting fundamentalist religious programs. Together, they took in an estimated $500 million in contributions a year. The two biggest figures were Falwell, host of the *Old Time Gospel Hour*, and Pat Robertson, organizer of the Christian Broadcasting Network and host of his own *700 Club* program. They completely eclipsed the older generation of fundamentalists leaders: Oral Roberts, Robert Schuller, and the most famous religious leader in the country, Billy Graham, who had advised presidents but had never been as aggressively conservative as the new breed.[10]

Paralleling the Religious Right was a network of secular neoconservative activist groups that had mastered the techniques of direct mail fund-raising. Richard Viguerie's operation mailed out more than 100 million pieces every year, serving conservative groups such as Citizens for Decent Literature and Gun Owners of America. Typical was a "profamily" letter asking frightening questions such as "Do you believe that children should have the right to sue their parents for being 'forced' to attend church?"[11] An important Viguerie client was Terry Dolan, organizer of the National Conservative Political Action Committee ("Nick-pac"). The third major figure, Paul Weyrich, created the Committee for the Survival of a Free Congress and in 1973 with the beer magnate Joseph Coors helped to found the Heritage Society, one of the first of several conservative think tanks that had a major influence on social policy over the next thirty years.

UNDERSTANDING REAGAN AND REAGANISM

In later years, Ronald Reagan was lionized by conservatives as the icon of modern conservatism, enjoying a status among Republicans paralleled by Franklin D. Roosevelt's among Democrats. The popular reputations of both presidents, however, were enveloped in fogs of mythology. Reagan, as we shall see, paid only lip service to the social issues of abortion and school prayer, and his biographer Lou Cannon dismissed his commitment on these issues as little more than a set of "throwaway lines." (Administration policy did change, however, when Edwin Meese became attorney general in 1985.) The enormous deficits created by his tax cuts, meanwhile, contradicted traditional conservative economic policies.[12] Although successfully projecting an image of defending moral values, in

Amendment," *NYT*, June 18, 1982. Tom Wicker, "The Baptist Switch," ibid., June 22, 1982. Bauer to Edwin L. Harper, June 22, 1982, Bauer Files, Box 3, RRPL. Aaron Haberman, "Into the Wilderness: Ronald Reagan, Bob Jones University, and the Political Education of the Christian Right," *The Historian* 67 (Summer 2005): 241. Flo Conway and Jim Siegelman, *Holy Terror: The Fundamentalist War on America's Freedoms in Religion, Politics and Our Private Lives* (Garden City, NY: Doubleday, 1982). Reagan's religion: Haynes Johnson, *Sleepwalking through History: America in the Reagan Years* (New York: W. W. Norton, 1991), p. 45; Garry Wills, *Reagan's America: Innocents at Home* (Garden City, NY: Doubleday, 1987).

10 Jeffrey K. Hadden and Anson Shupe, *Televangelism, Power, and Politics on God's Frontier* (New York: H. Holt, 1988). Alec Foege, *The Empire God Built: Inside Pat Robertson's Media Machine* (New York: John Wiley & Sons, 1996). Larry Martz with Ginny Carroll, *Ministry of Greed: The Inside Story of the Televangelists and Their Holy Wars* (New York: Weidenfeld & Nicolson, 1988).

11 Fund-raising letter: Conway and Siegelman, *Holy Terror*, p. 108.

12 "Senate Republicans Decide to Postpone 'Emotional' Debates," *NYT*, March 27, 1981; "Helms Says Senate May Consider Some Social Measures This Year," ibid. Lou Cannon, *Governor Reagan: His Rise to Power* (New York: Public Affairs, 2003). Lou Cannon, *President Reagan: The Role of a Lifetime* (New York: Public Affairs, 2000), p. 813. Robert Dallek, *Ronald Reagan: The Politics of Symbolism* (Cambridge, MA: Harvard University Press,

the Iran-Contra scandal he broke several laws and violated the long-standing American policy of refusing to negotiate with terrorists. And on the acquired immunodeficiency syndrome (AIDS) epidemic, his silence and refusal to act for five years undoubtedly resulted in tens of thousands of new, often fatal cases of infection.[13]

Reagan's critics consistently underestimated him, dismissing him as a former actor with no intellectual depth who repeated well-worn cliches about big government and the evils of communism. He was legendary for his disinterest in the details of public policy, and critics mocked his habit of telling stories that were pure fantasy. In a December 1983 speech to Medal of Honor winners he told a story about a World War II pilot who chose to crash and die with his wounded partner. The story actually was from the 1944 film *On a Wing and a Prayer*. Critics sneered but completely failed to understand the basis of Reagan's popular appeal. Alexander Haig, his first secretary of state, understood, explaining that Reagan was "imbued with very deep convictions, viscerally held." By 1980, the country had experienced Kennedy's assassination, the trauma of the Vietnam War that drove President Johnson from office, Watergate and Nixon's resignation, and the perceived ineptness of Presidents Ford and Carter. In that context, Reagan's plainspoken moral certitude had broad appeal. His genial style was far more effective in advancing conservative policies than Richard Nixon's hard-edged anger. Undoubtedly, his most skillful ploy was casting himself as the heir to Franklin D. Roosevelt, the friend of the common person. No less an authority on American politics than Bill Clinton understood Reagan's appeal. Twelve years away from the presidency, in a speech to the 1980 Democratic Party convention, he warned, "let us not underestimate Ronald Reagan. His voice is clear, consistent, and committed. His appeal is strong." Even some Democratic Party stalwarts were disturbed by their party's image of being beholden to special interest constituencies, including African Americans, women, and labor. The historian Arthur M. Schlesinger, Jr., biographer of FDR and adviser to later Democrats, summed it up in a book entitled *The Disuniting of America*.[14]

In fact, Reagan played the game of interest group politics as intensely as every other president. The White House Office of Public Liaison had become the home of outreach to interest groups on race, ethnicity, women, and religion, and Reagan's was the largest of

1984). Ronald Reagan, *The Reagan Diaries*, edited by Douglas Brinkley (New York: HarperCollins, 2007). The diaries shed little light on Reagan's thinking on key issues. Richard Reeves, *President Reagan: The Triumph of Imagination* (New York: Simon & Schuster, 2005). Wills, *Reagan's America: Innocents at Home*.

13 Haberman, "Into the Wilderness: Ronald Reagan, Bob Jones University, and the Political Education of the Christian Right," 241, 243. An excellent example of a truly fanciful analysis of Reagan's political philosophy is William Ker Muir, Jr., *The Bully Pulpit: The Presidential Leadership of Ronald Reagan* (San Francisco: Institute for Contemporary Studies, 1992).

14 Remarks at the Annual Convention of the Congressional Medal of Honor Society in New York City, December 12, 1983, APP. Stories: Haynes Johnson, *Sleepwalking through History*, p. 59, 165–6. Famously, his biographer Edmund Morris could not penetrate Reagan's seeming lack of substance, produced a ludicrous biography with fictional elements in response, and could not see the obvious point that Reagan's surface elements were the source of his political popularity: Edmund Morris, *Dutch: A Memoir of Ronald Reagan* (New York: Random House, 1999). Haig: Deborah Hart Strober and Gerald S. Strober, eds., *Reagan: The Man and His Presidency* (Boston: Houghton Mifflin, 1998), p. 111. Underestimation of Reagan: Dinesh D'Souza, *Ronald Reagan: How an Ordinary Man Became an Extraordinary Leader* (New York: Free Press, 1997), pp. 1–7, 73, 81. Reagan's character and background: Wills, *Reagan's America: Innocents at Home*. Clinton: "We Must Speak to America," August 14, 1980, in Stephen A. Smith, ed., *Preface to the Presidency: Selected Speeches of Bill Clinton, 1974–1992* (Fayetteville: University of Arkansas Press, 1996), pp. 23–7. Liberal discontent with "identity politics": Arthur M. Schlesinger, Jr., *The DisUniting of America: Reflections on a Multicultural Society* (New York: W. W. Norton, 1998).

any president of the period, twice the size of President Carter's. It included Jack Burgess for "ethnics," as office files labeled them, and Jacob Stein for Jews, Elizabeth Dole for women, and Luis Acle for the increasingly important Hispanic community. Nonetheless, Reagan successfully portrayed himself as the president of all the people, and not the hostage of special interest groups.[15]

The past as prologue: Reagan as governor

Reagan's two terms as governor of California from 1966 to 1974 provide illuminating insights into his presidency. Two years before the 1968 presidential election, he showed Richard Nixon how to win over worried Americans by condemning radical protests and "permissiveness" and presenting himself as the defender of order and traditional American values. He attacked student radicals and promised to clean up the "Mess at Berkeley," the University of California campus where the 1964 Free Speech movement was the first major student protest outside the southern sit-ins. Claiming the campus was dominated by a "minority of malcontents, beatniks, and filthy speech advocates," he bluntly warned radicals to "obey the rules or get out." The FBI covertly warned him of impending campus protests.[16]

Reagan's ambivalence about the 1967 California law liberalizing access to abortion was particularly revealing about his later performance as president. He signed the law, but with serious reservations. Public opinion was turning against criminal abortion laws in the mid-1960s, and California was the third state to liberalize its law. The Therapeutic Abortion Act permitted abortion in the case of rape or incest, where there was "substantial risk" of a deformed baby, and, most important, when the doctor thought that the pregnancy threatened the physical or mental health of the mother.

Reagan supported the bill, apparently believing it would never come to a final vote. When the Judiciary Committee surprised everyone by approving it 7–6, he was caught off guard and uncharacteristically indecisive. One biographer described him as being in "foreign territory," and at a May 9, 1967 press conference he appeared "lost at sea," giving confused and contradictory responses to reporters' questions. Although in his heart he opposed the bill, he felt obliged to honor an earlier commitment to several GOP legislators to support it. Thus, it is not entirely true, as some prochoice advocates later argued, that he supported abortion reform as governor. After the law went into effect, he was shocked and angered at the number of abortions under the mental health provisions, and he successfully opposed further liberalization in 1970. When he ran for president in 1980, New Right politics pushed him into an even stronger antiabortion posture.[17]

15 Dole Files, Box 19, RRPL. Hispanics: Acle, Concept Paper, Hispanic Appointments Task Force, n.d., Acle Files, Box 2, RRPL. A valuable perspective on the Office of Public Liaison is Joseph A. Pika, "The White House Office of Public Liaison," *Presidential Studies Quarterly* 39 (September 2009): 554–6.

16 "'Obey or Get Out' – Reagan," *San Francisco Chronicle*, December 3, 1966, clipping in Gubernatorial Papers, 1966 Campaign, Box 34, RRPL. Abundant materials on "law and order," "University of California," "pornography," and related issues: 1966 Campaign, Gubernatorial Files, RRPL. Cannon, *Governor Reagan*, pp. 271–3. "Reagan Demands Berkeley Inquiry," *NYT*, May 14, 1966. Ironically, when Reagan proposed to cut the university budget, one of the moderates on the University Board of Regents who worried about the impact on higher education was H. R. Haldeman, future Nixon aide and Watergate figure. FBI: "The Governor's Race," *San Francisco Chronicle*, June 9, 2002, with FBI documents.

17 Cannon, *Governor Reagan*, pp. 208–16. Reagan does not mention the law in his memoirs: Ronald Reagan, *Ronald Reagan: An American Life*, Pbk. ed. (New York: Pocket Books, 1992).

A WOMAN ON THE SUPREME COURT: SANDRA DAY O'CONNOR

"Sandra, I'd like to announce your nomination to the Court tomorrow." With that 6:10 p.m. phone call on July 7, 1981, President Reagan made history by nominating Sandra Day O'Connor to be the first woman on the U.S. Supreme Court.[18]

Not all of his supporters were happy with his choice. Prolife activists immediately opposed O'Connor for her past support for a liberalized Arizona abortion law. In his diary, Reagan noted with irritation, "Already the flack is starting and from my own supporters." The Moral Majority leader Falwell initially declared that "All good Christians should oppose O'Connor." The conservative activist Phyllis Schlafly accused her of being the "principal sponsor" of an "extremist" proposal to make women eligible for combat duty. Reagan employed his personal charm, however, and turned Falwell around. The Moral Majority leader then told other prolifers to "back off." The prolife opposition was understandable. On April 29, 1970, as an Arizona state senator and a member of its Judiciary Committee, O'Connor had voted to liberalize the state's abortion law. This fact was well known locally, and the abortion bill was covered in the local media at the time (the bill never passed). Dr. Carolyn Gerster, a Phoenix physician and prominent antiabortion leader, mentioned this history during O'Connor's nomination process, but to no effect.[19]

The O'Connor nomination revealed the low priority of abortion for Reagan and several of his top aides. In a brief July 1 White House meeting, Reagan blandly accepted her statement that she regarded abortion as "abhorrent," without pressing the issue and instead discussing their mutual interests in ranches and horses. A young White House staff lawyer was assigned to vet her, and he had two telephone conversations with her on July 6. He accepted at face value her statement that she had "no recollection of how she voted" on the abortion bill. The young attorney was Kenneth Starr, later famous if not notorious as independent counsel for his zealous pursuit of President Bill Clinton in the 1990s. Conservative senators fumed that O'Connor was "unresponsive" to questions about *Roe v. Wade* at her confirmation hearings, but to no avail. The Senate unanimously confirmed her, 99–0.[20]

O'Connor's nomination was rife with ironies. Reagan clearly chose her because she was a woman, despite his public opposition to affirmative action. During the 1980 campaign feminists attacked him for opposing the Equal Rights Amendment, and Reagan responded on October 14 by saying he would fill "one of the first Supreme Court vacancies" with a woman. Feminists dismissed it as a cynical ploy to offset their criticisms. Chief Justice Burger, who had reportedly been "totally opposed" to appointing a woman to the Court when President Nixon floated the idea in 1971, became an early and

18 Joan Biskupic, *Sandra Day O'Connor: How the First Woman on the Supreme Court Became Its Most Influential Justice* (New York: Ecco, 2005), p. 80.

19 Reagan, *The Reagan Diaries*, p. 28. "Reaction is Mixed," *NYT*, July 8, 1981. Biskupic, *Sandra Day O'Connor*, p. 58, citing *Arizona Republic* articles on April 29, 1970, April 30, 1970. Schlafley to "Senator" [form letter], August 21, 1981, Mary Elizabeth Quint Files, Box 1, RRPL. Falwell, Strober and Strober, *Reagan: The Man and His Presidency*, p. 85. A 2007 profile of Dr. Gerster is on the Arizona Right to Life Committee Web site: http://arizonarighttolife.org/Speakers_Bureau.html.

20 Starr to Attorney General, July 7, 1981, Meese Files, Box 7, RRPL. Gerster testimony and the July 7, 1981, Starr memo: Senate, Committee on the Judiciary, Hearings, Nomination of Sandra Day O'Connor, 9th Cong., 1st Sess., Sept. 9, 10, 11, 1981, pp. 280–2. The Starr investigation: Jeffrey Toobin, *The Nine: Inside the Secret World of the Supreme Court* (New York: Doubleday, 2007), p. 40. "Unresponsiveness": Theodore B. Olson to Robert A. McConnell, March 1, 1982, Wallinson Files, Box 4, RRPL.

vigorous O'Connor advocate. O'Connor's early legal career shared one important feature with that of Ruth Bader Ginsburg, who would join her on the Court in 1993. After graduating from law school (Columbia in Ginsburg's case; Stanford in O'Connor's) neither was able to get a job with a law firm. Their appointments to the Court dramatized the revolution in women's rights that had occurred in the intervening years.[21]

On the Court, O'Connor had a profound impact on the course of constitutional law. "Few associate justices in history," writes the journalist Jeffrey Toobin, "dominated a time so thoroughly or cast as many deciding votes as O'Connor." During her tenure, he adds, the Court "was in fact the O'Connor Court." She fashioned a centrist judicial philosophy that was conservative on most issues but deeply respected *stare decisis,* letting stand some important decisions protecting individual rights. Most important, she played the crucial role in abortion cases and prevented a reversal of *Roe v. Wade.*[22] The key to her influence was the alliance she fashioned with Justices Anthony Kennedy and David Souter, which moved Kennedy to the center on several key cases. (After she retired he swung back and gave the conservative bloc a 5–4 majority in key decisions.) Souter was instinctively libertarian and readily joined O'Connor's coalition, which was the major reason the much anticipated neoconservative revolution on the Supreme Court stalled for many years, particularly on abortion.

THE POLITICS OF ABORTION

Every year on January 22, the anniversary of *Roe v. Wade,* the prolife movement held a demonstration in Washington (an estimated seventy thousand people in 1984). President Reagan always met with their leaders privately but never once appeared in person at the rally. In 1983 he spoke from Camp David, and in 1984, according to his diary, he "went up to the W. H. balcony and waved to them." Reagan was primarily interested the issues that had mattered to him since before he ever ran for public office: taxes, government spending, fighting communism. In his memoirs, abortion and the other hot button social issues are simply not mentioned.[23]

In a declaration that terrified abortion rights activists, the 1980 GOP platform stated that "we affirm our support of a constitutional amendment to restore protection of the right to life for unborn children." Reagan was unenthusiastic about pressing the issue, but New Right leaders in Congress moved quickly on it, and Senator Jesse Helms immediately held hearings on both an antiabortion statute and a constitutional amendment in spring 1981. Both proposals had been around since the 1973 *Roe v. Wade* decision, but they now appeared to have a real possibility of passing. The Hatch Amendment (named after the Senate Judiciary Committee chair Orrin Hatch) read, "A right to abortion is not secured by this Constitution. The Congress and the several States shall have the concurrent power to restrict and prohibit abortions."[24] In a clear indication of the administration's real priorities,

[21] Toobin, *The Nine,* p. 38. Burger: Biskupic, *Sandra Day O'Connor,* pp. 72–3. Reagan campaign promise: "The Republican Defends Stance on Equal Rights and War Accusations," *NYT,* October 15, 1980.

[22] Biskupic, *Sandra Day O'Connor.* Toobin, *The Nine,* pp. 7, 38, 96.

[23] "Foes of Abortion Meet with Reagan," *NYT,* January 23, 1982. "Demonstrations Mark 10 Years of Legal Abortion," ibid., January 23, 1983. Reagan, *Reagan Diaries,* p. 214. Cannon, *The Role of a Lifetime,* p. 812.

[24] Republican Party platform of 1980, July 15, 1980, APP. James Bopp, Jr., *Restoring the Right to Life: The Human Life Amendment* (Provo, UT: Brigham Young University Press, 1984). Constitutional Amendments Relating to Abortion, Hearings, Subcommittee on the Constitution of the Committee on the Judiciary, United States

however, no administration official testified at the 1981 hearings. GOP Senate leaders did not want Helms even to hold the hearings. President Reagan publicly expressed support only after reportedly "bow[ing] to conservative pressure." Public opinion polls consistently found only about 20 percent supported a complete ban on abortion, while 60 percent supported some restrictions (such as parental notification for minors seeking abortions) while keeping it legal in most cases. Prochoice forces organized a broad-based coalition of religious, feminist, and civil libertarian groups. The issue of privacy and the potential government intrusion into intimate sexual matters gave pause to many moderates and conservatives. The Hatch Amendment failed in its first vote in September 1982, and again in two votes in 1983. That, according to one historian, was the "last serious attempt" to pass a constitutional amendment outlawing abortion.[25]

Many social conservative leaders were well aware of the administration's failure to deliver on its promises on abortion. Ronald Godwin, a Moral Majority official, recalled many meetings in the White House, but how, figuratively speaking, they always went in "through the side or back door of the White House," with the administration giving them "largely gestures." Godwin chided Falwell: "you don't ever cash in your chips." Falwell, however, was personally enchanted with Reagan and refused to pressure him. A telling statement was the administration's report celebrating its first year, *The Reagan Presidency: A New Beginning: A Review of the First Year, 1981*. Three pages of single-spaced bullets listed tax cuts, regulatory relief, and initiatives in foreign affairs but did not mention abortion or school prayer. A similar report for 1986 also did not mention any of the social issues.[26]

The pivotal Supreme Court abortion case was *Planned Parenthood v. Casey* in 1992. Although Reagan had been out of office for four years, his appointee Sandra Day O'Connor played the central role in preserving *Roe v. Wade*. The Pennsylvania law at issue in *Casey* included several requirements making it difficult to obtain an abortion: a twenty-four-hour waiting period, parental consent for minors, and a requirement that a married woman notify her husband prior to the procedure. Observers on all sides saw *Casey* as the Court's opportunity to overturn *Roe v. Wade*. There were four certain votes for reversing *Roe* (Chief Justice William Rehnquist, Byron White, Antonin Scalia, and Clarence Thomas), with Justices O'Connor and Kennedy as likely candidates for the deciding fifth vote. In a surprising decision, however, the Court accepted all of the Pennsylvania law except the husband notification requirement but reaffirmed *Roe* and the "central right" to an abortion. Justice O'Connor fashioned the compromise that persuaded Justices Kennedy and Souter to join her in the majority. Justice Scalia raged in a characteristically angry dissent, reiterating his argument that *Roe* was wrong "because the Constitution says absolutely nothing about it." But as Jeffrey Toobin observed, "It was O'Connor's Court now."[27]

Senate, 97th Cong., 1st Sess. 1981. Senate, Subcommittee on Separation of Powers, Judiciary Committee, Hearings, The Human Life Bill, 97th Cong., 1st Sess. 1981.

25 "Foes of Abortion Lose Senate Test," *NYT*, September 10, 1982. "Foes of Abortion Beaten in Senate on Amendment Bid," ibid., June 29, 1983. Haberman, "Into the Wilderness," 251.

26 Godwin: Strober and Strober, *Reagan: The Man and His Presidency*, pp. 104–5. Administration's position on social issues: John D. Lees, "Reagan and the Social Agenda," in John D. Lees and Michael Turner, *Reagan's First Four Years* (New York: Manchester University Press, 1988), pp. 193–205. *The Reagan Presidency: A New Beginning: A Review of the First Year, 1981* (Washington, DC: White House, 1982), Deaver Files, Box, 17, RRPL. Talking Points Memo: "1986 – Years of Decision," n.d., Luis Acle Files, OPL, Box 2, RRPL.

27 *Planned Parenthood v. Casey*, 505 U.S. 833 (1992). Toobin, *The Nine*, pp. 47, 50–3, 59.

Abortion: sex, science, and reproduction

The Reagan administration did yield to prolife pressure on several abortion-related issues. In 1984 alone, two dozen clinics were bombed, burned, or attacked in some way. The attacks could properly be described as domestic terrorism: an ideologically and religiously driven campaign of violence. Reagan administration officials rejected that interpretation and refused even to speak out against the violence (as did national right to life leaders). The FBI director, William Webster, said it was not terrorism because the attacks were not perpetrated by an "organized group" that claimed credit for them. "The objective is social," he explained, and therefore he did not "believe it currently meets our definition" of terrorism.[28]

The administration also attacked federal policies that were indirectly related to abortion. Title X of the 1970 Public Health Act providing federal funds for family planning services prohibited funds for abortion, but this restriction was not enough for conservative hard-liners. The Reagan administration expanded the prohibition in 1988 with a Health and Human Services regulation forbidding agencies even to discuss abortion as an alternative or to refer clients to abortion providers. Reproductive rights activists promptly labeled the ban a "gag order" and an infringement on medical professionals' First Amendment rights and their professional obligations to use their best medical judgment in treating patients. On this and many other policy issues, New Right hard-liners were strategically placed in federal agencies where they could revise official policies. The Supreme Court upheld the gag order in *Rust v. Sullivan,* 1991, by a vote of 5–4. Justice O'Connor voted to overturn the gag order but could not induce Kennedy or Souter to side with her in this case. In what became a predictable pattern of reversals, Bill Clinton repealed the gag order by executive order in January 1993, as one of his first acts in office; George W. Bush reinstated it in 2001; and Barack Obama repealed it again in 2009.[29]

Another long-running battle began in 1984, when the administration banned Agency for International Development (AID) funds for international organizations that even discussed abortion with their clients. Known as the Mexico City Policy, and to reproductive rights activists as the "international gag order," it joined the stem cell research ban as a political football: imposed by Republican presidents and repealed by Democrats, usually in one of their first acts in office.

Antiabortion activists moved beyond abortion to attack a range of sexuality-related policies, particularly teenage sexual activity and use of contraceptives. The 1981 Adolescent Family Life Act, which sailed through both houses of Congress without hearings over its implications, provided pregnancy prevention grants only to programs that did not advocate abortion. Initially, the administration awarded grants only to conservative and religious groups that incorporated explicit religious doctrine in their programs. The ACLU challenged this practice as a blatant violation of the separation of church and state. A district court declared the law unconstitutional, but the Supreme Court remanded the case for additional fact finding. In 1993, a long twelve years after the initial suit was filed,

[28] "Blasts Not on F.B.I. Terrorism List," *NYT*, December 5, 1984. "When Is a Terrorist Not Necessarily a Terrorist?" ibid., December 12, 1984. Warren M. Hern, "The Anti-Abortion Vigilantes," ibid., December 12, 1984.

[29] "Groups Challenging Abortion Rules," *NYT*, February 2, 1988. *Rust v. Sullivan*, 500 U.S. 173 (1991).

the ACLU and HHS reached a settlement under which grant recipients had to submit curricula in advance to ensure they did not promote religion.[30]

Advances in medical science introduced research on the transplant of fetal tissue into the abortion wars. In 1988 scientists at the National Institutes of Health sought approval from HHS for experiments involving the transplantation of fetal tissue. Pressured by anti-abortion forces who argued there was a link between fetal tissue and abortion, the Reagan administration in March 1988 imposed a temporary moratorium on federal funds for such research. Thus began another long political battle over an abortion-related policy. President George H. W. Bush's HHS secretary, Louis W. Sullivan, extended the moratorium indefinitely in 1989; Bill Clinton repealed it in 1993; George W. Bush reinstated it in 2001; and Barack Obama repealed it again in 2009.[31]

"Traditional values" on Women and families

As President Jimmy Carter's White House conference on families revealed, neoconservatives sought to restore what they believed to be "traditional" family values, which in practice meant attacking the idea of women's working outside the home, the ERA, birth control, abortion, and other aspects of contemporary American culture. New Right priorities in this regard created a political problem for the Reagan administration. Many Republican women supported abortion rights and the ERA and took for granted using birth control and pursuing professional careers, and this circumstance contributed to what was called the "gender gap." Polls indicated that Reagan trailed Democrats among women by about 10 percentage points. (In fact, slightly more women voted for Reagan than Carter in 1980.) The intensity of hostility to the administration surfaced at a regular meeting of the Women's Bureau Constituency in the Labor Department in late 1981. Many employees expressed their "distress" at the apparent "gutting" of civil rights enforcement with respect to women and racial minorities. When the White House spokesperson Wendy Borcherdt described plans for private industry programs for working women, "they just laughed." Some White House moderates suggested a commission on the status of women, but the conservative leader Phyllis Schlafly called it "counterproductive." Reagan refused to embrace completely the New Right women's agenda and created a President's Task Force on Legal Equity for Women in late 1981, saying he was opposed to the ERA but was "dedicated to eliminating discrimination against women."[32]

Reagan's women's equity initiative bore some fruit. For Women's Equality Day in August 1984, Defense Secretary Caspar Weinberger created a Departmental Task Force on Women's Equity. The task force later reported progress on pay equity, survivor benefit plans, and health benefits; the impact of reductions in force on women, who usually had the least seniority; and the establishment of women's career development programs. These actions continued President Carter' initiatives. In short, despite much

[30] *Kendrick v. Sullivan*, Civil Action 83-3175 (CRR), January 19, 1993, U.S. District Court, DC. Rebekah Saul, "Whatever Happened to the Adolescent Family Life Act?" *Guttmacher Report on Public Policy* 1 (April 1998): 5, 10–11.

[31] "Federal Agency Bars Implanting of Fetal Tissue," *NYT*, April 16, 1988.

[32] "Women Votes Are a Reagan Woe," *NYT*, November 19, 1981. Schlafley to Elizabeth Dole, April 3, 1981, Quint Files, Box 1, RRPL. Reagan Announcement, December 21, 1981, APP. Borcherdt to Elizabeth Dole, December 11, 1981, Dole Files, Box 33, RRPL.

public rhetoric against the ERA and feminism, administration pragmatists saw women as a powerful political constituency they needed to serve and advanced policies that would have been considered radical just a few years earlier.[33]

The bright line dividing Reagan conservatives from feminists and Democrats was the latter's emphasis on social services and formal legal equality for women. Conservatives sought to advance "family values" through opposition to abortion and by promoting economic growth. A 1988 report by Gary Bauer's Office of Policy Development, for example, argued that "family policy must be built upon a foundation of economic growth."[34]

A DEADLY SILENCE ON AIDS

A strange new disease began appearing around the world in the late 1970s. The first official notice in the United States of what became known as AIDS appeared in a June 5, 1981, Centers for Disease Control report. As evidence of a deadly epidemic mounted, President Reagan maintained a complete silence about it for four years, by which time thousands of people had died of the disease in the United States alone. In 1986 the National Academy of Sciences declared the federal government's response dangerously inadequate, predicted a "catastrophe," and called for a $2 billion national effort.[35]

Reagan's silence on AIDS was a direct result of Religious Right pressure. Merely acknowledging the existence of AIDS, they believed, meant implicitly approving of homosexuality. Jerry Falwell called AIDS "the wrath of God upon homosexuals." The conservative patriarch William F. Buckley, in a March 1986 *New York Times* interview, called for mandatory testing of gay men and tattooing them on the buttocks. Significantly, his extreme proposal fell on deaf ears, and despite the official silence of President Reagan there was no hysterical response to the AIDS epidemic. Notions of privacy had become fairly well established in the United States by then, and they had a major influence on public policy.[36]

Reagan had no personal dislike of homosexuals. During his years in Hollywood he certainly must have known and worked with many gays or lesbians in the movie industry. New Right activists in key administration positions drove official policy, however. The AIDS activist and playwright Larry Kramer met with the White House staffer Gary Bauer and found him terrifying, sensing that he "loathed" homosexuals. Reagan finally mentioned AIDS for the first time after the death of the actor Rock Hudson in October 1985. The death of a fellow actor they knew personally reportedly "shook" him and his wife, Nancy. Reagan mentioned AIDS again on February 5, 1986, but that same day

33 Department of Defense, Task Force on Equity for Women, n.d., Meese Files, Box 47, RRPL.

34 Family Working Group Charter: Meese to Bennett, March 4, 1986, Bauer Files, Box 1, RRPL. Office of Policy Development, Report to the President on the Family, July 8, 1988, Bauer Files, Box 1, RRPL. Reagan, Address before a Joint Session of Congress on the State of the Union, February 4, 1986, APP.

35 "Pneumocystis Pneumonia - Los Angeles," *Morbidity and Mortality Weekly Report* 30 (21): 250–2 (June 5, 1981), with later reports in Douglas A. Feldman and Julia Wang Miller, eds., *The AIDS Crisis: A Documentary History* (Westport, CT: Greenwood, 1998). Institute of Medicine, *Confronting AIDS: Directions for Public Health, Health Care, and Research* (Washington, DC: National Academy Press, 1986).

36 William F. Buckley, "Identify All the Carriers," *NYT*, March 18, 1986. "Federal Efforts on AIDS Criticized as Gravely Weak," ibid., October 30, 1986.

he proposed a budget cutting funding for AIDS research. Congress ignored him and approved more funding.[37]

In response to mounting pressure, Reagan finally appointed an AIDS Commission in June 1987. Gary Bauer urged Reagan not to appoint a homosexual to it because that would only "give homosexuality a stamp of approval." The commission was immediately engulfed in chaos, however, firing its executive director and then having several members quit because of the lack of progress. The ACLU, Public Citizen, and other groups sued the commission, charging that excluding homosexuals, the most affected group, violated the 1972 Federal Advisory Committee Act requiring that commissions be "fairly balanced." The commission's June 1988 report reflected current medical science, with no New Right condemnations of homosexuality, and was quite liberal on policy recommendations. It called for more research and public education about the disease, argued that HIV infection should be classified as a disability, and recommended stronger protections of the privacy rights of HIV-infected people. [38]

Not all Republicans were as completely in the grip of the New Right, and they saw AIDS as a major health problem. The most notable dissident was Vice President George H. W. Bush, who broke with Reagan on this issue and said, "we are facing a national and world emergency." Senator Robert Dole, the 1996 GOP presidential candidate, meanwhile, called for substantial federal spending, saying he did not care whether it needed to be $100 million or $2 billion. The key person on AIDS in the administration was Surgeon General C. Everett Koop. Although conservative on many policy issues, he remained true to his calling as a physician and refused to ignore the national medical crisis. After speaking out on use of condoms as a safe sex measure, however, he was frozen out by New Right hard-liners in the White House. Koop remembered that it was "impossible for me to ever get to the president." (Later, when no longer surgeon general, he enjoyed free access to President Bill Clinton.) Discussing condoms at all, much less with regard to homosexuality, was anathema for social conservatives. He further alarmed the White House when in a National Press Club speech he said he would counsel a pregnant woman who had tested positive for HIV about "all options available" to her, including abortion. The administration sent him a clear message "to keep out of that [issue]." Koop's official 1986 report on AIDS was notable for its candid treatment of the subject. HHS distributed more than 100 million copies of a pamphlet, *Understanding AIDS*, and some observers estimated that it was the most widely read book of the year.[39]

[37] Hollywood: Cannon, *Role of a Lifetime*, p. 819. Kramer: Strober and Strober, *Reagan: The Man and His Presidency*, p. 135. "Reagan Orders AIDS Report, Giving High Priority to Work for Cure," *NYT*, February 6, 1986. Cannon, *The Role of a Lifetime*, p. 814.

[38] Bauer to the President, June 30, 1987, Bauer Files, Box 2, RRPL. Executive Order 12601, Presidential Commission on Human Immunodeficiency Virus Epidemic, June 24, 1987, APP. "Leaders of AIDS Panel Quit amid Feuds and Criticism," *NYT*, October 8, 1987. "Suit Filed over Composition of the Federal Panel on AIDS," ibid., October 15, 1987. *Report of the Presidential Commission on Human Immunodeficiency Epidemic* (Washington, DC: June 24, 1988).

[39] "Bush Favors Requiring AIDS Test for Marriage License Applicants," *NYT*, April 9, 1987. Koop speech: Donald A. Clarke to Nancy J. Risque, re Dr. Koop's Speech, March 24, 1987, Bauer Files, Box 1, RRPL. C. Everett Koop, *Koop: The Memoirs of America's Family Doctor* (New York: Random House, 1991). Koop: Strober and Strober, *Reagan: The Man and His Presidency*, pp. 135–7. *Surgeon General's Report on Acquired Immune Deficiency Syndrome* (Washington, DC: U.S. Dept. of Health and Human Services, 1986). Centers for Disease Control, *Understanding AIDS: America Responds to AIDS* (Rockville, MD: HHS, 1988). "Surgeon General Urges Frank Talk to Young on AIDS," *NYT*, October 23, 1986.

President Reagan's silence on HIV/AIDS casts a shadow on his public image as the defender of moral values. Reported new cases of HIV infections and deaths soared until 1995, when 50,628 died of the disease, and then began a sharp decline. A 2008 Centers for Disease Control report attributed the reversal to the introduction of "highly active antiretroviral therapy." The administration's delay in acknowledging the epidemic and quickly supporting research and education efforts resulted in thousands of unnecessary infections and deaths.[40]

Despite President Reagan's silence on AIDS and hostility to homosexuality, however, lesbian and gay rights made slow but steady progress in many areas of American life. Wisconsin became the first state to outlaw discrimination on the basis of sexual orientation in 1982, and that year Laguna Beach, California, became the first city to elect an openly gay mayor. The total number of openly lesbian and gay elected officials steadily rose from 49 in 1991 to 495 in 2011. Rep. Gerry Studds of Massachusetts became the first openly gay member of Congress, announcing it on the floor of the House in 1983, and Rep. Barney Frank announced that he was gay in 1987. Berkeley, California, passed the first same-sex domestic partnership ordinance in 1984, and by 2010 twenty states and many cities and counties had enacted laws banning discrimination based on sexual orientation. As part of the Great Realignment, the two national political parties moved in opposite directions on homosexual issues. Jimmy Carter personally opposed discrimination in 1976, and the Democratic Party included an antidiscrimination plank in its 1980 platform. The Republican Party, meanwhile, remained firmly in the grip of antihomosexuality religious conservatives.[41]

ATTORNEY GENERAL MEESE'S RIGHT-WING AGENDA

The Moral Majority founder Jerry Falwell put it bluntly: Ed Meese "was our man there." The appointment of Edwin Meese as attorney general at the start of President Reagan's second term in 1985 resulted in a far more aggressive approach to the New Right's social agenda. As attorney general, he could act somewhat independently of Reagan's more moderate White House advisers.[42]

Meese's nomination served as a lightning rod for all the accumulated liberal criticisms of the administration. At his confirmation hearings, Senator Ted Kennedy minced no words, declaring that "the record of this administration over the past three years on issues affecting civil rights, women and the poor is a disgrace" and identifying Meese as "the architect of most, if not all" of the administration's policies. The Justice Department had "exploited every opportunity to roll back decades of progress on civil rights," had "brazenly politicized the Civil Rights Commission," and had opposed women's rights in cases before the Supreme Court. John Shattuck, director of the ACLU Washington office, submitted a lengthy report on the administration's civil rights record that explained the new dynamics of civil rights enforcement. Conservatives did not rely primarily on repealing existing laws, but instead on limiting their scope through administrative regulations

[40] Centers for Disease Control and Prevention, "HIV Surveillance – United States, 1981 – 2008," *Morbidity and Mortality Weekly Report* 60, (21): 689–93 (June 3, 2011).

[41] Data on elected officials: Victory Fund, Annual Reports. www.victoryfund.org. "For Gay Aspiring Politicians a Workshop on Winning Office," *NYT*, June 11, 2011.

[42] Falwell: Strober and Strober, *Reagan: The Man and His Presidency*, p. 64.

or simply not enforcing them at all. Civil rights forces found such approaches difficult to combat, as they lacked the high-profile quality of a bill before Congress or a Supreme Court case and typically involved complex matters of interpreting a statutory provision. Shattuck added that the administration had also "actively and repeatedly" fought voluntary efforts by state and local authorities to advance equality. Finally the administration cut or attempted to cut the budgets of the Legal Services Corporation, the Civil Rights Commission, and other agencies.[43]

The administration, for example, had not filed any suits related to conditions in facilities for the mentally ill or mentally retarded, emphasizing conciliation over litigation in this area. The Justice Department, meanwhile, had refused to participate when the district court expanded a suit against the Mississippi state prison to include county jails. On housing discrimination, it abandoned the "effects test" and substituted the more demanding "intent" test, as it had also tried to do with voting rights enforcement. On sex discrimination it sought to limit sharply the application of Title IX barring sex discrimination in educational programs. In the crucial Supreme Court case of *Grove City College v. Bell*, the administration successfully persuaded the Court that the penalty, cutting off federal funds, should apply only to the particular program involved rather than the institution as a whole.[44]

Architect of original intent

Arguably, Ed Meese's most lasting impact on the law was his role in promoting the doctrine of original intent, which conservative legal scholars developed as a counter to the liberal activism of the Warren Court. Original intent had the appeal of a general theory that applied to all constitutional matters without being tied to a particular issue such as race or school prayer. Thus, its advocates could argue that such key concepts as a wall of separation, privacy, and the *Miranda* warning were invalid because the Constitution did not specifically mention them and thus had been invented by liberal activist judges.[45]

Meese launched his campaign in a July 1985 speech to the American Bar Association (ABA), shortly after his confirmation, arguing that judges should "judge policies in light of principles, rather than remold principles in light of policies." The proper standard should be "the text of the document and the original intention of those who framed it." Most ominously for much of the body of Supreme Court decisions protecting civil liberties and civil rights, Meese squarely attacked the doctrine of incorporation, through which the various provisions of the Bill of Rights had been incorporated into the Fourteenth Amendment and made applicable to the states. He singled out the establishment clause, noting that it was not incorporated until the 1947 *Everson* decision, and saw it resting on an "intellectually shaky foundation." Quoting Justice William Rehnquist, he added that it "has no bases in the history of the [Fourteenth] amendment." Meese carefully did

[43] U.S. Senate, Judiciary Committee, Hearings, Nomination of Edwin Meese III to be Attorney General of the United States, 98th Cong, 2nd Sess., March 1, 2, 5, and 6, 1984, pp. 4–5. Statement of John Shattuck, National Legislative Director, and Muriel Morisey Spence, Legislative Counsel, American Civil Liberties Union, ibid., pp. 690–717.

[44] Shattuck, Testimony. *Grove City College v. Bell*, 465 U.S. 555 (1984).

[45] Leonard W. Levy, *Original Intent and the Framers' Constitution* (New York: Macmillan, 1988).

not mention *Brown v. Board of Education*, even though his argument clearly applied, because that would only invite a political firestorm he did not want.[46]

Meese's great achievement, as one observer put it, was to take an arcane legal concept "out of the pages of law reviews" and make it a matter of public debate. Some observers regard his ABA address as the "speech of his career."[47] Meese quickly sensed that he had struck a responsive chord and began an ambitious speaking campaign on the subject. He also promoted the Federalist Society, founded in 1982, which quickly became the center of conservative legal thinking and a recruiting ground for Republican presidents. On this issue Reagan's attorney general had a powerful and lasting impact on the law on civil liberties, both within the legal profession and among the general public, in a way that was very detrimental to the future of individual rights.

Politics and the attorney general

Meese's role as attorney general raised again the troubling question of whether a president should appoint to that powerful position a close personal friend or political adviser (or brother). Griffin Bell, President Jimmy Carter's attorney general, criticized Meese's appointment, pointing out that he had been White House counsel prior to his appointment. "It is very difficult for anyone to move from the White House to the Department of Justice," Bell argued, "because you will necessarily bring some of those entanglements with you." Meese, in fact, remained chair of the White House Policy Council while attorney general. Bell's critique applied with equal force to the previous attorneys general Robert Kennedy and John Mitchell, both of whom had been campaign directors for the presidents they served, and to the future attorney general Alberto Gonzales, who had been White House counsel to President George W. Bush and as attorney general acted more as a compliant friend than a source of independent legal judgment.[48]

Meese's war on pornography

The press conference had an almost comic air. Attorney General Meese on July 12, 1986, stood below the Spirit of Justice statue in the Justice Department, with her bare breasts in full view, as he announced the release of his antipornography commission report. Critics gleefully circulated photographs to make fun of both Meese and the report. (In January 2002, George W. Bush's attorney general, John Ashcroft, spent a reported eight thousand dollars for a curtain to cover the offending body parts.)[49]

46 Edwin Meese III, Speech to the American Bar Association, July 9, 1985," in *Major Policy Statements of the Attorney General: Edwin Meese III, 1985–1988* (Washington, DC: Department of Justice, 1989), pp. 1–8. Edwin Meese III, "Towards a Jurisprudence of Original Intent," *Harvard Journal of Law and Public Policy* 11 (1988): 5. Toobin, *The Nine*, p. 15. Two decades later, Justice Antonin Scalia provoked some controversy by refusing to answer whether *Brown* was wrongly decided. "Desegregation as Test in Constitutional Debate," *NYT*, November 10, 2009.

47 "Meese's Influence Looms in Today's Judicial Wars," *NYT* August 17, 2005.

48 Bell, OH, pp. 24–5, MCPA. Edwin Meese III, *With Reagan: The Inside Story* (Washington, DC: Regnery Gateway, 1992). He does not mention abortion, school prayer, original intent, or signing statements. Cornell W. Clayton, *The Politics of Justice: The Attorney General and the Making of Legal Policy* (Armonk, NY: M. E. Sharpe, 1992), pp. 48–88.

49 "The Story of "X," *NYT*, July 13, 1986. Maureen Dowd, "A Blue Burka for Justice," ibid., January 30, 2002.

Creation of the Attorney General's Commission on Pornography in spring 1985 was a major part of Meese's social agenda. As the first such effort since President Johnson's obscenity commission, it deeply alarmed civil libertarians about a possible new federal censorship effort. Appointments to the commission only heightened their fears. It was chaired by Henry Hudson, a zealous antipornography prosecutor from Virginia, and included James C. Dobson, head of the new Family Research Council, then just emerging as a powerful neoconservative voice. The commission's methods also disturbed social scientists. Particularly controversial was the handling of the evidence on the impact of violent pornography. "The available evidence," it concluded, "strongly supports the hypothesis that substantial exposure to sexually violent materials ... bears a causal relationship to antisocial acts of sexual violence." That conclusion seriously misrepresented existing research and was immediately challenged by the University of Wisconsin psychologist Edward Donnerstein, the leading expert on the subject. The commission's methods also raised serious legal issues. It sent letters to twenty-three companies informing that they were considered distributors of pornography and would be listed as such in the commission's final report if they did not contest the letter. *Playboy* and *Penthouse* magazines sued and won a ruling that the commission's action was unconstitutional, forcing the letter to be retracted. The owner of the 7-11 convenience store chain, however, caved in to the pressure and agreed to stop selling *Playboy*.[50]

In a surprising twist, the commission accepted the Supreme Court rulings on sexually explicit material. It asked rhetorically, "Is the Supreme Court Right?" and concluded that "its approach is most likely correct." Nonetheless, it advanced the Madisonian view that the First Amendment was intended to protect public debate over issues central to the democratic process and argued that much sexually explicit material was not "even remotely related to an exchange of views in the marketplace of ideas." It was a sophisticated argument advanced by some respected First Amendment scholars, but it potentially opened the door to restrictions on sexually oriented material.[51]

New York publishers declined to publish the commission's two-volume report, but a small Nashville firm issued a commercial version, which sold mainly to antipornography groups. Ironically, some conservative religious book stores refused to carry it, fearing that the language and graphic descriptions of sexual acts would offend their usual customers. A year later Meese formed the ten-person National Obscenity Enforcement Unit in the Justice Department. "Mr. Meese elevated obscenity to a top criminal justice priority," said H. Robert Showers, director of the new unit. [52]

[50] Attorney General's Commission on Pornography, *Final Report* (Washington, DC: U.S. Department of Justice, 1986). President's Commission on Obscenity and Pornography, *Report of the Commission on Obscenity and Pornography* (Washington, DC: Government Printing Office, 1970). Nixon's response, see Chapter 9 of this book. Daniel Linz, Steven D. Penrod, and Edward Donnerstein, "The Attorney General's Commission on Pornography: The Gaps between "Findings' and Facts," *American Bar Foundation Research Journal* 12, no. 4 (1987): 713–36. Marjorie Heins, *Sex, Sin, and Blasphemy: A Guide to America's Censorship Wars* (New York: New Press, 1993), pp. 69–71.

[51] Attorney General's Commission on Pornography, *Final Report*, "Is the Supreme Court Right?" pp. 260–9.

[52] "Some Say Meese Report Rates an 'X,'" *NYT*, October 21, 1986. "Justice Dept. Team Leading Broad Effort on Obscenity," ibid., August 22, 1987. Message to the Congress Transmitting Proposed Legislation on Child Protection and Obscenity Enforcement, November 10, 1987, APP.

A new assertion of presidential power: Signing statements

During the transition period following Reagan's victory in 1980, Dick Cheney advised chief of staff-to-be James Baker about the need to restore the authority of the presidency vis-a-vis Congress. Attorney General Meese played a key role in implementing that recommendation by elevating the status of presidential signing statements as an instrument of executive power. Signing statements were not new. As defenders of both Presidents Reagan and George W. Bush pointed out, presidents had issued them since the early days of the republic. As one analyst pointed out, however, they had always been "a relatively benign and largely ceremonial practice," often basically self-congratulatory press releases. Meese transformed their status through the clever strategy of persuading West Publishing in 1986 to publish them as part of the legislative history of statutes. This change, which he announced to Reagan's Domestic Policy Council on July 7, 1986 and which was hailed as a "great step," gave them powerful new legal significance.[53]

The transformation of signing statements marked a new chapter in the ongoing struggle between presidents and Congress. President Nixon had tried to thwart Congress by impounding (that is, not spending) appropriated funds and asserting executive privilege. Meese in particular felt the administration faced a "permanent government syndrome" that included entrenched and implacably hostile Democrats in Congress, the federal bureaucracies, and the news media. Signing statements remained a relatively low-level controversy under Reagan, not attracting the resistance that broad claims of executive privilege would have. They exploded into controversy when President George W. Bush escalated their use into a far more systematic assertion of presidential power. Philip J. Cooper, a leading expert on the subject, argues that over time they came to be "a potent, and politically very dangerous, tool of presidential direct action." President Bill Clinton used them as well, indicating that Democratic presidents faced with a hostile Congress sought ways to preserve presidential power.[54]

Mindful of President Nixon's humiliating defeat in the Supreme Court over executive privilege, Reagan did not assert it very aggressively. But in one little-noticed move that had serious long-term implications, just a few days before leaving office in January 1989 he issued Executive Order 12667 asserting the power of presidents to direct the National Archives to withhold documents of *former* presidents and also to consider requests by former presidents that documents be withheld from release. The order struck directly at the 1978 Presidential Records Act, which was passed in response to Nixon's attempt to withhold all of his presidential records and threatened to drop a veil of secrecy of unknown dimensions over the presidency. President George W. Bush extended its reach in a 2001 executive order, but a Supreme Court decision threw out the key provisions, and President Barack Obama revoked it by executive order in one of his first acts in office.[55]

[53] Cheney to Baker: Hayes, *Cheney*, pp. 161–3. "Great Step": T. Kenneth Krip to the President, Domestic Affairs Weekly Report, May 29, 1987, Christopher Cox Files, Box 2, RRPL. Meese to Domestic Policy Council, Administration Policy on Signing Statements," July 7, 1986, ibid., Box 3, RRPL.

[54] Meese statements: Meese, *With Reagan*, pp. 87–8, 119, 316, 322. Cooper, *By Order of the President*, p. 230. Phillip J. Cooper, *By Order of the President: The Use and Abuse of Executive Direct Action* (Lawrence: University of Kansas Press, 2002), pp. 201–2. Cooper places signing statements in the context of all forms of presidential power.

[55] Executive Order 12667, Presidential Records, January 18, 1989, APP. Executive Order 13233, Presidential Records, Further Implementation of the Presidential Records Act, November 1, 2001, APP. Obama: Executive Order 13489, Presidential Records, January 21, 2009, APP.

STORMING THE WALL OF SEPARATION

At a candle-lighting ceremony in the White House to promote prayer in school on September 25, 1982, President Reagan decried the "relentless drive to eliminate God from our schools." Through "twisted logic," he argued, the courts had turned the establishment clause on its head and infringed on "the freedom of those who choose to pray." He urged Congress immediately to approve the pending constitutional amendment permitting voluntary prayers.[56]

Beholden to the Religious Right, the Reagan administration was the most aggressively proreligion administration in modern American history, promoting a constitutional amendment permitting school prayer and vouchers for private and parochial school students and implementing religiously oriented programs on sexuality. As he did with other issues, Reagan framed religion in a way that had broad appeal. Unlike the fire-breathing leaders of the Religious Right, who alienated many people with statements such as Falwell's declaration that God does not hear the prayers of Jews, he posed as the genial voice of tolerance, casting the advocates of separation of church and state as the intolerant ones for refusing to respect religious belief. He invoked John F. Kennedy's 1960 campaign speech to the Houston ministers, emphasizing protection for free exercise of religion, while glossing over Kennedy's strong message on separation of church and state. The major goal for religious conservatives was a constitutional amendment to overturn the 1962 Supreme Court decision in *Engel v. Vitale* and allow prayer in public schools. Religious forces had been advocating an amendment ever since that decision, but none of the literally hundreds of proposed amendments had ever come close to serious consideration by Congress. Civil libertarians worried in early 1981 that an amendment might pass, given Reagan's popularity, the strength of the Religious Right, and Republican control of the Senate.[57]

A curious thing happened, however. A school prayer amendment not only never passed the Senate but had difficulty even getting a floor vote. Senator Jesse Helms began hearings in 1981, but the issue soon stalled. The key factor was President Reagan's lack of commitment to it. According to one historian, "for the most part [he] stayed out of the political fight." As was the case with the antiabortion amendment, he gave it lip service but put no real energy into it. The *New York Times* reported in September 1982 that he was "neutral" on the issue and was taking "no position" on a bill to strip the Supreme Court of jurisdiction over school prayer cases. Frustrated Religious Right leaders desperately tried to prod the White House. In a thinly veiled criticism, the Prayer Project warned that the amendment would fail "<u>unless we have the full and active support on [*sic*] the President, White House Congressional Liaison and Republican leadership in the House</u>" [underline in the original]. The Senate fell six votes short on a bill to end a liberal filibuster on the bill, and with that the antiprayer drive died.[58]

56 Remarks at a Candle-Lighting Ceremony for Prayer in Schools, September 25, 1982, APP.

57 Remarks at an Ecumenical Prayer Breakfast in Dallas, Texas, August 23, 1984, APP. U.S. Senate, Subcommittee on the Constitution of the Committee on the Judiciary, Constitutional Amendment Relating to School Prayer, Hearings, 97th Cong., 1st Sess. (1986).

58 Gary Jarmin, Prayer Project, to Morton Blackwell, School Prayer Amendment Strategy in Congress, July 20, 1982, Meese Files, Box 34, RRPL. "Reagan Neutral on Bid to Curb Court on Prayer," *NYT*, September 9, 1982; "School Prayer Advocates Lose Third Vote in Senate," ibid., September 23, 1982.

Reagan was not really a very religious person, certainly not in the manner of Presidents Jimmy Carter and George W. Bush. Moreover, key White House aides such as James Baker and Michael Deaver were old school Republicans, pragmatists interested in cutting taxes, increasing defense spending, and fighting communism. Social conservatives such as Gary Bauer occupied lower-level agency positions, where they advanced religion through administrative policies but did not control administration policy on high-profile issues. Additionally, the alarmed separationist community, which overlapped with the prochoice movement, mobilized an effective response both in Congress and in the arena of public opinion. Thus, the Senate rejected a proposed constitutional amendment to allow silent prayer in 1984 by an overwhelming vote of 85 to 15. Even advocates of a less drastic amendment to permit voluntary vocal prayer conceded they were five to ten votes short of the sixty-six needed for a constitutional amendment.[59]

One attempt to get around the wall of separation regarding aid to religious schools involved public funds for "remedial" and "enrichment" courses on mathematics, art, or music. Many of these classes, however, were taught in non-public school buildings leased by the state, and although some steps were taken to eliminate religious symbols in classrooms (no crucifixes, for example, and a sign reading "public school classroom"), the school buildings had obvious religious symbols and labels. The Reagan Justice Department filed an amicus brief in a private suit that challenged such programs, but the Supreme Court disagreed and in a 5–4 decision and declared the program in violation of the establishment clause. It noted the "pervasively sectarian nature" of the schools that associated the schools with religion.[60]

The Reagan administration also promised to find a way to provide financial support for private religious schools. Long an issue for Catholics, it was now important to Protestant fundamentalists with their network of private schools. To circumvent the Supreme Court's prohibition on direct aid to private religious schools, proponents devised the idea of tuition tax credits for parents who sent their children to private schools. Reagan and the Republicans were not alone on this issue. In the 1976 presidential election campaign, Jimmy Carter told the Chief Administrators of Catholic Education that he was "firmly committed" to finding some "constitutionally acceptable" way of providing aid for the parents of private school children. In 1980, candidate Reagan reminded the Catholic group that Carter had betrayed his promise over a 1978 tuition tax credit bill and promised to deliver where Carter had failed.[61]

The prospects for tuition tax credits looked very promising in early 1981, with neoconservatives such as Senator Jesse Helms in key Senate positions. Justice Department and Treasury Department officials warned that it would violate the separation of church and state and likely be declared unconstitutional, but the administration forged ahead with the Educational Opportunity and Equity Act in early 1982. Within just a few months, however, it backed off, just as President Carter had. Having won its cherished tax cut law the

59 Haberman, "Into the Wilderness," 251. "Bid to Sanction School Prayers Killed in Senate," *NYT*, March 16, 1984.

60 *Grand Rapids School District v. Ball*, 473 U.S. 373 (1985). Edward Keynes with Randall K. Miller, *The Court vs. Congress: Prayer, Busing, and Abortion* (Durham, NC: Duke University Press, 1989), pp. 199–203.

61 Lawrence J. McAndrews, "Late and Never: Ronald Reagan and Tuition Tax Credits," *Journal of Church and State* 42 (2000): 467–83; (Carter) p. 467.

year before and now facing large federal budget deficits, the administration was wary of further reductions in federal tax revenues. The decision was yet another indication of the White House's ambivalence about the New Right's agenda, and it sealed the fate of the bill. Reagan submitted another tuition tax credit bill in early 1983, but it was eventually killed by a vote of 59–38 in the Senate. In the 1984 presidential campaign, he did not even include the issue among his six points for improving education and did not mention it in his 1985 State of the Union Address. In the end, tuition tax credits became an unfulfilled promise, trumped by Reagan's emphasis on cutting taxes.[62]

WAR ON CRIME – AND ON CIVIL LIBERTIES

In a famous offhand remark, Ed Meese said, "If a person is innocent of a crime, then he is not a suspect."[63] The comment perfectly captured the Reagan administration's Alice in Wonderland view of the rights of criminal suspects. Turning the basic principle of a presumption of innocence on its head, Meese and conservative ideologues reasoned that if you were a suspect you were presumptively guilty, while ignoring the fact that innocent people are in fact arrested and detained. Law abiding people, in short, did not have to worry about removing constitutional constraints on the police, which were always attacked as "technicalities".

The Reagan administration's war on crime was basically a war on civil liberties, particularly Supreme Court decisions on the rights of suspects. Wasting no time, Reagan's first attorney general, William French Smith, created a Task Force on Violent Crime, which recommended limiting the right to bail for "dangerous" criminals, abolishing the insanity defense, restricting habeas corpus appeals, and, most important, creating a "good faith" exception to the exclusionary rule regarding illegal searches. Conservatives had been attacking the exclusionary rule since the 1961 *Mapp v. Ohio* decision. The task force recommended a federal law admitting evidence where the police officer may have conducted an illegal search but had acted in "good faith." To bolster its case, the White House Office of Legal Counsel (OLC) sponsored a study purporting to show that numerous criminal cases were "lost" because of excluded evidence, allowing dangerous criminals to go free. Criminologists immediately pounced on the report and pointed out that it used an improper baseline. The percentage of criminal cases rejected for prosecution because of the exclusionary rule was 0.8 percent rather than the 4.8 percent claimed by the OLC report. Virtually all other studies of the rule had also concluded that it had a minimal impact on prosecution.[64] In the end, Congress passed no new federal law, although the increasingly conservative Supreme Court carved out exceptions to the exclusionary rule.

[62] "Reagan to Offer a Plan to Provide Tuition Tax Credit," *NYT* April 13, 1982. Address before a Joint Session of the Congress on the State of the Union, February 6, 1985, APP.

[63] "Verdict Now, Trial Later," *NYT*, October 8, 1985 (quoting original interview in *U.S. News and World Report*).

[64] Attorney General's Task Force on Violent Crime, *Final Report* (Washington, DC: Department of Justice, 1981). Samuel Walker, *Sense and Nonsense about Crime, Drugs, and Communities: A Policy Guide*, 7th ed. (Belmont, CA: Wadsworth, 2011), pp. 206–7. Office of Legal Policy, *Report to the Attorney General on the Search and Seizure Exclusionary Rule* (Washington, DC: Department of Justice, 1988). *The Effects of the Exclusionary Rule: A Study in California* (Washington, DC: Department of Justice, 1983). Analysis in Walker, *Sense and Nonsense about Crime, Drugs, and Communities*, pp. 99–104.

The Reagan administration skillfully hitched its assault on the rights of criminal suspects to the new and popular crime victims' rights movement. The movement spoke directly to public resentment that crime victims had been forgotten by the criminal justice system, a point with much truth to it. Beginning in the 1970s, every state enacted some form of crime victims legislation. Many programs were worthy and long overdue, with no implications for civil liberties, such as victim compensation programs, counseling of victims, and shelters for domestic abuse victims.[65]

Tapping into this movement, Reagan created the President's Task Force on Victims of Crime. Its 1982 report endorsed most of the worthy proposals for helping crime victims but also reiterated the anti-civil liberties proposals in the violent crime report. And as with that report, criminologists found no empirical evidence directly linking, for example, limiting the right to bail to helping crime victims. Regarding bail, for example, research consistently found that criminals released on bail committed later crimes at a fairly low rate. Nor was it possible to predict which ones would reoffend and which ones would not. In the end, several of the anti-civil libertarian crime policy ideas gained ground, but the crime victims movement was not a major factor in that development.[66]

ROLLING BACK CIVIL RIGHTS ENFORCEMENT

When Reagan took office, the civil rights community feared a drastic weakening of civil rights enforcement. The 1980 GOP platform paid homage to equal opportunity but opposed affirmative action plans that included quotas, declaring that "equal opportunity should not be jeopardized by bureaucratic regulations and decisions which rely on quotas, ratios, and numerical requirements to exclude some individuals in favor of others."[67] Reagan's support among disaffected Democrats, especially white blue-collar workers, lay in their belief that they were the victims of preferential programs for racial minorities and women and that this approach represented reverse discrimination. While public controversy swirled around the politically sensitive issue of quotas, the most important actions by the Reagan administration involved the quiet nonenforcement of civil rights laws, as critics of Ed Meese argued at the time of his nomination for attorney general.

Reagan harbored no racial prejudice and in his memoirs expressed bewilderment and anger over the "myth" that he was a "bigot." He cited a 1931 incident at Eureka College when he helped to secure housing for two African-American fellow football teammates who had been denied rooms at a hotel. (The incident parallels similar encounters with discrimination by Richard Nixon and Gerald Ford as college students in the 1930s.) As an Iowa sports broadcaster in the 1930s, moreover, he criticized racial segregation in Major League Baseball and in Hollywood he quit a country club that did not admit Jews. Nor did he ever voice any of the vicious anti-semitism that Richard Nixon had often expressed. But as with Nixon, Reagan never understood that his policies and not his personal attitudes

65 Walker, *Sense and Nonsense about Crime, Drugs, and Communities*, pp. 202–2.

66 *President's Task Force on Victims of Crime, Final Report* (Washington, DC: Dept. of Justice December 1982). U.S. Department of Justice, *Attorney General's Task Force on Violent Crime: Final Report* (Washington, DC: Department of Justice, 1981). Critique of both reports: Walker, *Sense and Nonsense about Crime, Drugs, and Community*, pp. 180–99, 203–6.

67 1980 GOP platform, APP. Nicholas Laham, *The Reagan Presidency and the Politics of Race: In Pursuit of Colorblind Justice and Limited Government* (Westport, CT: Praeger, 1998).

were the source of the criticisms on civil rights. His vocal opposition to both the 1964 Civil Rights Act and the 1965 Voting Rights Act haunted him, years after both laws had become broadly accepted. In a highly publicized 1966 incident, he angrily stormed out of an California African-American Republican conference when someone mentioned the 1964 Civil Rights Act. Slamming down his notes as he left, he said, "I resent the implication that there is any bigotry in my nature."[68]

Reagan finessed the race issue as he did school prayer by skillfully presenting himself as the voice of tolerance and fair play. Just as he posed as the heir to Franklin D. Roosevelt, the friend of the common man, he associated himself with the civil rights icons Dr. Martin Luther King, Jr., and Rosa Parks, a maneuver that gave civil rights leaders fits. He defined them as heroes because of their inspiring individual efforts, with no reference whatsoever to the civil disobedience and mass demonstrations that had been so instrumental in bringing about racial progress. The great battle for equality, Reagan argued, was largely won, and only "traces" of discrimination remained.[69]

Despite invoking King's image, however, Reagan initially objected to making Martin Luther King's birthday a national holiday. In the face of strong public pressure for creating the holiday by 1983, administration figures considered alternatives, such as an American Heroes approach or a Day of National Observance, which would dilute the tribute to King. Finally realizing it was a losing battle, Reagan did an "about-face," endorsed the King holiday, and signed the bill making it federal law in November 1983.[70]

Tax exemption for discrimination? The Bob Jones University controversy

The most difficult civil rights issue for the Reagan administration involved Bob Jones University and the question of tax exemptions for private universities that engaged in race discrimination. The Internal Revenue Service had begun denying them tax exemptions in the 1960s, and President Nixon expanded the policy. Conservative activists fought back and inserted into the 1980 GOP platform a promise to "halt the unconstitutional regulatory vendetta launched by Mr. Carter's IRS Commissioner against independent schools."[71]

Bob Jones University, a Christian institution in Greenville, South Carolina, began admitting African Americans in 1971 but prohibited interracial dating among students. Reagan took up the issue before he became president, in November 1978 attacking the IRS for threatening "the destruction of religious freedom itself." Once he was in office,

68 Reagan, *An American Life*, pp. 52, 401–2. Lou Cannon, "Reagan's Southern Stumble," *NYT*, November 18, 2007. Cannon, *Governor Reagan*, pp. 122, 142–3, 264–5. "Reagan's Exit Stirs Negro GOP Parley," *NYT*, March 7, 1966.

69 Denise M. Bostdorff and Steven R. Goldzwig, "History, Collective Memory, and the Appropriation of Martin Luther King, Jr.: Reagan's Rhetorical Legacy," *Presidential Studies Quarterly* 35 (December 2005): 661–90.

70 Mel Bradley to Meese, Option Paper, August 3, 1983, Meese Files, Box 11, RRPL. "Aides Assert Reagan May Shift to Support Holiday," *NYT*, August 7, 1983. Remarks on Signing the Bill Making the Birthday of Martin Luther King, Jr., a National Holiday, November 2, 1983, APP.

71 Mark Taylor Dalhouse, *An Island in the Lake of Fire: Bob Jones University, Fundamentalism, and the Separatist Movement* (Athens: University of Georgia Press, 1996). Haberman, "Into the Wilderness." Statement opposing the administration's shift: U.S. Civil Rights Commission, *Discriminatory Religious Schools and Tax Exempt Status* (Washington, DC: United States Commission on Civil Rights, 1982). Republican Party platform of 1980. July 15, 1980, APP.

however, his top aides fell into a bitter dispute over the issue. Treasury Secretary Donald Regan wanted to maintain the existing policy, but Bruce Fein, a neoconservative activist who was now an associate deputy attorney general, took up the cause of Bob Jones University. When the dispute reached Reagan's desk, he scrawled on a memo, "I think we should" end IRS regulation of religious schools. Characteristically detached from the details, he did not inquire into the legal and political implications of this position. Consequently, on January 8, 1982, when the Treasury and Justice Departments reversed IRS policy, the reaction was swift and embarrassing to Reagan. About two hundred Justice Department lawyers and staff members signed a letter of protest, and twenty lawyers resigned. An angry and confused Reagan confided to his Diary, "I'm burned up" by the media stories on the case.[72]

Under fire, Reagan retreated, claiming he was "unalterably opposed to racial discrimination in any form," and proposed legislation to authorize formally the original IRS policy, which would end the objection that the IRS was acting without legal authority. His sudden shift was a rude slap at the Christian Right, and Bob Jones III, president of the university, denounced Reagan as a "traitor to God's people." A challenge by the university reached the Supreme Court in late 1982, but in yet another shift that reflected its internal divisions, the administration's brief called IRS policy an "egregious offense to religious liberty." In May 1983 the Court upheld the IRS in an 8–1 decision. Flags at Bob Jones University flew at half mast in protest, and Jerry Falwell denounced the decision as an "attack on religious liberty."[73]

The affair further illuminated the Reagan administration's complex relationship with the Religious Right. He courted them, rode into office on their votes, but often abandoned them on high-profile issues. Nonetheless, they refused to attack him. Politically, they had nowhere else to go; they knew this, and Reagan knew it too. Some analysts have argued that Reagan's failures only convinced many Religious Right leaders that they needed a long-term strategy of building a stronger grassroots political movement. That strategy would bear fruit in George W. Bush's two election campaigns where evangelicals provided critical support.

Attacking the Voting Rights Law and the Legal Services Corporation

The leading civil rights controversy in 1982 involved extension of the 1965 Voting Rights Law. The law had transformed southern politics, helping to elect innumerable African Americans to state and local offices. Civil rights leaders were understandably alarmed, then, when President Reagan in June 1981 asked Attorney General Smith for a comprehensive review of the law. Michael Uhlman, in the Office of Policy Development, told Meese in a characteristic neoconservative outburst that the "effects test," which the administration wanted to replace with the much stronger "intent test," "will invite litigation" and "tempt a Democrat-dominated federal bench to "redraw" the "political map." Activist

72 "200 in U.S. Agency Criticize Decision on Tax Exemptions," *NYT*, February 3, 1982. Reagan, *Reagan Diaries*, January 12, 1982, p. 62. Cannon, *The Role of a Lifetime*, pp. 521–2. On the reversal by the solicitor general, see Clayton, *The Politics of Justice*, pp. 55–6.

73 *Bob Jones University v. United States*, 461 U.S. 574 (1983). Roberts to Fred Fielding, January 4, 1984, Roberts Files, Box 6, RRPL.

judges, he warned, might claim they were supporting civil rights, but the real issue was "raw political power." The administration, however, quickly found that the law had broad political support, as had *Brown v. Board of Education.* Not renewing or even seriously limiting it would mean serious political trouble. The American Bar Association and other prestigious organizations joined the call to extend the law.[74]

Conservative ideologues in the administration argued for a more limited attack on the law, focusing on certain provisions, specifically Section 5 requiring local jurisdictions to "preclear" with the Justice Department any proposed changes in voting procedures that might "dilute" the African-American vote. Attorney General Smith told the Senate that ending preclearances was appropriate for jurisdictions that had "indeed removed past [discriminatory] practices." In the end, led by the liberal stalwart Senator Ted Kennedy, civil rights forces soundly rebuffed the Reagan administration, preserving the preclearance requirement and strengthening Section 2 to incorporate the results test. By very wide margins in both houses, Congress reauthorized the law for another twenty-five years. The battle, however, poisoned relations between the administration and the civil rights establishment. For the ceremony when Reagan signed the extension of the law extension, the administration pointedly did not invite Jesse Jackson and Coretta Scott King because they had "opposed virtually every initiative undertaken by this Administration."[75]

In a direct attack on low-income people, the Reagan administration set out to abolish the Legal Services Corporation (LSC). Created by Congress in 1974, the LSC grew out of 1960s War on Poverty programs that provided free legal services to the poor on such mundane issues as housing or credit problems. Conservatives hated the LSC because it often represented clients challenging landlords or other business interests. Reagan had a special animus against legal services from his days as California governor. In 1970 he had urged an end to all federal funding for legal services and vetoed one $1.8 million grant for the California Rural Legal Assistance (CRLA), which he deeply hated and accused of various misconduct. The government, he argued, should not fund "attempts to enforce a judicial resolution of political and public policy issues properly left to the electorate." A court eventually found his charges against CRLA unfounded.[76]

Reagan in 1981 proposed defunding LSC altogether. The agency, however, had strong political support, just as the Voting Rights Act did, and its allies rallied to its defense. The American Bar Association president, Reece Smith, organized a "March on Washington" that sent two hundred prominent lawyers to Washington to lobby for it. In the end, LSC survived, but greatly weakened. Congress reauthorized it in late 1981 with a 25 percent budget cut, a prohibition on lobbying by LSC staff, and a ban on class action suits. The latter was a particularly grievous setback, as advocates for the poor argued that class action

[74] Uhlman to Meese, October 16, 1981, Meese Files, Box 19, RRPL. Laughlin McDonald, *A Voting Rights Odyssey: Black Enfranchisement in Georgia* (New York: Cambridge University Press, 2003), pp. 174–81.

[75] Smith: *Extension of the Voting Rights Act*, Hearings, Subcommittee on Civil and Constitutional Rights of the Committee on the Judiciary, House of Representatives, 97th Cong., 1st Sess. (Washington, DC: Government Printing Office, 1982), pp. 66–72. Alexander Keyssar, *The Right to Vote: The Contested History of Democracy in the United States* (New York: Basic Books, 2000), pp. 287–93. Elizabeth Dole to Meese, Baker and Deaver, June 23, 1982, Meese Files, Box 31, RRPL.

[76] Kenneth F. Boehm and Peter T. Flaherty, *Why the Legal Services Corporation Must Be Abolished* (Washington, DC: Heritage Foundation, October 19, 1995). Reagan quote: "One More Narrow Escape," *Time*, November 23, 1981. A highly critical report on CLRA for Governor Reagan alleging "non-compliance," conduct unbecoming an attorney, "harassing and frivolous actions, and other abuses": California Office of Economic Opportunity, A Study and Evaluation of California Rural Legal Assistance, Inc. (1971), Gubernatorial Papers, Reports, RRPL.

suits were the most effective means of ending practices that affected large numbers of poor people. In another attack, Reagan sought to replace all the directors of the LSC. One of them was Hillary Rodham, wife of the future president Bill Clinton. She and her colleagues sued to keep their positions but lost. Reagan then appointed conservative directors.[77]

A weak record on racial minority appointments

The Reagan biographer Lou Cannon observes that as president Reagan was almost completely isolated from African Americans. In a dramatic reversal from the Carter administration, no African Americans held high-ranking positions in his administration. Secretary of Housing and Urban Development Samuel Pierce was an African American who served through both terms, but he was never an influential member of the administration, and in one publicized incident, Reagan did not even recognize him at a reception.[78]

Cannon's point was even more relevant to Reagan's appointments at the subcabinet level. A highly critical U.S. Civil Rights Commission report in 1983 contrasted his record with the "apparently unprecedented levels of women and minority men appointed by President Carter." Reagan's appointments to 980 top-level positions included only 8.2 percent minorities and 8 percent women, compared to Carter's record of 17 percent and 12 percent, respectively. The decline in diversity was particularly sharp at the Justice Department, an agency of particular concern to civil rights leaders, where racial minorities declined from 25 percent under Carter to only 5.3 percent under Reagan. The change was also great in the federal judiciary. Only 2.5 percent of Reagan's judicial appointments were African American, compared with 16 percent by Carter. The Civil Rights Commission concluded that it was "disappointed and concerned" about the administration's record.[79]

Reagan's most consequential African-American appointment was Clarence Thomas, who served first as assistant secretary for civil rights in the Department of Education and then as chair of the Equal Employment Opportunity Commission (where he opposed affirmative action). These positions built Thomas's resume and led to an appointment to the U.S. Supreme Court by President George H. W. Bush in 1991. Thomas was so conservative on race issues that civil rights leaders vehemently opposed his nomination to the Court.[80]

IRAN-CONTRA: THE ISSUE OF PRESIDENTIAL POWER RETURNS

Watergate replay, or Bush/Cheney prelude?

In televised congressional testimony in July 1987, Lt. Colonel Oliver North, heretofore an obscure member of the president's National Security Council, dramatically turned the tables on his inquisitors. Many liberals expected the hearings to be a replay

[77] *McCalpin v. Durant*, 247 US App.D.C. 45 (June 25, 1985); 766 F.2d 535.

[78] Cannon, *The Role of a Lifetime*, p. 521.

[79] U.S. Commission on Civil Rights, *Equal Opportunity in Presidential Appointments* (Washington, DC: Government Printing Office, 1983).

[80] Ken Foskett, *Judging Thomas: The Life and Times of Clarence Thomas* (New York: Morrow, 2004).

of Watergate: an exposé of secret illegal presidential actions that might even end with the president's removal. North, however, postured as a patriot defending national security and emerged as a conservative hero. North opened his testimony with a statement that became a virtual mantra in the new era of international terrorism: "I think it is very important for the American people to understand that this is a dangerous world."[81]

The hearings were an inquiry into the Iran-Contra scandal, a complex multifaceted scheme that included secretly selling military arms to Iran, in violation of federal law; secretly negotiating over the release of American hostages held in Lebanon, in violation of a long-standing pledge not to negotiate with terrorists; and using profits from the Iran arms sales to supply arms secretly to the rebel contras in Nicaragua, in violation of a specific congressional ban on such aid.[82] The scandal erupted in November 1986 and dominated the last two years of the Reagan administration, almost obscuring all other issues and exposing to withering public scrutiny Reagan's evident lack of knowledge about crucial administration actions. The affair triggered three separate investigations: the President's Tower Commission, chaired by Senator John Tower; a congressional investigation; and Special Prosecutor Lawrence Walsh's independent investigation. In the end, eleven administration officials were convicted of crimes related to the affair. President Reagan, however, emerged with his image only temporarily damaged.

The origins of the scandal lay in Reagan's determination to unleash the CIA and roll back international communism. Anti-communism was one of Reagan's longest-standing passions. He was a cold warrior of the old school (meaning the 1950s), seeing the Soviet Union as a great evil and the source of trouble all around the world. His neoconservative allies disdained President Jimmy Carter's emphasis on human rights in foreign policy. The Reagan aide Elliott Abrams, convicted for his role in the Iran-Contra scandal, explained that "the center of any human rights policy was going to be anti-communism."[83]

To lead the fight against international communism, Reagan chose William J. Casey to head the CIA. Casey was possibly even more old school than Reagan, having served in the Office of Strategic Services (OSS), predecessor to the CIA, during World War II. He fondly remembered those freewheeling days, when they operated with a complete absence of congressional oversight or media scrutiny, keeping a signed portrait of the OSS director William Donovan in his office. This experience put him squarely at odds with the post-Watergate standards of congressional oversight and closer media scrutiny of the CIA. He only invited trouble by voicing his contempt for Congress and its inquiring committees. As the CIA veteran Dewey Clarridge characterized it, Casey "had a lot of contempt ... for the Congressional bodies." At the Senate hearings on his nomination as director of the CIA, Casey was asked about reports that he planned to "unleash" the agency. He denied any such plans, told the committee that his agenda only involved "increasing the ability" of the agency to fulfill its responsibilities, and assured it that he would "comply fully with the spirit and the letter" of the congressional oversight process. The Senate confirmed him by a 95–0 vote. As events would prove, Casey lied. He did unleash the CIA, persuaded

[81] Oliver L. North, *Taking the Stand: The Testimony of Lieutenant Colonel Oliver L. North* (New York: Pocket Books, 1987).

[82] Theodore Draper, *A Very Thin Line: The Iran-Contra Affairs* (New York: Hill & Wang, 1991). Jane Mayer and Doyle McManus, *Landslide: The Unmaking of the President, 1984–1988* (Boston: Houghton Mifflin, 1988).

[83] Abrams: Strober and Strober, *Reagan: The Man and His Presidency*, p. 331.

President Reagan to loosen controls over the agency, and lied to or misled Congress on several occasions.[84]

Casey believed the Soviet Union was responsible for conflicts in Afghanistan, Cuba, Angola, and other trouble spots. As with most cold warriors, he refused to see conflicts as civil wars or nationalist uprisings. America's role in the world, moreover, was to keep the pressure on the Soviet Union by supporting anti-communist efforts anywhere and everywhere, regardless of whom it might entail as an ally. President Reagan agreed completely and eagerly accepted Casey's first major National Intelligence Estimate on "Soviet Support for International Terrorism." Covert action, Casey believed, was the best way to thwart Soviet activities around the world. President Carter had authorized CIA support for the mujahideen fighting Soviet occupation of Afghanistan, and Casey said, "This is the kind of thing we should be doing – only more." And more he did. On March 9, 1981, Reagan signed a presidential finding approving covert actions in Afghanistan, Cambodia, Granada, Cuba, Iran, Laos, Libya, and Nicaragua. Casey's initiatives had two disastrous results. First, they led to the Iran-Contra scandal; second, some of the mujahideen based in Pakistan became radical Islamists and eventually turned their anger toward the United States. One of them was a wealthy Saudi Arabian named Osama bin Laden.[85]

Reagan and Casey took advantage of the waning post-Vietnam belief in restraint in international affairs among the public and in Congress. It helped that the Senate Intelligence Committee was now chaired by the Republican Barry Goldwater, who had voted against creating the committee in the first place and now candidly said, "I don't believe in the Congress knowing too much intelligence." It was an attitude straight from the 1950s.[86]

One of the most remarkable aspects of Casey's tenure at the CIA was the number of experienced officials who at some point called him unfit for the job. Alexander Haig, Secretary of State under Reagan, challenged some of his covert action ideas, personally arguing with him that covert action should be "ancillary" to American foreign policy and not a dominant element. George Shultz, who followed Haig in office, later said flatly that Casey had "too much of an agenda" as CIA director, and that it is a mistake for the agency "to have an agenda," as opposed to "produc[ing] intelligence." The former president Gerald Ford flatly called him "not qualified," and the future president George H. W. Bush (himself CIA director for one year) thought he was an "inappropriate choice." Robert Gates, future head of the agency and secretary of defense, said he was "guilty of contempt of Congress from the day he was sworn in." When Shultz said, "I was mad at him at the end," it was because Casey had cut him and the State Department out of decision making on certain policies, notably Iran-Contra.[87]

Casey's appointment again raised the question of whether close political aides should be appointed attorney general or the head such critical agencies as the CIA and the FBI.

[84] Joseph E. Persico, *Casey: The Lives and Secrets of William J. Casey: From the OSS to the CIA* (New York: Viking, 1990), p. 209. Clarridge: Strober and Strober, *Reagan: The Man and His Presidency*, p. 74. Senate Select Committee on Intelligence, Hearing, *Nomination of William J. Casey*, 97th Cong., 1st Sess., January 13, 1981. On Casey at the CIA: Tim Weiner, *Legacy of Ashes: The History of the CIA* (New York: Doubleday, 2007), pp. 38–41.

[85] Persico, *Casey*, pp. 225, 264.

[86] Goldwater: Persico, *Casey*, p. 231.

[87] Criticisms in Weiner, *Legacy of Ashes*, pp. 376, 382. Haig criticisms: Persico, *Casey*, p. 273. Webster, OH, p. 44, MCPA.

He had been Reagan's campaign manager in the 1980 election, and neither one was about to question the other about a sensitive operation. In fact, they were too much alike in their views about America's role in the world.[88]

Immediately after being confirmed, Casey made a series of missteps that revealed his plans for unleashing the CIA. In early March 1981 someone leaked a draft of a White House proposal to allow CIA eavesdropping within the United States, causing a major uproar. Even Senator Daniel Moynihan, a member of the Intelligence Committee and strong Casey supporter, called the proposal "off the wall," and the administration quickly abandoned it. Two months later Casey proposed a law to allow the FBI to conduct "surprise" (that is, warrantless) searches of news media offices when they suspected plans to publish the names of covert CIA agents or other "sources of operational assistance." Predictably, the press expressed outrage at this threat to the First and Fourth Amendments, and Casey again backed off. Casey did succeed, however, in getting a new law making it a crime to disclose the names of covert CIA operatives. His other priority, exempting CIA operational files from the Freedom of Information Act, ran into significant opposition, but with President Reagan's support he got much of what he wanted. Total federal intelligence spending (including not just the CIA) increased by an estimated 125 percent between 1980 and 1989.[89]

Despite his initial blunders, Casey took charge of the CIA and bent it and American foreign policy to his will. When CIA analysts provided intelligence reports he did not like, he simply rewrote them. At his demand, Reagan gave him cabinet standing, the first CIA director to enjoy that status. He immediately dominated the National Security Planning Group and won approval for covert actions in Nicaragua, other Central American countries, Cuba, and several parts of Africa. (It was in the midst of a covert operation in Chad that Oliver North famously said, "Fuck the Congress.") To wound the Soviet Union, the CIA lavishly and uncritically funded the mujahideen fighting Soviet occupying forces in Afghanistan. Some of these individuals later became anti-American terrorists.[90]

Projecting American power and asserting presidential authority

On two occasions President Reagan used American military forces in ways that demonstrated both his eagerness to project American power around the world and the impotence of the 1973 War Powers Act in controlling presidential power. In the first and more controversial incident, Reagan sent U.S. marines to Lebanon in 1982 to join a multinational force seeking to resolve the civil war there. After some initial success, they withdrew, but Reagan sent them back a second time at the request of the Lebanese government. His unilateral decision to send troops raised the question of whether he violated the War Powers Act. The administration replied that the marines would not be engaged in "hostilities" as defined by the law. Events soon shattered this optimistic expectation, and marines became involved in shooting incidents. Disaster struck on October 23, 1983,

88 Casey as Reagan campaign manager: Persico, *Casey*, pp. 172–206.

89 "Intelligence Groups Seek Power to Gain Data on U.S. Citizens," *NYT*, March 10, 1981; "C.I.A. Aide Reassures Senate Panel," ibid., March 14, 1981. Persico, *Casey*, pp. 223–4. "C.I.A. Seeks Law for Surprise Searches of Newsrooms," *NYT*, May 9, 1981.

90 Weiner, *Legacy of Ashes*, pp. 376–7. Steve Coll, *Ghost Wars: The Secret History of the CIA, and bin Laden, From the Soviet Invasion to September 10, 2001* (New York: Penguin Books, 2005).

when a devastating bomb killed 241 marine and navy personnel. It was the largest number of marines killed on a single day since the bloody attack on Iwo Jima in World War II. Congress had approved a Lebanon reauthorization eleven days earlier, placing an eighteen-month limit on the use of troops. Reagan signed it but in words that anticipated the Bush administration twenty years later, declared that he did not "cede" any of his authority as commander in chief and explicitly denied that Congress could pass any law that would "impermissibly infringe" on a president's constitutional authority in this area. The American forces were removed in February 1984, but the underlying issue of presidential war power remained.[91]

In a second incident, Reagan on October 25, 1983, ordered seven thousand American troops to the island of Granada to protect Americans living there, including eight hundred medical students, and also because the CIA had reported communist activity on the island. Reagan summoned congressional leaders to the White House the night before troops were dispatched. Some complained that this did not allow sufficient time for proper consultation under the War Powers Act, but the law only required notification and not prior consultation. The U.S. forces were withdrawn on December 15, before the sixty-day deadline for an authorizing congressional resolution or declaration of war.[92]

These and other incidents clearly demonstrated that the 1973 War Powers Act was useless in preventing presidents from sending troops overseas. Subsequent presidents and their advisers understood the lessons very well. Bill Clinton sent troops into harm's way on several occasions, as did George W. Bush, and Barack Obama engaged U.S. forces in Libya in 2011, arguing that they were not engaged in hostilities, the same argument that Reagan had used.

Rolling back new controls over the intelligence agencies

At the Senate hearings on the Intelligence Reform Act on 1981, Senator Barry Goldwater expressed the contempt of conservatives for the post-Watergate controls over the intelligence agencies. "We have made ourselves the most public secret intelligence service in the world," he complained, adding that "this has to be stopped."[93]

In early 1984 a CIA covert action burst into public view and exposed the weakness of the new congressional oversight process. As part of the administration's crusade against the leftist Nicaraguan government, the CIA secretly planted mines in that nation's harbors. In March alone, seven vessels struck the mines, including ships from Japan and the Soviet Union. On March 8, Casey gave a two-and-a-half-hour briefing to the Senate Intelligence Committee. In one twenty-five-word sentence he referred to "magnetic mines" in three Nicaraguan harbors. The sentence was buried amid a list of other actions in such a way that a listener might easily think the mines were placed by the Nicaraguan

[91] David Locke Hall, *The Reagan Wars: A Constitutional Perspective on War Powers and the Presidency* (Boulder, CO: Westview Press, 1991). Statement on Signing the Multinational Force in Lebanon Resolution, October 12, 1983, APP. President Barack Obama also used the "not engaged in hostilities" argument in 2011 to argue that U.S. operations in Libya did not implicate the War Powers Act (see Chapter 15 of this book).

[92] Hall, *The Reagan Wars*, pp. 167–209.

[93] Senate Select Committee on Intelligence, Hearing, *Intelligence Reform Act of 1981*, July 21, 1981, 97th Cong., 1st Sess., p. 2.

Contras and not the CIA. The committee asked no questions about it, and Casey gave a similar one-sentence "briefing" to the House Intelligence Committee. Exactly one month later, Senator Goldwater was told the truth that the CIA had placed the mines. The staunch friend of the CIA exploded in anger and began to enter the information into the *Congressional Record*. That move was blocked, but the story immediately leaked to the press. Furious that he had not been properly briefed and feeling betrayed by Casey, whom he had supported so strongly, Goldwater fired off a stern letter of rebuke to the CIA director that ended with the pungent declaration "I am pissed off," a comment which only some newspapers printed.[94]

The episode quickly passed, but it dramatized the profound weakness of the congressional oversight process. Casey's March briefing occurred weeks if not months after the first mines had been planted. Moreover, the ambiguous one-sentence "briefing" hardly complied with the spirit of the law. Technically, the CIA had mentioned the mining on three separate occasions to congressional committees, in addition to individual senators and some Senate staff members. Casey certainly understood how his words could easily slip by busy senators. Senator Moynihan denounced Casey's actions as a "disinformation operation against our committee" and announced he was resigning from the Intelligence Committee. A contrite Casey apologized and talked him out of it.[95] The long-term result of the episode was that the CIA and future administrations learned that it was possible to manipulate the briefing process with hazy comments that technically complied with the law but did not provide meaningful detail.

"A neat idea": The Iran-Contra scandal begins

The Iran-Contra affair went wrong when Oliver North had a "neat idea." It began in October 1984 when President Reagan signed the second Boland Amendment barring any U.S. intelligence agency from assisting the contras, an anti-communist military opposition group in Nicaragua. Remembering Vietnam, Congress passed the Boland Amendment to assert its authority over foreign military operations. There were actually two Boland Amendments, the second broader in scope than the first, but with some ambiguity over what each required. Reagan signed both but promptly violated them. Casey and administration hard-liners were just as determined to reclaim presidential authority, had begun aiding the contras, and now sought ways to circumvent the law.[96]

At that very moment in an unrelated crisis, Reagan became very eager to secure the release of Americans (seven by late 1985) held hostage in Lebanon by Islamic militants. He was acutely aware of how the Iranian hostage crisis had damaged President Carter politically and was determined to free these hostages for this reason and also because he was genuinely moved by their fate. Several Mideast figures of dubious integrity surfaced and proposed a transfer of American arms to alleged "moderate" groups in Iran in exchange for the hostages. Such a deal would violate the long-standing American policy of not negotiating with terrorists, which Reagan had forcefully reiterated.

[94] Persico, *Casey*, pp. 371–8. "Pissed": "Explosion over Nicaragua," *Time*, April 23, 1984.

[95] Persico, *Casey*, pp. 377–8.

[96] Draper, *A Very Thin Line*, pp. 18, 23–5. *Report of the Congressional Committees Investigating the Iran-Contra Affair: With Supplemental, Minority, and Additional Views* (Washington, DC: Government Printing Office, 1987), pp. 343–6. "Moynihan to Quit Senate Panel Post in Dispute on C.I.A.," *NYT*, April 16, 1984.

American TOW missiles then began flowing to Iran through Israel. The CIA warned that the deal violated the arms export law, but Reagan on December 5, 1985, signed an official finding retroactively approving it. The finding also directed Casey not to inform Congress, another violation of the law. At a critical December 7, 1985, White House meeting, both Secretary of Defense Caspar Weinberger and Secretary of State George Shultz told him the arms deal was illegal and invited a host of other problems. Weinberger even wisecracked, "Visiting hours are Thursday," but Reagan was determined to free the hostages even at the (highly unlikely) risk of going to jail. "The American people," he replied, "will never forgive me if I fail to get those hostages out over this legal question."[97]

In the midst of these machinations, Oliver North came up with his "neat idea" of transferring surplus funds from the Iran arms deal to the Nicaraguan contras. Raising the price of arms in future deals would generate extra funds for both the contras and other future secret operations. Casey was excited because he had earlier mused about an off-the-books (and out of sight of Congress) source of funds for covert actions. In the Iran-Contra affair, this operation became known as The Enterprise. When the Iran-Contra affair was exposed, CIA director Casey, national security advisor John Poindexter, and Oliver North gave false testimony to Congress and began destroying an estimated five thousand documents. North called it a "shredding party." The affair raised questions about the role of the NSC. The Joint Congressional Committee later concluded that the NSC "was created to provide candid and comprehensive advice to the President" and not to conduct covert operations as it did in this instance.[98]

As the scandal unfolded, President Reagan gave a series of public statements that were alternatively vague, false, misleading, or mawkishly contrite. At a disastrous November 19, 1986, press conference horrified aides watched as Reagan made three statements that were not true and had to be immediately corrected. A week later, on November 25, after announcing that he had fired Oliver North and made other changes in his national security team, he abruptly ended the press briefing and turned it over to an unprepared Attorney General Meese. Reagan appointed the Tower Commission to investigate the affair, Congress created a joint Senate-House committee, and Meese appointed Lawrence Walsh as independent counsel to investigate possible criminal violations. For the moment, it looked like a Watergate deja vu.[99]

[97] December 7, 1985 meeting: Draper, *A Very Thin Line*, pp. 225–9. *Report of the Congressional Committees Investigating the Iran-Contra Affair*, pp. 139–244. Memoranda for Independent Counsel Lawrence Walsh in 1991 on the potential criminal liability of President Reagan and Vice President George H. W. Bush, and obtained under a FOIA request in 2011, found that Reagan knew in advance of each weapons shipment to Iran and the Bush knew about the mining of the harbors of Nicaragua. National Security Archive, *Iran Contra at 25: Reagan and Bush "Criminal Liability" Evaluations*, Electronic Briefing Book No. 365. www.gwu.edu/~NSAEBB365/index.htm.

[98] North, *Taking the Stand*. Oliver L. North with William Novak, *Under Fire: An American Story* (New York: HarperCollins, 1991). *Report of the Congressional Committees Investigating the Iran-Contra Affair*, p. 29; The Enterprise, pp. 289–317.

[99] The President's News Conference, November 19, 1986, APP. "Disarray Deepens," *NYT*, November 26, 1986. U.S. House of Representatives, Select Committee to Investigate Covert Arms Transactions with Iran, *Report of the Congressional Committees Investigating the IranContra Affair: With Supplemental Minority and Additional Views* (Washington, DC: Government Printing Office, 1987). Lawrence E. Walsh, *Iran-Contra: The Final Report* (New York: Times Books, 1994). [Tower Commission], *Report of the President's Special Review Board* (Washington, DC: Government Printing Office, 1987).

The congressional hearings were a disaster for Reagan's critics, as Oliver North successfully framed the issue in terms of protecting national security rather official misconduct. In the end, the Joint Congressional Committee's *Final Report* condemned the administration for "secrecy, deception, and disdain for law." In his memoirs, Reagan blandly insisted that "we were not trading arms for hostages, nor were we negotiating with terrorists," the facts of the case notwithstanding. The historian Theodore Draper, in the most thorough review of the affair pointed out that Congress did not examine its own failings in the events leading up to the scandal's discovery. The committee report claimed that "Congress was told almost nothing – and what it was told was false," but it did not discuss its failure to ask tough questions when being briefed. Oliver North later testified, "I didn't want to tell Congress anything"; he did not, and Congress did not press him. Elliott Abrams, convicted of two misdemeanors for withholding information, candidly explained the administration's tactic for dealing with Congress: unless Intelligence Committee members asked "exactly the right question, using exactly the right words, they weren't going to get the right answers."[100]

In a post mortem, the political scientist Loch Johnson, former staff member of the Church Committee, explained that the intelligence committees had largely failed in their "police patrol" function of providing continuous oversight and only roused themselves after the scandal broke for a "fire alarm" response. "Nothing is more important to effective oversight," he concluded, "than the will of individual lawmakers or executive overseers." That will was clearly lacking in the Iran-Contra scandal, as it would later regarding President George W. Bush's national security adventures.[101]

The Iran-contra scandal ended without any high drama similar to Watergate, although fourteen members of the administration were eventually indicted and eleven convicted for scandal-related crimes. Several had their convictions overturned on appeal, and on Christmas Eve 1992, a month before leaving office, President George H. W. Bush pardoned the former defense secretary Caspar Weinberger (two counts of perjury, one for obstruction of justice), Robert McFarlane (four misdemeanor counts of withholding information from Congress), and Elliott Abrams (two misdemeanor counts of withholding information), along with three others.[102]

The rise of Dick Cheney

The Iran-Contra affair was less a failed rerun of Watergate than a dress rehearsal for the far more serious abuses of presidential power under President George W. Bush fifteen years later. It was an ominous warning about the ability of an ideologically driven president to flout the law and the failure of the post-Watergate reforms in the face of a determined president.

[100] Reagan, *Ronald Reagan: An American Life*, p. 512. Draper, *A Very Thin Line*, pp. 596–7. *Report of the Congressional Committees*, pp, 21, 27, 31. Failure of Congressional investigation: Harold Hongju Koh, *The National Security Constitution: Sharing Power after the Iran-Contra Affair* (New Haven, CT: Yale University Press, 1990), particularly Ch. 1.

[101] Loch K. Johnson, "Governing in the Absence of Angels: On the Practice of Intelligence Accountability in the United States," pp. 57–78 (quote on p. 68), in Hans Born, Loch K. Johnson, and Ian Leigh, *Who's Watching the Spies? Establishing Intelligence Service Accountability* (Washington, DC: Potomac Books, 2005).

[102] Proclamation 6518 – Grant of Executive Clemency, December 24, 1992, APP.

In that regard, perhaps the most significant aspect of the affair was the Minority Report of the Joint Congressional Committee. Engineered by the Republican congressman Dick Cheney, it asserted an extreme view of presidential power in the area of foreign policy. While conceding that President Reagan and others made mistakes ("just that - mistakes in judgment and nothing more"), it accused Congress of "abuses of power and irresolution," which included "an aggrandizing theory of Congress' foreign policy powers" and an "ongoing state of political guerilla warfare over foreign policy" between Congress and the White House. Rejecting the Supreme Court justice Robert Jackson's influential opinion in the 1952 steel seizure case, which almost all observers regarded as the proper guide, the report flatly stated that Congress was "disabled" from passing laws (such as the Boland Amendment) that interfere with presidential power on foreign policy. The minority report was both a complete rejection of the post-Watergate controls over presidential power and the intelligence agencies and the clearest possible preview of Cheney's later role as vice president in the war on terrorism.[103]

The attack on unpopular ideas

Farley Mowat, the Canadian author of the best-selling book *Never Cry Wolf*, was denied a visa to enter the United States in 1985. The U.S. Immigration and Naturalization Service said he had been listed in a "lookout book" for "many, many years," and his case was covered by section 212A of the immigration law, which listed many grounds for denying entry, including anyone whose entry the secretary of state believed "would have potentially serious adverse foreign policy consequences" for the United States. Most observers believed he was denied a visa because he had protested U.S. cruise missile testing in Canada.[104]

Mowat was not the only well-known writer or activist denied entry to the United States by the Reagan administration. Hortensia Allende, widow of the assassinated president of Chile Salvadore Allende (the CIA was implicated in the coup), was also turned away. In a reversion to cold war era thinking, the Reagan administration made a concerted effort to deny visas to people espousing ideas it did not like. The administration ignored the 1978 McGovern Amendment which reversed the 1952 McCarran-Walter Act barring entry to people or ideas "prejudicial to the public interest." Lawsuits challenging the Reagan actions charged the government with violating the new law. The Supreme Court ruled against the administration in 1987, and in 1990 Senator Daniel Patrick Moynihan and Rep. Barney Frank sponsored an amendment that drastically limited the government's right to exclude people because of their views.[105]

And in the one major known violation of the post-Watergate restrictions on the FBI, the administration ordered the bureau to investigate CISPES (the Committee in Solidarity with the People of El Salvador) to determine whether it was directed by a foreign government. Reviving old cold war standards of guilt by association, the investigation went on for four years and covered legitimate First Amendment activities such as

103 *Report of the Congressional Committees Investigating the Iran Contra Affair*, p. 437.

104 "Author of 'Wolf' Book Barred," *NYT*, April 24, 1985. Farley Mowat, *My Discovery of America* (Boston: Atlantic Monthly Press, 1985).

105 James R. Edwards, Jr., *Keeping Extremists Out: The History of Ideological Exclusion, and the Need for Its Revival* (Washington, DC: Center for Immigration Studies, September 2005). ACLU, *Free Trade in Ideas: A Constitutional Imperative* (Washington, DC: Center for National Security Studies, May 1984). Jamie Kalven, "U.S. Visa Policy: The Machinery of Exclusion," *Bulletin of Atomic Scientists*, 43 (May 1987): 21–30.

a Washington demonstration against U.S. intervention in Central America and groups supporting CISPES. In 1988, the then-FBI director William Sessions conceded that the investigation had been an "aberration," and not standard bureau policy. Nonetheless, it became a model for investigations of alleged terrorist organizations in the years ahead.[106]

TRANSFORMING THE SUPREME COURT

It is the only instance when a Supreme Court nomination created a new verb in the English language. The hearings over President Reagan's nomination of Robert H. Bork in 1987 created the verb "to Bork," meaning to prevent someone from attaining an appointive office because of his or her background, character, or philosophy.[107]

President Nixon had promised to reorient the Supreme Court in a conservative "strict constructionist" direction, but the conservative revolution never fully materialized under Chief Justice Warren Burger. In fact, the Burger Court issued what is probably the most controversial decision of the late twentieth century with *Roe v. Wade*. On many other issues it upheld controversial Warren Court decisions and even broke new ground on women's rights. As the author Jeffrey Toobin put it, conservatives "could elect presidents, but they could not change the Court." The Reagan administration was determined to do what Nixon had not. Reagan himself had a vague notion of a nonactivist Court, but the crucial decisions were made by his conservative advisers, notably Ed Meese. In the selection of federal justices at all levels, one analyst concluded that with Meese the driving force, the Reagan administration was more preoccupied with the nominees' ideology than any since FDR.[108]

The retirement of Chief Justice Burger allowed Reagan to elevate Associate Justice William H. Rehnquist as his replacement. The nomination provoked a sharp ideological battle. Critics dredged up some of his early writings, including a 1952 memo he wrote as a clerk for Justice Robert Jackson arguing that *Plessy v. Ferguson* "was right and should be reaffirmed." Thirty years later, it was an embarrassing position. Rehnquist also wrote a 1957 article charging that a majority of justices on the Court were influenced by their left-wing clerks. The piece was an insult to some of the strongest-willed justices ever to serve on the Court. Rehnquist's voting record as associate justice warmed the hearts of conservatives. He was the justice least likely to overturn a law as violating the First Amendment, consistently favored weakening the wall of separation between church and state, and almost always favored the government over the rights of individuals. Despite the criticisms and the embarrassing old views, he was confirmed as chief justice by a vote of 65–33.[109]

106 "The FBI's Investigation of Central American Activists, 1981–1985," in David Cole and James X. Dempsey, *Terrorism and the Constitution* (New York: New Press, 2002), pp. 21–33.

107 William Safire, *Safire's New Political Dictionary: The Definitive Guide to the New Language of Politics* (New York: Random House, 1993), p. 76.

108 Toobin, *The Nine*, pp. 7, 17. Lincoln Caplan, "The Reagan Challenge to the Rule of Law," Sidney Blumenthal and Thomas Byrne Edsall, eds., *The Reagan Legacy* (New York: Pantheon, 1988), p. 231.

109 William Rehnquist, "A Random Thought on the Segregation Case" (1952), copy in Senate, Committee on the Judiciary, Hearings, Nomination of William H. Rehnquist and Lewis F. Powell, 92nd Cong., 1st Sess. (1971), p. 305. FBI: Tony Mauro, "Rehnquist FBI File Sheds New Light on Drug Dependence, Confirmation Battles," *Legal Times*, January 4, 2007.

The opportunity to move the Court in a conservative direction put the administration face to face with the question of exactly what it meant by "judicial activism," the standard conservative criticism of liberal Supreme Court decisions. A June 1986 memo asked, rhetorically, do we oppose judicial candidates "who embrace activism for conservative ends?" It concluded that "the only intellectually honest thing to do is to require that our candidate[s] renounce judicial activism, period." The point was well taken, but the administration ignored it and appointed justices who proved to be very activist in the pursuit of conservative ends.[110]

Overshadowed by the battle over Rehnquist was the nomination of Antonin Scalia to fill the seat vacated by Burger. Nomination fatigue undoubtedly explained the failure of Senate Democrats to mount any meaningful opposition, and the Senate unanimously confirmed Scalia, 98–0, with only five minutes of floor debate. He quickly became the most conservative justice on the Court (with the possible exception of Clarence Thomas, who joined the Court in 1991), an ideological firebrand on original intent and an unabashed activist in pursuit of conservative issues. Again and again he issued angry dissents criticizing his colleagues, which only isolated him on the Court and contrasted sharply with O'Connor's coalition building.[111]

The battle over Bork, 1987

Struggle over the future of the Supreme Court reached its peak in a titanic battle over the nomination of Robert H. Bork in summer 1987. The fight shaped the nomination process for the next two decades. Within hours of his nomination, Senator Ted Kennedy denounced Bork for opposing abortion and civil rights, conjuring up images of back alley abortions and racially segregated lunch counters. A coalition of civil rights, prochoice, and feminist groups quickly launched the most highly organized campaign against a Court nominee in history.[112]

Bork had indeed taken controversial positions on a number of issues and was a founder of the original intent philosophy, which was a clear threat to *Roe v. Wade,* and possibly even to *Brown v. Board of Education.* (In an angry book written after his rejection, he wrote that the landmark ruling was a "great and correct" decision but based on weak reasoning.) Bork's record gave his opponents much to feast on. A 1963 article in the *New Republic* questioned the constitutionality of parts of President Kennedy's civil rights bill, a position that set him apart from the national consensus on civil rights even then. Although Bork later said, "I no longer agree with that article," it now returned to haunt him and was probably more widely read in 1987 than it had been in 1963. Watergate also shadowed Bork. As the acting attorney general after both Attorney General Elliott Richardson and Deputy Attorney General William Ruckelshaus resigned when they refused to fire Special Prosecutor Archibald Cox, Bork carried out Nixon's order and fired Cox.[113]

110 Peter J. Wallinson, untitled memo circa June, 1986, Wallinson Files, Box 3, RRPL.

111 Richard A. Brisbin, Jr., *Justice Antonin Scalia and the Conservative Revival* (Baltimore: Johns Hopkins University Press, 1997). Henry J. Abraham, *Justices, Presidents, and Senators: A History of the U.S. Supreme Court Appointments from Washington to Bush II,* 5th ed. (Lanham, MD: Rowman & Littlefield, 2008), pp. 277–9.

112 Michael Pertschuk and Wendy Schaetzel, *The People Rising: The Campaign against the Bork Nomination,* Pbk. ed. (New York: Thunder's Mouth Press, 1989).

113 Robert H. Bork, *The Tempting of America: The Political Seduction of the Law* (New York: Free Press, 1990), Chs. 7, 8. A spirited rebuttal is Leonard W. Levy, *Original Intent and the Framer's Constitution* (New York Macmillan,

The Senate confirmation hearings over Bork became a televised national drama, drawing a higher level of public attention than any previous Court nomination. Finally, on October 23, the Senate rejected him by a vote of 42–58. Reagan then nominated justice Anthony M. Kennedy, who was confirmed with little controversy. As with Scalia's nomination, the Senate appeared to be too exhausted to wage another fight. Kennedy proved to be a very conservative justice on most issues and after Justice O'Connor's retirement in 2006 became even more consistently so.[114]

The epic struggle over Bork left a lasting legacy. It politicized judicial nominations as never before and shaped almost every subsequent Supreme Court nomination. Nominees went to great length to avoid answering direct questions about particular issues, particularly *Roe v. Wade*. Hearings became a charade, with nominees answering pointed questions with vague generalities that said nothing.[115] In the end, Reagan's appointments moved the Supreme Court sharply in a conservative direction. Scalia was the most conservative justice to serve in decades. Anthony Kennedy was also very conservative, although with occasional exceptions. Rehnquist was a far more conservative chief justice than Warren Burger had been. Only O'Connor's appointment was ideologically ambiguous. She broke the gender barrier on the Court, and while conservative on most issues, she preserved *Roe* and was a moderating force on other issues as well. All told, Reagan reshaped the Court in a way that President Nixon had promised but failed to do.

THE FIRST GEORGE BUSH

"A card-carrying member of the ACLU"

The GOP presidential candidate George H. W. Bush attacked his opponent as a "card-carrying member of the ACLU." For the first time in presidential history, the ACLU itself became a campaign issue, and civil liberties was reduced to three distorted and inflammatory issues: the American flag (both not saluting it and burning it), child pornography, and predatory criminals. The attack generated considerable attention, throwing the Democratic candidate Michael Dukakis on the defensive, from which he never recovered.[116]

Dukakis had indeed been a member of the ACLU and as Bush supporters pointed out had previously mentioned it himself. The attack succeeded in part because he failed to

1988). The most illuminating historical treatment is Jack N. Rakove, *Original Meanings: Politics and Ideas in the Making of the Constitution* (New York: Knopf, 1997). Robert Bork, "Civil Rights: A Challenge," *The New Republic* 149 (August 31, 1963): 80 (and Bork's explanation in *The Tempting of America*, pp. 80–1). "No longer agree": White House Talking Points [re Bork], n.d., Duberstein Files, Box 3, RRPL. Norman Vieria and Leonard Gross, *Supreme Court Appointments: Judge Bork and the Politicization of Senate Confirmations* (Carbondale: Southern Illinois University Press, 1998).

114 Ralph E. Shaffer, ed., *The Bork Hearings: Highlights from the Most Controversial Judicial Confirmation Battle in U.S. History* (Princeton, NJ: Markus Wiener Publishers, 2005). Vieira and Gross, *Supreme Court Appointments: Judge Bork and the Politicization of Senate Confirmations*. Bork's own bitter account: Bork, *The Tempting of America*, pp. 267–349.

115 Vieria and Gross, *Supreme Court Appointments*, pp. 247–54.

116 "Patriotism and the Pledge," *NYT*, August 27, 1988. "Bush Turns Heat on 'Liberal' Rival," ibid., August 27, 1988. Anthony Lewis, "On Civil Liberty," ibid., September 1, 1988. The Bush campaign team discovered that the ACLU was a hot button issue in focus groups in May: Haynes Johnson, *Sleepwalking through History*, pp. 395–6. David R. Runkel, ed., *Campaign for President: The Managers Look at '88* (Dover, MA: Auburn House, 1989), p. 286. Samuel Walker, *In Defense of American Liberties: A History of the ACLU* (New York: Oxford University Press, 1990), pp. 368–71.

respond with a positive affirmation of what civil liberties meant to him, never mentioning freedom of speech and press, equality, or privacy. Nor did he mention the number of times the ACLU of Massachusetts had sued him as governor of Massachusetts. Garry Wills, an astute commentator on American society, suggested that "Dukakis should have appeared with [ACLU] officers ... and joked about all the times they disagreed in the past, while asserting what makes America great is the preservation of free discussion and advocacy."[117] He did not, and his silence harmed his campaign and tainted the ACLU and civil liberties principles.

Bush also scored points against Dukakis over the case of Willie Horton. While serving a life sentence for murder in Massachusetts, Horton was released under a weekend furlough program and then committed a robbery and a rape. Bush exploited the case to label Dukakis "soft" on crime. The fact that Horton was African American and the rape victim white, meanwhile, added an incendiary racial dimension to the controversy. As with the ACLU issue, however, Dukakis failed to respond, for example by pointing out that furloughs were routine across the country or mentioning the very low failure rate), and the charge stuck.[118]

A Cynical Conservative

The first President George Bush famously suffered from a lack of what he himself called "the vision thing." More than any other Republican president or candidate in the modern era, George H. W. Bush was a thoroughly cynical conservative who altered his views to gain higher office. He entered politics in the 1960s as a moderate conservative, with liberal views on some issues. In 1980, he completely capitulated to the New Right to become Reagan's vice president. Despite a glittering resume (member of the House, Republican Party chair, CIA director), he lacked a clear political identity. In a 1988 interview he even conceded, "But ideas? I'm not what you would call your basic intellectual."[119]

To appease Texas conservatives in his first run for Congress in 1964, Bush opposed the Civil Rights Act, calling the public accommodation section "unconstitutional." The law, he said, was designed to protect 14 percent of the population, but he was concerned about the "other eighty-six percent." By 1968, however, he had a change of heart and as a member of the House supported the federal fair housing act, even though "almost all of my constituents were opposed to it." In a letter to a constituent, he explained that "the problem of discrimination troubled me deeply. I became particularly passionate on the issue after my tour in Vietnam where I saw young black soldiers fighting and dying, for love of their country while affluent white kids ran away or got deferred." It was a thoughtful observation, one that many opponents of the war expressed. His vote prompted a death threat in April 1968, and a week later he was booed at an angry

117 Garry Wills, "Introduction," in Editors of Time, *The Winning of the White House 1988* (New York: Time, 1988), p. 11.

118 Johnson, *Sleepwalking through History*, pp. 398–400. David C. Anderson, *Crime and the Politics of Hysteria: How the Willie Horton Story Changed American Justice* (New York: Times Books, 1995).

119 The "vision thing" quote apparently originated in a story, "Where Is the Real George Bush?" *Time*, January 26, 1987. A devastating portrait is in Randall Rothenberg, "In Search of George Bush," *New York Times Magazine*, April 3, 1988. Herbert S. Parmet, *George Bush: The Life of a Lone Star Yankee* (New York: Scribner's, 1997).

confrontation with four hundred people at Memorial High School. Nonetheless, he held his ground.[120]

Particularly revealing about Bush's political cynicism was his complete flip-flop on family planning. As a member of the House from 1967 to 1971, he made federal family planning programs one of his major issues – to the point where the powerful Democratic congressman Wilbur Mills jokingly labeled him "rubbers." He cosponsored a bill to end a ban on mailing contraceptives and was the principal sponsor of the 1971 Population Control and Research Act. He also commended Rep. Shirley Chisholm for her very early (pre-*Roe*) call for reform of existing criminal abortion laws.[121] His position was not surprising, since population control and family planning had traditionally been concerns for many elite Republicans, such as his father, the former Connecticut senator Prescott Bush. He threw these commitments aside in 1980, however, to win the vice presidential nomination.

Given his record, religious conservatives were not happy about his selection. Reagan told the Moral Majority leader Jerry Falwell to "talk to George about these things that bother you." He did, and Bush got the message about what positions were acceptable. Falwell did not want to pick a fight with Reagan and accepted Bush's apparent conversion. According to the Reagan aide James Baker, Reagan asked Bush only one question: "will you support my position on abortion?" He said he would and got the vice presidential nod. As president, Bush maintained the neoconservative policies of his predecessor. His resume included one year as CIA director under President Ford (1976–7), near the end of tumultuous period of revelations of agency misconduct. This aspect of is resume alarmed civil libertarians but few others. Upon becoming director in early 1976, he sent a memorandum to all CIA employees insisting on "strict adherence" to all laws, executive orders, and national security directives. Nonetheless, he was firmly wedded to maintaining secret operations. In a talk to CIA personnel on May 4, 1976, he acknowledged that the last year had been "rough" on the agency and "there will be changes" but held firm on key issues. Secrecy remained "essential"; congressional oversight was necessary, "but they must cooperate," he insisted, without explaining exactly how Congress should cooperate with the CIA. And on the crucial issue of covert operations, "I vote for retaining [the] capability." He never had William Casey's taste for aggressive secret operations, but in his year as CIA director he was willing to make only some concessions to the new era of accountability.[122]

Tangled appointments to the Supreme Court

George H. W. Bush made two appointments to the Supreme Court that could not have been more different in terms of civil liberties. The retirement of Justice William J. Brennan

120 Parmet, *George Bush: The Life of a Lone Star Yankee*, pp. 107–8. George H. W. Bush, *All the Best, G. Bush: My Life in Letters and Other Writings* (New York: Scribner, 1999), p. 107; 1964 Civil Rights Act: p. 88. Doro Bush Koch, *My Father, My President: A Personal Account of the Life of George H. W. Bush* (New York: Warner, 2006), pp. 55–7.

121 Parmet, *George Bush*, Ch. 9; "Rubbers," pp. 123–36.

122 Falwell: Strober and Strober, *Reagan: The Man and His Presidency*, p. 26; Baker: ibid., p. 26. Bush, Notes, Speech to CIA, May 4, 1976, Donated Materials, Personal Papers, CIA Files, Events and Appearances Files, Box 1, GHWBPL. See also "Memorandum for all CIA Employees," March 12, 1976; Speech, March 14, 1976, in Bush, *All the Best*, pp. 250–1.

in 1990 was easily the most serious blow to individual rights in many years. Brennan is today widely recognized as the intellectual architect of the Warren Court's revolution in constitutional law and in several key cases fashioned arguments that endured long into the conservative era on the Court. Most Court experts believe that Brennan was the real intellectual force in the "Warren" Court. Some even argue that Warren understood this and assigned Brennan many of the most important decisions. His 1,360 opinions include *Cooper v. Aaron* (1958), asserting the supremacy of Court decisions in the face of state opposition; *New York Times v. Sullivan* (1964), regarded as the most important modern statement on the meaning of free speech; *Baker v. Carr* (1962), applying the equal protection clause to the composition of congressional districts; and *Dombrowski v. Pfister* (1965), in which he created the phrase "chilling effect" on First Amendment freedoms.[123]

President Bush was eager to avoid a Bork-style nomination controversy and selected David H. Souter, a former member of the New Hampshire Supreme Court, who had been on the First Circuit Court of Appeals for only three months. His resume was so slim that he was labeled a "stealth" candidate. He had published exactly one law review article (and that was a tribute to someone rather than a discussion of a substantive issue) and had no meaningful record of opinions on the hot button issues of the day, particularly abortion. At his confirmation hearings, Souter engaged in the post-Bork game of evasion, in which Judiciary Committee members ask pointed questions about controversial issues and the nominee gives bland answers that reveal nothing. To the fury of conservatives, Souter turned out to be a liberal justice and a consistent member of the remaining civil libertarian bloc on the Court until his retirement in 2009.[124]

The retirement of Thurgood Marshall from the Court in 1991 dealt civil liberties another blow. It was also an event of enormous symbolic importance, as he was the first African American on the Court and before that the NAACP strategist and lead attorney in the historic *Brown v. Board of Education* decision. The vacancy immediately raised speculation about whether President Bush would replace him with another African-American justice. Bush did, and the result was another stormy nomination process.

Bush's choice of Clarence Thomas touched off the most bizarre Court nomination controversy in history. Thomas had served in several positions in the Reagan Administration, including as chair of the Equal Employment Opportunity Commission. Bush claimed that "the fact that he is black and a minority has nothing to do with this," but few believed him. Thomas had an extremely limited record on legal issues, although he was known to be a strong neoconservative. Virtually the entire civil rights establishment, including the NAACP and the Urban League, opposed him because of his opposition to affirmative action. The question of his judicial philosophy was completely sidetracked, however, by allegations against him of sexual harassment by the law professor Anita Hill. After protracted hearings that became a national soap opera, Thomas was narrowly confirmed by a 52–48 vote. On the bench, he joined Justice Antonin Scalia as the most extreme

123 Kim Isaac Eisler, *A Justice for All: William J. Brennan, Jr., and the Decisions That Transformed America* (New York: Simon & Schuster, 1993). Roger Goldman and David Gallen, *Justice William J. Brennan, Jr.: Freedom First* (New York: Carroll & Graf, 1994).

124 Committee on the Judiciary, United States Senate, *Nomination of David H. Souter to be Associate Justice of the Supreme Court of the United States*, Hearings, 101st Cong., 2nd Sess., 1990.

conservative justices on the Court, and in some cases he was the more conservative of the two.[125]

TWELVE YEARS OF NEOCONSERVATISM

The presidency of Ronald Reagan introduced the era of neoconservatism in American life., which included hostility to government action to end discrimination against people of color and women and an attack on the new tradition of separation of church and state. And as the Iran-Contra scandal highlighted, neoconservatives assaulted the new controls over the intelligence agencies and unilateral presidential action in foreign affairs. The anti-civil libertarian trends introduced by Reagan would reach their apex under President George W. Bush. Four months before Ronald Reagan left office, on September 11, 1988, the *New York Times* columnist Steven V. Roberts reviewed the president's record on the neoconservative social issues, finding them "Gone but Not Forgotten." The steam had gone out of the crusade for a ban on abortion, restoring prayer in school, and curbing pornography. "Not only has Congress lost its taste for the social agenda," he observed; "so, apparently, has Mr. Reagan." Gary Bauer, neoconservative activist and White House policy adviser, tried to put a brave face on the situation, maintaining, "We've come a lot farther down the road than most Washington pundits realize." He had a point. Reagan had achieved much by bypassing Congress and advancing conservative policies through administrative regulations (such as the abortion "gag order") and by appointing many conservative judges to lower federal courts.[126] The conservative congressman Dan Lundgren offered the very prescient comment that victory lay in the future: "The final chapter on Reagan's social policy will not be written for another 10 or 15 years." And, in fact, George W. Bush would take office exactly twelve years after Reagan left the White House and pursue a far more aggressive anti-civil libertarian set of policies, at home and abroad.

David Gergen, who served four different presidents and then had a career as a media political commentator, argued that Ronald Reagan's greatest legacy "is in how much he changed our minds."[127] Indeed. Reagan introduced the era of modern conservatism that dominated political discourse for thirty years and continued to have force after the election of Barack Obama in 2008. Most important, on national security he broke with the post-Vietnam attitude of restraint in foreign affairs in favor of aggressive anti-communism, which soon evolved into the war on terrorism and under George W. Bush included the worst assaults ever made on fundamental constitutional principles.

[125] Bush quote: Toobin, *The Nine*, p. 26. Jane Mayer and Jill Abramson, *Strange Justice: The Selling of Clarence Thomas* (Boston: Houghton Mifflin, 1994). Anita Hill, *Speaking Truth to Power* (New York: Doubleday, 1997). Kevin Merida and Michael A. Fletcher, *Supreme Discomfort: The Divided Soul of Clarence Thomas* (New York: Doubleday, 2007). Thomas's own memoir, at times belligerent or self-pitying: Clarence Thomas, *My Grandfather's Son: A Memoir* (New York: Harper, 2007). Henry J. Abraham, *Justices, Presidents, and Senators: A History of the U.S. Supreme Court Appointments from Washington to Bush II*. 5th ed. (Lanham, MD: Rowman & Littlefield, 2008), pp. 291–2. Vieria and Gross, *Supreme Court Appointments*, pp. 193–9 (evasive style: p. 196).

[126] Steven V. Roberts, "Reagan's Social Issues: Gone but Not Forgotten," *NYT*, September 11, 1988.

[127] David Gergen, "Ronald Reagan's Most Important Legacy," in Paul Boyer, ed., *Reagan as President: Contemporary Views of the Man, His Politics, and His Policies* (Chicago: Ivan Dee, 1990), p. 274.

13 Bill Clinton

The Divided Soul of a "New Democrat"

A "NEW DEMOCRAT" IN THE WHITE HOUSE

Liberals and civil libertarians had reason to rejoice when Bill Clinton entered the White House on January 20, 1993. After twelve years of conservative and anti–civil libertarian presidents, a new day seemed at hand. Clinton had pledged to support abortion rights and women's rights, had a unique rapport with African Americans, and in a remarkable campaign gesture promised to end the ban on homosexuals in the military.

Among all presidents to that time, Clinton had the best training in civil liberties. A graduate of Yale Law School who came of age politically in the Watergate years, he had taught constitutional law for a year (1973–4) at the University of Arkansas Law School (spending two weeks on *Roe v. Wade* and giving special attention to other women's rights issues). There were also good reasons for civil libertarians to be wary, however. Clinton defined himself as a "New Democrat" and was a leader of the centrist Democratic Leadership Council, organized after Ronald Reagan's massive reelection victory in 1984 committed to move the Democrats to the political center. Exactly what that meant for Clinton as president and for civil liberties remained to be seen.[1]

Bill Clinton was and remains an extraordinary complex person, in a league with Presidents Franklin D. Roosevelt and Lyndon Johnson. David Gergen, who served him and three other presidents, called him "a mass of contradictions." He was one of the best politicians of his generation, with a famous capacity to recover from defeat (after losing in his first run for elective office in 1974, after the Republicans captured control of Congress in 1994, and after the Monica Lewinsky scandal). Nonetheless, his reckless indiscretions, especially the Lewinsky affair, suggested someone at times with neither self-control nor political sense. The independent counsel Kenneth Starr found "substantial and credible information" that Clinton "obstructed justice" by "lying under oath" in the Paula Jones case. His subsequent impeachment by the House of Representatives in December 1998 tarnished his reputation for all time.[2]

1 David Maraniss, *First in His Class: The Biography of Bill Clinton* (New York: Simon & Schuster, 1996); on his law school teaching, pp. 287–94. Critical analysis of Clinton's New Democrat ideology and civil liberties: Floyd Abrams, "Clinton vs. the First Amendment," *NYT*, March 30, 1997. Robert Durant, "A 'New Covenant' Kept: Core Values, Presidential Communications, and the Paradox of the Clinton Presidency," *Presidential Studies Quarterly* 36 (September 2006): 345–72, finds consistency in Clinton's New Covenant values.

2 Maraniss, *First in His Class*. David Gergen, *Eyewitness to Power: The Essence of Leadership, Nixon to Clinton* (New York: Simon & Schuster, 2000), p. 251. *The Starr Report: The Findings of Independent Counsel Kenneth W. Starr on President Clinton and the Lewinsky Affair* (Washington, DC: PublicAffairs, 1998), p. 153. Clinton was also found in civil contempt for misleading testimony in the Jones case and was fined and later agreed to surrender his license to practice law in Arkansas for five years.

An event in the 1992 Democratic Party primaries provided a revealing clue to Clinton's handling of controversial civil liberties issues. In the middle of the crucial New Hampshire primary he flew back to Arkansas to ensure as governor the execution of Ricky Ray Rector, who many people argued should be spared because of his diminished mental capacity (an IQ of 64). Rector, in fact, did not seem to understand that he was to be executed, setting aside "for later" the dessert at his last meal. Clinton, however, knew well how Republicans had savagely and successfully attacked Michael Dukakis four years earlier for being "soft" on crime and was not going to let that happen to him.[3]

As president, Clinton compiled a very ambiguous record on civil liberties. On women's rights and abortion rights, including the politically very difficult issue of so-called partial birth abortions, no president had a better record. He had a personal rapport with African Americans that no other president ever matched, his appointments of African Americans to top positions surpassed those of any previous president, and he organized high-profile events to apologize for two historic incidents of racial injustice. At the same time, however, he aggressively pursued draconic crime policies that had a devastating impact on African Americans. A similar ambiguity characterized his approach to lesbian and gay rights. He made the first presidential appointments of openly lesbian and gay people but was forced to compromise on his promise about gays in the military. He enthusiastically supported two federal laws that drastically limited the right of habeas corpus, setting the state for further erosion of the historic right. On national security, he generally respected the post-Watergate reforms but also set some precedents that his successor George W. Bush pushed into lawlessness. Finally, his frequent use of executive orders to enact public policy, some troubling claims of executive authority, and his readiness to send American troops overseas (albeit with noble goals) without seeking congressional approval left a dangerous legacy regarding presidential power.

By his second term in office, the ACLU and several prominent First Amendment experts concluded that Clinton was a disaster. The ACLU president, Nadine Strossen, argued in 2000 that his "overall record is not good." The *New York Times*'s normally judicious Anthony Lewis went even further, accusing him of "the worst civil liberties record of any president in at least 60 years." The journalist Nat Hentoff added that no other president "has done so much damage to constitutional liberties as Bill Clinton." These hyperbolic criticisms were excessive, particularly when compared with Presidents Richard Nixon and Ronald Reagan's records and in light of Clinton's positive actions on several civil liberties issues. The First Amendment lawyer Floyd Abrams characterized the matter perfectly when he wrote, in both sadness and anger, that Clinton's record "is so disappointing because he knows better."[4] He did know better. Ever contradictory, Clinton advanced some civil liberties while also moving backward on others for political reasons.

3 "Arkansas Execution Raises Questions on Governor's Politics," *NYT*, January 25, 1992. William C. Berman, *From the Center to the Edge: The Politics and Policies of the Clinton Presidency* (Lanham, MD: Rowman & Littlefield, 2001), p. 12. Ten years later, the Supreme Court declared unconstitutional executing mentally retarded persons: *Atkins v Virginia*, 536 U.S. 304 (2002).

4 Quotes in Nadine Strossen, "Speech and Privacy," in Roger Pilon, ed., *The Rule of Law in the Wake of Clinton* (Washington, DC: Cato Institute, 2000), pp. 72, 77. Anthony Lewis, "Stand Up for Liberty," *NYT*, April 15, 1996. Floyd Abrams, "Clinton vs. the First Amendment," ibid., March 30, 1997.

TAKING OFFICE: INITIATIVES AND CRISES

The day after his inauguration in January 1993, Clinton fulfilled the hopes of civil libertarians by reversing several Reagan/Bush policies. By executive order he rescinded the 1988 gag order prohibiting agencies receiving Title X family planning funds from discussing, counseling, or making referrals regarding abortion. The rule, he flatly declared, "endangers women's lives and health." He also ended the 1988 moratorium on fetal tissue research, the ban on abortions in military hospitals, and a ban on importing RU-486, a nonsurgical alternative to abortion. In October, Attorney General Janet Reno reversed President Reagan's policy on the Freedom of Information Act, establishing a "presumption of disclosure."[5]

The first crisis: Gays in the military

Just five days after Clinton was sworn in, the Joint Chiefs of Staff asked for an urgent meeting to express their strong opposition to his campaign promise to allow homosexuals to serve openly in the military. At the meeting, the formidable General Colin Powell, chair of the Joint Chiefs, argued that it would be "prejudicial to good order and discipline" in the ranks. Clinton got nowhere arguing that the Pentagon had spent $500,000 in the past decade to remove seventeen thousand alleged homosexuals from military service. Even before taking office, he had already been advised that the issue would do him "great harm politically" and damage his relations with the military.[6]

Clinton's first major crisis in office involved both a high-profile civil liberties issue and a challenge to the politically powerful military. President Carter's initiatives on lesbian and gay rights, by comparison, had been low-visibility steps. The political power of the lesbian and gay rights community had been rising steadily since the Carter years, however, and the community had made considerable progress in many areas of American life during the Reagan and Bush years. Congressman Barney Frank, for example, became open about his homosexuality in 1987. Clinton actively courted this growing constituency. David Mixner, an old friend, was a member of his campaign's National Executive Committee and helped raise an estimated $4 million in contributions from the gay community. (In 1988, Dukakis had refused to accept a reported $1 million Mixner had raised.) Roberta Achtenberg worked on the Democratic Party platform and on July 13, 1992, became the first open lesbian to address a major party convention.[7]

Congress was just as strongly opposed to gays' serving in the military as the Joint Chiefs and was reportedly in open "revolt" against Clinton's plan. Both the House of

[5] Memorandum on the Title X "Gag Rule" January 22, 1993, APP. "Clinton's Departure," *NYT*, January 24, 1995. Attorney General Janet Reno, Memorandum for Heads of Departments and Agencies, The Freedom of Information Act, October 4, 1993, APP.

[6] John Holub to President-elect Clinton, Homosexuals in the Armed Services, January 14, 1993, Neuwirth Files, Box 4, FOIA 2006-0227-F, WJCPL. Bill Clinton, *My Life. V. 2, The Presidential Years*, Pbk. ed. (New York: Vintage Books, 2005), pp. 20–5.

[7] David Mixner, *Stranger among Friends* (New York: Bantam Books, 1996). Clinton did not mention Mixner in his memoirs, *My Life*. Achtenberg: David Mixner and Dennis Bailey, *Brave Journeys: Profiles in Gay and Lesbian Courage* (New York: Bantam Books, 2000), pp. 193–209.

Representatives and the Senate passed resolutions opposing it. Clinton fully understood that Congress could easily overrule any executive order he issued on the matter. Faced with certain defeat, Clinton tried to salvage something with a compromise. On January 29, after only nine days in office, he directed the secretary of defense to develop an acceptable policy in six months. The result was the "Don't Ask, Don't Tell" policy, adopted on July 19, 1993, under which the military would discharge any service member who engaged in homosexual conduct or stated that he or she was homosexual or bisexual but would not ask anyone directly about his or her sexual orientation. Clinton conceded that "it is not a perfect solution.... And it certainly will not please everyone." It was an embarrassing defeat in the first weeks of his presidency. In his memoirs he wrote, "In the short run, I got the worst of both worlds," displeasing both sides.[8]

Despite the "Don't Ask, Don't Tell" debacle, Clinton was the first president to appoint openly lesbian or gay people to important federal positions – an estimated 150 in all. Lesbian and gay activists organized Coalition 93 to recruit applicants for top jobs. Most prominently, Roberta Achtenberg was nominated as assistant secretary for housing and urban development and became the first openly homosexual person to face a Senate confirmation hearing. After several days of very contentious hearings, with the conservative senators Jesse Helms and Trent Lott voicing strenuous objections, she was confirmed by a vote of 58–31. It was a historic first.[9]

The most publicized nomination involved Clinton's 1999 choice of James C. Hormel as ambassador to Luxembourg. (He was a grandson of the founder of the Hormel meat packing company, creator of SPAM). With a University of Chicago Law School degree and a term as assistant dean of the school, he was no less qualified than many other ambassadorial appointments. When conservative senators blocked the nomination, Clinton made a recess appointment, making Hormel the first openly gay ambassador in American history.[10]

Clinton also honored his commitment to his gay supporters with strong and public support for federal action on AIDS, completely reversing President Reagan's hesitant and delayed response. He created an Office of National AIDS Policy in 1993, hosted the first White House conference on AIDS in December 1995, and substantially increased federal funding for AIDS research. Also, he responded favorably to the Congressional Black Caucus's call for a declaration of national emergency on AIDS in the African-American community (which by then accounted for 40 percent of all new cases), announcing a "severe and ongoing health crisis" in October 1998. That move and related health measures represented some of Clinton's most significant actions on behalf of African Americans.[11]

[8] "Lawmakers Revolt on Lifting Gay Ban in Military Service," *NYT*, January 26, 1993. Memorandum on Ending Discrimination in the Armed Forces. January 29, 1993, APP. Remarks Announcing the New Policy on Homosexuals in the Military. July 19, 1993, APP. Clinton, *My Life*, V. 2, p. 24.

[9] "Housing Nominee Is Attacked," *NYT*, May 21, 1993. Mixner and Bailey, *Brave Journeys: Profiles in Gay and Lesbian Courage*, pp. 193–209.

[10] "Clinton Appoints Gay Man as Ambassador as Congress Is Away," *NYT*, June 5, 1999.

[11] Remarks to the White House Conference on HIV and AIDS, December 6, 1995, APP. Statement on Emergency Funding for the HIV/AIDS Initiative in Minority Communities, October 28, 1998, APP. Materials on AIDS programs in DPC, Jennings Files, Box 1, WJCPL.

DOMA: The same-sex marriage controversy

If Bill Clinton thought he had finessed the issue of gay rights with the "Don't Ask, Don't Tell" policy, he was wrong. As the lesbian and gay rights movement continued to gain strength, its expectations for full equality soared to levels undreamed of only a few years before. In 1996, the previously unthinkable issue of a legal right to same-sex marriages burst onto the political scene when it appeared that Hawaiian courts might recognize same-sex marriage. It was an election year, and social conservatives mounted a full-bore attack on what they called an assault on the sanctity of marriage. Clinton was again caught between his commitments to a constituency and powerful political opposition.[12]

Republicans promptly saw gay marriage as another "wedge" issue to use against Clinton and the Democrats and pushed for laws banning it in the states and in Congress. One result was the federal Defense of Marriage Act (known as DOMA), holding that no state had to recognize a legal same-sex marriage from another state and prohibiting recognition of same-sex marriages in federal benefit programs. The bill passed by the overwhelming margins of 85–14 in the Senate and 342–67 in the House. The day the Senate voted, however, it also rejected a ban on discrimination in employment by only one vote, 50–49. Such a close vote in an election year was a clear sign that lesbian and gay rights had made some significant inroads at the national level.[13]

Clinton signed the Defense of Marriage Act into law in September 1996 with a statement that characteristically tried to please both sides. For his liberal supporters he began with a strong statement opposing "discrimination of any kind, including discrimination against gay and lesbian Americans." For conservatives he quickly added that he had "long opposed government recognition of same-gender marriages." The statement simply papered over the fact that not recognizing same-sex marriages was both a deeply hurtful insult and a form of discrimination. He did, however, call on Congress to pass the Employment Non-Discrimination Act, which the Senate had defeated by a single vote, making him the first president to endorse such legislation. (Interestingly, Clinton did not mention DOMA in his autobiography.)[14]

DOMA was not just a symbolic issue. It had an enormous impact on federal policies affecting the daily lives of ordinary Americans. In 1997 the General Accountability Office identified 1,049 federal statutes in which rights, benefits, or privileges were affected by marital status, and a follow-up report in 2004 found another 120 provisions passed in the intervening seven years. DOMA affected such widely used programs as Social Security benefits, food stamps, Medicare and Medicaid, veterans' pensions, educational assistance, federal employee retirement benefits, and immigration law. For the most part, however, these mundane but nonetheless practical consequences were ignored in the national debate over same-sex marriage.[15]

In May 1998, Clinton issued Executive Order 13087 adding homosexuals to federally protected classes. The terse May 28 order was not accompanied by any public statement explaining his support for the measure, but he was under savage attack because of the

12 "Fearing a Toehold for Gay Marriages, Conservatives Rush to Bar the Door," *NYT*, March 6, 1996.

13 "Senators Reject Both Job-Bias Ban and Gay Marriage," *NYT*, September 11, 1996.

14 Statement on Same-Gender Marriage, September 20,1996, APP.

15 *GAO to Honorable Bill Frist, Defense of Marriage Act: Update to Prior Report, January 23, 2004*, GAO-04-353R. The GAO changed its name to General Accountability Office in 2004.

Lewinsky affair and elections were just months away. For all his compromises, Clinton advanced lesbian and gay rights in important ways.[16]

A SPECIAL RAPPORT: BILL CLINTON AND AFRICAN AMERICANS

When the African-American comedian Chris Tucker joked about Clinton's being "the first black president" at the 1999 Congressional Black Caucus dinner, everyone laughed and no one took offense. Nothing was more remarkable about Bill Clinton than his special personal rapport with African Americans. Lyndon Johnson delivered far more in the way of landmark legislation, but his relationship with the black community was a matter of shared political goals, with none of the personal affection that Clinton enjoyed.[17]

Testimonials to Clinton's "special bond" came from all across the African American community. The civil rights attorney Johnnie Cochrane said he was "the most comfortable Caucasian about black people that most of us have ever seen." In an August 1998 poll, Clinton scored a 93 percent approval rating among African Americans, four points higher than the Reverend Jesse Jackson, arguably the most prominent civil rights activist at that time. Most observers felt his background made the difference: a southerner who grew up amid segregation and understood different racial experiences and a personal history as the child of a broken home who was raised by a single parent. This gave him a special empathy with the struggles of the less fortunate. At Yale Law School, the small number of black students usually ate at a separate table. One day Clinton just sat down with them and started talking. Some of the African-American students were initially put off by this seemingly presumptuous white guy but were quickly won over by his conversational ease, humor, and stories about growing up as a white southerner. In his year teaching at the University of Arkansas Law School, he was extremely popular with all students, because of his informal style and easy grading, but he made special efforts to help African-American students.[18]

When elected governor of Arkansas in 1978, he broke barriers by appointing an unprecedented number of African Americans to positions in his administration and by inviting them to official social events, a tradition-breaking move in Arkansas at that time. One of his appointees recalled that he was always "pushing the buttons" on race. Richard Mays, whom he appointed as the first African American on the state Supreme Court, recalled a party where Clinton was the only white person, "and you could not tell in any way that there was discomfort." As president, he did the same, inviting many African Americans to White House events and speaking every year at the Congressional Black Caucus dinner.[19]

16 Executive Order 13087 – Further Amendment to Executive Order 11478, Equal Employment Opportunity in the Federal Government, May 28, 1998, APP.

17 The incident and the speech: DeWayne Wickham, *Bill Clinton and Black America* (New York: Ballantine, 2002). See also Darlene Clark Hine, "African Americans and the Clinton Presidency: Reckoning with Race, 1992–2000," in Todd G. Shields, Jeannie M. Whayne, and Donald R. Kelley, eds., *The Clinton Riddle: Perspectives on the Forty-Second President* (Fayetteville: University of Arkansas Press, 2004), pp. 79–91.

18 Yale Law School and University of Arkansas: Maraniss, *First in His Class*, pp. 238–9, 293–4. Wickham, *Bill Clinton and Black America* (Cochrane, p. 40).

19 Recollections of Shackelford and Mays: Michael Takiff, *A Complicated Man: the Life of Bill Clinton as Told by Those Who Know Him* (New Haven, CT: Yale University Press, 2010), pp. 81–2.

Clinton's appointments of African Americans exceeded those of President Jimmy Carter, who had the best record to that time. The Harvard Law professor Charles Ogletree commented about the cabinet, "you've never seen as many African American men and women in significant positions." Appointees included Ron Brown as commerce secretary and Hazel O'Leary as secretary of energy. In eight years he appointed sixty-one African Americans as federal judges, compared with seventeen by Reagan and Bush in their twelve years. He also appointed twenty-three Hispanics compared with twenty-two by Reagan and Bush. Other high-level appointments included Bob Nash as White House personnel director, Bettie Currie as his personal secretary, and Maggie Williams as First Lady Hillary Clinton's chief of staff.[20]

The power of symbolic events

As did Lyndon Johnson, Clinton understood the power of symbolic events and organized two that resonated significantly with African Americans. Particularly moving was his official apology for the Tuskegee Syphilis Experiment. From 1932 to 1972 the U.S. Public Health Service project allowed 399 African Americans infected with syphilis to remain untreated while physicians studied the progression of the disease. They were never informed of their diagnosis, told that they were subjects in a government study, or informed that by the mid-1940s penicillin was available as a treatment. Most outrageously, when local draft boards directed fifty subjects to seek penicillin treatment, study directors intervened to prevent it. Even when ethical questions were raised in 1966, the American Medical Association and the African American National Medical Association urged the experiment be continued. The Public Health Service investigator Peter Buxton finally leaked the story to the *New York Times* for a front-page article on July 26, 1972. (The experiment was one of several ethical abuses that began coming to light in the late 1960s and led to the current federal guidelines on the protection of human subjects.)[21]

The Tuskegee experiment remained little known to most white Americans, apart from historians and medical ethicists. Nonetheless, in a courageous gesture, President Clinton invited eight survivors to the White House on May 16, 1997, when he apologized on behalf of the entire country. "[M]any Americans would prefer not to remember," he advised, "but we dare not forget. It was a time when our Nation failed to live up to its ideals … it is in remembering that past that we can build a better present and a better future." It was a powerful statement about a shameful episode in American history, unmatched by any other president.[22]

Four months later, Clinton paid tribute to the heroes of the 1957 integration of Central High School in Little Rock, Arkansas, in which President Eisenhower finally sent federal troops to ensure compliance with a federal court integration order. On September 25, 1997, he celebrated the fortieth anniversary of the crisis with a ceremony in Little Rock

20 African American appointments: Wickham, *Bill Clinton and Black America*, appendix, pp. 290–310 (Ogletree, p. 118).

21 Remarks in Apology to African-Americans on the Tuskegee Experiment, May 16, 1997, APP. "Syphilis Victims in U.S. Study Went Untreated for 40 Years," *NYT*, July 26, 1972. James H. Jones, *Bad Blood: The Tuskegee Syphilis Experiment* (New York: Free Press, 1993).

22 "Clinton Regrets 'Clearly Racist' U.S. Study," *NYT*, May 19, 1997.

that included all nine of the original students. In moving words, he empathized with the students who had initially been turned away from Central High amid threats to their lives. "On September 4th, 1957, Elizabeth Eckford walked to this door for her first day of school, utterly alone. She was turned away by people who were afraid of change.... And America saw her, haunted and taunted for the simple color of her skin." Clinton recalled that he was eleven years old, living just fifty miles away in Hot Springs, and that he never attended a school with an African American until he went to college. He concluded with a call to finish the job on civil rights: "Forty years later, we know there are still more doors to be opened." He then posed for photographs of himself inside Central High, symbolically opening the door to members of the original Little Rock None. As did the Tuskegee ceremony, the event demonstrated his remarkable capacity for empathy for the victims of injustice.[23]

The Lani Guinier fiasco

Despite his rapport with African Americans, political calculations at times led Clinton to acts that damaged his reputation on race relations. The most publicized episode occurred in his first months in office when he nominated the Yale Law professor Lani Guinier for assistant attorney general for civil rights. An African American and classmate at Yale Law School, Guinier had been an active civil rights litigator and had even participated in a voting rights suit against Clinton when he was governor of Arkansas. Most importantly, she had written extensively on voting rights and had proposed some elaborate voting arrangements to facilitate greater African-American representation in elective offices.

The day after her nomination, the neoconservative activist Clint Bolick attacked her as a "quota queen" in the *Wall Street Journal*. Her nomination never recovered. Making the rounds of Senate Judiciary Committee members and explaining that some of her proposals were used by private corporation boards, she found no support. Leading Democrats, including Senator Joe Biden, Judiciary Committee chair, also backed away. Finally realizing he did not have the votes, Clinton phoned her and said, "Lani, I have decided to withdraw your nomination.... You made the best case I can imagine, but you didn't change my mind." Pulling the rug out from under a prominent civil rights activist so early in his administration damaged Clinton's image on race relations. The episode, moreover, occurred in the midst of the controversy over gays in the military and the embarrassing withdrawal of his first two choices for attorney general, raising questions about his leadership abilities. Civil rights leaders saw it as retreat under fire, while conservatives saw that he could be bullied if attacked hard enough on a hot button issue. The episode also revealed something about Clinton's character. Guinier later wrote that neither Bill nor Hillary Clinton ever spoke to her again. Many observers noted that he was averse to such conflict.[24]

[23] Remarks on the 40th Anniversary of the Desegregation of Central High School in Little Rock, Arkansas, September 25, 1997, APP. "In Little Rock, Clinton Warns of Racial Split," *NYT*, September 26, 1997.

[24] Lani Guinier, *Lift Every Voice: Turning a Civil Rights Setback into a New Vision of Social Justice* (New York: Simon & Schuster, 1998), pp. 25, 125; the nomination process is covered in pp. 21–166. Clinton's account: Clinton, V. 2, *My Life*, pp. 75–6

"Mend it, but don't end it": Wrestling with affirmative action

On race, President Clinton also had to face the thorny issues of affirmative action and quotas in employment and college admissions. Like President Carter before him, he was caught between his African-American constituents and strong public opposition to racial preferences. He would have preferred to avoid the issue, but the Supreme Court forced his hand with a June 1995 decision (*Adarand Contructors v. Pena*) challenging minority set-asides in government contracts. As it had since *Bakke* in 1978, the Court steered a delicate course through conflicting constitutional principles, upholding the concept of affirmative action but ruling that racial preferences could be used but only where there was a compelling state interest and where no nonrace remedy was adequate. Civil rights advocates considered this extremely high standard difficult if not impossible to meet. The decision only reinforced their feeling that the Court and the country were turning their backs on racial equality.[25]

Politically torn, Clinton tried to devise a middle-of-the-road course, choosing the National Archives as a symbolic setting for a major address on the subject on July 19, 1995. "There could be no better place" for this discussion, he pointed out, than the building that housed both the Declaration of Independence and the Constitution, the "bedrocks of our common ground." Almost half the speech was devoted to a history of the civil rights movement, and he singled out Congressman John Lewis, who had been beaten in the 1965 Selma voting rights march, in the audience as person who had "put his life on the line" for civil rights. And in a statement that became an administration refrain, Clinton declared, "Affirmative action has been good for America." It did not, he added, mean an "unjustified preference of the unqualified over the qualified of any race or either gender." He also stated his opposition to "numerical quotas" and the "selection or rejection of any employee or student solely on the basis of race or gender without regard to merit." To those who thought affirmative action was no longer needed, he cited examples of the "persistence" of "bigotry," such as a recent report on discrimination in black home loan applications and the ninety thousand employment discrimination suits filed the previous year. He ended with a slogan, "Mend it, but don't end it," and set forth four principles for mending affirmative action: no quotas, no reverse discrimination, no preferences for unqualified people, and ending programs once they have succeeded.[26]

The speech was a heroic effort, but on close inspection it papered over all the hard questions. Did "no quotas" rule out goals and timetables, and would there be absolutely no counting of job applicants by race? If so, what exactly did affirmative action mean? He opposed reverse discrimination, but fierce opponents of affirmative action saw any kind of race-conscious programs to be just that. In the end, it was not clear what new approach Clinton really proposed. In this regard, the *New York Times* story on his 1997 Little Rock speech had noted that he offered no specifics on the current school integration situation, despite worsening de facto segregation, particularly in the North. The nation's race

[25] *Adarand Constructors v. Pena*, 515 U.S. 200 (1995). Administration's response: DPC, Warnath Files, Box 1, WJCPL.

[26] Remarks at the National Archives and Records Administration, July 19, 1995, APP. Clinton, *My Life*, V. 2, pp. 258–61.

problem was indeed very deep, and apart from high-profile symbolic events, President Clinton offered few if any specific proposals to address it.

The Clinton administration did little to advance school desegregation. Congress had passed three separate amendments to prohibit the use of federal funds for busing of students. Clinton was well aware of these laws and the depth of congressional and public opposition to busing, and so he simply did not talk about it. Instead, he proposed to revise the 1965 Elementary and Secondary Education Act with a new formula to provide more federal assistance to poor schools. Members of the House, however, quickly realized that at least half of them would lose money for schools in their districts, and they steadily watered down his proposal.[27]

A failed initiative on race

"Consider this," Bill Clinton asked his San Diego audience in June 1997. "We were born with a Declaration of Independence which asserted that we were all created equal and a Constitution that enshrined slavery." Hoping to change the national debate over race, Clinton launched a presidential initiative on the issue on June 14, 1997, between the Tuskegee Experiment and Little Rock events. He acknowledged America's diversity ("And more than ever, we understand the benefits of our racial, linguistic, and cultural diversity in a global society") and outlined a plan for "a great and unprecedented conversation about race" that would transcend old, and in his view sterile debates. (Ironically, the idea of a national dialogue on race had been originally proposed in 1993 by Lani Guinier, his failed nominee as assistant attorney general for civil rights.)[28]

To chair his President's Initiative on Race, Clinton selected the renowned African-American historian John Hope Franklin. As it embarked on a series of "town meetings" across the country, however, the initiative immediately became embroiled in a series of bitter controversies over its own agenda regarding affirmative action. Neoconservatives led by Harvard's Abigail Thernstrom accused it of deliberately excluding any serious debate on the issue. Clinton attended the first town meeting, in Akron, Ohio, on December 3, 1997, and pointedly called on Thernstrom, who had been belatedly added to the initiative. He strode over to where she was sitting and asked her whether she favored abolishing the army's affirmative action program, which had helped the early career of General Colin Powell. It was a good question, and Thernstrom tried to dodge it. In the end, however, Clinton may have scored debating points that day, but the initiative generated no meaningful dialogue or constructive recommendations on the issue.[29]

[27] Lawrence J. McAndrews, "Talking the Talk: Bill Clinton and School Desegregation," *International Social Science Review* 79 (2004): 87–107.

[28] Remarks at a Commencement Luncheon at the University of California San Diego in La Jolla,June 14, 1997, APP. President's Initiative on Race, *One America in the 21st Century: Forging a New Future* (Washington, DC: Advisory Board to the President's Initiative, 1998). Claire Jean Kim, "Clinton's Race Initiative: Recasting The American Dilemma," *Polity* XXXIII (Winter 2000): 175–97. John Goering, "An Assessment of President Clinton's Initiative on Race," *Ethnic and Racial Studies* 24 (May 2001): 472–84. Guinier, *Lift Every Voice*, pp. 273–311 (on a "conversation" on race); p. 308 (suggestion to Clinton in 1993).

[29] "Clinton, at Meeting on Race, Struggles to Sharpen Debate," *NYT*, December 4, 1997. "In Akron, Dialogue but Few Changes," ibid. Transcript of encounter: Remarks in a Roundtable Discussion on Race in Akron, December 3, 1997, APP. Race initiative materials: Federal Records, President's Advisory Board on Race, WJCPL.

The initiative's final report, *One America in the 21st Century: Forging a New Future,* was in two respects very different from its two predecessors, Gunnar Myrdal's 1944 *An American Dilemma* and the 1968 Kerner Commission Report. First, it acknowledged the deep cultural differences in America based on race and ethnicity (but not, importantly, innate biological differences), which the two previous reports had implicitly assumed would dissolve in the face of education and the experience of integration. Second, it recommended more "dialogue," cross-racial discussions about cultural differences. The report, however, dodged all of the fundamental social and economic problems interwoven with race that faced the nation and offered no substantive proposals regarding the stark racial inequalities in employment, education, housing, health care, and criminal justice. This lack of serious policy recommendations stands as a grave mark against the Initiative itself and Clinton's overall record on race, offsetting his very strong appointments and symbolic events.

Whatever its merits, the initiative's report never had a chance of getting any public attention. It was released in September 1998 just one week after Special Prosecutor Kenneth Starr's much anticipated report on Clinton and the Monica Lewinsky scandal. With the nation's attention totally focused on the president's misdeeds and possible impeachment, it instantly disappeared.[30]

Despite the failure of the race initiative to chart any new courses on public policies, Clinton had in fact launched a number of positive initiatives from the minute he took office. Some of the most important, as we have already mentioned, involved health care. These included funding and HHS programs related to sickle-cell anemia and racial disparities in prenatal care, diabetes, and breast and cervical cancer. As with his initiative on the AIDS crisis in the African-American community, these efforts stood in stark contrast to the indifference of the Reagan administration.[31] Clinton's policies on crime, as we shall see, were very contradictory, having both very destructive and some positive impacts on the African-American community.

FIGHTING CRIME, ERODING CIVIL LIBERTIES

Years later, Clinton had second thoughts. In 2008 he admitted he had been wrong on his policies regarding imprisonment. The occasion was a symposium marking the fortieth anniversary of the Kerner Commission report on the 1960s urban riots. "I regret more than I can say that we didn't do more" to reduce the racial disparities in sentencing for crack cocaine. "I think it's a cancer," he added. The damage was done, however, and much of it done by his policies.[32]

The heart of the problem was Clinton's vigorous pursuit of the wars on crime and drugs, which arose from his centrist New Democrat outlook. He and others in the Democratic Leadership Council were acutely conscious of how Republicans had used the crime issue against their party, from Richard Nixon's "law and order" rhetoric in 1968 to George

30 Favorable view of the Initiative: John Goering, "An Assessment of President Clinton's Initiative on Race," *Ethnic and Racial Studies* 24 (May 2001): 472–84.

31 Race and health materials in DPC, Jennings Files, Boxes 1, 29, WJCPL.

32 Bill Clinton, Keynote Address, Kerner at 40, University of Pennsylvania, February 19, 2008, APP. Jeffrey Rosen, "A Card Carrying Civil Libertarian," *NYT*, March 1, 2008.

H. W. Bush's cynical use of the Willie Horton issue in the 1988 campaign. Determined not to let it happen again, they embraced strong anticrime stands.[33]

The centerpiece of Clinton's crime program was the 1994 Violent Crime Control Act, a large and complex law with both good and bad civil liberties elements. The worst provisions involved sentencing. In his 1994 State of the Union Address, Clinton endorsed the pernicious idea of "three strikes and you're out," under which persons convicted of their third felony would receive a life sentence. The idea swept the country, and several states enacted variations of it. Almost all criminologists were appalled at this draconian, meat ax approach to sentencing, which did not take into account the seriousness of particular felony convictions. In California, which used its law more aggressively than any other state (most prosecutors sensibly found ways to evade their state laws), sophisticated research found that it had no impact on crime. Clinton's law also provided federal financial incentives for states to increase incarceration. Half of the $9.7 billion for prison construction was available to states that adopted "truth in sentencing" laws designed to ensure that violent offenders serve 85 percent of their nominal sentence. The 85 percent requirement addressed the long-standing conservative argument that dangerous criminals were released from prison early through parole and thereby allowed to prey again on the public. The national prison population soared 55 percent during the Clinton years, from 850,000 in 1992 to 1,318,333 eight years later. The crime rate also experienced a historic drop in these years. Conservatives credited longer prison terms for this decrease, but most criminologists cited the economic boom, community policing, and other factors. The financial incentives in the 1994 law encouraged states, which house 87 percent of all prisoners, both to build more prisons and to extend the actual time served. These changes fell hardest on African Americans, and in high crime neighborhoods arrest and long prison terms became a common experience.[34]

With regard to drugs, a particularly egregious case of racial disparity involved the provision in the Federal Sentencing Guidelines that involved a one hundred to one disparity in sentencing for crack versus powder cocaine. The guidelines mandated the same sentence for possession of 5 grams of crack cocaine, which African Americans mostly used, and 500 grams of powder cocaine, which was favored by whites. Criminologists denounced the disparate racial impact, but Clinton took a hard line and opposed a 1995 Sentencing Commission recommendation to eliminate the disparity. An official Justice Department statement reiterated the argument that "crack is a more dangerous and harmful substance" than powder cocaine. Two years later, in a meeting with African-American journalists, Clinton said he supported change but then proposed only reducing the disparity from one hundred to one to ten to one. Once out of office, he conceded that it had been politically impossible to get any change through Congress, but this overlooked his own active support for the disparity, which seemed clearly politically motivated.[35]

[33] Strossen, "Speech and Privacy," 70–1.

[34] Alfred Blumstein and Joel Wallman, eds., *The Crime Drop in America* (New York: Cambridge University Press, 2006). Samuel Walker, *Sense and Nonsense about Crime, Drugs, and Communities*, 7th ed. (Belmont, CA: Wadsworth Cengage, 2011), pp. 3 9.

[35] JoAnn Harris, Department of Justice Position Statement, Cocaine and Federal Sentencing Policy, February 1, 1995, DPC, Reed Files, Box 77, WJCPL. DeWayne Wickham, "The Real Cost of Prisons," *USA Today*, Weblog, March 8, 2008.

The most well-known part of the 1994 crime law was the $9 billion in federal funds for hiring 100,000 additional police officers and for community policing. It happened that the Clinton years witnessed the greatest decline in serious crime since the FBI began recording data in the 1930s. Murders in New York City, San Diego, and other cities plunged to levels not seen since the early 1960s. Criminologists debated the causes of this historic achievement, and there is no convincing evidence that the seventy thousand additional officers who were actually funded by the 1994 law had any direct effect. To the extent that the 1994 law encouraged community policing programs and better relations between the police and neighborhood residents, programs in some cities did have a positive impact on race relations.[36]

The 1994 crime bill also included $1.6 billion for programs related to violence against women, the first serious federal effort in this regard. Funds supported shelters for battered women, treatment programs for male batterers, and reforms to ensure that prosecutors took seriously crimes of violence against women. The Violence against Women initiative was the first significant federal effort in that regard, and it reflected Clinton's larger commitment to women's issues.[37]

Attacking police misconduct

The one provision of the 1994 Violent Crime Control Act that advanced racial justice was section 14141, authorizing the Justice Department to bring civil suits against police departments where there was a "pattern or practice" of citizens' rights violations. Such suits were designed to effect organizational reform and establish meaningful accountability measures (thus seeking to change "rotten barrels" rather than prosecuting individual "rotten apples"). The Clinton Justice Department used section 14141 to sue and reach settlements with about twenty law enforcement agencies, including the Pittsburgh, Los Angeles, Cincinnati, and Washington, D.C., police departments (and the New Jersey State Police, for racial profiling in traffic stops). Although almost all the departments initially dragged their feet in implementing the mandated reforms, the eventual results were promising. The court-appointed monitor for the New Jersey State Police, for example, concluded in 2007 that the department had "become self-monitoring and self-correcting to a degree not often observed in American law enforcement." The monitors in Cincinnati and Washington, D.C., reported similar results. It remains to be seen whether these reforms would be sustained over time, but for the moment the improvements appeared very significant.[38]

Because the victims of the police abuses addressed by federal litigation were almost always African Americans or Latinos, the effort was one of the most direct and tangible benefits to the historic victims of injustice. In this regard it represented precisely the kind of specific policy initiative Clinton's Initiative on Race failed to recommend.

36 Blumstein and Wallman, eds., *The Crime Drop in America*. Walker, *Sense and Nonsense about Crime, Drugs, and Communities*, pp. 3–35.

37 National Research Council, *Advancing the Federal Research Agenda on Violence against Women* (Washington, DC: National Academy Press, 2004).

38 Materials on police misconduct: DPC, Reed Files, Box 86, WJCPL. Samuel Walker and Morgan Macdonald, "An Alternative Remedy for Police Misconduct: A Model State "Pattern or Practice Statute," *George Mason Civil Rights Law Journal* 19 (Summer 2009): 479–552.

Undermining the right of habeas corpus

Clinton's criminal justice initiatives also included two of the worst parts of his general civil liberties record in the form of assaults on the right of habeas corpus. The 1996 Prison Litigation Reform Act restricted prisoners' access to the courts in ways that, according to Human Rights Watch, "apply to no other persons." It drastically limited the ability of prisoners to challenge harmful and unconstitutional conditions in prisons and injuries suffered at the hands of prison staff. The law applied not just to convicted prisoners, but also to persons in jail awaiting trial who had not yet been found guilty of any crime. Even worse, it also applied to children and juveniles being held in detention. The law required prisoners to exhaust all administrative remedies before petitioning a federal court; simply missing a filing deadline would disqualify an appeal. Additionally, to file a claim of mental or emotional injury, a prisoner first had to show physical injury. The law specifically restricted the authority of federal courts to order changes regarding prison overcrowding or other unconstitutional conditions and in this regard set back twenty-five years of prisoners' rights litigation that had brought about significant improvements in prison conditions.[39]

The Prison Litigation Reform Act was fully consistent with the "court-stripping" proposals advanced by conservatives since the 1950s in response to Supreme Court decisions protecting individual rights, with regard to anti-communist measures, school prayer, pornography, school busing, and abortion. By endorsing the law, President Clinton and many Democrats in Congress embraced this long-standing conservative position and in this instance denied a vulnerable group of people the basic right of access to the courts.[40] The law had a dramatic impact on prisoners' rights litigation. Six years later, prisoner lawsuits had declined by almost half (43 percent), despite a 23 percent increase in the number of prisoners. The ballooning prison population, which was in part encouraged by Clinton's policies, aggravated overcrowding in state prisons, with all the attendant problems of prison violence and inadequate resources, which the federal courts were now less able to address.

The second attack on habeas corpus was in the 1996 Antiterrorism and Effective Death Penalty Act. Some of the antiterrorism provisions had been proposed by President Reagan in 1984 but rejected by Congress. The political mood changed significantly over the next decade, however, and President Clinton, not wanting to appear soft on terrorism or domestic criminals, particularly in an election year, embraced many of these proposals. The law criminalized "material support" for terrorism, a very expansive concept that could include financial support for humanitarian programs that were only indirectly related to a terrorist group. It also authorized the government to exclude or deport foreign nationals whom it believed were associated with groups the secretary of state designated as terrorist. Secret evidence, moreover, could be used in deportation hearings before a new special court. Finally, the law expanded the federal government's wiretap authority, permitting "roving" wiretaps on a person and not a specific place as in the past. The

39 Human Rights Watch, *No Equal Justice: The Prison Litigation Reform Act in the United States* (New York: Human Rights Watch, 2009). Prisoners' right movement: Samuel Walker, *In Defense of American Liberties: A History of the ACLU* (New York: Oxford University Press, 1990), pp. 310–12.

40 Edward Keynes and Randall K. Miller, *The Court vs. Congress: Prayer, Busing, and Abortion* (Durham, NC: Duke University Press, 1989).

constitutional law expert David Cole and a colleague called the law one of "the worst assaults on civil liberties in decades."[41]

A White House memo revealed that the administration fully understood the civil liberties implications of the bill, particularly those that "would undercut meaningful federal habeas reviews and raise profoundly troubling constitutional issues." It expressed concern about attacks from liberals and civil libertarians and recommended dropping language in Clinton's signing statement that "could be used against us" politically. The language remained in the statement, with Clinton optimistically – and quite naively – expressing the hope that courts would interpret the law in accordance with traditional American ideals.[42]

The habeas corpus provisions of the law, which had nothing to do with terrorism, were not in Clinton's original bill but added later by the conservative senator Orrin Hatch. Prisoners under sentence of death were given only six months to file habeas corpus petitions, while other prisoners would have a year. Signing the bill, Clinton explained that he had "long sought to streamline Federal appeals" in death penalty cases, decrying the fact that "for too long" "endless death row appeals have stood in the way of justice." His original preference had always been to allow one and only one appeal, with a one-year deadline. Civil libertarians, horrified and disappointed in Clinton, saw this as yet another "court-stripping" measure that denied justice to convicted offenders. Clinton's attacks on habeas corpus had enormous long-term consequences, preparing the ground, certainly in the minds of members of Congress, for President George W. Bush's attack on the historic right in the war on terrorism just a few years later.[43]

Defending justice

Despite his policies on crime and drugs that severely damaged poor and African-American and Latino communities, Clinton took one important step to ensure justice for the poor. Reversing President Reagan's attempt to abolish the Legal Services Corporation, he proposed to increase its budget. This did not only reflect a sincerely felt commitment to helping the poor; he had a personal connection with the LSC. First Lady Hillary Clinton had been a member of the LSC board, and in fact had sued to prevent her removal by President Reagan. At the twenty-fifth anniversary celebration of the LSC in July 1999 he said he had been "never more proud of anything than her service" to it.[44]

Clinton also ended the Reagan administration's indifference to violent attacks on abortion clinics and their staff. He publicly condemned the "senseless violence" of the bombing that killed an off-duty police officer at a Birmingham, Alabama, family planning clinic in January 1998 and dispatched federal agents to assist in the investigation. Two weeks after the October 23, 1998, murder of Dr. Barnett Slepian, an abortion provider in Buffalo, New York, by an antiabortion fanatic, Attorney General Janet Reno created

[41] David Cole and James X. Dempsey, *Terrorism and the Constitution: Sacrificing Civil Liberties in the Name of National Security*, Rev. ed. (New York: New Press, 2006), Chs. 8, 9, and 10, pp. 107–46 (quote on p. 135).

[42] Bruce Reed to the President, May 3, 1995; Bruce Reed to Todd Stern, April 23, 1996, DPC, Reed Files, Box 76, WJCPL. Clinton, Signing Statement, April 24, 1996, APP.

[43] Statement on Signing the Antiterrorism and Effective Death Penalty Act of 1996, April 24, 1996, APP. "Clinton Signs Measure on Terrorism and Death Penalty Appeals," *NYT*, April 25, 1996. The Supreme Court unanimously upheld provisions of the law in *Felker v. Turpin*, 518 U.S. 651 (1996).

[44] Remarks by the President and the First Lady, July 27, 1999, APP.

the Task Force on Violence against Health Care Providers. The task force included staff from the Civil Rights Division, the FBI, the Bureau of Alcohol, Tobacco, and Firearms, and other federal agencies.[45]

STANDING FIRM ON ABORTION RIGHTS AND WOMEN'S RIGHTS

Abortion was the one issue on which President Clinton deserves the highest marks for defending a very difficult civil liberties issue. On his first full day as president in 1993 he issued an executive order rescinding the gag order banning federal funds to international agencies that were involved in any way with abortions.[46]

The hardest issue Clinton faced involved the so-called partial birth abortions. These very late term abortions (medically known as intact dilation and extraction, or IDX) involve special medical circumstances and represent only 0.2 percent of all abortions in the United States (the term "partial birth" is in fact a political slogan created by the anti-abortion movement). Antiabortion forces cited the fact that in some cases the fetus is viable and charged that it therefore involved a "killing."

In two acts of considerable political courage, President Clinton vetoed bills banning IDX abortions in 1995 and 1997. It would have been easy for him to let the bills become law. They had overwhelming support in Congress, and he could also have argued that because the procedure was so rarely used, the overall impact of a ban would be minimal, with the basic right of abortion preserved. Nonetheless, he refused to compromise and went out of his way to identify publicly with women who had undergone the procedure. In his April 10, 1996, veto message he commented, "I have just met with five courageous women and their families, and I want to thank the Lines, the Stellas, the Watts, the Costellos, and the Ades all for meeting with me." He pointed out that they represented different religious faiths. Congress again passed a partial birth abortion ban in 2003, which President George W. Bush signed and the Supreme Court upheld in 2006.[47]

Clinton's record on all women's issues was very strong, not just with abortion, and particularly so with regard to appointments to top federal positions. In addition to appointing a record percentage of women to the lower federal courts, he named Ruth Bader Ginsburg as the second woman on the Supreme Court and Janet Reno as the first woman to be U.S. attorney general. Reno, his third choice for the job (all three were women), was never really a member of the Clinton inner circle and, as we shall see, was a stickler for legal procedures on some crucial national security issues.

One important initiative involved strengthening child support collection efforts. With Executive Order 12953 on February 27, 1995, Clinton attempted to establish the executive branch of the federal government as a "model employer" on this issue. The order required all federal agencies "to cooperate fully" in child support enforcement and

45 Statement on the Bombing of a Family Planning Clinic in Birmingham, Alabama, January 29, 1998, APP. U.S. Department of Justice, Civil Rights Division, National Task Force on Violence Against Health Care Providers, *Overview* (Updated, July 25, 2008).

46 "A Flurry of Edicts," *NYT*, January 23, 1993.

47 Remarks on Returning without Approval to the House of Representatives Partial Birth Abortion Legislation, April 10, 1996, APP. Message to the House of Representatives Returning without Approval Partial Birth Abortion Legislation, October 10, 1997, APP. *Gonzales v Carhart*, 550 U.S. 124 (2007).

collection efforts by providing information to its employees about remedies available to them and to process wage withholding actions consistent with federal law.[48]

Clinton also supported and signed into law the Family and Medical Leave Act in early February 1993. President George H. W. Bush had twice vetoed similar bills. Compared with long-standing policies in European countries, the law was pathetically weak, allowing only unpaid rather than paid leave for family-related matters, but it was at least a modest step forward in this country in terms of tangible support for families.[49]

Despite his strong record on women's issues, Clinton squandered his support among women with the Lewinsky affair, and Al Gore paid the price in the 2000 election. Some analysts estimated that Gore's support among married women was 6 percentage points lower than Clinton's in 1996, in part because the disgusted Gore kept Clinton away from the campaign. Active support by a scandal-free Clinton might well have won several states for Gore where the vote was very close.

PRESERVING THE WALL OF SEPARATION IN PUBLIC SCHOOLS

Perhaps more than any other president, Bill Clinton took specific actions to clarify the bitterly controversial issue of separation of church and state in the public schools and in the federal workplace. Considerable misunderstanding prevailed about what the Supreme Court's decisions on school prayer required and did not require, much of it the result of deliberate distortion by religious conservatives. As a southern Protestant, Clinton had a position on religious liberty that closely paralleled that of Jimmy Carter and Lyndon Johnson, and all three inherited the southern Protestant tradition of a strong commitment to separation of church and state. The ACLU President, Nadine Strossen, who was fiercely critical of Clinton on free speech and privacy issues, gave him an "especially high" rating on religious liberty.[50]

On July 12, 1995, Clinton directed his secretary of education, Richard Riley, to develop a comprehensive report on what kinds of religious activities were and were not permitted in schools. The August 1995 report, *Religious Expression in Public Schools*, was distributed to all public schools throughout the country. It carefully distinguished between student-initiated actions, such as praying before eating lunch or reading the Bible during free time, which were permissible, and school-sponsored activities, which were not. The report's singular contribution was to put to rest the oft-repeated allegation by religious fundamentalists that the Supreme Court had completely expelled religion from public schools. A wide array of religious and civil libertarian groups applauded the report. In retrospect, the real question was why no previous administration had developed such guidance for public school officials and the public. Clinton followed up with additional explanatory reports for both teachers and parents in 1997; he also issued a set of guidelines on religious expression in the federal workplace.[51]

48 Executive Order 12953 – Actions Required of All Executive Agencies to Facilitate Payment of Child Support, February 27, 1995, APP.

49 Statement on Signing the Family and Medical Leave Act of 1993, February 5, 1993, APP.

50 Nadine Strossen, "Speech and Privacy," 69.

51 Materials in DPC, Reed Files, Box 94, WJCPL. Memorandum on Religious Expression in Public Schools, July 12, 1995, APP. Office of the White House, Guidelines on Religious Exercise and Religious Expression in the Federal Workplace, August 14, 1997. U.S. Department of Education, *Teachers Guide to Religion in Public Schools* (1997). Clinton, *My Life*, V. 2, p. 258.

CLINTON AND THE FIRST AMENDMENT

Nothing better illustrated Clinton's New Democrat approach to the First Amendment and other difficult civil liberties issues than his position on flag burning. The issue erupted into national controversy after Supreme Court decisions in 1989 and 1990 declaring unconstitutional first a Texas and then a federal flag burning law. The decisions provoked a drive in Congress to ban flag desecration by amending the First Amendment. Clinton was deeply torn between, on the one hand, the constitutional principles that as a former law school professor he understood better than any modern American president and, on the other hand, his political instincts, which told him defending flag burning was terribly unpopular. He made it clear that he was proud of his "long and vocal record" on protecting the flag. As Arkansas governor he had supported flag protection legislation and initiated a Flag Respect program in the state's public schools. After the Supreme Court decisions, he remained steadfastly opposed to a constitutional amendment to protect the flag, fully understanding that, as a 1995 staff memo put it, "The Bill of Rights has *never* been amended." As a centrist, he hoped instead to craft a law that would pass Supreme Court review, but the staff memo conceded that it "cannot be achieved." He was finally spared having to make a decision when the controversy faded away.[52]

The most sweeping peacetime censorship law in American history

Clinton's centrist ambivalence was also evident in his response to the 1996 Communications Decency Act (CDA), arguably the most sweeping censorship law in American history. It reached far beyond such historic outrages as the 1798 Alien and Sedition Acts, the 1917 Espionage Act, and the 1918 Sedition Act, which covered only a narrow, albeit important range of political speech -criticizing the government. The key provisions of the CDA, however, sought to protect children from "indecent" and "patently offensive" materials on the Internet and cable television and in that respect covered an enormous range of words that would inevitably be used in sex education, discussions of birth control and abortion, and homosexuality.[53]

As an amendment to Title V to the Telecommunications Act in 1995, the CDA created a serious dilemma for Clinton because the main part of the law deregulating the communications industry was a very high priority for him and Vice President Al Gore. The final bill passed the Senate in June 1995 by an overwhelming vote of 84–16. Moreover, the CDA provisions were framed in terms of protecting children from unwanted and inappropriate sexual materials, a goal that was difficult to challenge with a presidential election the following year. With neoconservatives' championing "family values," few politicians were willing to stand for First Amendment principles at the risk of being labeled soft on pornography and indifferent to the welfare of children.

President Clinton was deeply ambivalent about the CDA, once again caught between constitutional principles and political calculations. In 1996 he had begun "tacking" to

52 Abner Mikva and Chris Cerf, Memorandum to the President, Re [Walter] Dellinger Testimony on Flag Burning Amendment, June 3, 1995, DCP, Warnath Files, Box 10, WJCPL.

53 On the earlier laws, see Geoffrey R. Stone, *Perilous Times: Free Speech in Wartime from the Sedition Act of 1798 to the War on Terrorism* (New York: W. W. Norton, 2004).

the center, as his own aides put it, to blunt criticisms from social conservatives on issues such as pornography. Testifying on the bill, administration officials acknowledged the CDA's potential impact on the First Amendment and privacy but did not formally oppose it. They did warn that the provisions criminalizing material beyond the prevailing legal definition of "obscenity" raised series constitutional questions.[54]

Signing the bill into law at the Library of Congress, in another symbolic moment, Clinton pointedly referred to Thomas Jefferson and touted the "revolutionary" telecommunications reform as comparable to the creation of the interstate highway system fifty years before. He specifically objected to the provisions on "abortion-related speech and information" and reiterated this in a formal signing statement. The Justice Department had advised him that it was a violation of the First Amendment and would not enforce it. It is significant that Clinton confined his objections to abortion-related materials and said nothing about the threat of censorship of other materials related to sexuality and health. (Notably, his signing statement promise not to enforce part of a new law passed with little criticism. When his successor George W. Bush made many similar promises in signing statements on numerous national security issues, there was an enormous controversy.)[55] We can only speculate on what position Clinton would have taken on the CDA had it been a separate bill, divorced from the high-priority telecommunications deregulation. Given his willingness to compromise on other politically volatile issues, however, one suspects that he would have supported it.

Literally within hours after Clinton signed the bill into law, a coalition led by the ACLU that included a wide range of women's health, lesbian and gay rights, and anticensorship groups sought an injunction against the CDA. Federal courts subsequently held the law unconstitutional at every level, including the Supreme Court on June 26, 1997, in *Reno v. ACLU*. The Court held the terms "indecent" and "patently offensive" to be impermissibly vague and asked rhetorically whether the managers of Web sites could be confident that discussions of birth control, homosexuality, or prison rape would not violate the law. It cited safe sex education materials by the group Critical Path, written in "street language" for teenagers. Although the law provided good faith exceptions for Web sites that made reasonable efforts to restrict access by age, the Court found that given the nature of the Internet, no method existed for verifying the age of a Web user. Fundamentally, the CDA was "a content based regulation of speech," and legitimate efforts to protect children do not justify an "unnecessarily broad suppression" of speech directed toward adults.[56]

Disturbing threats to privacy

Civil libertarians were also alarmed by the Clinton administration's enthusiasm for measures, couched in terms of social reform or antiterrorism policy, that threatened

[54] Administration Concerns Regarding S. 652: The Telecommunications Competition and Deregulation Act of 1995, U.S. House of Representatives, Subcommittee on Telecommunications and Finance, Hearings, 104th Cong., 1st Sess. 1995.

[55] Statement on Signing the Telecommunications Act of 1996, February 8, 1996, APP. Jeremy Lipschultz, *Broadcast and Internet Indecency: Defining Free Speech* (New York: Routledge, 2008), pp. 104–15.

[56] "Communications Bill Signed, and the Battles Begin Anew, "*NYT*, February 9, 1996. *Reno v. ACLU*, 521 U.S. 844 (1997). Marjorie Heins, *Not in Front of the Children, "Indecency," Censorship, and the Innocence of Youth* (New Brunswick, NJ: Rutgers University Press, 2007), pp. 157–79. Mike Godwin, *Cyber Rights: Defending Free Speech in the Digital Age* (New York: Times Books, 1998), pp. 260–93.

individual privacy. The 1996 Welfare Reform Law, for example, required employers to collect personal information about new employees. Clinton's failed health care reform effort of 1993–4 included data collection procedures and a unique personal identifier that could easily become a national ID number.[57]

The administration also enthusiastically supported the so-called clipper chip, which many people saw as a serious threat to privacy. Announced in 1993, the clipper chip was an encryption device to be installed on telephones, with the government holding in escrow a decryption "key." Vice President Al Gore, who had a special interest in technology issues, touted the clipper chip as "a law and order issue," since criminals could use encryption to hide their illegal activities. The application to international terrorism was also obvious.[58]

The clipper chip roused fierce opposition from privacy and civil liberties groups. Many were new organizations that had sprung up in response to the revolution in communications technology, notably the Electronic Frontier Foundation and the Electronic Privacy Information Center. Technical problems with the encryption process also bedeviled the proposal (the original design was not available for peer review by scientists), along with concerns that it could set back American international competitiveness in technology if other countries objected to it. Some conservatives in Congress, such as the Missouri senator John Ashcroft, also opposed the clipper chip (although he would take a very different position on surveillance when be became attorney general under President George W. Bush). By 1996, the proposal was dead and abandoned. Nonetheless, it demonstrated the Clinton administration's fascination with technology and eagerness to ignore privacy considerations in the name of law enforcement. [59]

TROUBLING ASSERTIONS OF PRESIDENTIAL POWER

Before Bush: Presidential signing statements

A front-page story in the *Boston Globe* in April 2006 provoked a national controversy over President George W. Bush's use of presidential signing statements. By then Bush had issued more than five hundred such statements announcing his intent not to enforce portions of new laws because they violated his constitutional authority as president. The story provoked wide accusations that it represented an imperious power grab. Bush's defenders pointed out that presidents had long used signing statements, including Bill Clinton, who issued 105 covering 140 sections of different laws during his eight years in office. It was the highest number to that time, and more than the estimated 71 by Ronald Reagan. Clinton's use of signing statements had been largely unremarked, but the 2006 controversy over Bush drew attention to the fact that he too had made strong assertions of presidential power through signing statements, executive orders, and claims of executive privilege.[60]

[57] Strossen, "Speech and Privacy," 73–5.
[58] Statement by the Press Secretary, April 16, 1993, APP. Statement by the Vice President, February 4, 1994.
[59] Strossen, "Speech and Privacy."
[60] "Bush Challenges Hundreds of Laws," *Boston Globe*, April 30, 2006. The reporter's expanded work: Charlie Savage, *Takeover: The Return of the Imperial Presidency and the Subversion of American Democracy* (Boston: Little, Brown, 2007), p. 237. Matthew Crenson and Benjamin Ginsberg, *Presidential Power: Unchecked and Unbalanced* (New York: W. W. Norton, 2007), p. 200.

Democrats did not object to Clinton's signing statements for the simple reason that he used them to advance liberal social policies they supported. The 1996 Defense Appropriations Act, for example, required the military to discharge anyone who tested positive for HIV. Clinton issued a signing statement saying he would not enforce this provision, calling it "blatantly discriminatory and highly punitive to service members and their families." The administration aggressively defended the practice. Walter Dellinger, head of the Office of Legal Counsel from 1993 to 1996, wrote a crucial memorandum in November 1993 arguing that "the President may declare in a signing statement that a provision of the bill before him is flatly unconstitutional, and that he will refuse to enforce it." "This advice," he added, is "consistent with the views of the Framers."[61]

In the 2006 controversy, the Bush administration cited Dellinger's memorandum. When the ABA condemned Bush, Dellinger responded with a thoughtful *New York Times* op-ed piece emphasizing the complexity of the issue. Particularly troublesome is that while presidents can always veto unconstitutional bills, they typically have many provisions, most of which are acceptable and often necessary. (The 1996 Telecommunications Act, with its CDA provisions, was an excellent example.) The key issue, he argued, is not the principle of refusing to execute objectionable laws, but the Bush administration's "sweeping claims of unilateral executive power." That point was well taken, but it still left no meaningful guidance on exactly when a president's rejection of Congress crossed the line or how many such rejections were excessive.[62]

Making policy through executive orders

Clinton was even more aggressive in asserting presidential power to make social policy through executive orders than he was through signing statements, issuing a total of 364, for an average of 45.5 per year, or almost one a week. This figure is actually low among post-Watergate presidents. Jimmy Carter had the highest annual average, at 80 per year, until George W. Bush arrived in the Oval Office.[63]

As with signing statements, Clinton used executive orders to advance liberal social policies that Congress would not support. This became particularly important after Republicans captured control of Congress in 1994. Executive Order 12954 in March 1995, for example, prohibited federal contractors from replacing strikers with new workers: "contracting agencies shall not contract with employers that permanently replace lawfully striking employees" (it was later struck down by the District of Columbia Court of Appeals). With Executive Order 13087 Clinton added homosexuals to federal protected classes of employees, including Washington, D.C., the Postal Service, and civilian

61 Statement on Signing the National Defense Authorization Act for Fiscal Year 1996, February 10, 1996, APP. Crenson and Ginsberg, *Presidential Power*, p. 199. Clinton cited President Roosevelt's signing statement in the 1940s *Lovett* case (see Chapter 4 of this book). *United States v. Lovett*, 328 U.S. 303 (1946). Walter Dellinger, Assistant Attorney General, The Legal Significance of Presidential Signing Statements, November 3, 1993, *Opinions of the Office of Legal Counsel* (Washington, DC: Department of Justice, 1993–4), V. 17, pp. 131–41. Philip J. Cooper, *By Order of the President: The Use and Abuse of Executive Direct Action* (Lawrence: University Press of Kansas, 2002).

62 American Bar Association, Task Force on Presidential Signing Statements and the Separation of Powers Doctrine (Chicago: ABA, 2006). Walter Dellinger, "A Slip of the Pen," *NYT*, July 31, 2006.

63 Todd F. Gaziano, *The Use and Abuse of Executive Orders and Other Presidential Directives* (Washington, DC: Heritage Foundation, February 21, 2001), p. 13.

employees of the military who were not covered by the Don't Ask, Don't Tell policy. (It exempted the intelligence agencies, the FBI, the CIA, and the NSA, however.) Executive Order 13166 on Improving Access to Services for Persons with Limited English Proficiency required federal agencies and any organization receiving federal funds to ensure that its services were available to people with only limited command of English. With immigration changing the face of America, it was a major step in the direction of inclusiveness. Clinton expanded the 1906 Antiquities Act through an executive order to protect parts of the environment from development and issued Executive Order 13061 to establish the American Heritage Rivers Initiative, protecting rivers. Executive Order 12898, meanwhile, proclaimed a policy on environmental racism and directed federal agencies to investigate the problem.[64]

Liberal Democrats applauded Clinton for strong presidential leadership in all of these instances. In January 1993, for example, the *New York Times*'s Thomas L. Friedman wrote that they signaled a radical ideological shift in the role of government. When President Reagan had used executive orders, they reflected his conservative belief that government was the problem; Clinton's actions, on the other hand, represented government as an "active, not passive" force in dealing with vital issues. Criticisms of Clinton's assertions of presidential power were almost entirely confined to very conservative groups such as the Heritage Foundation, the Cato Institute, and Phyllis Schlafly's Eagle Forum, all of which accused him of abusing presidential power. With the advent of President George W. Bush in 2001, however, the two sides flip-flopped, with liberals voicing outrage and Republicans falling silent on the exercise of unilateral presidential power.[65]

The issue of executive orders took a particularly revealing turn after Clinton left office. In his last days in office, he barred development in millions of acres of federal lands in ten western states, holding that they were protected by the 1906 Antiquities Act. President Bush denounced this move in the 2000 presidential election, but in a 2003 Supreme Court case, he ordered Solicitor General Ted Olson to defend Clinton's action in order to preserve the underlying principle of presidential authority. In short, Bush was quite willing to sacrifice a specific policy issue to preserve the broader principle of executive power.[66]

Secrecy and executive privilege: A mixed record

On the issue of secrecy, the Clinton record was very mixed. Attorney General Janet Reno in October 1993 issued a memorandum to all departments and agencies that the Freedom of Information Act created a "presumption of disclosure." The directive explicitly reversed

64 Executive Order 12954 – Ensuring the Economical and Efficient Administration and Completion of Federal Government Contracts, March 8, 1995, APP. Crenson and Ginsberg, *Presidential Power*, p. 196. Executive Order 13087 – Further Amendment to Executive Order 11478, Equal Employment Opportunity in the Federal Government, May 28, 1998, APP. Executive Order 13166 – Improving Access to Services for Persons with Limited English Proficiency, August 11, 2000, APP. Douglas W. Kmiec, "Expanding Executive Power," in Roger Pilon, ed., *The Rule of Law in the Wake of Clinton* (Washington, DC: Cato Institute, 2000), pp. 50–7.

65 Thomas L. Friedman, "Clinton's Departure," *NYT*, January 24, 1993. Gaziano, *The Use and Abuse of Executive Orders and Other Presidential Directives*. William J. Olson and Alan Woll, *Executive Orders and National Emergencies: How Presidents Have Come to 'Run the Country' by Usurping Legislative Power*, Policy Analysis No. 358 (Washington, DC: Cato Institute, October 28, 1999). Phyllis Schlafly, *Power Grab by Executive Order* (Eagle Forum, August 5, 1998). Crenson and Ginsberg, *Presidential Power: Unchecked and Unbalanced*, p. 19.

66 Crenson and Ginsberg, *Presidential Power*, p. 201.

President Ronald Reagan's 1981 guidelines, which had favored nondisclosure. Agency FOIA officers should release documents "whenever possible," Reno directed, unless there were some indication of potential "harm" to the United States. Reno's directive was a positive step back to the original purposes of openness in the FOIA law.[67]

At the same time, however, Clinton made claims of executive privilege that evoked eerie memories of Richard Nixon. The executive privilege expert Mark Rozell cites thirteen separate cases when Clinton asserted the claim, "an astounding number" in his view, which was "far more than all of the other post-Watergate presidents combined." Moreover, many were dubious claims involving political issues or criminal investigations and not legitimate national security issues.[68]

The worst example arose in the Monica Lewinsky scandal, which exploded in December 1997. Kenneth Starr had been appointed independent counsel in 1994 to investigate Clinton's role in the Whitewater affair, a tangled Arkansas real estate deal (no investigating body ever found any wrongdoing by either Bill or Hillary Clinton). When Starr plunged into the Lewinsky affair, Clinton invoked executive privilege to block interviews with White House staff. The Clinton attorney Charles Ruff argued that because the investigation involved events during the president's term in office, the "matter is inextricably intertwined with the daily presidential agenda, and thus has a substantial impact on the president's ability to discharge his obligations." One commentator observed, "It is hard to imagine a more dubious use of executive privilege." In particular, there was no national security issue at stake. Judge Norma Holloway Johnson rejected Clinton's claim and the investigation proceeded. Holloway's decision on May 5, 1998, marked the first time since the Supreme Court's Nixon tapes case that a president lost an executive privilege claim in court.[69]

In addition to the Lewinsky-related claim of executive privilege, Rozell cites cases involving the investigations of firings of White House travel office staff, of bribery allegations against Agriculture Secretary Mike Espy, a controversial White House antidrug memo, and materials on U.S. policy toward Haiti. Although some of the investigations were undoubtedly politically motivated, that did not justify a claim to withhold documents. Rozell concludes with the damning indictment that a comparison of Presidents Nixon and Clinton is "apt." Both asserted the privilege to conceal personal wrongdoing or other embarrassing information, and both "gave executive privilege a bad name," making it difficult for subsequent presidents "to reestablish the legitimacy of this constitutional power."[70]

In an early 1994 memo, the White House Special Counsel Lloyd Cutler argued that executive privilege should be used "only after careful review," where it is "necessary to protect Executive Branch prerogatives," and when it extends only to the president and

[67] Reno, Memorandum for Heads of Departments and Agencies, The Freedom of Information Act, October 4, 1993. http://www.justice.gov/oip/foia_updates/Vol_XIV_3/page3.htm.

[68] Mark J. Rozell, *Executive Privilege: Presidential Power, Secrecy, and Accountability*, 3rd ed. Rev. and Updated (Lawrence: University of Kansas Press, 2010), pp. 123–47. This book discusses nine cases; in earlier work Rozell cites thirteen.

[69] Mark J. Rozell, "Something to Hide: Clinton's Misuse of Executive Privilege," *PS: Political Science and Politics* 32 (September 1999): 550–3. "Ruff's Argument for Executive Privilege," *Washington Post*, May 28, 1998. "President Is Denied Executive Privilege," *Washington Post*, May 6, 1998.

[70] Rozell, "Something to Hide," 551. Rozell, *Executive Privilege*, 3rd ed. The term "executive privilege" does not appear in the index to Clinton's memoirs, *My Life*, v. 2.

not to departments or agencies. Most important, Cutler argued that in "investigations of personal wrongdoing by governmental officials, it is our practice not to assert executive privilege." Clinton abandoned these principles for what Rozell terms a "very broad view that all White House communications are presumptively privileged."[71]

In the 1994 ethics investigation of bribery allegations against the agriculture secretary, Mike Espy, the independent counsel in June 1997 requested eighty-four documents. The White House claimed executive privilege and refused to turn them over. The court of appeals eventually ordered the documents released. In another case, a House of Representatives committee requested a memo by the FBI director, Louis Freeh, criticizing the administration's antidrug policy. Attorney General Janet Reno and the White House refused to turn it over, claiming it represented advice to the president rather than a bureau policy statement. In the highly publicized "travelgate" affair, meanwhile, in which the White House fired seven staff members in the White House travel office, the White House refused to give Congress three thousand documents. The issue involved no valid reasons for a claim of executive privilege.[72]

The Lewinsky scandal: Echoes of Watergate

Bill Clinton's presidency will be forever tainted by the Monica Lewinsky scandal: his sexual dalliances with her in the White House, his failure to tell the truth in public statements and under oath, and his impeachment by the House of Representatives on December 19, 1998 (but acquittal by the Senate).[73] The scandal raised several civil liberties issues that resonated with the Watergate scandal more than twenty years earlier. In addition to executive privilege, there was the question of whether a sitting president is above the law.

The tawdry accusations against Clinton included the case of Paula Jones, who alleged that Clinton had sexually harassed her on May 8, 1991, in Little Rock, Arkansas. In response to her damage suit against him in 1994, the White House asserted both executive privilege and the broader claim that as a sitting president Clinton was temporarily immune from such legal actions. (Clinton did not ask for complete immunity, but only for postponement until he was no longer president.) The solicitor general argued that the demands of the case posed "serious risks for the institution of the Presidency." In *Clinton v. Jones,* however, the Supreme Court unanimously rejected that argument, holding that "the president is subject to judicial process in appropriate circumstances." It was unpersuaded that the case would unleash a flood of frivolous litigation and said Congress could enact appropriate legislation, if needed. Clinton's two Court appointees, Ruth Bader Ginsburg and Stephen Breyer, voted against him.[74]

Predictably, Clinton denounced the Court's decision in his memoirs as "one of the most politically naive decisions the Supreme Court has made in a long time." The legal analyst Jeffrey Toobin also wrote that Justice John Paul Stevens's opinion that the Jones suit would not consume much of the president's time was an "epically incorrect prediction." In fact, the case did consume a good bit of Clinton's time and energy, although it is

71 Rozell, "Something to Hide," 551.
72 Rozell, "Something to Hide," 551–2.
73 Nicol C. Rae and Colton C. Campbell, *Impeaching Clinton: Partisan Strife on Capitol Hill* (Lawrence: University of Kansas Press, 2004).
74 *Clinton v. Jones*, 520 U.S. 682 (1997).

difficult to separate Jones's case from the burgeoning Lewinsky scandal. Presidential time aside, however, there remained the question of whether a sitting president is above the law, in the sense of being immune from conventional legal proceedings. Nixon's efforts to thwart investigations of Watergate were on many people's minds in this case. The ACLU, which had called for Nixon's impeachment, submitted an amicus brief on behalf of Jones, arguing that the Nixon case "stands for the proposition that despite the distraction that will inevitably flow, the President can be compelled to provide evidence, including testimony, in a criminal case." The events of subsequent years have not supported the fears of Clinton and his defenders about the president's being consumed by lawsuits. [75]

The second echo of Watergate involved Kenneth Starr's investigation of Clinton's sexual improprieties in the first place, which went far beyond his original mandate regarding the Whitewater deal. The independent counsel law made the office almost unaccountable to anyone but its own judgment. (Formally, Starr did request and receive approval to expand his investigation of perjury and obstruction of justice in January 1998.) In fact, Starr's investigation was heavily shaped by partisan political considerations. The key questions about Clinton's sexual escapades, which led to his lying to a grand jury, were fed to Starr by a group of ideologically driven anti-Clinton operatives in elite law firms.[76]

Starr's questionable tactics do not excuse President Clinton, however. His reckless sexual activity began long before he entered the White House. He certainly knew that he had political enemies after him, and he certainly should have known that as president he was exposed to unsparing scrutiny. Yet, his behavior persisted, and most importantly he did lie to the grand jury. Nonetheless, the obsessive Starr investigation confirmed earlier warnings about the dangers of an unaccountable independent counsel. Griffin Bell, President Jimmy Carter's attorney general, had warned about the danger of complete independence: "It's a bad law.... There's no oversight at all." And in a very prescient observation, he predicted that "the American people will come to regret this." Clinton certainly did, as did most Democrats and many other Americans. Congress allowed the Independent Counsel Act to expire quietly in 1999.[77]

In 2000, the conservative Cato Institute published a collection of essays, *The Rule of Law in the Wake of Clinton*, covering a wide range of domestic and foreign policy issues, all highly critical of his expansive and in their view constitutionally questionable approach to presidential power. Douglas Kmiec, who had served in the Office of Legal Counsel under President Reagan, wrote that "Executive Power [is] a Duty, Not [a] Grant" [of power]. The "take care" clause of the Constitution was "meant to deny the president a suspending or dispensing power," such as had been exercised by English kings. He ended with the sober warning "If we are to preserve our liberties against an overweening executive, the American people must insist that future presidents be more respectful of constitutional limits than William Clinton has been during his tenure." Read today in the wake of President George W. Bush's even greater claims of presidential power, his warning takes on special meaning. Bush as President completely ignored it, and with rare

[75] ACLU *amicus* brief, *Clinton v. Jones*: http://www.aclu.org/content/aclu-amicus-brief-clinton-v-jones. Jeffrey Toobin, *A Vast Conspiracy: The Real Story of the Sex Scandal That Nearly Brought Down a President* (New York: Random House, 1999), pp. 115–17. Clinton, *My Life*, V. 2, p. 393. Toobin, *The Nine*, pp. 116–18.

[76] Toobin, *A Vast Conspiracy*. Kenneth W. Starr, *The Starr Report: The Findings of Independent Counsel Kenneth W. Starr on President Clinton and the Lewinsky Affair* (New York: PublicAffairs Press, 1998).

[77] Bell, OH, p. 23, MCPA.

exceptions conservatives refused to criticize his actions. As the journalist Charlie Savage put it in his book on Bush, "The tenure of President Clinton, like that of Carter before him, showed that presidential power is not a partisan issue."[78]

CONFRONTING INTERNATIONAL TERRORISM

Only in retrospect does Osama bin Laden loom over the Clinton presidency. At the time, very few Americans perceived the sponsor of the September 11, 2001, terrorist attacks as a serious threat to the security of the United States, and few had even heard his name. President Clinton and his chief terrorism aide Richard Clarke did know his name and saw him as a real threat. Their response illuminates the conflicting considerations on how to deal with international terrorism while respecting established law.

After 9/11, the debate over its origins became marked by partisan finger pointing. Clinton's critics and defenders of President George W. Bush accuse him of failing to act in the face of evident danger and therefore being partly responsible for the terrorist attacks. The official 9/11 commission found no serious merit to that charge. Clinton's pre-9/11 actions deserve careful examination if only because they contrast so sharply with his successor's. (The release of still-classified documents in the years ahead will undoubtedly clarify and change current assessments.) There is no doubt that Clinton was very alert to the threat of international terrorism and responded with some aggressive antiterrorist measures. On August 20, 1998, for example, he ordered the bombing of terrorist facilities in Afghanistan and Sudan, specifically referring to "Usama bin Laden, perhaps the preeminent organizer and financier of international terrorism in the world today." (Cynics noted that he had testified before the grand jury about the Lewinsky scandal on August 17 and that the bombing was a "wag the dog" effort to distract attention from his personal problems. A bombing attack against Iraq in December that year revived accusations of a "wag the dog" effort because of the pending impeachment vote. The Secretary of Defense had to answer questions before a closed session of the House on December 16, with nearly all members present.) Significantly, his administration was fully cognizant of the legal culture that had grown up around national security and placed constraints on intelligence gathering, covert actions, and presidential power. The Bush administration, by contrast, had utter contempt for that same legal culture. At the same time, however, the Clinton administration embraced some measures that went to the brink of the law and in some instances set dangerous precedents for his successor in the White House.[79]

President Clinton received a rude introduction to the threat of international terrorism, and of Osama bin Laden in particular, just five days after he was sworn in. On January 25, 1993, two CIA employees were shot and killed outside agency headquarters. One month later, terrorists bombed the World Trade Center in New York City. In response, Clinton initiated several important antiterrorism steps and made the return of terrorists to the

[78] Douglas W. Kmiec, "Expanding Executive Power," in Roger Pilon, ed., *The Rule of Law in the Wake of Clinton* (Washington, DC: Cato Institute, 2000), pp. 47, 61. Savage, *Takeover*, p. 63.

[79] The indispensable discussion of the changing legal culture surrounding national security is Jack Goldsmith, *The Terror Presidency: Law and Judgment inside the Bush Administration* (New York: W. W. Norton, 2007). Clinton, Address to the Nation on Military Action against Terrorist Sites in Afghanistan and Sudan, August 20, 1998, APP. December incident: Takiff, *A Complicated Man*, pp. 363–5.The "wag the dog" concept was popularized in a motion picture of the same name released in early 1998.

United States for trial the "highest priority." Concern about terrorism remained steady throughout his presidency. The public was unaware of most of this, as it was preoccupied with domestic policy issues, including the debacle over Clinton's health care proposal, the Republican capture of Congress in 1994, and the Lewinsky scandal.[80]

The key figure in the administration's antiterrorist efforts was Richard Clarke, who served in various intelligence positions under Presidents Reagan and George H. W. Bush, and later briefly under George W. Bush. One account characterizes Clarke and a few others as "the Jeremiads," a small beleaguered group arguing that al-Qaeda posed a major threat to American security. Clinton elevated him to counterterrorism specialist with the National Security Council, expanding his role and giving him a seat on the Principals Committee, which reviewed national security issues. Clarke's experience under four presidents, of both political parties, makes his a particularly authoritative voice. Notably, in January 2001 he warned the Bush administration about possible attacks on the United States, and in summer 2001 he desperately but unsuccessfully tried to convince President Bush and Secretary of State Condoleeza Rice that an al-Qaeda attack was imminent.[81]

On three occasions in the Clinton years - in 1996, 1998, and 2000 - the possibility of capturing or killing bid Laden arose. In early 1996, for example, the government of Sudan wanted him out of their country and negotiated with the United States over arresting him. The administration declined, and some controversy surrounds this refusal. Clinton's critics argue that it was a great lost opportunity, which could have prevented both the USS *Cole* bombing in 2000 and the 9/11 tragedy. The 9/11 commission, however, concluded, "we have not found any reliable evidence to support the Sudanese claim" that they were willing to turn him over to American authorities. The administration's hesitancy arose not from indifference to terrorism, but from a proper concern about the legality and practical consequences of successfully kidnapping or killing someone like bin Laden. Many officials thought that having a CIA agent kill him on the spot would violate President Gerald Ford's 1976 ban on assassinations. An agent could kill him in self-defense, they conceded, but this only raised the inevitable questions about what circumstances would constitute self-defense, and whether any such claim would be seen as a cover story. A successful kidnapping, meanwhile, raised a host of difficult questions how any such person would be treated once in American custody, as the country learned after George W. Bush became president.[82]

Attention has also focused on a 1998 episode when bin Laden was allegedly at Tarnak Farms in Afghanistan. The CIA vigorously advocated kidnapping him and prepared a formal Memorandum of Notification on it. The 9/11 Commission Report found that

80 "Gunman Kills 2 Near C.I.A. Entrance," *NYT*, January 26, 1993.

81 Richard A. Clarke, *Against All Enemies: Inside America's War on Terror* (New York: Free Press, 2004), pp. 227–38. "Jeremiad": Stephen Grey, *Ghost Plane: the True Story of the CIA Torture Program* (New York: St. Martin's, 2006), p. 131. Thomas H. Kean and Lee H. Hamilton, *The 9/11 Commission Report: Final Report of the National Commission on Terrorist Attacks upon the United States* (Washington, DC: Government Printing Office, 2004), pp. 254–65.

82 The conservative attack on Clinton: Richard Miniter, *Losing Bin Laden: How Bill Clinton's Failures Unleashed Global Terror* (Washington, DC: Regnery, 2003). The 9/11 Commission found failures among many government agencies but did not single out the Clinton administration for special blame: Kean and Hamilton, *The 9/11 Commission Report*, p. 110. Trevor Paglen and A. C. Thompson, *Torture Taxi: On the Trail of the CIA's Rendition Flights* (Hoboken, NJ: Melville House, 2006), pp. 21–7.

this idea "brought to the surface all of the unease about paramilitary covert action that had become ingrained, at least among some CIA senior managers." Justice Department officials were very uncertain about the legality of a kidnapping. When the CIA's Counter Terrorism Center briefed Attorney General Reno and the FBI director, Louis Freeh, in May 1998 it told them the plan had only a 30 percent chance of success. The national security advisor, Sandy Berger, asked several pointed questions regarding the dependability of the Afghans who would be involved in the plan and what would happen if the kidnap succeeded. In particular he expressed doubts about the strength of the evidence against bin Laden and worried that he might be acquitted if taken to the United States for trial. In the face of all these questions, the kidnap plan was abandoned.[83]

Berger's doubts highlight the very different approaches of the Clinton and Bush administrations to international terrorism on one fundamental point. The Clinton administration consistently viewed international terrorism as a law enforcement problem, in which actions are governed by established legal procedures. This included both the legality of killing bin Laden and Berger's concerns about a criminal trial. The Bush administration, however, redefined international terrorism as a military problem. Many knowledgeable observers now argue that the change crossed a legal rubicon by placing key issues such as interrogation tactics outside the framework of established due process procedures. Most important, it allowed the administration to invoke the president's commander in chief powers as the basic source of legal authority. Critics argue that the Clinton administration was paralyzed by concerns about legality, but years later, in view of the legal, moral, and practical morass arising from the Bush administration's lack of respect for the law, the Clinton team's caution seemed both legally correct and pragmatic.[84]

Stepping onto the slippery slope: "Rendering to justice"

The agonizing administration debates over kidnapping bin Laden involved the CIA program known as rendering to justice: kidnapping international criminals and taking them to the United States to stand trial. (The most famous modern rendition was Israel's kidnapping of the Nazi Adolph Eichman in 1960.) The Bush administration transformed this program into one of its greatest horrors, known as extraordinary rendition, in which the CIA secretly kidnapped alleged terrorists and had some of them tortured. Renditions originated on a limited scale in the Clinton administration.[85]

[83] Kean and Hamilton, *The 9/11 Commission Report*, pp. 163–8. In 2004, it was discovered that Sandy Berger had illegally removed classified documents from the National Archives in October 2003, prior to testifying before the 9/11 commission. Copies of the documents remained available elsewhere and no documents were completely lost, according to the Justice Department, but other officials maintain that it is possible that some originals disappeared. In 2005 he pleaded guilty to a misdemeanor, was sentenced to two years probation, was fined $50,000, was stripped of his security clearance for three years, and later surrendered his law license. The incident casts a cloud over Berger's tenure as national security adviser and some aspects of President Clinton's response to terrorism. "Report Details Archives Theft by Ex-Adviser," *NYT*, December 21, 2006.

[84] From a criminal justice to a military process: Jane Mayer, *The Dark Side: The Inside Story of How the War on Terror Turned into a War on American Ideals*, Pbk. ed. (New York: Anchor Books, 2009), p. 52, and surrounding text.

[85] Hannah Arendt, *Eichmann in Jerusalem: A Report on the Banality of Evil* (New York: Viking, 1963).

The exact date when rendering to justice began is not entirely clear, but in the mid-1990s it began on a limited and controlled basis, reflecting the administration's law enforcement approach to terrorism. To its credit, the Clinton administration agonized at great length over the idea of renditions, recognizing that it stood at the borderline of the law where important issues were ill defined. Attorney General Reno insisted that each candidate for rendition have an outstanding criminal warrant, and that he or she be brought to trial. Significantly, no renditions were done for the purpose of making someone available for interrogations, as was the case with the Bush administration. Presidential Decision Directive 39, on June 21, 1995, "Return of Indicted Terrorists to the U.S. for Prosecution," authorized using "all legal means available" to remove or deport terrorists from the United States. If the host country did not cooperate, suspects would be rendered without their cooperation, subject to "the procedures outlined in NSD-77" (which remains classified). The CIA's Michael Scheuer testified to Congress in 2007, "I authored it, then ran and managed" the program from August 1995 to June 1999, during which time somewhere between thirteen and more than two dozen people were rendered. The journalist Stephen Grey persuasively argues that they began as a compromise between the administration's refusal to use troops to seize people and the CIA's lack of any other alternative. In his account, CIA veterans saw renditions as only one small tool in their repertoire and a complement to other means of dealing with terrorism. Only under President George W. Bush did they escalate into a major and essentially uncontrolled program.[86]

Richard Clarke provides a firsthand account of renditions under Clinton and the intense internal debates surrounding it. "By the mid-1990s," he wrote, these snatches were becoming routine CSG [Counterterrorism Security Group] activity." When he proposed a snatch in 1993, the White House counsel, Lloyd Cutler, strenuously argued to Clinton that it would violate international law. Clinton, according to Clarke, was leaning in that direction until Vice President Al Gore arrived late at the meeting. After hearing a summary of the arguments, Gore laughed and said it was a "no-brainer." "Of course it's a violation of international law," he went on. "That's why it's a covert action. The guy is a terrorist. Go grab his ass." Clarke further argues that President Clinton "approved every snatch that he was asked to review."[87] In the end, the Clinton administration did not step very far onto the slippery slope with renditions, but it took a few cautious steps and in doing so set the stage for the Bush administration to plunge into lawlessness and torture.

After the 9/11 terrorist attack, there was much controversy over the so-called wall that Attorney General Reno erected between intelligence investigations and criminal

[86] Louis Fisher, "Extraordinary Rendition: the Price of Secrecy," *American University Law Review* 57 (2008): 1418–20, citing the Congressional testimony of FBI Director Louis Freeh, CIA Director Geroge Tenet, and Scheuer. Stephen Grey, *Ghost Plane: The True Story of the CIA Torture Program* (New York: St. Martin's, 2006), Ch. 6, pp. 129–52; especially the legal history of renditions reaching back to the 1980s (pp. 134–5); the Clinton directives and their immediate aftermath (pp. 136–9); renditions as only one tool (pp. 132, 152). Mayer, *The Dark Side*, pp. 101–38. The White House, Presidential Decision Directive 39, June 21, 1995. Available at http://www.fas.org/irp/offdocs/pdd39htm.

[87] Clarke, *Against All Enemies*, pp. 143–5. In an admittedly partial list of sixteen Clinton era renditions, six of the first seven involved renditions to the United States. Of the next nine, however, five were rendered to Egypt, widely reputed to torture its detainees and a favorite rendition destination for the Bush administration. Grey, *Ghost Plane*, appendix, pp. 269–83.

investigations of suspected terrorists. Clinton critics argue that the wall prevented the sharing of information among different parts of the Justice Department and therefore obstructed the possible capture of Mohamed Atta, the 9/11 leader. The charge is a potentially powerful indictment, but it has no basis in fact.[88]

The "wall" was actually a metaphor for a complex set of administrative regulations designed to control intelligence gathering within the United States. The regulations were another post-Watergate reform that sought to prevent abuses by the intelligence agencies and had been developing for more than a decade before Bill Clinton became president. The goal was to ensure that information from intelligence gathering efforts did not contaminate criminal prosecutions against the same subject because of the lower standard required for the former. The document cited by conservative critics of Janet Reno is a 1995 memorandum by the deputy attorney general, Jamie Gorelick. In fact, the memorandum required the sharing of information, subject to approval by higher Justice Department officials. It explicitly directed that certain information "will be disseminated" and be "promptly considered for dissemination". The Bush administration, moreover, reaffirmed the Gorelick memorandum in August 2001, a month before the 9/11 attacks. In the years before those attacks, there was indeed a serious failure of information sharing among the intelligence agencies, but the 9/11 commission concluded that the memorandum was "misunderstood and misapplied." FBI agents in the field believed they were forbidden to share information, and no one ever corrected their impression and ordered cooperation. At the same time, the FBI director, Louis Freeh, never made national security a bureau priority and faced resistance from parts of the deeply ingrained institutional culture of the FBI. Moreover, Freeh failed to install an up-to-date communications technology system in the bureau and establish procedures for analyzing information from agents in the field. The 9/11 commission reached the devastating conclusion that as a result "the FBI lacked the ability to know what it knew." The important point of the controversy over the "wall" is that it illustrates the Clinton administration's law enforcement approach to terrorism and the care it took to follow legal procedures in investigations. The Gorelick memo, for example, was especially concerned with complying with the FISA law and avoiding even the appearance of circumventing it.[89]

Clinton and the power to go the war

Clinton's dispatch of American military forces around the world on several occasions prompted some controversy, raising again the Vietnam era question of presidential war powers, but it never rose to the level of a major crisis. In September 1994 he sent sixteen thousand troops to restore order in Haiti; in 1995 he sent twenty thousand ground troops to Bosnia as part of a sixty-thousand-member UN military force to implement a UN peace plan; in March 1999, he sent thirty-one thousand service people to undertake

[88] Conservative attacks regarding "the wall," see Heather MacDonald, "FBI Handcuffed," *New York Post*, October 27, 2002.

[89] Memo: Gorelick to Mary Jo White, et al., Instructions on Separation of Certain Foreign Counterintelligence and Criminal Investigations [Classified "Secret"; declassified April 10, 2004]. Copies widely available on the Web. Kean and Hamilton, *The 9/11 Commission Report*, pp. 77–80. Kate Martin, "Justice Department Fails to Address 9/11 Intelligence Failures," *Watching Justice* (New York: Open Society Institute, April 19, 2004).

air operations in Serbia to prevent ethnic cleansing of Albanians; and in Kosovo Clinton supported a NATO bombing campaign in 1999 and committed seven thousand ground troops as part of a NATO peace-keeping force.[90]

In the case of Haiti, Clinton did not request authorization from Congress, nor even consult it regarding the dispatch of American troops. Ten prominent constitutional scholars, including Gerald Gunther, Lawrence Tribe, and Philip Kurland, sent a letter protesting the action. Walter Dellinger, head of the Office of Legal Counsel, replied with a letter to GOP senators setting forth three justifications: The use of troops was implicit in congressional approval in the 1994 Defense Appropriation Act; the president had notified Congress of his plans; and it was not a "war," because a legitimate government in Haiti had invited America to send troops. One analyst labeled these arguments "slim legal reeds."[91]

Clinton justified his military actions as humanitarian or nation-building efforts. Interestingly, a conservative legal scholar and expert on the subject by the name of John Yoo concluded in 2000 that "no president in recent times has had a quicker trigger finger" and argued that Clinton acted without congressional authority. Just a year later, Yoo would head President Bush's Office of Legal Counsel and in that capacity wrote memos arguing that the president of the United States when acting as commander in chief had virtually unlimited power.[92]

MODERATE LIBERTARIANS TO THE SUPREME COURT

Citing her "pioneering work in behalf of the women of this country," President Clinton on June 14, 1993, appointed Ruth Bader Ginsburg as only the second woman to sit on the Supreme Court. Her "truly historic record of achievement" included arguing six women's rights cases before the Supreme Court, five of which she won (including the breakthrough *Reed v. Reed* and *Frontiero v. Richardson* cases).[93] At the time she was a judge on the U.S. Court of Appeals for the District of Columbia, to which President Jimmy Carter had appointed her in 1980.

In important respects, Ginsburg's achievement resembled Thurgood Marshall's. Just as he had transformed American law as legal director of the NAACP Legal Defense Fund (arguing and winning *Brown v. Board of Education*), Ginsburg, as the founding director of the ACLU Women's Rights Project, had broken new ground on women's rights. Her appointment was an indication of how far the women's movement had progressed in a little more than twenty years, as she moved from the principal advocate of a radical new idea in the law to a seat on the highest court in the land. As had Sandra

[90] Richard Sale, *Clinton's Secret Wars: The Evolution of a Commander in Chief* (New York: Thomas Dunne Books, 2009).

[91] David M. O'Brien, "Clinton's Legal Policy and the Courts: Rising from Disarray or Turning Around and Around?" in Colin Campbell and Bert A. Rockman, eds., *The Clinton Presidency: First Appraisals* (Chatham, NJ: Chatham House, 1996), pp. 126–62. 154–5.

[92] A particularly interesting critique of Clinton's use of the military, especially considering the author's role in the George W. Bush administration, is by John Yoo, "The Imperial President Abroad," in Pilon, ed., *The Rule of Law in the Wake of Clinton*, pp. 159–79.

[93] Remarks Announcing the Nomination of Ruth Bader Ginsburg to Be a Supreme Court Associate Justice, June 14, 1993, APP.

Day O'Connor, her colleague on the Court, she had been unable to obtain a job with a law firm after graduating from Columbia University Law School tied for first in her class (where she was the first woman to edit the law review). Later, however, she became the first woman awarded tenure on the Columbia Law School faculty. Given her ACLU background, it was considered likely that she would be asked pointed questions about her views on civil liberties issues. At her confirmation hearings, however, she did not answer questions on the hot button issues of abortion, gay rights, and church and state. Some observers labeled this tactic the "Ginsburg precedent," although it would be more accurately called the post-Bork precedent. Since the bitter conflict over his unsuccessful 1987 nomination, all Court nominees had avoided commenting on the more controversial issues. In 2005, when the Bush chief justice nominee John Roberts also did not answer questions on sensitive issues, Ginsburg called his position "unquestionably right."[94]

For his second appointment, Clinton chose Stephen Breyer, who had previously served as counsel to the Senate Judiciary Committee under Ted Kennedy. Clinton saw him as a moderate liberal pragmatist, and that proved to be a good prediction of his record on the Court.[95]

A remarkable record with the lower courts

With respect to appointments to the lower federal courts, President Clinton succeeded in setting new records on both diversity and quality. More than half of all his appointments were women or racial and ethnic minorities: 31 percent women, 24 percent African Americans, and 8.5 percent Hispanic. One appointee, Deborah Batts, an African American, former assistant U.S. attorney, and former law professor, was the first open lesbian ever appointed a federal judge. Her sexual orientation did not become an issue in her confirmation process, however.[96] Clinton's choices, moreover, involved no compromise with quality. Two-thirds (65 percent) received the American Bar Association's highest rating of "well qualified," the highest percentage of any president since the ABA began rating nominees in the 1950s.[97]

Despite this outstanding record, some liberals and libertarians were not happy, as he did not impose any strict jurisprudential test in selecting his nominees. This was in sharp contrast to the Reagan/Bush approach and that of many other presidents. The political scientist David M. O'Brien concluded that Clinton seemed more interested in diversity and quality than ideology. He quoted the Ninth Circuit Court of Appeals judge Stephen Reinhardt's argument that Presidents Reagan and Bush consciously sought to change the orientation of the federal courts and that Clinton had the same opportunity, but "he blew it."[98]

[94] Michael Comiskey, "The Usefulness of Senate Confirmation Hearings for Judicial Nominees: The Case of Ruth Bader Ginsburg," *PS: Political Science and Politics* 27 (June 1994): 224–7. Toobin, *The Nine*, pp. 69–73.

[95] Toobin, *The Nine*, pp. 79–81.

[96] O'Brien, "Clinton's Legal Policy and the Courts," pp. 138–9. "Deborah A. Batts," Federal Judicial Center, *Biographical Directory of Federal Judges*: www.fjc.gov.

[97] O'Brien, "Clinton's Legal Policy and the Courts," table 4.3, p. 137.

[98] Ibid.,pp. 140–2.

A CONTRADICTORY PRESIDENT

Bill Clinton ranks with Franklin D. Roosevelt and Lyndon Johnson as one of the most complex and contradictory people ever to serve as president of the United States. On civil liberties he was like the proverbial little girl: When he was good he was very, very good; and when he was bad, he was equally disappointing. On abortion, women's rights, church and state separation, and lesbian and gay rights his record was outstanding. He staunchly defended reproductive rights, including even the very controversial "partial birth" abortion procedure. He advanced women's rights in a number of other areas as well, including the first federal programs related to violence against women, and with his many appointments of women to high office, including the federal courts. With regard to the separation of church and state he resisted New Right pressures for prayer in school and published the first meaningful federal guidelines on which kinds of religious expression in public schools were permitted and which were forbidden by the Supreme Court. On gay rights he fully supported federal action on the HIV crisis, ending President Reagan's late and inadequate response. He initiated the issue of gays' serving openly in the military, only to face fierce opposition from the military and Congress, and had to settle for the compromise "don't ask, don't tell" policy, which satisfied almost no one. Overall, on these issues he had a generally excellent record.

On racial justice, however, Clinton's record was extremely contradictory. He famously had an unmatched rapport with African Americans, one of the best records on appointments to high office, and a special knack for organizing symbolic events that educated the public about America's shameful racist history on the 1957 Little Rock crisis and the Tuskegee Syphilis Experiment). On substantive policy, however, he failed in two very important respects. His high-profile Initiative on Race offered nothing in the way of policies to address the persistent inequalities in employment, education, crime, or other areas. Even worse, Clinton's New Democrat pandering to public hysteria about crime and drugs included support for sentencing policies that had direct and terribly adverse consequences for the African-American community.

On other civil liberties issues, Clinton's record was as disturbing as his liberal and civil libertarian critics argued. Particularly bad was his enthusiasm for limiting the right of habeas corpus, setting a precedent that his successor in the White House would take even further. On the First Amendment Clinton yielded to his political instincts in not taking strong stands against the Communications Decency Act and efforts to ban flag burning. Finally, he embraced limitations on privacy in the name of law enforcement.

On national security issues, Clinton's record is particularly ambiguous. Very alert to the rising threat of international terrorism, and al-Qaeda in particular, he directed a response that was aggressive but nonetheless carefully attuned to the new legal culture surrounding the intelligence agencies and the powers of the president. His record in this regard looks much better today than it did at the time, mainly because of his successor's record. At the same time, however, Clinton repeatedly made claims regarding presidential power that were troubling in and of themselves and prepared the ground for abuses by the Bush administration. With both signing statements and executive orders he advanced liberal social policies only by setting himself over and above the will of Congress. He also dispatched American troops overseas, always with good humanitarian intentions but with disregard for the War Powers Act.

Bill Clinton presided over a period of economic prosperity, balanced budgets for several years, and the longest decline in serious crime on record. After the economic crash of 2007-8, these years would be fondly remembered. It was his own fault that he so deeply damaged his reputation with the Lewinsky scandal that still tarnished his reputation. Several prominent liberals criticized Clinton's record on civil liberties because, as they put it, he knew better. He did know better and although he had the best sense of individual rights of any president since Lyndon Johnson, his political instincts too often led him in the wrong direction.[99]

[99] Some analysts argue that the Lewinsky scandal cost Al Gore the 2000 election because a disgusted Gore kept Clinton on the sidelines in the campaign. Gore's vote among married women declined 6 percent compared with Clinton's in 1996. Takiff, *A Complicated Man*, pp. 392–7.

PART IV

Civil Liberties in the Age of Terrorism

14 George W. Bush

A Systematic Assault on the Constitution

OVER TO "THE DARK SIDE"

Five days after the terrorist attacks on the United States on September 11, 2001, Vice President Richard Cheney appeared on NBC's *Meet the Press* and explained that in responding to terrorism, "We also have to work, though, sort of the dark side, if you will."[1] Little did Americans realize what that meant for civil liberties and the rule of law.

President George W. Bush's war on terrorism involved a war on the Constitution, with unprecedented claims of presidential power, an attack on the principle of separation of powers, suspension of the right of habeas corpus for terrorist detainees, repudiation of the Geneva Conventions, and illegal spying on Americans. The administration's actions sent grave questions of constitutional law to the U.S. Supreme Court in a series of historic confrontations, but they also had a human face. One belonged to Brandon Mayfield, a Portland, Oregon, attorney and army veteran, arrested for alleged involvement in a terrorist bombing in Spain. FBI agents secretly entered his home and office under "sneak and peek" warrants authorized by the 2001 PATRIOT Act; arrested him on May 6, 2004, and initially refused to tell his family why he was arrested or where he was being held. Even after Spanish authorities told the FBI the key fingerprint did not match, they held him for another two weeks. Finally conceding its colossal mistake, the bureau released him, and the government awarded him a $2 million settlement.[2] His case was one of many violations of law affecting Americans and people in other countries.

The war on terrorism was only one part of the Bush administration's assault on civil liberties. Bush took office with a far deeper debt to the Religious Right than had Ronald Reagan. He became a born again Christian in 1985 at age thirty-nine, and his crusading faith was completely unlike Reagan's diffidence, or Jimmy Carter's Christian humility. The administration aggressively promoted government-sponsored religious programs; largely abandoned civil rights enforcement; imposed political criteria for federal appointments, particularly in the Justice Department; and declared a virtual "war" on science, banning stem cell research, censoring government reports, and politicizing appointments. These actions alone would make Bush one of the worst presidents ever on civil liberties.

When the administration took office in January 2001, the attorney general nominee John Ashcroft was the lightning rod for its liberal critics. A devout evangelical Christian, he was "the most visible symbol" of the administration's commitment to the Religious

[1] Cheney, *Meet the Press*, September 16, 2001. Transcript available on the Web. In 1954, the Doolittle Commission investigating the CIA argued, "There are no rules in such a game.... Hitherto acceptable norms of human conduct do not apply ... [and] longstanding American concepts of 'fair play' must be reconsidered." See Chapter 6 of this book.

[2] Eric Lichtblau, *Bush's Law: The Remaking of American Justice* (New York: Pantheon Books, 2008), pp. 65–74.

Right. He regarded himself as "a marked man" at his confirmation hearings because of his religiosity, as well as his civil rights record, which included opposing both school integration in St. Louis while governor of Missouri and an African-American judicial nominee while in the Senate. Although firmly opposed to abortion, he nonetheless explained at his hearings that *Roe v. Wade* was established law and an attorney general had an obligation to uphold it. His answers persuaded few critics, however, and he was finally confirmed by a vote of 52–to 48, one of the narrowest margins in history.[3]

Confirming his critics' fears, he led an 8:00 a.m. Bible study groups each day at the Justice Department. While entirely voluntary, the sessions nonetheless suggested that open expression of Christian faith had a preferred place in the administration. All of the initial criticisms, however, were overwhelmed by the 9/11 terrorist attacks. Ashcroft vowed "never again" and, with one notable exception, approved all of the administration's illegal actions in the war on terrorism. The best that can be said of Ashcroft as attorney general is that he was not as bad as his successor, the completely hapless and compliant Alberto Gonzales, whose main qualification for the job was his personal loyalty to President Bush.[4]

A passive president; an aggressive vice president

In a candid account of his own role in the Bush administration, Jack Goldsmith observed that the president was "an invisible presence" in the drama over antiterrorism policies. As head of the Office of Legal Counsel (OLC) in 2003 and 2004, he courageously put his career on the line by revoking earlier OLC memos authorizing torture. With only rare exception, he observed, Bush approved policies drafted by Vice President Cheney and his small coterie, failing either to ask probing questions or to seek outside advice and apparently not understanding the radical implications of the torture authorization or his claims of presidential power.[5]

Bush as president was possibly even more detached from policy details than President Reagan had been. The journalist Lou Cannon, author of two excellent books on Reagan, found abundant evidence of Bush's faults in his earlier careers as a baseball executive and governor of Texas: an excessive loyalty to subordinates, passivity in certain crucial moments, an unwillingness to face hard facts, a refusal to seek a broad range of advice on key policies or do much reading on his own, a pollyannish view of the world, and a short attention span. In one illustrative instance, Bush reportedly was upset when Condoleeza Rice described a situation as "complex."[6]

[3] John Ashcroft, *Never Again: Securing America and Restoring Justice* (New York: Center Street, 2006), "A Marked Man," pp. 39–64. Nancy V. Baker, *General Ashcroft: Attorney at War* (Lawrence: University Press of Kansas, 2006), pp. 20–6.

[4] "Visible symbol": Esther Kaplan, *With God on Their Side: How Christian Fundamentalists Trampled Science, Policy, and Democracy in George W. Bush's White House* (New York: New Press, 2004), p. 34. Bible study: Ashcroft, *Never Again*, pp. 98–100.

[5] Jack Goldsmith, *The Terror Presidency: Law and Judgment inside the Bush Administration* (New York: W. W. Norton, 2007), p. 213. Jane Mayer, *The Dark Side: The Inside Story of How the War on Terror Turned into a War on American Ideals*, Pbk. ed. (New York: Anchor Books, 2009), pp. 62–3. Cheney: see Chapter 10 of this book.

[6] Lou Cannon and Carl M. Cannon, *Reagan's Disciple: George W. Bush's Troubled Quest for a Presidential Legacy* (Washington, DC: Public Affairs, 2008), pp. 231, 235; "complex" comment, p. 237.

Nonetheless, Bush survived politically, winning reelection in 2004 despite the revelations of the grotesque treatment of prisoners in the Abu Ghraib prison in Iraq earlier that year. Part of his success was the refusal of leading Democrats to challenge his worst policies for fear of being labeled soft on terrorism. In the 2004 elections, the Democratic candidate John Kerry never mentioned Abu Ghraib. Additionally, after 9/11, Bush had the quality that had worked so well for Reagan, what the historian Sean Wilentz called his "simple, unflinching eloquence" and an air of moral certitude in the face of a national crisis. In a revealing incident shortly after he turned to religion in 1985, his mother, the former first lady Barbara Bush, was so worried about his rigidity that she asked the Reverend Billy Graham to counsel her son. Graham was alarmed at what he found, and warned the future president, "never play God."[7] As president however, Bush never indicated any doubt about his actions.

The driving force behind the worst abuses of civil liberties on national security was Vice President Dick Cheney, who has justly been called the most powerful vice president in history. Every account portrays him as the unrelenting advocate of the most extreme claims of presidential power, "enhanced" interrogation tactics that constituted torture, and illegal wiretapping. He was aided by a small clique of neoconservative loyalists, especially his assistant, David Addington. The journalist Charlie Savage observes that there were two groups of people in the administration. Bush people, such as Alberto Gonzales and Harriet Miers, were loyal to Bush and inexperienced in the ways of Washington. Cheney people, meanwhile, were ideologically driven and had long Washington experience, which allowed them to outmaneuver the Bush people easily. Lawyers in the Justice, State, and Defense Departments and the CIA who expressed reservations about questionable policies were either browbeaten into silence or excluded from key decisions. The result was a virtual coup d'etat within the administration, an event unprecedented in American presidential history.[8]

Bush demanded action in response to 9/11, and Cheney and his colleagues were ready. Cheney had clearly signaled his views on presidential power as chief of staff to President Gerald Ford in 1974, in the 1987 minority report of the Iran/Contra scandal investigation, and his advice to the incoming George H. W. Bush administration in 1988. Having spent the previous twenty-seven years honing a belief in unfettered presidential power on national security matters, as the *New York Times* reporter James Risen put it, Cheney and his neo-conservative allies took power with "an agenda that was ready-made for the world of September 12."[9]

[7] Sean Wilentz, "Worst President in History," *Rolling Stone*, April 21, 2006. Cannon and Cannon, *Reagan's Disciple*, pp. 252–3. Kerry: Mayer, *The Dark Side*, p. 304. Graham: Bill Minutaglio, *First Son: George W. Bush and the Bush Family Dynasty* (New York: Three Rivers, 1999), p. 289.

[8] Stephen F. Hayes, *Cheney: The Untold Story of America's Most Powerful and Controversial Vice President* (New York: HarperCollins, 2007). "Cheney, Others OK'd Harsh Interrogations," *Associated Press*, April 11, 2008. Goldsmith, *The Terror Presidency*, p. 213. Mayer, *The Dark Side*, pp. 323–4. Bush/Cheney people: Charlie Savage, *Takeover: The Return of the Imperial Presidency and the Subversion of American Democracy* (Boston: Little, Brown, 2007), p. 7. Joel K. Goldstein, "Cheney, Vice Presidential Power, and the War on Terror," *Presidential Studies Quarterly* 40 (March 2010): 102–39 on long-term changes in the institutional role of the vice-presidency.

[9] James Risen, *State of War: The Secret History of the CIA and the Bush Administration*, Pbk. ed. (New York: Free Press, 2007), p. 221.

9/11: THE WORLD OF CIVIL LIBERTIES CHANGES

Civil liberties in America changed profoundly at exactly 8:46 a.m. eastern time on September 11, 2001, when hijacked American Airlines Flight 11 crashed into the north tower of the World Trade Center in New York City. Seventeen minutes later, another plane crashed into the south tower, and an hour later, both towers collapsed, killing almost three thousand people. A third hijacked plane crashed into the Pentagon in Washington, D.C., and a fourth crashed in rural Pennsylvania.[10]

The terrorist attacks provoked fear across the country and unleashed an unprecedented assault on civil liberties. The public fully supported the resulting anti-terrorism policies devised by the Bush administration and Congress. Cofer Black, head of the CIA's Counterterrorism Center, told a Senate committee, "All I want to say is that there was a 'before' 9/11 and 'after' 9/11. After 9/11 the gloves come off." On September 14, Bush declared a national emergency. Other presidents had declared national emergencies, but Bush's declaration was essentially an empty formality. Far more important were a series of secret presidential orders that took the administration over to Cheney's "dark side." On September 17, Bush signed a secret finding directing the CIA to kill or capture al-Qaeda members, and a September 25 Office of Legal Counsel memo by John Yoo argued that Bush's actions as commander in chief were "unreviewable" by Congress or the courts. An October 23 Yoo memo, meanwhile, justified the use of military force against terrorist activities *within* the United States and held that in such actions the administration "need not follow the exact procedures that govern [normal] law enforcement operations," that the warrant requirement of the Fourth Amendment did not apply, and that "First Amendment speech and press rights may also be subordinated to the overriding need to wage war successfully."[11] No president had ever claimed such sweeping authority to suspend the Bill of Rights.

In only one of several steps toward greater secrecy, Ashcroft issued new guidelines on the Freedom of Information Act on October 12, significantly reversing the policy established by the Clinton administration in 1993. While giving rhetorical support to the principles of FOIA, it advised that agency heads "carefully consider" the importance of confidentiality to "efficient" government operations and assured them the Justice Department would "defend your decisions." And on November 5, the Office of Legal Counsel approved "searches for intelligence purposes" in a way that effectively bypassed the FISA court created in 1978 for the sole purpose of supervising such searches. These new policies were the first steps in what would become an obsessive practice of secrecy

[10] Thomas H. Kean and Lee H. Hamilton, *The 9/11 Commission Report: Final Report of the National Commission on Terrorist Attacks upon the United States*, Authorized ed. (New York: W. W. Norton, 2004).

[11] Cofer Black, Testimony, Congressional Joint Inquiry into 9/11, September 26, 2002. Bush, Proclamation 7463 – Declaration of National Emergency by Reason of Certain Terrorist Attacks, September 14, 2001, APP. John Yoo, The President's Constitutional Authority to Conduct Military Operations against Terrorists and Nations Supporting Them, September 25, 2001. www.justice.gov/olc/warpowers925.htm. John Yoo, RE: Authority for Use of Military Force to Combat Terrorist Activities within the United States [underline in original], October 23, 2001: http://www.justice.gov/olc/docs/memomilitaryforcecombatus10232001.pdf. Documents cited throughout this chapter are widely available. See Mark Danner, *Torture and Truth: America, Abu Ghraib, and the War on Terror* (New York: New York Review of Books, 2004), and the National Security Archive, Torture Archive, Selection of Key Documents: http://www.gwu.edu/~nsarchiv/torture_archive/index.htm.

in the Bush administration; bypassing the FISA court, meanwhile, would explode into a major controversy in late 2005.[12]

On the morning of September 12, President Bush turned to Attorney General John Ashcroft and said, "Don't ever let this happen again." Ashcroft said he "took it personally" and vowed, "Never again," putting the Justice Department in a "war mode" on November 7. Participants described a "fevered climate" inside the administration, with "constant crisis-atmosphere meetings." FBI agents interviewed more than eight thousand Arab Americans, with no pretext other than their national origins. The arrival of FBI agents at workplaces threw a cloud of suspicion over innocent people. The Arab-American Anti-Discrimination Committee reported more than seven hundred violent attacks by other citizens on Arab Americans in the first nine weeks after 9/11. There were eighty incidents of people being removed from commercial aircraft because of their appearance or words, eight hundred cases of employment discrimination, and numerous accounts of denial of services. And in the most chilling attack on dissent since the Nixon administration, Attorney General Ashcroft told the Senate on December 6 that administration critics were giving "ammunition to America's enemies."[13]

The atmosphere resembled the response to Pearl Harbor sixty years earlier, with a toxic brew of war and stereotyping of "foreign" elements. There was no wholesale roundup of Muslims or Arab Americans similar to the evacuation of the Japanese Americans, but in important respects, the Bush administration's actions were a far more insidious attack on civil liberties than Roosevelt's. The worst actions were secret - initially, anyway - and whereas the evacuation of the Japanese Americans was understood to be a temporary measure, the war on terrorism was essentially a war without end.

Unleashing the surveillance society: The PATRIOT Act

Six weeks after 9/11, Congress passed the PATRIOT Act (officially the Uniting and Strengthening America by Providing Appropriate Tools Required to Intercept and Obstruct Terrorism Act). In the atmosphere of panic, few if any members of Congress read the entire 342-page bill, which passed with little serious discussion of the sweeping implications of many of its provisions. Exactly one senator, Russ Feingold, Democrat of Wisconsin, dared to vote against it, and only sixty-six voted against it in the House of Representatives.[14]

The assaults on civil liberties in the PATRIOT Act included so-called sneak and peek search warrants, national security letters, roving wiretaps, looser restrictions for Foreign Intelligence Surveillance Act (FISA) court wiretaps, expanded power of the government

[12] Attorney General Ashcroft, Memorandum for Heads of all Federal Departments and Agencies, The Freedom of Information Act, October 12, 2001. www.doj.gov/foia/foia.pdf. John C. Yoo, Authority of the Deputy Attorney General under Executive Order 12333, November 5, 2001. www.justice.gov/olc/at Opinions.

[13] Ashcroft, *Never Again*, p. 130. "Ashcroft Plan Would Recast Justice Dept. in a War Mode," *NYT*, November 9, 2001. Risen, *State of War*, pp. 61, 65, 221. Arab-American Anti-Discrimination Committee, *Report on Hate Crimes and Discrimination against Arab-Americans: The Post September 11 Backlash, September 11, 2001–October 11, 2002* (Washington, DC: ADC, 2003). "Ammunition": "Ashcroft Defends Antiterror Plan: Says Criticism May Aid U.S. Foes," *NYT*, December 7, 2001.

[14] David Cole and James X. Dempsey, *Terrorism and the Constitution*, Rev. ed. (New York: New Press, 2006), pp. 195–218. Howard Ball, *The USA Patriot Act of 2001: Balancing Civil Liberties and National Security: A Reference Handbook* (Santa Barbara: ABC-CLIO, 2004).

to seize business and financial records, and authority to access electronic data and read e-mail subject line Web search patterns, all without warrants. The "sneak and peek" search provision authorized federal agents to enter a home or office and seize items without immediately informing the subject. Brandon Mayfield, the Portland, Oregon, attorney mistakenly arrested as a terrorist suspect, learned how terrifying and abusive this authority could be. One day in April 2004 his wife told him their front door was bolted in a way that made it difficult for her to enter. They also noticed window blinds closed in uncustomary ways, and when the hard drive on Mayfield's office computer started crashing, his tech-savvy son told him someone had removed it and reinstalled it incorrectly.[15]

Brandon Mayfield's trauma was one of the few that attracted much attention – largely because he was a native born American of European background. As the *New York Times* reporter Eric Lichtblau observed, "The thousands of Muslim men jailed by American authorities in the early months and years after 9/11 registered but a blip on the American psyche." Most Americans did not care: "They were foreign-looking men, with foreign-sounding names."[16]

National security letters (NSLs) are administrative subpoenas allowing the FBI to order a person or organization to turn over "any tangible things" it believes are related to international terrorism. As administrative actions, NSLs do not require warrants and are therefore an end run around the Fourth Amendment. NSLs were actually not new. Administrative subpoenas were created in 1978 with the Right to Financial Privacy Act authorizing seizure of financial records. In fact, several war on terrorism procedures had been in existence for some years in one form or another. Administrative subpoenas expanded over the years and, including the PATRIOT Act, are authorized by five separate federal statutes. Predictably, the number of NSLs escalated dramatically. According to the Justice Department's inspector general, the FBI issued nearly 200,000 NSLs between 2003 and 2006, with many involving serious abuses.[17]

A particularly offensive aspect of NSLs was the FBI's authority to "gag" anyone receiving one, forbidding him or her to tell anyone about the letter. The most celebrated NSL gag order was imposed on the Library Connection, a consortium of twenty-six Connecticut libraries, demanding their circulation records in 2005. Gagged, the librarians were unable to speak out about their own case or participate in the debate over the PATRIOT Act reauthorization in late 2005 and 2006. Inevitably, word of the case leaked out and was reported in the *New York Times,* but the librarians could not comment on the story. An ACLU suit on behalf of Library Connection challenging the constitutionality of the gag order eventually prevailed, and the FBI finally withdrew both the gag order and the demand for library records. In a separate case, a district court in New York declared NSL provisions unconstitutional.[18]

[15] Lichtblau, *Bush's Law,* pp. 65–72.

[16] Lichtblau, *Bush's Law*, p. 65.

[17] Charles Doyle, *National Security Letters in Foreign Intelligence Investigations: A Glimpse of the Legal Background and Recent Amendments,* RS 22406 (Washington, DC: Congressional Research Service, Updated March 28, 2008).

[18] ACLU, *America's Surveillance Society* (New York: ACLU, 2008), p. 3. Connecticut case, *Doe v. Ashcroft,* and related issues: American Library Association web site: www.ala.org. Herbert N. Foerstel, *Refuge of a Scoundrel: The Patriot Act in Libraries* (Westport, CT: Libraries Unlimited, 2004).

A culture of suspicion, spying, and secrecy

The Bush administration also promoted a deeply insidious culture of suspicion through several dubious proposals. It first devised TIPS (Terrorism Information and Prevention System) to encourage Americans to spy on each other. Workers in service industries, such as postal carriers and telephone repair people, would be encouraged to report "suspicious" behavior. The Justice Department Web site assured that "these workers will use their common sense" but provided no guidelines regarding suspicious conduct. TIPS recalled the American Protective League in World War I, when private citizens carrying Justice Department badges seized young men they thought were avoiding the draft, acting entirely on their own prejudices. TIPS was quickly exposed, outraging even conservatives such as the Texas Republican congressman Dick Armey. Congress banned it in the 2002 Homeland Security Act.[19]

Determined to expand domestic surveillance, the administration then came up with Total Information Awareness (TIA), created by the Defense Advanced Research Projects Agency (DARPA; famous for developing the Internet). TIA was a massive data mining program that would search individual Americans' financial, travel, and health records to look for "suspicious" patterns. The moving force behind TIA was John Poindexter, President Ronald Reagan's national security director, who had been convicted of several offenses in the Iran-Contra scandal. TIA was also too much for Congress, which killed it in a 2003 defense appropriations bill.[20]

The Pentagon, meanwhile, developed a secret surveillance program, TALON (Threat and Local Observation Notices), in 2003, which asked civilian and military Pentagon employees to report "suspicious" activity near defense facilities. After NBC News exposed the program in late 2005, an ACLU freedom of information request found that the Pentagon database included traditional antiwar protests by such groups as the pacifist American Friends Service Committee and many local organizations. The Defense Department Inspector General reported there were about 13,000 TALON reports by early 2006, but in the face of public criticisms, but the following year an Under Secretary of Defense recommended that the program be terminated.[21] The administration also developed "watch lists" naming people as suspected terrorists or sympathizers. The no-fly list, for example, barred listed individuals from commercial air flights. By 2009, the secretary of homeland security claimed there were only twenty-five hundred names on the list, but critics charged there were as many as thirty thousand to fifty thousand names. The criteria for being listed were vague, people had no way of knowing they were on the list, and, if they did, they had great difficulty in getting off it. In an incident that exposed how ludicrous the program was, Senator Ted Kennedy in August 2004 said he had been delayed at airports because of names on the list similar to his.[22]

19 Operation Tips: Terrorism Information and Prevention System. www.citizencorps.gov/tips.html. America Protective League: see Chapter 2 of this book, in the section on "Governt-sponsored vigilantism."

20 Cole and Dempsey, *Terrorism and the Constitution*, pp. 226–7. Poindexter's role in the Iran-Contra scandal: Theodore Draper, *A Very Thin Line: The Iran-Contra Affairs* (New York: Hill & Wang, 1991).

21 Inspector General, Department of Defense, The Threat and Local Observation Notice (TALON) Report Program, Report No. 07-INTEL-09 (June 27, 2007). ACLU, *No Real Threat: The Pentagon's Secret Database on Peaceful Protest* (New York: ACLU, 2007).

22 "Senator? Terrorist? A Watch List Stops Kennedy at Airport," *NYT*, August 20, 2004.

The fascination with data mining led in 2003 to a set of Fusion Centers, a joint Homeland Security and Justice Department venture combining data from both government and private sources that would be mined for suspicious activity patterns. By 2009 there were at least nine active Fusion Centers, including facilities in Virginia, Michigan, and Arizona. Data mining was another strategy that did not originate with the war on terrorism. Computer technology had already made it a widespread practice in both government and private industry. A 2004 General Accounting Office (GAO) report, for example, found 131 operational and 68 planned data mining efforts in 128 federal agencies. About half were related to improving agency service or performance, and 24 were directed toward fraud, waste, and abuse. Fourteen specifically involved "analyzing intelligence and detecting terrorist activities."[23]

The culture of suspicion cultivated by the administration encouraged a revival of political spying by state and local law enforcement agencies, which had been exposed and largely ended in the 1970s. In one outrageous case, the Maryland State Police placed fifty-three peace activists on a terrorism-related watch list. They included members of the Pledge of Resistance, an antiwar group; the Baltimore Coalition against the Death Penalty; and several nuns involved with these groups. No police reports indicated any suspected criminal activity.[24]

The common theme running through all of the domestic surveillance programs was a disdain for the Fourth Amendment and individual privacy. Other presidential administrations had spied on Americans, but none ever approached the Bush administration's determined, systematic efforts. President Nixon's wiretapping involved small, sporadic efforts by comparison. Congress generally supported the Bush programs. It overwhelmingly passed the PATRIOT Act but did prohibit both TIPS and TIA. The American public had few reservations. In a December 2001 ABC News poll, 90 percent of Americans supported the administration's actions in the war on terrorism, and only 6 percent objected.[25]

Foreign visitors whose ideas or associations the government did not like also fell under suspicion in a revival of ideological exclusion reminiscent of the cold war and the Reagan administration. Tariq Ramadan, a Swiss citizen and noted Muslim scholar who had taught at Oxford University and other leading universities, was unable to teach at Notre Dame University in 2004 when the administration revoked his visa on the grounds of "providing material support to terrorist organizations." *Foreign Policy* magazine ranked him eighth among the one hundred most influential contemporary intellectuals in the world. The ACLU and other groups sued to end his exclusion, and he eventually was granted a visa and spoke in New York City in 2010.[26]

In the end, the massive, multipronged effort to identify terrorists not only violated civil liberties but was ineffectual and did not make America any safer. In 2006, for example,

[23] General Accounting Office, *Data Mining: Federal Efforts Cover a Wide Range of Uses*, GAO-04-548 (Washington, DC: General Accounting Office, May 2004).

[24] ACLU, *America's Surveillance Society*. www.aclu.org. "Spying Uncovered. Documents Show State Police Monitored Peace and Anti-Death Penalty Groups," *Baltimore Sun*, July 18, 2008. ACLU, *No Real Threat*. 1970s exposes: Frank J. Donner, *Protectors of Privilege: Red Squads and Police Repression in Urban America* (Berkeley: University of California Press, 1990).

[25] Summary of public opinion polls, 2001–7, "War on Terrorism," PollingReport.com.

[26] ACLU, "Tariq Ramadan among Many Writers and Scholars Denied Entry on Basis of Political Views," Press Release, March 24, 2009. www.aclu.org. Ramadan on the heterogenous nature of Islam: Tariq Ramadan, *Western Muslims and the Future of Islam* (New York: Oxford University Press, 2004).

the Justice Department declined to prosecute a staggering 87 percent of the international terrorism cases referred by the FBI. There was a sharp spike in referrals in 2002, obviously in reaction to 9/11, followed by an equally dramatic decline in 2003, from 355 cases to 66. By 2008 the number had fallen to what it had been in 1999, well before 9/11.[27]

Republicans loyally supported their president and were joined by most Democrats in Congress as well. The only conservatives to protest the assaults on civil liberties were Far Right ideologues who were less committed to GOP party loyalty. The former Georgia congressman Bob Barr, for example, worked with the ACLU in opposing the PATRIOT Act. But even the Federalist Society, a bastion of conservative legal thought, said almost nothing about Bush's extraordinary claims of unlimited presidential power. The Safe and Free Coalition fashioned by the ACLU in the immediate wake of 9/11 included Phyllis Schlafly's Eagle Forum and other conservative groups. The libertarian Ron Paul, GOP candidate for president in 2008, warned that the threat to "liberty and privacy is very real." Although fairly limited in scope and impact, the conservative protests were nonetheless a significant development. During the cold war, for example, conservatives stood by silently in the face of assaults on freedom of speech and association.[28]

Gradually, as the immediate shock of the 9/11 attacks receded, and the abuses of the PATRIOT Act and other Bush administration actions came to light, grassroots opposition began to emerge. The Bill of Rights Defense Committee, closely allied with the ACLU, organized local governments to pass resolutions opposing the act. The Denver City Council enacted the first to mention the PATRIOT Act specifically on March 18, 2002, denouncing the law, affirming the principle of freedom from unreasonable searches and seizures, and directing that a copy of the resolution be sent to President Bush. By mid-2008, 414 local, county, and state governments had passed resolutions opposing the PATRIOT Act, with efforts under way in another 274 communities.[29]

SECRET – AND NOT SECRET – ABUSES OF PRESIDENTIAL POWER

John Yoo's October 23, 2001, OLC memo advised that in the war on terrorism, even "First Amendment speech and press rights may also be subordinated to the overriding need to wage war successfully." The defining feature of the Bush administration's war on terrorism was its sweeping theory of presidential power, far exceeding anything claimed by any previous president. Vice President Cheney had been ruminating on this subject for a quarter of a century and had publicly articulated his views in the minority report in the 1987 Congressional Iran-Contra investigation[30] Yoo opened by declaring that actions against terrorists operating in the United States "need not follow the exact procedures that govern law enforcement operations." The current threat of international terrorism is "unprecedented in recent American history." Since "Al-Qaeda is not

[27] ACLU, *Reclaiming Patriotism: A Call to Reconsider the Patriot Act* (New York: ACLU, 2009), p. 13. www.aclu.org.

[28] ACLU coalition: Nadine Strossen, "Preserving Safety and Freedom Post 9-11," *Journal of the Institute of Justice and International Studies*, 3 (2003): 1–7.

[29] Denver City Council, Resolution 13, March 18, 2002, with other resolutions and documents on the Web site of the Bill of Rights Defense Committee: www.bordc.org.

[30] Yoo and Delahunty, RE: Authority for Use of Military Force to Combat Terrorist Activities within the United States, October 23, 2001. Mayer, *The Dark Side*, p. 9 (on the Geneva Conventions); p. 47 (on presidential power).

a nation" the United States was not bound by either domestic or international law in dealing with it. Thus, as writer Jane Mayer points out, "America became the first nation ever to authorize violations of the Geneva Conventions." Finally, Yoo argued that the United States had been attacked and had a fundamental "right of self-defense." (The Bush administration itself repudiated the extraordinary October 23, 2001, memo in its last months, on October 6, 2008.)[31]

At one point in 2002, the administration considered sending U.S. troops to Buffalo, New York, to arrest suspected al-Qaeda terrorists. The 1878 Posse Comitatus Act prohibited use of the military in domestic law enforcement situations, but officials cited Yoo'S October 23, 2001, memo to argue that this would be a national security–related and therefore military operation rather than a conventional law enforcement action. Defining war on terrorism actions as military ones marked a radical departure from President Clinton's administration, which had maintained a law enforcement approach, with all the standards of due process that required. As Bush later explained in his memoirs, "On 9/11 it was obvious the law enforcement approach to terrorism had failed." A bitter debate ensued deep within the administration, with Cheney and his allies arguing for using troops. Bush finally rejected the idea and ordered the FBI to make the arrests. It was one of the few occasions when he asserted himself as president and rejected a Cheney proposal.[32]

Secret and illegal: warrantless wiretapping of Americans

It seemed to be an instant replay of December 1974, twenty-one years earlier, when a front-page story in the *New York Times* exposed secret CIA spying on Americans. This time, an equally sensational *Times* front-page story on December 16, 2005, exposed a program of illegal spying on Americans by the National Security Agency. The story revealed that the Bush administration had willfully violated the 1978 Foreign Intelligence Surveillance Act (FISA), one of the landmarks of the post-Watergate reforms.[33]

FISA actually accommodated the intelligence agencies in many ways, particularly an emergency provision that allowed a warrantless wiretap for seventy-two hours before seeking a warrant, and over the years, the FISA court was extraordinarily generous to the government, rejecting exactly 5 of 22,990 warrants between 1979 and 2006. The mere existence of the FISA court, of course, may have forced prosecutors to improve the quality of their requests, and perhaps not even to request wiretaps in an unknown number of cases. NSA and the Bush administration, however, chafed at FISA constraints, particularly because they blocked "data mining" or "link analysis" that advances in computer technology made possible.[34]

[31] Yoo and Delahaunty, Memorandum for Alberto R. Gonzales, Re: Authority for Use of Military Force to Combat Terrorist Activities within the United States, October 23, 2001. Steven G. Bradbury, Memorandum for the Files, RE October 23, 2001, OLC Opinion Addressing the Domestic Use of Military Force to Combat Terrorist Activities, October 6, 2008. http://www.gwu.edu/~nsarchiv/torturingdemocracy//documents/20081006.pdf.

[32] "Bush Weighed Using Military in Arrests," *NYT*, July 25, 2009. George W. Bush, *Decision Points* (New York: Crown Books, 2010), p. 154.

[33] "Bush Lets U.S. Spy on Callers without Courts," *NYT*, December 16, 2005. Ch. 2, Risen, *State of War*, pp. 39–60. Hersh: "Huge CIA Operation Reported in US against Antiwar Forces, Other Dissidents during Nixon Years," *NYT*, December 22, 1974.

[34] William French Smith, Attorney General to Director of the Administrative Office of the United States Courts, April 22, 1981 (1980 FISA Annual Report). Congressional Research Service, *The Foreign Intelligence Surveillance Act: A Brief Overview of Selected Issues, Updated* (Washington, DC: CRS, February 8, 2008).

The NSA illegal spying program was another direct result of 9/11. Just twenty-three days after the terrorist attacks, on October 4, President Bush authorized it in a secret order. It was so secret that most top national security officials did not even know about it. The *Times* reporter Eric Lichtblau argues that it was another Dick Cheney brainchild and was fully consistent with his belief that Congress could not limit a president's power on national security when he acted as commander in chief. Yoo dutifully provided an elaborate legal rationale to justify it. The *Times*'s James Risen argues that the Bush administration spying "swept aside nearly thirty years of rules and regulations" over national security wiretaps. By the time it stopped, an estimated seven hundred people outside the United States and five hundred inside had been illegally wiretapped.[35]

In one of the few known instances when he exercised independent judgment, President Bush had some reservations about violating the FISA law and approved it only on the condition that the Justice Department continually review the program and that the attorney general reauthorize it every forty-five days. This requirement would eventually lead to an astonishing hospital room confrontation in 2003 that has no known precedent in American history. Radical changes in communications technology made possible the illegal NSA spying program – and facilitated its exposure. The majority of international telephone and e-mail communications now travel in digital form, and because of the American lead in the industry, most of the traffic passes through the United States at some point. Government surveillance, therefore, only requires the giant telecommunications companies (the "telecoms") to allow government agents to install the necessary equipment. All but one of the companies cooperated with NSA (only QWEST refused). Using private companies, however, greatly raised the risk that an employee would discover the wiretapping and blow the whistle – which is exactly what happened. Mark Klein, an AT&T technician in San Francisco, discovered an NSA official in the building one day, learned about a supersecret Room 641A, and finally came across documents describing the company's cooperation with the NSA. He then heard of similar things from technicians at other ATT facilities around the country, and soon the secret was out.[36]

Lichtblau's exposé, meanwhile, had its own disturbing history, which revived old questions about the role of the media in national security issues. The Bush administration learned about his reporting in advance and put intense pressure on *Time*s editors and publisher to prevent them from publishing it, summoning the publisher Arthur Sulzberger, Jr., and the editor William Keller to the White House. Keller "vividly" recalled being told they would be responsible for the next terrorist attack if they published the story. The administration bluntly argued that the story would benefit al-Qaeda. The pressure worked, and the story did not appear before the 2004 presidential election, when it might have affected the outcome. A year later, the *Times* again planned to publish the story, and White House pressure resumed, including a meeting at the White House in December 2005. When the editors learned that the administration might seek a federal court injunction to stop publication, in a replay of President Nixon's injunction to halt publication of the *Pentagon Papers* in 1971, the editors quickly posted the

35 The October 4 memorandum was still secret in late 2011. Risen, *State of War*, pp. 42, 54.

36 The other instance was his refusal to send military troops to Buffalo, New York, despite Vice President Cheney's urging and a John Yoo OLC memorandum providing legal justification. Klein: Lichtblau, *Bush's Law*, p. 139.

story on its Web site. In the new digital world of publishing, there were no printing presses to stop.[37]

President Bush blatantly lied to the American people about the NSA spying. In an April 2004 speech in Buffalo, New York, he assured his audience that any federal wiretap "requires a court order." As Lichtblau recounts the speech, Bush dramatically chopped the air with his left hand: "We're talking about getting - chop - a court order - chop." The gesture may have impressed the audience, but Bush was lying, and he knew it.[38]

Actually, a number of different people and agencies had learned about the NSA spying. Some FBI officials stumbled across it accidentally within a month. And in a move that was either subtle or brazen, Attorney General John Ashcroft informed Royce Lamberth, chief judge of the FISA court, about it in fall 2001. Lamberth, however, did nothing about this blatantly illegal bypassing of his court. Congress also failed to exercise proper oversight. The administration duly briefed the Senate and House intelligence committees, as required. After the *Times* exposé, however, the Senate Democratic minority leader, Tom Daschle, and others accused the CIA of not fully explaining the spying program.[39]

President Bush's requirement that he review and renew the spying program every forty-five days led to one of the most bizarre confrontations in American presidential history. When Jack Goldsmith became head of the Office of Legal Counsel in March 2003, he was horrified by the crucial OLC memos on war powers, torture, and the NSA spying. Finding them "legally flawed, tendentious in substance and tone, and overbroad and thus unnecessary," he decided in late 2003 he "must withdraw and replace" them. He and Deputy Attorney General James Comey persuaded Attorney General Ashcroft not to reauthorize the NSA spying program, and for the first time the Bush administration faced a serious revolt within its ranks.[40]

At this critical moment, Ashcroft was rushed to the hospital for emergency surgery to remove his gallbladder. On March 10, the day of his surgery, Comey informed the White House he would not reauthorize the NSA spying. A furious Vice President Cheney moved to overrule him. Late that night, Comey learned that the White House counsel, Alberto Gonzales, and the chief of staff, Andrew Card, were headed to the hospital to see Ashcroft, despite a ban on all visitors. Correctly suspecting their intent, he immediately called the FBI director, Robert Mueller, and told him to meet him at George Washington Hospital. Racing through the city with emergency lights flashing and running up the stairs at the hospital, Comey managed to beat Gonzales and Card to Ashcroft's room. He quickly saw that Ashcroft was in no condition to conduct any business, much less decide a serious legal matter. Gonzales and Card then walked in and, ignoring Comey, presented Ashcroft with the reauthorization for his signature. In what is probably one of the most principled acts by any attorney general, Ashcroft told them, "I'm not the Attorney General"

37 Lichtblau, *Bush's Law*, pp. 204–11. Pentagon Papers case: see Chapter 9 of this book. White House meeting: Bill Keller, "The Boy Who Kicked the Hornet's Nest," *New York Times Magazine*, January 30, 2011, p. 38.

38 Remarks in a Discussion of the PATRIOT Act in Buffalo, New York, April 20, 2004, AP. Lichtblau, *Bush's Law*, p. 159.

39 Lichtblau, *Bush's Law*, pp. 166–7.

40 Goldsmith, *The Terror Presidency*, pp. 177–82, explains that legal constraints limit his ability to explain events fully, but he is explicit in condemning the Bush administration for choosing secrecy rather than a developing a flexible and legal approach. Lichtblau, *Bush's Law*, p. 175–6.

and pointed to Comey. Civil libertarians had regarded Ashcroft as a threat because of his overt profession of Christian faith, but this one act transforms his reputation as attorney general. At the time of his resignation, in an internal memo, Comey paid Ashcroft a high tribute: "when it came to crunch-time, he stood up, even from an intensive care hospital bed." "That backbone," he lamented, "is [now] gone." The incident revealed the administration's contempt for the rule of law and its disregard even for the personal health of one of its own top officials.[41]

Undeterred by the lack of a reauthorization, the White House went ahead with the NSA program the next day. Comey and several other Justice Department officials revolted and drafted letters of resignation. Finally realizing that a major crisis was about to erupt, President Bush asked to meet privately with Comey and Mueller. After hearing their arguments against the spying program, he told them, "Do what the [Justice] Department thinks is right." The writer Jane Mayer quotes an insider who said, "I tend to think no one had ever told him the truth before." Vindicated, Comey and his staff wrote new controls for the NSA program to limit future abuse.[42]

A month after the *Times*'s exposé, the attorney general, Alberto Gonzales, defended the NSA spying program in a speech at Georgetown University Law Center. Drawing on an OLC memo, he argued that the September 2001 Congressional Authorization for Use of Military Force (AUMF) empowering the administration to "use all necessary and appropriate force" against terrorism covered "intelligence collection inside the United States," as a "traditional incident of war." Most likely, few senators supporting the authorization thought it amended FISA. The FISA process, Gonzales added, was too slow to cope with urgent terrorist situations, completely ignoring the emergency procedure allowing temporary seventy-two-hour warrantless surveillance.[43]

Despite public outrage over the illegal NSA spying, Congress not only refused to end it, but actually expanded the government's powers. The 2008 FISA Amendments Act granted retroactive immunity from civil suits to the telecommunication corporations for collaborating with the NSA (at least forty suits had been filed), allowed the government to destroy records about the program, and increased the time limit for warrantless wiretaps from forty-eight hours to seven days. In a revealing index of congressional support for the war on terrorism, the bill passed the Senate 69–28 and 293–129 in the House. The ACLU charged that the law "legalizes mass, untargeted and unwarranted spying" on communications, and that "no president should have [such] unchecked power.[44]

The irony of the Bush administration's obsession with secrecy is that it was intended to cover up policies that so outraged much of the public that it led to unprecedented disclosures of government actions. The resulting leaks, Freedom of Information Act requests (the ACLU alone obtained "hundreds of thousands" of documents, according to staff

41 Lichtblau, *Bush's Law*, pp. 179–85. Mayer, *The Dark Side*, pp. 289–91. Comey to Chuck Rosenberg, April 28, 2005. http://www.gwu.edu/~nsarchiv/torturingdemocracy/documents/20050428.pdf.

42 Mayer, *The Dark Side*, pp. 264–8, 291. Lichtblau, *Bush's Law*, p. 184.

43 Alberto Gonzalez, "Prepared Remarks for Attorney General Alberto R. Gonzalez at the Georgetown University Law Center, January 24, 2006. www.fas.org. Office of Legal Counsel, Legal Authorities Supporting the Activities of the National Security Agency Described by the President, January 19, 2006. www.justice.gov/olc/ at Opinions.

44 ACLU, Talking Points on the 2008 FISA Amendments Act of 2008, July 1, 2008: www.aclu.org.

lawyers), investigative journalism stories, and Congressional investigations yielded more documents about the inner workings of the Bush administration than any other recent president.

THE WORLD, AMERICA, AND VICE PRESIDENT CHENEY

The administration's claims of sweeping presidential powers should have been no surprise. The argument had been developing for a quarter of a century among a small group of neoconservative ideologues, with Dick Cheney as the moving force. As the *New York Times* reporter James Risen put it, he and his allies arrived in the White House with an agenda for reasserting presidential power at home and American power around the world. Cheney himself saw his national security agenda as "a restoration, if you will, of the power and authority of the president." Determined, well versed in the issues, and skilled in bureaucratic in-fighting, he completely outmaneuvered President Bush.[45]

Cheney first set forth his view of presidential power in late 1974 when he was chief of staff for President Gerald Ford. Until then, most political observers had seen him as a nonideological political technician, with ambitions but little substance. Watergate apparently changed him, and the December 1974 exposé of CIA domestic spying pushed him even further. Worried about the impact of congressional investigations, Cheney put his thoughts on yellow legal note paper. Most important, the administration needed to head off "congressional efforts to *further encroach on the Executive branch* [emphasis added]." Twenty-six years later as vice president, he pursued that goal with unrelenting zeal.[46]

As a congressman from Wyoming from 1979 to 1989, Cheney compiled one of the most conservative voting records in the House, opposing virtually all civil liberties and liberal social policies. He voted for constitutional amendments to ban abortion and busing students to achieve racial integration, opposed a ban on housing discrimination against families and children, fought the Clean Water Act, and voted ten times against federal nutrition programs.[47]

Cheney's view of presidential powers was rooted in a broad vision of America's role in a post-cold war world. The collapse of the Soviet Union in the late 1980s, he and other neoconservatives believed, left the United States as the dominant economic and military world power. In a fateful leap, they then argued that the United States had both the right and an obligation to use its power around the world, including in unilateral military interventions. Two other crucial leaps followed. First, they argued that the president has unlimited authority in matters of foreign policy and national security, citing the 1936 *United States v. Curtiss-Wright* Supreme Court decision, which called the president the "sole organ" of foreign policy (although many legal experts argue that the decision has been misinterpreted by advocates of presidential power). Second, and even more cru-

45 Risen, *State of War*, p. 221. Hayes, *Cheney*. Lou Dubose and Jake Bernstein, *Vice: Dick Cheney and the Hijacking of the American Presidency* (New York: Random House, 2006). John Nichols, *The Rise and Rise of Richard B. Cheney* (New York: New Press, 2005). Bob Woodward, "Cheney Upholds Power of the Presidency," *Washington Post*, January 20, 2005.

46 Hayes, *Cheney*, pp. 71–2, 88. Cheney, Notes, circa 1974, Cheney Files, Box 6, GFPL.

47 Hayes, *Cheney*, pp. 122–203. Nichols, *The Rise and Rise*, pp. 90–3.

cially, they argued that neither the Congress nor the courts could limit that power. All of the worst Bush abuses of power flowed from these assumptions.[48]

President Bush embraced the idea of preemptive war, appropriately, in a June 1, 2002, commencement address at West Point. The old cold war doctrines of deterrence and containment were no longer adequate to the new world of international terrorism, he advised. The "new threats require new thinking," and Americans must "be forward looking and resolute, [and] be ready for preemptive action."[49] It was a clear signal that the administration was preparing to invade Iraq.

Cheney's first full-blown statement of his view of presidential power appeared in the 1987 minority report in the congressional investigation of the Iran-Contra scandal. In addition to denying any violations of law by the Reagan administration, the report argued that it was "unconstitutional for Congress to pass laws intruding" on the powers of the Commander in Chief." This included not only the Boland Amendment at issue in the scandal, but also the 1973 War Powers Act and other controls that had developed in the post-Watergate period. Years later, Cheney was very proud of the minority report. When the illegal NSA spying was exposed in 2005, he told reporters, "If you want to understand why this program is legal ... go back and read my Iran-Contra report."[50]

ASSERTING PRESIDENTIAL POWER: THREE AVENUES

To implement Cheney's view of presidential power, the Bush administration seized on three existing avenues: the theory of the unitary executive, presidential signing statements, and the theory of state secrets. It carried the first two to radical extremes, and with the third simply extended a dangerous principle used by several previous presidents.

In a November 5, 2002, signing statement, President Bush announced that he would enforce six sections of the law only as he saw fit, "consistent with the constitutional authority of the President to supervise the unitary executive branch."[51] The fact that the law involved federal education research, with utterly no national security implications, revealed the administration's zeal in asserting presidential power.

The "soft" version of the theory of the unitary executive is a perfectly reasonable truism: the president, for example, appoints the secretary of defense and directs the Defense Department and military policy. The Bush administration, however, embraced the "strong" version, which holds that neither Congress nor the courts can limit the power of the president as commander in chief. The theory surfaced in academic legal circles in the 1980s and had been used by the Reagan administration. Thus it was not something cobbled together after 9/11. The law professor Dawn Johnsen, a critic of the strong

48 Louis Fisher, *Presidential War Power* (Lawrence: University Press of Kansas, 1995). John Yoo provided the principal legal rationales for the Bush view of presidential power, and many commentators have noted his failure to address the *Youngstown Steel* case. The case is briefly mentioned in John Yoo, *The Power of War and Peace: The Constitution and Foreign Affairs after 9/11* (Chicago: University of Chicago Press, 2005), p. 6, but then not addressed explicitly.

49 Commencement Address at the United States Military Academy in West Point, New York, June 1, 2002, APP.

50 Daniel K. Inouye and Lee H. Hamilton, *Report of the Congressional Committees Investigating the Iran-Contra Affair, with the Minority Views* (New York: Times Books, 1988), pp. 371–459. Cheney 2005 quote in Sean Wilentz, "Mr. Cheney's Minority Report," *NYT*, July 9, 2007.

51 Statement on Signing Legislation to Provide for Improvement of Federal Education Research, Statistics, Evaluation, Information, and Dissemination, and for Other Purposes, November 5, 2002, APP.

version, found that by early 2008, President Bush had invoked the theory 363 times. It had been rejected by the Supreme Court in a 1988 case upholding the 1978 Independent Counsel Act, but like a bull in the constitutional china shop, the Bush administration simply ignored the decision and continued to invoke the theory.[52]

A front-page story by Charlie Savage in the *Boston Globe* on April 30, 2006, meanwhile, set off a separate uproar over President Bush's assertions of presidential power. The *Globe* reported that he had issued more than 750 signing statements declaring he would not enforce portions of newly enacted laws, including affirmative action, defense regulations, whistle-blower protection for federal employees, and everything related to national security. Bush's extraordinary use of signing statements had been discussed a year earlier by the presidential power expert Philip J. Cooper in an academic journal. He observed that few people had noticed, even though the evidence was in plain sight. Savage's exposé in the *Globe* changed all that.[53]

Signing statements were not new. The administration aggressively defended them, citing among other justifications their long history reaching back at least to President James Monroe. Traditionally, however, they were little more than press releases celebrating a new law. In the mid-1980s, President Reagan's attorney general, Edwin Meese, enhanced their legal status, and Reagan issued an estimated 250 statements. President Bill Clinton also used them many times, indicating that Democratic as well as Republican presidents sought to protect and even expand executive power. With President Bush, it was not the number of signing statements, but his aggressive use of them on every conceivable issue, which clearly signaled a very broad view of presidential power. Opaque legalese disguised the real meaning of any particular statement. Thus, for example, Bush's December 30, 2005, statement saying he would enforce section 8104 of a Defense Department appropriations act only as he saw fit did not reveal to the nonexpert that he was repudiating the McCain Amendment banning torture – arguably one of the most consequential of all his signing statements.[54]

The *Boston Globe* story provoked widespread alarm about a presidential power grab. An American Bar Association Task Force Report condemned the administration's practice "as contrary to law and our constitutional system of separation of powers." The scholar Phillip J. Cooper labeled them "A Different Kind of Line Item Veto." At a Senate

52 Steven G. Calabresi and Christopher S. Yoo, *The Unitary Executive: Presidential Power from Washington to Bush* (New Haven, CT: Yale University Press, 2008). Ronald Reagan, Statement on Signing the Federal Debt Limit and Deficit Reduction Bill, September 29, 1987, APP. Dawn E. Johnsen, "What's a President to Do? Interpreting the Constitution in the Wake of Bush Administration Abuses," *Boston University Law Review* 88 (April 2008): 395–419. *Morrison v. Olson*, 487 U.S. 654 (1988).

53 "Bush Challenges Hundreds of Law," *Boston Globe*, April 30, 2006. Savage, *Takeover*, pp. 228–49. Phillip J. Cooper, "George W. Bush, Edgar Allen Poe, and the Use of Abuse of Presidential Signing Statements," *Presidential Studies Quarterly* 35 (September 2005): 515–53. Phillip J. Cooper, *By Order of the President: The Use and Abuse of Executive Direct Action* (Lawrence: University of Kansas Press, 2002), pp. 199–230, which puts signing statements in the context of other forms of presidential power.

54 John P. Elwood, Presidential Signing Statements, Statement before the House Committee on the Judiciary, January 31, 2007. www.justice.gov/olc at Opinions. Reagan: Chapter 12 of this book, in the section on "A New Assertion of Presidential Power: Signing Statements." Interpretation sympathetic to Bush: Christopher S. Kelley, "Contextualizing the Signing Statement," *Presidential Studies Quarterly* 37 (December 2007): 737–48. Signing statements in the context of other forms of presidential power: Cooper, *By Order of the President*, pp. 199–230. Statement on Signing the Department of Defense, Emergency Supplemental Appropriations to Address Hurricanes in the Gulf of Mexico, and Pandemic Influenza Act, 2006, December 30, 2005, APP.

Judiciary Committee hearing, on June, 27, 2006, Senator Patrick Leahy declared, "We are at a pivotal moment in our Nation's history . . . with a President who makes sweeping claims for almost unchecked Executive Power." Even the law professor Steven Calabresi, who had first urged greater use of signing statements in 1985 as a member of the Reagan administration, eventually criticized Bush, as did the conservative law professor Douglas Kmiec, director of the OLC under Reagan, who denounced Bush's practices as "provocative." Kmiec, it should be noted, was also one of the few conservatives to criticize the Bush administration's excessive use of executive privilege. [55]

In truth, signing statements involve complex matters of law and policy. A president is certainly justified in saying he or she would not enforce a section of a law that is clearly illegal (such as a blatant violation of free speech), without having to veto the entire bill. As is often the case, a bad provision is included in a larger bill with other urgent priorities (such as a defense appropriation). Even the ABA Task Force did not provide objective principles for distinguishing between proper and improper use of signing statements.

A third assertion of presidential power involved the theory of state secrets, in which the administration refused to disclose certain documents in court cases, claiming their release would reveal information damaging to national security. State secrets was also not a new concept, and presidents had been using it quietly for decades. The Supreme Court established the doctrine in the 1953 *United States v. Reynolds* case, in which the widows of three civilian engineers killed in the crash of an Air Force B-29 bomber sued the government for negligence. The government withheld a crucial air force report on the crash on the grounds that it would reveal important secrets. When the report was finally released in 2000, it clearly established air force negligence and contained no secrets. The case had little immediate impact, and over the next twenty-three years there were only four reported cases involving state secrets claims.[56] Everything changed in the 1970s, however, and the claim was invoked in fifty-one reported cases in the following twenty-four years, largely in response to international terrorism. Ironically, the change was prompted by the 1974 Supreme Court case on President Richard Nixon's White House tapes. By limiting the scope of executive privilege as a way of withholding important information, the Court encouraged subsequent administrations to find alternative rationales. Two Democratic presidents (Carter and Clinton) and two Republicans (Reagan and George H. W. Bush) used this new secrecy option, reflecting a bipartisan commitment to secrecy.

In short, the Bush administration made extraordinary claims of executive authority, but in almost every case it built on precedents from both Democratic and Republican presidents. To be sure, George W. Bush carried each one to extremes, but the underlying problem was not simply Bush but an inherent drive for secrecy among presidents in a dangerous world of international threats.

[55] American Bar Association, *Task Force on Presidential Signing Statements and the Separation of Powers Doctrine* (Chicago: ABA, 2006). www.abanet.org. "ABA Condemns President Bush's Use of Signing Statements," Associated Press, August 9, 2006. The ABA did not recommend abolishing signing statements, but instead proposed regulations to curb their abuse. Calabresi and Kimiec comments: Savage, *Takeover*, pp. 243–4. Doug Kmiec, "Executive (Over) Privileged – Must the Abuse Continue," *Convictions*, July 14, 2008. www.slate.com/blogs/convictions/archive/2008/07/14/.

[56] Louis Fisher, *In the Name of National Security: Unchecked Presidential Power and the Reynolds Case* (Lawrence: University Press of Kansas, 2006). Barry Siegel, *Claim of Privilege: A Mysterious Plane Crash, A Landmark Supreme Court Case, and the Rise of State Secrets* (New York: HarperCollins, 2008).

THE DARK SIDE: RENDITION, DETENTION, AND TORTURE

Vice President Cheney was not being flippant in his September 16, 2001, comment that the country would have to go over to "the dark side" in the war against terrorism.[57] He meant it, and he was the driving force behind the Bush administration's plunge into a set of secret, illegal, and even barbaric practices of international kidnappings, secret prisons (which critics labeled the "American Gulag"), denial of habeas corpus, indefinite detention of terrorist suspects, and torture. These outrages were justified by legal memos that horrified independent attorneys, secrecy, and blatant lying to the public.

The American "torture taxi": Extraordinary rendition

Khalid El-Masri was one of the human faces of the Bush administration's abuses of power. A German citizen born in Kuwait to Lebanese parents, he was kidnapped by CIA agents in Macedonia on January 23, 2004, in an extraordinary rendition. Masked, black-clad CIA agents stripped him naked, beat him, drugged him through an anal suppository (a degrading practice designed to reinforce the sense of helplessness), and flew him to a CIA prison in Afghanistan known as the "Salt Pit," where he was interrogated. In his case, they had the wrong person. Finally recognizing its mistake five months later, the CIA flew him to Albania and dumped him on a street in the dead of night. As many as three thousand people were allegedly seized on the streets around the world and sent either to foreign countries or to secret CIA prisons. The exact number of those rendered may never be known, including how many died. The victims literally disappeared from the rule of law and became essentially stateless people, with no legal rights or access to any court of law. As an April 2006 Amnesty International report characterized the policy, they were "beyond the protection of the law" and "the perpetrator[s] above it."[58]

Extraordinary rendition encapsulated the Bush administration's secrecy, claims of extraordinary presidential power, and contempt for the rule of law, including American laws and international agreements. On September 17, 2001, six days after the 9/11 attacks, President Bush signed a secret presidential finding authorizing the CIA to "kill, capture, and detain" al-Qaeda members. Arguably, the finding violated President Gerald Ford's 1976 executive order forbidding assassinations. A March 13, 2002, OLC memo argued that "our constitutional history and practice confirms" that the president as commander in chief has "exercised exclusive and virtually unfettered control over the disposition of enemy soldiers and agents captures in time of war." Neither the Geneva Conventions or the Convention against Torture restrict the commander in chief power of the president.[59]

Initially, the CIA took rendition victims to sympathetic countries, particularly Egypt, which some called "torture central," where it assumed they would be tortured. Soon,

[57] Cheney, Transcript, *Meet the Press*, September 16, 2001, www.msnbc.msn.com.

[58] Stephen Grey, *Ghost Plane: The True Story of the CIA Torture Program* (New York: St. Martin's, 2006), pp. 79–102. Trevor Paglen and A. C. Thompson, *Torture Taxi: On the Trail of the CIA's Rendition Flights* (Cambridge, UK: Icon Books, 2007). Amnesty International USA, *Below the Radar: Secret Flights to Torture and Disappearance* (New York: Amnesty International, April 5, 2006), pp. 2, 8. Mayer, *The Dark Side*, pp. 282–7.

[59] As of November 2011 the September 17, 2001, finding has not been made public. Grey, *Ghost Plane*, p. 149. Office of Legal Counsel, RE: The President's Power as Commander in Chief to Transfer Captured Terrorists to the Control and Custody of Foreign Nations, March 13, 2002. Released by the Obama Administration, March 2, 2009.

however, the agency decided it needed its own prisons and created secret "black sites" in cooperative countries such as Poland, the Czech Republic, Germany, Jordan, and Thailand. Officials in these countries denied any knowledge of the secret prisons, but a 2006 European Union (EU) report exposed official collaboration and revealed a total of 1,245 rendition flights to EU countries. The concept of extraordinary rendition is not recognized in international law, and human rights experts argue that it violates Article 3 of the United Nations Convention against Torture, which forbids sending a person to a country "where there are substantial grounds" for believing that he might be tortured. Article 2 of the convention forbids torture itself. The United States ratified the convention on October 21, 1994, and thus the Bush administration violated American law with extraordinary renditions that led to torture.[60]

The Bush administration did not invent renditions. They began on a far more limited basis, possibly in the late 1980s, and expanded in 1995 under President Clinton. Suspects, however, were initially taken to the United States for trial – literally "rendered to justice" – and Clinton's attorney general, Janet Reno, insisted there be an outstanding warrant for the person. (Eventually, however, some were sent to other countries under Clinton.) The Bush administration threw those strictures aside and seized anyone it believed was a terrorist, sending them to neither the United States nor a court of law. Countries accepting them gave pro forma assurances they would not be tortured, but it is generally believed that U.S. officials knew they would[61]

The CIA secretly transported people in aircraft registered to dummy private corporations. Private planes did not attract the attention military aircraft would, but they left extensive paper trails in the form of company incorporation papers, business addresses, names of corporate officials, and flight plans, all with signatures. Dogged journalists exposed the deceit. The signature of "Colleen A. Bornt," for example, appears on various documents in different handwritings, and "she" was a nonexistent CIA "ghost." People at the nominal headquarters of Premier Executive Transport Services, at 339 Washington St., Dedham, Massachusetts, refused to talk to investigative reporters. The flights of Premier's Gulfstream V N379P plane were tracked from flight records, and it became known as the "Guantanamo Express."[62]

AN INTERNATIONAL DISGRACE: TORTURE

"The war on terrorism is a new kind of war," the White House counsel Alberto Gonzales advised President Bush in a secret January 25, 2002, memo. Bush had said the same thing in public remarks on September 17, 2001, just a week after the 9/11 attacks. The United States, therefore, did not have to abide by the Geneva Conventions in its treatment of captured terrorist suspects. The memo justified the most grotesque violations of law and

60 "Torture Central," Grey, *Ghost Plane*, p. 42. Paglen and Thompson, *Torture Taxi*, pp. 21, 27, 174; Ch. 4, "Dark Prisons" 125–51. Council of Europe, *Secret Detentions and Illegal Transfers of Detainees Involving Council of Europe Member States: Second Report* (11 June 2007). Mayer, *The Dark Side*, "Inside the Black Sites," pp. 139–81.

61 Paglen and Thompson, *Torture Taxi*, pp. 21, 26, 63–4, 66. Clinton: see Chapter 13 of this book. Eichmann rendition: Hannah Arendt, *Eichmann in Jerusalem: A Report on the Banality of Evil* (New York: Viking Press, 1963).

62 Paglen and Thompson, *Torture Taxi*, pp. 42–6, 53. Amnesty International, *Below the Radar*, pp. 23–4, 29–30. Grey, *Ghost Plane*, Ch. 5, pp. 105–28.

human rights principles: torture. Bush approved Gonzales's memo on February 7, 2002: "I accept the legal conclusion of the Department of Justice ... that none of the provisions of Geneva apply to our conflict with al-Qaeda." He then appeared to soften his position and assure critics by stating that "our values as a nation ... call for us to treat detainees humanely." But in a sleight of hand that only careful readers noticed, he explained that the "Armed Forces shall continue to treat detainees humanely," specifically omitting the CIA from this stricture.[63]

Critics believe the March 28, 2002, capture in Pakistan of Abu Zubaydah, the first so-called high-value suspect seized by the CIA, was "the critical precedent" that "triggered everything." President Bush described him as al-Qaeda's "chief of staff, " and the CIA was determined to get as much information as possible from him. This forced the administration to confront the legality of what it euphemistically called "harsh interrogation" tactics, and what others called torture.[64]

The January 2002 memo, together with the other so-called torture memos, highlight the special nature of Bush administration "lawlessness." Cheney, his aide David Addington, and John Yoo were not oblivious to the rule of law. Quite the contrary, they were highly conscious of the new legal culture surrounding presidential power and international human rights. The purpose of all the "torture memos" was to provide elaborate legalistic rationales for what they knew flew in the face of established legal principles and humanitarian standards. The new legal culture had permeated the Justice Department, the Pentagon, the State Department, and even the CIA. Many Pentagon officials opposed torture for all the reasons cited by Gonzales in his January memo, particularly its impact on military discipline. FBI agents observing interrogations at Guantanamo were deeply disturbed by what they witnessed and opposed water boarding and related techniques. The pervasiveness of the new legal culture was the very reason Cheney operated with such obsessive secrecy, as he needed to cut out of decision-making procedures the lawyers in the other agencies who objected to harsh interrogation techniques.[65]

In practice, the approved harsh interrogation included a range of techniques, generally used in combination and over extended periods, that were designed to isolate, disorient, confuse, exhaust, and create a feeling of hopelessness. Detainees were stripped naked; held in isolation, with extremes of heat and cold; deprived of sleep; shackled in painful "stress" positions; threatened with dogs (a highly offensive act in Muslim culture), or subjected to other culturally offensive actions; and subjected to very loud music. The most controversial technique was water boarding, which became the focal point of American and international outrage. The procedure of pouring water over a prone person

[63] "Ashcroft Defends Antiterror Plan: Says Criticism May Aid U.S. Foes," *NYT*, December 7, 2001. Gonzales to Bush, Decision Re Application of the Geneva Convention on Prisoners of War to the Conflict with Al Qaeda and the Taliban, January 25, 2002, Danner, *Torture and Truth*, pp. 83–7. Bush to Vice President, et al, Humane Treatment of al Qaeda and Taliban Detainees, February 7, 2002, in ibid., pp. 105–6. Another valuable collection of documents: Karen J. Greenberg and Joshua L. Dratel, eds., *The Torture Papers: The Road to Abu Ghraib* (New York: Cambridge University Press, 2005). In a separate secret memo Gonzales held that the Convention against Torture, ratified by Congress in 1994 and thereby American law, applied only within the United States and not to actions overseas, thereby exempting Bush administration practices. Savage, *Takeover*, p. 213.

[64] Risen, *State of War*, 22–7; quotes, p. 27.

[65] Risen, *State of War*, p. 32.

to create the feeling of drowning has been condemned as torture by everyone from military authorities to human rights activists. Khalid Sheikh Mohammed (often referred to as "KSM"), an admitted mastermind of the 9/11 attacks, was reportedly water boarded 183 times by the CIA; Abu Zubaida was water boarded 83 times in one month of 2002. (There is some controversy over the exact figures, but not about the fact of water boarding.) The Bush administration claimed KSM divulged vitally important information, but to their embarrassment he later recanted his torture-induced statements.[66]

The most notorious of the "torture memos, dated August 1, 2002, spun a web of legalese arguing that to qualify as torture any treatment had to be specifically intended to be torture, be conducted over an extended period, and involve pain of such intensity as to be "akin to that which accompanies serious physical injury such as death or organ failure." The memo added, however, that "even if" the acts in question amounted to torture the president has unlimited power to approve interrogation techniques as commander in chief, and that "any effort" to apply the Convention Against Torture and interfere with "the President's direction of such core war matters as the detention and interrogation of enemy combatants would be unconstitutional."[67] In short, the president as commander in chief is beyond the reach of either the Congress or the Supreme Court, and the memo denied the fundamental principle of separation of powers that is the foundation of American constitutional democracy. It is doubtful that President Bush fully understood the implications of this and other key memos, but it is absolutely certain that Vice President Cheney did. The Pulitzer Prize-winning reporter Anthony Lewis characterized the memos as "like the advice of a mob lawyer to a mafia don on how to skirt the law and stay out of prison." Three months after taking office, the Obama administration formally withdrew the August 1, 2000, torture memo.[68]

As public outrage over torture mounted at home and abroad, President Bush simply lied about it, just as he did with NSA spying. When he sent Congress a bill to create military commissions on September 6, 2006, he declared, "I want to be absolutely clear with our people and the world: the United States does not torture. It's against our laws, and it's against our values. I have not authorized it, and I will not authorize it." In his own mind, he was telling the truth, because the August 1 memo told him the techniques in questions were not torture. Apart from administration loyalists, no one was persuaded. The International Committee of the Red Cross concluded in 2007 that the United States was indeed engaging in torture, and that CIA agents in their secret prisons engaged in "cruel, inhumane or degrading" practices that violated the Geneva Conventions.[69]

[66] "Detainee's Harsh Treatment Foiled No Plots," *Washington Post*, March 29, 2009. OLC conclusion that water boarding did not constitute torture: Jay S. Bybee to John Rizzo, Re Interrogation of Al Qaeda Operative, August 1, 2002, National Security Archives, Key Documents.

[67] Jay Bybee, Memorandum for Alberto R. Gonzales, August 1, 2002, RE: Standards of Conduct for Interrogation Under 18 USC ## 2340-2340A, Danner, *Torture and Truth*, pp. 115-66.

[68] Anthony Lewis, "Making Torture Legal," *New York Review of Books* (July 15, 2004). David J. Barron, Assistant Attorney General, Withdrawal of Office of Legal Counsel CIA Interrogation Opinions, April 15, 2009. http://www.justice.gov/olc/2009/withdrawalofficelegalcounsel.pdf.

[69] Remarks on the War on Terror, September 6, 2006, APP. International Committee of the Red Cross, Strictly Confidential, *ICRC Report on the Treatment of Fourteen 'High Value Detainees' in CIA Custody* (Washington, DC: ICRC, February 2007). Mark Danner, "U.S. Torture: Voices from the Black Sites," *New York Review of Books* (April 9, 2009).

Significant public outrage over torture did not really arise until 2004, in response to the Abu Ghraib photos depicting American abuse of Iraqi prisoners. In the immediate aftermath of the 9/11 attacks, however, even respected, normally liberal voices endorsed torture by Americans. In November 2001 *Newsweek*'s Jonathan Alter wrote that it's "Time to Think about Torture." A few days later, the Harvard Law professor Alan Dershowitz, a prominent civil libertarian, recommended torture administered under judicial "torture warrants," which he argued would justify it. That these voices would even consider torture indicates the powerful impact of the 9/11 attacks on American thinking about civil liberties.[70]

The consequences: From Gitmo to Abu Ghraib

All pretense of denial about abusive practices evaporated in March 2004 when horrific photographs surfaced of Iraqi prisoners being abused by Americans in the military Abu Ghraib prison in Baghdad. The now-infamous images depicted human pyramids of naked men, prisoners led around on dog leashes, and the most notorious image of a hooded prisoner standing on a box with electric wires dangling from his body.[71]

The Abu Ghraib abuses were a direct consequence of the original torture authorization. The secretary of defense, Donald Rumseld, in early 2003 gave Major General Geoffrey Miller a verbal order to "Gitmoize" Iraq in order to obtain more useful intelligence. When Miller arrived in Baghdad on August 31 with a seventeen-member "Tiger Team," torture "migrated" around the world. The military blamed the Abu Ghraib abuses on a few "bad apples," but in December 2008 the Senate Armed Services Committee concluded that officials had "solicited information on how to use aggressive techniques" and then "authorized their use."[72] As many critics had argued, moreover, torture produced worthless intelligence, with victims confessing what their captors wanted to hear. Shafiq Rasul recanted his confession, as did Ibn al Shaykh al-Libbi, who had been water boarded. President Bush touted the evidence obtained from Khalid Sheikh Mohammed and Abu Zubaydah as extremely valuable in his September 6, 2006, speech, but KSM later recanted his statements. The *Washington Post* in 2009 reported that Abu Zubaida gave false and misleading evidence under torture. Even the CIA director, George Tenet, finally conceded they got nothing "solid" from KSM, but in his 2010 memoirs Bush continued to insist that the extreme interrogation techniques "proved highly effective."[73]

Torture also created serious legal and practical problems about what to do with detainees who were tortured, consigning them to a legal limbo, where the United States could not bring them to trial because of the abuses and yet was afraid to release them.

70 Jonathan Alter, "Time to Think about Torture," *Newsweek*, 11/5/01. Alan M. Dershowitz, "Is There a Torturous Road to Justice?" *Los Angeles Times*, November 8, 2001. Mark Bowden, "The Dark Art of Interrogation," *Atlantic Monthly* (October 2003). Grey, *Ghost Plane*, pp. 148–9.

71 Photographs and documents: Danner, *Torture and Truth*.

72 Mayer, *The Dark Side*, 235, 240–1. Danner, *Torture and Truth*. U.S. Senate Armed Services Committee Inquiry into the Treatment of Detainees in U.S. Custody (December 12, 2008), p. xii. Janis L. Karpinski, *One Woman's Army: The Commanding General of Abu Ghraib Tells Her Story* (New York: Miramax, 2005).

73 "Detainee's Harsh Treatment Foiled No Plots," *Washington Post*, March 29, 2009. "Illusions Fueled Rough Handling of Qaeda Figure," *NYT*, April 18, 2009. Mayer, *The Dark Side*, pp. 277, 325. Risen, *State of War*, p. 33. Savage, *Takeover*, pp. 218–19. Effectiveness of torture: Grey, *Ghost Plane*, pp. 141–4. George W. Bush, *Decision Points* (New York: Crown, 2010), p. 169.

Jamie Gorelick, a Justice Department official in the Clinton administration and a member of the 9/11 commission, explained, "It's a big problem.... In criminal justice, you either prosecute the suspects or let them go. But if you've treated them in ways that won't allow you to prosecute them you're in this no-man's land. What do you do with these people."[74] President Barack Obama would inherit this problem and quickly find that he could not close Guantanamo as quickly as he initially promised.

Jack Goldsmith steps in

"They're going to be really mad," the Justice Department attorney Patrick Philbin told the OLC head Jack Goldsmith as they drove to the White House in December 2003. "They've never been told 'no.'" He was right. Although some administration officials had objected, none ever fought the Bush administration over its detention and torture policies. And so when Goldsmith told them he was withdrawing the torture memos, Cheney and his aide David Addington exploded in fury. Addington crudely told Goldsmith, "The blood of the hundred thousand people who die in the next attack will be on *your* hands."[75]

A few key administration officials had objected to some of the worst policies. On January 11, 2002, the State Department lawyer William H. Taft IV (great-grandson of President William H. Taft) advised John Yoo that "the most important factual assumptions" in the draft of a forthcoming memo and "its legal analysis are seriously flawed." Two weeks later, Colin Powell warned the White House counsel, Alberto Gonzales, of the very dangerous consequences of repudiating the Geneva Conventions. These and other critics were either ignored, cut out of the decision-making process, or browbeaten by Cheney or Addington.[76]

Goldsmith stands as the real hero of the Bush administration. A conservative who generally supported the administration's actions, he was also a principled legal scholar who was appalled by the unprofessional legal reasoning in John Yoo's memos. Literally within hours after assuming office, Goldsmith received a phone call from the White House counsel Gonzales asking whether the Geneva Conventions applied. Examining the key memos over the next few weeks, he found them deeply flawed, and in December 2003, after much agonizing, he decided to begin withdrawing them.[77]

Goldsmith's actions highlight the special role of the Office of Legal Counsel. Most Americans had not even heard of it, but over the years it had become the lawyer for presidential administrations – the Justice Department's conscience, as some put it – with the power to approve or disapprove presidential actions. Thus, when Goldsmith "withdrew" the torture memos, his act was accepted as having the force of law. In

[74] Gorelick quoted in Mayer, *The Dark Side*, p. 111.

[75] Goldsmith, *The Terror Presidency*, p. 41 (Philbin); p. 71 (Addington).

[76] William H. Taft, IV to John C. Yoo, January 11, 2002, Your Draft Memorandum of January 9. See also Taft to Counsel to the President, February 2, 2002. http://www.torturingdemocracy.org/documents/20020111.pdf. Colin Powell to Counsel to the President, January 26, 2002, Draft Decision Memorandum for the President on the Applicability of the Geneva Convention to the Conflict in Afghanistan. http://www.torturingdemocracy.org/documents/20020126.pdf.

[77] Goldsmith, *The Terror Presidency*, pp. 151–61. Jeffrey Rosen, "Conscience of a Conservative," *New York Times Magazine*, September 9, 2007. Goldsmith generally approved of Bush's policies and felt they could have been accomplished through proper legal procedures.

theory, a president could ignore the OLC, and Goldsmith even told Bush that, but Bush dared not take that step. Vice President Cheney raged in protest, but in vain. In his memoir, Goldsmith provides an illuminating discussion of the enormous change in the legal culture surrounding presidential power between World War II and the Bush presidency. When Franklin D. Roosevelt was president, there was little if any law governing presidential power, and FDR had essentially a free hand, for example, in his decisions on the Japanese Americans and the German saboteurs. The 1949 Geneva Conventions, the 1952 Supreme Court decision on President Truman's seizure of the steel mills, the Convention against Torture, and other legal constraints simply did not exist. They did exist by Bush's time, however, and his disregard for them alone qualifies him as the worst president ever on civil liberties.[78]

Congress finally rose up in 2005 to ban torture, but the Bush administration undermined it through another of its assertions of presidential power. In response to the Abu Ghraib scandal, the Republican senator John McCain, who had been tortured while a prisoner in the Vietnam War, sponsored the 2005 Detainee Treatment Act, prohibiting the mistreatment of detainees and limiting interrogation techniques to those specified in the *U.S. Army Field Manual for Human Intelligence*. Vice President Cheney made three trips to Congress in a desperate attempt to stop the bill. At one point he proposed having it apply to the military but not the CIA. McCain adamantly refused. The law, however, accepted the Bush position that federal courts had no authority to hear habeas corpus petitions from detainees regarding torture. Bush made a tactical retreat and signed the bill, mainly because he knew he had an ace in the hole. And so at 8:00 p.m. Friday, December 30, 2005 – prime time for burying a controversial announcement – the White House quietly released a signing statement saying that it would enforce section 8104 of the law regarding interrogations "in a manner consistent with the President's constitutional authority as Commander in Chief ... and to supervise the unitary executive branch." The word "torture" did not appear, and a nonspecialist would not know that President Bush was vowing to ignore one of the most hotly debated mandates ever enacted by Congress. Congress, however, did not have the stomach for a principled stand on this grave issue. In 2006 it reversed itself, passing the Graham-Levin Amendment allowing the use of evidence obtained through torture. The historian Alfred McCoy has argued that the amendment made torture the official policy of the U.S. government. In short, Congress was eventually complicit in approving the most offensive part of the Bush war on terrorism.[79]

Only some Europeans objected to the U.S. renditions and torture. The Spanish prosecutor Baltasar Garzon investigated possible war crimes charges against six American officials, including Cheney and Yoo. And in 2009, the Milan, Italy, prosecutor Armondo Spataro won convictions of twenty-three CIA-related Americans for the kidnapping in Italy of Abu Omar and his rendition to Egypt in 2003.[80]

78 Goldsmith, *The Terror Presidency*, pp. 32–9; the point is central to Goldsmith's entire book. See also: Jack L. Goldsmith and Cass R. Sunstein, "Military Tribunals and Legal Culture: What a Difference Sixty Years Makes," *Constitutional Commentary* 19 (2002): 288.

79 Bush, Signing Statement, December 30, 2005, APP. Alfred W. McCoy, *A Question of Torture: CIA Interrogation, from the Cold War to the War on Terrorism* (New York: Metropolitan Books, 2006).

80 Steven Hendricks, *A Kidnapping in Milan: The CIA on Trial* (New York: W. W. Norton, 2010).

THE SUPREME COURT CONFRONTS PRESIDENTIAL POWER

"Gitmo," the U.S. Military Detention Camp at Guantanamo Bay, Cuba, became the symbol of the Bush administration's violations of the Constitution and human rights and eventually the focus of a monumental legal struggle between the White House and the Supreme Court over fundamental constitutional questions of presidential power. In four historic decisions, the Court, while conceding much to the administration, decisively ruled key administration policies unconstitutional.

The first twenty prisoners arrived at Guantanamo on January 11, 2002, and the total eventually reached an estimated 775 people. The administration used the ill-defined category of "unlawful enemy combatants" for the detainees; that meant they were not prisoners of war subject to the Geneva Conventions and would be tried by the military commissions Bush created in November 2001. The commissions' procedures appalled legal experts and human rights activists by rejecting many established principles of American law: denying the right of habeas corpus; admitting coerced testimony, even if obtained by torture; allowing secret evidence that the defense could not challenge; and a definition of war crimes that included new categories of conduct. In announcing the commissions, President Bush asserted that "it is not practicable" to apply "the principles of law and the rules of evidence" used in ordinary criminal cases to terrorism suspects. This statement reflected the assumption that the war on terrorism was a military rather than a traditional criminal law matter and that this was "a different kind of war."[81]

The first detainee case to reach the Supreme Court involved a habeas corpus petition filed by Yaser Esam Hamdi, a U.S. citizen captured in Afghanistan in 2001 and detained indefinitely as an unlawful enemy combatant. Despite his citizenship, the administration claimed he had no right to an attorney or access to American courts. The latter point raised the issue of habeas corpus, the cornerstone of Anglo-American law since the Magna Carta was signed in 1215. In a stunning 8–1 decision on June 28, 2004, the Court in *Hamdi v. Rumsfeld* soundly rebuked the administration. Justice Sandra Day O'Connor framed the core issue in the war on terrorism, writing that it is "vital that our calculus not give short shrift to the values that this country holds dear or to the privilege that is American citizenship." It is in the "most challenging and uncertain moments" "that we must preserve our commitment at home to the principles for which we fight abroad." And most important, "we necessarily reject the Government's assertion that separation of powers principles mandate a heavily circumscribed role for the courts in such circumstances ... [and most important] a state of war is not a blank check for the President when it comes to the rights of the Nation's citizens." [82]

In a companion case the same day (*Rasul v. Bush*), the Court held that the prison camp at Guantanamo was not beyond the reach of American law, rejecting another key

[81] Risen, *State of War*, pp. 27–33. Joseph Margulies, *Guantanamo: And the Abuse of Presidential Power* (New York: Simon & Schuster, 2007). Military Order – Detention, Treatment, and Trial of Certain Non-Citizens in the War on Terrorism, November 13, 2001, APP. Donald Rumsfeld, Military Commission Order, March 21, 2002. http://www.defense.gov/news/Mar2002/d20020321ord.pdf.

[82] *Hamdi v. Rumsfeld*, 542 U.S. 507 (2004). Even Justice Antonin Scalia, generally an enthusiastic supporter of strong executive power, was outraged, and in a blunt opinion wrote "indefinite imprisonment at the will of the Executive" attacks "the very core of liberty."

administration position. The right of habeas corpus, it declared, lay "deep into the genius of our common law." Additionally, not only was the United States not at war with the nations of the defendants (two Australians, twelve Kuwaitis), but they had committed no aggressive acts against the United States and had never had access to any judicial tribunal. The Court was not finished. Two years later, in *Hamdan v. Rumsfeld*, it ruled that the Bush military commissions violated both the Uniform Code of Military Justice and the Geneva Conventions, and that the president had no authority to create military commissions without congressional approval. The 2005 Detainee Treatment Act had stripped the federal courts of jurisdiction over detainees, but in a 5–3 decision, the Court asserted its jurisdiction and held that the administration did not have the authority to set up the commissions without the approval of Congress.[83]

Hamdan forced the administration to scramble to salvage its treatment of the Guantanamo detainees. At its urging, and in the midst of an off-year election campaign, Congress passed the 2006 Military Commissions Act. Section 6 specifically denied enemy combatants the right of habeas corpus. With elections just weeks away, Congress hesitated to defend constitutional principles for fear of being labeled soft on terrorists. The law passed the Senate 65–35, with only one Republican voting against it; Democrats split 21–32 (plus one independent), while the House passed the law 250–170. An amendment to guarantee the right of habeas corpus was defeated by a very narrow margin of 51–48.

The Bush administration was not above petty retaliation against those who challenged it. In recognition of the historic significance of the *Hamdan* decision, Hamdan's attorney was named one of the one hundred most influential lawyers in America by the *National Law Journal*. The navy responded by discharging him under its "up or out" policy."[84]

A challenge to the Military Commissions Act that reached the Supreme Court involved Lakhdar Boumediene, a naturalized citizen of Bosnia and Herzegovina who was seized in Bosnia for a suspected plot to bomb the American embassy there. His appeal was supported by a remarkable twenty amicus briefs, including briefs from the ABA, the ACLU, a group of retired military officers, several retired federal judges, and the UN High Commission on Human Rights. In a close 5–4 decision, with Justice Anthony Kennedy writing for the majority, the Court held that the right of habeas corpus applies to persons designated as enemy combatants, even if they are not American citizens, in a remarkable extension of the right. If the government suspends that right, it argued, it must provide an alternative remedy, and Kennedy called the existing combatant status review tribunals "inadequate." In a powerful assertion of its prerogatives and yet another rebuke to the administration, the Court held that "to hold that the political branches may switch the constitution on or off at will would lead to a regime in which they, not this court, 'say what the law is.'"[85]

With the four decisions in *Hamdi, Rasul, Hamdan*, and *Boumediene*, the Supreme Court emerged as the most consistent – indeed, the only – defender of fundamental civil

[83] *Rasul v. Bush*, 542 U.S. 466 (2004). *Hamdan v. Rumsfeld*, 548 U.S. 557 (2006). Jonathan Mahler, *The Challenge: Hamdan v. Rumsfeld and the Fight over Presidential Power* (New York: Farrar, Straus & Giroux, 2008).

[84] "Hamdan Navy lawyer denied promotion, will leave US military," *Jurist*, October 10, 2006.

[85] *Boumediene v. Bush*, 553 U.S. 723 (2008). The legal scholar Ronald Dworkin called the *Boumediene* decision "one of the most important Supreme Court decisions in recent years," representing a "landmark change" by recognizing for the first time that the right of habeas corpus applies to aliens imprisoned by the U.S. Ronald Dworkin, "Why It Was a Great Victory," *The New York Review of Books*, 55 (August 14, 2008).

liberties among the three branches of government. The very conservative Rehnquist/ Roberts Court acquitted itself far better than had the liberal Roosevelt Court in World War II in the Japanese-American and the German saboteurs cases. Despite their profound legal significance, however, the four cases did not grip the public the way the 1971 *Pentagon Papers* or the 1974 Nixon White House tapes cases had. Not only did they involve very abstract legal principles, but, probably more important, the principal figures were suspected terrorists rather than a major newspaper or a sitting president. Few Americans thought that the constitutional issues at stake really affected them.

AUTHORIZATION TO GO TO WAR

A week after the 9/11 attacks, Congress passed the Authorization for Use of Military Force, specifically "against those responsible for the recent attacks against the United States." Just a few weeks later, on October 7, 2001, the Bush administration invaded Afghanistan to deny Osama bin Laden and al-Qaeda a safe haven there. Secretly, the Bush administration would use this authorization for other actions, including illegal spying by the National Security Agency. Iraq rather than Afghanistan was the administration's real target, however. Neoconservative hard-liners like Cheney had urged removing Iraq's Saddam Hussein for many years and now somehow envisioned that his removal would lead to introducing democracy to the entire Middle East. As Peter Bienart writes in *The Icarus Syndrome*, neoconservatives believed that as the only world superpower the United States had the power and the right to carry democracy to the rest of the world. Bienart labels this argument the "Hubris of Dominance," similar to Woodrow Wilson's idea of making the world safe for democracy.[86]

The plans to invade Iraq placed the administration face to face with the 1973 War Powers Act. Although the administration regarded the law as an illegitimate constraint on presidential power, it nonetheless felt required to seek a congressional resolution, which it obtained with the Authorization for Use of Military Force against Iraq. The administration's main arguments in support of it were later exposed as lies: that Hussein was developing weapons of mass destruction and that al-Qaeda operatives were "known to be in Iraq." After some concessions to please Democrats, Congress passed the authorization on October 16, 2002. by large margins: 77–23 in the Senate and 296–133 in the House. Democrats in Congress were almost perfectly divided over it. Senator Ted Kennedy spoke for most liberal opponents when he said there were too many unanswered questions about how any war would be waged, its likely cost, and the lack of an exit strategy. Democrats with presidential aspirations, however, voted for it, including both the future vice president, Joe Biden, and the future presidential aspirant Hillary Clinton, who called it "probably the hardest decision I've ever had to make." The future president, Barack Obama, then an Illinois state senator, opposed invading Iraq.[87]

[86] Authorization for Use of Military Force Against Terrorists, September 18, 2001. P.L 107–40. Peter Beinart, *The Icarus Syndrome: A History of American Hubris* (New York: Harper, 2010).

[87] *Authorization for Use of Military Force against Iraq*, P. L. 107–243 (October 16, 2002). "A Lopsided Victory," *NYT*, October 11, 2002. Revelations of the administration's lies about weapons of mass destruction and Saddam's support for al-Qaeda fueled calls for Bush's impeachment. Elizabeth Holtzman and Cynthia L. Cooper, *The Case for Impeachment of George W. Bush: A Practical Guide for Concerned Citizens* (New York: Nation Books, 2006), pp. 43–86.

The administration's lies over the Iraq authorization, moreover, may be compared with President Lyndon Johnson's misrepresentation of events in the Gulf of Tonkin in August 1964 to obtain a congressional resolution justifying expanded military actions in Vietnam. The Iraq War soon became as unpopular as the Vietnam War, but that was only after it too became a military fiasco. In the critical months between the 9/11 terrorist attacks and the Iraq invasion, however, only a minority in Congress was willing to question the administration's case for war, and with only a few exceptions, the news media accepted it uncritically.

The Bush administration's war on terrorism was a civil liberties disaster of epic proportions. The administration violated American and international law, undermined core principles of American constitutional democracy, made the United States an international pariah over torture, and repeatedly lied to the American people. Almost lost in the bitter controversies over these issues were the attacks on civil liberties with regard to domestic policies. These too were arguably worse than those of any previous president. To these, we now turn our attention.

A RELIGIOUS CRUSADE AT HOME

A week after taking office, Bush issued Executive Order 13199 creating the White House Office of Faith-Based and Community Initiatives. The office reflected Bush's idea of "compassionate conservatism," in which faith-based groups were "indispensable in meeting the needs of poor Americans and distressed neighborhoods." Although Bush claimed that his effort "recognizes the need there be separation of church and state," his administration aggressively developed programs that advanced fundamentalist Christian doctrine. The attack on the wall of separation between church and state far exceeded the worst previous assault, that by President Ronald Reagan.[88]

George Bush was the most passionately religious person to occupy the White House since Jimmy Carter. Both were "born again" Christians but stood at opposite ends of the spectrum with regard to faith and public policy. Carter had been a lifelong Baptist and held firmly to the traditional Southern Baptist commitment to separation of church and state. Bush, on the other hand, was a recent convert, having been born again as an evangelical Christian in 1985 at age thirty-nine. He embraced the Religious Right view that government should actively promote religion. Some analysts estimated that 40 percent of his 2000 electoral support was from evangelicals, compared with only 12 to 15 percent of President Reagan's support in 1980 and 1984. Karl Rove, his key political strategist, based their 2004 reelection campaign on mobilizing the evangelical vote, and it was probably the pivotal factor in Bush's reelection.[89]

The administration paid its political debt to the Religious Right by showering leading evangelicals with federal funds. Pat Robertson's Operation Blessing received a

[88] Executive Order 13199 – Establishment of White House Office of Faith-Based and Community Initiatives, January 29, 2001, APP. George W. Bush, *Record of Accomplishment... Policy Addresses of President George W. Bush Speeches* (Washington, DC: Bush-Cheney '04, 2004), p. 285. Executive Order 13279 – Equal Protection of the Laws for Faith-Based and Community Organizations, December 12, 2002, APP.

[89] Esther Kaplan, *With God on Their Side: How Christian Fundamentalists Trampled Science, Policy, and Democracy in George W. Bush's White House* (New York: New Press, 2004), p. 75. James Moore and Wayne Slater, *Rove Exposed: How Bush's Brain Fooled America* (Hoboken, NJ: Wiley, 2006).

three-year $1.5 million grant, and Chuck Colson, who had gone to prison for his role in the Watergate scandal, shared $22.5 million for his Prison Fellowship.[90] In addition to rewarding its friends, the faith-based initiative was consistent with the neoconservative political agenda of reducing the size of government by promising more private charities to help the poor. It also responded to long-standing Catholic and conservative Protestant arguments that Supreme Court decisions on separation of church and state discriminated against them with regard to receiving government funds. In December 2002 Bush issued Executive Order 13279 requiring that "no organization should be discriminated against on the basis of religion or religious belief in the administration or distribution of Federal financial assistance under social service programs." In June 2007, moreover, an OLC memo held that the 1993 Religious Freedom Restoration Act permitted religious organizations to discriminate in favor of fellow believers when hiring employees.[91]

AN ANTIHOMOSEXUAL AGENDA – WITH SOME ODD COMPROMISES

Three months after taking office, President Bush appointed Scott Evertz to head the Office of National AIDS Policy. The surprising aspect was not that Bush maintained the AIDS office created by President Clinton, but that Evertz was openly gay and a chapter president of the Log Cabin Republicans, the gay rights caucus within the GOP. Given his evangelical Christian beliefs and political debt to the Religious Right, Bush regarded homosexuality as a sin and vigorously opposed legalizing same-sex marriages. In practice, however, his record on gay rights issues was quite mixed. Early on, he appointed four openly gay people to federal posts, including the ambassador to Romania, who moved into the embassy with his same-sex partner. The silence about this among Christian conservatives was in stark contrast to the uproar over President Bill Clinton's nomination of an openly gay ambassador in 1999. Bush also signed a bill allowing domestic partners in Washington, D.C., to register formally their relationships with the local government. This ended a nine-year federal bar to a local city ordinance. Finally, Bush made a very strong and public commitment to help people with AIDS, including creating a Global AIDS Trust Fund in May 2001 with $200 million in federal funds for medical research, treatment, and assistance to families.[92]

It was curious that Bush's Religious Right supporters did not protest these actions. In part, they undoubtedly accommodated themselves to the growing acceptance of

90 Kaplan, *With God on Our Side*, pp. 34, 52. Cynthia Brown, ed., *Lost Liberties: Ashcroft and the Assault on Personal Freedom* (New York: New Press, 2003).

91 Executive Order 13199, January 29, 2001, APP. Executive Order 13279, December 12, 2002, APP. Marvin Olasky, *Compassionate Conservatism: What It Is, What It Does, and How It Can Transform America* (New York: Free Press, 2000), represents the views of the movement's most prominent advocate. Office of Faith-Based Initiatives, *The Quiet Revolution: The President's Faith-Based and Community Initiative: A Seven-Year Progress Report* (2008). Amy E. Black, Douglas L. Koopman, and David K. Ryden, *Of Little Faith: The Politics of George W. Bush's Faith-based Initiatives* (Washington, DC: Georgetown University Press, 2004). Request for Review and Withdrawal of June 29, 2007, Office of Legal Counsel Memorandum Re: RFRA. Letter to AG Holder, September 17, 2009, ACLU Press Release.

92 "President Bush Names Scott Evertz as National AIDS Policy Coordinator," Log Cabin Republican News, April 9, 2001. Www.lcrga.com/news/scott-evertz-office-national-aids-policy/200104091442.sht. Lou Chibbaro, Jr., "Mixed Reviews on Lesbian and Gay Rights for Bush's First Year," in Citizens' Commission on Civil Rights, *Rights at Risk: Equality in an Age of Terrorism* (Washington, DC: Citizens' Commission on Civil Rights, 2002), pp. 219–25.

same-sex culture in American society. But as had been the case with President Reagan, they simply chose not to criticize their president, who served their interests on so many other issues. Traditional conservatives, after all, refused to criticize Bush for his extreme claims of presidential power, which violated their long-standing principles.

The issue of same-sex marriage was another matter, however, and Bush took a strong stand against it. In 2004 he proposed a constitutional amendment to define marriage as between a man and a woman. This would go far beyond the 1996 Defense of Marriage Act, which only allowed states not to recognize same-sex marriages from other states. The proposal did not go anywhere, and there is good reason to suspect that it was nothing more than an election year ploy to placate hard-line antigay forces. He made the proposal again in early 2006, another election year, but also gained no political traction.[93]

"BUSH LEAGUE SCIENCE": THE WAR ON SCIENCE

The National Park Service ordered copies of Tom Vail's *Grand Canyon: A Different View* for its bookstores in July 2003. The book presented a fundamentalist Christian view of the origins of the canyon, denying the established scientific position that the rocks are two billion years old and the canyon itself six million years old. Leading geologists protested the sponsorship of blatantly nonscientific material, but the Religious Right mobilized in support of the book, which stayed in the bookstores. The incident was just one of many in a campaign that critics labeled a Bush administration "war on science."[94]

Much of the war on science focused on issues of sexuality. In 2002, a Centers for Disease Control Fact Sheet on condoms disappeared from the CDC Web site. Similarly, a CDC effort on Programs That Work (PTW) on contraceptives was abruptly discontinued. At the National Institutes of Health, recipients of grants related to HIV and pregnancy prevention learned that their grants were in jeopardy. Hearings by Congressman Henry Waxman produced a list of almost three hundred grants that were threatened or cancelled, along with clearly biased comments about certain programs. In June 2002, for example, the National Cancer Institute posted a statement on its Web site indicating a "possible link" between abortion and breast cancer, citing "conflicting" scientific studies. Public outcry forced the institute to remove the posting and to restore its original position that there was no scientific evidence of such a link.[95]

The administration aggressively promoted abstinence-only sex education for teenagers. President Bill Clinton's 1996 Welfare Reform Act had included $50 million for abstinence education, but programs did not incorporate specific religious doctrine. The Bush administration changed that, with federally funded programs giving false information about the effectiveness of contraception, claiming that condoms fail to prevent the spread of sexually transmitted diseases 31 percent of the time. It also provided misinformation

[93] Remarks Calling for a Constitutional Amendment Defining and Protecting Marriage, February 24, 2004, APP. "Bush Calls for Ban on Same-Sex Marriages," February 25, 2004. "Bush Re-Enters Gay Marriage Fight," *Washington Post*, June 3, 2006.

[94] Kaplan, *With God on Our Side*, pp. 90–2. "Bush League Science": Ch. 14, Chris Mooney, *The Republican War on Science* (New York: Basic Books, 2005).

[95] Mooney, *Republican War on Science*, pp. 236–37."Bush Policies Hurt AIDS Prevention, Groups Say," *Washington Post*, October 1, 2002. Kaplan, *With God on Our Side*, pp. 97–100, 120–1. "HIV Prevention Group Says That Bush Administration Is Targeting Their Work," *Associated Press*, October 1, 2002.

about the risks of sterility from having an abortion, while the idea that life begins as conception was presented as an established scientific fact, rather than a view rejected by most religious faiths. Materials also presented as fact cultural stereotypes about the sexes, for example, that women need financial support and men need admiration.[96]

In early 2004, the nation's leading scientists publicly protested the political war on science. They included more than sixty prominent scientists and former government science officials, and twenty Nobel Prize winners. A Union of Concerned Scientists (UCS) statement declared that the administration had "manipulated" the principle of an "objective and impartial perspective" on important policy questions in order to push its political agenda. Additionally, the administration had placed people who were "professionally unqualified" or had clear conflicts of interest in official positions. Some existing science advisory committees had been disbanded, because some of the members were politically unacceptable, and the administration had censored or suppressed government reports. One case involved the physicist William R. Miller, who was named to an advisory panel with the National Institute of Drug Abuse. In the vetting process he was asked about his position on abortion and whether he had voted for President Bush. His answers were unacceptable, and his nomination was dropped. The UCS "A to Z Guide to Political Interference in Science" listed antiscience actions by the administration on sex education, HIV/AIDS education, endangered salmon, global warming, and more.[97]

Bush also reversed President Clinton's policy on stem cell research, in August 2001 restoring limits first imposed by his father's administration. His policy trod a fine line between his antiabortion constituents, who believed that destroying an embryo for research purposes took a human life, and the overwhelming majority of the scientific community, which supported stem cell research. Bush banned federally funded research on any stem cells created after the date of his announcement but permitted research on the estimated sixty-four cell lines that already existed. In 2006 he used his first veto to reject a bill overturning his ban. Continuing what had become a standard political ritual, Barack Obama reversed the ban in 2009 in one of his first acts as president.[98]

POLITICIZING THE JUSTICE DEPARTMENT

Ever since John Mitchell's tenure as President Richard Nixon's attorney general, when he went to prison for his involvement in the Watergate scandal, thoughtful observers had warned about presidents' appointing political aides or personal friends to that critical law enforcement position. Presidents Gerald Ford and Jimmy Carter accepted the lesson, appointing attorneys general who defined themselves as politically independent and who on occasion rejected White House pressures. Bush's two attorneys general, however, politicized the office and stand out as perhaps the worst in modern times.

John Ashcroft, attorney general in Bush's first term, fully supported policies breaching the separation of church and state, aggressively used the questionable sections of the

[96] U.S. House of Representatives, Committee on Government Reform, *The Content of Federally Funded Abstinence-Only Education Programs. Prepared for Rep. Henry A. Waxman* (December 2004).

[97] Union of Concerned Scientists, *2004 Scientist Statement on Restoring Scientific Integrity to Federal Policy Making* (February, 2004). www.ucsusa.org. Mooney, *Republican War on Science*, p. 227. Union of Concerned Scientists, *The A to Z Guide to Political Interference in Science* (2008). www.ucsusa.org.

[98] Address to the Nation on Stem Cell Research From Crawford, Texas, August 9, 2001, APP.

PATRIOT Act, and (with the one notable exception discussed earlier) never objected to administration war on terrorism policies. In congressional testimony in later 2001, he warned that people who questioned the administration's policies in the war on terrorism gave aid and comfort to the enemy. Alberto Gonzales, White House counsel in Bush's first term before becoming attorney general in early 2005, was possibly the most hapless person ever to hold the office. He and Bush valued personal loyalty above all else, and Gonzales was particularly eager not to ask critical questions or present Bush with different points of view on critical issues. As White House counsel, he approved every proposal on the war on terrorism, regardless of established legal precedent. In his January 2005 Senate confirmation hearings, he repeatedly said he did not remember signing certain documents and refused to take responsibility for his most controversial actions. Asked about the notorious August 2002 torture memo, Gonzales weakly replied, "I don't recall today whether or not I was in agreement with all of the analysis."[99]

Reshaping civil rights enforcement

"Justice Dept. Reshapes Its Civil Rights Mission," headlined the *New York Times* on June 14, 2007. In addition to downgrading enforcement of existing laws on race and sex discrimination, the Bush administration added a prominent new issue to its agenda. To serve its commitment to the Religious Right, it launched a major attack on religious discrimination. The special counsel for religious discrimination, created in 2002, focused almost entirely on free exercise of religion cases involving limitations on religious activities. Civil libertarian principles underpinned these cases, including, for example, zoning laws restricting the location of houses of worship and denial of equal access to religious groups in public facilities. The department also defended the rights of Muslims to wear religious headdresses and filed charges in bias crimes against mosques and individual Muslims. The Justice Department, however, completely ignored violations of the establishment clause of the First Amendment – if only because the administration itself was engaged in those violations.[100]

With regard to sex discrimination, the administration attacked established Title IX standards prohibiting sex discrimination in higher education. In October 2006 it reversed prior interpretations prohibiting segregating classes and other activities by sex, with the proviso that "the single-sex nature of the class or extra-curricular activity is substantially related to achieving that objective," and that institutions "*may* [emphasis added] be required to provide a substantially equal single-sex class or extra-curricular activity to the excluded sex."[101]

The Justice Department also abandoned one of the major initiatives of the Clinton administration, litigation against systemic police misconduct. Section 14141 of the 1994 Violent Crime Control Act gave the Justice Department authority to bring civil suits against

[99] Bill Minutaglio, *The President's Counselor: The Rise to Power of Alberto Gonzales* (New York: Rayo, 2006). U.S. Senate, Committee on the Judiciary, Confirmation Hearing on the Nomination of Alberto Gonzales to be Attorney General of the United States, January 6, 2005, p. 57.

[100] "Justice Dept. Reshapes Its Civil Rights Mission," *NYT*, June 14, 2007. Department of Justice, Civil Rights Division, Special Counsel for Religious Discrimination, *Religious Freedom in Focus* (c2008) [summary of principal cases, February 2004–March–April 2008].

[101] *CFR*, October 25, 2006 (effective November 24, 2006).

police departments where there is a "pattern or practice" of abuse of citizens' rights. The principal victims in such cases were African Americans and Latinos, and thus the program represented a major civil rights initiative. The Bush Justice Department, however, ended this effort, investigating only a few police departments after 2003 and bringing no cases against big city departments, where the most significant police abuse problems existed.[102]

The most politically contentious civil rights issue by the last years of the Bush administration was immigration. With an estimated 12 million undocumented immigrants (most from Mexico) an aggressive antiimmigrant movement arose across the country. The immigration issue posed a serious political dilemma for President Bush and the Republican Party, however, as it wanted to appease the strong antiimmigrant forces within the party while not offending the increasingly important Latino vote. Complex legislation promising "comprehensive immigration reform" was proposed but failed to gain any traction as the immigration debate became increasingly inflamed.

The Bush administration did, however, introduce many abuses into immigration enforcement, including lengthy detention of undocumented people awaiting deportation and rules for immigration courts that violated standards of due process. In one of the most outrageous moves, Attorney General Ashcroft in September 2001 ordered that immigration courts be closed to the public. The move was another response to the 9/11 attacks and reflected the administration's mania for secrecy.

Politicizing appointments

To a degree unmatched by any previous administration, the Bush administration politicized hiring in the Justice Department. The effort went far beyond traditional political patronage in top policy making positions and reached down into career civil service positions that had long been insulated from politics, flagrantly imposing political criteria for even the lowest-level positions. The worst abuses occurred within the Civil Rights Division. After public outrage forced an investigation, the Justice Department's own inspector general in 2008 identified the deputy attorney general, Bradley Schlozman (who served from May 2003 to June 2005), as the worst offender. He "inappropriately considered political and ideological affiliations in hiring experienced attorneys in the [five] sections he supervised and entry-level attorneys throughout the Division for the Attorney General's Honors Program." Additionally, in the assignment of cases, he "favored applicants with conservative political or ideological affiliations" over those "with civil rights or human rights experience whom he considered to be overly liberal." Many of his new hires lacked any civil rights experience related to their jobs. Taking a direct role in the interview process, he inquired, for example, into whether one applicant was a member of the ACLU. The applicant was not and was hired even though the section head objected for other reasons. Career attorneys also suffered for their political views. Schlozman criticized some as "disloyal" and "not on the team" and said they needed to be moved to make room for "real Americans."[103]

102 Samuel Walker and Morgan Macdonald, "An Alternative Remedy for Police Misconduct: A Model State Pattern or Practice Statute," *George Mason University Civil Rights Law Journal* (2009): 479–552.

103 Department of Justice, Office of the Inspector General, *An Investigation of Allegations of Politicized Hiring and Other Improper Personnel Actions in the Civil Rights Division* (July 2, 2008), pp. 17, 23–4, 35.

Particularly notorious was the role of Monica Goodling, briefly the Justice Department's White House liaison. Like many young conservatives in the administration, she was dedicated and hardworking, but also a zealous conservative Christian, educated entirely at conservative religious institutions: Messiah College and Pat Robertson's Regent University Law School. An investigation concluded that she "violated both federal law and Department policy ... when she considered political or ideological affiliations in hiring decisions." She freely admitted refusing to approve one attorney for a counterterrorism unit because his wife was a Democratic Party activist.[104]

The greatest scandal involved the firing of seven U.S. attorneys by the attorney general on December 7, 2006. All were original Bush appointees and loyal Republicans, and six of the seven had recently received outstanding performance evaluations. It was soon revealed, however, that they had been the subject of complaints by local GOP officials about their failure to pursue certain cases: Carol Lam had allegedly been "lax" in handling immigration cases in Southern California, the New Mexico attorney David Iglesias did not file charges regarding alleged Democratic Party voter fraud cases, and so on. The scandal quickly became public, and Democrats in Congress launched investigations. The administration invoked executive privilege in refusing to turn over White House documents on the matter. E-mails, however, surfaced showing consultations between the White House and the Justice Department about removing certain U.S. attorneys as early as 2005. Attorney General Gonzales acknowledged mistakes but denied any wrongdoing. President Bush also admitted mistakes but loyally supported his attorney general.[105]

In all, the damage Gonzales inflicted on the Justice Department was incalculable. One department official said, "It will take fifty years to undo the damage that he did to the place." After leaving office, he had much difficulty finding a job as an attorney, and a Spanish court began investigating him and five others for possible war crimes.[106]

THE SUPREME COURT: THE CONSERVATIVE REVOLUTION FINALLY ARRIVES

In the summer of 2005, Justice Sandra Day O'Connor announced her plan to retire from the Supreme Court. Although she had been a consistently conservative justice on most issues, she had also played a pivotal moderate role on several key issues. Particularly important, she fashioned a coalition with Justices David Souter and Anthony Kennedy that preserved the core of *Roe v. Wade* in the critical 1992 *Planned Parenthood v. Casey* decision. She also voted to declare unconstitutional the Texas homosexual sodomy law. She also delivered a sharp rebuke to the Bush administration in *Hamdi*, declaring that

[104] Department of Justice, Office of the Inspector General, *An Investigation of Politicized Hiring by Monica Goodling and Other Staff in the Office of the Attorney General* (Washington, DC: Department of Justice, July 28, 2008), pp. 45, 50.

[105] Department of Justice, Office of the Inspector General, An Investigation into the Removal of Nine U.S. Attorneys in 2006 (Washington, DC: Department of Justice, September 2008). www.justice.gov/oig/ at Special Reports. Paul D. Clement, Solicitor General and Acting Attorney General, to The White House, Assertion of Executive Privilege Concerning the Dismissal and Replacement of U.S. Attorneys, June 27, 2007. www.justice.gov/olc/ at Opinions. David Iglesias, "Why I Was Fired," *NYT*, March 21, 2007.

[106] Lichtblau, *Bush's Law*, p. 157. "Spanish Court Weighs Inquiry on Torture for 6 Bush-Era Officials," *NYT*, March 29, 2009.

"a state of war is not a blank check for the president when it comes to the rights of the nation's citizens." The most dramatic illustration of her influence on the Court was the fact that after her departure Justice Kennedy joined the conservative majority in a number of 5–4 decisions on major issues.[107]

To fill O'Connor's seat, President Bush nominated John Roberts in July 2005. When Chief Justice Rehnquist died in September, Bush withdrew the nomination and resubmitted Roberts's name for the chief justice position. The Roberts confirmation hearings followed the now-well-established post-Bork ritual, as he offered only bland generalities to probing questions about abortion and other hot button issues. He testified that *Roe v. Wade* was "the settled law of the land" and that his personal views would not prevent him from "fully and faithfully applying that precedent." As a member of the Reagan and Bush administrations he had coauthored a brief saying *Roe* was "wrongly decided" and should be overruled. In a 2007 partial birth abortion case, however, he refused to join Justice Clarence Thomas's call for repealing *Roe*. He also testified that *Brown v. Board of Education* had "vindicat[ed] the vision of justice that the framers enacted in the Constitution." Yet, in two crucial 2007 decisions he ruled against two school desegregation plans and in a declaration pregnant with meaning for all race-conscious remedies wrote that "[t]he way to stop discrimination on the basis of race is to stop discriminating on the basis of race." With regard to presidential power, the journalist Charlie Savage noted that Justice Rehnquist had been an old school conservative who remembered the battles against President Roosevelt's and Truman's claims of power, but that Roberts was a Reagan era neoconservative who believed passionately in untrammeled executive power. The difference would have powerful implications for many crucial constitutional issues raised by the Bush administration.[108]

To fill the remaining vacancy, Bush named Samuel A. Alito, a judge on the Third Circuit Court of Appeals. As an assistant attorney general in the Reagan administration, he had been a New Right hard-liner, among other things a strong advocate of presidential signing statements. Applying for the position, he cited Barry Goldwater as an important influence and expressed concerns about Warren Court decisions. Perhaps most indicative of the impact of his social views, when the Third Circuit decided the *Casey* abortion case, Alito accepted the constitutionality of the Pennsylvania requirement that wives notify their husbands before having an abortion. The Supreme Court rejected that provision when it upheld most of the Pennsylvania law in 1991. He was narrowly confirmed by the Senate in a 58–42 vote and went on to join Roberts as an extremely conservative justice.[109]

107 Jeffrey Toobin, *The Nine: Inside the Secret World of the Supreme Court* (New York: Doubleday, 2007). Joan Biskupic, *Sandra Day O'Connor: How the First Woman on the Supreme Court Became Its Most Influential Justice* (New York: ECCO, 2005).

108 "Roberts Avoids Specifics on Abortion Issue," *Washington Post*, September 15, 2005. *Gonzales v. Carhart*, 550 U.S. 124 (2007). *Parents Involved in Community Schools v. Seattle School District No. 1*, 551 U.S. 701 (2007). Alliance for Justice: *Fact Sheet: The Impact of Justice: Roberts and Alito on the Bench* (Washington, DC: Alliance for Justice, n.d.). Savage, *Takeover*, p. 261.

109 Samuel A. Alito, Jr., to The Litigation Strategy Working Group, Using Presidential Signing Statements to Make Fuller Use of the President's Constitutionally Assigned Role in the Process of Enacting Law, February 5, 1986, Office of Legal Counsel, U.S. Department of Justice. "Alito Once Made Case for Presidential Power," *Washington Post*, January 2, 2006.

THE MOST SWEEPING ASSAULT ON THE CONSTITUTION

President George W. Bush perpetrated the most systematic violations of civil liberties of any modern president. To be sure, at first glance his actions might seem less damaging than those of some of his predecessors. He did not suppress all dissent, as Woodrow Wilson had done in World War I; did not put Americans in concentration camps, as Franklin D. Roosevelt did; and he was not driven from office for obstructing justice, as Richard Nixon was. In other important respects, however, Bush's abuses were a far more fundamental long-term threat to American democracy than anything done by these other presidents. Wilson and Roosevelt understood that their actions were temporary war measures. Bush struck at the very principle of the separation of powers, the core of the American idea of constitutional democracy, and the right of habeas corpus, the most ancient right in Anglo American law. His argument that the president as commander in chief is above the reach of Congress and the courts is the most sweeping assertion of unilateral presidential power ever made. Justice Robert Jackson's words in both *Korematsu* and the steel seizure cases appear profoundly prophetic. As he put it in *Korematsu*, a principle unchecked by constitutional limitations "lies about like a loaded weapon, ready for the hand of any authority that can bring forward a plausible claim of an urgent need." And in the steel seizure case Jackson wrote that President Truman's action originated "in the individual will of the President," and that no one "knows the limits of the power that he may seek to exert in this instance." These were prophetic words that fifty years later were an ominous warning about the potential long-term damage done by the Bush administration.[110]

In many respects, Bush looms as a pathetic figure, because he really did not appear to understand the full implications of his own policies. In his memoirs, he justified his decision on torture because "the lawyer said it was legal." The man who proudly called himself "the decider" simply passed the buck. In truth, Vice President Dick Cheney, widely seen as the most powerful vice president in history, engineered the worst of the Bush administration policies. He fully understood what the policies on torture and spying involved and had for twenty-five years championed unfettered presidential power. One commentary on Bush's war on terrorism occurred in early February 2011, three years after he left office. He reportedly cancelled a trip to Switzerland out of fear that he might be charged with war crimes by Swiss authorities. (Under the principle of universal jurisdiction, a state may prosecute someone for crimes that did not occur within its boundaries but which it regards as a crime against all people.) No other president had ever faced the possibility of such an international disgrace.[111]

The war on terrorism was only one part of Bush's assaults on civil liberties. On domestic policies the administration aggressively promoted Christian religious doctrine, waged a war on science that threatened the very canons of science itself, and crudely injected politics into the Department of Justice and other federal agencies. For these reasons alone, Bush would be a strong contender for the dubious honor of being the worst president ever on civil liberties. As they left office, President Bush and Vice President Cheney were unrepentant and unapologetic. Just two weeks before leaving office in January 2009

[110] Jackson, Dissent in *Korematsu v. United States,* 323 U.S. 214 (1944).

[111] "Bush Trip To Switzerland Called Off amid Threats of Protest, Legal Action," *Washington Post,* February 6, 2011.

Cheney declared, "And I don't believe we violated anybody's civil liberties." And in his memoirs, published in 2011 he adamantly continued to maintain that the CIA's enhanced interrogation techniques were not torture and had obtained valuable information about terrorist activities.[112] He was not being disingenuous; he genuinely believed the administration had neither violated civil liberties nor tortured anyone..

The fault dear Brutus – Beyond Bush and Cheney

How, then, did Bush and Cheney get away with such systematic violations of established constitutional principles? The answer raises very troubling questions about American democracy. Bush had the full support of Congress and the American people in the war on terrorism. In November 2001, two months after the 9/11 terrorist attacks, 88 percent of Americans approved of his handling of terrorism, while a lonely 9 percent were opposed. The national mood closely resembled that in the period immediately after Pearl Harbor when all but a few Americans uncritically accepted the evacuation and internment of the Japanese Americans. The public also tolerated the violations of civil liberties during World War I and the cold war. By 2007, approval of war on terrorism policies had fallen to 41 percent, with a bare majority of 51 percent disapproving. As the *New York Times*'s Risen observed, however, that was mainly because "the war in Iraq had turned into a debacle."[113] Concern about civil liberties in the war on terrorism among the general public remained uncertain. The lesson appears to be that in a time of national emergency, Americans are quite willing to set aside constitutional principles in the name of national security. This is particularly true if the president in any given crisis manipulates public fears, or lies to the public, or fails to articulate the core values of American constitutional democracy.

For its part, Congress failed to defend civil liberties in the war on terrorism. It rushed through the PATRIOT Act with essentially no debate immediately after 9/11 and has never repealed any of its major provisions. True, Congress objected immediately to the administration's TIPS and TIA surveillance proposals, but it may be that those programs appeared to strike at the privacy of ordinary Americans rather than suspected "others" people viewed as the real terrorist threats. The *Washington Post* reporter Tom Ricks characterized the failure of Congress with a chapter entitled "The Silence of the Lambs." The *New Yorker*'s Jane Mayer added that Congress "all but abdicated." When briefed on secret administration actions, members of the intelligence committees never asked the probing questions they should have asked, and it seems they really did not want to ask. Only after public opinion turned against Bush and the Iraq War did Democrats in Congress complain that they had been misled.[114] As had been the case with the Iran-Contra affair under President Reagan, Bush's war on terrorism indicated that an ideologically driven

[112] CBS News, *Face the Nation*, January 4, 2009. Dick Cheney, with Liz Cheney, *In My Time: A Personal and Political Memoir* (New York: Threshold Editions, 2011), pp. 357–62.

[113] Risen, *State of War*, pp. 227, 229. *CBS News Poll*, November, 2001, October 12–16, 2007. Other polls found similar results. Www.pollingreport.com/terror.htm.

[114] "Few In Congress Questioning President over Civil Liberties," *NYT*, December 5, 2001. Thomas E. Ricks, *Fiasco: The American Military Adventure in Iraq* (New York: Penguin, 2006), Ch. 6, pp. 85–111. Mayer, *The Dark Side*, p. 300. The failure of Congress to exercise oversight authority: Harold Hongju Koh, *The National Security Constitution: Sharing Power after the Iran-Contra Affair* (New Haven, CT: Yale University Press, 1990), pp. 16–21.

administration can – at least temporarily – secretly override the elaborate post-Watergate controls over presidential power and the intelligence agencies.

The media also bear their share of responsibility for the Bush abuses. To be sure, several reporters and news media distinguished themselves with impressive investigations and exposés: the *New York Times* reporters Eric Lichtblau and James Risen exposed the NSA secret warrantless wiretapping program; Charles Savage of the *Boston Globe* exposed the abuse of signing statements; the *New Yorker*'s Jane Mayer reworked her original stories into her book *The Dark Side* on the CIA's horrific extraordinary rendition program and what it led to. Others certainly belong on this list. As Risen himself later admitted, however, "We in the media were no doubt swept up in that same national mood of fear and outrage." The *New York Times* itself held up publication of the NSA spying story for an entire year and in perhaps the most notorious failure of all, gave front page space to Judith Miller's uncritical articles promoting the administration's arguments for going to war with Iraq.[115]

The Supreme Court, on the other hand, distinguished itself by rejecting the administration's most extreme assertions of presidential power in the *Hamdi, Rasul, Hamdan,* and *Boumediene* cases. Although dominated by very conservative justices and hostile to a wide range of established civil liberties principles, the Court established a far better record on constitutional principles in a time of national crisis than the famously liberal Roosevelt Court on the Japanese-American cases in World War II.

The *New York Times* columnist Frank Rich in late 2007 properly placed responsibility squarely on the American people. "We can continue to blame the Bush administration for the horrors of Iraq," he wrote. "But we must also examine our own responsibility for the hideous acts committed in our name." Recalling World War II, he saw the problem as "The 'Good Germans' among Us," all the people who did not speak out.[116] He could have quoted the great journalist Edward R. Murrow, who quoted Shakespeare in speaking out during a civil liberties crisis a half-century earlier. In his famous criticism of the anti-communist demagogue Senator Joe McCarthy, Murrow intoned, "The fault dear Brutus is not in our stars but in ourselves." In the end, it was not just Bush; it was the American people.

[115] Lichtblau, *Bush's Law*, p. 12.
[116] Frank Rich, "The 'Good Germans' among Us," *NYT*, October 14, 2007.

15 Conclusion

Reflections on Presidents, Civil Liberties, and Democracy – with Observations on Barack Obama

AMERICA TRANSFORMED: THE RIGHTS REVOLUTION

When the Woodrow Wilson administration convicted the socialist Eugene V. Debs for opposing the war in 1918 and sentenced him to prison for ten years, there was no First Amendment law protecting his right to dissent. When President Wilson imposed racial segregation on federal employees after taking office in 1913, there was no law barring race discrimination in employment. The Comstock Act in those years barred from the mail information about birth control, abortion, and contraceptive devices. Homosexuality was barely whispered about in private. Public schools across the country imposed Protestant religious doctrine on students in official ceremonies. In short, a century ago the legal protection of civil liberties as we know it today did not exist. The public and private lives of Americans were constricted in ways that people today can scarcely imagine and would not tolerate.

A rights revolution has transformed American society over the past one hundred years. The growth of freedom Americans enjoy is not strictly a matter of the formal law; it also includes habits and expectations that govern our daily lives and reflect our expectations about what constitutes a free society. It is possible today for people to read, write, speak, buy a home where they want to live, attend a school or university, work, love, and marry in ways unimaginable in President Wilson's day. Historians typically characterize the vast transformation of modern society in terms of industrialization, urbanization, and globalization. The rights revolution properly belongs on that list.[1]

PRESIDENTS AND THE RIGHTS REVOLUTION

Sadly, this book indicates that American presidents played little active role in the rights revolution and have been poor custodians of the Bill of Rights and the values it embodies. Several presidents perpetrated some of the worst assaults on the rights of Americans. Wilson suppressed dissent in World War I, Franklin D. Roosevelt interned 117,116 Japanese Americans, Richard Nixon obstructed justice to protect his own criminal conduct, and George W. Bush attacked the fundamental principle of the separation of powers and the historic right of habeas corpus. No president unequivocally defended freedom of speech for an unpopular group or idea, and only one president ever publicly

[1] Samuel Walker, *The Rights Revolution* (New York: Oxford University Press, 1998). Although it is well beyond the scope of this book, we should add that the post-World War II international human rights movement represents the global dimension of the rights revolution.

spoke out in defense of the constitutional rights of criminal suspects. As we will explain in more detail later, American democracy itself is at the heart of this problem. Popularly elected presidents inevitably respond to the powerful anti-civil libertarian impulses in American society. At the same time, however, countervailing popular forces have in recent years provided strong support for some civil liberties issues. The relationship between democracy and civil liberties, in short, is extremely complex.

Only one president ever risked his political career in defense of constitutional rights. Harry Truman aggressively advanced a civil rights program in 1946–8, knowing it would jeopardize his reelection chances in 1948. His stand on behalf of racial justice was far in advance of public opinion, including even the views of white northerners. Lyndon Johnson accomplished far more in terms of civil rights, engineering passage of both the 1964 Civil Rights Act and the 1965 Voting Rights Act, but the politics of civil rights had changed dramatically by then. His opposition to wiretapping and support for immigration reform, the rights of criminal suspects, and federal funding for family planning make him the greatest civil libertarian president. He enjoyed a rising tide of popular support on most of these issues, however, and did not really have to take an unpopular stand, as Truman did.

Our review of presidents and civil liberties from Woodrow Wilson to the present inevitably raises the question of the current White House occupant, Barack Obama. He was elected on a wave of revulsion against his predecessor's policies on the Iraq War, government secrecy, failure to enforce civil rights laws, opposition to abortion rights and the rights of lesbian and gay people, a war on science, and the political uses of federal agencies. In his first two days in office civil libertarians cheered Obama's actions to ban torture and close secret CIA prisons, a promise to close the notorious Guantanamo Bay detention center, and ends to bans on stem cell research and abortion advocacy in foreign aid programs. Enthusiasm soon gave way to disappointment, however, as it became clear that he was unwilling to pursue many civil liberties issues and even maintained some of his predecessor's most offensive national security policies. A stinging July 2010 ACLU report rebuked him for continuing to use some of Bush's worst war on terrorism policies, including embracing the "legal architecture" underpinning those policies. The ACLU followed a year later with a report attacking his policies on secrecy. (His promise regarding Guantanamo Bay, it must be said, was thwarted by Congress.) [2] Obama's supporters wrestled with how to explain the gap between the promise and the performance.

Obama also disappointed many of his supporters on other issues besides national security. Many liberals felt he was too friendly to Wall Street, depending too much on their campaign contributions. He shocked environmentalists with a major retreat on ozone regulations in September 2011. On lesbian and gay rights issues he seemed of two minds, with no clear or consistent position, ending "Don't Ask, Don't Tell" in the military and supporting a repeal of the federal Defense of Marriage Act, but also refusing to endorse same-sex marriage in principle. African Americans were deeply troubled by his refusal to speak out directly on race and his failure to address the impact of the recession

[2] "Legal architecture": ACLU, *Establishing a New Normal: National Security, Civil Liberties, and Human Rights under the Obama Administration: An 18-Month Review* (New York: ACLU, July 2010). www.aclu.org. FBI powers: *NYT*, June 14, 2011. ACLU, *Drastic Measures Required* (New York: ACLU, 2011).

on their community. The Latino community also felt he had failed to honor 2008 campaign promises, while remaining silent on their issues. Obama in his relationship with constituent groups began to resemble Jimmy Carter. Both presidents did far more on the respective issues than their predecessors but were caught in a dynamic of greater expectations of supporters. Obama was far more restrained on national security than Bush, more committed to regulating the financial community, was stronger on the environment and lesbian and gay rights, and so on. But in each case he disappointed by doing less than each constituent group expected.[3]

The history of presidents and civil liberties examined in this book puts Obama's performance in perspective. His actions, as is the case with all presidents, are a product of many factors, which include a president's personality and political style but also the larger political and economic environment, the very nature of civil liberties, and the institution of the presidency. Examining these factors illuminates the place of civil liberties in a constitutional democracy and how presidents respond to the controversies that arise.

PRESIDENTS AND CIVIL LIBERTIES

Contradictions may be the norm with respect to presidents and civil liberties. Franklin D. Roosevelt's record is forever tarnished by his internment of the Japanese Americans. Yet, he also did much to advance civil liberties: his attorney general, Frank Murphy, created the forerunner of today's Civil Rights Division in the Justice Department; his 1941 Four Freedoms speech was the first presidential endorsement of freedom of speech and religion by a modern president; his appointments to the Supreme Court fashioned the first important body of constitutional law protecting individual rights. Harry Truman stands out for his strong record on civil rights: desegregating the armed services and creating the first presidential civil rights commission. Yet, his 1947 Federal Loyalty Program was a terrible assault on freedom of belief and association, establishing guilt by association as official government policy and preparing the ground for McCarthyism. His appointments to the Supreme Court were embarrassingly mediocre, and they contributed to a number of important anti–civil libertarian decisions in the 1940s and early 1950s. Dwight D. Eisenhower refused to condemn Senator Joe McCarthy and failed to endorse the Supreme Court's *Brown v. Board of Education* decision on school desegregation. Nonetheless, his administration actively pursued racial integration in Washington, D.C., achieving more in his first year in office than Truman had in seven and a half years. Ike also appointed several federal judges in the South who did yeoman work in enforcing school integration under *Brown*. Most famously, two of Eisenhower's Supreme Court appointments, Earl Warren and William Brennan, were leaders of the Court's great expansion of civil liberties in the late 1950s and 1960s. Lyndon Johnson, the greatest civil libertarian president, nonetheless ordered the FBI to spy on civil rights activists, directed the CIA to spy on Americans in 1967, and lied to Congress about the events in the Gulf of Tonkin in August 1964 to obtain an authorization to escalate American military actions in Vietnam. In short, we should not be surprised to find contradictions in President Obama's record on civil liberties.

[3] "Pushing a Liberal Agenda, with Democrats as Target," *NYT*, June 8, 2010. "Stung by Obama, Environmentalists Weigh Options," *NYT*, September 4, 2011. Comparison with Carter: see Chapter 11 of this book.

Nor should we be surprised to find that Obama has disappointed his strongest supporters. Woodrow Wilson championed reforms to enhance the democratic process, yet suppressed freedom of speech and press, the very foundations of democracy. Franklin D. Roosevelt was the beloved champion of the "common man," and yet he was indifferent to the rights of working people on the Wagner Act, labor's "Magna Carta." John F. Kennedy raised expectations about civil rights but took no action until compelled to do so in 1963 by massive demonstrations in the street. Richard Nixon promised to transform the Supreme Court, but his appointees sustained judicial activism, most notably in *Roe v. Wade.* Ronald Reagan publicly opposed abortion and supported school prayer but never put any effort behind conservative congressional efforts on those issues.

Many of Obama's friends criticized him for failing to take forceful leadership on crucial issues. He let Congress wage the battle over health care reform in 2009 and on the debt crisis in 2011. After the law was enacted, moreover, he and Democratic Party congressional leaders did not conduct a national campaign emphasizing how it helped people and families with particular medical problems. This failure allowed Republicans to demonize the law and him in terms of a threatening "Obamacare." Some observers saw him seeking to be the detached mediator between contending forces. Many presidents have failed to lead or use the bully pulpit of the White House when strong leadership, if only public statements, would have had a significant impact. Wilson failed to speak out against vigilante violence by superpatriots and racist elements. Roosevelt could have called for tolerance in the wake of Pearl Harbor, pointing out that it was the Nazis who put entire groups of people in concentration camps, and avoided the tragedy of evacuation and internment. Dwight D. Eisenhower refused to criticize Senator Joe McCarthy by name and refused to endorse *Brown v. Board of Education.* Ronald Reagan maintained a deadly silence in the face of the AIDS crisis, failing to mobilize a meaningful federal response to a national health emergency. Other examples abound.[4]

On some notable occasions, presidents did understand the power of the White House bully pulpit. Roosevelt's Four Freedoms speech in January 1941 remains one of the most eloquent statements by a president on behalf of freedom of speech and religious liberty, delivered at a critical moment in a world beset by totalitarianism and war. As a candidate, John F. Kennedy gave the most forceful and thorough discussion of religious liberty by anyone who ever served as president in modern times. He also completely transformed his image on civil rights with a single speech, his June 1963 televised address proposing a federal civil rights law. More than any other president, Lyndon Johnson saw himself as schoolmaster to the nation. In his historic 1965 voting rights speech he gave a homily on freedom of speech and assembly, and when signing the 1966 Bail Reform Act he explained that there is no conflict between the constitutional rights of criminal suspects and effective crime control. As a candidate in 2008, Obama gave a speech on race that was one of the best discussions of this difficult subject by any candidate or president.

Personality and political style certainly explain some presidential behavior. Historians have long wrestled with the incredibly complex personalities of Franklin D. Roosevelt, Lyndon Johnson, Richard Nixon, and Bill Clinton, to name only the most extreme cases, and how they affected their respective performances. Woodrow Wilson's self-righteousness

[4] This theme is developed in Samuel Walker, "Great Speeches Presidents Did NOT Give – and Should Have," Presentation, University of Nebraska at Omaha, September 2009.

and rigidity famously contributed to his disastrous handling of the Versailles Treaty ratification crisis and were also factors in his dismissing criticisms of his handling of dissent during World War I. FDR's famous political instincts served him well in many instances, but they included a blithe disregard for legal principles, as in the case of his decision on the Japanese Americans. Truman's capacity to make bold decisions allowed him to use the atomic bomb, desegregate the military, fire General Douglas MacArthur, and seize the steel mills. Richard Nixon's "dark side" - his paranoia and belief that powerful "establishment" forces were out to get him - contributed directly to Watergate and his ultimate resignation in disgrace. Ronald Reagan's eternally sunny optimism was the key to his political success, while Bill Clinton's reckless sexual activities damaged and nearly derailed his entire presidency.

And so it is with Obama. Although he inspired his supporters in the 2008 campaign with grand rhetoric about "hope" and "change," when he took office it soon became apparent that he was a moderate who believed in compromise and bipartisanship. One commentator observed that bipartisanship was the closest thing his administration had to an ideology. Curiously, he remained wedded to that approach in the face of the most ferociously partisan opposition the country had seen since Roosevelt and the New Deal in the 1930s. He was a moderate in the most immoderate times. In the fierce debate over health care reform through 2009, he remained aloof from the battle, letting it play out in Congress. On the budget debates of 2010 and 2011 he disappointed many supporters by seeming too eager to compromise with the Republicans in Congress. In April 2011, the liberal economist and *New York Times* columnist Paul Krugman commented that Obama and his advisers seemed to think he could win reelection by being "conciliatory and reasonable," when what the country wants is "a president who believes in something, and is willing to take a stand." David Bromwich in the *New York Review of Books* observed in mid-2011, "He retains the wish to be seen as a man above party." In 2012, however, Obama's State of the Union address indicated a tougher and more partisan stand against the Republicans on questions of the economy and the budget.[5]

One consequence of Obama's seeming detachment as president through 2011 is that he did not seem able to connect with ordinary Americans. The ability to do so was the hallmark of Franklin D. Roosevelt's leadership style. Common people adored him even though he himself was a very wealthy member of the American elite. Similarly, Ronald Reagan persuaded many ordinary Americans (and lifelong Democrats) that he spoke for them. Obama seemed to have that capacity as a candidate but not as president. In this regard he tended to resemble Jimmy Carter: a highly intelligent person, with many good ideas, who could not convince ordinary people that he understood and cared about their situation.

Whatever their personality, however, presidents work in the broader political, economic, and international context. Woodrow Wilson was handed the European war, while Roosevelt took office with the nation already in the depths of the depression and was later handed another world war. John F. Kennedy did not anticipate the explosion of the civil rights movement. The surprise 9/11 terrorist attacks became the central factor in the

[5] David Bromwich, "Obama: His Words and Deeds," *New York Review of Books*, May 22, 2011. Paul Krugman, "The President Is Missing," *NYT*, April 11, 2011.

presidency of George W. Bush. None of these presidents chose these conditions, however much their personalities may have shaped their responses to them.

In this regard, the central fact of Obama's presidency has been the economic recession that struck just as he was taking office. The economy lost 800,000 jobs the very month he took the oath of office. Only Herbert Hoover had such bad luck with the economy. Had the recession begun a year earlier, in late 2007, it would have been blamed on Bush, and Obama and the Democrats would have swept the 2008 elections by huge margins, in a replay of Roosevelt and 1932. Presidents, however, do not control the business cycle any more than they control foreign wars, and the test of their leadership is their capacity to respond to the situation they face. The recession fueled a ferocious conservative and antiincumbent political movement, of which the Tea Party was only the most extreme manifestation, that threw Obama completely on the defensive and derailed most of his original objectives. It aggravated the debt crisis that by 2011 completely changed the American political dialogue.

The question of race

Perhaps nothing is more complex and curious than the issue of Obama and race. The agonizing issue of America, race, and presidents has its own complex and changing history. Democrats in the first half of the twentieth century were beholden to the powerful southern segregationist bloc. Wilson imposed segregation in the federal agencies; Roosevelt failed to support the emerging civil rights movement. Republicans in those years were often stronger on civil rights than Democrats. In early 1960 Martin Luther King was not the only civil rights leader who thought Richard Nixon was the better choice than John F. Kennedy. After doing virtually nothing for two and a half years, however, Kennedy transformed his image with his June 1963 television speech proposing a federal civil rights bill. By the 1970s, the issue of race became more subtle and complex. Democratic presidents have been stronger in appointing African Americans to federal positions and more committed to enforcing civil rights laws. When Ronald Reagan sought to limit the Voting Rights Act in 1982, congressional Democrats mobilized public support and strengthened the law. The political alignment on several racial issues became ambiguous in the years after 1965. Democrats nominally supported affirmative action, while Republicans opposed it, but no prominent Democrat ever endorsed the use of quotas in employment or college admissions. Democrats have also opposed the use of busing to achieve school integration just as strongly as have Republicans. Bill Clinton had extraordinary rapport with African Americans but embraced imprisonment policies that had a severely adverse effect on their community. Although race related policies have become more complex, race remains a major issue in politics, and certainly in presidential politics.

The election of Barack Obama, it quickly turned out, was filled with ironies with respect to race. Most obviously, it was a truly historic moment for America, with the country apparently turning the corner and overcoming its legacy of racism and electing an African-American president. The *New York Times* highlighted a postelection column by Frank Rich, characterizing the election with a subhead reading, "America Did More Than Elect a Black President" on November 4, 2008.[6] The election was a strong statement that

[6] Frank Rich, "It Still Felt Good the Morning After," *NYT*, November 9, 2008.

for a majority of the voters at least, race was no longer a factor in choosing a president. It paralleled the 1960 election when John F. Kennedy's victory proved that the country's long-standing anti-Catholic prejudice had finally waned. Perhaps the most meaningful image on election night was that of the Reverend Jesse Jackson in the crowd in Chicago with tears in his eyes. Although he had himself run for the Democratic nomination, one suspects that he never really expected to see an African American actually elected president in his own lifetime.

At the same time, however, Obama's election evoked a powerful racist backlash. Anti-Obama fervor expressed itself in the so-called birther movement. Polls found that about a quarter of the American people believed that he was not born in America. The belief that he is an alien, maintained in the face of a Hawaiian birth certificate and media records of his birth, can only be attributed to a powerful feeling that he is not a legitimate president, and that in turn is fueled by racism.[7] About 20 percent of Americans believe that he is a Muslim. This idea also persists in the face of the evidence of the highly publicized controversy over inflammatory remarks by his Christian pastor, the Reverend Jeremiah Wright, in the 2008 campaign. One can legitimately ask, if race does not explain the continuing strength of these anti-Obama beliefs in the face of clear evidence to the contrary, what other factor does?[8] Many previous presidents were hated when in office, notably Roosevelt. But arguably, not even he faced such widespread and passionate belief that he was not a legitimate president.

Obama, however, has been very reluctant to address the issue of race, and particularly the racially based challenges to his legitimacy as president. The *New York Times*, for example, reported in September 2009, "As Race Debate Grows, Obama Steers Clear of It." And on his 2011 visit to Brazil he avoided the issue despite the fact that he had reportedly "inspired millions" there "because of his African heritage." This choice has been particularly curious, because when he does address race he is spectacularly successful. In the 2008 campaign, his March 18 speech in response to the controversy that arose over inflammatory racial remarks by his Chicago pastor Jeremiah Wright is rivaled only by Lyndon Johnson's 1965 voting rights speech as the best speech on race by any president or candidate for office. The singular contribution of the speech was to note the continually changing context of race in America, and argue how tired cliches that posit no change are counterproductive, and how America's future is always ours to choose. And in 2010, when he finally addressed the controversy over his birth certificate, the issue almost completely vanished.[9]

CIVIL LIBERTIES AND DEMOCRACY

To understand presidents and civil liberties fully, we need to look beyond individual presidents and their personal characteristics and look at the place of civil liberties in American democracy. By their very nature, civil liberties involve unpopular issues: the dissenter's right to criticize the government in wartime, freedom of the press for the

7 "Born in the U.S.A.: The Facts about Obama's Birth Certificate," factcheck.org, updated, November 1, 2008.

8 "Polls Show More Americans Think Obama Is a Muslim," *Washington Post*, August 19, 2010.

9 "As Race Debate Grows, Obama Steers Clear of It," *NYT*, September 17, 2009. "President Underscores Similarities with Brazilians, but Sidesteps One," ibid., March 20, 2011. Barack Obama, "A More Perfect Union," March 18, 2008.

novel with graphic sexual violence, freedom for "hate speech" attacking racial or religious groups, the right of the vicious criminal to a fair trial, the right of an international terrorist to constitutional protections. In earlier decades in America, it was impossible to discuss openly either abortion or same-sex relationships. In a democracy, presidents (and candidates for Congress) either avoid defending such unpopular issues or pander to majority opinion with anti–civil libertarian positions.

The very unpopularity of difficult civil liberties issues highlights why we have a Bill of Rights. The authors of the Bill of Rights understood that it was necessary to take certain controversies out of the political arena and beyond the reach of popular majorities. The proverbial "tyranny of the majority" is not a scholarly abstraction, but rather the substance of the long history of the denial of individual rights in America. Alexis de Tocqueville, one of the most astute observers of America, noted this problem in his classic 1833 work, *Democracy in America*.[10]

With this in mind, it is hardly surprising that the Supreme Court, the least democratic institution in our constitutional democracy, has been so important in advancing individual rights. Although the Court did not undertake this role until the late 1930s, it has been central to the modern rights revolution. And in another manifestation of the underside of democracy, the political response to controversial Court decisions has been predictably hostile. Partisans on the losing side of controversial decisions have attacked the Court as an undemocratic elite. Southern segregationists attacked the Court after *Brown v. Board of Education*; advocates of school prayer sought a constitutional amendment to overturn the school prayer decision, as did abortion opponents after *Roe v. Wade*; and many liberals have discussed ways to negate recent decisions by a conservative Court, including notably *Citizens United v. Federal Election Commission* (2010) on campaign finance.[11]

To attribute the growth of rights entirely to the Courts, however, is to miss a much deeper dynamic. The Supreme Court, after all, only responds to cases brought before it, and which it agrees to hear and the arguments raised in the various briefs. The larger question is, How do controversial civil liberties cases arise in the first instance? They are brought by individuals or groups and today usually with the support of an advocacy group. The issues and the arguments in the briefs do not appear out of thin air. With only rare possible exception, they reflect broader currents of thought about rights. Courts, and the Supreme Court in particular, are affected in one way or another by these social and intellectual currents. (This is not to say that the Court responds to public opinion in some simplistic fashion, however. The relationship between the two is extremely complex and beyond the scope of this discussion.) In short, even the very undemocratic U.S. Supreme Court is a part of the larger context of an evolving democracy.

As this book makes clear, respect for civil liberties is not a matter of Democrats versus Republicans. Presidents of both parties have perpetrated some of the worst violations of civil liberties We have already discussed Woodrow Wilson suppression of dissent in World War I, Roosevelt's internment of the Japanese Americans, Nixon's obstruction of justice in the Watergate scandal, and George W. Bush's abuses in the war on terrorism. Since the Great Realignment that began in the late 1970s, however, the differences between

10 Alexis de Tocqueville, *Democracy in America* (Garden City, NY: Doubleday, 1969), Part II, Chapter 7.

11 See, most recently, James MacGregor Burns, *Packing the Court: The Rise of Judicial Power and the Coming Crisis of the Supreme Court* (New York: Penguin, 2009).

the two major parties on civil liberties are much stronger than ever before. Democratic presidents have supported abortion rights, women's rights, and lesbian and gay rights and have opposed prayer in public schools and restrictions on sexually related materials more than have Republicans. They have also been generally more restrained with regard to national security, presidential power, and the intelligence agencies than GOP presidents (although not always enough to satisfy civil libertarians). r The remarkable aspect of the last thirty-five years in American history is the extent to which civil liberties issues have been the central controversies in American politics.

The special case of national security

National security, and all of the constitutional issues it raises, represents a very special case, and one with a long history, with regard to presidents and civil liberties. The most consistent pattern in the assaults on civil liberties by American presidents involves national security, during shooting wars, cold wars, and the current war on terrorism. Wilson suppressed freedom of speech and press during World War I because he genuinely believed that dissent undermined the war effort. Roosevelt authorized the evacuation of the Japanese Americans because he feared a Japanese invasion of the West Coast after the Pearl Harbor attack. Truman created his loyalty program because he was convinced there were communists and other disloyal people employed in federal agencies. Reagan unleashed the intelligence agencies, imposed greater government secrecy, and approved the secret and illegal Iran-Contra deal because he believed international communism seriously threatened the United States. George W. Bush claimed extraordinary presidential power, approved torture, and undermined the right of habeas corpus because he saw terrorism as an immediate threat to the survival of the nation. Richard Nixon, in this regard, stands alone because his abuses of power involved personal and political motives.

Public disgust over the Vietnam War and Richard Nixon's abuses of power led to a watershed in the law and public policy regarding both the intelligence agencies and presidential power. The resulting reforms included the War Powers Act, the Foreign Intelligence Surveillance Act (FISA), a ban on CIA assassinations, and two new congressional intelligence committees. Presidents Ford and Carter generally complied with these new controls, but others chafed at them. Ronald Reagan took office determined to roll them back and flouted them and broke other laws in the Iran-Contra scandal. Bill Clinton respected some of the controls but also made a number of unwarranted claims of presidential power, including ignoring the War Powers Act. George W. Bush and Dick Cheney waged a direct assault on the authority of both Congress and the courts to limit the prerogatives of the president when acting as commander in chief. All of the presidents in the post-Watergate period made at least some claim of secrecy, and none renounced the power to conduct covert actions overseas.

Obama quickly developed a mixed record on national security. He reversed several of Bush's most offensive national security policies in his first days in office but maintained others. He continued to invoke the state secrets doctrine and did not renounce covert actions. Most notably in 2011 he rejected arguments that his actions in the revolution in Libya violated the 1973 War Powers Act, on the dubious grounds that Americans were not engaged in "hostilities" within the meaning of the law. Some legal scholars, moreover, rejected the administration's argument that American actions were authorized through the United Nations and NATO. The administration's embrace of bombings by pilotless drones, moreover, seemed to portend warfare without geographic limits. Obama and Attorney General Eric Holder seemed willing to compromise the right of terrorist suspects to a standard *Miranda* warning on their right to remain silent. Whether this represented their true belief about how to prosecute such cases or an attempt to avoid attacks from congressional Republicans was not clear.[12]

The Obama administration's increase in the use of pilotless drone aircraft and the closely related issue of targeted killing of individuals deeply troubled human rights activists in the United States and abroad. Drone technology offered the prospect of seemingly limitless military attacks around the world. The administration's embrace of it resembled the enthusiasm for covert actions during the cold war, when Democratic and Republican administrations alike saw it as a very low cost and seemingly efficient way of accomplishing certain international goals without the cost, publicity, or delay of conventional military actions. The targeted killing of the American-born militant Anwar al-Awlaki in September 2011 raised the troubling question of the power to kill a U.S. citizen without any due process. Such killing of foreign nationals might, in certain situations, violate the prohibition on assassinating foreign leaders. In short, while the Obama administration was certainly far more restrained on national security issues than that of George W. Bush, some actions have raised new and troubling questions.[13]

The evidence in this book puts Obama in perspective on national security. The preference for security over liberty is almost inherent in the office of the presidency. The world looks very different from the Oval Office than it does from the campaign trail or other elective office, and Obama is only the latest president to experience this radical change of perspective. Woodrow Wilson ran for reelection on the slogan that he "kept us out of war," but within five months he took the United States into World War I. Lyndon Johnson ran for reelection in 1964 promising not to send Americans to fight a war in Asia but soon sent troops to Vietnam (and appears to have been planning to do so all along). Obama campaigned against the Iraq War and then disappointed supporters when he did not remove American troops quickly from Iraq and greatly escalated the use of drone bombings in Afghanistan, Pakistan, and elsewhere.[14]

No president wants to be blamed for another Pearl Harbor or 9/11 attack, and the dynamics of the office push them toward what they regard as the "safe" position regarding potential threats against the country. Security has consistently trumped the defense of civil liberties principles. On a purely human level, presidents feel the awesome responsibility of the office to defend the country and protect American lives. It is naive to expect otherwise. George Tenet, director of the CIA under George W. Bush, has provided in his memoirs the most revealing insight into how national security considerations impinge

12 "White House Defends Continuing U.S. Role in Libya Operation," *NYT*, June 16, 2011. Louis Fisher, Statement to Senate Foreign Relations Committee, June 28, 2011. Available at the Constitution Project. "House Rebukes Obama for Continuing Libyan Mission without Consent," *NYT*, June 4, 2011. "Holder Backs a Miranda Limit for Terror Suspects," *NYT*, May 9, 2010. "Courts Test Miranda Rights Limits in Terror Cases," *NYT*, November 23, 2011.

13 "C.I.A. Strike Kills U.S.-Born Militant in a Car in Yemen, ibid, October 1, 2011. Peter W. Singer, *Wired for War: The Robotics Revolution and Conflict in the Twenty-First Century* (New York: Penguin, 2009).

14 "A Covert Assault on Terror Widens in Asia and Africa," *NYT*, August 15, 2010.

on the presidency. Every day, he recalled, hundreds of possible national security threats reach the CIA. "You could drive yourself crazy," if you took them all as immediate threats, he explained. Presidents get a partial summary of these possible threats in their daily brief, and we can only imagine how it affects their thinking. Presidents feel an awesome responsibility to protect the country and have equally awesome powers at their disposal. And as the ACLU president Susan Herman warns, "all presidents will believe that they personally can be trusted to use their vast powers wisely."[15]

Powerful political forces also help drive the preference for security over liberty. Popular fears about threats to national security, often manipulated by politicians, have been a key element in many of the worst violations of civil liberties, notably with the Japanese Americans, in the cold war, and in the war on terrorism. The opposition party is always ready to jump at the chance to portray the incumbent as weak in protecting the nation. One thinks of John F. Kennedy's criticizing President Eisenhower in 1960 for the "missile gap," which American intelligence had secretly confirmed did not exist. In recent decades, Republicans have been particularly successful in portraying themselves as stronger on national security than Democrats, and Democrats have made strenuous efforts to prove they are not.

The Pentagon, the CIA, the NSA, and the FBI, moreover, have vested institutional interests in arguing that real threats exist and that they should be granted authority to thwart them. Such steps never involve a close reading of the Bill of Rights. We do not know the extent to which CIA officials exaggerate those hundreds of threats that George Tenet describes. The Pentagon and the intelligence agencies also have powerful allies in Congress and the media who are eager to champion their cause and attack a president who appears weak. In his long heyday, the FBI director J. Edgar Hoover cultivated allies in the news media and manipulated them to exaggerate domestic communist threats to the nation. From its first days the CIA developed a very cozy relationship with the leading news media, and the agency had little meaningful oversight from Congress. The Iran-Contra scandal in the 1980s and much of the war on terrorism after 2001 indicate that Congress is reluctant to use aggressively the oversight authority it gained in the post-Watergate reforms.

Public opinion also constrains presidential decisions in the national security arena, although in complex ways. If the American people generally have a weak and inconsistent commitment to civil liberties, it is certainly weakest on national security. It is sobering to recall how few Americans protested Roosevelt's evacuation and internment of the Japanese Americans. In the 1950s public opinion polls strongly supported measures directed against alleged subversives that violated freedom of speech and association. Most recently, after 9/11 about 90 percent of Americans initially supported President George W. Bush's war on terrorism (although admittedly they were initially not aware of the secret and most offensive aspects of that war).[16] The only hopeful aspect of these chapters of American history is that while public opinion was easily stampeded at first, the passage of time and revelations of abuses had a corrective effect, although the impact has generally been slow and incomplete.

[15] George Tenet, *At the Center of the Storm: My Years at the CIA* (New York: HarperCollins, 2007), p. 232. Susan N. Herman, *Taking Liberties: The War on Terror and the Erosion of American Democracy* (New York: Oxford University Press, 2011), p. 191.

[16] *CBS News Poll*, November 2001.

Public opinion, however, is a very malleable entity and can be shaped by presidential leadership, for good or ill. Presidents, unfortunately, have too often failed critical tests of their special responsibility in times of crisis. As we already indicated, presidents have used the bully pulpit of their office only occasionally on civil liberties issues. It is not unreasonable to argue that FDR could have persuaded the country to accept a more restrained policy regarding the Japanese Americans, one based on individualized suspicion. Truman, meanwhile, could have at least attempted a policy on suspected communists in government based on individualized suspicion of illegal activities, rather than guilt by association. George W. Bush could have implemented a more narrowly tailored antiterrorist policy that respected the Constitution. Had he made the effort, moreover, he probably could have persuaded the public on policies that were more respectful of civil liberties while adequate for national security.[17] In each of these cases, the history of this country could have been very different had the president actively defended the principles in the Bill of Rights. We cannot, therefore, assume that public opinion is a fixed entity.

The capacity of presidents to shape public opinion is, of course, constrained by the political context in which they work. FDR faced powerful isolationist feeling in the late 1930s, despite the rising threat of Hitler in Europe. Kennedy deferred to a national reluctance to act on civil rights, until massive demonstrations in the streets dramatically altered the public mood. From the 1970s onward, every Democratic Party president opposed busing of public school students for racial integration and endorsed "tough" anticrime policies in response to public attitudes on these two issues. Nonetheless, Truman's strong leadership on civil rights in the period 1946–8 provides an important exception to the rule. As we have suggested, a good part of the discontent with Obama among his supporters reflects their feeling that he has not tried wholeheartedly to use the power of his office to shape the political dialogue, on national security and other issues.[18]

AN ALTERNATIVE INTERPRETATION OF DEMOCRACY AND RIGHTS

It has long been a truism that democracy in America is the great enemy of civil liberties.[19] Yet, the evidence in this book suggests a more complex and fluid interpretation, one that recognizes a constantly changing social and political environment and in which democratic forces in some important instances support certain civil liberties. It is a more hopeful view that is rooted in important civil liberties developments of recent decades.

As a part of the Great Realignment of the late 1970s, several civil liberties issues gained a significant measure of popular acceptance. Beginning in the 1960s, they built political constituencies to which presidents and other politicians must inevitably respond.[20]

17 With regard to Truman, it is a question of whether he could have survived politically with a more limited policy. On Bush, Jack Goldsmith argues for a constitutionally correct policy on terrorism in *The Terror Presidency*. On what presidents failed to do, see Samuel Walker, "Great Speeches Presidents Did NOT Give – and Should Have." The question of how different Al Gore would have been in responding to the 9/11 terrorist attacks can be the subject of a fascinating, although ultimately unresolvable debate.

18 See the relevant chapters for the presidents named here.

19 De Tocqueville, *Democracy in America*, Part II, Chap. 7. John Stuart Mill, *On Liberty*. Federalist No. 10, James Madison, Alexander Hamilton, and John Jay, *The Federalist Papers*.

20 The most important advocate of this interpretation, which posits popular support for civil liberties against the elitist view that only the courts can protect them, is the historian Paul L. Murphy, *The Meaning of Freedom of Speech: First Amendment Freedoms from Wilson to FDR* (Westport, CT: Greenwood Press, 1972), pp. 3–10, Introduction," (especially pp. 9–10).

Lyndon Johnson secured passage of the 1964 Civil Rights Act and the 1965 Voting Rights Act in large part because by then racial justice had won a measure of political support across the country. This represented a dramatic change from just a few years earlier. Women's equality also gained a new legal and political status, and by the mid-1970s, women were a powerful constituency in the Democratic Party, as were African Americans. Democratic presidents from Jimmy Carter onward have been generally stronger supporters of women's rights issues than Republicans (although quite accepting of women in high positions who nonetheless support the conservative agenda).

The Supreme Court's historic *Roe v. Wade* decision affirming a constitutional right to abortion transformed the American political landscape. No president prior to *Roe* endorsed, or for that matter even discussed, abortion rights. The politics of reproductive rights quickly changed, however. Jimmy Carter, although personally ambivalent about abortion itself, staunchly opposed outlawing it, as did all subsequent Democratic Party presidents and candidates. Abortion proved to be an even more polarizing issue than women's rights, with Republicans embracing the antiabortion position.

A New York City police raid on the gay bar Stonewall in 1969 marked the birth of yet another rights movement, an organized effort for the rights of lesbian and gay people. Prior to that night, homosexuality was a virtually unmentionable topic in American public life. Several decades later, after much organizing, litigation, and political activity, many states and cities have laws prohibiting discrimination on the basis of sexual orientation, the courts have banned discrimination in a number of areas, and same-sex marriages are legal in five states, a development that was unthinkable as recently as the 1980s.[21] Lesbian and gay activists have become another important constituency within the Democratic Party. Jimmy Carter was the first president to invite their representatives to the White House in 1977. Bill Clinton took the bold step in the 1992 campaign of promising to end discrimination against gays in the military, although it proved to be one he could not keep as soon as he took office.

Finally, as a result of major demographic changes and political organizing, the Latino community has become a force with considerable political influence. The result is that while both the Democratic and Republican Parties have constituencies demanding tougher immigration enforcement (far stronger within the GOP), national party leaders are very wary of offending the growing Latino vote.

The experience of these rights movements indicates that some civil liberties issues do move from the status of unpopular into the political mainstream. The democratic process, in short, can work to expand and protect certain individual rights. Recognizing this process challenges the standard elitist interpretation of how civil liberties advance. Elitist elements - activist organizations, creative attorneys, the Supreme Court - may be crucial in the early years of a movement, but at a certain point public opinion can and does change, with the consequent impact on local and national politics.[22]

[21] David Carter, *Stonewall: The Riot That Sparked the Gay Revolution* (New York: St. Martin's, 2004).

[22] It is impossible in this regard to imagine the growth of free speech without taking into account the ACLU, the growth of civil rights law without the NAACP, and the expansion of religious liberty and other important rights without the now largely forgotten role of the Jehovah's Witnesses between the late 1930s and early 1950s. Samuel Walker, *In Defense of American Liberties: A History of the ACLU* (New York: Oxford, 1990). Richard Kluger, *Simple Justice* (New York: Vintage Books, 1976). Shawn Francis Peters, *Judging Jehovah's Witnesses: Religious Persecution and the Dawn of the Rights Revolution* (Lawrence: University Press of Kansas, 2000).

Even on national security, the democratic process has achieved some significant, albeit imperfect, gains since the 1970s. Exposure of CIA and FBI abuses in the mid-1970s led to the first meaningful controls over the intelligence agencies, notably the 1978 Foreign Intelligence Surveillance Act and the creation of intelligence oversight committees in both houses of Congress. The 1973 War Powers Act was one of several attempts to limit presidential power on foreign affairs. Subsequent events proved that these controls were imperfect (and in the case of the 1973 War Powers Act, probably a complete failure). Nonetheless, they redefined law and policy regarding many issues related to presidential power and the intelligence agencies, putting an end to the era when so many critical actions of our government were completely beyond public scrutiny and legal controls. The extreme secrecy engineered by Vice President Cheney in the Bush administration, in fact, sprang from his awareness of the new legal controls and the knowledge that he could circumvent them only in secret.[23]

In short, the democratic process in the last several decades has resulted in centers of political support for a number of once-taboo civil liberties issues. The idea that democracy is inherently hostile to civil liberties is both simplistic and not supported by the historical record.

FINAL THOUGHTS: A CONVERSATION ABOUT AMERICA

What, in the end, do we learn from studying presidents and civil liberties? Given the complexity of the issues and the contradictions that mark the records of so many presidents, we argue that any attempt to rank the presidents, for example, into "great," "near great," and so on, is futile. Meaningful comparisons would require placing a comparative value on various incidents. How much, for example, is the Japanese-American internment "worth"? This would require a quantification of historical events that would be impossible. The study of presidents and civil liberties, as does the study of history generally, enhances our understanding of today's world by putting it in perspective. This is particularly true today when national politics has become so bitterly partisan. But there is more. Studying presidents and civil liberties is a conversation about America, about who we are, our basic values, and what we expect of our leaders.

When historians rank George Washington, Abraham Lincoln, and Franklin D. Roosevelt as the only three "great" presidents, they are making judgments that these chief executives provided wise and effective leadership at critical moments in our history, and that they honored and in some instances defined America's values.[24] Washington is esteemed for establishing practices as the first president that have served the country well, including refusing to accept any exalted title, eschewing any military aura, delivering an annual message to Congress, declining to run for a third term. Lincoln is revered for his leadership during the Civil War, for issuing the Emancipation Proclamation, and for his

Arguably, the first historian to suggest popular support for certain civil liberties was Paul Murphy in *The Meaning of Freedom of Speech*, pp. 9–10.

23 Jack Goldsmith, *The Terror Presidency: Law and Judgment inside the Bush Administration* (New York: W. W. Norton, 2007). On the secrecy, which was largely engineered by Vice President Dick Cheney, see Goldsmith, *The Terror Presidency*; Jane Mayer, *The Dark Side: The Inside Story of How the War on Terror Turned into a War on American Ideals*, Pbk ed. (New York Anchor Books, 2009).

24 James Lindgren and Steven G. Calabresi, "Rating the Presidents of the United States, 1989–2000: A Survey of Scholars in Political Science, History, and Law," *Constitutional Commentary*, 18 (Winter 2001): 583–605.

Gettysburg Address, which historians have long regarded as perhaps the finest statement of the meaning of America. Roosevelt gave people hope during the Great Depression and provided strong and wise leadership during World War II. Different presidents, the historians are saying, might well have made very different decisions, and in each case the result would have meant a very different and less worthy course for American history.

By the same token, when this book criticizes Woodrow Wilson for suppressing freedom of speech during World War I, it represents a judgment that the First Amendment occupies a central place in American constitutional democracy, and that he was certainly wrong in failing to honor the values it embodies. When this book criticizes Harry Truman for his federal loyalty program, it is a judgment that the principle of guilt by association that it embodied is illegitimate and did great harm to the country. Recognizing his leadership on civil rights at a critical moment, meanwhile, is a statement about the importance of that issue in American life. And so it continues with other presidents and other issues.

Implicit in these judgments are political debates that raise fundamental questions about our values as a constitutional democracy. Are there limits to free speech during wartime? If so, what are those limits? Do some forms of advocacy genuinely imperil national security? In the case of the Japanese Americans, few if any Americans today would argue that any group should lose their liberties simply because of their race. We have reached that consensus only because that tragedy has forced us as a nation to consider that question. The question remains, however, of what kinds of actions the government can permissibly take after an attack that kills thousands of people. The 9/11 terrorist attacks raised those questions anew, and the debate over the actions of the Bush administration – and now the Obama administration – continues. This is not a narrow political debate, but one that addresses the very scope of government authority in a constitutional democracy in a dangerous world.

All presidential decisions on civil liberties issues are made in the context of political considerations. FDR's evacuation order was prompted in large part by political pressure from the West Coast. Truman's loyalty program was designed in part to fend off Republican attacks that he was soft on communism. The basic question becomes one of our expectations regarding presidential leadership. To what extent should we expect a president to rise above politics and take a courageous but politically risky position on a matter of constitutional rights? The same consideration holds with regard to President Eisenhower's refusal to denounce McCarthy by name. He refrained in part so as not to attack a fellow Republican and alienate McCarthy's supporters. Again, given the recklessness of McCarthy's tactics, to what extent should we expect Eisenhower to have risen above partisan considerations and publicly challenged a destructive force in American life?

In so many of the major incidents covered in this book, many Americans wish presidents had chosen different courses of action. We cannot remake history, of course, but that is not now the point. The important point is that in discussing the choices they made in their times of crisis, we define not just our personal values but the values we hold dear for the country. Thus, the discussion of presidents and civil liberties becomes a dialogue about our most important values: freedom of speech, tolerance, racial justice, procedural fairness, and respect for the principles in the Constitution and the Bill of Rights. In the course of these discussions, we should not shy away from making judgments about presidents for their performance. Indeed, making judgments is the point of the exercise.

Taking into account the complexities and contradictions in the performances of various presidents, moreover, heightens our sense of the richness and complexity of both American history and contemporary political life. One of the worst aspects of the poisoned culture of contemporary politics is its fierce and blind partisanship, which reduces everything to an oversimplified black and white dimension. Reclaiming an appreciation for the complexity of politics and the conflicting pressures on our presidents provide a valuable tempering perspective on current events. That, after all, is what the study of history has always done.

Sources

PRESIDENTIAL LIBRARIES

George H. W. Bush Presidential Library

- Donated Materials
  - Personal Papers
- Subject Files
  - Human Rights

Jimmy Carter Presidential Library

- Domestic Policy Staff Files
- Hamilton Jordan Files
- Louis Martin Files
- Office of the Counsel Files
- Office of Public Liaison Files
- Office of Sarah Weddington Files
- Oral Histories
  - Lloyd Cutler, Exit Interview
  - Stuart Eizenstat, Exit Interview
  - Hendrick Hertzberg, Exit Interview
  - Robert Lipshutz, Exit Interview
  - Sarah Weddington, Exit Interview

William J. Clinton Presidential Library

- Clinton Administration History Project
  - Central Intelligence Agency
  - Department of Justice
- Domestic Policy Council
  - Bruce Reed Files
  - Chris Jennings Files
  - Carole Rasco Files
  - Ira Magaziner Files
  - Kendra Brooks Files
  - Stephen Warnath Files
- National Security Council Files
  - Samuel Berger Files

Richard A. Clarke Files
President's Foreign Intelligence Advisory Board Files
President's Advisory Board on Race
President's Counsel's Office
Bruce Lindsey Files

Dwight D. Eisenhower Presidential Library

DDE Records as President Papers
Herbert Brownell Papers
Official Files
Special Assistant for National Security Affairs files
White House Central Files
E. Frederic Morrow Papers
Ann C. Whitman Files
Administration Series
Herbert Brownell Files
DDE Diary
William P. Rogers Files
Ann C. Whitman Diary
Ann C. Whitman Diary
Oral Histories
Herbert Brownell
Gordon Gray
John McCone
E. Frederic Morrow
Maxwell Rabb
Ann C. Whitman

Gerald Ford Presidential Library

Philip Buchen Files
Cabinet Meeting Minutes, 1974–1977
James Cannon Files
Richard Cheney Files
Congressional Relations Office
Counsel to the President Files
Counselors to the President Files
Council Staff
Domestic Affairs Assistant/Domestic
Ford Pre-Presidential Speeches
Robert Hartmann Files
Patricia Lindh and Jeanne Holm Files
Vernon Loen and Charles Leppert Files
National Security Advisor/NSC Staff Files
National Security Council Minutes
President Ford's Daily Diary, 1974–1977

Presidential Handwriting Files
Public Liaison Office
Stanley S. Scott Files
  Richard Cheney Files
White House Central Files
  Human Rights
  Judicial Legal

Herbert Hoover Presidential Library

Campaign and Transition Papers
Commerce Department Papers
Presidential Papers
Oral History
  See Miller Center for Public Affairs

Lyndon B. Johnson Presidential Library

Administrative Histories
Aides Files
  Ramsey Clark Papers
Daily Diary
House of Representatives File
National Security File
National Youth Administration File
Records from Federal Government Agencies
Task Force Reports
Telephone Conversations
White House Central Files
  Confidential File
  Subject File
Oral Histories
  McGeorge Bundy
  Horace Busby
  Douglass Cater
  Ramsey Clark
  Tom Clark
  Clark Clifford
  William E. Colby
  Cartha D. DeLoach
  James Farmer
  Abe Fortas
  Arthur Goldberg
  Rev. Billy Graham
  Sarah T. Hughes
  Nicholas Katzenbach
  Harry McPherson
  Burke Marshall
  Louis Martin

Clarence Mitchell
Lawrence F. O'Brien
Drew Pearson
A. Philip Randolph
Earl Warren

John F. Kennedy Presidential Library

Richard Goodwin Papers
Robert F. Kennedy Papers
Ed Guthman Papers
Nicholas Katzenbach Papers
Francis Keppel Papers
Burke Marshall Papers
Esther Peterson Papers
Pierre Salinger Papers
Theodore Sorensen Papers
James Wine Papers
Harris Wofford Papers
Pre-Presidential Papers
President's Office Papers
White House Central Files

Oral Histories

Joseph W. Alsop
Ross Barnett
Richard M. Bissell
Horace Busby
Wilbur Cohen
Richard Cardinal Cushing
C. Douglas Dillon
Angier Biddle Duke
Allen W. Dulles
Gerald Ford
Felix Frankfurter
Nicholas Katzenbach
Francis Keppel
Martin Luther King
John E. Moss
John Siegenthaler
James Wine
Harris Wofford

RFK Oral History Project

Ramsey Clark
Burke Marshall

Richard Nixon Papers (then at the National Archives)

- Commission on Obscenity and Pornography
- Exit Interviews
  - Charles W. Colson
- Grand Jury Testimony and Files, 1975
- President's Office Files
  - Annotated News Summaries
  - President's Handwriting Files
- President's Personal File
  - Memoranda From the President
- White House Central Files
  - Subject Files
    - Campus Disorders
    - Equality
    - Human Rights
    - Women
- White House Special Files
  - Patrick Buchanan Files
  - Charles W. Colson Files
  - John Ehrlichman Files

Ronald Reagan Presidential Library

- Gubernatorial Papers
  - 1966 Campaign Files
  - Cabinet Office Files
  - Education Unit Files
- Presidential Papers
  - Luis Acle Files
  - Gary Bauer Files
  - Christopher Cox Files
  - Michael Deaver Files
  - Elizabeth Dole
  - Kenneth W. Duberstein Files
  - Fred Fielding Files
  - Stephen Galebach Files
  - Edwin Meese Files
  - Oliver North
  - John Poindexter Files
  - Mary Elizabeth Quint Files
  - John G. Roberts Files
  - Peter Wallinson Files
- White House Counsel Files (Meese)
- White House Office of Political Affairs
- White House Office of Public Affairs

Franklin D. Roosevelt Presidential Library

- Francis Biddle Papers
- John Carter Franklin File
- Stephen T. Early Papers
- Official File
- President's Personal File
- President's Secretary's File
- Eleanor Roosevelt Oral History Project
  - Pauli Murray
  - Esther Peterson
  - Joseph Rauh
  - James Rowe
- Eleanor Roosevelt Papers

Harry S. Truman Presidential Library

- Charles Sawyer Papers
- Dean Acheson Papers
- Eleanor Bontecu Papers
- Tom Clark Papers
- George M. Elsey Papers
- Philleo Nash Papers
- Post-Presidential Papers
- President's Secretary Files
- Sidney Souers Papers
- White House Central Files
- Oral Histories
  - Dean Acheson
  - Karl Bendetsen
  - Richard M. Bissell
  - Eleanor Bontecu
  - David Bruce
  - John Franklin Carter
  - Clark Clifford
  - Jonathan Daniels
  - George M. Elsey
  - Gordon Gray
  - Milton Kayle
  - E. W. Kenworthy
  - James Loeb
  - Max Lowenthal
  - Philleo Nash
  - Joseph Rauh
  - James Rowe
  - Stephen J. Spingarn
  - John R. Steelman
  - Earl Warren

Tom Clark
William H. Hastie

GENERAL SOURCES

American Presidency Project, University of California at Santa Barbara.
National Security Archive. George Washington University. www.gwu.edu/~nsarchiv/.
The New York Times, 1851–. Online edition.
United States. Department of State. *Foreign Relations of the United States*.
Library of Congress
Albert S. Burleson Papers
Calvin Coolidge Papers
Felix Frankfurter Papers
Warren G. Harding Papers
Harold L. Ickes Papers
Frank Murphy Papers
A. Philip Randolph Papers
Joseph L. Rauh Papers
Francis B. Sayre Papers
Harlan Fiske Stone Papers
Moorefield Storey Papers
National Woman's Party Papers
Oral History
Harry Blackmun
Maj. Gen. Jeanne Holm (Ret.)
Foreign Affairs Oral History Project
David Blakemore
Julia Child
Esther Peterson
Laurence Silberman
James Wine

LIBRARIES, ARCHIVES, INDIVIDUAL, AND ORGANIZATIONAL PAPERS

American Civil Liberties Union Records, Princeton University
American Civil Liberties Union Files.
American Civil Liberties Union Records: The Roger Baldwin Years, 1917–1950 Microfilm edition (Wilmington, DE: Scholarly Resources, 1996). [Cited as ACLUP-MF (1996).
American Civil Liberties Union Records and Publications, 1917–1975), Microfilm edition. (Glen Rock, NJ: Microfilming Corporation of America, 1977). [Cited as ACLUP-MF (1977). ACLU Web site: www.aclu.org
American Rhetoric. www.americanrhetoric.com
Assassination Archive Research Center. www.aarc.org
Bell, Griffin. Oral History. University of Georgia. Richard B. Russell Oral History Documentary Collection.
Bethune, Mary McLeod. Papers. Microfilm ed. Frederick, MD: University Publications of America, 1997.

Biddle, Francis. Papers. Georgetown University.
Blackmun, Harry. Oral History. National Public Radio.
California, University of. Regional Oral History Office (ROHO). Bancroft Library.
  Earl Warren Era in California, 1925–1953.
    Herbert Brownell, et al., Earl Warren: The Chief Justiceship.
    Warren Burger.
    Earl Warren.
  Japanese-American Relocation Reviewed.
    Interviews
      Tom Clark.
      Edward Ennis.
      Mike Masaoka.
      James Rowe.
  Ronald Reagan Era in California, 1966–1974.
    Republican Campaigns and Party Issues, 1964–1976.
  Suffragists.
    Alice Paul.
    Burnita Shelton Matthews.
    Jeannette Rankin.
    The Suffragists: From Tea Parties to Prison.
Central Intelligence Agency.
Center for the Study of Intelligence. Www.cia.gov/library/center-for-the-study-of-intelligence/index.html
  Electronic Reading Room.
Civil Rights in Mississippi Digital Archive, (CRMDA), University of Southern Mississippi.
Clark, Tom. Oral History. University of Kentuck. Fred M. Vinson Oral History Project.
Columbia University Oral History Collection.
  Roger Baldwin
  Archibald Cox
  Milton Eisenhower
  Oval Faubus
  Robert H. Finch
  Erwin Griswold
  Learned Hand
  Herbert Hoover
  Ben W. Huebsch
  Francis Keppel
  Arthur Larson
  John J. McCloy
  Frederic Morrow
  John Lord O'Brian
  Esther Peterson
  Maxwell Rabb
  Eleanor Roosevelt
  Frances B. Sayre
  Leverett Saltonstall

G. David Schine
Upton Sinclair
Elbert Tuttle
Congress of Racial Equality (CORE). Papers.
Microfilm edition. Frederick, MD: University Publications of America, 1981–1984.
DENSHO: The Japanese American Legacy Project. Densho Digital Archive. www.densho.org/archive/.
Douglas, William O. Oral History [online]. Princeton University
Federal Bureau of Investigation
Electronic Reading Room [ERR].
Roger Baldwin
FBI Undercover Operations
Gay Activist Alliance
John F. Kennedy
Joseph P. Kennedy
Robert F. Kennedy
Martin Luther King
Ku Klux Klan
Thurgood Marshall
National Organization for Women
George W. Norris
A. Philip Randolph
Paul Robeson
Eleanor Roosevelt
J. Edgar Hoover, Official and Confidential File, Microfilm edition.
Southern Christian Leadership Conference. Communist Infiltration of the SCLC. FBI Investigation File. (Wilmington, DC: Scholarly Resources, 1983).
Surveillance of Radicals in the United States, 1917–1941. Frederick, MD: University Publications of America, 1984.
First Amendment Center. www.firstamendmentcenter.org.
www.livingroomcandidate.org
King, Martin Luther Papers. Clayborne Carson, ed.. Berkeley: University of California Press, 1992–2005.
Levi, Edward H. Papers. University of Chicago.
Memory Hole, The. www.memoryhole.org
Miller Center of Public Affairs, University of Virginia.
Herbert Hoover Oral History.
Oral History Interviews.
Martin Anderson
Howard Baker
Griffin Bell
Lloyd Cutler
Stuart Eizenstat
Hendrick Hertzberg
Lyn Nofziger
Gerald Rafshoon

George P. Shultz
William H. Webster
Anne Wexler
Presidential Speech Archive.
Murphy, Frank Papers. University of Michigan. Bentley Library.
Murray, Pauli. Papers. Schlesinger Library. Radcliffe Institute for Advanced Study. Harvard University.
National Association for the Advancement of Colored People. Papers. Library of Congress. Microfilm edition.
National Security Council, Minutes of the, First Supplement. Microfilm ed. (Frederick, MD: University Publications of America, 1988).
Oral Histories of the South. University of North Carolina.
Jimmy Carter
Bill Clinton
Leslie W. Dunbar
Virginia Durr
Orval Faubus
Clark Foreman
Al Gore, Sr.
John Lewis
Pauli Murray
Claude Pepper
Daniel Pollitt
John Seigenthaler
Strom Thurmond
Schorr, Daniel. Oral History. National Public Radio.
Stimson, Henry L. Diaries. Yale University. Micofilm edition.
Swarthmore College Peace Collection.
Edward W. Evans Papers.
Fellowship of Reconciliation Papers.
Joint Amnesty Committee Papers.
John Nevin Sayre Papers.
Virtual Vietnam Archive. Vietnam Center and Archive. Texas Tech University.
www.watergateinfo.org
Women's Bureau, United States. Records of the Women's Bureau of the Department of Labor, 1918–1965. Microfilm ed.. Frederick, MD: University Publications of America, 1986–.
Women's History Research Center, Women and the Law, Microfilm edition. Berkeley, CA: 1974.

Index